NOURISHING TRADITIONS

The Cookbook that Challenges Politically Correct Nutrition and the Diet Dictocrats

Sally Fallon
with Pat Connolly and Mary G. Enig, Ph.D.
Cover Design by Kim Waters Murray
Illustrations by Marion Dearth

NOURISHING TRADITIONS

The Cookbook that Challenges
Politically Correct Nutrition
and the Diet Dictocrats

A Note to the Reader: The ideas and suggestions contained in this book are not intended as a substitute for appropriate care of a licensed health practitioner.

Published by:
ProMotion Publishing
3368 F Governor Drive, Suite 144
San Diego, CA 92122
1-800-231-1776

ISBN
1-887314-15-6

PRINTED IN THE UNITED STATES OF AMERICA

The authors thankfully acknowledge permission to print excerpts from the following:

From AGELESS REMEDIES FROM MOTHERS KITCHEN by Hanna Kroeger, Copyright © 1981, Reprinted by permission of the author.

From LES ALIMENTS FERMENTES TRADITIONNELS. UNE RICHESSE MECONNUE by Claude Aubert, Copyright © 1985; DIS-MOI COMMENT TU CUISINES, JE TE DIRAI COMMENT TO TE PORTES by Claude Aubert, Copyright © 1987; and DES CRUDITES TOUTE L'ANNEE by Annelies Schoneck, Copyright © 1988, Reprinted by permission of Terre Vivante, Mens, France.

From CHOLESTEROL AND YOUR HEALTH by Christopher Mudd, M.S., J.S., Copyright © 1990. Reprinted by permission of the author.

From A DIET OF TRIPE by Terence McLaughlin, Copyright © 1978, Reprinted by permission of David & Charles, Publishers.

From EAT RIGHT TO LIVE LONGER by Cass Igram, M.D., Copyright © 1989, The American Institute of Curative Nutrition. Reprinted by permission of the author.

From ENZYMES FOR HEALTH AND LONGEVITY by Edward Howell, M.D., Copyright © 1980. Reprinted by permission of the National Enzyme Company.

From ENZYME NUTRITION by Edward Howell, M.D., Copyright © 1985. Reprinted by permission of Avery Publishing Group, Inc.

From FIGHTING THE FOOD GIANTS by Paul Stitt, Copyright © 1990. Reprinted by permission of the author.

From FLAX OIL AS A TRUE AID AGAINST ARTHRITIS, HEART INFARCTION, CANCER AND OTHER DISEASES by Johanna Budwig, © 1992. Reprinted by permission of Apple Publishing Company.

From FOOD IS YOUR BEST MEDICINE by Henry G. Bieler, MD Copyright © 1965 by Henry G. Bieler. Reprinted by permission of Random House, Inc.

From THE FOOD PHARMACY by Jean Carper. Copyright © 1988 by Jean Carper. Used by permission of Bantam Books, a division of Bantam Doubleday Dell Publishing Group, Inc.

From THE FOOD PHARMACY GUIDE TO GOOD EATING by Jean Carper. Copyright © 1991 by Jean Carper. Used by permission of Bantam Books, a division of Bantam Doubleday Dell Publishing Group, Inc.

From A FOREST JOURNEY by John Perlin, Copyright © 1989. Reprinted by permission of W.W. Norton & Company, Inc.

From THE GOOD LAND by Patricia Mitchell, Copyright © 1992, Reprinted by permission of the author.

From HANDBOOK OF INDIGENOUS FERMENTED FOODS, Keith Steinkraus, Ed., Copyright © 1983. Reprinted by permission of Marcel Dekker.

From THE KELLOGG REPORT by Joseph D. Beasely, M.D. and Jerry J. Swift, M.A., Copyright © 1989. Reprinted by permission of the authors.

From THE LOG OF CHRISTOPHER COLUMBUS by Robert H. Fuson. Original English language edition published by International Marine Published Company, Camden, Maine, U.S.A., Copyright © 1987 by Robert H. Fuson, all Rights Reserved. Reprinted by Permission of McGraw Hill, Inc. Professional Book Group.

From THE MILK OF HUMAN KINDNESS IS NOT PASTEURIZED by William Campbell Douglass, M.D., Copyright © 1985; SECOND OPINION; and EAT YOUR CHOLESTEROL by William Campbell Douglas, M.D. Reprinted by Permission.

From "NEW" TRITION by George Meinig, D.D. S., Copyright © 1987, Reprinted by permission of the author.

From NOURISHING WISDOM by David Marc, Copyright © 1991 by David Marc. Reprinted by permission of Bell Tower, a division of Crown Publishers, Inc.

From NUTRITION ALMANAC by J Kirshmann, Copyright © 1990. Reprinted by permission of McGraw-Hill, Inc.

From NUTRITION AND PHYSICAL DEGENERATION by Weston A. Price, Copyright © 1989; THE FRIENDLY BACTERIA by William H. Lee, R.Ph. and Ray C. Wunderlich, Copyright © 1991; DR. NEWBOLD'S TYPE A TYPE B WEIGHT LOSS by H.L. Newbold, M.D., Copyright © 1991; YOUR BODY IS YOUR BEST DOCTOR by Melvin E. Page, D.D.S. and Leon Abrams, Jr., Ph.D., Copyright © 1991; VICTORY OVER DIABETES by William H. Philpott, M.D. and Dwight K. Kalita, Ph.D., Copyright © 1983; OCTACOSANOL, CARNITINE AND OTHER "ACCESSORY" NUTRIENTS by Jeffrey Bland, Ph.D., copyright © 1982; SOLVED, THE RIDDLE OF ILLNESS by Stephen E. Langer, M.D. and James Scheer, Copyright © 1995; and NUTRITION FOR TOTS TO TEENS by Emory W. Thurston, Ph.D., Sc.D. Copyright © 1979. Published by Keats Publishing Inc., New Canaan, CT. Reprinted by Permission.

From ORTHOMOLECULAR PSYCHIATRY; and HOW TO LIVE LONGER AND FEEL BETTER by Linus Pauling, Ph.D. Reprinted by permission of the Linus Pauling Institute of Science & Medicine, Palo Alto, California.

From SEASALT'S HIDDEN POWERS by Jacques DeLangre, Copyright © 1992. Published by Happiness Press, Magalia, California. Reprinted by Permission.

From SMART FOR LIFE by Michael D. Chafetz. Copyright © 1992 by Michael D. Chafetz. Used by permission of Viking Penguin, a division of Penguin Books USA, Inc.

From SUPERIMMUNITY FOR KIDS by Leo Galland and Dian Dincin Buchman. Copyright © 1988 by Copestone Press, Inc. Used by permission of Dutton Signet, a division of Penquin Books USA, Inc.

From SUGAR BLUES by William Dufty, Copyright © 1975. Reprinted by permission of the author.

From "Adding extra bacteria. . . ", *New Scientist*. Reprinted by permission of The New Scientist.

From "Can Foie Gras Aid the Heart? A French Scientist Says Yes" by Molly O'Neill, 11/17/91; "A Treasure Hunt For Korean Foods" by Elaine Louie, 5/11/94; and "Study Shows Viral Mutation Due to Nutritional Deficiency" by Warren Leary, 5/1/95 *The New York Times*, Copyright © 1991/94/95 by the New York Times Company. Reprinted by Permission.

From "Corn: Builder of Cities" by Mary Talbot Fall/Winter 1991 from *Newsweek* © 1991, Newsweek, Inc. All rights reserved. Reprinted by Permission.

From "Egg yolk as a source of long-chain polyunsaturated fatty acids in infant feeding" by Artemis P. Simopoulos and Norman Salem, Jr. *American Journal of Clinical Nutrition*, Vol 55, 1992. Reprinted by permission of the American Society for Clinical Nutrition and the authors.

From "Facts on Fats and Oils"; and *Search For Health* by Tom Valentine. Reprinted by permission of the author.

From "Fish Sauces Add a Subtle Grace Note", by John Willoughby and Chris Schlesinger, *The New York Times*, March 1994. Reprinted by permission of The New York Times.

From "Free radical pathology in age associated diseases: Treatment with EDTA chelation therapy, nutrition and anti-oxidants" by E.M. Cranton, M.D. and J.P. Frackelton, M.D. *Journal of Holistic Medicine* Spring/Summer 1984. Reprinted by Permission of the Journal of Holistic Medicine.

From *Health Freedom News*. Reprinted by permission of the National Health Federation.

From "Infant Formula" July 28, 1995. Reprinted by permission of Community Nutrition Institute, Washington, D.C.

From "Lower cholesterol increases risks of violent death", reprinted by permission of Reuters.

From "Low serum cholesterol and suicide" by Hyman Engelberg, M.D., *The Lancet*, March 21, 1992. Reprinted by permission of The Lancet, Ltd.

From "The Margarine Masquerade" by Judith DeCava, *Journal of the National Academy of Research Biochemists*, September 1988. Reprinted by permission of the National Academy of Research Biochemists, Inc.

From *Price Pottenger Nutrtion Foundation Journal*. Reprinted by permission of the Price Pottenger Nutrition Foundation.

From "Synergy in the Garden" by Jim Duke, Ph.D., *Organic Gardening* July/Aug 1995. Reprinted by Permission of RODALE'S ORGANIC GARDENING magazine. Copyright 1995. Rodale Press, Inc. U.S.A. All rights reserved. For a one-year subscription send $25.00 to Organic Gardening, 33 E. Minor St. Emmaus, PA 18098.

From "Tripe is Losing its Savor in the Land of Offal as Innards Prices Soar" by Peter Gumbul, *The Wall Street Journal*, 11/11/93. Reprinted by permission of The Wall Street Journal © Dow Jones & Company, Inc. All Rights Reserved Worldwide.

From "Vegetarianism: An Anthropological/Nutritional Evaluation" by H. Leon Abrams, Jr. Vol. 2, No. 2, 1980, *Journal of Applied Nutrition*. Reprinted by permission of the author.

From "When he was a boy in Japan. . . ," *Palisades Citizens News*. Reprinted by permission of the Palisades Citizens Association.

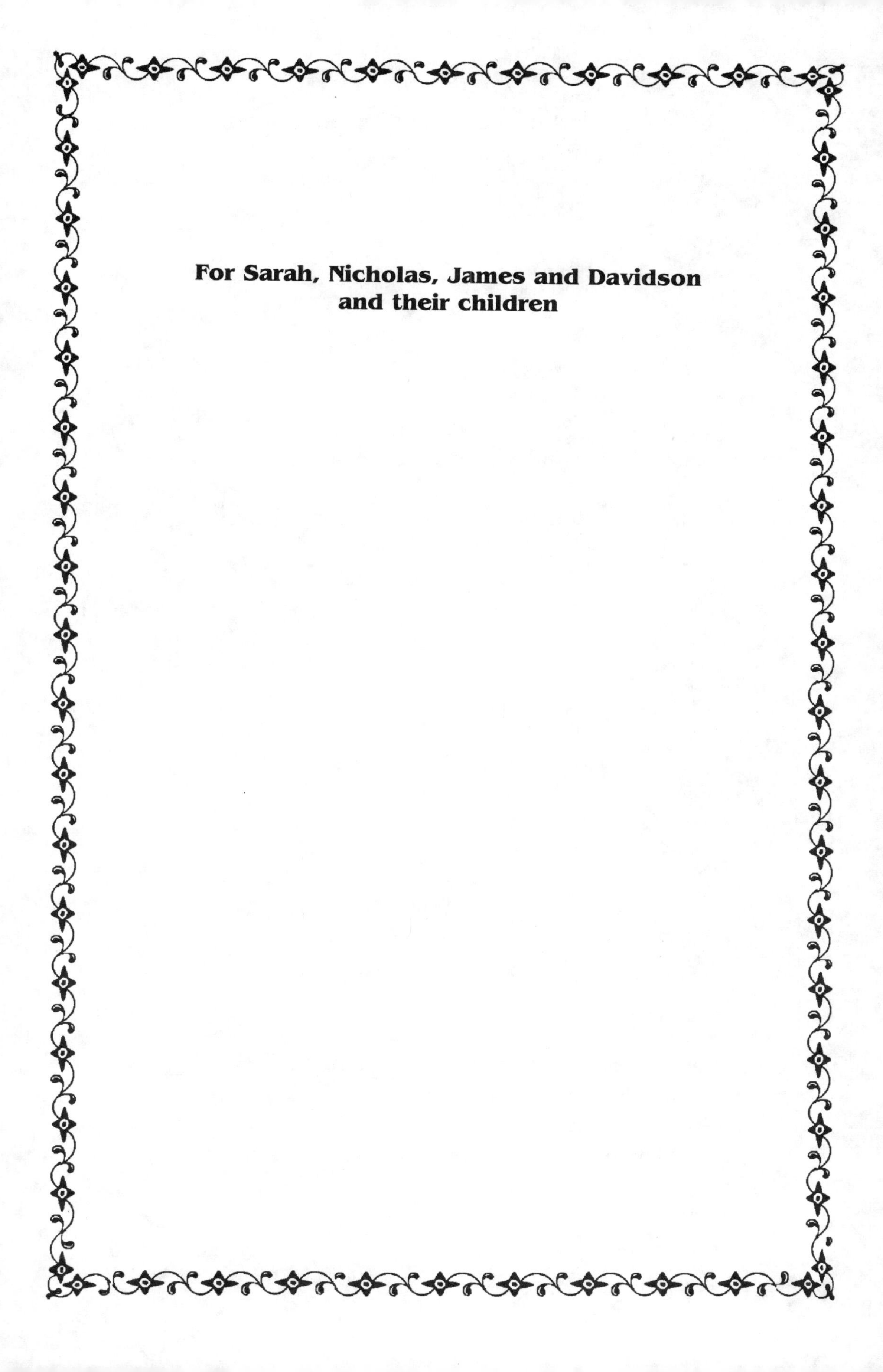

For Sarah, Nicholas, James and Davidson and their children

ACKNOWLEDGEMENTS

The authors are grateful to Mary Ann Gregory, whose suggestion planted the seed for this book; to those who watered it with their encouragement and help including Dr. Alsop Corwin, H. Leon Abrams, Jr., Stephen Acuff, Patrick Van Mauck, Dr. Meira Fields, Leyla Uran, Zeynep Gur, Tamas and Hajna Dakun, Pam Howell, Jeffrey Dearth, Jim and Christine Murphy, Valerie Curry, Charlie Votaw, Richard Thomas, Tom Dix, Cy Nelson, Randolph and Ginny Aires, Carmen and George Denby, Trudy Fallon, Jon Cutler, Supat Sirivicha, Ira Wexler, Chris Archila, Vladimir Ratsimer, Lynn Greaves, Kurt Reiman, Fred Gregory, Dr. Artemis Simopoulos, Bill Shawn, Christopher Hartman, Bob White, Diana Vivian, Mary Hudson and Milka Halama; and to John Fallon whose support and enthusiasm never faltered.

Particular thanks goes to Maggie Wetzel who always used butter.

We also wish to thank those who contributed recipes: Maggie Wetzel, Harry Wetzel and Katie Wetzel; Mary Ann Gregory; John Desmond; Rosemary Barron; Sally Hazell Fallon, Ann Marie Fallon and Tom Fallon; Philomena Aparacio; Madaline Curry; Moustafa and Lynn Soliman; Sue Rogers; Carole Valentine; Audrey Powell; Maribel Kim; Vivian Mason; June Shields; Marie Meyer; Taiwo Obi; Thomas Connelly; Isabel Molin; Maria de Lourdes Campos; Tony Rossi, Mary Jo Bierline; Emily Sagar; Karen Acuff; Soroor Ehteshami; Maria Noguera and Marie Claude Leduc.

CONTENTS

PREFACE

Technology is a generous benefactor. To those who have wisely used his gifts he has bestowed freedom from drudgery, freedom to travel, freedom from the discomforts of cold, heat and dirt, and freedom from ignorance, boredom and oppression. But father technology has not brought us freedom from disease. Chronic illness in industrialized nations has reached epic proportions because we have been dazzled by his stepchildren—fast foods, fractionated foods, convenience foods, packaged foods, fake foods, embalmed foods, ersatz foods—all the bright baubles that fill up the shelves at our grocery stores, convenience markets, vending machines and even health food stores.

The premise of this book is that modern food choices and preparation techniques constitute a radical change from the way man has nourished himself for thousands of years and, from the perspective of history, represent a fad that not only has severely compromised his health and vitality, but may well destroy him; and that the culinary traditions of our ancestors, and the food choices and preparation techniques of healthy nonindustrialized peoples, should serve as the model for contemporary eating habits, even and especially during this modern technological age.

The first modern researcher to take a careful look at the health and eating habits of isolated traditional societies was a dentist, Dr. Weston Price. Fifty years ago, Dr. Price traveled the world over to observe population groups untouched by civilization, living entirely on local foods. While the diets of these peoples differed in many particulars, they contained several factors in common. Almost without exception, the groups he studied ate liberally of seafood or other animal proteins and fats in the form of organ meats and dairy products; they valued animal fats as absolutely necessary to good health; and they ate fats, meats, fruits, vegetables, legumes, nuts, seeds and whole grains in their natural, unrefined state. A high portion of these primitive diets consisted of raw foods, of both animal and vegetable origin.

In all of these groups—from isolated Irish and Swiss, from Eskimos to Africans—Dr. Price observed superb health in almost every member of the tribe or village. They were free of chronic disease, dental decay and mental illness; they were strong, sturdy and attractive; and they produced healthy children with ease, generation after generation.

Dr. Price found many occasions to compare these healthy primitives with their civilized counterparts, living on the products of the industrial revolution—refined grains, canned foods, pasteurized milk and sugar. In these peoples, he found rampant tooth decay, diseases both infectious and degenerative, and infertility. Children born to primitives who had adopted the white man's diet had crowded and crooked teeth, narrowed faces, deformities of bone structure, susceptibility to infectious illness and chronic disease. Studies too numerous to count have confirmed Dr. Price's observations that the civilized diet, particularly the Western diet of refined carbohydrates and devitalized fats and oils, undermines and despoils our God-given genetic inheritance of physical perfection and vibrant health.

Later research on the diets of primitive and nonindustrialized peoples has focussed on their food preparation techniques. Almost universally among these peoples, grains, milk products and often vegetables, fruits and meats are allowed to ferment or pickle before they are eaten. These pickling techniques preserve foods so that they are available during periods of scarcity, but unlike modern preservation methods, which deaden and denature our foods, this process of lacto-fermentation makes nutrients in these foods more available, and supplies the intestinal tract with health-promoting lactic acid and lactic-acid-producing bacteria.

Another technique found universally in ethnic cuisines is the use of gelatin-rich meat broths with cooked food. The archives of our medical libraries contain many studies on the beneficial effect of gelatin taken on a daily or frequent basis, but these studies are ignored even as methods for making rich broths are forgotten.

Technology can be a kind father, but only in partnership with his mothering, feminine partner—the nourishing traditions of our ancestors. These traditions require us to apply more wisdom to the way we produce and process our food, and yes, more time in the kitchen, but they give highly satisfying results—delicious meals, increased vitality, robust children and freedom from the chains of acute and chronic illness. The wise and loving marriage of modern invention with the sustaining, nurturing food folkways of our ancestors is the partnership that will transform the Twenty-First Century into an age of gold; divorce hastens the physical degeneration of the human race, cheats mankind of his unlimited potential, destroys his will and condemns him to the role of undercitizen in a totalitarian world order.

INTRODUCTION

In no period of our history as a nation have Americans been so concerned about the subject of diet and nutrition. Yet if we accept the premise that what we eat determines our health, then we must add the observation that in no period of our history as a nation have Americans eaten so poorly, a statement that the most cursory survey of current statistics can prove.

Although heart disease and cancer were rare at the turn of the century, today these two diseases strike with increasing frequency, in spite of billions of dollars in research to combat them, and in spite of tremendous advances in diagnostic and surgical techniques. In America, one person in three dies of cancer, one in three suffers from allergies, one in ten will have ulcers and one in five is mentally ill. Continuing this grim litany, one out of five pregnancies ends in miscarriage and one quarter of a million infants are born with a birth defect each year. Other degenerative diseases—arthritis, multiple sclerosis, digestive disorders, diabetes, osteoporosis, Alzheimers, epilepsy and chronic fatigue—afflict a significant majority of our citizens, sapping the energy and the very life blood of our nation. Learning disabilities such as dyslexia and hyperactivity afflict seven million young people. These diseases were also extremely rare only a generation or two ago.

Today, chronic illness afflicts nearly half of all Americans and causes three out of four deaths in the United States. Most tragically, these diseases, formerly the purview of the very old, now strike our children and those in the prime of life.

Americans spend one dollar out of every fourteen for medical services or over $800 billion yearly, more than the national deficit, the food bill and the profits of all US corporations combined. Yet, we have little to show for this tremendous drain on our resources. Medical science has not even been able to lengthen our life-span. Fewer persons alive at 70 today survive until 90 than 40 years ago, the longer average life-span being due to saving the lives of children through improved sanitation. And those who do survive past 70 are often a helpless burden to their families, rather than useful members of society. New killer viruses now command newspaper headlines and even infectious diseases such as TB, whose control has been a notable achievement of orthodox medicine, are making a comeback, this time in forms resistant to allopathic drugs.

POLITICALLY CORRECT NUTRITION

Clearly something is very wrong, even though many Americans have been conscientious about following the dietary advice of the experts. They take exercise seriously; many have stopped smoking; consumption of fresh vegetables has increased; many have reduced their intake of salt; and a good portion of Americanshave cut back on red meats and animal fats. But none of these measures has made a dent in the ever increasing toll of degenerative disease. We buy foods labeled low-fat, no cholesterol, reduced sodium, thinking they are good for us. Why, then, are we so sick?

The premise of this book is that the advice of the Diet Dictocrats—what they tell us and, just as important, what they don't tell us—is wrong. Not 100% wrong. There is a certain amount of truth in their pronouncements, enough to give them credibility, but not enough to save us from the sufferings of chronic disease.

Who are the Diet Dictocrats? In general they are doctors, researchers and spokesmen for various government and quasi-government agencies such as the Food and Drug Administration; the American Medical Association; prestigious hospitals and research centers such as Sloan-Kettering and the National Institutes of Health; university medical schools and nutrition departments; and large philanthropic organizations like the National Heart and Lung Institute and the American Cancer Society, ostensibly dedicated to combatting our most serious diseases. Based on what we read in the newspapers and national magazines, these organizations speak with one voice. "Exercise, eat vegetables, stop smoking, reduce salt," they say, "and cut back or eliminate animal fats and red meat." Most recently, the Department of Agriculture issued new nutritional guidelines in the form of a pyramid, calling for a diet based on grains—bread, pasta, cereal and crackers—along with fruits and vegetables. The guidelines recommend only moderate amounts of protein foods—meat, fowl, fish, nuts and legumes—and strictly limited consumption of sweets and fats.

The new guidelines have their good points. They are right, for example, in calling for a reduction in sweets in the American diet. We must recognize and applaud progress wherever we find it. Since 1923, when a US Farmers Bulletin recommended one pound of sugar per person per week, consumers have heard numerous government reassurances that sugar was harmless. During the last few years these soothing voices have fallen quiet as the evidence against sugar continues to mount. As far as we are aware, the new Department of Agriculture guidelines represent the first time a government agency has warned us against eating too much sugar. Whether the popular press will emphasize this feature of the Food Pyramid remains to be seen.

The new food guidelines rightly give fruits and vegetables their due, placing them just above grains. For many years, the establishment said little about fruits and vegetables; the American Cancer Society even went so far as to publicly deny the role of fresh vegetables in preventing cancer. Research has proven them wrong and fruits and vegetables are now receiving just recognition.

But several dangerous errors are built into the edifice of the Food Pyramid. First, the new guidelines imply that everyone can eat the same foods in the same proportions and be healthy. According to Department of Agriculture recommendations, grains should be the basis of our diet; but many people do very poorly on grains.

Others cannot tolerate dairy products. These intolerances are due to genetic and other factors. Secondly, the pyramid calls for reduced fats without addressing the dangers of low-fat diets. Finally, the new guidelines perpetuate the myth that fats, carbohydrates and proteins have equal nutritional properties no matter how much or how little they are processed. The experts make no distinction between whole grains and refined, between food grown organically and those grown with pesticides and commercial fertilizers; between raw milk and pasteurized; between fresh and rancid fats; between fresh and processed fruits and vegetables; between range-fed meats and those raised in crowded pens; between natural and battery-produced eggs, between foods that nourished our ancestors and new-fangled products that dominate the marketplace.

This is Politically Correct Nutrition. It singles out foods grown by independent producers—eggs and beef—but spares the highly profitable and powerful grain cartels, vegetable oil producers and food processing industry; it sacrifices old-fashioned butter on the altar of the latest nutritional fad, but spares highly processed milk products and ice cream; it gives lip service to the overwhelming evidence implicating sugar as a major cause of our degenerative diseases but spares the soft drink industry; and it raises not a murmur against the refining of flour, the hydrogenation of vegetable oils and the adulteration of our foods with harmful preservatives, flavorings and coloring agents.

The Diet Dictocrats are strangely silent about the ever increasing trend toward food processing and the devitalization of America's rich agricultural bounty. Food processing is the largest manufacturing industry in the country, and hence the most powerful. This industry naturally uses its financial clout to influence the slant of university research and the dictates that come from government agencies. A 1980 study showed that almost half the leading officials at the FDA had previously worked for organizations the agency is mandated to regulate. The universities have equally powerful ties to the food processing industry. A good example is Harvard University where Dr. Frederick Stare, head of the nutrition department for many years, began his career with several articles delineating nutritional deficiencies caused by white flour; and a study on Irish priests that positively correlated a high intake of vegetable oils with heart disease, while exonerating animal fats as a cause. Soon after he became department head, however, the university received several important grants from the food processing industry. Dr. Stare's articles and weekly newspaper columns then began assuring the public that there was nothing wrong with white bread, sugar and highly processed foods. He recommended one cup of corn oil per day for heart disease and in one article he even suggested Coca Cola as a snack!

Many nutritional cookbooks have been written according to the Diet Dictocrats' politically correct guidelines, including all those approved by the American Heart Association. A good example is the best selling *Eater's Choice* by Dr. Ron Goor and Nancy Goor. A brief introduction rehashing a few politically correct studies, said to implicate saturated fats as the cause of heart disease, is followed by pages of recipes just loaded with sugar and white flour. The authors assure us that the best thing we can do for our hearts is to replace butter with margarine and eliminate eggs and red meat from our diet, in spite of the fact that most studies, honestly evaluated, show that such a diet is not only useless but also harmful.

FATS

Fats from animal and vegetable sources provide a concentrated source of energy in the diet; they also provide the building blocks for cell membranes, for hormones and for prostaglandins. In addition, they act as carriers for important fat-soluble vitamins A, D, E and K. Dietary fats are needed for the conversion of carotene to vitamin A and for a host of other processes.

Politically Correct Nutrition is based on the assumption that we should reduce our intake of fats, particularly saturated fats from animal sources. Fats from animal sources contain cholesterol, presented as the villain of the civilized diet.

The theory—and it is only a theory—that there is a direct relationship between the amount of saturated fat in the diet and the incidence of coronary heart disease, as well as certain types of cancer, was proposed by a researcher named Ancel Keys in the late 1950's. Numerous subsequent studies have questioned his data and conclusions. Nevertheless, Keys' articles received far more publicity than those contradicting him. The vegetable oil industry and food processing industries, the main beneficiaries of the saturated fat/heart disease connection, began promoting and funding further research designed to support Keys' theories.

The most well-known advocate of the low-fat diet was Dr. Nathan Pritikin. Actually Pritikin advocated eliminating sugar, white flour and all processed foods from the diet, and recommended the use of fresh raw foods, whole grains and a strenuous exercise program; but it was the low-fat aspects of his regime that received the most attention in the media. Adherents found that they lost weight and that their blood cholesterol levels and blood pressure declined. The success of the Pritikin diet was probably due to a number of factors having nothing to do reduction in dietary fat —weight loss alone, for example, will precipitate a reduction in blood cholesterol levels—but Pritikin soon found that the fat-free diet presented many problems, not the least of which was the fact that people just could not stay on it. Those who possessed enough will power to stay fat-free for any length of time developed a variety of health problems including low energy, difficulty in concentration, depression, weight gain and signs of mineral deficiencies.[1] Pritikin may have saved himself from heart disease but his low-fat diet did not spare him from cancer. He died, in the prime of life, of leukemia. We shouldn't have to die of either disease.

After problems with the no-fat regime became apparent, Pritikin introduced a small amount of fat from vegetable sources into his diet—something like 10% of the total caloric intake. Today the Diet Dictocrats advise us to limit fats to 25-30% of the caloric intake (12 to 15 % of the diet by weight). A careful reckoning of daily fat intake, and avoidance of animal fats, is presented as the key to perfect health.

The experts assure us that the theory that animal fat consumption causes coronary heart disease is backed by abundant evidence. Most people would be surprised to learn that there is, in fact, very little evidence to support the contention that a diet low in cholesterol and saturated fat actually reduces death from heart disease or in any way increases one's life-span. Consider the following:

Before 1920, coronary heart disease was rare in America, so rare that when a young internist named Paul Dudley White introduced the German electrocardiograph to his colleagues at Harvard University, they advised him to concentrate on a more profitable branch of medicine. The new machine revealed the presence of arterial blockages, thus permitting early diagnosis of coronary heart disease; but in those days clogged arteries were a medical rarity, and White had to search for patients who could benefit from his new technology. During the next forty years, however, the incidence of coronary heart disease rose dramatically, so much so that by the mid-fifties, heart disease was the leading cause of death among Americans. Today heart disease causes 40% of all US deaths. If, as we have been told, heart disease results from the consumption of saturated fats, one would expect to find a corresponding increase in animal fat in the American diet. Actually the reverse is true. During the sixty year period from 1910 to 1970, the proportion of traditional animal fat in the American diet declined from 83% to 62%, and butter consumption plummeted from 18 pounds per person per year to 4. During the past eighty years, dietary cholesterol intake has increased only 1%. During the same period the percentage of dietary vegetable fat in the form of margarine, shortening and refined oils increased about 400% and the consumption of sugar and processed foods increased about 60%.[2]

The Framingham Heart Study is often cited as proof of the cholesterol/animal fat theory. This study began in 1948 and involved about 6,000 people from the town of Framingham, Massachusetts. Two groups were compared at five year intervals—those who consumed little cholesterol and saturated fat and those who consumed large amounts. Today, after 40 years, the current director of this study admits, "In Framingham, Mass, the more saturated fat one ate, the more cholesterol one ate, the more calories one ate, the lower the person's serum cholesterol. . . we found that the people who ate the most cholesterol, ate the most saturated fat, ate the most calories, weighed the least and were the most physically active."[3] The study did show that those who weighed more and had higher blood cholesterol levels were more at risk for future coronary heart disease; but weight gain and cholesterol levels had an inverse correlation with fat and cholesterol intake in the diet.[4]

In a multi-year British study involving several thousand men, half were asked to reduce saturated fat and cholesterol in their diets, to stop smoking and to increase the amounts of unsaturated oils such as margarine and vegetable oils. After one year, those on the "good" diet had 100% more deaths than those on the "bad" diet, in spite of the fact that those men on the "bad" diet continued to smoke! But in describing the study, the author ignored these results and gave a politically correct conclusion: "The implication for public health policy in the U.K. is that a preventive programme such as we evaluated in this trial is probably effective. . ."[5]

The US Multiple Risk Factor Intervention Trial, sponsored by the National Heart and Lung Institute, compared mortality rates and eating habits of over 12,000 men. Those with "good" dietary habits (reduced saturated fat and cholesterol, reduced smoking, etc.) showed a marginal reduction in total coronary heart disease rates, but their overall mortality from all causes was higher. Similar results have been obtained in several other studies. The few studies that indicate a correlation between fat reduction and a decrease in coronary heart disease mortality also document a concurrent increase in deaths from cancer, brain hemorrhage, suicide and violent death.[6]

The Lipid Research Clinics Coronary Primary Prevention Trial (LRC-CPPT), which cost 150 million dollars, is the study most often cited by the experts to justify the low-fat diet. Actually, dietary cholesterol and saturated fat were not tested in this study as all subjects were already on a low-cholesterol, low-saturated-fat diet. Instead, the study tested the effects of a cholesterol-lowering drug. Statistical analysis of the results indicated a 24% reduction in the rate of coronary heart disease rate in the group taking drugs compared with the placebo group; however, non-heart disease deaths in the drug group increased—deaths from cancer, stroke, violence and suicide.[7] Even the claim that a diet low in saturated fat and cholesterol reduced heart disease is suspect. Independent researchers who tabulated the results of this study found *no* significant statistical difference in the coronary heart disease death rate between the two groups.[8] However both the popular press and medical journals touted the LRC-CPPT survey as the long-sought proof that animal fats are the cause of heart disease, America's number one killer.

While it is true that researchers have induced heart disease in animals by giving them extremely large dosages of cholesterol—amounts ten times that found in the ordinary human diet—several population surveys squarely contradict the cholesterol-heart disease connection. A survey of 1700 patients with hardening of the arteries, conducted by the famous heart surgeon Michael DeBakey, found no relationship between the level of cholesterol in the blood and the incidence of atherosclerosis.[9] A survey of South Carolina adults found no correlation with blood cholesterol levels and "bad" dietary habits such as use of red meat, animal fats, fried foods, butter, eggs, whole milk, bacon, sausage and cheese.[10] A Medical Research Council survey showed that men eating butter ran half the risk of developing heart disease as those using margarine.[11]

Mother's milk contains a higher portion of cholesterol than almost any other food. It also contains over 50% of its calories as fat, much of it saturated fat. Both cholesterol and saturated fat are essential for growth in babies and children, especially development of the brain.[12] Yet, the American Heart Association is now recommending a low-cholesterol, low-fat diet for children! Commercial formulas are low in saturated fats and some are almost completely devoid of cholesterol. A recent study linked a low-fat diet with failure to thrive in children.[13]

Numerous surveys of traditional populations have yielded information that is an embarrassment to the Diet Dictocrats. For example, a study comparing Jews living in Yemen, whose diets contain fats solely of animal origin, to Jews living in Israel, whose diets contain margarine and vegetable oils, revealed little heart disease in the former group but high levels of both heart disease and diabetes in the latter.[14] (The study also noted that the Yemenite Jews consumed no sugar but those in Israel consumed it in amounts equaling 25 to 30% of total carbohydrate intake.) A comparison of populations in northern and southern India revealed a similar pattern. People in northern India consume 17 times more animal fat but have an incidence of coronary heart disease 7 times lower than people in southern India.[15] The Masai and kindred tribes of Africa subsist largely on milk and beef. They are free from coronary heart disease, and have excellent blood cholesterol levels.[16] Eskimos eat liberally of animal fats from fish and marine animals. On their native diet they are disease-free, and exceptionally hardy.[17] Several Mediterranean societies are free of heart and circulatory disease even though fat comprises up to 70% of their caloric intake. The inhabitants of Crete use large amounts of unrefined olive oil in cooking and on all foods. They are remarkable for their good health and longevity.[18] A study of Puerto Ricans revealed that although they consume large amounts of animal fat, they have a very low incidence of colon and breast cancer.[19] None of these studies is mentioned by those urging restriction of saturated fats.

The relative good health of the Japanese, who have the longest life-span in the world, is generally attributed to a low-fat diet. Although the Japanese eat few dairy fats, the notion that their diet is low in fat is a myth; rather it contains moderate amounts of animal fats from eggs, chicken, beef, seafood and organ meats. With their fondness for shellfish and fish broth, eaten on a daily basis, the Japanese probably consume more cholesterol than most Americans. What they do *not* consume is a lot of vegetable oil, white flour or processed food (although they do eat white rice.) Those who point to Japanese statistics to promote the low-fat diet fail to mention that the Swiss live almost as long on one of the fattiest diets in the world. Tied for third in the longevity stakes are Austria and Greece—both with high-fat diets.[20]

As a final example, let us consider the French. Anyone who has eaten his way across France has observed that the French diet is just loaded with saturated fats in the form of butter, eggs, cheese, cream, liver, meats and rich pates. Yet the French have a lower rate of coronary heart disease than many other western countries. In the United States, 315 of every 100,000 middle aged men die of heart attacks each year; in France the rate is 145 per 100,000. In the Gascony region, where goose and duck liver form a staple of the diet, this rate is a remarkably low 80 per 100,000.[21] This phenomenon has recently gained international attention and has been dubbed the *paradoxe francais*. (The French do suffer from many degenerative diseases, however. They eat large amounts of sugar and white flour and little in the way of whole grains; and in recent years have succumbed to the time-saving temptations of processed foods.)

Clearly something is wrong with the theories we read in the popular press (and used to bolster sales of "low-fat" concoctions and cholesterol-free foods.) The notion that saturated fats *per se* cause heart disease as well as cancer is not only facile, it is just plain wrong. But it *is* true that some fats are bad for us. In order to understand which ones, we must know something about the chemistry of fats

Fats—or lipids—are a miscellaneous grouping of organic substances that are not soluble in water. Most fat in our bodies and in the food we eat is in the form of triglycerides, that is, three fatty acid chains attached to a glycerol molecule. Elevated triglycerides in the blood have been positively linked to proneness to heart disease but these triglycerides do not come directly from dietary fats; they are made in the liver from any excess sugars that have not been completely burned. The source of these excess sugars is any food containing carbohydrates, but particularly refined sugar and processed carbohydrates.

In simple terms, fatty acids are chains of carbon atoms with hydrogen linkages. A fatty acid is called saturated when all available carbon bonds are occupied by a hydrogen atom. Monounsaturated fatty acids have two carbon atoms double-bonded to each other and therefore lack two hydrogen atoms. The single unsaturated fatty acid most commonly found in our food is oleic acid, the main component of olive oil. Polyunsaturated fatty acids have two or more pairs of carbon double bonds and therefore lack four or more hydrogen atoms. The two polyunsaturated fatty acids found most frequently in our foods are double unsaturated linoleic acid with two double carbon bonds (also called omega-6); and triple unsaturated linolenic acid with three double bonds (also called omega-3).

All fats and oils, whether of vegetable or animal origin, are some combination of saturated fatty acids, monounsaturated fatty acids (oleic acid) and the polyunsaturates linoleic and linolenic acid. In general animal fats such as butter, lard and tallow contain about 50% saturated fat and are solid at room temperature. Vegetable fats from northern climates contain a preponderance of polyunsaturated fatty acids and are liquid at room temperature. But vegetable oils from the tropics are highly saturated. Coconut oil, for example, is 92% saturated. These fats are liquid in the tropics, but hard as butter in northern climes. Highly saturated tropical oils such as coconut and palm oil are not harmful, as the popular press would lead us to believe. These fats and oils have nourished healthy populations, free of heart disease, for millennia.[22] Vegetable oils are more saturated in hot climates because the increased saturation helps maintain stiffness in plant leaves. Olive oil with its preponderance of oleic acid is the product of a temperate climate. It is liquid at warm temperatures but hardens when refrigerated.

Researchers classify fatty acids not only according to their degree of saturation but also by their length. Short chain fatty acids have 4 to 6 carbon atoms; medium length fatty acids have 8 to 12; long chain fatty acids have 14 to 18 carbon atoms and very long chain fatty acids have 20 to 24 carbon atoms. Saturated fats vary in length from short to long—butter and coconut oil contain a large portion of short and medium chain fatty acids, while stearic acid, the main component of beef fat, is a long chain fatty acid with 18 carbons. Oleic acid, linoleic acid and linolenic acid also have 18 carbons. Very long chain fatty acids, such as those found in fish oils and organ tissues, tend to be highly unsaturated, with four, five and even six double bonds.

Short and medium chain fatty acids have several interesting properties. Unlike the longer chain fatty acids which are absorbed by the lymph system and must be acted on by the bile salts, short chain fatty acids are absorbed directly through the portal vein to the liver. As they do not need to be acted upon by the bile salts, these short and medium chain fatty acids supply quick energy. In general, the body uses the longer chain fatty acids, including the longer chain saturated fatty acids, to construct membranes and vital hormone-like substances, to create electric potentials and move electric currents.

It is the longer chain fatty acids that are stored in the adipose tissue, particularly oleic and linoleic acid.[23] Thus butter and coconut oil, which contain a significant portion of short and medium chain fatty acids, do not contribute to weight gain as much as olive oil and vegetable oil.[24] The short and medium chain fatty acids also have anti-microbial and anti-fungal properties in the intestinal tract; they have anti-tumor properties and help strengthen the immune system,[25] while an excess of polyunsaturated fatty acids stimulates tumor growth.[26]

Unsaturated omega-3 and omega-6 fatty acids are called essential fatty acids or EFA's because the body cannot manufacture them, at least not in the form in which they occur in foods. Researchers vary in their estimates of the amount of polyunsaturated fatty acids needed in the diet, giving figures as low as 0.5% and as high as 15%, but recent scientific evidence supports the lower range and has led knowledgeable researchers to recommend limiting our intake of polyunsaturates to 4% of the caloric total, in approximate proportions 1 1/2 % omega-3 linolenic acid and 2 1/2 % omega-6 linoleic acid.[27] EFA consumption in this range is found in native populations whose intake of polyunsaturated oils comes from the small amounts found in pulses, grains, green vegetables, fish, olive oil and animal fats, but not from commercial vegetable oils. What we find in the American diet is a high intake of polyunsaturates—something like 10% to 30% of the total caloric intake—far more than the majority of primitive groups. Worse, most of these polyunsaturates are in the form of double unsaturated omega-6 linoleic acid, with very little of vital triple unsaturated linolenic acid. Recent research has revealed that too much omega-6 in the diet can interfere with the desaturase enzymes that produce longer chain highly unsaturated fatty acids, which are the precursors of important prostaglandins.[28] These are localized tissue hormones that direct many processes in the cells. When the production of prostaglandins is compromised by excess omega-6 in the diet, coupled with too little omega-3, serious problems result including inflammation, hypertension, irritation of the digestive tract, depressed immune function, sterility, cell proliferation, cancer and weight gain.[29] Other studies indicate that excessive unsaturated fatty acids in the diet of infants can interfere with brain development and with learning and behavior.[30] In contrast, dietary saturated fats contribute to optimal utilization of essential fatty acids.[31] Thus, although not called essential, saturated fats are absolutely necessary in the diet, not only for the role they play in enhancing EFA utilization, in supplying quick energy, and in their immune system enhancing characteristics, but also because of the important vitamins they carry.

A number of researchers argue that Americans are deficient in omega-3 linolenic acid, which is necessary for cell oxidation, and for the proper metabolizing of important sulphur-containing amino acids.[32] The three double bonds in this fatty acid create a natural and powerful electron cloud that plays a vital role in many of the body's chemical processes, including the production of prostaglandins. This same feature makes linolenic acid extremely susceptible to rancidity. It is the first polyunsaturate to be damaged during high temperature refining and the process of hydrogenation; and modern agricultural and industrial practices have reduced the amount of omega-3 fatty acids in commercially available vegetables, eggs, fish and meat. For example, organic eggs can contain omega-3 and omega-6 fatty acids in the beneficial ratio of approximately one-to-one; but commercial supermarket eggs can contain as much as nineteen times more omega-6 than omega-3![33]

A serious problem with the polyunsaturate family, and particularly linolenic acid, is its instability. With their double carbon bonds, these fatty acids tend to polymerize, that is bond with each other, and bond with other molecules. They are also more easily rendered rancid when subjected to heat, oxygen and moisture as in cooking and processing. Rancid oils are characterized by free radicals in the double bond—that is, single atoms or clusters with an unpaired electron in an outer orbit. These compounds are extremely reactive chemically. They have been characterized as "marauders" in the body for they attack cell walls and red blood cells, and cause damage in DNA/RNA strands, thus triggering mutations in tissue, blood vessels and skin. Free radical damage to the skin causes wrinkles and premature aging; free radical damage to the tissues and organs sets the stage for tumors. Is it any wonder that tests and studies have repeatedly shown a high correlation between cancer and the consumption of polyunsaturates?[34] New evidence links exposure to free radicals with premature aging, with auto-immune diseases such as arthritis and to Parkinson's disease, Lou Gehrig's disease, Alzheimers and cataracts.[35]

When free radical damage occurs in blood vessels, the body's natural healing substance steps in to repair the damage—that substance is cholesterol. Cholesterol is a high-molecular-weight alcohol that is manufactured in the liver. Among its many important roles, cholesterol acts as a precursor to vital hormones like adrenaline, estrogen and progesterone and to steroids that protect against heart disease and cancer; it is a precursor to vitamin D and to bile salts; cholesterol forms a part of lipid membranes in cells, acting as a stabilizer and entering the cells in unusually high amounts to give them stiffness if the diet is too high in polyunsaturates (which is why a diet high in polyunsaturated oils may cause a drop in serum cholesterol.). Recent research shows that cholesterol plays a role as an anti-oxidant.[36] Finally, cholesterol is needed as a receptor for serotonin in the brain.[37] Low serotonin levels have been linked to aggressive and violent behavior, depression and suicidal tendencies.

Most of the body's supply of cholesterol is manufactured by the liver—only a small amount of this vital tissue healing substance comes from dietary sources. Of the cholesterol we ingest, only about one-third is absorbed through the intestines; but the cholesterol that is excreted plays an important role in maintaining the health of the intestinal wall.[38]

Cholesterol is not the cause of heart disease but, as an anti-oxidant and the body's tissue healing substance, fights against free radicals in the blood and helps plug arterial damage they cause (although the arterial plaques themselves contain very little cholesterol.) However, like fats, cholesterol may be damaged by exposure to heat and oxygen. This damaged or oxidized cholesterol seems to promote both injury to the arterial cells as well as a pathological build-up of plaque in the arteries.[39] Damaged cholesterol is found in powdered eggs and milk and in meats and fats that have been heated to high temperatures in frying and other high-temperature processes.

High serum cholesterol levels are an indication that the body needs cholesterol to protect itself from high levels of altered, free-radical-containing fats; high cholesterol levels may also be an indication of poor thyroid function (hypothyroidism). Hypothyroid individuals are particularly susceptible to infections, heart disease and cancer.[40] Thus the correlation between high blood cholesterol levels with heart disease and cancer may actually be a correlation between these killer diseases and poor thyroid function. When thyroid function is poor, often the result of a diet high in sugar and low in nutrients, the body floods the blood with cholesterol as an adaptive and protective mechanism, providing a superabundance of the materials needed to heal tissues and produce protective steroids. Just as a large police force is needed in a locality where crime occurs frequently, so cholesterol is needed in a poorly nourished body to protect the individual from a tendency to heart disease and cancer. Blaming coronary heart disease on cholesterol is like blaming the police for murder and theft in a high crime area.

While serum cholesterol levels provide an inaccurate indication of future heart disease, high levels of homocysteine, a protein metabolite, have been positively correlated with pathological build-up of plaque in the arteries. Folic acid, vitamin B6, vitamin B12 and choline are nutrients that lower serum homocysteine levels.[41]

The best way to treat heart disease, then, is not to focus on lowering cholesterol—either by drugs or diet—but to bolster thyroid function through an improved diet that provides usable iodine; to eliminate free-radical-containing foods that cause the body to need constant repair; and to avoid vitamin and mineral deficiencies that make the artery walls more prone to ruptures and the build-up of plaque. Coronary heart disease is a deficiency disease—brought on by a diet low in nutrients and high in harmful free radicals.

It is important to understand that of all substances ingested by the body, it is polyunsaturated oils that are most easily rendered dangerous by food processing, especially unstable omega-3 linolenic acid. Consider the following processes inflicted upon naturally occurring fats before they appear on our tables:

- **Extraction:** Oils naturally occurring in fruits, nuts and seeds must first be extracted. In the old days this extraction was achieved by a slow-moving stone press. But oils processed in large factories are obtained by crushing the oil bearing seeds and heating them to 230 degrees. The oil is then squeezed out at pressures from 10 to 20 tons per inch, thereby generating more heat. During this process the oils are exposed to damaging light and oxygen. In order to extract the last 10% or so of the oil from crushed seeds, processors then treat the pulp with one of a number of solvents—gasoline, hexane, benzene, ethyl ether, carbon disulfide, carbon tetrachloride or methylene chloride. The solvent is then boiled off, although up to 100 parts per million remain in the oil. These solvents, themselves toxic, also retain the toxic pesticides adhering to seeds and grains before processing begins.

High temperature processing causes the weak carbon bonds of the unsaturated fatty acids, especially triple unsaturated linolenic acid, to break apart, thereby creating dangerous free radicals. In addition, anti-oxidants including fat soluble vitamin E, which protect the body from the ravages of free radicals, are neutralized or destroyed by high temperatures and pressures. BHT and BHA, both suspected of causing cancer and brain damage, are always added to these oils, to replace vitamin E and other natural preservatives destroyed by heat.

There *is* a safe modern technique for extraction that drills into the seeds and extracts the oil and its precious cargo of anti-oxidants under low temperatures, with minimal exposure to light and oxygen. These unrefined oils will remain fresh for a long time if stored in the refrigerator in dark bottles. Extra virgin olive oil is produced by crushing olives between stone or steel rollers. This process is a gentle one that preserves the integrity of the fatty acids and the numerous natural preservatives in olive oil. If the olive oil is packaged in an opaque container, it will retain its freshness and precious store of anti-oxidants for many months.

Hydrogenation: This is the process that turns polyunsaturates, normally liquid at room temperature, into a fat that is solid at room temperature—margarine and shortening. To produce them, manufacturers begin with the cheapest oils—soy, corn or cottonseed—already rancid from the extraction process. These oils are then mixed with tiny metal particles—usually nickel oxide. Nickel oxide is very toxic when absorbed and is impossible to totally eliminate from margarine. The oil with its nickel catalyst is then subjected to hydrogen gas in a high pressure, high temperature reactor. Next, soap-like emulsifiers and starch are squeezed into the mixture to give it a better consistency; the oil is yet again subjected to high temperature when it is steam-cleaned. This removes its horrible odor. Margarine's natural color, an unappetizing grey, is removed by bleach. Coal-tar dyes and strong flavors must then be added to make it resemble butter. Finally the mixture is compressed and packaged in blocks or tubs, ready to be spread on your toast.

Margarine and other partially hydrogenated oils are even worse for you than the highly refined vegetable oils from which they are made, because of chemical changes that occur during the hydrogenation process. Under high temperatures, the nickel catalyst causes the hydrogen atoms to change position on the fatty acid chain. Before hydrogenation, two hydrogen atoms occur together on the chain, causing the chain to bend slightly and creating an electron cloud at the site of the double bond. This is called the *cis* formation, the configuration most commonly found in nature. With hydrogenation, one hydrogen atom is moved to the other side so that the molecule straightens. This is called the *trans* formation, rarely found in nature. These man-made *trans*-fats are toxins to the body, but unfortunately your digestive system does not recognize them as such. Instead of being eliminated, the *trans*-fats are incorporated into the body's cell membranes as if they were *cis*-fats—your cells actually become hydrogenated! Once in place, *trans*-fatty acids with their misplaced hydrogen atom wreak havoc in cell metabolism. These altered fats actually block the utilization of essential fatty acids, causing many deleterious effects ranging from sexual dysfunction, increased blood cholesterol and paralysis of the immune system.[42] In the 1940's, researchers found a strong correlation between cancer and the consumption of fat—the fats used were hydrogenated fats, not naturally saturated fats.[43] (Until recently, the confusion between hydrogenated fats and naturally saturated fats has persisted not only in the popular press, but in scientific data bases, resulting in much error in study results.) Consumption of hydrogenated fats is associated with a host of other serious diseases, not only cancer but also atherosclerosis, diabetes, obesity, immune system dysfunction, low birth weight babies and birth defects, sterility, difficulty in lactation and problems with bones and tendons[44], yet hydrogenated fats continue to be promoted as health foods. Margarine's popularity represents a triumph of advertising duplicity over common sense. Your best defense is to avoid it like the plague.

Homogenization: This is the process whereby the fat particles of cream are strained through tiny pores under great pressure. The resulting fat particles are so small that they stay in suspension rather than rise to the top of the milk. This makes the fat and cholesterol more susceptible to rancidity and oxidation, and some research indicates that homogenized fats may contribute to heart disease.[45]

The media's constant attack on saturated fats is extremely suspect. Claims that butter causes chronic high cholesterol values have not been substantiated by research—although some studies show that butter consumption causes a small, temporary rise—while other studies have shown that stearic acid, the main component of beef fat, actually lowers cholesterol.[46] Margarine, on the other hand, provokes chronic high levels of protective cholesterol and has been linked to both heart disease and cancer.[47] Butter has received so much adverse propaganda that we have lost sight of the fact that it has long been a valuable component of many traditional diets, containing the following vital nutrients:

Fat Soluble Vitamins: These include vitamins A (retinol), D and E as well as all their naturally occurring constituents needed to obtain maximum effect. Butter is America's best source of these essential vitamins. In fact, vitamin A from butter is more easily absorbed and utilized than from other sources.[48] (These fat soluble vitamins are relatively stable and survive the pasteurization process.) When Dr. Weston Price studied the diets of primitive peoples around the world, he found that butter was a staple in many native diets. (He did not find any primitive peoples who consumed polyunsaturated oils.) The groups he studied particularly valued the deep yellow butter produced by cows feeding on spring pasturage. Their natural intuition told them that its life-giving qualities were especially beneficial for children and expectant mothers. When Dr. Price analyzed this spring butter he found that it was exceptionally high in all fat soluble vitamins, particularly vitamin A. These vitamins act as catalysts to mineral absorption—without them, according to Dr. Price, we are not able to utilize the minerals we ingest, no matter how abundant they may be in our diets. Vitamins A and D are essential for growth, for healthy bones, and for proper development of the brain and nervous systems. Vitamin E, also plentiful in butter, is a precursor of sex hormones. Many studies have shown the importance of butter fat in maintaining normal reproductive powers; its absence results in "nutritional castration"—the failure to bring out male and female sexual characteristics. As butter consumption in America has declined, sterility rates and homosexuality have increased. In test animals, butter substitutes are unable to promote growth or sustain reproduction.[49]

Not all of the groups Dr. Price studied ate butter; but all the groups he observed went to great lengths to obtain foods high in fat soluble vitamins—fish, fish eggs, organ meats, blubber of sea animals and insects. Without knowing the names of the vitamins contained in these foods, isolated traditional societies recognized their importance in the diet and liberally ate foods containing them. They rightly believed that they were necessary for fertility and the growth of children. When Dr. Price analyzed the contents of these foods, he found that native diets consistently provided about ten times more fat soluble vitamins than the American diet. (This ratio is probably more severe today as Americans have reduced animal fats.) Dr. Price realized that these fat soluble vitamins promoted the beautiful bone structure, wide palate, flawless uncrowded teeth, and handsome, well-proportioned faces that he found universally in isolated primitives. American children in general do not eat fish or organ meats, at least not to any great extent, and blubber and insects are not a part of the western diet; many will not eat eggs. The only good source of fat soluble vitamins in the American diet, one sure to be eaten, is butterfat. Butter added to vegetables and spread on bread, and cream added to soups and sauces, ensure proper assimilation of the minerals and water soluble vitamins in vegetables, grains and meat.

- **The Wulzen Factor:** Called the "anti-stiffness" factor, this is a steroid or cortisone-like chemical present in raw animal fat. Researcher Wulzen determined that this substance protects humans and animals from calcification of the joints—degenerative arthritis—as well as hardening of the arteries, cataracts and calcification of the pineal gland.[50] Several independent researchers have confirmed her findings. Calves fed pasteurized milk or skim milk develop joint stiffness and do not thrive. Their symptoms are reversed when raw butterfat is added to the diet. Pasteurization destroys the Wulzen factor—it is present only in *raw* butter, cream and whole milk.

- **The X Factor:** Discovered by Dr. Price, the X factor is a catalyst which, like vitamins A and D, helps the body absorb and utilize minerals. The X factor is found in organ meats, to a lesser extent in other animal fats and has been detected in organically grown, unprocessed corn oil. It may exist in other high-quality, minimally processed vegetable oils. Butter can be an especially rich source of the X factor but quantities are substantially lower in dairy cows fed cottonseed meal or high protein soy-based feeds instead of green grass.[51] Fortunately, the X factor is not destroyed by pasteurization.

- **Arachidonic Acid:** A polyunsaturate containing four double carbon bonds, found in small amounts in animal fats, but not in vegetable fats. Arachidonic acid is a precursor to important prostaglandins and other vital substances.

- **Short and Medium Chain Fatty Acids:** Butter contains about 15% short and medium chain fatty acids. This type of saturated fat does not need to be emulsified by bile salts, but is absorbed directly from the small intestine to the liver, where it is converted into energy. These fatty acids also have anti-microbial, anti-tumor and immune system supportive properties, especially 12-carbon lauric acid, a medium chain fatty acid not found in other animal fats. Highly protective lauric should be called a conditionally essential fatty acid because it is the one saturated fat that the body does not make itself.[52] We must obtain it from one of two dietary sources—butter or tropical oils. Propionic acid and butyric acid, very short chain fatty acids, are all but unique to butter. These have anti-fungal properties as well as anti-tumor effects.[53]

- **Omega-6 and omega-3 polyunsaturates:** These occur in butter in small but equal amounts. This perfect balance between linoleic and linolenic acid prevents the kind of problems associated with the overconsumption of omega-6 fatty acids.

- **Conjugated Linoleic Acid:** Butterfat also contains a form of rearranged linoleic acid called CLA that has strong anti-cancer properties.[54]

- **Lecithin:** Lecithin is a natural component of butter. It is known to assist in the proper assimilation and metabolization of cholesterol and other fat constituents.

- **Cholesterol:** Mother's milk is high in cholesterol because it is essential for growth and development. Cholesterol is also needed to produce a variety of steroids that protect against cancer, heart disease and mental illness.

- **Glycosphingolipids:** This special category of fat protects against gastrointestinal infections, especially in the very young and the elderly. For this reason, children who drink skimmed milk have diarrhea at rates three to five times greater than children who drink whole milk.[55]

- **Trace Minerals:** Many trace minerals are incorporated into the fat globule membrane of butterfat, including manganese, zinc, chromium and iodine. In mountainous areas far from the sea, iodine in butter protects against goiter and other thyroid problems. Butter is extremely rich in selenium, a vital anti-oxidant, containing more per gram than herring or wheat germ.

One frequently voiced objection to the consumption of butter and other animal fats is that they tend to accumulate environmental poisons. Fat soluble poisons such as DDT do accumulate in fats; but water soluble poisons such as antibiotics and growth hormones accumulate in the water fraction of milk and meats. Vegetables and grains also accumulate poisons. Aflatoxin, a fungus that grows on grain, is one of the most powerful carcinogens known. It is correct to assume that all of our foods, whether of vegetable or animal origin, may be contaminated. The solution to environmental poisons is not to eliminate animal fats, so essential to growth, reproduction and overall health, but to seek out organic meats and butter, as well as vegetables and grains. These are becoming increasingly available in health food stores and supermarkets.

Before leaving this complex but vital subject of fats, it is worthwhile examining the composition of vegetable oils with a view to determining their usefulness and appropriateness in food preparation:

- **Olive oil:** 75% oleic acid, the stable monounsaturated fat, along with 13% saturated fat, 10 % omega-6 linoleic acid and 2% omega-3 linolenic acid. The high percentage of oleic acid makes olive oil ideal for cooking and salads. Extra virgin olive oil is also rich in anti-oxidants. Olive oil has withstood the test of time; it is the safest oil you can use, but don't overdo. The longer chain fatty acids found in olive oil are more likely to contribute to the build- up of body fat than the short and medium length fatty acids found in butter.

- **Peanut oil:** 48% oleic acid, 18% saturated fat and 34% omega-6 linoleic acid. Like olive oil, peanut oil is relatively stable, and therefore appropriate for stir-frys on occasion. But the high percentage of omega-6 presents a danger, so use of peanut oil should be strictly limited.

Sesame Oil: 42% oleic acid, 15% saturated fat, and 43% omega-6 linoleic acid. Sesame oil is similar in composition to peanut oil and is recommended for frying in some diets. However, the high percentage of omega-6 militates against frequent use.

Safflower, Corn, Sunflower, Soybean and Cottonseed Oil: All contain over 50% omega-6, with only minimal amounts of omega-3. Safflower oil contains almost 80% omega-6. Researchers are just beginning to discover the dangers of excess omega-6 oils in the diet, whether rancid or not. Use of all these oils should be strictly limited. They should never be consumed after they have been heated, as in cooking, frying, baking, etc. However, mother's milk is rich in omega-6 fatty acids and unrefined sunflower oil, which is more stable than the other omega-6 oils, has a place as a supplement in infant feeding.

Canola oil: 5% saturated fat, 57% oleic acid, 23% omega-6 and 10%-15% omega-3. Canola oil is the newest oil on the market. The canola oil seed was developed from the rape seed, a member of the mustard family. Rape seed is unsuited to human consumption because it contains a very long chain fatty acid called erucic acid, which in large quantities is associated fibrotic lesions in the heart. Canola oil was bred to contain little if any erucic acid, and has drawn the attention of nutritionists because of its high oleic acid content. But there are some indications that canola oil presents dangers of its own. It has a high sulphur content, and goes rancid easily. Baked goods made with canola oil develop mold very quickly. The omega-3 fatty acids of processed canola oil contain *trans* fatty acids, similar to those in margarine, and possibly more dangerous to the health.[56] Canola oil presents a number of dangers and should be avoided completely.

Flax Seed oil: 9% saturated, 18% oleic acid, 16% omega-6 and 57% omega-3. With its extremely high omega-3 content, flax seed oil provides a remedy for the omega-6/omega-3 imbalance so prevalent in America today. Not surprisingly, Scandinavian folk lore values flax seed oil as a health food. New extraction and bottling methods have minimized rancidity problems. It should always be kept refrigerated, never heated! Add a spoonful to salad dressings for a small but daily infusion of linolenic acid with its triple-carbon-bond electron cloud.

Palm, Palm Kernel and Coconut Oils: These tropical oils contain between 80% and 90% saturated fats along with small amounts of oleic acid and linoleic acid. Of the total saturated fat content, over two-thirds is in the form of short and medium chain fatty acids (often called medium chain triglycerides). Of particular interest is lauric acid, found in large quantities in both coconut oil and in mother's milk. This fatty acid has strong anti-fungal and anti-microbial properties. Palm, palm kernel and coconut oils protect tropical populations from bacteria and fungus so prevalent in their food supply; as third world nations in tropical areas have switched to polyunsaturated vegetable oils, the incidence of intestinal disorders and immune deficiency diseases has increased dramatically. Because coconut oil contains lauric acid, it is often used in baby formulas. These oils are extremely stable and can be kept at room temperature for many months without becoming rancid. It is a shame we do not use these oils for cooking and baking—the bad rap they have received is the result of intense lobbying by the vegetable oil industry.[57] Red palm oil has a strong taste that most will find disagreeable (although it is used extensively throughout Africa) but coconut oil is excellent for baking purposes—it makes wonderful cookies. White palm kernel oil was formerly used as shortening and in the production of commercial French fries; the saturated fat scare has forced most manufacturers to abandon this safe and healthy oil in favor of artificially saturated hydrogenated soybean, corn and cottonseed oils—the waste products of America's three biggest crops.

In summary, our choice of fats and oils is one of extreme importance. Most people, especially infants and growing children, benefit from more fat in the diet rather than less. But the fats we eat must be chosen with care. Avoid all processed foods containing new-fangled hydrogenated fats and polyunsaturated oils. Instead use traditional oils like extra virgin olive oil and unrefined flax seed oil. Acquaint yourself with the merits of coconut oil for baking. And finally, use good old-fashioned butter, not margarine, with the happy assurance that it is a wholesome—indeed, an essential—food for you and your whole family.

Organic butter, extra virgin olive oil, and cold processed flax oil in opaque containers are available in health food stores and gourmet markets. Coconut oil is often sold in the cosmetic section of such stores. (See Sources for a recommended supplier of unrefined fats and oils by mail order.)

CARBOHYDRATES

All green plants produce carbohydrates—starch and sugar—in their leaves through the action of sunlight, carbon dioxide and water. Sugar comes in many forms. Sucrose, or common table sugar, is a disaccharide that breaks down during digestion into the simple sugars glucose and fructose. Glucose is the primary sugar in the blood; fructose is the primary sugar in fruit and refined corn syrup. Other common disaccharides are maltose (malt sugar) and lactose (milk sugar). Any word ending in *-ose* is a sugar.

Complex sugars are longer chain sugars composed of fructose and other simple sugars. Relatively short complex sugars called stachyose and farrinose occur in beans and other legumes; longer ones occur in certain plant foods like the Jerusalem artichoke and seaweed. Unlike herbivorous animals, humans lack enzymes needed to break down these sugars into their simple components; however, some individuals have certain beneficial flora in the large intestine that will perform this task.

In contrast, most humans are able to digest starch, a polysaccharide composed exclusively of glucose molecules. During the process of cooking, chewing and especially through prolonged enzymatic action during digestion, the starches are broken into separate glucose molecules. Glucose enters the bloodstream via the small intestine where it supplies energy wherever the body needs it—for accomplishing cellular processes, for thinking, or for moving an arm or a leg. As the body uses glucose for all its processes, it can be said that sugar is essential to life. But the body does not need to ingest sugar, or even large quantities of carbohydrates, to produce it. Certain primitive groups such as the Eskimos, the pre-Colombian plains Indians, and the medieval inhabitants of Greenland, subsisted on a diet composed almost entirely of animal products—protein and fats. Examination of the skulls of these groups shows a virtual absence of tooth decay and hence a high general level of health on a diet almost completely devoid of carbohydrate foods.

Only during the last century has man's diet included a high percentage of *refined* carbohydrates. Our ancestors ate fruits and grains in their natural, unrefined state. In nature, sugars and carbohydrates—the energy providers—are linked together with vitamins, minerals, enzymes, proteins and fiber—the body-building components of foods. In whole form, sugars and starches support life; but refined carbohydrates are inimical to life because they are devoid of these body-building elements. Digestion of refined carbohydrates calls on the body's own store of vitamins, minerals and enzymes for proper metabolization. When B vitamins are absent, for example, the breakdown of carbohydrates cannot take place, yet most B vitamins are removed during the refining process.

The refining process strips grains, vegetables and fruits of both their B vitamin and mineral component. Refined carbohydrates have been called "empty" calories. "Negative" calories would be a more appropriate term because consumption of refined calories depletes the body's precious reserves. Consumption of sugar and white flour may be likened to drawing on a savings account. If continued withdrawals are made, faster than new funds are put in, the account will eventually become depleted. Some people may go longer than others without overt suffering, but eventually all will feel the effects of this inexorable law. If you were fortunate enough to be born with an excellent constitution, you may be able to eat unlimited quantities of sugar with relative impunity; but your children's or your grandchildren's inheritance will be one of impoverished reserves.

The all-important level of glucose in the blood is regulated by a finely-tuned mechanism involving insulin secretions from the pancreas, and hormones from several glands including the adrenal glands and the thyroid. When sugars and starches are eaten in their natural, unrefined form, they are digested slowly and enter the bloodstream at a moderate rate for a period of several hours. If the body goes for a long period without food, this mechanism will call upon reserves stored in the liver. When properly working, this marvelous blood sugar regulation process provides the cells with a steady, even supply of glucose. The body is kept on an even keel, so to speak, both physically and emotionally.

But when refined sugars and starches are consumed, we have an entirely different story. They tend to enter the blood stream in a rush, causing a sudden spurt in blood sugar levels. The body's regulation mechanism kicks into high gear, flooding the bloodstream with insulin and other hormones to bring the blood sugar levels down to acceptable levels. Repeated onslaughts of sugar will eventually disrupt this finely-tuned process, causing some elements to remain in a constant state of activity, and others to become worn out and therefore inadequate to do the job. The situation is worsened by the fact that a diet high in refined carbohydrates will also be deficient in vitamins, minerals and enzymes, those body-building elements that keep the glands and organs in good repair. When the endocrine system thus becomes disturbed, numerous other pathological conditions soon manifest—degenerative disease, allergies, obesity, alcoholism, drug addiction, depression and behavioral problems.

Disrupted regulation results in blood sugar that habitually remains either higher or lower than the narrow range under which the body is designed to function. A person with abnormally high blood sugar is a diabetic; a person whose blood sugar regularly drops below normal is a hypoglycemic. These two diseases are really two sides of the same coin and both stem from the same cause—excess consumption of refined carbohydrates. The diabetic lives in danger of blindness, gangrene in the limbs, heart disease and diabetic coma. Insulin injections can protect the diabetic from sudden death by coma but, unless the diet improves, cannot halt the progressive deterioration of the cornea, the tissues and the circulatory system. Low blood sugar opens a veritable Pandora's box of symptoms ranging from seizures, depression and unfounded phobias to allergies, headaches and chronic fatigue.

Hypoglycemics are often advised to eat something sweet when they feel the symptoms of low blood sugar, for sugar rushes into the bloodstream and gives a temporary lift. This policy is misguided for several reasons. First, as the calories are empty, the body-building reserves are further depleted. Second, the roller-coaster cycle of high blood sugar, sent too low by faulty regulating mechanism, is further perpetuated. And finally, the brief period of high blood sugar sets in motion a harmful process called glycation, the bonding of amino acids to sugar molecules when the blood sugar concentration is too high. These abnormal proteins are then incorporated into the tissues and can do enormous damage, especially to the long-lived proteins in the lens of the eye and the myelin in the fatty insulating sheath around the nerves.[58] The collagen of skin, tendons and membranes is also damaged by these glycated proteins. This process takes place in everyone who eats sugar, not just diabetics.

Strict abstinence from sugar and very limited use of refined flour is good advice for everyone. We must remember that these skeletonized products were virtually unknown in the human diet before 1600, and never used in great quantities before the present century. Our physical nature is such that we need foods that are whole, not skeletonized and denatured, to grow, to prosper and to reproduce. As the consumption of sugar has increased, so have all the "civilized" diseases. In 1821 the average sugar intake in America was 10 pounds per person per year; today it is 170 pounds per person, over one fourth the average caloric intake. Another large fraction of all calories comes from refined flour and refined vegetable oils.[59] This means that less than half the diet must provide all the nutrients to a body that is under constant stress from its intake of sugar, refined flour and rancid and hydrogenated vegetable oils. Herein lies a major cause of the vast increase in degenerative diseases that plague modern America.

Until recently, the Diet Dictocrats denied the role of sugar as a cause of disease. Few establishment spokesmen will admit that sugar consumption has anything to do with heart disease; and some have adopted the breathtaking stance that sugar has not been proven to cause diabetes. "If we didn't prefer foods with added sugar, it would not be added," says Dr. Frederick Stare, former chairman of the Department of Nutrition at Harvard University's School of Public Health. "Remember, eating is one of the real pleasures of life as well as a necessity... for most people, sugar helps other things taste better... Sugar calories are not different from other calories, from calories obtained from protein, starch, fat or alcohol." Harvard's Department of Nutrition receives the bulk of its funding from the food processing industry, and nothing contributes to the profits of the food processing industry so much as sugar—cheap, easily produced and stored, of infinite shelf life, its sweetness a convenient mask for the flavorless, overprocessed concoctions to which it is added. Sugar is the food processors' best preservative. It blocks various forms of decay-causing bacteria by tying up the water in which they grow.

Scientific evidence against sugar has been mounting for decades. As early as 1933 research showed that increased consumption of sugar caused an increase in various disease conditions in school children.[60] Sugar, especially fructose, has been shown to shorten life in numerous animal experiments.[61] Sugar consumption has recently been cited as the root cause of anorexia and eating disorders.[62] In the 1950's, British researcher Yudkin published conclusive findings that excessive use of sugar was associated with the following conditions: release of free fatty acids at the aorta, rise in blood cholesterol, rise in triglycerides, increase in adhesiveness of the blood platelets, increase in blood insulin levels, increase in blood corticosteroid levels, increase in gastric acidity, enlargement of the liver, hypertrophy of the adrenals, and shrinkage of the pancreas.[63] Numerous subsequent studies have positively correlated sugar consumption with heart disease.[64] These results are far more unequivocal than the more tenuous association with heart disease and saturated fats. Researchers Lopez in the 1960's and the Ahrens in the 1970's have repeatedly pointed out the fallacy of the fat theory for coronary heart disease but their work has not received recognition by government agencies or by the press. The food processing industry—America's largest industry—has a tremendous interest in confining this research to scientific publications stored in the basements of our medical libraries. If the public were made aware of the dangers of refined carbohydrate consumption, and took steps to reduce it, this powerful industry would shrink to a fraction of its size. You don't need animal fats to produce junk food; but you do need vegetable oils, white flour and sugar.

More plagues than heart disease can be laid at sugar's door. A survey of medical journals in the 1970's produced findings implicating sugar as a causative factor in kidney disease, liver disease, shortened life-span, increased desire for coffee and tobacco, as well as atherosclerosis and coronary heart disease.[65] Sugar consumption is associated with hyperactivity, behavior problems, lack of concentration and violent tendencies.[66] Sugar consumption encourages the overgrowth of candida albicans, systematic fungi in the digestive tract, causing it to spread to the respiratory system, the tissues and internal organs. Sugar consumption is positively associated with cancer in humans and test animals.[67] Tumors are known to be enormous sugar absorbers. Research indicates that it is the fructose, not the glucose, moiety of sugar that is the most harmful, especially for growing children.[68] Yet the greatest increase in sugar consumption during the last two decades is from high fructose corn syrup used in soft drinks, ketchup and many other fabricated foods.

Last, but not least, sugar consumption is the cause of bone loss and dental decay. Tooth decay and bone loss occur when the precise ratio of calcium to phosphorus in the blood varies from the normal ratio of 4 parts phosphorus to 10 parts calcium. At this proportion, all blood calcium can be properly utilized. Dr. Melvin Page of Florida demonstrated in numerous studies that sugar consumption causes phosphorus levels to drop and calcium to rise.[69] Calcium rises because it is pulled from the teeth and the bones. The drop in phosphorus hinders the absorption of this calcium, making it unusable and therefore toxic. Thus, sugar consumption causes tooth decay not because it promotes bacterial growth in the mouth, as most dentists believe, but because it alters the internal body chemistry.

Orthodox nutritionists admit that sugar causes tooth decay, although they may be mistaken about just why this is so, but their warnings to avoid tooth decay by limiting sweets are disingenuous. Most people would be willing to pay the price for bad teeth as long as they did not have to stop eating sugar. After all, teeth can be repaired or replaced. But poor teeth are always the outward sign of other types of degeneration in the body, degeneration that cannot be repaired by mechanical means.

Sweetness in fruits, grains and vegetables is an indication that they are ripe and therefore have reached maximum vitamin and mineral content. The naturally sweet foods from which sugar is extracted—sugar beet, sugar cane and corn—are particularly high in nutrients such as B vitamins, magnesium and chromium. All of these seem to play an important role in the blood sugar regulation mechanism. These nutrients are discarded—or made into animal feed—when the raw product is refined into sugar. Refining strips foods of vital nutrients while concentrating sugars, thus allowing us to fill our body's energy requirements for energy without obtaining the nutrients needed for body-building, digestion and repair.

Whole grains provide Vitamin E, B vitamins in abundance, and many important minerals, all of which are essential to life. These too are discarded in the refining process. Fiber—indigestible cellulose that plays an important role in the digestion and elimination— is also eliminated. Refined flour is commonly fortified but this is of little value. Fortification adds a handful of synthetic vitamins and minerals to white flour and polished rice after a host of essential factors have been removed or destroyed. Some of the vitamins added during the fortification process may even be dangerous. Some researchers believe that excess iron from fortified flour can cause tissue damage, and other studies link excess or toxic iron to heart disease.[70] Vitamins B1 and B2 added to grains without B6 lead to imbalances in numerous processes involving B vitamin pathways. The safety of bleaching agents, almost universally applied to white flour, has never been established.

Moderate use of natural sweeteners is found in many traditional societies. We therefore recommend that you satisfy your sweet tooth by eating fully ripened fruit in season and by limited use of certain natural sweeteners high in vitamins and minerals such as raw honey, date sugar, dehydrated cane sugar juice (commercially available as Sucanat) and maple syrup. Avoid all refined sugars including table sugar, so-called raw sugar or brown sugar (both composed of about 96% refined sugar), corn syrup, fructose and large amounts of fruit juice.

We recommend the use of a variety of whole grains, but with an important caveat. Whole grains contain a substance called phytic acid in their bran. Phytic acid combines with iron, calcium, phosphorus and zinc in the intestinal tract so that these minerals cannot be absorbed.[71] Traditional societies usually soak or ferment their grains before eating them, processes that neutralize phytates and, in effect, pre-digest grains so that all their nutrients are more available.[72] Sprouting, overnight soaking and old-fashioned sour leavening can accomplish this important pre-digestion in our own kitchens. Many people who are allergic to grains will tolerate them well when they are prepared according to these procedures. Proper preparation techniques also help break down complex sugars in legumes, making them more digestible.

Whole grains that have been processed by high heat and pressure to produce puffed wheat, oats, and rice are actually quite toxic and have caused rapid death in test animals.[73] We do not recommend rice cakes, a popular snack food. Grains that have been slurried and extruded at high temperatures and pressures to make little flakes and shapes that are sold as breakfast cereals should also be avoided. Most, if not all, nutrients are destroyed during processing and they are very difficult to digest.

Most people who have "got religion" about nutrition have learned through experience that sugar and white flour are inimical to good health; and they know how difficult it is to give these things up in a society whose eating habits are based on them. It is relatively easy to replace margarine with butter and refined polyunsaturates with extra virgin olive oil because these fats taste so much better; but sugar and white flour, being mildly to severely addictive, are harder to give up. Try replacing white flour products with a variety of whole grains, properly prepared, and limiting sweets to occasional desserts made from natural sweeteners. It may take time, and you will almost certainly have set-backs, but in the end your will-power and persistence will reward you with the good health that is everyone's natural heritage.

PROTEINS

Proteins are the building blocks of the animal kingdom. The human body assembles and utilizes about 50,000 different proteins to form organs, nerves, muscles and flesh. Enzymes—the managers and catalysts of all the body's processes—are specialized proteins. So are antibodies.

All proteins are combinations of just 22 amino acids, eight of which are considered essential nutrients for humans. When the essential amino acids are present in the diet, the body can usually build the other non-essential amino acids. However, if just one essential amino acid is low or missing, the body is unable to synthesize the other proteins it needs, even when overall protein intake is high. Of particular importance to the health of the brain and nervous system are the sulphur-containing amino acids—methionine, cysteine and cystine—found most plentifully in eggs and meat. Some individuals cannot manufacture amino acids considered "non-essential", such as taurine and carnitine, but must obtain them from dietary sources.

Protein is essential for the formation of hormones, for the process of blood clotting, and the formation of milk during lactation. Protein helps regulate the acid-alkaline balance of tissues and blood. When protein is lacking in the diet, there is a tendency for the blood and tissues to become either too acid or too alkaline, depending on the acidity or the alkalinity of the foods we eat. Improper acid-alkaline balance is often a problem among vegetarians.

Just as animal fats are our only sources of Vitamins A and D and other body-building factors, so also animal protein is our only source of complete protein. All of the essential amino acids, and many considered "non-essential", are present in animal products. Sources of protein from the vegetable kingdom contain only incomplete protein, that is they lack one or more essential amino acids, even when overall protein content is high. The body must have all the amino acids in order to use any of them. The two best sources of protein in the vegetable kingdom are legumes and cereal grains, but all plant foods are low in tryptophan, cystine and threonine. Legumes such as beans, peanuts and cashews are high in the amino acid lysine but low in methionine. Cereal grains have the opposite profile. In order to obtain the best possible protein combination from vegetable sources, pulses and grains must be eaten together. Most grain-based cuisines instinctively incorporate this principle. For example, corn and beans are staple fare in Mexican cuisine, as are chick peas and whole wheat in the Middle East and rice and soy bean products in the Orient.

Vegetarianism has recently achieved political correctness, and nutritionists advocating a restriction or complete elimination of animal products garner good reviews in the popular press. Their influence is reflected in the new Food Pyramid but the scientific evidence, honestly evaluated, argues against relying too heavily on grains and pulses as sources of protein, or for severely reducing animal products.

Our primitive ancestors subsisted on a diet composed largely of meat and fat, augmented with vegetables, fruits and nuts. Studies of their remains reveal that they possessed excellent bone structure, heavy musculature and flawless teeth. Agricultural man added milk, grains and legumes to this diet. These foods allowed him to pursue a more comfortable life-style than the hunter-gatherer, but at a price. In his studies of primitive peoples, Dr. Price found that those whose diets consisted largely of grains and legumes, while far more healthy than civilized moderns, nevertheless had more caries than those living primarily on meat and fish. Skulls of prehistoric peoples subsisting almost entirely on vegetable foods have teeth containing caries and abscesses, and show evidence of tuberculosis as well.[74]

A more recent study by Dr. Cheraskin corroborates Dr. Price's observations. He surveyed 1040 dentists and their wives. Those who had the lowest number of problems and diseases as measured by the Cornell Medical Index had the most protein in their diets. The healthiest consumed an average of 125 grams per day, similar to the protein intake of stone age man.[75] The claim that high protein diets cause bone loss is supported neither by scientific research or anthropological surveys.[76] Inadequate protein intake leads to loss of myocardial muscle and may therefore contribute to coronary heart disease.[77] However, protein cannot be adequately utilized without dietary fats. That is why protein and fats occur together in eggs, milk, fish and meats. A high protein, low-fat diet can cause many problems including too-rapid growth and depletion of vitamin A and D reserves.

Anthropologist William Haviland's studies of Mayan remains lead to interesting conclusions about the long-term effects of a diet devoid of animal products. He found that the average male skeleton was about 165 centimeters during the early period of the civilization, when meat was readily available. During the later periods, the height of the average lower class male declined to 157 centimeters—about the height of the average Pygmy—while at the same time, the average height of males from the ruling class increased to about 170 centimeters. The lower class subsisted mostly on corn and beans while the ruling classes were able to supplement their diet with small amounts of scarce animal protein.[78] Will such extreme class differentiation divide the American population if it follows the guidelines of the new Food Pyramid—either through ignorance or by necessity?

The claim is often made that animal products shorten life-span but the most cursory look at long-lived ethnic groups will show that this is not the case. Russians from the Caucasus Mountains, an area famous for longevity, eat fatty meat and whole milk products frequently. Studies of Georgian populations show that those who have the most meat and fat in their diets live the longest.[79] Inhabitants of Vilcabamba in Equador, known for their longevity, consume a variety of animal foods. The long-lived people of Hunza consume animal protein in the form of goat milk products. On the other hand, the vegetarian inhabitants of southern India have one of the shortest life-spans in the world.[80]

Not only is it difficult to obtain adequate protein on a diet devoid of animal products; such a diet often leads to deficiencies in many important minerals as well. This is because such a diet will lack the fat-soluble catalysts needed for mineral absorption. Furthermore, phytates in grains make their mineral content of calcium, iron, zinc, and magnesium difficult to utilize. Unless the grains are properly prepared to neutralize phytates, the body may be unable to assimilate these minerals. Zinc, iron, calcium and other minerals from animal sources are more easily and readily absorbed.

We should not overestimate the dangers of deficiencies in these minerals. The effects of calcium and iron deficiency are well know, those of zinc less so. Even a small lack of zinc in the diet of pregnant animals results in offspring with deformities such as club feet, cleft palates, domed skulls, and fused and missing ribs. In humans zinc deficiency often results in impaired mentality, and mental retardation. In men, zinc depletion leads to decreased fertility. Man's best source of zinc is animal products.

Vitamin B12 occurs *only* in animal products. The body stores a supply of vitamin B12 that can last from two to five years. When this supply is depleted, B12 deficiency diseases result. These include anemia, nervous disorders such as panic attacks, schizophrenia and hallucinations, sudden or temporary loss of function of a limb, weakness, numbness of hands and feet, loss of balance and impaired eyesight. B12 deficiency has been found in breast-fed infants of strict vegetarians.[81] It has been claimed that fermented soybean foods contain B12, but studies show that these are not absorbed by humans.[82] Whether spirulina—a blue-green algae valued for its high protein, vitamin and mineral content—contains vitamin B12 is a matter of debate. Some claim that spirulina contains substances that actually block the assimilation of B12.

Because grains and pulses eaten alone cannot supply complete amino acids, vegetarians must take care to balance the two at every meal. Vegetarian diets also tend to be deficient in phosphorus as meat is the principle source of phosphorus for most people. This is another reason that vegetarianism has been linked to tooth decay. Vegetarians often have difficulty maintaining the proper acid-alkali balance in the blood and tissues because adequate protein and minerals are needed for this regulation.

Careful examination of mammalian physiology and eating habits reveals that none of the higher animals can be called strictly vegetarian. All primates eat some form of animal food. Gorillas—mistakenly labeled vegetarian—eat insect eggs and larvae that adhere to leaves and fruit. Other primates eat crickets, flies, rodents, small antelope and other animals. Neither can cattle and other ruminants be labeled strictly vegetarian because they always take in insect life adhering to the plants they eat, and because their stomachs and intestinal tracts contain enormous amounts of protozoa. These microscopic animals help digest grasses and in turn are digested and utilized by the cow. Only during the present modern age has any group of humans been able to follow a diet strictly free of animal products. In less sanitary times, there were always insect parts in the food supply. Small insects with their larva or eggs left on plant foods prevent B12 deficiency anemia among Hindus in India. Hindus also eat milk products and some sects consume termites. When these Hindus move to England, where the food supply is subject to strict cleanliness regulations, the incidence of pernicious anemia increases dramatically.[83]

Current wisdom dictates that Americans should at least reduce their consumption of red meats and the dark meat of birds, because these meats contain more saturated fat than fish or white poultry meat, but even this stricture is ill-advised, especially for those who tend to be anemic. Red meat is rich in mineral salts such as iron and zinc, both of which play an important role in the body's use of essential fatty acids; and as we have seen, problems of saturated fat consumption have been greatly exaggerated. Furthermore, high protein diets require increased amounts of vitamin

A. Meat should always be eaten with its fat, otherwise deficiencies occur.

A few highly publicized studies have claimed a link between consumption of meat and saturated fats with cancer, especially cancer of the colon.[84] Studies showing an animal product-cancer correlation can be faulted on two counts. First, the data bases combined saturated fats from animal sources with hydrogenated fats, known to be carcinogenic;[85] and second, these studies did not include sugar and refined flour in their surveys, even though researcher Lopez and others have shown that in so-called civilized countries, high meat consumption and high sugar intake often occur together.[86] Actually, the pathway for cancer of the colon is known to researchers. It involves high levels of omega-6 linoleic acid and hydrogenated fats, which in the presence of carcinogens and acted on by certain enzymes in the cells lining the colon, lead to tumor formation.[87] This explains the fact that in industrialized countries, where there are many carcinogens in meat, and where consumption of vegetable oils and sugar is high, meat-eating has been associated with cancer; but in traditional societies, where the foods are more pure and sugar and vegetable oils are not consumed, meat eating is not associated with cancer. A chorus of establishment voices, including the American Cancer Society, the National Cancer Institute and the Senate Committee on Nutrition and Human Needs, claims that animal fat is linked with other cancers of various types. Yet when researchers from the University of Maryland analyzed their data, they found that vegetable fat was correlated with cancer and animal fat was not.[88]

Animal products, then, are important sources of body-building elements in the diet. Animal fats supply vitamin A and vitamin D and animal protein is rich in mineral salts, vitamin B6 and vitamin B12. The primitive tribes studied by Dr. Price especially valued certain high-vitamin animal products like organ meats, butter, fish eggs and shellfish for growing children and for parents of both sexes during their child-bearing years. They also ate a certain amount of their animal protein raw.

Animal fats and gelatin-rich bone broths both spare protein.[89] Individuals who must restrict protein consumption for budgetary reasons, should include liberal amounts of good quality animal fats and meat broth in their diets.

We have already seen that both fats and carbohydrates can be devitalized by processing and refining. This is also true of proteins. Isolated protein powders made from soy, whey, casein and egg whites are currently popular as basic ingredients in diet beverages and many so-called health food products. These proteins are obtained by a high temperature process that over-denatures the proteins to such an extent that they become virtually useless,[90] while increasing nitrates and other carcinogens.[91] Protein powders are often consumed as part of a low-fat diet and can thereby lead to depletion of vitamin A and D reserves. Soy protein isolates are high in mineral-blocking phytates and potent cancer-causing and growth-inhibiting enzyme blockers.[92]

Any discussion of meat eating should include the observation that temporary abstinence from animal products seems to be a healthful habit. This is reflected in the dietary laws of many religions, and in the practices of primitive peoples who engage in periods of sparse eating or complete fasting, often in late winter or early spring when food is scarce. This wisdom is justified by the fact that meatless diets often prove beneficial in the treatment of cancer and other diseases such as arthritis, kidney disease and gout. Some people have noted improvement of various conditions when they stop eating animal products. But problems arise when the practice is continued for too long. These include caries, bone loss, nervous disorders and reproductive problems. Strict vegetarianism is particularly dangerous for growing children and for women—and men—during their child-producing years.

We must be careful as well, not to blindly extrapolate from the habits of meat-eating primitive peoples. There is a great deal to be learned from their dietary habits but the fact is that we are not fundamentally cave men, but beings with a divine component to our natures. The desire to abstain from animal products, found so often in those of a spiritual nature, may in fact be a longing for a return to a former, more perfect state of consciousness that was ours before our souls took embodiment in the material plane. This longing leads to the notion that our bodies and souls can be purified, or that one can achieve spiritual enlightenment, through a meatless diet. Saintly individuals are often drawn to strict vegetarian habits, and some have been able to sustain themselves on a diet free of animal products for fairly long periods of time. (Some have even lived on no food at all; for many years St. Therese Neumann of Bavaria consumed only the consecrated host. Similar well-documented examples are found in the lives of Catholic and Hindu saints.) Even so, it is a mistake to think that meat eaters lack spirituality—many highly spiritual people eat meat regularly. Perhaps they instinctively realize that when we eat animal products we are accepting, reverently and humbly, the requirements of the earthly body temple in which the soul is temporarily housed, even as we look forward to the day when we have completed our earthly assignment and our souls will be freed to return to a higher condition, one in which we will no longer be dependent on foods provided by the animal kingdom. Seen in this light, strict vegetarianism can be likened to a kind of spiritual pride that seeks to "take heaven by force," and to shirk the earthly duties for which the physical body was created.

The rare St. Therese's on our planet usually lead celibate and contemplative lives. But most of us were born to live and work in the world, and share the responsibility for producing healthy children. Animal products are essential for optimum growth and healthy reproduction. If you feel compelled to adopt the life of a saint or a sage, and are drawn to vegetarianism, we urge you to wait until your later years to do so, when the period of growth and procreation is accomplished, and then to avoid fanaticism in its practice. If you choose not to eat red meat nor to serve it to your family, make sure to supply your loved ones with good quality dairy products and an adequate supply of sea foods. If your religious beliefs proscribe both fish and meat, then a good supply of high quality dairy products and eggs is essential. If your budget prevents plentiful consumption of animal products, it is important to supplement a balance of grains and pulses with at least a small amount of animal products each day, including animal fats rich in vitamins A and D. Animal studies indicate that animal protein in the amount of one sardine per person per day, combined with protein from grains and pulses, is generally sufficient to maintain reproduction and adequate growth.[93]

The amount of meat you include in your diet depends on your genetic makeup and on hormonal factors. Some people do not produce enough hydrochloric acid in their stomachs to handle large amounts of meat well. Some researchers claim that our need for protein declines in later years. Requirements for individual essential amino acids vary enormously. For example, dark-skinned peoples may need more tryptophan, found in eggs and dairy products, as this essential amino acid is used in the production of melanin; deficiencies may lead to insomnia, hyperactivity and other nervous disorders. Some individuals have high requirements for carnitine, a non-essential amino acid found plentifully in lamb or beef, because they have difficulty manufacturing enough of it for proper functioning of the heart.

Our endorsement of animal products must be tempered with this important caveat: The meat, milk and eggs in our supermarkets are highly contaminated and vastly inferior in nutritional quality to those available to our ancestors just a few decades ago. Modern cattle raising techniques include the use of steroids to make meat more tender, and antibiotics that allow cattle to survive in crowded feed lots. Many cattle supplying steaks to the American table have never seen the open range, and calves raised for veal are often confined to crates for the whole of their pathetic short lives. Diseased animals routinely pass inspection and find their way into the food supply. Chickens are raised in crowded pens, often under artificial light both night and day, and fed on substandard food. They too must be guarded from infection by antibiotics. Their eggs are inferior in nutritional qualities to those of free-range, properly nourished hens. According to the renowned cancer specialist Virginia Livingston-Wheeler, most chicken and nearly half the beef consumed in America today is cancerous and pathogenic. Her research has convinced her that these cancers are transmissible to man.[94]

Some have argued that cows and sheep require pasturage that could be better used to raise grains for starving millions in third world countries. This argument ignores the fact that a large portion of our earth's dry land is unsuited to cultivation. The open range, and desert and mountainous areas, yield their fruits in grazing animals. A far more serious threat to humanity is the monoculture of grains and legumes, which tends to deplete the soil and requires the use of artificial fertilizers and pesticides. The educated consumer and the enlightened farmer together can bring about the return of the mixed farm, where cultivation of fruits and vegetables is combined with the raising of livestock and fowl in a manner that is efficient, economical and environmentally friendly. For example, chickens running free in garden areas eat insect pests, while providing high-quality eggs; sheep grazing in orchards obviate the need for herbicides; and cows grazing in woodlands and other marginal areas provide rich, unpolluted milk, making these lands economically viable for the farmer. It is not animal cultivation that leads to hunger and famine, but unwise agricultural practices and monopolistic distribution systems.

We don't recommend that you stop eating meat but we do suggest that you be careful of your supply. Make an effort to obtain organic beef, lamb and chicken. Better yet, try to find a source for buffalo and game. Buffalo and venison (deer, antelope, etc.) are raised on the open range, and their nutritional properties, including their fatty acid profile, are superior. The same goes for game birds such as duck, geese, pheasant, and wild turkey. Learn to eat the organs of land animals as well as the muscle meats—primitive peoples studied by Dr. Price consistently prized organ meats for their health giving properties. Eggs from free-range chickens are available at most health food stores. Make a habit of eating fish, especially cold water deep sea fish, as often as possible. They are rich in omega-3 fatty acids, fat soluble vitamins and many important minerals including iodine, selenium and magnesium. Dr. Price was amazed to find that primitive land-locked peoples made great efforts to obtain food from the sea.

Two types of meat are best eaten only occasionally, or completely avoided —these are pork and shellfish. Investigations into the effects of pork consumption on blood chemistry have revealed serious changes for several hours after pork is consumed.[95] The pork used was organic, free of trichinosis, so the changes that occurred in the blood were due to some other factor. In the laboratory, pork is one of the best mediums for feeding the growth of cancer cells. The prohibitions against pork found in the Bible and the Koran thus may derive from something other than a concern for parasite contamination.

Parasite contamination and pollutants are, however, good reasons for being careful about shellfish such as scallops, clams, and oysters, and to a lesser extent shrimp, crab and lobster. For the same reason, scavenger-type fish such as catfish are best avoided. Be sure of your source before you buy shellfish, otherwise you risk food poisoning and allergic reactions.

Ocean going fish that contain mercury also contain substances called alkylglycerols that remove mercury from the body; but organically bound mercury in fish from industrially polluted waters is toxic and has caused deformities and mental deficiency in the children of Japanese women who ate mercury-contaminated fish from Minamata Bay. A similar contamination poisoned natives near the Hudson Bay in Canada.

Research indicates that meats cooked at very high temperatures contain elevated amounts of carcinogens.[96] Meat should be eaten raw, rare, or braised in liquid. Avoid highly processed meats such as sausage, luncheon meats and bacon. Nitrites, nitrates and other common meat preservatives added to these products are potent carcinogens, linked to cancer of the esophagus, stomach, large intestine, bladder and lungs. Over-consumption of preserved meats can also lead to degeneration of the heart muscle.

Charcoal grilled meats and smoked foods contain chemicals called polycyclic aromatic hydrocarbons that are used to induce cancer in laboratory animals; yet our ancestors ate liberally of smoked meats and fish without suffering from the cancer plague, and primitive man cooked his meat over an open fire. There are probably factors in the primitive diet that give protection against these carcinogens. Modern man is best advised to eat smoked and barbecued meats sparingly.

MILK & MILK PRODUCTS

What about milk? Among nutritionists, there is no other subject that arouses so much controversy. While our hunter-gatherer ancestors did not use milk products, there are many agricultural societies that depend on milk of cattle, sheep, goats, horses, water buffalo and camels for their animal protein and value this "white blood" for its life-sustaining properties. Yet many people are strongly allergic to milk—in fact milk is the most frequent allergy found among people tested for food sensitivities. One cause of this allergy is the absence of intestinal lactase, an enzyme that digests lactose, or milk sugar. All baby animals produce lactase but production of the enzyme declines and disappears soon after weaning. In humans, a mutation or recessive gene allows the continued production of lactase in some individuals. In an isolated population that is forced to depend on milk products for animal protein, those with this gene would have an advantage. If a gene for the persistence of lactase had a frequency of five percent in such a population, in 400 generations its frequency would have risen to sixty percent assuming that those who possessed it had one percent more children per generation than intolerant individuals.[97] Natural selection is the mechanism for adapting isolated populations to the food available to them. But modern man is highly peripatetic and no society in the western world is composed entirely of people whose ancestors come from the immediate region. Only thirty to forty percent of the world's population produces lactase in adulthood.

Another reason that milk is often poorly tolerated is that milk protein—called casein—is one of the most difficult proteins for the body to break down. Once again, the process of natural selection will result in a population more able to digest casein if milk and milk products are part of the traditional diet.

Whether or not you tolerate milk products thus depends on your genetic makeup and your ancestral heritage. If your ancestors came from the milk drinking regions of Europe, such as the Alps or the British Isles, then it is likely that you possess the gene for adult lactase production and therefore tolerate milk products quite well. If your ancestors came from the seacoast regions, or from the New World, the likelihood of your possessing the necessary enzyme is less.

The practice of fermenting or souring milk is found in almost all traditional cattle herding groups. This process partially breaks down lactose and pre-digests casein. The end products—kefir, yoghurt, clabber, etc.—are often well tolerated by those who cannot drink fresh milk. Butter and cream contain little lactose or casein and are usually well tolerated in their natural state. Even so, fermented or soured butter and cream are more digestible. Those with an extreme intolerance for milk protein can take butter in the form of ghee or clarified butter, from which the milk solids have been removed. Cheese, which consists of highly concentrated casein, is well tolerated by some, and best completely avoided by others. Cheeses made from raw milk contain a full complement of enzymes and are therefore more easily digested than cheeses made from pasteurized milk. Natural cheeses, whether from pasteurized or unpasteurized milk, will be more digestible when eaten raw. Processed cheeses contain emulsifiers, extenders, phosphates and hydrogenated oils; they should be strictly avoided.

While some lucky people are genetically equipped to digest milk in all its forms, the milk sold in your supermarket is bad for everybody, partly because the modern cow is a freak of nature. In order to produce cows that give enormous quantities of milk, farmers have succeeded in breeding animals with abnormally active pituitary glands. The pituitary gland not only produces hormones that stimulate the production of milk; it also produces growth hormones. Recently the FDA approved a genetically engineered growth hormone for cows, to be given by injection. These hormones are identical to those produced by the pituitary gland in today's genetically manipulated cows. This practice will simply add to the high level of bovine growth hormones that have been present in our milk for decades. These hormones are present in the water fraction of the milk, not in the butterfat. Babies receive growth hormones from their mothers through their mothers' milk. Small amounts of these hormones are necessary but a superfluity can result in growth abnormalities. Excessive pituitary hormones are also associated with tumor formation and some studies link milk consumption with cancer. The freak pituitary cow is prone to many diseases. She almost always secretes pus into her milk and needs frequent doses of antibiotics.

An equally serious problem with today's milk is the fact that it is pasteurized. We have been taught that pasteurization is a good thing, a method of protecting ourselves against infectious diseases, but closer examination reveals that its merits are highly exaggerated. The modern milking machine and stainless steel tanks, along with efficient packaging and distribution, make pasteurization totally unnecessary for the purposes of sanitation. And pasteurization is no guarantee of cleanliness. All outbreaks of salmonella from contaminated milk in recent decades—and there have been many—have occurred in pasteurized milk.[98] This includes a 1985 outbreak in Illinois that struck 14,316 people causing at least one death. The salmonella strain in that batch of pasteurized milk was found to be genetically resistant to both penicillin and tetracycline.[99] Raw milk contains lactic-acid-producing bacteria which protect against pathogens. Pasteurization destroys these helpful organisms, leaving the finished product devoid of any protective mechanism should undesirable bacteria inadvertently contaminate the supply.

But that's not all that pasteurization does to milk. Heat alters milk's amino acids lysine and tyrosine, making the whole complex of proteins less available; it promotes rancidity of unsaturated fatty acids and causes vitamin loss. Vitamin C loss in pasteurization usually exceeds 50%; loss of other water-soluble vitamins can run as high as 80%; the Wulzen or anti-stiffness factor is totally destroyed. Pasteurization alters milk's mineral components such as calcium, chlorine, magnesium, phosphorus, potassium, sodium and sulphur as well as many trace minerals, making them less available. There is some evidence that pasteurization alters lactase, making it more readily absorbable. This, and the fact that pasteurized milk puts unnecessary strain on the pancreas to produce digestive enzymes, may explain why milk consumption in civilized societies has been linked with diabetes.[100]

Last but not least, pasteurization destroys all the enzymes in milk—in fact, the test for successful pasteurization is absence of enzymes. These enzymes help the body assimilate all body-building factors, including calcium. That is why those who drink pasteurized milk may suffer nevertheless from osteoporosis. Lipase in raw milk helps the body digest and utilize butterfat and some have speculated that the rise in heart disease in the West is due to the fact that pasteurization destroys this enzyme.[101] After pasteurization, chemicals may be added to suppress odor and restore taste. Artificial vitamin D, shown to be toxic to the arteries and kidneys, is added. The final indignity is homogenization which has been linked to heart disease.

Powdered milk is added to the most popular varieties of commercial milk—one-percent and two-percent milk. Commercial dehydration methods oxidize cholesterol in powdered milk, rendering it harmful to the arteries. High temperature drying also creates large quantities of nitrate compounds, which are potent carcinogens.

Modern pasteurized milk, devoid of its enzyme content, puts an enormous strain on the body's digestive mechanism. In the elderly, and those with milk intolerance or inherited weaknesses of digestion, this milk passes through not fully digested. Undigested milk particles can clog the tiny villi of the small intestine and become like rancid cheese, preventing the absorption of vital nutrients and promoting the up-take of toxic substances. The result is allergies, chronic fatigue and a host of degenerative diseases.

All the healthy milk-drinking populations studies by Dr. Price subsisted on raw milk, raw cultured milk or raw cheese from normal animals eating fresh grass or fodder. It is very difficult to find this kind of milk in America. In California and Georgia, raw milk was formerly available in health food stores. Intense harassment by state sanitation authorities has all but driven raw milk from the market in these states, in spite of the fact that it is technically legal. Even when available, this milk suffers from the same drawbacks as most supermarket milk—it comes from freak-pituitary cows, often raised in crowded pens on dry feed. In some states you can buy raw milk at the farm. If you can find a farmer who will sell you raw milk from old fashioned scrub cows, or from Jersey or Guernsey cows, allowed to feed on fresh pasturage, then by all means avail yourself of this source. Some stores now carry pasteurized, but not homogenized, milk from cows raised on natural feed. Such milk may be used to make cultured milk products like yoghurt, cultured buttermilk and cultured cream. Cultured buttermilk, which is low in casein but high in lactic acid, is often well tolerated by those with milk allergies, and gives excellent results when used to soak whole grain flours for baking. If you cannot find good quality raw milk, you should limit your consumption of milk products to cultured milk, cultured buttermilk, whole milk yoghurt, butter, cream and raw cheese—which are available in all states. Much imported cheese is raw (look for the words "milk" or "fresh milk" on the label) and of very high quality.

VITAMINS & MINERALS

The discovery of the first vitamins, in the early 1900's, began the era of modern interest in diet and nutrition. Pioneering chemists found that certain "unknown substances" in food were essential to life. They discovered that fat soluble A and water soluble B vitamins were necessary to prevent diseases like rickets, beriberi and pellagra; and that vitamin C, a factor present in many fresh foods, prevented scurvy. By the 1930's, a great many more vitamins had been discovered and their effects catalogued. Public interest in the subject was intense, and articles on vitamins often appeared in magazines and newspapers.

The discovery of new vitamins has not stopped since the early days of research, and the subject of food science has proved to be far more complex than anyone at first imagined. The early discoveries led some researchers to conclude that all vitamins necessary to life could be supplied in their isolated form, as vitamin pills. We now know that vitamins do not exist as single compounds, but as parts of a complex of compounds, each part contributing to the whole. For example, vitamin C used to treat scurvy and other deficiency conditions is more effective when given in natural form that includes minerals, rutin and other analogs.[102]

As many as seventeen water soluble vitamins labeled B have been discovered, present in different proportions in different foods, but all working together synergistically; vitamin D has as many as twelve components;[103] vitamin P has at least five components. Most vitamins, it seems, produce optimum results in the presence of certain naturally occurring "co-factors" such as trace minerals, enzymes and coenzymes, as well as other vitamins.

As vitamins have been isolated, so have the various minerals in our foods. The short list of macro-minerals—calcium, chlorine, magnesium, phosphorus, potassium, and sodium—now shares the research spotlight with a longer list of essential trace minerals. These are needed only in minute amounts, but their absence nevertheless results in many disease conditions. The number of trace minerals known to be essential to life now exceeds thirty and some researchers believe that for optimum health the body needs to ingest every substance found in the earth's crust. Along with familiar trace minerals such as iron and iodine, the body also needs others, not so well known, like cobalt, germanium and boron.

The early view that inorganic minerals could be effectively taken in tablet form or added as "enrichments" to white bread has also undergone revision in recent decades. The body best recognizes and absorbs minerals in organic form, present in food with numerous co-factors.

The bewildering array of factors in foods now known to be essential has led nutritionists to recognize the futility of providing all factors necessary to life in pill form. While supplementing the diet with certain isolated vitamins and minerals has proven beneficial for many disease conditions, the best source of vitamins for most of us is properly prepared whole foods. For this reason, the importance of eating foods that are rich in vitamins and minerals cannot be underestimated.

Vitamin and mineral content of food varies enormously with farming methods.[104] Nitrogen fertilizers produce initial high yields, in part by pulling minerals from the soil. In time, commercially fertilized soils become depleted, and the foods grown on them suffer accordingly. The revival of interest in compost and natural fertilizers, rich in minerals including trace minerals, is due in part to the realization that healthy soil is the basis of health for all life forms. Scientific assays have shown large differences in vitamin and mineral content between foods grown with nitrogen fertilizers and food grown organically. For example, cabbage can vary in its iron content from 94 parts per million to 0 parts per million; tomatoes can vary in iron content from 1,938 parts per million to 1 part per million. Vitamin A content of butterfat varies with the season as well as the soil; even the protein portion of grains and legumes will vary with soil fertility. Some commercially raised oranges have been found to contain *no* vitamin C!

Food processing affects vitamin content to varying extents. Some vitamins are heat sensitive while others survive heating fairly well. Steaming and waterless methods of cooking preserve vitamins better than rapid boiling and vegetables cooked in acidic liquid preserve vitamins better than those cooked in an alkaline medium. Oxidation is a prime cause of vitamin loss. Cold temperatures and freezing have little effect on vitamin content, and air or sun drying preserve or even enhance nutrient content; long periods of high heat used in canning are destructive to some vitamins, but not all. Some methods of food preservation and processing actually make nutrients more available—these include simmering bones in acidic liquid to made broth, culturing of dairy products, sprouting and certain methods of pickling, fermenting and leavening.

The Diet Dictocrats have set minimum daily requirements for a few key vitamins and minerals but many investigators feel that these standards are far too low. These critics contend that minimum daily requirements are sufficient to prevent acute deficiencies but not enough to support optimum health, especially as individual requirements for specific vitamins and minerals vary widely. In fact, a typical profile of nutrient requirements is one in which the individual has average needs with respect to most vitamins and minerals, but requirements far in excess of average for a few specific nutrients.[105] Consumption of sugar, refined flour and hydrogenated fats, and of alcohol, tobacco and many drugs, all deplete the body of nutrients, resulting in higher vitamin and mineral requirements for users. Stress of any sort causes the body to use up available nutrients at a faster than normal rate.

Space permits only a most cursory summary of the major nutrients in our foods. Many books have been written on the specific roles of vitamins and minerals and their use in the treatment of disease. See Appendix D if you wish to explore this subject further.

Vitamin A: This all-important vitamin is a catalyst on which innumerable biochemical processes depend. According to Dr. Price, neither protein nor minerals can be utilized by the body without vitamin A from animal sources.[106] Vitamin A also acts as an anti-oxidant, protecting the body against pollutants and free radicals, hence against cancer. Vitamin A stimulates the secretion of gastric juices needed for protein digestion, plays a vital role in the building of strong bones and rich blood, contributes to the production of RNA and is needed for the formation of visual purple. Sources of preformed vitamin A (called retinol) include butterfat, liver and other organ meats, seafood and fish liver oils. Provitamin A or carotene is also a powerful anti-oxidant. It is found in all yellow, red, orange or dark green fruits and vegetables. Carotenoids are converted to Vitamin A in the upper intestine. Vegetarians claim that the body's requirement for vitamin A can be met with carotenes from vegetable sources but many people—particularly infants, diabetics and individuals with poor thyroid function—cannot make this conversion.[107] Furthermore, studies have shown that our bodies cannot convert carotenoids into vitamin A without the presence of fat in the diet.[108] Dr. Price discovered that the diets of healthy primitives contained at least ten times more vitamin A from animal sources than those of civilized men. The high vitamin A content of their diets insured them excellent bone structure, wide and handsome faces with plenty of room for the teeth, and ample protection against stress of all types. However, high amounts of Vitamin A can also be toxic, especially to those with impaired liver function and those whose diets are otherwise poor. Antibiotics, laxatives and cholesterol-lowering drugs interfere with Vitamin A absorption.

Vitamin B: All the water soluble B vitamins work as a team to promote healthy nerves, skin, eyes, hair, liver, muscle tone, and cardiovascular system; they protect from mental disorders, depression and anxiety. Deficiency of the B vitamin complex can result in the enlargement and malfunction of almost every organ and gland in the body. The best source of B vitamins is whole grains —refinement thus wastes this essential source. They are also found in fresh fruits, vegetables, nuts, legumes, seafood, and organ meats; they can also be produced by intestinal bacteria. B1 (thiamine) was the first water soluble vitamin to be discovered. Deficiency leads to the disease beriberi. Recent evidence indicates that B1 deficiency is the root cause of anorexia and other eating disorders.[109] It is essential for the manufacture of hydrochloric acid and has been used to treat constipation, sea sickness, fatigue, herpes and multiple sclerosis. Sugar consumption rapidly depletes vitamin B1. Deficiencies of B2 or riboflavin are rare as this vitamin occurs plentifully in most foods. Deficiency of B3 or niacin results in the disease pellagra, characterized by dermatitis, dementia, tremors and diarrhea. The amino acid tryptophan can be converted to niacin and has been used to treat a variety of symptoms indicative of niacin deficiency. Recent studies have revealed that vitamin B6 or pyridoxine, found mostly in animal products, contributes to the proper functioning of over one hundred enzymes. Deficiencies in B6 have been linked to diabetes, nervous disorders and coronary heart disease. They are widespread in the US because excess B1 and B2, added to white flour, interferes with B6 function, and because Americans no longer have access to one of the best sources of this heat-sensitive nutrient—raw milk. The B vitamin folic acid counteracts cancer by strengthening the chromosomes; folic acid deficiency can result in babies born with neural tube deformities like spinal bifida. B12 is needed to prevent anemia and nervous disorders as well as maintain fertility and promote normal growth and development. It is found only in animal products. B15 (pangamic acid) and B17 (nitrilosides) protect against cancer; the former is found in grains and seeds, the latter in grasses, sprouts, buckwheat and the seeds of many fruits. Traditional diets are much richer in nitrilosides than our own.

Vitamin C: A water soluble vitamin most well known for its use in treatment of the common cold, it is needed for a host of processes including tissue growth and repair, strength of capillary walls, lactation and adrenal gland function. It is vital for the formation of collagen, the body's structural substance. Vitamin C is found in citrus fruits and many other fresh fruits and vegetables. Linus Pauling has promoted the use of megadoses of Vitamin C for schizophrenia as well as for the common cold. It promotes healing of wounds and is a powerful antioxidant. Massive doses of vitamin C have been used to cure drug addiction. New evidence suggests that vitamin C works synergistically with vitamin E. Hypoglycemics and individuals on a high-protein diet require more vitamin C as these conditions interfere with the metabolism of ascorbic acid. It is found in many fruits and vegetables, and in certain animal organs. It is destroyed by heat. Alcohol and many common drugs including aspirin and oral contraceptives may reduce vitamin C levels in the body.

Vitamin D: Along with vitamin A, vitamin D is needed for calcium and phosphorus absorption and thus is essential to healthy bones and teeth and to normal growth. Its role in many other mechanisms has recently been recognized. Vitamin D acts as a powerful steroid hormone, igniting widescale gene activity in the skin, pancreas, parathyroid gland, breast and ovaries. Deficiency can cause rickets and myopia. The body manufactures vitamin D in the presence of sunlight—cholesterol is an important element in this pathway—but nevertheless requires additional amounts from food. It is found almost exclusively in animal sources—butterfat, eggs, liver, organ meats, seafood and fish liver oils. Artificial vitamin D added to milk has been linked to hyperactivity and other allergic reactions.

Vitamin E: This fat soluble vitamin is needed for circulation, tissue repair and healing. It seems to help in the treatment of fibrocystic conditions, sterility, PMS, muscular dystrophy and in retarding the aging process. A powerful antioxidant, it works in concert with certain trace elements, notably selenium and zinc, to prevent cancer and cardiovascular disease. A vital role of vitamin E is the deactivation of free radicals. Increased ingestion of polyunsaturated oils requires greater amounts of vitamin E in the diet. It is found in unrefined vegetable oils, butter, organ meats, grains, nuts, seeds, legumes, and dark green leafy vegetables.

- **Vitamin K:** This fat-soluble compound is needed for blood clotting and may play a role in bone formation. Vitamin K given to post-menopausal women helps prevent bone loss. It is found in liver, egg yolks, grains, and cruciferous and dark leafy vegetables.

- **Vitamin P:** Also called bioflavonoids, these water soluble compounds enhance the absorption of vitamin C to promote healing and to protect the structure of blood capillaries. They have an anti-bacterial effect, stimulate bile production, lower cholesterol levels, regulate menstrual flow and help prevent cataracts. One of the bioflavonoids, rutin, has been shown to have a sedative-stimulant effect on the brain. Sources include peppers, grapes, buckwheat and the white peel of citrus fruits.

As for minerals, it is important to remember that the body best absorbs these nutrients in organic, ionized form; and in the presence of adequate vitamins A and D from animal sources. Both deficiencies and surfeit of the various minerals can cause disease conditions. That is why it is so important to depend upon a varied and healthy diet for our minerals, rather than to take them as supplements. The following six minerals are called macro minerals because they are needed in relatively large quantities.

- **Calcium:** Not only vital for strong bones and teeth, calcium is also needed for the heart and nervous system, and for muscle growth and contraction. Calcium helps prevent the accumulation of too much acid or too much alkali in the blood. Calcium is found abundantly in many foods—meats, seafood, dark green vegetables and nuts, as well as in dairy products and bone broths—but it is often difficult to absorb and utilize. Both iron and zinc can inhibit calcium absorption, as can excess phosphorus and magnesium. Phytic acid in the bran of grains that have not been soaked, fermented, sprouted or naturally leavened will bind with calcium and other minerals in the intestinal tract, making these minerals less available. Sufficient vitamin D is needed for calcium absorption, as is a proper potassium/calcium ratio in the blood. Consumption of sugar and stress both pull calcium from the bones.

- **Chlorine:** Chlorine is widely distributed in the body in compound form with sodium or potassium. It helps regulate the correct balance of acid and alkali in the blood and the passage of fluids across cell membranes. It is needed for the production of hydrochloric acid, and hence for protein digestion. Chlorine is also essential to proper growth and functioning of the brain. The most important source of chlorine is salt but traces are found in many foods. Lacto-fermented beverages and meat broths both provide a good source of easily-assimilable chlorine.

- **Magnesium:** This mineral is essential to enzyme activity, to calcium and potassium uptake, to nerve transmission and bone formation, and to carbohydrate and mineral metabolism. It is magnesium, not calcium, that helps form hard tooth enamel, resistant to decay. Like calcium and chlorine, magnesium also plays a role in regulating the acid-alkaline balance in the body. High magnesium levels in drinking water have been linked to resistance to heart disease. Although it is found in many foods, including dairy products, nuts, vegetables, fish, meat and seafood, deficiencies are common in America due to soil depletion, poor absorption and lack of minerals in much drinking water. A diet high in carbohydrates, oxalic acid in foods like raw spinach, and phytic acid found in whole grains can lead to deficiencies. An excellent source of usable magnesium is beef, chicken or fish broth. High amounts of zinc and vitamin D increase the body's need for magnesium. Magnesium deficiency can result in coronary heart disease, chronic weight loss, obesity, fatigue, epilepsy and impaired brain function. Chocolate cravings are a sign of magnesium deficiency.

Phosphorus: The second most abundant mineral in the body, phosphorus is needed for bone growth, kidney function and cell growth. It also plays a role in maintaining acid-alkali balance in the blood. Phosphorus is found in many foods but in order to be properly utilized, it must be in proper balance with magnesium and calcium in the blood. Excessive levels of phosphorus in the blood can lead to cravings for sugar and alcohol; too little phosphorus inhibits calcium absorption and can lead to osteoporosis. Best sources are animal products, whole grains, pulses and nuts.

Potassium: Potassium and sodium work in concert in all body processes. Inner cell fluids are high in potassium while fluids outside the cell are high in sodium. Thus potassium is important for a healthy nervous system and for many chemical reactions within the cells. Potassium is helpful in treating high blood pressure. It is found in a wide variety of nuts, grains and vegetables. Excessive use of salt along with inadequate intake of fruits and vegetables can result in a potassium deficiency.

Sodium: As all body fluids contain sodium, it can be said that sodium is essential to life. It is needed for many biochemical processes in the body including regulation of water balance, distribution of fluids on either side of cell walls, stimulation of nerves, contraction and expansion of muscles and the regulation of acid-alkali balance. However, excess sodium can result in high blood pressure, potassium deficiency, and liver, kidney and heart disease; symptoms of deficiency include confusion, low blood sugar, weakness, lethargy and heart palpitations. Meat broths and zucchini are excellent sources.

Although needed in only minute amounts, trace minerals are essential for many biochemical processes. Often it is a single atom of a trace mineral, incorporated into a complex protein, that gives the compound its specific characteristic—iron as a part of the hemoglobin molecule, for example, or any of a number of trace minerals as the distinguishing component of specific enzymes. The following list is not meant to be exhaustive, but merely indicative of the complexity of bodily processes, and their dependence on well-mineralized soil and food.

- **Boron:** Needed for healthy bones. Found in fruits, especially apples, leafy vegetables, nuts and grains.

- **Chromium:** Needed for glucose metabolism and hence for the maintenance of proper blood sugar levels, as well as for the synthesis of cholesterol, fats and protein. Most Americans are deficient in chromium because they eat so many refined carbohydrates. Best sources are animal products, molasses, nuts, whole wheat, eggs and vegetables.

- **Cobalt:** Works with copper to promote assimilation of iron. A cobalt atom resides in the center of vitamin B12. Best sources are animal products. Cobalt deficiency occurs most frequently in vegetarians.

- **Copper:** Aids in the formation of bone, hemoglobin and red blood cells. Needed for healthy nerves, a healthy immune system and collagen formation, copper works in balance with zinc and vitamin C. Along with manganese, magnesium, silver and iodine, copper plays an important role in memory and brain function. The best and most easily assimilated source is liver followed by nuts, molasses and oats. Copper deficiency is widespread in America. Copper deficiency combined with high fructose consumption has particularly deleterious effects on infants and growing children.

- **Germanium:** A newcomer to the list of trace minerals now known to be essential to optimum health. Germanium-rich foods help combat rheumatoid arthritis, food allergies, elevated cholesterol, fungal and viral infections and cancer. Germanium attaches itself readily to oxygen and transports it to parts of the body where it is needed. Certain foods will concentrate germanium if it is found in the soil—garlic, ginseng, mushrooms, onions and the herbs aloe vera, comfrey, and suma.

- **Iodine:** Although needed in only minute amounts, iodine is essential for numerous body processes such as fat metabolism, thyroid gland function, and the production of sex hormones. Muscle cramps are a sign of deficiency as are cold hands and feet, proneness to weight gain, poor memory, constipation, depression and headaches. It seems to be essential for mental development. Iodine deficiency has been linked to mental retardation, to coronary heart disease, to susceptibility to polio and to breast cancer. Sources include most sea foods, unrefined sea salt, kelp and other sea weeds, fish broth, butter, pineapple and dark green vegetables. Certain vegetables such as cabbage and spinach can block iodine absorption when eaten raw. Requirements for iodine vary widely. In general, those whose ancestors come from seacoast areas require more iodine than those whose ancestors come from inland regions. Proper iodine utilization requires sufficient levels of vitamin A, supplied by animal fats.

Iron: As part of the hemoglobin molecule, iron is vital for healthy blood; iron also forms an essential part of many enzymes. Iron deficiency is associated with poor mental development and problems with the immune system. It is found in eggs, fish, liver, meat and green leafy vegetables. Iron found in animal protein is more readily absorbed than iron in vegetable foods. Recently researchers have warned against inorganic iron used to supplement white bread as this form of iron cannot be utilized by the body and its build-up in the blood and tissues is essentially a build-up of toxins. Elevated amounts of inorganic iron have been linked to heart disease and cancer.

Manganese: Needed for healthy nerves, a healthy immune system and blood sugar regulation, manganese also plays a part in the formation of mothers' milk, and in the growth of healthy bones. Deficiency may lead to trembling hands, seizures and lack of coordination. High milk consumption may lead to manganese deficiency as calcium can interfere with manganese absorption. Phosphorus antagonizes manganese as well. Best sources are pecans and other nuts, seeds, whole grains and butterfat.

Molybdenum: Needed in small amounts for nitrogen metabolism, iron absorption, fat oxidation and normal cell function. Best sources are lentils, liver, beans, grains, legumes and dark green leafy vegetables.

Selenium: A vital antioxidant that acts with vitamin E to protect the immune system, and maintain healthy heart function. It is vital for pancreatic function and tissue elasticity and has been shown to protect against radiation and toxic minerals. Deficiency can lead to muscle breakdown, but an excess may lead to cancer. Best sources are butter, Brazil nuts, seafood, and grains.

Silicon: Needed for healthy bones and connective tissue. Silicon rich foods and broth will hasten bone repair after a fracture. Best sources are leafy green vegetables and whole grains.

Sulphur: Part of the chemical structure of several amino acids, sulphur aids in many body processes. It helps protect the body from infection, blocks the harmful effects of radiation and pollution and slows down the aging process. Sulphur-containing proteins are the building blocks of cell membranes. Some researchers believe that an overabundance of sulphur can be harmful. Sulphur is found in cruciferous vegetables, eggs, milk and animal products.

Vanadium: Needed for cellular metabolism and the formation of bones and teeth, it also plays a role in growth and reproduction and helps control cholesterol levels in the blood. Deficiency has been linked to cardiovascular and kidney disease. Buckwheat, unrefined vegetable oils, grains and olives are the best sources. Vanadium is difficult to absorb. It is inhibited by tobacco.

Zinc: Called the intelligence mineral, zinc is required for mental development, for healthy reproductive organs, particularly the prostate gland, for protein synthesis and collagen formation. Zinc is also involved in the blood sugar control mechanism and thus protects against diabetes. Zinc is needed to maintain proper levels of vitamin E in the blood. Inability to taste or smell is a sign of zinc deficiency. High levels of phytic acid in cereal grains and legumes block zinc absorption. Zinc deficiency during pregnancy can cause birth defects. As oral contraceptives diminish zinc levels, it is important for women to wait at least six months after discontinuing the pill before becoming pregnant. Best sources include fish, legumes, meats, oysters, nuts, seeds and ginger.

Not all minerals are beneficial. Lead, cadmium, mercury, aluminum and arsenic are poisons to the body, at least in their inorganic form. These come from polluted air, water, soil and food; lead finds its way into the water supply through lead pipes. Sources of aluminum include processed soy products, aluminim cookware, refined table salt, deodorants and antacids. Baking powder is another source of aluminim and should be avoided. Amalgam fillings are the principle source of toxic mercury in the system—linked to Alzheimers and a number of other disease conditions. The anti-oxidants—vitamin A, carotenes, vitamin C, vitamin E and selenium—all protect against these toxins and help the body to eliminate them.

ENZYMES

An important branch of twentieth century nutritional research, running parallel to and equal in significance to the discovery of vitamins and minerals, has been the discovery of enzymes and their function. Enzymes are complex proteins that act as catalysts in almost every biochemical process that takes place in the body. Their activity depends on the presence of adequate vitamins and minerals. Many enzymes incorporate a single molecule of a trace mineral—such as copper, iron or zinc—without which the enzyme cannot function.

In 1930, when enzymes first came to the attention of biochemists, some 80 were identified; today over 5,000 have been discovered. Enzymes fall into one of three major classifications. The largest classification is the metabolic enzymes which play a role in all body processes including breathing, talking, moving, thinking, behavior and maintenance of the immune system. A subset of these metabolic enzymes acts to neutralize poisons and carcinogens such as pollutants, DDT and tobacco smoke, changing them into less toxic forms that the body can eliminate. The second category is the digestive enzymes, of which there are about 22 in number. Most of these are manufactured by the pancreas. They are secreted by glands in the duodenum (a valve that separates the stomach from the small intestine) and work to break down the bulk of partially digested food leaving the stomach.

The enzymes we need to consider when planning our diets are the third category, the food enzymes. These are present in raw foods and they initiate the process of digestion in the mouth and upper stomach. Food enzymes include proteases for digesting protein, lipases for digesting fats and amylases for digesting carbohydrates. Amylases in saliva contribute to the digestion of carbohydrates while they are being chewed, and all enzymes found in food continue this process while it rests in the upper or cardiac portion of the stomach. The upper stomach secretes no digestive juices whatsoever, but acts much like the crop of a bird or the first stomach of ruminant animals. It can be described as a sort of holding tank where the enzymes present in raw foods do their work on what we have eaten before this more or less partially digested mass passes on to the lower stomach, about 30 minutes after food is ingested. Hydrochloric acid secretion occurs only in the lower stomach and is stimulated by the passage of food from the upper to lower stomach.[110] (This hydrochloric acid does not digest meat, as is commonly believed, but activates the enzyme pepsinogen to its active form pepsin that digests protein.)

Enzyme research has revealed the importance of raw foods in the diet. The enzymes in raw food help start the process of digestion and lower the body's need to produce digestive enzymes. All enzymes are deactivated at a wet-heat temperature of 118 degrees Fahrenheit, and a dry-heat temperature of about 150 degrees. It is one of those happy designs of nature that foods and liquid at 117 degrees can be touched without pain, but liquids over 118 degrees will burn. Thus we have a built-in mechanism for determining whether or not the food we are eating still contains its enzyme content.

A diet composed exclusively of cooked food puts a severe strain on the pancreas, drawing down its reserves, so to speak. If the pancreas is constantly overstimulated to produce the enzymes that ought to be in foods, the result over time will be inhibited function. Humans eating an enzyme-poor diet, comprised primarily of cooked food, use up a tremendous amount of their enzyme potential in the outpouring of secretions from the pancreas and other digestive organs. The result, according to the late Dr. Edward Howell, is a shortened life-span, illness, and lowered resistance to stress of all types. He points out that humans and animals on a diet comprised largely of cooked food have enlarged pancreas organs while other glands and organs, notably the brain, actually shrink in size. His research also uncovered the fact that the body recycles enzymes by absorbing them through the intestine and colon and transporting them in the blood back to the upper intestine to be used again.[111] The body is thus designed to conserve its precious enzyme stores.

Dr. Howell formulated the following Enzyme Nutrition Axiom: The *length of life* is inversely proportional to the rate of exhaustion of the *enzyme potential* of an organism. The increased use of food enzymes promotes a *decreased rate* of exhaustion of the enzyme potential.[112] Another rule can be expressed as follows: Whole foods give good health; enzyme-rich foods provide limitless energy

Almost all traditional societies incorporate raw, enzyme-rich foods into their cuisines—not only vegetable foods but also raw animal proteins and fats in the form of raw dairy foods, raw muscle and organ meats, and raw fish. These diets also traditionally include a certain amount of cultured or fermented foods, which have an enzyme content that is actually enhanced by the fermenting and culturing process. The Eskimo diet, for example, is composed in large portion of raw fish that has been allowed to "autolate" or "pre-digest", that is, become putrefied or semi-rancid; to this predigested food they ascribe their stamina. The culturing of dairy products, found almost universally among pre-industrialized peoples, enhances the enzyme content of milk, cream, butter and cheese. Ethnic groups that consume large amounts of cooked meat usually include fermented vegetables or condiments such as sauerkraut and pickled carrots, cucumbers and beets with their meals. Oriental cultured soybean products, such as *natto* and *miso*, are another good source of food enzymes if these foods are eaten unheated. Even after being subjected to heat, fermented foods are more easily assimilated because they have been pre-digested by enzymes. In like manner, meats that have been well-aged or marinated present less of a strain on the digestive mechanism because of this pre-digestion.

Grains, nuts, legumes and seeds are rich in enzymes, as well as other nutrients, but they also contain enzyme inhibitors. Unless deactivated, these enzyme inhibitors can put an even greater strain on the digestive system than cooked foods. Sprouting, soaking in warm acidic water, leavening, culturing and fermenting, all found in traditional societies, are processes that deactivate enzyme inhibitors, thus making all the enzymes and nutrients in grains, nuts and seeds more readily available.

Most fruits and vegetables contain few enzymes; exceptional plant foods noted for high enzyme content include extra virgin olive oil and other unrefined oils, raw honey, grapes, figs and many tropical fruits including avocados, dates, bananas, papaya, pineapple, kiwi and mangos.

SALT, SPICES & ADDITIVES

Many topics under the rubric of nutrition are fraught with controversy and the subject of salt is no exception. It has been fashionable in recent years for nutritionists to restrict the use of salt and this is one proscription that medical orthodoxy has endorsed. Early research uncovered a correlation of salt intake with high blood pressure but subsequent studies indicated that salt restriction may harm more people than it helps. A large study conducted in 1983 found that dietary salt did not have any significant effect on blood pressure in the majority of people. In some cases, salt restriction actually raises blood pressure.[113]

The need for salt varies according to the individual. People with weak adrenal glands lose salt in their urine and must have plentiful salt in the diet; but for others, excessive salt consumption causes calcium to be excreted in the urine, and hence can lead to osteoporosis. Some nutritionists contend that salt stimulates the glands in much the same way as sugar, and can thus lead to a host of degenerative illnesses. A salt-free diet will often cure acne and oily skin. Excessive salt in the diet depletes potassium. On the other hand, salt is a powerful enzyme activator. Dr. Edward Howell, noted enzyme researcher, observed that those who lived on a diet composed almost entirely of raw foods, like the Eskimo, do not need salt in their diets; but those who subsist on a diet largely composed of cooked foods require salt to activate enzymes in the intestines. With few exceptions, all traditional cultures use some salt. Primitive peoples living far from the sea or other salt sources burn sodium-rich marsh grasses and add the ash to their food.

Salt is also important for its chloride component, needed for the manufacture of hydrochloric acid, proper functioning of the brain and nervous system and for many other processes. Some researchers believe that salt is essential to the digestion of carbohydrate foods as well.

Most discussions of salt ignore the issue of salt processing. Few people realize that our salt—like our sugar, flour and vegetable oils—is highly refined; it is the product of a chemical and high temperature industrial process that removes all the valuable magnesium salts as well as trace minerals naturally occurring in the sea. To keep salt dry, salt refiners adulterate this "pure" product with several harmful additives, including aluminum compounds. Along with an iodine compound, processors add two other chemicals to commercial table salt. One is a stabilizer, dextrose, which turns the salt a purplish color. The other is a bleaching agent which restores whiteness to the salt. According to some researchers, these additives prevent salt from combining with body fluids so that it becomes toxic and a strain on the kidneys.[114] This may be why the late physician Henry Bieler found evidence of sodium starvation in the tissues of people who consumed large amounts of salt.[115]

Even most so-called sea salt is produced by industrial methods. The best and most health-promoting salt is extracted by the action of the sun on seawater in clay-lined vats. Its light grey color indicates a high moisture and trace mineral content. This natural salt contains only about 82% sodium chloride; it contains about .5% all-important magnesium salts and nearly 80 trace minerals. Moreover, as it has not been heated to high temperatures, the minerals remain in ionized form, and hence are easily assimilated. The best and purest commercially available source of this salt is the natural salt marshes of Brittany, where it is "farmed" according to a centuries old method. (See Sources.) Red sea salt from Hawaii is also an excellent product, but it is not readily available in the continental US.

Natural sea salt is a rich source of iodine, the absence of which leads to goiter and many other conditions of an underactive and malfunctioning thyroid gland. Iodized salt will often relieve the overt symptoms of goiter—it will cause the thyroid gland to shrink back to normal or near-normal size—but it does not prevent other thyroid malfunctions such as obesity, low vitality, fragile teeth and bones, various sexual and mental problems, and proneness to heart disease and cancer. There is evidence that the form of iodine added to iodized salt passes through the body very quickly, sometimes within 20 minutes, and therefore does little long-term good. Natural sea salt contains from 30 to 1200 times more iodine than "enriched" salt, and this iodine is in organic, usable form that stays in the body for 48 hours or more, long enough to nourish the thyroid gland.[116]

Broth made from animal bones and meat is a another good source of both sodium and iodine as well as magnesium, potassium and important trace minerals. Broth made from fish carcasses and fish heads is rich in additional substances that nourish the thyroid gland and protect the body from the deleterious effects of unsaturated fatty acids.[117] Thus it is an essential component in the diet of those who frequently eat oily fish, such as the Japanese. Properly made, broth is also a source of gelatin which research has shown to be an excellent aid to digestion and assimilation of cooked foods.[118] The food provider with an eye for nutrition, as well as good taste, will make these broths a staple in her repertoire.

What about spices? Once again there is debate among nutritionists. One school of thought claims that spices stimulate the glands and should always be avoided; others point out that spices make our food taste good, and render it more digestible by stimulating the saliva. Spices are good sources of magnesium and other minerals. Certainly it would be a shame to forego the rich cornucopia of spices that modern transport brings to our markets. A compromise position allows spicy foods in moderation to those who are healthy; but those whose glands have been worn out by many years of poor diet may have to adopt bland fare in order to regain and maintain their well-being. Fresh herbs are less stimulating and should be used whenever possible—they are rich in vitamins, minerals and other health-promoting factors.

Monosodium glutamate is an additive that has been soundly condemned by the health food profession and for good reason. Glutamate is a neurotoxic substance that causes many adverse reactions. In sensitive individuals these manifest as dizziness, violent diarrhea and even anaphylactic shock. Longer term and more insidious consequences of MSG ingestion include Parkinsons and Alzheimers in adults and neurological damage in children. Animal studies have linked MSG with brain lesions, retinal degeneration and obesity.[119]

The powerful MSG industry lobby has been able to allay the publics fears about MSG by pointing out that monosodium glutamate is derived from the amino acid glutamic acid, a non-essential amino acid that occurs plentifully in meat broths and fermented products like soy sauce and *miso*. It is glutamic acid that gives these foods their rich, meat-like taste. However, the form of glutamic acid in homemade meat broths is a naturally occurring isomer that is absorbed very slowly from the intestines and rarely causes allergic reactions; but the glutamate in MSG is not a naturally occurring isomer. It is absorbed almost instantly from the mouth, lungs and stomach into the bloodstream. All foods containing MSG should be avoided, as well as hydrolyzed protein, which also contains glutamate and produces the same effects.[120] A great many processed foods contain MSG or hydrolyzed protein, especially soy-based concoctions and those sold as meat broth substitutes.

About the hundreds of other additives, preservatives, colorings and artificial flavorings added to processed foods we can only say, avoid them as much as possible. The healthy body produces enzymes that deactivate many of these substances; but when the body is overloaded with junk food, and its enzyme production over-taxed, it cannot marshal the resources needed to neutralize this onslaught of poisons. Unpublished research indicates that while small amounts of additives taken one at a time may be relatively harmless, these same small amounts when combined can have severely toxic effects.[121]

It is important to distinguish between food processing techniques that preserve or enhance the nutrients in food, and those that deplete them. In general, freezing preserves most of the nutrients in food; pickling, fermenting and culturing according to traditional methods, enhance the availability of many nutrients by increasing enzyme activity. Sun drying is an age-old method for preserving foods that conserves and even enhances nutrients. But processes involving high temperatures and added chemicals should be avoided as much as possible. This includes pasteurization, high temperature drying, high temperature and pressure processing of grains and oils, and solvent extraction of oils. Irradiation does not heat foods to high temperatures but nevertheless alters large portions of their nutrients.[122] Feeding studies show that irradiated foods cause mutagenic blood abnormalities in children.[123]

Canned foods should play a limited role in your cooking, not only because vitamins are destroyed but because canned foods lack enzymes. Fresh vegetables are almost always preferable with the exception of tomatoes. Tomatoes for canning are picked at the peak of ripeness, with a carotene content much higher than most fresh tomatoes sold in stores. Carotene survives the canning process although some other vitamins may not. Thus, limited use of canned tomato products is acceptable. Canned legumes such as kidney beans and chick peas will contain the same nutrients as those which have been boiled on your own stove, but they may not have undergone the all-important soaking process to neutralize phytates, so their use should be limited.

Whenever possible, buy organically grown meats and vegetables (but you needn't make a fetish about it.) Organically produced food is free from most harmful pesticides and is generally higher in vitamin and mineral content. Organically produced foods are becoming more available—organic grains and legumes can be purchased at most health food stores, and the supply of organic fruits and vegetables increases each year. It is particularly important to buy organic potatoes and onions. Regular commercial potatoes and onions have been treated with sprout inhibitors that cause cellular changes in test animals. Avoid thin-skinned fruits that have come from long distances—they usually have been treated with chemicals of questionable safety.

BEVERAGES

Most books on nutrition have little to say about what we drink; yet our choice of beverages plays an important role in determining our health.

A primary factor contributing to the scourge of degenerative diseases plaguing this nation is the national love affair with soft drinks. Americans consumed 43 gallons of soft drinks per person in 1990, nearly double the amount of 1970. Soft drinks have found their way into the hands of tiny children, and into vending machines in our public schools. We have become the Pepsi degeneration.

What's wrong with soft drinks? Just about everything. First, they are loaded with sweeteners—usually high fructose corn syrup—or sugar substitutes, notably aspartame. We have already discussed the deleterious effect of refined sugar, particularly fructose, on every organ and system in the body. The sugar in soda pop is nothing but naked calories and acts as an anti-nutrient. Sugar in soft drinks, more than any other source, contributes to what has become a national addiction to sweet foods of all kinds. It is estimated that sugar in soft drinks accounts for 35% of all US sugar consumption.

Sugar substitutes do nothing to reduce the dependence or craving for sweet tasting foods and tests have shown that sugar substitutes don't even help you lose weight—some people actually gain weight when they drink diet sodas.[124] Furthermore, they have their own dangers. The most widely used artificial sweetener—aspartame or Nutra-sweet—has been associated with numerous health problems including dizziness, visual impairment, severe muscle aches, numbing of extremities, pancreatitis, high blood pressure, retinal hemorrhaging, seizures and depression. It is suspected of causing birth defects and chemical disruptions in the brain. Researchers at Utah State University found that even at low levels, aspartame induces adverse changes in the pituitary glands of mice.[125] The pituitary gland is the master gland upon which the proper functioning of all the body's processes depend.

When aspartame is digested it breaks down into the amino acids phenylalanine and aspartic acid, plus methanol. Methanol, or wood alcohol, is a known poison. Methanol is also found in fruit juices and our regulatory agencies have seized on this fact to assure us that the ethanol by-product of aspartame is not harmful. They fail to point out that the methanol content of diet soft drinks is 15 to 100 times higher than that of fruit juices. In any event, the safety level of methanol has never been determined.

In addition to sugar, most soft drinks contain phosphoric acid—this is what gives them their kick. Phosphoric acid blocks the absorption of calcium and magnesium in the intestines thus contributing directly to fragile, easily-fractured bones in children, and osteoporosis or bone loss in adults. Magnesium deficiency also contributes to impairment of the immune system, fatigue, high blood pressure and many other ailments.

Many soft drinks also contain caffeine. Caffeine and its related substance theobromine (from tea and cocoa), have a similar effect on the body as sugar. They stimulate the adrenal glands to release an adrenaline-like substance which in turn causes the liver to release sugar into the blood stream. This is what gives you the "lift" when you drink coffee, tea, Coke or Pepsi. The problem is that the delicate blood sugar regulation mechanism cannot long tolerate the constant stimulation of habitual caffeine ingestion. Often the blood sugar lowering mechanisms over-react, causing low blood sugar and its concomitant complaints of chronic fatigue, dizziness, depression, allergies and behavioral disorders. Caffeine-containing drinks irritate the lining of the stomach and cause an increase in stomach acid. They affect the nervous system, leading to insomnia and restlessness. Prolonged use of caffeine can contribute to any one of a number of serious diseases such as cancer, bone loss, mental disorders and birth defects. Caffeine's effects on the nervous system are most pronounced in children—yet cola drinks have become standard fare for America's youth. It has been said that if coffee were introduced as a new drug today, it would not receive FDA approval. It is best to avoid all sources of caffeine—not just colas but also coffee and tea, decongestants, pep pills, aspirin, diuretics and—we're sorry to say—chocolate.

As a final blow, soft drink manufacturers polish off their creation with a variety of artificial flavorings, colorings and preservatives, most of which have dubious claims to safety. The entire brew is a concoction of chemicals designed to sap our physical and mental health. Soda pop is the veritable drink of the devil. If you choose to make an effort to improve the eating habits of your family, here is the place to begin, this is the place to make a stand. Don't buy soft drinks, don't keep them around and do everything you can to discourage your children from drinking them.

The list of drinks to avoid is a long one—soft drinks, sugared drinks, coffee, tea, and cocoa. Pasteurized, homogenized milk belongs on this list. To this group must be added one more, fruit juices, because the process of juicing fruit concentrates its sweetness. There is as much sugar in a glass of orange juice as there is in a candy bar —and all of it is fructose, which is more harmful than the sucrose of sugar. Consumption of apple juice has been linked to failure to thrive in infants.[126] Excessive consumption of fruit juices can also upset the acid-alkaline balance of the body, causing the urine to become alkaline rather than acid. Even over-consumption of vegetable juices, which are not sweet, can cause an imbalance. Fresh fruit is delicious and healthful in moderate amounts, but overindulgence in fruit can cause severe mineral deficiencies. Our natural appestats prevent us from eating too much fruit at one time, but in fruit juice we get concentrated sweetness in several quick gulps. A glass of fruit juice may contain the sugar equivalent of dozens of pieces of fruit. Furthermore, most fruit juice is filtered and pasteurized, hence skeletonized, much like refined sugar and white flour. Fruit juice consumption should be limited to an ounce or two at a time, diluted with water, so that you do not take in any more fructose than you would consume in one piece of fruit.

What kind of water should we drink—distilled or purified, bottled or tap, hard or soft? The evidence points to hard water, which is water rich in mineral ions, as being of great value in promoting overall health. Several studies have shown that the rate of coronary heart disease is lower in localities where hard water is available. Areas of the world noted for the longevity of local inhabitants—notably the Caucasus, Hunzaland and Vilcabamba in South America—are all watered by richly mineralized run-off from high glaciers. The water in these areas contains so much mineral residue in the form of silt that it is milky or cloudy.

A comparative study of the water in Deaf Smith County, Texas with that of Dallas produced an interesting profile of drinking water's ideal components. Deaf Smith County residents are famous for their good teeth and bone structure; they have few fractures even in advanced age. X-rays of both people and cattle show unusual size and density of bone structure; cross sections of long bones are approximately 50% greater in thickness than those of people living in other regions. By contrast, bones of Dallas County residents break easily and heal slowly. Analysis of the water in both counties reveals the surprising fact that calcium in Dallas County water is six times as high as that in Deaf Smith County. But Deaf Smith County water is eight times higher in iodine, two times higher in magnesium, and contains numerous trace minerals that are absent from Dallas County water.[127] It seems that the magnesium and trace minerals, especially iodine, contribute to enzymatic processes that go into creating strong and healthy bones; and magnesium is incorporated into the bone itself, contributing to its strength. Several other studies have yielded positive correlations between softness of water in a locality and incidence of coronary heart disease.

Water that has been softened is water that has been shorn of its valuable mineral content. Water softeners function by activating sodium molecules. These sodium ions combine with other minerals in the water and are then removed. The use of softened water is highly correlated with an increased incidence of cancer, heart attacks and strokes.[128]

Unfortunately, most water supplies are contaminated by a number of harmful chemicals, either as a result of run-off from farms and gardens, or because they are deliberately treated with chlorine or fluorides. Fluoridated water should be avoided at all costs—it contributes to bone loss, bone deformities, cancer and a host of other illnesses—and offers little real protection against tooth decay.[129] Bottled mineral water varies widely in quality and is not necessarily free from contaminants.

What is the solution? There is no perfect source of water for most of us, but the best solution seems to be tap water that has been treated with a filter. A filter that uses compressed carbon will remove all heavy metals, chlorine, and other impurities but leaves valuable mineral ions such as calcium, magnesium, iodine, silicon, and selenium. It is less effective for fluorides and nitrates. These can be removed with a reverse osmosis water treatment unit. Unfortunately, this process removes beneficial minerals as well. It is important to add trace minerals in liquid or powder form to filtered water, especially water treated by reverse osmosis. This will enrich your water and give you the closest approximation possible to the kind of deep well or high mountain water associated with a robust constitution and long life. (See Sources for suppliers of water treatment units and trace mineral preparations.)

How much water should we drink? Conventional wisdom calls for six to eight large glasses per day, but Oriental medicine teaches that this is a dangerous practice which puts undue strain on the kidneys. The food we eat contains a great deal of water and water is also a by-product of carbohydrate metabolism. There is some evidence that an additional six to eight glasses of water can lead to mineral losses. Researchers from both East and West warn that excessive liquids taken at meals dilute stomach acid and put undue stain on the digestive process. A good rule is to avoid drinking large amounts of liquid from one half hour before a meal to two hours after. It is also wise to avoid liquids that are too hot or too cold. Iced water with a meal makes digestion very difficult.

A study of beverages from around the world reveals that traditional societies frequently consume lacto-fermented beverages made from fruits, the sap of trees, herbs and grains.[130] These drinks are valued for medicinal qualities including the ability to relieve intestinal problems and constipation, encourage lactation, strengthen the sick, and promote overall well-being and stamina. Above all, these drinks are considered superior to plain water in their ability to relieve thirst during physical labor. Many vitamins and minerals are lost through perspiration. Modern research has discovered that a liquid containing small amounts of sugars and electrolytes of minerals (mineral ions) is actually absorbed faster than plain water, and has the added advantage of rapidly replacing minerals lost in sweat.[131] This research was used to promote commercial sports drinks, high-sugar, additive-laced concoctions containing small amounts of electrolytes. But natural lactic-acid fermented drinks contain numerous valuable minerals in suspension, and small amounts of sugar, along with lactic acid and beneficial lactobacilli, all of which promote good health in many ways, while at the same time cutting the sensation of thirst.

Both modern soft drinks and plain water are poor substitutes for these health-promoting traditional beverages. Taken with meals they contribute to thorough and easy digestion of food; taken after physical labor they rapidly replace lost mineral ions to give an energizing lift that renews rather than depletes the body's reserves. The day when every town and hamlet in America produces its own distinctive lacto-fermented brew, made from the local products of woods and fields, will be the day when Americans see the dawning of a new age of good health and well-being along with a new era of economic vitality based on small-scale local production rather than on large-scale monopolistic control of the food processing industry.

On the subject of alcoholic beverages, the evidence is also inconsistent. Certainly the problem of alcoholism is enormous, particularly in the United States, where there are some 15 to 20 million alcoholics, or about one in every ten people. Alcoholics are more prone to all diseases and to accidents than the normal population, and tend to die young. On the other hand, several traditional societies, noted for the longevity and good health of their citizens, consume moderate amounts of beer or wine made from grapes, bananas or other fruit. These wines tend to have a lower alcohol content than modern wines and beers and are consumed only at certain times of the year, such as harvest festivals. Research indicates that moderate consumption of alcohol, particularity wine, may prevent heart disease; one oft-quoted study indicates that those who drink moderately—one to two glasses per day—in general live longer than those who over-indulge, and than those who do not drink at all, but this may be due to the fact that such people tend to be moderate in all their habits and may be able to better afford a more nutritious diet. Other studies link even moderate alcohol consumption with breast cancer.[132]

The religions of the world differ in their laws on alcohol consumption but all are in agreement that those on a mystical path, or those who have chosen a life of devoted service, should refrain entirely from alcoholic beverages. If you do drink, we urge you to partake only of wine or unpasteurized beer with meals in very moderate amounts, and to refrain from all alcoholic beverages from time to time. Pregnant women should not consume alcohol. (If you use wine in cooking, but want to be sure that the alcohol has evaporated, boil the sauce to which it has been added, uncovered, for about ten minutes.)

The problem of alcoholism is allied to the problem of nutrition in general. The root cause of alcoholism is a deficiency of B vitamins, trace minerals and the amino acid glutamine.[133] Some practitioners find that alcoholics improve when grains are removed from their diets.[134] Thus the best diet for the alcoholic is one that is high in B vitamins, devoid of all grains and sugars, and rich in high protein foods such as eggs and meat. . . not exactly the diet promoted by the Department of Agriculture and its new food pyramid!

It is common for former alcoholics to replace alcoholic drinks with sweets and soft drinks without realizing that sugar plays havoc with the intestinal flora, fostering overgrowth of candida albicans and other fungi. Under certain conditions these pathogenic yeasts actually convert sugars in the gut to alcohol! There are well documented cases of inebriation caused by sugar consumption and candida overgrowth in persons who do not drink alcohol.[135] The alcoholic, in turning to sugar, is often supplying himself with alcohol throughout the day!

Alcohol-free beer and wine are high in carbohydrates and should also be avoided by those attempting to give up alcoholic beverages. Often they still contain .5% alcohol and the taste of these wines and beers may perpetuate the longing for alcohol. As they have been boiled to remove alcohol, they have been shorn of their enzyme content, which is a health-promoting, compensating factor in wine and unpasteurized beer.

The recipes for traditional lacto-fermented beverages we present in this book constitute an alternative not only to soft drinks but to alcoholic beverages as well. We offer the theory that the craving for alcohol, as well as the craving for soft drinks, stems from an ancient collective memory of the kind of lacto-fermented beverages still found in primitive societies. These beverages give a lift to the tired body by supplying mineral ions depleted through perspiration, and make food taste more agreeable and satisfying by supplying lactobacilli, lactic-acid and enzymes needed for easy and thorough digestion.

ABOUT FOOD ALLERGIES, FOOD CHOICES & FOOD COMBINING

For many people, the presence of food allergies and the necessity to restrict food choices tarnish the joy of eating. Food allergies afflict a large portion of our population and can cause such diverse complaints as sneezing, itching, arthritis, nervous disorders, concentration problems, insomnia, headaches, and chronic fatigue. More recently, diseases like cancer, diabetes, multiple sclerosis and schizophrenia have been linked to food allergies. Often allergy sufferers find that they are allergic to the very foods they eat frequently and like the most.

Allergy tests have revealed sensitivities to every food commonly eaten but most prevalent are allergies to milk products and grains—precisely the two foods added to man's diet when he changed from a hunter-gatherer life-style to one of cultivation and domestication. The proteins of grain and milk, namely gluten and casein, are two of the hardest proteins to digest. This is one reason that traditional cultures almost invariable soak or sprout grains and culture their dairy products before eating them. Milk allergies also stem from the body's inability to produce the enzyme lactase, required to break down lactose or milk sugar. Up to 70% of the world's population, by some estimates, is genetically incapable of producing lactase. The process of fermenting or culturing milk products breaks down a portion of the lactose but there still remains a large group that cannot tolerate milk products in any form. Some people are allergic to the high levels of the amino acid tyramine found in cheddar-type cheeses. Orientals, in particular, tolerate milk products very poorly.

On the other hand, Orientals tolerate grains better than other population groups, perhaps because of the length of time Oriental societies have subsisted on grains. Those members of Oriental societies unable to thrive on grains have long since been selected out through shortened life-span and reduced fertility. This selection process may be the reason that Orientals have longer intestines than other races; and that the pancreas and salivary glands of Orientals are up to 50% larger as a function of body weight that those of Westerners.[136] These traits allow them to digest grains more fully and contribute to their high tolerance for rice, millet, and wheat.

The comparatively smaller salivary glands, pancreas and intestines of the Westerner often make it difficult for him to tolerate grains, especially gluten-containing grains such as wheat, corn, oats, rye and barley. Grain sensitivities are often found in peoples whose ancestors came from seacoast regions. Gluten intolerance is associated with a family history of alcoholism, arthritis, Down's syndrome, and mental disorders such as schizophrenia and dementia.[137] Gluten intolerance has been linked with B6 deficiency.

People with poor adrenal function are often unable to tolerate carbohydrates in any form. A smaller group of people cannot tolerate meat, due to suppressed or absent hydrochloric acid production in the stomach. This may be due to a deficiency of vitamin B6 and zinc, both needed for the production of pancreatic enzymes, or of insufficient chloride due to a low-salt diet. Hydrochloric acid production often decreases with age, rendering meats less well tolerated by the older generation.

People who suffer from an underactive thyroid condition often do best on a diet in which fats, especially unsaturated fats, are restricted, while others, notably hypoglycemics and individuals prone to seizures, benefit from a diet that is comparatively high in fats.

Some individuals are sensitive to foods from the nightshade family—tomatoes, potatoes, eggplant and peppers—and react with sore and painful joints, leading to arthritis. Certain fruits containing aspirin-like compounds called salicylates, such as tomatoes, almonds, apricots, peaches and nectarines, have been shown to contribute to hyperactivity and asthma in some children. Citrus fruits, especially in the form of commercial orange and grapefruit juice, frequently cause allergies. Heavily yeasted foods such as vinegar, barley malt, alcoholic beverages, commercially pickled foods, soy sauce, Worcestershire sauce, and aged cheeses should be avoided by those suffering from chronic yeast infection.[138]

As easy way to determine whether you are allergic to a certain food is the following: Avoid the suspected food for at least four days. Then eat a moderate amount of it on an empty stomach. Test your pulse before and after eating the food. If your pulse rises more than a few beats per minute, or if you have any adverse reaction, you are probably allergic to it.[139] We should always be alert to symptoms of food intolerance—rashes, fatigue, insomnia, headaches, joint pain, hoarseness, etc. These are nature's warning signals and it is the wise individual who heeds them.

Genetic predisposition is a major cause of allergies; another cause is poor diet in general, resulting in digestion that is less than thorough. A diet deficient in animal fats and other body-building factors during infancy and childhood may lead to weaknesses in the intestinal walls, the so-called "leaky gut syndrome" in which partially digested food particles pass into the blood stream. Another contributing factor is enzyme exhaustion. Consumption of sugar and caffeine stresses the adrenal glands and adrenal exhaustion is a prime cause of allergies. Sugar and refined carbohydrates in the gut can lead to an overgrowth of candida albicans fungi. This naturally occurring fungus breaks down dead or inert foods in the intestines. With over-consumption of dead foods such as refined carbohydrates, these organisms multiply uncontrollably. Vinegar and other heavily yeasted foods also encourage candida overgrowth in some people. These yeasts actually change form, attach themselves to the walls of the intestine and grow outward, causing holes in the intestinal wall that allow undigested food and toxins, including toxins produced by candida albicans, to enter the bloodstream. These toxins and undigested food particles will then trigger allergic reactions, especially when the immune system is weak or the body is under stress.

A final cause of food allergies is the present day tendency to eat exclusively foods from just a few types or families. Of the 4,000 or so edible plant species that have fed human societies at one time or another in the past, only 150 are widely cultivated today and just three of them provide 60 percent of the world's food.[140] Today most peoples' choice of foods is limited to about thirty families and for some people, the choice is even more restricted. It is not unusual for some children to confine themselves to pizza and hot dogs, or to peanut butter and jelly sandwiches; or for those following the macrobiotic diet to consume mostly rice and soybean products with a few vegetables. Thus their food sources are limited to one or two animal or a handful of vegetable foods. Such a diet will not only be deficient in many nutrients, but the constant call for the enzymes needed to digest these few foods can very well lead to the exhaustion of that specific digestion mechanism. The exclusive use of just a few foods thus can lead to severe food addictions—every bit as harmful and as difficult to break as addictions to drugs or alcohol. These food addictions, with their concomitant allergic reactions, nurture the biochemical disruptions that lead to more serious degenerative diseases.

If you have food allergies or sensitivities—and many people do—you will have to eliminate some categories of food from your diet. The best defense against allergies to begin with is a varied and healthful diet from which all refined and stimulating foods—sugar, white flour, refined and hydrogenated vegetable oils, refined salt and caffeine—have been eliminated, and which supplies the intestinal tract with lactic-acid producing bacteria and food enzymes on a frequent basis.

Along with allergies, our genetic inheritance, our constitutional type, our age, our race, our blood type, our occupation, the climate in which we live and our state of health all have a bearing on what we should eat. Elderly people and invalids, whose digestive mechanisms have been compromised or are in decline should pay special attention to getting a good supply of enzymes in their diet and should favor foods that have been pureed, prepared with meat broths or pre-digested, like soaked gruels and porridges. Growing children and pregnant women need plenty of fat-soluble vitamins found in butter, cream, fish and fish eggs, eggs and organ meats. Those living in cold climates also need more of these vitamin-A-rich foods. Those who do hard physical labor may need a steady supply of animal products in the diet; but those who lead a contemplative life often find overconsumption of animal products, especially red meat, a hindrance. The wisdom of the ancients teaches us that there are appropriate times for both feasting on rich foods and for fasting on the simplest of fare.

Periodic fasting is an age-old method for restoring and maintaining health. Fasting on meat or vegetable broth or on lacto-fermented vegetable juices allows our enzyme-producing and digestive mechanisms to rest, so that other enzyme systems can work at repairing, detoxifying and healing. Many ancient physicians recommended a mono-diet for the sick, such as ten days of rice gruel. Hippocrates often prescribed a diet consisting only of raw milk for those suffering from TB or psoriasis. Cleansing fasts work best when carried out in conjunction with a program of intestinal cleansing through enemas or colonics.

What about food combining? Are there some foods that should be eaten together, and others that should not? The theory that various types of food should not be eaten together, but confined to separate meals, was introduced at the turn of the century by Dr. W. H. Hay. He stated that since starches and sugars require alkaline conditions for complete digestion, and proteins require acid conditions, they should not be eaten together. Later he decided that acidic fruits must not be eaten with starches and sugars, nor with protein. This diet received renewed interest with the publication of *Fit for Life* by Harvey and Marilyn Diamond, and many people say they have been helped by this system. The authors advocate eating starches and proteins at different meals; further, they recommend beginning the day with fruit only, eating starches at lunch, and saving protein foods for the evening meal. As proof of the importance of proper food combining, they cite research showing that protein and starches taken together are not fully digested. To clinch their argument, they point out that legumes —foods which contain both starch and protein—often cause indigestion.

There are several problems with the assumptions behind this food combining system. The assertion that the body is unable to digest protein and starches together is just plain wrong. The healthy body is entirely equipped to do just that. Most protein digestion occurs in the lower stomach which is an acidic environment; starches are then digested in the small intestine with its alkaline environment. In addition, there is predigestion of both protein and starches in the upper stomach, and this digestion is more or less thorough in relation to the food enzymes available from food and saliva. (Gelatin-rich broth also contributes to a thorough digestion of both proteins and starches.) In addition, protein digestion occurs in the small intestine by proteases secreted at the duodenum.

Beans cause digestive problems, not because they contain protein and starches together, but because they contain two complex sugars, farrinose and stachyose, which are not easily broken down by enzymes normally found in the intestines. Beans and other legumes will be more digestible if soaked for a long period before cooking as this process begins the breakdown of these starches. Beans properly prepared have provided nourishment to peoples all over the globe and can be easily digested by most people. Actually there is no food on earth that is a pure starch or a pure protein. Even meat contains some sugar and all acidic fruits contain starch.

A final argument against food combining derives from the fact that we find no such strictures among traditional societies whose intuitive wisdom has dictated food choices that have kept them healthy for generations. A few examples culled from the research of Dr. Price will suffice: The diet of isolated Swiss villagers consisted of milk products eaten with rye bread; primitive Gaelic peoples subsisted on fish and oats; natives of the Caribbean consumed seafood along with starchy tubers of the manioc family; Indians in the Andes mountains ate potatoes with small animals and seafood; Polynesians consumed starchy tubers, fruit and seafood. Semitic peoples combined meat and milk products with grains. Primitive peoples, with their unerring native wisdom, put no restrictions on combining starches and proteins or even fruits and proteins—they couldn't afford to and they didn't need to.

It must be said, however that some people find they have more energy when they avoid certain food combinations, possibly a sign that their digestive systems have been compromised through poor diet and improper food preparation techniques. Milk products with meat and citrus fruits with grains seem to be the most frequent problem-causing combinations. Many find they do not tolerate raw fruit eaten with other foods. An individual determination of improper food combinations can only be accomplished on a trial and error basis.

No discussion of food choices would be complete without a consideration of macrobiotics. The macrobiotic diet system, said to be based on the ancient Chinese text *The Yellow Emperor's Classic of Internal Medicine*, was introduced to the West by George Ohsawa, and popularized by several gifted writers. It is an extension of the ancient Chinese world view that all energies and all objects in the cosmos can be classified as either yin (female) or yang (male). With its system of facial diagnosis and treatment based upon correspondences of specific foods to various organs and conditions, it has many similarities to the medieval doctrine of the four humors, which has recently enjoyed something of a resurgence in Europe. Such intuitive and non-invasive methods can be very useful to the medical practitioner, especially when combined with more orthodox diagnostic techniques that are grounded in the scientific method.

According to the marcobiotic system, sugar is the most yin food, followed by fruit juices, honey, tropical fruits, acid fruits, dairy products and vegetables of the nightshade family; pork is the most yang food, followed by beef, game, poultry, eggs and fish. Vegetables and legumes are slightly yin while grains are slightly yang. Rice, revered by Orientals as the perfect food, is said to be in the center—with perfect balance of yin and yang energies.

Ohsawa repeatedly warned about dangers of refined foods like sugar and white flour. He had excellent short-term results with this diet—in spite of the fact that it did not eliminate smoking—both in Japan and in the West.

Unfortunately, Ohsawa confused many people by his extreme statements and unclear food guidelines (only a small portion of his writing was directly concerned with food) and he is generally remembered for the strict brown rice diet, a cleansing regime for the sick. Michio Kushi then developed his "standard macrobiotic diet" which gave more precise macrobiotic food recommendations. People more easily understood the Kushi presentation and he is the best known of all macrobiotic advocates. Natural sea salt, fish broth and fermented vegetables are allowed but not stressed as necessary components of the diet. Kushi permitted a small portion of white meat fish occasionally, *if desired*, claiming that a totally vegetarian fare would cover all nutritional needs. This claim cannot be supported by scientific evidence. Kushi's more extreme claims—that a strict brown rice diet would bring spiritual enlightenment, and that diets based entirely on local foods would bring peace to the planet—defy common sense.

The particulars of Kushi's diet can be faulted on several counts. First, as most adherents omit fish broth, and many also omit fermented vegetables, it often lacks both gelatin and food enzymes and can therefore be difficult to digest, especially for the Westerner who, with a shorter intestinal tract, smaller pancreas and smaller salivary gland than the Oriental, does better on grains that have been soaked or fermented, or cooked in gelatin-rich broth. For this reason, candida infection, intestinal discomfort and low energy are frequent complaints among many macrobiotic adherents. Dishes containing *seitan*—unfermented wheat gluten—can pose real problems to those with gluten intolerance. Secondly, this restrictive version of macrobiotics does not supply all-important fat soluble vitamins A and D. Predictably, children born and raised in households where this diet was rigorously applied suffered from small stature and rickets.[141] In adults, dangerously low cholesterol levels resulting in depression, poor concentration and even strokes and cancer have been associated with programs that call for the elimination of animal proteins and fats, and an over-reliance on vegetable oils—programs found in many macrobiotic cookbooks, and indeed in numerous health-oriented cookbooks. A third problem is the danger of certain mineral deficiencies, especially zinc deficiency, from a heavy reliance on grains that have not been soaked or fermented. In short, second generation macrobiotics is an artificial diet not found in any traditional society anywhere in the world, which as an alternative to junk food often gives good results in the beginning but which leads to widespread deficiencies in the long term.

A new breed of macrobiotic practitioners has bravely admitted the faults of Kushi's interpretation, and now sees macrobiotics as an open-ended system, subject to progressive revelation. Many macrobiotic cookbooks now include recipes for oily fish and eggs and a number of counselors have begun to recommend butter and other dairy products, especially for children. We submit that the principles presented in this book, including the use of gelatinous broth, fermented foods including soaked and soured grains, natural sea salt, and a more scientific approach to the subject of fats would ensure Ohsawa's promised benefits, without requiring those drawn to macrobiotics to abandon any of their basic principles.

Two important foods in the macrobiotic diet require additional comment: soybeans and seaweed. Soy beans are high in phytates and contain potent enzyme inhibitors that are only deactivated by fermentation and not by ordinary cooking.[142] These inhibitors can lead to protein assimilation problems in those who consume unfermented soy products frequently.[143] Soybeans must not be used like kidney beans in soups and other dishes, but only as *miso*, *natto*, *tempeh* etc. It is also a mistake to rely on tofu or bean curd as a protein food because of its high phytate content.[144] Those who wish to eat tofu would be wise to imitate the Japanese who eat small amounts of tofu in fish broth. Soy milk, often substituted for cow's milk, also has a high phytate content and can lead to mineral deficiencies.[145] Seaweeds are found in many native diets. They are an excellent source of minerals but they also contain long chain complex sugars, similar to those found in the Jerusalem artichoke, which some individuals are unable to digest. These undigested sugars may cause an overgrowth of candida albicans and other problems with the intestinal flora.[146] Furthermore, many commercial seaweeds are treated with pesticides and fungicides on drying racks. Those who consume seaweeds frequently should be careful of their supply, and should simmer them for a long period to begin the breakdown of the long-chain sugars found in all sea vegetables. (For unsprayed seaweeds, see Sources.)

The principles of nourishing traditions presented in these pages—the importance of whole foods, the need for raw foods; the advantages of fish and meat broths and of lacto-fermentation for grains, vegetables and beverages, the proper choice of fats and the universal requirement for sufficient fat soluble vitamins—can and should be applied not only to macrobiotics but to every diet—Oriental, Middle Eastern, African, Latin American, European, and plain old American. The living laboratory of human society has demonstrated that diets based on these wise and ancient principles, regardless of specific ingredients, promote optimum physical and mental well being, and healthy offspring, generation after generation.

GUIDE TO FOOD SELECTION

A sound approach to food selection, one that we think will serve you better than the Food Pyramid, divides our choices into three distinct categories: **Nourishing Traditional Foods, Compromise Foods** and **New-Fangled Foods**. Eat a varied diet of foods chosen from the **Nourishing Traditional Foods** category. The proportion of animal foods, grains, dairy products, fruits and fats you choose will depend on your ethnic heritage, your constitution, your age, your occupation, the climate in which you live and your specific food sensitivities and allergies. Healthy people can eat foods in the **Compromise Foods** group occasionally in moderate amounts. **New-Fangled Foods** are best avoided by everybody.

NOURISHING TRADITIONAL FOODS

Proteins: Fresh, organically raised meat including beef, lamb, game, chicken, turkey, duck and other fowl; organ meats from organically raised animals; seafood of all types from deep sea waters; fish eggs; fresh, organic eggs; fermented soy products.

Fats: Fresh butter and cream, preferably raw and cultured; beef, lamb, chicken and duck fat; extra virgin olive oil; unrefined flax seed oil in small amounts; coconut oil and other tropical oils.

Dairy: Raw, cultured organic dairy products such as yoghurt, piima milk, kefir and raw cheese.

Carbohydrates: Whole grain products properly treated for the removal of phytates such as sourdough and sprouted grain bread, soaked or sprouted cereal grains; soaked and fermented pulses and legumes including lentils, beans, and chickpeas; sprouted or soaked seeds and nuts; fresh fruits and vegetables; fermented vegetables.

Beverages: Filtered, high-mineral water; lacto-fermented drinks made from grain or fruit; herb teas; meat stocks and vegetable broths.

Condiments: Natural sea salt; raw vinegar; spices; and fresh herbs.

COMPROMISE FOODS

Protein: Pork, shellfish, fresh or shallow water fish, commercially raised beef, lamb, turkey and chicken; barbecued or smoked meats; battery eggs, tofu.

Fats: Unrefined peanut and sesame oils; lard.

Dairy: Raw, uncultured milk; pasteurized cultured milk products; pasteurized cheeses.

Carbohydrates: Whole grains not treated for phytates such as quick-rise breads and pasta; unbleached white flour; canned pulses; thin-skinned fruits and vegetables imported from long distances; canned tomato products; well-cooked, unsprayed seaweeds; natural sweeteners such as honey, maple syrup, sucanat, and date sugar.

Beverages: Wine or unpasteurized beer in moderation with meals; dilute fruit juices.

Condiments: Commercial salt; pasteurized vinegar; canned condiments; soy sauce made with commercially refined salt.

NEW-FANGLED FOODS

Protein: Processed meats containing additives and preservatives such as luncheon meat, salami, and bacon; hydrolyzed protein and protein isolates; soy milk

Fats: All highly-processed vegetable oils, margarine, tub spreads and vegetable shortenings; fat substitutes; deep fried foods; low-fat products.

Dairy: Pasteurized, homogenized commercial milk; ultra-high temperature cream and milk; processed cheeses.

Carbohydrates: Bleached and "fortified" white flour products; commercial dry cereals; granolas; refined sugar in all forms such as dextrose, fructose and corn syrup; irradiated fruits and vegetables; most canned products; chocolate.

Beverages: Soda pop; distilled or pasteurized alcohol products; full strength fruit juices; coffee, tea and cocoa.

Condiments: Commercial baking powder; MSG; artificial flavors, additives and colors; chemically produced food preservatives; aspartame.

A WORD on EQUIPMENT

Modern equipment takes old-fashioned drudgery out of traditional cooking—but it is important to make wise choices. Choose stainless steel rather than aluminum cookware. Acidic or salty foods cooked in aluminum will cause this toxic metal to be dissolved into food. Recent research has linked aluminum with Alzheimers disease and many investigators feel that aluminum from cookware contributes to other diseases as well.[147] Aluminum is a cumulative toxin and all care should be taken to avoid taking it in any form.

Unfortunately, as some people have gotten the message about aluminum, and have exchanged their inexpensive aluminum pans for the more expensive stainless steel variety, aluminum cookware has crept back in at the top end, so to speak, in the form of spun aluminum cookware for the gourmet market. Don't buy it. It looks great, but it is just as dangerous as less expensive aluminum ware.

It is important also to use baking pans and cookie sheets made of stainless steel—these are available at cookware stores, at a cost not much greater than the aluminum and coated varieties. (See Sources.)

Glass, enamel and cast iron cookware are fine. An old-fashioned heavy cast iron frying pan is a must for all sauteing and stir-frys. These pans need never be washed but merely rinsed in hot water and dried with paper towels. A cast iron pan, well-seasoned in this manner, will never stick; and food cooked in heavy cast iron is much less likely to burn than food cooked in the thickest stainless steel.

Use a wooden cutting board—it is much less likely to harbor pathogenic bacteria than the plastic variety. For the same reason it is preferable to store food in glass rather than plastic containers.

A set of good knives is essential. Serrated knives of various lengths are best for bread and vegetables—those made by Cutco (see Sources) are excellent and keep their cutting edge for years. Tempered steel knives that can be honed are best for meats. A fish filleting knife with a medium-length, flexible blade, and a long, flexible round-ended carving knife comprise the two basics. A thick bladed knife in tempered steel for chopping will round out your collection.

Next on the list of equipment is a good all-purpose food processor with a full complement of blades—what did we do before this labor saving device made its way into our kitchens? For slicing, grating, chopping, mixing and blending, the food processor is invaluable, allowing us to prepare traditional dishes that once required extensive hand labor—chopping parsley for tabouli, grinding chickpeas for hummus, making a julienne of vegetables, processing perfect mayonnaise. The food processor handles these prosaic chores with ease. Choose one with an attachment that allows you to add oils drop by drop—essential for making mayonnaise and pesto sauce.

For soups we recommend a hand-held blender—this is what the French use to make their evening *potage*. The soup is blended right in the pot, thus saving time and dishes to wash. A mixer, either hand-held or counter top variety, is a handy gadget to have if you do any baking, but a wire whisk and a little muscle power will accomplish the same tasks.

For lacto-fermented vegetables and chutneys you will need a collection of wide-mouth quart-sized mason jars and a wooden pounder. For lacto-fermented beverages you will need some half-gallon-sized glass containers with air-tight seals.

If you bake frequently, you will want to buy a grain mill. This allows you to have fresh flour when you need it. (Whole grain flour quickly goes rancid after grinding.) A small hand mill can be bought for about $100. Motor-driven mills are more expensive, but serious cooks will find that they are worth it. The grinding surface should be true stone and not a synthetic version. A good choice is the Jupiter Mill, manufactured in Germany. (See Sources). The grinding surface is hard granite. It has adjustable settings which allow you to both crack grains, and grind them into fine flour. A stainless steel milling attachment allows you to grind oily seeds and sprouted grains. A smaller mini-mill is useful for grinding spices and flax seeds.

Two good staple snacks for large families are home-made applesauce and fresh popcorn. Apple sauce is best made with a *Moulin A Legumes*. A similar American device is called the Foley Food Mill but the French version, with its removable bottom and blade, is much more serviceable. For popcorn, consider investing in a popper so that your children can prepare this nutritious snack by themselves. (Store bought popped pop-corn is not only rancid—it is loaded with commercial salt and vegetable oils.)

One piece of modern equipment we do *not* recommend is the microwave oven. Unfortunately the microwave achieved instant popularity without much prior research having been carried out to study the effects of eating microwaved food. In consequence, one large experiment involving an unwitting populace is now in progress. The small amount of research done on the effects of eating microwaved food has produced some frightening conclusions. Research carried out in Australia as well as in the United States has revealed that the microwave may have unfavorable effects on fats and proteins, making them more difficult to assimilate. More recent research carried out in Switzerland revealed that the microwave caused changes in vitamin content and availability. Eating microwaved food results in abnormal blood profiles in test-persons, profiles similar to those that occur in the early stages of cancer.[148] An especially dangerous practice is using the microwave for heating baby's bottle. We recommend that you resist using the microwave at all costs. If you don't have one, don't buy one; if you already have a microwave, unplug it and find some other use for it —they are quite handy for storing vases. If you must have some rapid-cooking mechanism try the Jet Stream oven (see Sources), which cooks food quickly using convection currents. The Jet Stream does not compromise the taste of food, as the microwave does, and it will even brown chickens and roasts.

We are also skeptical of the pressure cooker—another relative newcomer to the culinary scene. Pressure cooking of grains allows them to become soft enough for consumption long before the all-important process of neutralizing phytates is complete. A heavy flame-proof casserole of good quality enamel over cast iron is ideal for grains, as well as for stews. Traditional cuisines always call for a long, slow cooking of grains and legumes.

PARTING WORDS

Modern man, faced with a dazzling array of modern products, is naturally tempted by their convenience and glitz. He would prefer not to worry about how his foods are processed or what they contain; he would prefer not to spend time preparing nutritious food the way his ancestors did. But the inevitable consequence of this insouciance is the host of the debilitating diseases now endemic in our society.

With traditions forgotten, the tool that allows modern man to regain his health and vitality is knowledge—knowledge of the fruits of honest scientific inquiry as well as new-found familiarity with culinary customs of times past. The cook, the food provider and parents of young children can no longer afford to be misled by what passes for nutritional wisdom in the popular press, especially as so much orthodox advice—magnified, simplified and twisted by publicity for processed foods—is partially or totally wrong. We urge you to keep abreast of research conducted by independent researchers and holistic doctors, especially as it sheds light on the nourishing traditions of our ancestors.

Then call on your reserves of ingenuity and creativity to translate that knowledge into delicious meals in whatever culinary tradition may appeal to you and your family. We must not lose sight of the fact that the fundamental requirement of the food we eat is that we like it. The healthiest food in the world does us no good if we must gag it down because it tastes bad.

Our food should satisfy our four basic tastes—salt, sour, bitter and sweet. These tastes are meant to guide us to the foods we need, but they are easily suborned by ignorance or lack of will. Satisfy the salt taste with natural sea salt or traditional meat broths that also provide magnesium and vital trace minerals, instead of products laced with MSG or drenched in commercial salt; please the sour taste bud with old-fashioned fermented foods that provide the enzymatic by-products of the culturing process, rather than with pasteurized condiments and alcohol; gratify the bitter taste bud with the dark green vegetables and herbs that are valued in every traditional society, so rich in vitamins and minerals, instead of coffee and tea; and delight the sweet tooth with fruits at their peak of ripeness, and with natural sweeteners high in nutrients, rather than refined sugar products.

To make us healthy, our food must taste good; it must be digestible; and it must be eaten in peace. Even whole foods, properly prepared according to traditional methods, do us no good if we eat them with a grudge; they will not confer health on the man who does not forgive. It is the loving heart who will find, in the pages that follow, guidelines for providing an abundance of all the nutrients we need to live healthy, happy and productive lives.

KITCHEN TIPS AND HINTS

- Wash all fruits and vegetables to remove pesticides and other impurities. Dr. Bonner's Sal Suds (see Sources), hydrogen peroxide and chlorox bleach (about 1/2 cup per sinkful) are all recommended for pesticide removal. Be sure to rinse well.

- To ripen tomatoes, peaches and other thin-skinned fruits, set them well separated in a sunny spot on a tray lined with paper towels. When soft enough, transfer to refrigerator.

- Do not add garlic to sauteing onions or other vegetables, because it has a tendency to burn. Add garlic after you have added your liquid--stock, wine, stir-fry sauce, tomatoes, etc.

- Always use unsalted butter. Those who like their butter salty can sprinkle sea salt on later.

- Use only unrefined sea salt.

- Use extra virgin olive oil and butter for cooking. Occasional use of peanut oil for stir frying is permissible.

- Always skim stock, sauces, soups, legumes and stews. Many impurities rise to the top with the foam. Add spices and seasoning to stock, sauces, soups, pulses and stews after skimming.

- Use only organic lemons and oranges when grating the rinds for zest.

- Sauces and stews containing wine should be allowed to boil, uncovered, for at least 10 minutes, to ensure all alcohol is evaporated.

- Grow your own herbs if you have garden space. If not, at least grow thyme in a pot. Nothing beats fresh thyme for flavor.

- To dry lettuce, watercress or parsley, wash well, shake dry and place in a pillow case (in the case of lettuce) or small cloth bag (in the case of watercress or parsley). Tie up and place in your washing machine. Run on the last spin cycle to remove water by centrifugal force.

- To peel tomatoes and other thin-skinned fruits, bring a pan of water to a boil. Using a slotted spoon, dip tomatoes in, one at a time, for about 5 seconds each. Skin should peel off easily. To seed tomatoes, cut in half at the equator, hold tomato half in palm of hand and gently squeeze out seeds.

- To peel large amounts of garlic, place whole bulbs in the oven and bake at 300 degrees until the individual cloves open. Remove from oven and remove individual cloves.

- Always dry meat well before browning or it will stew rather than brown. Throw out browning fat when all pieces have browned and add more fat to pan if necessary to saute vegetables.

- Always put meat juices back into sauces and stews--they are rich in important amino acids.

- The most delicious sauces are made by the process of "reduction"--that is by boiling down stock so that the quantity reduces. The sauce becomes thick and the flavors concentrated. If your stock is rather thin to begin with, you may want to add a tablespoon or two of gelatin (see Sources) to hasten the thickening process. For a final thickening, use arrowroot--not flour. Mix 2 tablespoons arrowroot with 2 tablespoons water. Spoonful by spoonful add mixture to sauce, stews or clear soups until desired thickness is obtained. Sauce will maintain clarity and flavor.

- When beating eggwhites and cream, best results will be obtained by using a wire whisk, rather than an electric beater. Beat eggwhites in a very clean stainless steel or glass bowl with a pinch of salt.

- Keep your kitchen uncluttered and your counters clear. Store only items you use on a daily basis in your kitchen cupboards and leave as much working space as possible on your counters. Wipe counters after each task, to provide a clean space for the next. Easy access to the tools and utensils you need, and clean, clear counter space, help make cooking a joy rather than a chore.

- Dishwasher powder is extremely poisonous and should be used with great care. Use half the recommended amount and only for one cycle of the dishwasher. Do not fill the second cycle receptacle with dish powder, but let it be a rinse cycle, so that your dishes are rinsed twice. If you are caring for a cancer patient or anyone who is very sick, wash their dishes by hand in a mild liquid soap and rinse well.

- When preparing a meal, always think ahead to what must be done for the next two meals; put grains and pulses to soak, and meats to marinate, as necessary. Our readers will notice that the food preparation methods we recommend call for considerable advance planning—not a bad habit to cultivate in life.

- Throw away all boxed breakfast cereals. Start your day with soaked oatmeal or other grain, whole grain dishes such as pancakes or muffins, eggs, fish, nut milks, broth or homemade soup.

- Aim for a diet that is 50% raw or enzyme-enhanced. Raw foods include vegetables, fruits, meats, fats and milk products.

- A good rule is to start your evening meal with a dish containing enzymes—either a salad with homemade dressing, raw meat or fish, or soup containing cultured cream. If your next course includes a sauce made from gelatin-rich stock, easy digestion and a peaceful night's sleep will be assured.

- If the meal you serve consists entirely of cooked foods, then a lacto-fermented condiment is a must.

- Keep sweets to a minimum, even natural sweets.

REFERENCES

1. Gittleman, Ann Louise, MS *Beyond Pritikin*, 1980, Bantam Books, New York
2. US Department of Agriculture statistics quoted in Douglass, William Campbell, MD *The Milk of Human Kindness is Not Pasteurized*, 1985 Copple House Books, Lakemont, Georgia, 184; and in Beasley, Joseph D, MD and Jerry J Swift, MA *The Kellog Report*, 1989 The Institute of Health Policy and Practice, Annandale-on-Hudson, New York, 144
3. Castelli, William, *Archives of Internal Medicine*, 1992
4. Hubert, H, et al, *Circulation*, 1983 67:968
5. Rose, G, et al, *Lancet*, 1983 1:1062-1065
6. *JAMA*, September 24, 1982 248(12):1465
7. *JAMA*, 1984 251:359
8. Kronmal, R, *JAMA*, April 12, 1985 253 (14):2091
9. *JAMA*, 1964 189:655-59
10. Lackland, DT, et al, *Journal Nutrition* November 1990 120:11S:1433-1436
11. *Nutrition Week* Mar 22, 1991 21:12:2-3
12. Alfin-Slater, R B and L Aftergood, "Lipids", *Modern Nutrition in Health and Disease*, Chapter 5, 6th ed, R S Goodhart and M E Shils, eds, Lea and Febiger, Philadelphia 1980, p 131
13. Smith, M M, MNS RD and F Lifshitz, MD *Pediatrics* Mar 1994 93:3:438-443
14. Cohen, A, *American Hebrew Journal*, 1963, 65:291
15. Malhotra, S, *Indian Journal of Industrial Medicine*, 1968, 14:219
16. Kang-Jey Ho, et al, *Arch eological Pathology*, 1971, 91:387
17. Price, Weston, DDS *Nutritional Degeneration,* 1945 Price Pottenger Nutrition Foundation, Inc., La Mesa, California, 59-72
18. Carper, Jean, *Food Pharmacy Guide to Good Eating,* 1991 Bantam Books, New York, New York, 34-35 (Olive oil Crete)
19. Fernandez, N A *Cancer Res* 1975 35:3272; Martines, I, et al, *Cancer Res* 1975 35:3265
20. Moore, Thomas J, *Lifespan: What Really Affects Human Longevity*, 1990 Simon and Schuster, New York
21. *New York Times*, November 17, 1991
22. A study of South Pacific Islanders who consumed large amounts of coconut oil showed no coronary heart disease, Prior, I, et al, *American Journal of Clinical Nutrition* 1981, 34:1552
23. Levels of linoleic acid in adipose tissues reflect the amount of linoleic acid in the diet. Valero, et al, *Annals of Nutritional Metabolism,* Nov/Dec 1990 34:6:323-327; Felton, C v, et al, *Lancet* 1994 344:1195-96
24. *American Journal of Clinical Nutrition* 1992 56:616-622; Pan, David A, et al, *Nutrient Metabolism*, American Institute of Nutrition, 1993 512
25. Kabara, J J, *The Pharmacological Effects of Lipids,* J J Kabara, ed, The American Oil Chemists Society, Champaign, IL 1978 pp 1-14; Cohen, L A et al, *J Natl Cancer Inst* 1986 77:43
26. *Journal Nutrition* Feb 1990 120:2:148-157

27. *Lipids* 1985 20:4:227
28. *Food Technology*, October 1988, 134; *Lipids*, 1985 20:4:227
29. Horrobin, D F, *Reviews in Pure and Applied Pharmacological Sciences* Vol 4, 1983 Freund Publishing House 339-383; Devlin, T M, ed,*Textbook of Biochemistry*, 2nd Ed., 1982 Wiley Medical, 429-430
30. Harmon, D, et al, *Journal of the American Geriatrics Society* 1976 24:1: 292-8 and Meerson, Z, et al,*Bulletin Experimental Biological Medicine* 1983 96:9:70-71
31. Garg, M L, et al, *FASCB Journal* 1988 2:4:A852
32. Galland, Leo,*MD Superimmunity for Kids*, 1988 Copestown Press, New York and Valentine, Tom, *Search for Health*, January/February 1993 1:3:41-45
33. Simopoulos, A P, amd Norman Salem *Am J of Clin Nutr 1992 55:411-4*
34. A review of studies showing correlation of high polyunsaturate consumption with increased incidence of cancer is found in Mudd, Chris, *Cholesterol and Your Health*, 1990 American Lite Co, Oklahoma City
35. Machlin, I J and A Bendich, *FASEB Journal* 1987 1:441-445
36. Cranton, E M, MD and J P Frackelton, MD,*Journal of Holistic Medicine*, Spring/ Summer 1984.
37. Engelberg, Hyman, *Lancet*, March 21, 1992 339:727-728
38. Alfin-Slater, *op cit*, p 134
39. Addis, Paul, *Food and Nutrition News*, March/April 1990, 62:2:7-10
40. Barnes, Broda and L Galton,*Hyprthyroidism, The Unsuspected Illness*, 1976 T Y Crowell, New York
41. Ubbink, J B, *Nutrition Reivews* Nov 1994 52:(11) 383-393
42. *Science News Letter*, Feb 1956; Schantz, E J, et al,*Journal of Dairy Science* 1940 23:181-89. A summary of other research is found in DeCava, Judith *Journal of the National Academy of Research Biochemists*, September 1988 1053-1059
43. Enig, Mary G PhD, *Nutrition Quarterly*, 1993 Vol 17, No 4
44. *Ibid.* Unpublished research indicates that trans fatty acids incorporated into the growth plates of bones lead to problems with tendons and joints, personal communication, Mary G. Enig PhD
45. Zikakis, et al, *Journal of Dairy Science*, 1977 60:533; Oster, *American Journal of Clinical Research*, April 1971, Vol II, No 1
46. *Journal American College Nutrition* April 1991 10:2:93-106; Enig, et al,*Federation Proceedings*, July 1978 37:9:2215-2220
47. *Journal American College Nutrition, Ibid.*, and *Nutrition Week* Mar 22, 1991 21:12:2-3
48. Fraps, G S, and A R Kemmerer, *Texas Agricultural Bulletin* Feb 1938 No 560
49. Schantz,*op cit*
50. *American Journal of Physical Medicine,* 1941, p 133;*Physiological Zoology*, 1935 8:457
51. Personal communication, Pat Connolly, Executive Director, Price Pottenger Nutrition Foundation
52. Enig, Mary, Ph.D., "Health and Nutritional Benefits from Coconut Oil and its Advantages over Competing Oils", COCOTECH XXXII, Cochin, Inida July 17-21, 1995.

53. Prasad, K N, *Life Science*, 1980, 27:1351-8; Gershon, Herman and Larry Shanks, *Symposium on the Pharmacological Effect of Lipids*, Jon J Kabara Ed, American Oil Chemists Society, Champaign, Illinois 1978 51-62
54. Belury, M A *Nutrition Reviews* April 1995 53:(4)83-89
55. Koopman, J S, et al, *AJPH* 1984 74 (12):1371-1373
56. Personal communication, Mary G Enig, Ph D
57. Personal communication, Mary G. Enig, Ph D. This lobbying is largely channeled through the Institute for Shortening and Edible Oils.
58. Furth, Anna and John Harding, *New Scientist*, September 1989 44-47
59. Beasley, *op cit* 144-145
60. Paton, J, *British Medical Journal* 1933 1:738
61. Howell, Edward, MD *Enzyme Nutrition* 1985 Avery Publishing Group, Inc Wayne, NJ, 88, 104; Fields, M *Proc Soc Exp Biol Med* 1984 175:530-537
62. Douglas, W C, MD, *Second Opinion*, May 1995 Vol V, No 5
63. Yudkin, J *Lancet* 1957 11:155-62; Yudkin, J, et al, *Ann Nutr Metab* 1986 30(4):261-66; Yudkin, J et al (eds) *Sugar: Chemical, Biological and Nutritional Aspects of Sucrose* 1971 Daniel Davey, Hartford, CT
64. This research is summarized in Mudd, *op cit*
65. Howell, *op cit*
66. These studies are summarized in Beasely, *op cit*, 132. See also, Yudkin, John, Dr, *Sweet & Dangerous*, 1973 Bantam Books, New York, NY
67. Beasley, *op cit* 129
68. Fields, *op cit*
69. Page, Melvin, DDS, *Degeneration, Regeneration*, 1949 Nutritional Development, St. Petersburg, FL
70. Sullivan, J L, *Lancet*, June 13, 1981 1239; Gutteridge, J M et al, *Biochem Journal* 1982 206:605-9
71. Reinhold, John G, *Ecology of Food and Nutrition*, 1972 I:187-192
72. Aubert, Claude, *Les Aliments Fermentes Traditionnels. Une Richesse Meconnue* 1985 Terre Vivante, Paris, France, 35; Steinkraus, Keith H, ed, *Handbook of Indigenous Fermented Foods*, 1983 Marcel Dekker, Inc, New York, NY
73. Stitt, Paul, *Fighting the Food Giants*, 1981, Natural Press, Manitowoc, WI 62
74. Abrams, H Leon, *Journal of Applied Nutrition*, 1980 32:2:70-71
75. Cheraskin, E, et al, *Journal Orthomolecular Psychiatry*, 1978 7:150-155
76. *British Journal Nutrition* Sep 1986 56:2:341-348; *Federation Proceedings* Nov 1986; 45:12:2758-2762; *American Journal Clinical Nutrition* June 1983 37:6:924-929
77. *Canadian Medical Journal* Oct 1, 1986 135:7:753-8
78. Haviland, W A, *American Antiquity*, 1967 32:316-325
79. Pitskhelauri, G Z, Dr, *The Long Living of Soviet Georgia*, 1982 Human Sciences Press, New York, NY
80. Abrams, *op cit*
81. *Nutrition Reviews*, 1979 37:142-144 (check)
82. Specker, B L, et al, *Am J Clin Nutr* 1988 47:89-92; Berg H van den, et al, *Lancet* 1988 1:242-3; Herbert, V *Am J Clin Nutr* 1987 46:387-402
83. *Nature's Way,* 1979 10:20-30
84. A good example is the Willard study which received extensive press coverage. A

seriously flawed data base invalidates the conclusion that dietary saturated fat and meat consumption contributes to cancer of the colon. Willlard, Walter C et al, *New England Journal of Medicine*, December 13, 1990 1664-1671

85. Enig, Mary G, Ph D *Townsend Letter for Doctors,* December, 1993 1214-1215
86. Mudd, *op cit*
87. Merrill, Alfred J, et al, *Annual Review Nutrition* 1993 13:539-559
88. Enig, Marg G, Ph D, et al, *Federation Proceedings*, July 1978 37:9:2215-2220
89. Gotthoffer, N R, *Gelatin in Nutrition and Medicine*, 1945 Grayslade Gelatin Co, Greyslake, IL; Burton, B T and W R Foster, *Human Nutrition* 4th ed, McGraw-Hill Book Co, 1988 p 85
90. Wallace, G M *J Sci Fd Agri* Oct 1971:526-35
91. Rackis, J J, et al, *Qual Plant Foods Hum Nutr* 1985 35:225
92. *Ibid*, 232
93. Aubert, Claude, *Dis-Moi Comment Tu Cuisines, Je Te Dirais Comment Tu te Portes* 1987 Terre Vivant, Paris, France, 114
94. Livingston-Wheeler, Virginia, MD, *Conquest of Cancer: Vaccines and Diet,* 1984 F. Watts, New York, NY
95. Personal communication, Dr Olympia Pinto, Rio de Janeiro. Using both phase contour and dark field microscopicy, Dr. Pinto has studied the blood profiles of patients and medical students consuming pork. He has had difficulty finding subjects for long term studies because both patients and medical students voluntarily discontinued pork consumption after initial blood asseys.
96. Adamson, R H, *Cancer Prevention* Nov 1990 1-7; Bjeldanes, L F, et al, *J Agriculture Food Chem* 1983 31:18-21
97. Holzman, Neil A, et al, *Modern Nutrition in Health and Disease*, 6th ed. (Goodhart and Shils, eds) 1980 Lea and Febiger Philadelphia, PA, 1193-1219
98. Douglass, *The Milk of Human Kindness, op cit*, 82-101
99. Beasley, *op cit*, 174
100. *New England Journal of Medicine*, July 1992 327:5:348-9
101. Howell, *op cit*, 145-146
102. Baker, Herman and Oscar Frank, *Journal of the International Association of Preventative Medicine*, July 1982 19-24
103. Price, *op cit*, 278
104. Smith, Bob, *Journal of Applied Nutrition* 1993 45:1
105. Burton, B T, ed *The Heinz Handbook of Nutrition*, 1959 McGraw Hill, New York, NY
106. Price, *op cit* Dr. Price referred to vitamins A and D as "fat soluble activators"
107. Dunne, Lavon J, *Nutrition Almanac*, 3rd ed, 1990 McGraw Hill, New York, NY
108. Solomans, N W, and J Bulox, *Nutr Rev* July 1993 51:199-204
109. Douglas, *Second Opinion, op cit*
110. Howell, *op cit*, 54
111. Howell, Edward, *Enzymes for Health and Longevity*, 1980 Omangod Press, Woodstock Valley, CT
112. Howell, *Enzyme Nutrition, op cit*, xv
113. Holden, Robert A, et al, *JAMA,* July 15, 1983 250:3:356-369
114. DeLangre, Jacques, *Seasalt's Hidden Powers,* 1992 Happiness Press, Magnolia, CA

115. Bieler, H, MD, *Food is Your Best Medicine,* 1965 Ballantine Books, NY, NY
116. DeLangre, *op cit*
117. Peat, Ray, PhD, *Health Freedom News,* September 1993, 33-34
118. These studies are summarized in Gotthoffer, *op cit*
119. Samuels, J L, and A, Ph D, *Search for Health,* Sep/Oct 1993 2:1:28-47
120. *Ibid;* Samuels, J L, and A, Ph D, *Townsend Letter for Doctors,* Nov 1995
121. Personnal Communication, Mary G. Enig, Ph D
122. Elias, P S and A J Cohen, *Radiation Chemistry of Major Food Components* 1977 Elsevier Biomedical Press, NY
123. Bhaskaram, C and G Sadasivan, *Am J Clin Nutr* Feb 1975 28:130-35
124. Stellman, S D and L Garfinkel, *Appetite* 1988 11:85-91
125. Roberts, H J, MD, *Natural Food and Farming* March/April 1992, 23-34
126. Smith, M M, *op cit*
127. Myers, John, MD, *Metabolic Aspects of Health*, 1979 Discovery Press, Kentfield, CT
128. Sherman, W C, *Food and Nutr News* Feb 1977 48(3):3; Foster, H D *Lancet* Sept 12 1987 2(8559):633
129. Yiamouyiannis, John, *Fluoride, The Aging Factor*, 1986 Health Action Press, Dellaware, OH
130. Steinkraus, *op cit*
131. American Gastroenterological Association *Physiology of Intestinal Fluid and Electrolyte Absorption*, 1980 Milner-Fenwick, Baltimore, MD
132. *Journal National Cancer Institute* May 5, 1993 85:9:722-7
133. Williams, Roger J, MD, *The Prevention of Alcoholism Through Nutrition*, 1981 Bantam Books, New York, NY
134. Igram, Cass, MD Eat Right or Die Young, 1989 Literary Visions, Inc, Cedar Rapids, Iowa, 134
135. Crook, William G, *The Yeast Connection*, Random House, New York, NY 1983, 221-222
136. Howell, *Enzymes for Health and Longevity*, *op cit*, 111
137. Reading, Dr. Chris, *Your Family Tree Connection: Genealogy and Health* 1984 Keats Publishing, Inc, New Canaan, CT
138. Lorenzani, Shirley S, Ph D, *Candida, A Twentieth Century Disease*, 1986 Keats Publishing, New Canaan, CT
139. For a more detailed description of allergy testing using the pulse test Coca, Arthur F, *The Pulse Test*, 1982 Lyle Stuart, Inc., Secaucus, NJ
140. "Nuturing a Cornucopia of Potential", *Washington Post*, October 26, 1993
141. Abrams, *op cit;* Dagnelie, Pieter C, et al, *American Journal of Clinical Nutrition* 1990 51:202-208
142. *Journal Food Science* Jan/Feb 1984 49:1:199-201
143. Katz, S, *Nutritional Anthropology*, 1987 Alan R. Lin, Inc, NY, NY 1987 47
144. *Nutrition Research* Jan 1989 9:1:127-132
145. Lonnerdal, Bo, Ph D, *Am J Clinical Nutrition,* November 1984 40:1064
146. Personal communication, Mary G Enig, Ph D
147. Weiner, Dr. Michael, *Reducing the Risk of Alzheimer's,* 1987 Scarborough House Publishers, Chelsea, MI
148. Valentine, Tom, *Search for Health* September/October 1992 1:1:2-13

MASTERING THE BASICS

CULTURED DAIRY PRODUCTS

Cultured or fermented dairy products play a role in many traditional cuisines. In fact, only in the West is milk consumed in a "natural" or unfermented state and this Occidental practice is relatively new. Before the age of industrialization, Europeans consumed milk as yoghurt, cheese, clabber or curds and whey. Without pasteurization or refrigeration, milk sours and separates spontaneously. This is due to the process of lacto-fermentation during which lactic-acid-producing bacteria begin digesting or breaking down both milk sugar (lactose) and milk protein (casein). When these friendly bacteria have produced enough lactic acid to inactivate all putrefying bacteria, the milk is effectively preserved from spoilage for several days or weeks, and in the case of cheese, which undergoes further fermentation of a different type, for several years.

Yoghurt is the fermented milk product with which we are most familiar in the West. It comes originally from Bulgaria. Unlike spontaneously soured milk, yoghurt is produced by first heating milk and then adding a culture. In Russia, a popular beverage is *kefir*, a slightly effervescent, mildly alcoholic beverage of fermented cow, goat or sheep milk. *Koumiss*, another Russian beverage popular in the eastern regions, is made from mare's milk. Scandinavian countries produce a cultured milk product in wooden barrels called *longfil* which keeps for many months. The Norwegians make a variety of *longfil* called *kjaeldermelk* which they produce in caves. In the Middle East, milk is soured in special containers to produce *laban*. In India, milk from cows or water buffalo is soured to produce *dahi*, which the Indians consume with every meal. The Masai tribesmen of Africa consume milk as their principal food—always in soured or cultured form.

In Europe, soured milk products are still extensively used. Sour or fermented cream—*creme fraiche*—is an indispensable ingredient in soups and sauces. The delicious sour butter of France and Germany is made from churning fermented cream. Cultured butter needs no salt and its high enzyme content makes it easy to digest. Cream cheese and cottage cheese are traditionally made by allowing the fermentation process to continue for several days until the white curds or casein-containing portion of the milk separates from the whey. When this cream cheese is weighted down or inoculated with further cultures, it undergoes an additional fermentation process resulting in many different types of cheese. Modern cheese makers consider whey a waste product but in earlier times it was used to produce a variety of other fermented foods and beverages.

Like the process of sprouting grains, fermentation of milk results in numerous beneficial changes. Fermentation breaks down casein or milk protein, one of the most difficult proteins to digest. Culturing restores many of the enzymes destroyed during pasteurization including lactase, which helps digest lactose or milk sugar; and numerous enzymes which helps the body absorb calcium and other minerals. Lactase produced during the culturing process allows many people who are allergic to natural milk to tolerate fermented milk products. Both vitamin B and vitamin C content of milk increase during fermentation. Another product of lacto-fermentation, hydrogen peroxide, helps transport oxygen to the cells. Research has shown that regular consumption of cultured dairy products lowers cholesterol and protects against bone loss. Finally, cultured dairy products provide friendly bacteria and lactic acid to the digestive tract. These friendly creatures and their by-products keep pathogens at bay, guard against infectious illness and aid in the fullest possible digestion of all food we consume. Perhaps this is why so many traditional societies value fermented milk products for their health promoting-properties and insist on giving them to the sick, the aged and to nursing mothers. In the absence of high-technology sanitation systems, lacto-fermented dairy foods, as well as beverages and vegetables, provide essential protection against infectious disease.

A great many recipes in this book call for fermented dairy products in the form of cultured milk, cultured cream or *creme fraiche*, natural cream cheese and yoghurt. We also use cultured whey to make fermented vegetables, chutneys, beverages and grain dishes.

The recipes presented here are designed to allow you to produce fermented dairy products in your own kitchen with a minimum of difficulty. They require no special equipment other than a simple room thermometer. Most are made using a Finnish culture called *piima*, an inexpensive powder that can be kept in your refrigerator (see Sources). Piima culture is derived from the milk of cows that feed on the butterwort plant. Centuries ago, Scandinavian farmers discovered that milk clabbered better when their cows consumed this herb.

The piima culture is a foolproof way to ferment dairy products but the process does require a constant ambient temperature of 72 to 75 degrees. You will avoid much frustration by purchasing a simple room thermometer and finding a place in your home where the temperature always stays within this range, such as a closet or cupboard with a light bulb or a shelf over a refrigerator or near a heating vent. Once you have located a spot where the piima culture can do its work, the rest is easy. It pays to make milk culturing part of your routine so that you always have on hand the products you need for healthy and appetizing meals.

STARTER CULTURE

1 cup good quality cream
1 envelope piima culture (see Sources)

You will need a culture to produce the other fermented products in this chapter. Start with the best quality cream you can find, such as the thick old-fashioned cream available at health food stores and gourmet food shops. Raw cream is best, but pasteurized cream will do. Do not use ultrapasteurized cream—it does not contain enough nutrients to support your culture.

Find a place in your house where the temperature is a fairly constant 72-75 degrees. If the temperature is below 69 degrees, the culture will become stringy and slimy. If the temperature is more than 75 degrees, the culture will separate and sour.

Place the cream in an impeccably clean glass jar. It is very important to avoid contamination by airborne bacteria or by aerosols, sprays, paint fumes, dusts, molds, yeast and insecticides. Stir in the piima powder and cover tightly. Leave in a 72-75 degree location for about 24 hours. Transfer to refrigerator.

A small amount of this culture can now be added to milk and cream to produce the other fermented products in this chapter. The culture will keep well chilled for several months. Always test it with your nose before using. If it smells bad, throw it out and start again.

The tradition of preserving foods, enhancing their nutritive value, and making them more interesting to eat through fermentation is a very ancient one. A form of yogurt was said to have been revealed to Abraham by an angel, and the starter particles of kefir, a substance similar to yogurt but thin enough to be drinkable, are called "grains of the Prophet Mohammed", the Prophet having been credited with their introduction. William H. Lee PhD *The Friendly Bacteria*

The fermentation of milk makes it more assimilable to persons with lactose intolerance because a large part of the lactose is transformed into lactic acid; and because the presence of the enzyme lactase in fermented milk products helps break down lactose in the digestive tract. Furthermore, a portion of the milk protein (casein) is decomposed, liberating the amino acids of which it is formed. Research shows that proteins in yoghurt are digested twice as quickly as those of non-fermented milk. Claude Aubert *Les Aliments Traditionnels Fermentes*

During fermentation of milk products, thirty to forty percent of the lactose is broken down so that the high lactose content is reduced. However, a special enzyme activity also takes place. Fermented products that are not pasteurized or heated in ways that destroy enzyme activity have significant levels of enzymes that contribute to the digestion of lactose in the intestine. Dr. Betty Kamen *Health Freedom News*

PIIMA CREAM

1 pint good quality cream
1 tablespoon starter culture (page 76)

Cream cultured with the piima culture is similar to French *creme fraiche*, but has, we think, a better flavor. Use the best quality cream you can find. Raw cream is best but pasteurized will do. Do not use ultrapasteurized cream. Place cream in a clean glass container. Add the starter, cover tightly, and place in a spot where the temperature is a stable 72-75 degrees for 20 to 24 hours. It will have thickened slightly. Chill well. When cool the cream becomes quite firm. Piima cream will keep in the refrigerator for several weeks. It may develop a thin yellowish or pinkish crust—simply remove this with a spoon.

Piima cream is delicious in soups, sauces and desserts and more digestible than natural cream due to its high enzyme content.

Each isolated Swiss valley or village has its own special feast days of which athletic contests are the principal events. The feasting in the past has been largely on dairy products. The athletes were provided with large bowls of cream as constituting one of the most popular and healthful beverages, and special cheese was always available. . . their cream products took the place of our modern ice cream. . . it is reported that practically all skulls that are exhumed in the Rhone Valley, and indeed, practically throughout all of Switzerland where graves have existed for more than a hundred years, are found with relatively perfect teeth; whereas the teeth of people recently buried have been riddled with caries or lost through this disease. Weston Price DDS *Nutrition and Physical Degeneration*

PIIMA MILK

1 quart fresh whole milk, non-homogenized
1 tablespoon starter culture (page 76)

Use the best quality milk you can find. Raw milk is best but pasteurized will do. Try to find milk from a dairy that feeds its cows natural feed and does not keep them confined in pens. Do not use ultrapasteurized or homogenized milk. Place milk in a clean glass container. Add the starter, stir or shake well, cover tightly, and place in a spot where the temperature is a stable 72-75 degrees for 20 to 24 hours. Cultured milk does not thicken as does yoghurt, but remains rather liquid. Chill well. Use in the preparation of many grain dishes, in baby formula (page 561) or as an enzyme-rich and easily digested substitute for pasteurized milk.

[The Rosickys] had been at one accord not to hurry through life, not to be always skimping and saving. They saw their neighbours buy more land and feed more stock than they did, without discontent. Once when the creamery agent came to the Rosickys to persuade them to sell him their cream, he told then how much the Fasslers, their nearest neighbours, had made on their cream last year.

"Yes," said Mary, "and look at them Fassler children! Pale, pinched little things, they look like skimmed milk. I'd rather put some colour into my children's faces than put money into the bank" Willa Cather *Neighbour Rosicky*

In isolated Swiss villages, a limited amount of garden stuff is grown, chiefly green foods for summer use. While the cows spend the warm summer on the verdant knolls and wooded slopes near the glaciers and fields of perpetual snow, they have a period of high and rich productivity of milk. The milk constitutes an important part of the summer's harvesting. While the men and boys gather in the hay and rye, the women and children go in large numbers with the cattle to collect the milk and make and store cheese for the following winter's use This [raw] cheese contains the natural butter fat and minerals of the splendid milk and is a virtual storehouse of life for the coming winter.

These people. . . recognize the presence of Divinity in the life-giving qualities of the butter made in June when the cows have arrived for pasturage near the glaciers. [The priest] gathers the people together to thank the kind Father for the evidence of his Being in the life-giving qualities of butter and cheese made when the cows eat the grass near the snow line. This worshipful program includes the lighting of a wick in a bowl of the first butter made after the cows have reached the luscious summer pasturage. This wick is permitted to burn in a special sanctuary built for that purpose. The natives of the valley are able to recognize the superior quality of their June butter, and, without knowing exactly why, pay it due homage. Weston Price DDS *Nutrition and Physical Degeneration*

CULTURED BUTTER AND BUTTERMILK

Makes 1/2 pound butter and 2 cups buttermilk

1 quart piima cream (page 77)

Cultured butter is available in many health food stores and gourmet markets—but it is quite expensive. It is very easy to make your own cultured butter at a lower cost, with its welcome by-product, cultured buttermilk.

Place cultured cream in your food processor fitted with a steel blade and process until butter forms. Transfer to a bowl and press out the buttermilk with a wooden spoon or paddle. Pour buttermilk into a separate container and reserve for baking. When no more buttermilk comes out of the butter, lift it out of the bowl and pat it dry with paper towels. Place butter in a crock or molds. Cover with plastic wrap and chill well.

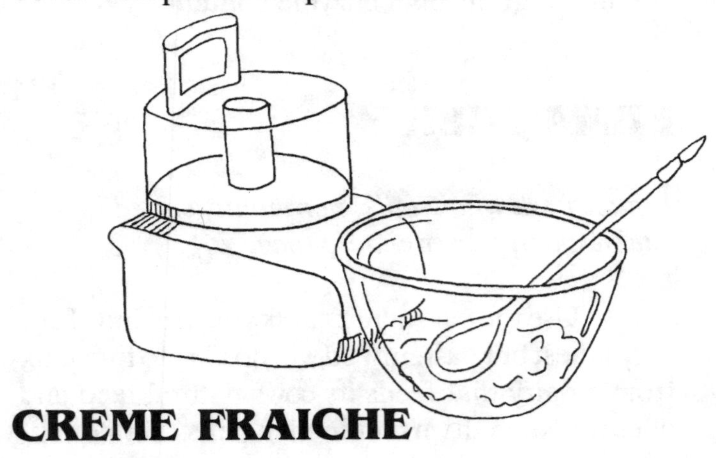

CREME FRAICHE

1 pint good quality cream
1 tablespoon cultured buttermilk

French *creme fraiche* is very similar to piima cream. Use the best quality cream you can find—not ultrapasteurized. Place in a clean glass container. Add buttermilk, cover tightly and place in a warm spot for 20 to 24 hours. Chill well.

YOGHURT

1/2 cup good quality commercial plain yoghurt, or 1/2 cup yoghurt from previous batch
1 quart fresh whole milk, non-homogenized
a candy thermometer

If you use a lot of yoghurt, it is advisable to make your own for the rather technical reason that fresh yoghurt contains lactic acid in which the (+) or "right-handed" form predominates; whereas in older yoghurt the (-) or "left-handed" form predominates. The (+) form of lactic acid in yoghurt is most beneficial to the human organism while the (-) form may have adverse effects.

Yoghurt is easy to make—neither a yoghurt maker nor a special culture is necessary. Start with the best quality milk you can find. Raw milk is best but pasteurized milk will do. Do not use ultrapasteurized or homogenized milk.

Gently heat the milk to 180 degrees and allow to cool to about 110 degrees. Stir in yoghurt and place in a covered glass or stainless steel container. Place in a warm oven (about 150 degrees, or a gas oven with a pilot light) overnight. In the morning transfer to the refrigerator.

Metchnikoff attributed the relative long life span and freedom from disease of Bulgarian peasants to their consumption of sour milk containing a lactic acid bacillus. . . However, his assumption took no account of a far better explanation. Dairy products form a large proportion of the diet in certain countries. Before the era of pasteurization, dairy products were utilized in the raw condition, since their palatability does not improve by heat-treatment, as is the case with many food materials. When a large share of the calory requirement was supplied by raw milk, raw butter and raw cheese, not only did the organism receive a daily quota of enzymes, but the enzyme content of the tissues was not so heavily drawn upon as in those countries where the preponderance of the diet consisted of heat-treated foods. Therefore, the Bulgarian peasants, many of whom Metchnikoff found to live to the century mark in their mountainous abode, might be expected to have a long life span because their enzyme reserve is more slowly used up during the course of living. Edward Howell MD *Enzymes for Health and Longevity*

Various researchers have learned that children and certain adults can beat allergies by taking the supplement lactobacillus acidophilus, the friendly bacteria found in yoghurt [and other fermented foods. One published study revealed that every allergic child who volunteered to be tested was deficient in lactobacillus acidophilus, a condition corrected, in most instances, by taking this supplement. John Shelly *Health Freedom News*

CREAM CHEESE AND WHEY

Makes 2 cups cream cheese and 5 cups whey

2 quarts fresh milk, non-homogenized
2 tablespoons starter culture (page 76)

It is worth making your own cream cheese as the commercial variety is produced by putting milk under high pressure, not by the beneficial action of lactic-acid-producing bacteria. We call for its use in a number of recipes. The whey that is a by-product is a very useful product. Used as a starter for lacto-fermented vegetables, it allows you to produce consistently successful results with a reduced amount of salt; and those who cannot tolerate milk protein even in cultured form can substitute whey mixed with water in many of our recipes for baked goods.

Follow the directions for piima milk (page 77), but allow the milk to stand in a warm place for 2 or 3 days, until it separates. The separated milk should smell sweet, not sour. If the odor is at all unpleasant, discard and start again.

Line a large strainer set over a bowl with several layers of cheese cloth or a clean linen dish towel. Pour in the separated milk. The whey will run into the bowl and the milk solids will stay in the strainer. After several hours, tie up the cheese cloth or linen towel with the milk solids inside, being careful not to squeeze. Tie this little sack to a wooden spoon placed across the top of a bowl or pitcher so that more whey can drip out of the bag. When the bag stops dripping, the cheese is ready. Store whey in a mason jar and cream cheese in a covered glass container. Refrigerated, the cream cheese will keep for about 2 months and the whey for about 6 months.

Old Par, [an English peasant] who lived to the age of 152 years and 9 months, existed and even thrived on a diet of "sub-rancid cheese, and milk in every form, coarse and hard bread, and small drink, generally sour whey," as William Harvey wrote. . . "On this sorry fare, but living in his home, free from care, did this poor man attain to such length of days." Terence McLaughlin *A Diet of Tripe*

Whey is such a good helper in your kitchen. It has a lot of minerals. One tablespoon of whey in a little water will help digestion. It is a remedy that will keep your muscles young. It will keep your joints movable and ligaments elastic. When age wants to bend your back, take whey. . . With stomach ailments, take one tablespoon whey three times daily, this will feed the stomach glands and they will work well again. Hanna Kroeger *Ageless Remedies from Mothers Kitchen*

FERMENTED VEGETABLES & FRUITS

It may seem strange to us that in earlier times, people knew how to preserve vegetables for long periods without the use of freezers or canning machines. This was done through the process of lacto-fermentation. Lactic acid is a natural preservative which inhibits putrefying bacteria. Starches and sugars in vegetables and fruits are converted into lactic acid by lactic-acid-producing bacteria, of which there are many species. These lactobacilli are ubiquitous, present on the surface of all living things, and especially numerous on the leaves and roots of plants growing in or near the ground. Man needs only to learn the techniques for controlling and encouraging their proliferation to put them to his own use, just as he has learned to put certain yeasts to use in converting the sugars in grape juice to alcohol in wine.

The ancient Greeks understood that important chemical changes took place during this type of fermentation. Their name for it was "alchemy". Like the fermentation of dairy products, preservation of vegetables and fruits by the process of lacto-fermentation has numerous advantages beyond those of simple preservation. The proliferation of lactobacilli in fermented vegetables enhances their digestibility and increases vitamin levels. These beneficial organisms produce numerous helpful enzymes as well as antibiotic and anti-carcinogenic substances. Their main by-product, lactic acid, not only keeps vegetables and fruits in a state of perfect preservation, but also promotes the growth of healthy flora throughout the intestine. Other alchemical by-products include hydrogen peroxide, a potent blood and tissue oxygenator, and small amounts of benzoic acid.

A partial list of lacto-fermented vegetables from around the world is sufficient to prove the universality of this practice. In Europe, the principle lacto-fermented food is sauerkraut. Described in Roman texts, it has been prized for its delicious taste as well as medicinal properties for many centuries. Cucumbers, beets and turnips are also traditional foods for lacto-fermentation. Less well known are ancient recipes for pickled herbs and leaves such as sorrel and grape leaves. In Russia and Poland one finds pickled green tomatoes, peppers and lettuces as well. The practice of lacto-fermentation is also found throughout the Orient. The peoples of Japan, China and Korea make pickled preparations of cabbage, turnip, eggplant, cucumber, onion, squash and carrot. Korean *kimchi,* for example, is a lacto-fermented condiment of cabbage, other vegetables and seasonings, that is eaten on a daily basis and no Japanese meal is complete without a portion of pickled vegetable. American tradition includes many types of relishes—corn relish, cucumber relish, watermelon rind—all of which were no doubt originally lacto-fermented products. The pickling of fruit is less well known but nevertheless found in many traditional cultures. The Japanese prize pickled *umeboshi* plums and the peoples of India traditionally fermented fruit with spices to make chutneys.

Lacto-fermented condiments are easy to make. Fruits and vegetables are first washed and cut up, mixed with herbs or spices and then pounded briefly to release juices. They are then mixed with a solution of salt water and placed in an air tight container. Salt inhibits putrefying bacteria for several days until enough lactic acid is produced to preserve the vegetables for many months. The amount of salt can be reduced or even eliminated if whey is added to the pickling solution. Rich in lactic acid and lactic-acid producing bacteria, whey acts as an inoculant, reducing the time needed for sufficient lactic acid to be produced to insure preservation. Use of whey will ensure consistently successful pickling; it is essential for pickling fruits. During the first few days of fermentation, the vegetables are kept at room temperature; afterwards they must be placed in a cool dark place to ensure preservation.

It is important to use the best quality organic vegetables, sea salt and filtered or pure water for lacto-fermentation. Lactobacilli need plenty of nutrients to do their work and if the vegetables are deficient, the process of fermentation will not proceed. Likewise if your salt or water contains impurities, the quality of the final product will be jeopardized.

Lacto-fermentation is an artisanal craft that does not lend itself to industrialization. Results are not always predictable. For this reason, when the pickling process became industrialized, many changes were made that rendered the final product more uniform and more saleable, but not necessarily more nutritious. Chief among these was the use of vinegar for the brine, resulting in a product that is more acidic and not necessarily beneficial when eaten in large quantities; and of subjecting the final product to pasteurization, thereby effectively killing all the lactic-acid-producing bacteria and robbing consumers of their beneficial effect on the digestion.

The recipes presented in this chapter are designed to be made in small quantities in your own kitchen. They require no special equipment apart from wide-mouth quart-sized mason jars and a wooden pounder. We recommend adding small amount of whey to each jar of vegetables to ensure that your results are consistently satisfactory. Concentrated whey and dried whey can be purchased at health food stores but the whey you make yourself (page 80) will be far superior because it still contains its valuable enzyme content.

About 1 inch of space should be left between the top of your vegetables with their liquid and the top of the jar, as the vegetables and their juices expand slightly during fermentation. Be sure to close the jars very tightly. Lacto-fermentation is an anaerobic process and the presence of oxygen, once fermentation has begun, will ruin the final product.

We have tried to keep these recipes as simple as possible without undue stress on ideal temperatures or precise durations. In general, a room temperature of about 72 degrees will be sufficient to insure a lactic acid fermentation in about 2 to 4 days. More time will be needed if your kitchen is colder, and less if it is very warm. After 2 to 4 days at room temperature, the jars should be placed in a dark, cool spot, ideally one with a temperature of about 40 degrees. In days gone by, containers of lacto-fermented vegetables were stored in cellars or caves. A wine cellar or small refrigerator kept on a "warm" setting is ideal; failing that, the top shelf of your refrigerator will do. Lacto-fermented fruit chutneys need about 2 days at room temperature and should always be stored in a refrigerator.

Lacto-fermented vegetables increase in flavor with time—according to the experts, sauerkraut needs at least six months to fully mature. But they also can be eaten as soon as they are ready for cold storage—after 3 or 4 days in jars. Lacto-fermented fruits and preserves should be eaten within two months of preparation.

Do not be dismayed if little spots of white foam appear at the top of the pickling liquid. They are completely harmless, and can be lifted off with a spoon if you like. The occasional batch that goes bad presents no danger—the smell is so awful that nothing on earth could persuade you to eat it.

Lactic-acid fermented vegetables and fruit chutneys should have a pleasant odor and a mildly acidic flavor. They are not meant to be eaten in large quantities but as condiments. They go beautifully with meats and fish of all sorts, as well as with pulses and grains. They are easy to prepare and they confer health benefits than cannot be underestimated.

Scientists and doctors today are mystified by the proliferation of new viruses—not only the deadly AIDS virus but the whole gamut of human viruses that seem to be associated with everything from chronic fatigue to cancer and arthritis. They are equally mystified by recent increases in the incidence of intestinal parasites and pathogenic yeasts, even among those whose sanitary practices are faultless. Could it be that in abandoning the ancient practice of lacto-fermentation, and in our insistence on a diet in which everything has been pasteurized, we have compromised the health of our intestinal flora and made ourselves vulnerable to legions of pathogenic microorganisms? If so, the cure for these diseases will be found not in inoculations, drugs or antibiotics, but in a restored partnership with the many varieties of lactobacilli, our symbionts of the microscopic world.

Of all the organic acids, lactic acid is the one that best inhibits the proliferation of bacteria that cause putrefaction, but it does not bring about in the body the over-acidifying action of certain other acids that form when one eats meat, eggs, sugar or cheese. While other products of the fermentation process, like alcohol and acetic acid, must be decomposed and eliminated, lactic acid can in large part be used by the body. Annelies Schoneck *Des Crudites Toute L'Annee*

Organic acids present in fermented milk and vegetable products play an important role in the health of old people as they aid a digestive system that is growing more and more feeble. Annelies Schoneck *Des Crudites Toute L'Annee*

After two or three days of lacto-fermentation, vegetables begin to soften and certain substances in them begin to decompose. If the vegetables contain nitrates—often the case after a summer with little sun—they are broken down. . . If all goes well, the lactic-acid producing bacteria take over and the process of acidification begins. New substances are formed, notably . . . choline and, above all, lactic acid. This acidification insures the conservation of the vegetables. . . but the fermentation of the aromas doesn't come about until a later stage, during storage. Lacto-fermentation is not only a means of conserving foods but also a procedure for ennobling them, as proved by their taste and aroma. Annelies Schoneck *Des Crudites Toute L'Annee*

SAUERKRAUT

Makes 1 quart

4 cups shredded cabbage, loosely packed
1 teaspoon juniper berries
1/2 teaspoon cumin seeds
1/2 teaspoon mustard seeds
2 teaspoons sea salt
2 tablespoons whey (if not available, add an additional 1 teaspoon salt)
1 cup filtered water

In a bowl, mix cabbage with juniper berries, cumin and mustard seeds. Mash or pound with a wooden pounder for several minutes to release juices. Place in a quart-sized wide-mouth mason jar and pack down with the pounder. Mix water with salt and whey and pour into jar. Add more water if needed to bring liquid to top of cabbage. There should be about one inch of space between the top of the cabbage and the top of the jar. Cover tightly and keep at room temperature for about 3 days. Transfer to cold storage. The sauerkraut can be eaten immediately, but it improves with age.

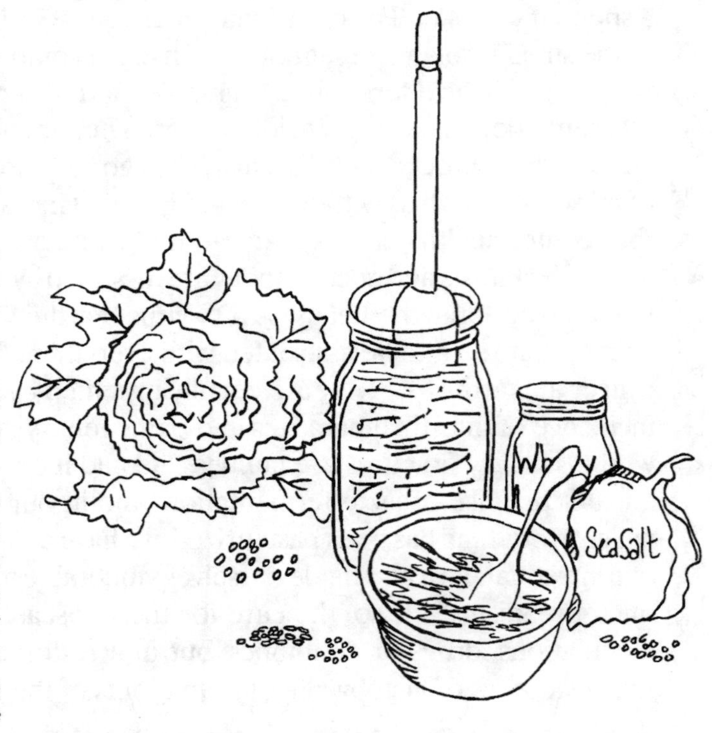

CORTIDO

(Latin American Sauerkraut)
Makes 2 quarts

1 whole cabbage, cored and shredded
1 cup grated carrots
2 medium onions, quartered lengthwise and very finely sliced
2-3 teaspoons dried oregano
1/4-1/2 teaspoon red pepper flakes
1 teaspoon sea salt
2 tablespoons whey (optional)
4-6 cups pineapple vinegar (page 142) or equal parts water and raw wine vinegar

This delicious spicy condiment goes beautifully with Mexican and Latin American food of all types. It is traditionally made with pineapple vinegar but can also be prepared with a mixture of raw wine vinegar and water. Like traditional sauerkraut, cortido improves with age.

In a large bowl mix cabbage with carrots, onions, oregano and red chile flakes. Pound several minutes with a wooden pounder to release the cabbage juices. Put cabbage mixture into two quart-sized mason jars and press down with pounder. There should be about 1 inch of space between the top of the cabbage and the top of the jar. Mix salt and whey with liquid and pour over cabbage. Add more water if needed to bring level of liquid to the level of cabbage. Cover tightly and leave at room temperature for about 3 days before transferring to cold storage.

Among all the vegetables that one can conserve through lacto-fermentation, cabbage has been man's preferred choice. . . . Here is how it was prepared in the olden days, according to Anna Nilssonn: "As children, we always looked forward to the day they made sauerkraut. Two men seated themselves face to face, and, straddling a barrel, held between them a large tool for shredding the cabbage. The little box that the cabbage fell into went back and forth between them to the rhythm of a song they chanted. Then arrived the moment that all of us children were waiting for. When they sang the refrain, one of the men would jump nimbly into the cask, scatter a handful of salt over the grated cabbage, and stamp down with his feet." But sauerkraut was known at a much more ancient time. . . In China, they fermented cabbage 6000 years ago. In ancient Rome, sauerkraut had a reputation as a food that was easy to digest. Even at that period, there were already two known methods for lacto-fermenting vegetables according to descriptions. . . given by Pliny (about 50 B.C.). The first method consisted in mashing the cut-up cabbage in great earthenware containers which were then hermetically sealed. The second consisted of mixing different vegetables, including wild herbs, and covering them with a solution of salt water. This mixture was called *compositur* or "mixture". Tiberius always carried a barrel of sauerkraut with him during his long voyages to the Middle East because the Romans knew that the lactic acid it contained protected them from intestinal infections. Annelies Schoneck *Des Crudites Toute L'Annee*

KIMCHI

(Korean Sauerkraut)
Makes 2 quarts

1 head green or Napa cabbage, cored and shredded
1 bunch green onions, chopped
1 cup grated carrots
1/2 cup grated daikon radish (optional)
1-2 tablespoons freshly grated ginger
3 cloves garlic, peeled and minced
1/2 teaspoon dried chile flakes
2 teaspoons sea salt
2 tablespoons whey (if not available, use an additional 2 teaspoons salt)
1/2 cup filtered water

Place vegetables, ginger and red chile flakes in a bowl and mash down with wooden pounder to release juices. Stuff into 2 quart-sized wide-mouth mason jars and press down with pounder. The top of the vegetables should be 1 inch below top of jar. Mix water with whey and salt and pour over cabbage mixture. Add additional water if needed to bring liquid to top of cabbage. Cover tightly. Keep in a warm place for 2 to 3 days before transferring to cold storage.

One striking observation [of ethnic cuisines] is that rarely are meals eaten without at least one fermented food, often a drink. In France, if one took away bread, cheese, ham, sausage, wine and beer, all produced through fermentation, our meals would be much impoverished.

In colder countries sauerkraut, cucumbers, *cornichons* (always fermented in the old days), other vegetables and many types of fish preserved by fermentation are always served. In Japan, it's not a meal without *miso*, soy sauce and pickles, all fermented products. In India, they drink soured milk every day, practically at every meal.

In Indonesia they eat *tempeh*, in Korea *kimchi* (a kind of sauerkraut) and in Africa porridge of fermented millet or cereal beers. In Moslem countries these fermented drinks are forbidden but they eat bread, dishes made with fermented pulses and milk products.

Without being indispensable, a small amount of some raw fermented food (preferably lacto-fermented) helps the digestion. This is especially true when the meal is a bit heavy. It isn't by chance, nor merely for the pleasure of taste, that we eat *cornichons* with *charcuterie*. Claude Aubert *Dis-Moi Comment Tu Cuisines*

TSUKEMONO

(Japanese Sauerkraut)
Makes 1 quart

1 small head green or Napa cabbage, cored and shredded
1 bunch green onions, chopped
2 tablespoons soy sauce
2 tablespoons fresh lemon juice
2 tablespoons whey (if not available, use an additional 1 teaspoon salt)
1 teaspoon sea salt

This is traditionally made with a culture of rice bran, but whey serves an identical purpose and is more easily obtained. Place vegetables in a bowl and mash down with wooden pounder. Stuff into a quart-sized wide mouth mason jars and mash down with pounder. Top of vegetables should be 1 inch below top of jar. Mix whey, salt, vinegar, lemon juice and soy sauce and pour over cabbage mixture. Add additional water if needed to bring liquid to top of cabbage. Cover tightly. Keep at room temperature for 2 to 3 days before transferring to cold storage.

Lets hear it for eggplant, squash, green beans, spinach and cabbage! All of these vegetables seem to ward off stomach cancer, according to a recent analysis in China. Scientists studied the eating habits of 482 residents of Heilongjiang Province; half had stomach cancer; half did not. Those free of cancer much preferred spinach, squash, eggplant, green beans, and especially cabbage. In fact the amount of cabbage deemed protective against stomach cancer was minuscule, according to researchers—a mere one-third cup of raw cabbage or two tablespoons of cooked cabbage per day. [In China, cabbage is often eaten pickled. SWF] Jean Carper *The Food Pharmacy Guide to Good Eating*

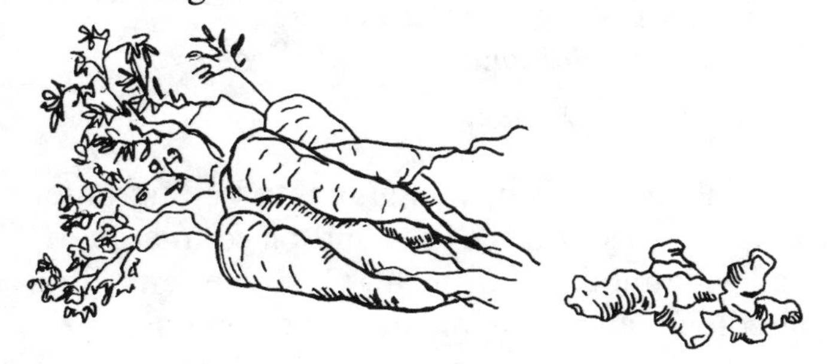

GINGER CARROTS

Makes 1 quart

4 cups grated carrots, loosely packed
1 tablespoon fresh ginger, grated
2 teaspoons sea salt
2 tablespoons whey (if not available, add an additional 1 teaspoon salt)

These are the best introduction to lacto-fermented vegetables we know; the taste is delicious and the sweetness of the carrots neutralizes the acidity that some people find disagreeable when first introduced to lacto-fermented vegetables. Ginger carrots go well with fish and with highly spiced meats.

In a bowl, mix all ingredients and pound with wooden pounder to release juices. Place in a quart-sized wide-mouth mason jar and press down with the wooden pounder. There should be about an inch of space between the top of the carrots and the top of the jar. Cover tightly. Leave at room temperature about 2-3 days before transferring to cold storage.

Sauerkraut owes its reputation in part to the famous navigators of past centuries. For his second round-the-world voyage, Captain Cook loaded 60 barrels of sauerkraut onto his ship. After 27 months at sea, 15 days before returning to England, he opened the last barrel and offered some sauerkraut to some Portuguese noblemen who had come on board. . . they carried off the rest of the barrel to give some to their friends. This last barrel was perfectly preserved after 27 months, in spite of changes in climate and the incessant rocking of the ship. The sauerkraut had also preserved sufficient quantities of vitamin C to protect the entire crew from scurvy. Not one case occurred during the long voyage even though this disease usually decimated crews on voyages of this length. Claude Aubert *Les Aliments Fermentes Traditionnels*

Listen to your ancestors. Listen to modern science. If there is a single bit of dietary advice that can boost your defenses against disease easily, quickly and safely it is: eat more onions, garlic and peppers!... Since the beginning of civilization humankind has used garlic, onions and peppers as natural medicines. The scientific validity behind that practice is becoming clear.

In tests on humans garlic has been found to lower cholesterol; raise good-type HDL cholesterol; lower blood pressure; produce more NK (natural killer) cells in the blood, cells that help fight off infections and tumors; inhibit blood platelet stickiness, reducing the risk of blood clots; destroy infection-causing bacteria and viruses; cure encephalitis; and reduce the risk of certain cancers. Jean Carper *The Food Pharmacy Guide to Good Eating*

PEASANT'S LUNCH

Sour Dough Bread with Cultured Butter

Raw Cheddar Cheese

Pickled Herring

Pickled Garlic
Pickled Cucumbers

Kvass

PICKLED PEARL ONIONS

Makes 1 quart

2 pounds pearl onions
1 cinnamon stick
1 small nutmeg, cracked open
2 teaspoons whole cloves
1 tablespoon juniper berries
1 teaspoon green peppercorns
several sprigs fresh tarragon
2 teaspoons sea salt
2 tablespoons whey (if not available, use an additional 1 teaspoon salt)
1 cup filtered water

Peel onions by plunging into boiling water for about 10 seconds. Peel and place in a quart-sized wide-mouth mason jar. Combine remaining ingredients and pour mixture over onions. Add more water if necessary to cover onions. Liquid should come to within 1 inch of top of jar. Cover tightly. Keep at room temperature for 3 days before transferring to cold storage.

PICKLED GARLIC

Makes 1 quart

about 12 heads garlic
2 teaspoons dried oregano
2 teaspoons sea salt
2 tablespoons whey (if not available, use an additional 1 teaspoon salt)

Set garlic heads in a 300 degree oven and bake until heads open and cloves can be easily removed. Place cloves in a quart-sized wide mouth mason jar. Mix oregano, salt and whey with 1/2 cup of water. Pour over garlic. Add more water to bring level of liquid to the top of the garlic. Cover tightly and keep at room temperature for 2 or 3 days before removing to cold storage.

PICKLED CUCUMBERS

Makes 1 quart

4-5 pickling cucumbers or 15-20 gherkins
1 tablespoon mustard seeds
2 tablespoons fresh dill, snipped
2 teaspoons sea salt
2 tablespoons whey (if not available, use an additional 1 teaspoon salt)
1 cup filtered water

Wash cucumbers well and place in a quart-sized wide-mouth mason jar. Combine remaining ingredients and pour over cucumbers. Add more water if necessary to bring level of liquid to about 1 inch below the top of the jar. Cover tightly. Keep at room temperature for 3 days before transferring to cold storage.

Variation: Pickled Cucumber Slices

Wash cucumbers well and slice at 1/4 inch intervals. Proceed as above. Pickles will be ready for cold storage after 2 days at room temperature.

Lacto-fermented cucumbers and *cornichons* [small cucumbers] are very refreshing and far less acid than pickles conserved in vinegar—one never grows tired of them. In classic cooking, these cornichons always go with meat courses and with sausages and preserved meats; a wise habit since this vegetable is able to dissolve precipitates of uric acid and thus prevents the formation of stones, often caused by meats and sausages, foods rich in uric acid Claude Aubert *Les Aliments Fermentes Traditionnels*

Using the food of the host as a culture medium, the quantity of enzymes produced by these countless bacteria must be considerable and they are placed at the selective disposal of the organism. It cannot be denied that bacteria are efficient and prolific enzyme producers since highly active bacterial enzymes are being used regularly in industry. Edward Howell MD *Enzymes for Health and Longevity*

Almanzo felt a little better when he sat down to the good Sunday dinner. Mother sliced the hot rye'n'injun bread on the breadboard by her plate. Father's spoon cut deep into the chicken pie; he scooped out big pieces of thick crust and turned up their fluffy yellow under-sides on the plate. He poured gravy over them; he dipped up big pieces of tender chicken, dark meat and white meat sliding from the bones. He added a mound of baked beans and topped it with a quivering slice of fat pork. At the edge of the plate he piled dark-red beet pickles. And he handed the plate to Almanzo. Laura Ingalls Wilder *Farmer Boy*

Among the many minerals contained in the beet, one must cite first of all iron and copper, important trace minerals; but also calcium, phosphorus, potassium and sodium. Under certain types of agriculture, the amount of sugar in the red beet can be more than 5 %. These natural sugars and the minerals that the beet contains are in balanced proportions and make of the beet an especially precious food. Beets help reestablish numerous functions of the body and a diet based on beets has an incontestable curative effect. Beets are permitted to diabetics and are used in cancer therapies. Because of its dark red color, the beet has for a long time been considered a blood restorative and a food that strengthens the entire organism. The beet should appear often on our tables. Annelies Schoneck *Des Crudites Toute L'Annee*

PICKLED BEETS

Makes 1 quart

3 1/2 cups beets, peeled and coarsely chopped
seeds from 2 cardamom pods (optional)
2 teaspoons sea salt
2 tablespoons whey (if not available, use an additional 1 teaspoon salt)
1 cup filtered water

A certain amount of care must be taken with beets as their high sugar content may encourage alcoholic as well as lactic acid fermentation. Do not grate or cut the beets with a food processor—this releases too much juice and the fermentation process will proceed too quickly, so that it favors formation of alcohol rather than lactic acid; instead coarsely chop with a sharp knife or cut into a 1/4 inch julienne if you have the patience. Place beets in a quart-sized wide-mouth mason jar. Combine remaining ingredients and pour over beets. Add more water if necessary to cover beets completely. Cover tightly. Keep at room temperature for 2 days before transferring to cold storage.

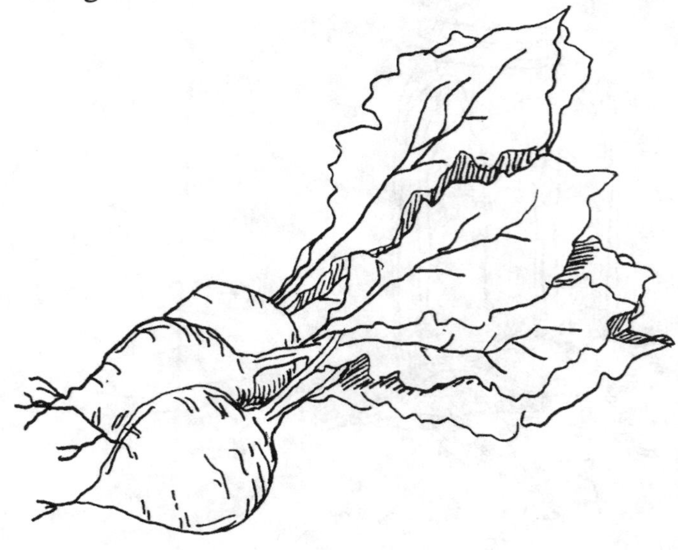

PICKLED DAIKON RADISH

Makes 1 quart

4 cups grated daikon radish, loosely packed
2 teaspoons sea salt
1 tablespoon soy sauce (optional)
2 tablespoon wheys (if not available, use an additional 1 teaspoon salt)

Place all ingredients in a bowl, mix well and pound with wooden pounder to release juices. Place radish mixture in a one-quart wide-mouth mason jar. Press down lightly with a wooden pounder. Cover tightly and keep at room temperature for 2 days before transferring to cold storage.

The daikon radish is greatly prized in the Orient as a digestive aid. Fermented daikon radish, or *takuan*, is commonly served with macrobiotic food. Tests have shown it to be especially high in lactobacilli. It is also valued as a diuretic, as a decongestant and as a source of substances that inhibit cancer. Folk wisdom claims the daikon rids the body of accumulated fats. SWF

PICKLED TURNIPS

Makes 1 quart

2 1/2 cups turnips, peeled, quartered and sliced
3/4 cup beets, peeled, quartered and sliced
1 medium onion, peeled, quartered and sliced
2 teaspoons sea salt
2 tablespoons whey (if not available use an additional 1 teaspoon salt
1 cup filtered water

Mix vegetables and place in a wide-mouth quart-sized mason jar. Press down with wooden pounder. Mix water with salt and whey and pour over vegetables. Add more liquid, if needed, to cover the turnip mixture. Cover tightly and keep at room temperature for 3 days before transferring to cold storage.

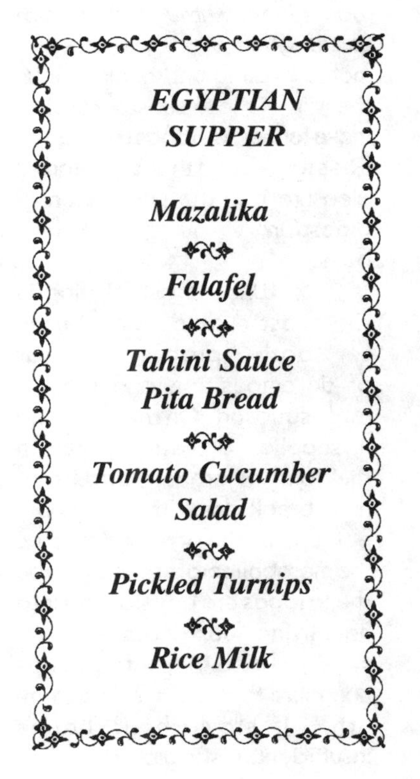

PICKLED RED PEPPERS

Makes 1 quart

about 24 thick red peppers, seeded and cut into quarters
2 teaspoons sea salt
2 tablespoons whey (if not available, use an additional 1 teaspoon salt)
1/2-1 cup filtered water

This delicious Mediterranean condiment is worth all the trouble of roasting and peeling.

Place pepper quarters skin side down in an oiled pyrex pan in a 450 degree oven until skin darkens and begins to buckle. Remove to a platter and place under a plastic bag for about 10 minutes. Using a sharp knife, carefully remove skin. Pack the peppers into a quart-sized wide-mouth mason jar. Mix whey and salt with water and pour into jar. Add more water if needed to completely cover the peppers. Keep at room temperature for 3 days before transferring to cold storage.

PICKLED GRAPE LEAVES

Makes 1 quart

2 dozen grape leaves
1 tablespoon sea salt
4 tablespoons whey (if not available, use an additional 1 tablespoon salt)
2 cups filtered water

If you have a grape vine in your garden or live near a vineyard, you may want to try these. Pickled grape leaves are used to make dolmas (page 235).

Wash leaves well. Place water, salt and whey in a large bowl. Soak the leaves in the liquid for about 1 hour. Place all the leaves together and roll up. Stuff into a quart-sized wide-mouth mason jar. Pour in enough soaking liquid to cover leaves. Keep at room temperature for 2 days before transferring to cold storage.

The digestive process has two distinct features; one is the breaking down of ingested foods; the other is the building up of nutrients needed by the body. If the breaking down is incomplete, the building up cannot proceed correctly. In reality we nourish ourselves not by what we eat but by what we are capable of breaking down and transforming into nutrients the body can use. Of great importance in this process is the role played by the aromatic substances that are formed during lacto-fermentation. The aroma of lacto-fermented foods is the by-product of certain substances present in infinitesimal amounts, but essential for the ultimate assimilation of the food to the body. Hippocrates expressed this principle with the words *Suavia nutriunt*—that which smells good nourishes and promotes healing and health. Thus the role of these substances that make fermented foods taste good goes far beyond that of gustatory pleasure and the stimulation of digestion, to our general well being.

What is astonishing is that lactic acid contributes to both processes—that of decomposition and that of reconstruction. On the one hand it supplies digestive juices in the form of organic acids that help break down the foods we eat, and on the other it activates the metabolic processes whereby these foods are transformed into new living substances.

Lacto-fermented foods normalize the acidity of the stomach. If stomach acidity is insufficient, it stimulates the acid producing glands of the stomach and in cases where acidity is too high it has the inverse effect. Lactic acid helps break down pro-

CORN RELISH

Makes 1 quart

3 cups fresh corn kernels
1 small tomato, peeled, seeded and diced
1 small onion, finely diced
1/2 red pepper, seeded and diced
2 tablespoons cilantro leaves
1/4-1/2 teaspoon red pepper flakes
2 teaspoons sea salt
2 tablespoons whey (if not available, use an additional 1 teaspoon sea salt)
1 cup filtered water

In a large bowl mix corn, tomato, onion, red pepper, cilantro and red pepper flakes. Press lightly with wooden pounder to release juices. Place in a quart-sized wide mouth mason jar. Mix water with salt and whey and pour into jar. Add more liquid, if needed, to cover the corn. Corn plus liquid should be about 1 inch below the top of the jar. Cover tightly. Leave at room temperature for 2 days before transferring to cold storage.

TOMATO PEPPER RELISH

Makes 1 quart

4 ripe tomatoes, peeled, seeded and chopped
1 bunch green onions, chopped
1 green pepper, seeded and chopped
1-2 jalapeno chiles, seeded and chopped
1 bunch cilantro, chopped
2 cloves garlic, mashed
2 tablespoons whey
2 teaspoons sea salt
1 cup filtered water

Place all vegetables in a bowl and mix thoroughly. Place in a wide-mouth quart-sized mason jar and press down lightly with wooden pounder. Mix water with salt and whey and pour into jar. Add more liquid, if needed to completely cover the tomato mixture. Cover tightly and keep at room temperature for 2 days before transferring to cold storage.

teins and thus aids in their assimilation by the body. It also aids the assimilation of iron. The decomposition in the stomach of the organic forms of iron depends on the quantity of hydrochloric acid present as well as the amount of vitamin C, which is why sauerkraut and other lacto-fermented vegetables rich in this vitamin have such a favorable influence. . . Lactic acid activates the secretions of the pancreas which is particularly important for diabetics. . . Sauerkraut contains large quantities of choline, a substance that lowers blood pressure and regulates the passage of nutrients into the blood. . . Choline has another interesting property in that it aids the body in the metabolism of fats. If choline is lacking, fats accumulate in the liver. . . Sauerkraut also contains acetylcholine which has a powerful effect on the parasympathetic nervous system. It helps reduce blood pressure, slows down the rate of heartbeat, and promotes calmness and sleep. As acetylcholine is destroyed by cooking, raw sauerkraut and its juice is preferable to cooked. Acetylcholine also has a beneficial effect on the peristaltic movements of the intestine. Sauerkraut and other lacto-fermented vegetables thus are recommended for constipation. . .There is often the tendency to look for exterior infectious agents as the cause of illness. We forget that the intestine that is functioning poorly leads to serious consequences for the whole body. This is why, since most ancient times, lactic acid was used to clean the intestine. Different types of lacto-fermented juices were used as preferred remedies against typhus and other illnesses of this type. The most recent

FERMENTED TARO ROOT

(Poi)
Makes about 3 cups

2 pounds taro root
2 teaspoons sea salt
2 tablespoons whey

Taro and related tubers are found throughout the tropical world—in Africa, the West Indies and in Polynesia. Explorers discovered that the natives ate root vegetables after they had been buried in the ground and fermented for several days to several months!

Poke a few holes in the tubers and bake in an oven at 300 degrees for about 2 hours or until soft. Peel and mash with salt and whey. Place in a bowl, cover and leave at room temperature for 24 hours. Place in an airtight container and store in the refrigerator. This may be spread on bread or crackers like cream cheese. It also makes an excellent baby food.

Variation: Fermented Sweet Potato

Use *2 pounds sweet potatoes* instead of taro root.

POTATO CHEESE

Makes about 4 cups

4 cups cooked potatoes, peeled
2 cups piima milk (page 77)
1 tablespoon salt

This recipe for fermented potatoes comes from *The American Frugal Housewife*, published in 1833. Mix ingredients well in food processor. Place in a covered bowl and leave at room temperature for about 2 days. Place in a large strainer, lined with cheesecloth or a clean linen towel. Tie the cheesecloth or towel in a bundle to a spoon, hung over a jug or bowl, so the "cheese" can drain. When draining stops, transfer to an air tight container and store in the refrigerator.

research has confirmed this beneficial action of lactic acid producing bacteria. . .

The mucus membranes of the intestinal tract are protected by bacteria which create an acid environment in which the pathogenic bacteria cannot multiply. The whole digestive tract harbors a complex bacteriological flora that varies from one part to the next. The lactic acid producing bacteria are characterized by the fact that they survive the transition from the stomach to the small intestine and they are still active when they reach the large intestine. . . Recent research has shown that lactic acid producing bacteria can prevent the growth of coliform bacteria and agents of cholera from establishing themselves in the intestine. Even certain carcinogenic substances are inhibited and inactivated. . . In effect, the state of our intestinal flora contributes not only to the absorption of nutrients and the functioning of the intestine but also to our ability to resist infections. Annelies Schoneck *Des Crudites Toute L'Annee*

The harvesting was easy, as Ekwefi had said. Ezinma shook every tree violently with a long stick before she bent down to cut the stem and dig out the tuber. . . When they had harvested a sizable heap they carried it down in two trips to the stream, where every woman had a shallow well for fermenting her cassava.

"It should be ready in four days or even three," said Obiageli. "They are young tubers." Chinua Achebe *Things Fall Apart*

SALSA

Makes 1 quart

4 medium tomatoes, peeled, seeded and diced
2 small onions, finely diced
1/4 cup diced chile pepper, hot or mild
1 bunch cilantro, chopped
1 teaspoon dried oregano
juice of 2 lemons
2 teaspoons sea salt
2 tablespoons whey (if not available, use an additional 1 teaspoon salt)
1/2-1 cup filtered water

Mix all ingredients except water and place in a quart-sized wide mouth mason jar. Press down lightly with a wooden pounder. Add enough water to cover vegetables. Cover tightly and keep at room temperature for 2 days before transferring to cold storage.

There is a discernible undercurrent of opinion among practicing medical men that a certain amount of raw, uncooked food in the diet is indispensable to the highest degree of health. Assuming that the proteins, fats, carbohydrates, minerals, and vitamins are equally available for nutrition in raw and cooked food, any demonstrable nutritional superiority of raw food must then be ascribed to the "live" quality of raw food, and when this live quality is subjected to analysis, it is shown to consist of, or be possessed of, no other property than that possessed by enzymes. Edward Howell MD *Enzymes for Health and Longevity*

KETCHUP

Makes 1 quart

3 cups canned tomato paste, preferably organic
1/4 cup whey
1 tablespoon sea salt
1/2 cup maple syrup
1/4 teaspoon cayenne pepper
3 cloves garlic, peeled and mashed
1/2 cup homemade fish sauce (page 143) or commercial fish sauce

Mix all ingredients well. Place in quart-sized wide-mouth mason jars and leave at room temperature for about 2 days. Transfer to refrigerator.

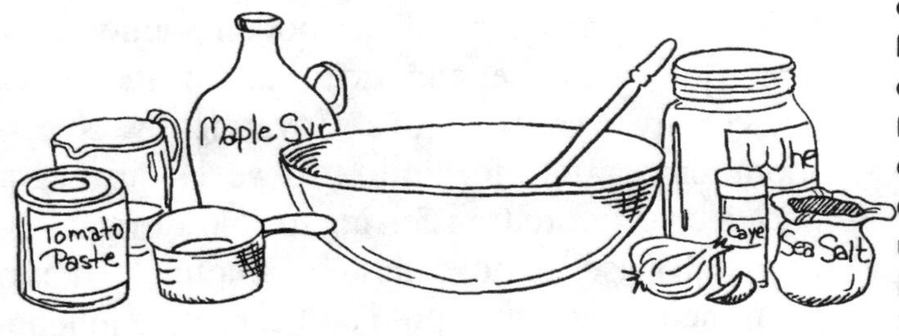

Ketchup provides us with an excellent example of a condiment that was formerly fermented and therefore health promoting, but whose benefits were lost with large scale canning methods and a reliance on sugar rather than lactic acid as a preservative. The word ketchup derives from the Chinese Amoy dialect *ke-tsiap* or pickled fish-brine or sauce, the universal condiment of the ancient world. The English added things like mushrooms, walnuts, cucumbers and oysters to this fermented brew; Americans added tomatoes from Mexico to make tomato ketchup. Writing in 1730, Dean Swift mentions ketchup as one of several fermented foods favored by the English. "And for our home-bred British cheer,/ Botargo [fish roe relish], catsup and cabiar [caviar]." A return to ancient preservation methods would transform America's favorite condiment from a health liability to a beneficial digestive aid. SWF

Hot foods have been used to treat pulmonary diseases since antiquity... Egyptian medical writings recommended mustard in respiratory therapy. Hippocrates prescribed vinegar and pepper as respiratory drugs. .. Galen, favored the use of garlic for chest pain. In the Middle Ages mustard was a potion used against asthma, coughs and chest congestion. ... In 1802 the English physician Herberden recommended garlic and mustard seed, among other agents, to treat asthma. Oriental medicine uses capsicum peppers, black pepper, mustard, garlic, turmeric and other spices to treat colds, sinusitis, bronchitis, and asthma. Russians use horseradish to cure colds. Jean Carper *The Food Pharmacy*

In the third century A.D. the Romans believed that the lemon was an antidote for all poisons, as illustrated by the tale of two criminals thrown to venomous snakes; the one who had eaten a lemon beforehand survived snakebite, the other died. So great is the reputation of the lemon that, so the story goes, it became an accompaniment for fish in the belief that if a fishbone got stuck in the throat, the lemon juice would dissolve it. Lemon juice has long been heralded as a diuretic, diaphoretic, and astringent... Lemons and limes gained fame for their ability to prevent scurvy. .. lemon juice is an antioxidant because of the vitamin C. And lemon peel exhibits remarkable antioxidant activity unrelated to vitamin C... In a screening of plants with ability to kill roundworms in humans, lemon extract was effective. Lemon oil can also kill fungi. Jean Carper *The Food Pharmacy*

MUSTARD

Makes 2 cups

6 ounces mustard seeds
1/2 to 1 cup filtered water
2 tablespoons whey
2 teaspoons sea salt
juice of 1 lemon
2 cloves garlic, mashed (optional)
1 tablespoon honey (optional)
2 tablespoons whole mustard seeds (optional)

Grind mustard seeds to a fine powder in a mini-grinder. Mix 1/2 cup water with whey and salt and blend with mustard powder. Blend in optional ingredients. Add more water to obtain desired consistency. Place in a pint-sized jar and cover tightly. Let sit at room temperature 2 days before transferring to cold storage.

PRESERVED LEMON

Makes 1 quart

5 organic lemons, preferable thin-skinned variety
3 tablespoons sea salt
3 cinnamon sticks, broken up
2 tablespoons whey (if not available,
use an additional 2 tablespoons salt)
juice of 2 lemons

This delicious fermented condiment comes from Morocco.

Wash lemons well, slice thinly and cut slices into quarters. Toss in a bowl with salt and cinnamon sticks. Place in a quart-sized wide-mouth mason jar and press down lightly with a wooden pounder. Mix lemon juice with whey and add to jar. Add more water if necessary to cover lemons. Cover tightly. Keep at room temperature for up to two weeks, turning jar once a day, before transferring to cold storage.

To use, remove desired amount of lemon from the jar. Remove pulp and cut into a julienne. This is delicious in any recipe calling for lemon zest.

MINT CHUTNEY

Makes 3 cups

2 cups fresh mint leaves
1 medium onion, peeled and coarsely chopped
4 cloves garlic, peeled and coarsely chopped
4 jalapeno chiles, seeded and chopped
2 teaspoons cumin seeds, toasted in oven
2/3 cup crispy almonds (page 487), chopped
2 teaspoons sea salt
2 tablespoons whey (if not available, use an additional 1 teaspoon salt)
1 cup filtered water

Place all ingredients except salt, whey and water in food processor and pulse a few times until finely chopped but not paste-like. Place in a quart-sized wide mouth mason jar and press down lightly with wooden pounder. Mix salt and whey with water and pour into jar. Liquid should come to the top of the chutney. Cover tightly. Keep at room temperature for 2 days before transferring to refrigerator. This should be eaten within 2 months.

CHERRY CHUTNEY

Makes 1 quart

4 cups ripe cherries, pitted and quartered
1/2 teaspoon coriander seeds
1/2 teaspoon whole cloves
grated rind of 1 orange
juice of 1 orange
1/8 cup sucanat
1/4 cup whey
2 teaspoons sea salt
1/2 cup filtered water

Mix cherries with spices and orange rind and place in a quart-sized wide-mouth mason jar. Press down lightly with a wooden pounder. Mix remaining ingredients and pour into jar. Add more liquid if necessary to cover the fruit. Cover tightly and leave at room temperature for 2 days before transferring to refrigerator. This should be eaten within 2 months.

All cultures have used herbs for medicinal purposes as well as to flavor foods. Sadly, many fresh herbs sold in supermarkets have high levels of pesticides. Best to grow herbs in your own garden. Mint is especially easy to grow and is a most refreshing herb for summer meals. Extracts of various species of mint are said to relieve digestive disorders, headaches and viral infections. SWF

JUNE DINNER

Summer Salad

Basic Baked Chicken with Cherry Chutney

Corn on the Cob

Sauted Zucchini

Merengues with Strawberries and Whipped Cream

When we buy vegetables, we are often deceived by their color and appearance whereas their aroma, taste and consistency tell us more about their quality. And quality is of paramount importance if we want to preserve these vegetables through lacto-fermentation; lactic acid producing bacteria need a great many vitamins and minerals that only vegetables rich in these elements can supply. This is why when foods are successfully lacto-fermented, we can be assured of their inherent nutritional quality. Annelies Schoneck *Des Crudites Toute L'Annee*

FRUIT CHUTNEY

Makes 1 quart

3 cups fresh peaches, pears, apples, mango or papaya
1/2 cup filtered water
grated rind of 2 lemons
juice of 2 lemons
1/8 cup sucanat
2 teaspoons sea salt
1/4 cup whey
1/2 cup crispy pecans (page 485), chopped
1/2 cup dark raisins
1 teaspoon ground cumin
1/2 teaspoon red pepper flakes
1/2 teaspoon dried green peppercorns, crushed
1/2 teaspoon dried thyme
1 teaspoon fennel seeds
1 teaspoon coriander seeds

Mix water, lemon juice, lemon rind, salt and whey. Peel fruit and cut up into lemon juice mixture. Mix with nuts, raisins, herbs and spices and place into a quart-sized wide mouth mason jar. Press down lightly with pounder. Fruit mixture should be 1 inch lower than the top of the jar. Add more water if necessary to bring liquid to the level of the fruit mixture. Cover tightly. Keep at room temperature for 2 days before transferring to refrigerator. Should be eaten within 2 months.

The pineapple is a native of South America. It is an unusual fruit in that it forms when the fruits of a hundred or more separate flowers coalesce. It has a high sugar content and a delicious flavor. Pineapple is high in fiber and contains carotenoids, B-complex vitamins and vitamin C. Pineapple also contains a unique enzyme called bromelain that decomposes protein. This enzyme works not only in the acid present in the stomach, but also in the alkaline environment of the intestine and been used to treat a number of diseases including, heart disease, rheumatoid arthritis, injuries, edema, pneumonia and scleroderma. It is claimed to shorten labor and reduce appetite.

According to Professor Francisco Villaroel of Bolivia, pineapple is a powerful remedy for chest ailments, jaundice, arteriosclerosis, anemia and cerebral problems such as neurasthenia, melancholia and loss of memory.

Pineapple is rich in manganese which is necessary for strong bones and a healthy nervous system. Recent studies have revealed that women with osteoporosis have about one-third less manganese in their blood than healthy women. The manganese in pineapple is in a particularly absorbable form.

The enzyme bromelain in pineapple is what makes other fruit become soggy when mixed with pineapple. Surprisingly, pineapple that has been lacto-fermented does not become soggy, but retains its crispness. With its protein-digesting bromelain content, lacto-fermented pineapple chutney is the perfect accompaniment for meat dishes of all types. SWF

PINEAPPLE CHUTNEY

Makes 1 quart

1 small pineapple
1 bunch cilantro, coarsely chopped
1 tablespoon freshly grated ginger
2 tablespoons fresh lime juice
1 teaspoon sea salt
1/4 cup whey
1/2 cup filtered water

Mix pineapple, cilantro and ginger and place in a quart-sized wide mouth mason jar. Press down lightly with a wooden pounder. Mix lime juice, sea salt and whey with water and pour over pineapple. Add more water if needed to bring liquid to top of pineapple. Cover tightly. Keep at room temperature for 2 days before transferring to refrigerator. Should be eaten within 1 month.

Variation:

Add *1 small red onion, 1/2 red pepper* and *1 jalapeno pepper, all finely chopped.*

Imported mangoes, corn syrup, sugar, distilled vinegar, salt, raisins, lime juice, dextrose, tamarind extract, caramel coloring, spices, natural flavors and dehydrated onions.

See Appendix B for Answer

PAPAYA CHUTNEY

Makes 1 quart

3 cups ripe papaya, peeled and cubed
1 tablespoon ginger, grated
1 red pepper, seeded and cut into a julienne
1 small onion, chopped
1 jalapeno chile, seeded and chopped (optional)
1/2 cup fresh mint leaves, cut into pieces
1 bunch cilantro, chopped
1/8 cup sucanat
1/2 cup lime juice
2 teaspoons sea salt
1/4 cup whey
1/2 cup filtered water

Mix papaya with ginger, peppers, onion, mint and cilantro and place in a quart-sized wide-mouth mason jar. Press down lightly with a wooden pounder. Mix remaining ingredients and pour into jar. Add more liquid if necessary to cover the fruit. Cover tightly and leave at room temperature for 2 days before transferring to refrigerator. This should be eaten within 2 months.

Variation: Mango Chutney

Use *3 cups firm mango, peeled and cubed,* instead of papaya.

The papaya hails from the American tropics. The papaya tree is fast-growing and short-lived; it looks like a palm tree with a tuft of large leaves at the top. Some papayas weigh as much as twenty pounds—perhaps this is why Columbus called the papaya tree the "melon tree". Most commercially available papayas in America come from Hawaii but they are also grown in Florida, Mexico and Puerto Rico. Papayas picked green will ripen at room temperature. They are rich in carotenoids and vitamin C as well as potassium and phosphorus. They contain a unique protein digestion enzyme which is used commercially as a meat tenderizer—hence the wisdom of taking papaya chutney with meats. Save the papaya seeds to make papaya pepper (page 143), which is also rich in enzymes and an excellent substitute for black pepper. SWF

RAISIN CHUTNEY

Makes 1 quart

3 cups yellow raisins, soaked in warm water for 1 hour
20 black peppercorns
1/2 teaspoon red pepper flakes
2 tablespoons coriander seeds
1 tablespoon cumin seeds
1 tablespoon anise seeds
1 tablespoon freshly grated ginger
4 cloves garlic, peeled and coarsely chopped
1 bunch fresh cilantro, stems removed
2 teaspoons salt
1/4 cup whey
1 cup filtered water

Place garlic and cilantro in food processor and pulse a few times. Drain raisins and add to food processor along with seeds and ginger. Pulse a few times until the mixture becomes a coarse paste. Transfer to a quart-sized wide-mouth mason jar and press down lightly with wooden pounder. Mix salt and whey with water and pour into jar. You may need to poke a few holes in the chutney to allow liquid to percolate through. Liquid should just cover raisin mixture. Cover tightly. Keep at room temperature for 2 days before transferring to refrigerator.

There is something fascinating about microorganisms. They are everywhere: in the air, in water, in our food, on our bodies, in our bodies, invisible and without number, capable of multiplying with extraordinary rapidity, agents of illness and even of death, but also the foundation of life and health.

Microorganisms frighten us: aren't these germs responsible for deadly scourges (tuberculosis, plague, cholera, typhoid)? Aren't they responsible for serious food contamination?

Down with the one-celled organism, we say! Long live disinfection! Germicides, fungicides, antibiotics, antiseptics, sterilization, freezing—we lack no weapons in the war against germs. Medicine, agriculture and the food industry make use of them all.

[We should] consider not how to kill microorganisms, but rather how to make them our friends and allies; how to use them in ways that encourage their proliferation in our foods. We should consider how to put to use the numerous types of microorganisms that, far from contaminating what we eat, improve its flavor and nutritive value in such a way as to turn simple foodstuffs into true natural remedies.

Grains, pulses, vegetables, fruits and milk—these are the foods that can be transformed by fungus and bacteria, using very ancient procedures, in such a way as to confer on them qualities they initially lacked, as well as to preserve them without the aid of modern industrial processes. Claude Aubert *Les Aliments Fermentes Traditionnels*

APRICOT BUTTER

Makes 2 quarts

4 cups unsulphured dried apricots
1 tablespoon sea salt
1/4 cup whey
1/8-1/4 cup raw honey

Cook apricots until soft in filtered water. Let cool slightly and transfer with a slotted spoon to food processor. Process with remaining ingredients and place in a quart-sized wide-mouth mason jar. Cover tightly and let stand at room temperature for 2 days before transferring to refrigerator. Should be eaten within 2 months.

Variation: Apple Butter
Use *dried apples* instead of apricots
Variation: Pear Butter
Use *dried pears* instead of apricots.

The apricot is cherished in the Himalayan kingdom of Hunza (the land of Shangri-La in the novel and film *Lost Horizon*) as a source of health and exceptional longevity. The people eat prodigious amounts of a type of wild apricot called *khubani*. Scientists have seriously proposed there is truth to the apricot's mystical reputation. Indeed, Nobel-prize winner G. S. Whipple in 1934 hailed the apricot as "equal to liver in hemoglobin regeneration.". . . apricots are high on the list of fruits and vegetables likely to help prevent certain cancers. . . because apricots, like other bright-orange fruits or vegetables, contain highly concentrated amounts of beta carotene, a form of vitamin A that is spectacularly successful in lab tests in thwarting certain cancers, including lung and skin. Jean Carper *The Food Pharmacy*

ORANGE MARMALADE

Makes 1 quart

3-4 organic oranges, preferably Seville oranges
1/4 cup sucanat
2 teaspoons salt
1/4 cup whey
1/2 cup filtered water

This makes a thin, rather than a gooey, marmalade, but the taste is delicious. Slice oranges very thinly and cut slices into quarters. Place in a quart-sized wide mouth mason jar and press down lightly with a wooden pounder. Combine remaining ingredients and pour over oranges. Add more water if necessary to cover oranges completely. Cover tightly. Leave at room temperature for 3 days before transferring to cold storage. If marmalade develops spots of white mold on the top, simply remove them with a spoon.

Variation: Kumquat Marmalade
Use *about 2 dozen kumquats* instead of oranges.

Oranges are famous for their high vitamin C content. They also contain potassium and some calcium. The interior white membrane is a good source of bioflavanoids, so essential to the health of the blood capillaries. Seville oranges are prized for the flavor of their skin, which folklore claims has medicinal properties.

Before the days of refrigerated ships, oranges from Spain came to Northern Europe in the form of marmalade. Originally marmalade was a lacto-fermented food! The oranges were mixed with salt water and pressed into large casks. The long sea voyage gave them plenty of time to ferment and develop rich flavors. Sugar was too expensive to be added in large quantities, so marmalade was traditionally quite tart. SWF

BERRY PRESERVES

Makes 1 quart

4-5 cups fresh berries such as blueberries, blackberries or raspberries or a mixture
2 teaspoons sea salt
1/4 cup sucanat
1/4 cup whey
1 cup filtered water

These are excellent on pancakes and waffles. You can use any summer berry except strawberries, which are too acid for lacto-fermentation purposes. This makes a syrup, rather than a thick jam and is delicious on pancakes.

Wash berries, place in a quart-sized wide-mouth mason jar and mash down lightly with a wooden pounder. Combine remaining ingredients and pour over berries. Add more water if necessary to completely cover berries. Cover tightly. Leave at room temperature for 2 days before transferring to the refrigerator. Should be eaten within one month.

Strawberries, blackberries, raspberries, and to a lesser extent blueberries, cranberries, grapes, apples, Brazil nuts, walnuts and cashews all contain the anticancer compound ellagic acid, says Dr. Gary D. Stoner, a pathologist at the Medical College of Ohio.

Ellagic acid is an antioxidant that helps detoxify cancer-causing agents in several different ways. It may block the activation of carcinogens, inhibit the carcinogen itself, or keep the DNA in cells from undergoing mutation.

For example, in one test, ellagic acid blocked damage in human and mouse lung cells dosed with cancer-causing agents. The strawberry acid stopped from 45 to 70 percent of the genetic damage to the cells.

Strawberries are particularly rich in ellagic acid. It's high in both the pulp and the seeds. So if you strain the berries, tossing out the seeds, you also throw away some of the berry's anticancer capabilities. Jean Carper *The Food Pharmacy Guide to Good Eating*

SPROUTED GRAINS, NUTS & SEEDS

Credit for discovering the value of sprouted seeds traditionally goes to the Chinese who learned to germinate legumes many centuries ago. They carried mung beans on their ocean going ships, sprouted them throughout their voyages and consumed them in sufficient quantities to prevent scurvy. The Chinese instinctively knew that there was a certain something missing in non-germinated seeds and grains that was produced during the sprouting process—that substance is vitamin C.

But it is a mistake to think that the values of sprouted grain were unknown in the West. For centuries, beers of all sorts have been made with germinated grains. Certain old French cookbooks recommend sprouting dried peas before using them in soups. Bulgur, used extensively in Middle Eastern cooking, is made by coarsely grinding sprouted wheat. According to enzyme specialist Dr. Edward Howell, in the past we ate most of our grains in partially germinated form. Grain standing in sheaves and stacks in open fields often began to sprout before it was brought into storage. Modern farming techniques prevent grains from germinating before they reach our tables.

The process of germination not only produces vitamin C, but also changes the composition of grain and seeds in numerous beneficial ways. Sprouting increases vitamin B content, especially B2, B5 and B6. Carotene increases dramatically—sometimes eightfold. Even more important, sprouting neutralizes phytic acid, a substance present in the bran of all grains, which inhibits absorption of calcium, magnesium, iron and zinc; sprouting also neutralizes enzyme inhibitors present in all seeds. These inhibitors can neutralize our own precious enzymes in the digestive tract. Complex sugars responsible for intestinal gas are broken down during sprouting and a portion of the starch in grain is transformed into sugar. Sprouting inactivates aflatoxins, potent carcinogens found in grains. Finally, numerous enzymes that help digestion are produced during the germinating process.

Sprouted grains should be a regular feature of the diet, and they can be used in numerous ways—in salads, sandwiches, vegetable dishes, as breakfast cereals and as additions to breads and baked goods. However, we must warn against overdoing on *raw* sprouted grains as raw sprouts also contain irritating substances that keep animals from eating the tender shoots. These substances are neutralized in cooking. Sprouted grains should usually be eaten lightly steamed or added to soups and casseroles.

No special equipment is required to transform grains and seeds into sprouts—just wide-mouth quart-sized mason jars with a round of window screen material cut to fit into the lid of the jar, replacing the solid insert.

The method for sprouting all grains and seeds is the same—only the length of time needed to accomplish full germination varies with the size and nature of the seed. Simply fill a mason jar one-third full with any grain or seed. Add water to the top of the jar and screw on the top with its screen insert. Allow the grains to soak overnight and pour off the water. Rinse the grains well—you can do this without removing the top. Invert the jar and let it sit at an angle so it can drain, and to allow air to circulate. The grains should be rinsed every few hours, or at least twice a day. In one to four days the sprouts will be ready. Rinse well, shake out excess moisture, and replace the screen insert with the solid section of the lid. Store the sprouts in the refrigerator.

Almost any grain or seed can be sprouted—wheat, barley, dried beans, flax seeds, radish seeds, onion seeds, chia seeds, chick peas, and almonds. Fragile seeds such as pumpkin and sunflower also sprout nicely. If you buy these already hulled, try to find them in nitrogen packs, as this method of packing inhibits the detrimental effects of fat oxidation. Nuts that have been removed from their shells cannot be sprouted, but an overnight soaking in warm, salted water will neutralize sprout inhibitors and phytates. (See Snacks, page 484.)

There is only one seed we do *not* recommend in sprouted form (or in any form) and that is—surprisingly—alfalfa! After mung beans, alfalfa is the variety of sprout that has caught on in the health food world. Unfortunately, it seems that all the praise heaped on the alfalfa sprout was ill advised. Tests have shown that alfalfa sprouts inhibit the immune system and can contribute to inflammatory arthritis and lupus. Alfalfa seeds contain an amino acid called canavanine which can be toxic to man and animals when taken in quantity. (Canavanine is not found in mature alfalfa plants; it is apparently metabolized during growth.) Primitive societies have always avoided eating the alfalfa seed, even when it was readily available. They used the mature alfalfa plants for fodder, but recognized that the seed and tender young plant were not suitable for human consumption. (That old traditional wisdom again—we ignore it at our peril!)

GRAINS (WHEAT, RYE, BARLEY)

Rinse 2 to 3 times per day. Sprouts are tiny and white. They will be ready in 3 to 4 days, reaching a maximum length of 1/4 inch. Use to make bulgur (page 436) or add to salads and breads.

BUCKWHEAT

Begin with whole buckwheat seeds that have *not* been toasted. Rinse 2 to 3 times per day. Tiny sprouts are ready in 2 days. Use to make kasha (page 438).

BEANS (KIDNEY, LIMA, BLACK)

Rinse 3 to 4 times per day. Ready in about 3 days, when sprout is 1/4 inch long. Beans should then be cooked. Sprouted beans will cook in much less time than beans that have been merely soaked.

BEANS (MUNG, SOY AND ADZUKI)

Fill jar only 1/4 full. Rinse 4 or more times per day. Sprouts will be ready in about 4 days. Mung bean and soy bean sprouts are ready when 2 inches long; the adzuki bean sprout is ready at 1 inch.

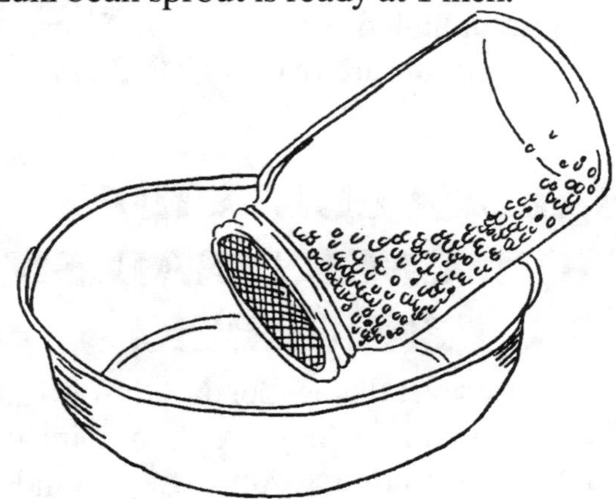

Germination increases the enzyme activity as much as six times. This is due to proteolytic release of the enzymes by inactivation of the enzyme inhibitors found in all seeds. Soaking the seeds allows proteases within to neutralize the inhibitor and release the enzymes from bondage. During the years 1930 to 1940 chemists spoke of free and bound enzymes in seeds. It was found that such enzymes as protease and papaine soaked in water with the seeds, released the "sleeping" enzymes from bondage. In 1944 when enzyme inhibitors were discovered in seeds the mystery was cleared up. Edward Howell MD *Enzymes for Health and Longevity*

Any seed can be made to germinate by increasing its moisture and holding it at the proper temperature. Resting seeds contain starch, which is a storage product and a source of future energy when conditions become ideal for the seed to germinate and grow into a plant. In nature, seeds sometimes must rest or hibernate for months or years before conditions become satisfactory for them to grow. Enzymes are present in the resting seed but are prevented from being active by the presence of enzyme inhibitors. Germination neutralizes the inhibitors and releases the enzymes. Enzyme inhibitors are part of the seed machinery and serve a purpose. But these inhibitors are out of place in our bodies. They could stop our own enzymes from working. Edward Howell MD *Enzymes for Health and Longevity*

Before the advent of factory farms, grain was partially germinated, but modern grain consists of dormant (resting) seeds. . . In former times grain was harvested and sheaved. The sheaves were put into shocks and were gathered and built into stacks which stood in the field for several more weeks before threshing. During this period of weathering in the field the grain seeds were exposed to rain and dew which soaked into the sheaves. The grain could pick up this moisture and, with heat from the sun, conditions were ideal for favoring a degree of germination and enzyme multiplication in the grain. The modern combine harvester removes the grain from the stalk immediately after cutting and permits it to be hauled away to the granary. Hence, there is no weathering and consequent enzyme development, resulting in a mature but dormant seed. Edward Howell MD *Enzymes for Health and Longevity*

Sprouting accomplishes a veritable pre-digestion of grains. Phytic acid, which blocks the absorption of calcium and magnesium, is largely decomposed. So are certain sugars which cause intestinal gas. Part of the starch is transformed into sugars and numerous enzymes that aid digestion are produced. Claude Aubert *Dis-Moi Comment Tu Cuisines*

ALMONDS

Sprouted almonds are much more digestible than untreated ones. Rinse 3 times per day. Ready in 3 days. Sprout is merely a tiny white appendage, about 1/8 inch long.

LENTILS

Rinse 3 times a day. Sprout 3 to 4 days until sprout is 1/4 inch long. Steam or cook lightly.

SUNFLOWER SEEDS

These are among the most satisfactory seeds for sprouting. Sunflower sprouts are just delicious in salads, but they must be eaten very soon after sprouting is accomplished, as they soon go black. Try to find hulled sunflower seeds packed in nitrogen packs. Rinse 2 times per day. Ready in 12 to 18 hours, when sprout is just barely showing. Use in High Enzyme Salad (page 177).

PUMPKIN OR MELON SEEDS

Rinse 3 times per day and sprout for about 3 days until sprout is 1/4 inch long. Seeds merely soaked for 12 hours, and then lightly toasted are a traditional Mexican food called pepitas (page 485).

SESAME SEEDS

Use unhulled sesame seeds. Rinse 4 times daily. Tiny sprouts are ready in 2 to 3 days.

SMALL SEEDS (CHIA, ONION, CRESS, RADISH, FLAX, FENUGREEK)

Rinse several times per day. Sprouts are ready in 3 to 4 days when they are 1 to 2 inches long. Sprouted small seeds are wonderful on sandwiches.

STOCKS

A lamentable outcome of our modern meat processing techniques, and our hurry-up, throw-away life-style, has been a decline in the use of meat, chicken and fish stocks in food preparation. In days gone by, when the butcher sold meat on the bone rather than as individual filets, and whole chickens rather than boneless breasts, our thrifty ancestors made use of every part of the animal by preparing stock or bouillon from the bony portions. Meat and fish stocks are found almost universally in traditional cuisines—French, Italian, Chinese, Japanese, African, South American, Middle Eastern and Russian; but the use of homemade meat broths to produce nourishing and flavorful soups and sauces has almost completely disappeared from the American culinary tradition.

Properly prepared, meat stocks are extremely nutritious, containing the minerals of bone, cartilage, marrow and vegetables as electrolytes, and hence in easily-assimilated form. In particular, wine or vinegar added during cooking supplies the acid needed to draw minerals, particularly calcium, magnesium and potassium, into the broth.

Stock is also of great value because it supplies hydrophilic colloids to the diet. Organic molecules are colloids. In raw form, these molecules attract liquids—they are hydrophilic. Thus when we eat a salad or some other raw food, the hydrophilic colloids attract digestive juices for rapid and effective digestion. Colloids that have been heated are hydrophobic—they repel liquids, making cooked foods harder to digest. However, the proteinaceous gelatin in meat broths has the unusual property of attracting liquids—it is hydrophilic—even after it has been heated. The same property by which gelatin attracts water to form desserts like Jello, allows it to attract digestive juices to the surface of cooked food particles.

The public is generally unaware of the large body of research that has been done on the beneficial effects of gelatin taken with food. Gelatin acts first and foremost as an aid to digestion and has been used successfully in the treatment of many intestinal disorders including hyperacidity, colitis and Crohn's disease. Although gelatin is by no means a complete protein, containing only amino acids arginine and glycine in large amounts, it acts as a protein sparer, allowing the body to more fully utilize the complete proteins that are taken in. Thus, gelatin-rich broths are a must for those who can afford only meager diets. Gelatin also seems to be of use in the treatment of many chronic disorders including anemia and other diseases of the blood, diabetes, muscular dystrophy and even cancer. Other important ingredients that go into broth are amino acids; cartilage, which recently has been used with remarkable results in the treatment of cancer; and collagen, used to treat rheumatoid arthritis and other ailments.

In folk wisdom, rich chicken broth—the famous Jewish penicillin —is a valued remedy for colds and flu. The 12th-century physician Moses Maimonides prescribed chicken broth as a treatment for colds and asthma. Science has in fact confirmed that broth helps prevent and mitigate infectious diseases. The wise food provider, who uses gelatin-rich broth on a daily or at least a frequent basis, provides continuous protection from these unfortunate conditions.

Fish stock, made from the carcasses and heads of fish, is especially rich in minerals including all-important iodine. Even more important, stock made from the heads, and therefore the thyroid glands of the fish, supplies thyroid hormone and other substances that nourish the thyroid gland. Four thousand years ago, Chinese doctors rejuvenated aging patients with a soup made from the thyroid glands of animals. According to ancient texts, this treatment helped patients feel younger, gave them more energy and often restored mental abilities. During the reign of Queen Victoria, prominent London physicians prescribed special raw thyroid sandwiches to failing patients. Very few of us could eat such fare with relish, but soups and sauces made from fish broth are absolutely delicious—a remedy that no convalescent could refuse. According to researcher Dr. Broda Barnes, at least 40% of all Americans suffer from a deficiency of the thyroid gland with its accompanying symptoms of fatigue, weight gain, frequent colds and flu, inability to concentrate, depression and a host of more serious complications like heart disease and cancer. We would do well do imitate our brothers from the East by including fish broth in the diet as often as possible.

The wonderful thing about fish and meat stocks is that, along with conferring many health benefits, they also add immeasurably to the flavor of our food. In European cuisines, rich stocks form the basis of those exquisite, clear, thick, smooth, satisfying and beautifully flavored sauces that seem to be produced by magic The magic is in the stock, made from scratch with as much care and attention to detail as the final dish. Those who have had the privilege of visiting the kitchens of fine restaurants in France, have observed pots of pale broth simmering on the back burners of huge cookstoves. When this insipid-looking liquid is enriched with herbs or wine, and reduced by boiling down, the effects of the gelatin and flavors of meat and bone become concentrated. The result is a wonderful sauce, both nutritious and delicious. It is worth taking time and putting effort into making meat stocks on a regular basis. Your family will gain innumerable health benefits; and you will earn a reputation as an excellent cook.

The test of whether your stock contains liberal amounts of gelatin is carried out by chilling the broth. If the broth turns firm when refrigerated, then the stock has been properly prepared. If the stock is still runny when cold, it means you have not cooked it long enough or added enough vinegar. You may add a little powdered gelatin (see Sources) if your broth is too runny.

Stock can be made in bulk and stored until needed. Clear stock will keep about five days in the refrigerator, longer if reboiled; and will keep several months in the freezer. You may find it useful to store stock in pint-sized or quart-sized containers in order to have sufficient amounts on hand for sauces and stews. If space is at a premium in your freezer, you can reduce the stock by boiling down for several hours until it becomes very concentrated and syrupy. (This reduced, concentrated stock is called*fumee*.) Store in small containers or zip lock bags. Frozen *fumee* in zip lock bags is easily thawed by putting the bags under hot running water. Add water to thawed *fumee* to turn it back into stock Be sure to mark the kind of stock you are storing with little stick-on labels—they all look alike when frozen.

FISH STOCK

An oil researcher spent 100 days eating what he considered to be the "Eskimo diet," seal blubber and mackerel paste. He observed that his blood lipid peroxides . . . reached a level 50 times higher than normal. . . [and] his sperm count had gone to zero. Evidently, he didn't have a very thorough understanding of the Eskimo way of life. In most traditional cultures, the whole animal is used for food, including the brain and the endocrine glands. Since unsaturated fats inhibit thyroid function, and since Eskimos usually have a high caloric intake but are not typically obese, it seems that their metabolic rate is being promoted by something in their diet, which might also be responsible for protecting them from the effects experienced by the oil researcher. People who eat fish heads (or other animal heads) generally consume the thyroid gland, as well as the brain. The brain is the body's richest source of cholesterol, which, with adequate thyroid hormone and vitamin A, is converted into the steroid hormones pregnenolone, progesterone and DHEA, in proportion to the quantity circulating in blood in low density lipoproteins. . . DHEA is known to be low in people who are susceptible to heart disease or cancer and all three of these steroids have a broad spectrum of protective actions. Thyroid hormone, vitamin A and cholesterol, which are used to produce the protective steroids, have been found to have a similarly broad range of protective effects, even when used singly. Ray Peat, PhD *Health Freedom News*

3 or 4 whole carcasses, including heads, of non-oily fish such as sole, turbot, rockfish or snapper
2 tablespoons butter
2 onions, coarsely chopped
1 carrot, coarsely chopped
several sprigs fresh thyme
several sprigs parsley
1 bay leaf
1/2 cup dry white wine or vermouth
1 tablespoon vinegar

Ideally fish stock is made from the bones of sole or turbot. In Europe, you can buy these fish on the bone. The fish monger skins and filets the fish for you, giving you the filets for your evening meal and the bones for making the stock and final sauce. Unfortunately, in America sole arrives at the fish market as filets, already boned. But snapper, rock fish and other non-oily fish work equally well and a good fish merchant will save the carcasses for you if you ask him. As he normally throws these carcasses away, he shouldn't charge you for them. Be sure to take the heads as well as the body of the carcass—these are especially rich in iodine and fat soluble vitamins. Do not use the carcasses of oily fish such as salmon, sword fish or tuna.

Melt butter in a large stainless steel pot. Add the vegetables and cook very gently, about 1/2 hour, until they are soft. Add wine and bring to a boil. Add the fish carcasses and cover with cold, filtered water. Add vinegar. Bring to a boil. Take the time to carefully skim off the scum and impurities as they rise to the top. Tie herbs together and add to the pot. Reduce heat, cover and simmer for at least 4 hours or overnight. Remove carcasses with tongs or a slotted spoon and strain the liquid into pint-sized storage containers for refrigerator or freezer.

This stock forms the basis for all the fish sauces in this book. The carrot will add a delicate sweetness to the stock when it has been reduced. Do not be tempted to add more carrots to the stock or your final sauce will be too sweet!

ORIENTAL FISH STOCK

2 medium fish carcasses, including heads, of non-oily fish such as turbot, rockfish or snapper
Shells (and heads if available) from 3/4 pound fresh shrimp (reserve shrimp for other uses)
2-3 quarts filtered water
1/4 cup vinegar
3 stalks celery, chopped
4 cloves garlic, peeled and chopped
1-inch fresh ginger, peeled and chopped
1 teaspoon black pepper corns

Place carcasses, shrimp shells, water and vinegar in a large stainless steel pot. Bring to a boil and skim. Add remaining ingredients. Simmer, covered, for at least 4 hours or overnight. Strain into a bowl and refrigerate, or into smaller containers and freeze.

When he was a boy in Japan, Itoh learned from his mother to use all parts of a fish, including the eyes, roe and bones. After World War II it was necessary to conserve food, so they made broth from bones that were then retrieved, dried, eaten salted as a crispy snack. . . One type of appetizer, Nimono, means "cooked in broth." This is one of the most difficult skills to acquire and each chef takes much pride in developing an individual style with broths. *Palisades Citizens News*

The value of gelatin in the treatment of diseases of the digestive system has long been recognized. Uffelmam, in 1891 referred to the use of gelatin in certain cases of gastric catarrh, especially in hyperacidity. Weil, Lumiere and Pehu found, by direct clinical practice, that gelatin acted better and more rapidly than bismuth and tannin and their derivatives in remedying infant diarrhea which had not developed as far as infant cholera. . . These workers believed that gelatin acted to cause a mechanical neutralization of the intestinal poisons. . . Mann. . . was impressed with the value of gelatin in the cure of colitis. . . Herzberg pointed out that he had employed gelatin, in the simple form of a concentrated calves' foot broth, with excellent results in diarretic condition of children and adults, in cases of abdominal typhus and in dysentery. N.R Gotthoffer *Gelatin in Nutrition and Medicine*

Fish broth will cure anything.
South American Proverb

BEEF STOCK

about 6 pounds beef marrow and knuckle bones
1 calves foot, cut into pieces (optional)
5 pounds meaty rib or neck bones
4 or more quarts cold filtered water
1/4 cup vinegar
3 onions, coarsely chopped
3 carrots, coarsely chopped
3 celery stalks, coarsely chopped
several sprigs of fresh thyme, tied together
1 teaspoon dried green peppercorns, crushed
l bunch parsley

Good beef stock must be made with several sorts of beef bones: knuckle bones and feet impart large quantities of gelatin to the broth; marrow bones impart flavor and the particular nutrients of the bone marrow; and meaty rib or neck bones add color and flavor.

Place the knuckle and marrow bones and optional calves foot in a very large pot and cover with water. Let stand for one hour. Meanwhile, place the meaty bones in a roasting pan and brown at 350 degrees in the oven. When well browned, add to the pot along with vinegar and vegetables. Pour fat out of roasting pan, add cold water, set over a high flame and bring to a boil, stirring with a wooden spoon to deglaze. Add this liquid to the pot. Add additional water, if necessary, to cover the bones, but the liquid should come no higher than within one inch of the rim of the pot, as the volume expands slightly during cooking. Bring to a boil. A large amount of scum will come to the top and it is important to remove this with a spoon. After you have skimmed, reduce heat and add the thyme and crushed peppercorns.

Simmer stock for at least 12 and as long as 72 hours. Just before finishing, add the parsley. Let it wilt and remove stock from heat.

The beginnings of gelatin therapy are buried in antiquity; reference to its use as a hemostatic agent in China in the first century is found in the writings of San Han Ron (204 AD). . . Ono stating that gelatin has been used as a hemostatic agent in China and Japan from prehistoric times. Homberger also referred to its use in China an Japan during the first century for stopping nose bleeding by inhaling the powdered form, and for "bleeding of the stomach, the urogential organs, the uterus. . . the intestines and the rectum." Dutton likewise noted frequent reference to the early use of gelatin, both internally and externally, in the Chinese pharmacology. . .In 1759 a report was made by an anonymous writer in Nurmberg on the use of gelatin in dysentery, at the same time indicating that gelatin had been employed for a long time as a source of nourishment for weak patients. Bishoff in 1805 referred to its use in wasting away diseases and in dysentery and deplored the forgotten use of "this ancient remedy". N.R Gotthoffer *Gelatin in Nutrition and Medicine*

You will now have a pot of rather repulsive looking brown liquid containing globs of gelatinous and fatty material. It doesn't even smell particularly good. But don't despair. After straining you will have a delicious and nourishing clear broth that forms the basis for many other recipes in this book.

Remove bones with tongs or a slotted spoon. Strain the stock into a large bowl. Let cool in the refrigerator and remove the congealed fat that rises to the top. Reheat and transfer to storage containers. Note: Your dog will love the leftover meat and bones.

Variation: Lamb Stock

Use *lamb bones*, especially lamb neck bones. This makes a delicious stock.

Variation: Venison Stock

Use *venison meat and bones*. Be sure to use the feet of the deer, and a section of antler if possible.

If man did not cook his food, there would be no need for the addition of any hydrophilic colloid [gelatin] to his dietary. Uncooked foods contain sufficient hydrophilic colloids to keep gastric mucosa in excellent condition. As we live largely on cooked food, problems arise. An old description of the stomach contents portrays them in layers, each layer assuming its position by virtue of its specific gravity: meat first, then vegetables and fruits . . .and finally the water layer with its scum of fat. According to this view, these layers churn around in sufficient gastric juices to digest the meal in one and one-half hours to four hours if all goes well. If these gastric contents are then removed and examined, the aqueous layer is strongly acid, though the degree of acidity differs with the individual. If we add a hydrophilic colloid of excellent hydration capacity to the diet portrayed above, a definite change takes place in the stomach contents. If they are withdrawn for analysis, a gluey mass is recovered. It is not sour as are the stomach contents without the gelatin; it does not show any acidity until the colloid is broken down. Under these conditions, digestion is generally distributed throughout the mass rather than layered. F. M. Pottenger, Jr. MD *Hydrophilic Colloid Diet*

Good broth resurrects the dead.
South American Proverb

CHICKEN STOCK

Know Your Ingredients

Name This Product #2

Salt, hydrolyzed vegetable protein, corn syrup solids, sugar, beef fat, monosodium glutamate (flavor enhancer), dextrose (corn sugar), onion powder, water, garlic powder, caramel color, natural flavorings, disodium guanylate & disodium inosinate (flavor enhancers), partially hydrogenated vegetable oil (soybean oil and/or palm oil and/or cottonseed oil), artificial color.

See Appendix B for Answer

Why is chicken soup superior to all the things we have, even more relaxing than "Tylenol?" It is because chicken soup has a natural ingredient which feeds, repairs and calms the mucous lining in the small intestine. This inner lining is the beginning or ending of the nervous system. It is easily pulled away from the intestine through too many laxatives, too many food additives . . . and parasites. Chicken soup. . . heals the nerves, improves digestion, reduces allergies, relaxes and gives strength. Hanna Kroeger *Ageless Remedies from Mother's Kitchen*

1 whole chicken or 2 to 3 pounds of bony chicken parts such as necks, backs, breastbones and wings
gizzards from one chicken (optional)
feet from the chicken (optional)
4 quarts cold filtered water
1 tablespoon vinegar
1 large onion, coarsely chopped
2 carrots, peeled and coarsely chopped
3 celery stalks, coarsely chopped
1 bunch parsley

If you are using a whole chicken, remove the fat glands, and the gizzards from the cavity. By all means, use chicken feet if you can find them—they are full of gelatin. (Jewish folklore considers the addition of chicken feet the secret to successful broth.) Place chicken or chicken pieces in a large stainless steel pot with the water, vinegar and all vegetables except parsley. Bring to a boil and remove scum that rises to the top. Cover and cook for 12 to 24 hours. The longer you cook the stock, the richer and more flavorful it will be. About five minutes before finishing the stock, add parsley. This will impart additional mineral ions to the broth.

Remove from heat and take out the chicken or pieces with a slotted spoon. If you are using a whole chicken, let cool and remove chicken meat from the carcass. Reserve for other uses such as chicken salads, enchiladas, sandwiches or curries. (The skin and smaller bones, which will be very soft, may be given to your dog or cat.) Strain the stock into a large bowl and reserve in your refrigerator until the fat rises to the top and congeals. Skim off this fat and reserve the stock in covered containers in your refrigerator or freezer.

Variations: Turkey Stock and Duck Stock

Prepare as chicken stock using *turkey wings and drumsticks* or *duck carcasses from which the breasts, legs and thighs have been removed*. These stocks will have a stronger flavor than chicken stock and will profit from the addition of *several sprigs of fresh thyme tied together* during cooking. Be sure to refrigerate and defat these stocks before using. The reserved duck fat is highly prized for cooking purposes.

It was a rare winter when there was not an outbreak of diphtheria in Hayfield or Back Creek or Timber Ridge. . . Doctor Brush rode with his saddle-bags all day long from house to house, never bothering to wash his hands when he came or went. His treatment was to scour throats with a mixture of sulphur and molasses, and to forbid his patients both food and water. [Both of Mrs. Blake's girls, Betty and Mary, got diphtheria that winter.] While Fairhead was walking up and down the yard, he kept an eye on the windows of Mrs. Blake's upstairs bedroom. As soon as the candle-light shone there, it would be time for him to go help with the girls. He circled the house, picked up some sticks from the wood-pile, and was about go into the kitchen when he saw through the window something which startled him. A white figure emerged from the stairway and drifted across the indoor duskiness of the room, It was Mary, barefoot, in her night-gown, as if she were walking in her sleep. She reached the table, sank down on a wooden chair, and lifted the bowl of chicken broth in her two hands. . . She drank slowly, resting her elbows on the table. . . Fairhead knew he ought to go in and take the soup from her. But he was unable to move or to make a sound. . .

Mary slept all night. When Mrs. Blake came in at four in the morning and held her candle before the girl's face, she knew that she was better. . .

But Betty died, just slipped away without a struggle, like she was dropping asleep.
Willa Cather *Sapphira and the Slave Girl*

CLARIFIED STOCK

2 quarts defatted stock
2 egg whites, lightly beaten

For most recipes, clarification is unnecessary. If you want a perfectly clear stock, however, add egg whites and bring to a boil, whisking with a wire whisk. When the stock begins to boil, stop whisking. Let boil for 3 to 5 minutes. A white foam, gradually becoming a spongy crust, will form on the surface. Off heat, lift off the crust and strain the stock through a strainer lined with several layers of cheese cloth.

QUICK STOCK

1 can Health Valley chicken or beef stock or frozen, store-bought beef, chicken or fish stock
1 tablespoon gelatin (See Sources)

This lacks the flavor and nutritive properties of homemade stock, but will do in emergencies. Mix liquid stock with gelatin, bring to a boil and proceed with your recipe.

SALAD DRESSINGS

In recent decades, misinformation and confusion about fats has led many dieticians and nutritionists to advise against salad dressings. Our salads should be dressed with plain lemon juice, they say, in order to avoid an excess of fats in the diet. The problem is that a salad with nothing more than a squeeze of lemon juice is virtually inedible. As a result of this well-meaning advice, many health conscious individuals have cut back on salads, or have eliminated them altogether.

It is certainly true that we should avoid all *bottled and commercial* salad dressings, even the so-called health food ones, as well as any concoction for salads labeled "low-fat". These dressings are invariably made with cheap, low-quality oils that have been stripped of their nutrients and rendered dangerously rancid by high temperature or solvent extraction processes. Bottled dressings are further adulterated with many ingredients that should not pass between human lips, including stabilizers, preservatives, artificial flavors and colors, not to mention refined sweeteners. These expensive blends of empty calories are bad for everybody, young and old, and should not be allowed in our cupboards.

But homemade salad dressings, made with extra virgin olive oil plus raw vinegar or lemon juice, are the best coat that any self-respecting salad can put on. Olive oil supplies vitamin E and a cornucopia of anti-oxidants, while both olive oil and raw vinegar provide a wide spectrum of enzymes, right at the start of your meal where they belong. Fresh herbs and garlic, anchovies, cultured cream, raw cheese, raw egg yolk and homemade mayonnaise added to dressings all have a contribution to make, both to enzyme and vitamin content and to exciting flavors that whet the appetite and encourage us to eat our salads down to the last bite.

Good dressings take very little time to make. Our basic salad dressing can be put together in less than half a minute and requires no more equipment that a fork and a small bowl. With a little practice you will learn to make it without measuring. Most of our other dressings are variations on the basic recipe. Salad dressings are one of the easiest things in the whole culinary repertoire to master and they pay substantial dividends in health benefits for very little effort expended.

For all of our dressings we recommend extra virgin olive oil as a base, along with a small amount of unrefined flax seed oil. Olive oil provides oleic acid, a very stable mono-unsaturated fatty acid. Studies have repeatedly shown that olive oil provides numerous health benefits, including protection from heart disease and cancer. If the oil has been correctly processed, it will still contain its original content of lipase, the enzyme needed to digest fats. Use Italian olive oil for the best taste. Extra virgin olive oil with a green hue will be richest in nutrients and anti-oxidants.

Along with olive oil, we recommend adding a tablespoon or so of unrefined flax seed oil, the best vegetable source of omega-3 fatty acids (linolenic acid). Flax oil is extremely susceptible to rancidity so be sure to buy unrefined flax seed oil in dark bottles that have been kept in cold storage. We recommend Omega brand for best quality.

We strongly advise you to avoid the many polyunsaturated oils touted as health foods, such as soy, sunflower, corn and safflower, even cold pressed versions of these products. These oils have a very high omega-6 component. Surfeit of omega-6 interferes with enzymes needed to produce prostaglandins and thus may contribute to impaired immune function and to a host of other diseases. Canola oil is high in omega-3 but it goes rancid easily and research indicates that it may present other health hazards. Canola oil has yet to stand the test of time and is best avoided.

Two of our dressings offer a particularly synergistic combination of omega-3 fatty acids and sulphur-containing proteins—our blue cheese dressing and the tahini dressing. Roquefort cheese made from sheeps milk has a high content of protective lauric acid.

Americans and Europeans differ on the question of proportions of oil to vinegar in salad dressings. Americans tend to make their dressings in a proportion of three parts oil to one part vinegar; the French use five parts olive oil to one part vinegar, a combination that most Americans find too oily. We have taken the middle ground and give proportions of four parts oil to one part vinegar. You can adjust these proportions to suit your taste.

Those who suffer from candida overgrowth should avoid vinegar until their condition has ameliorated. Cultured whey (page 80), beet kvass (page 568) or fresh lemon juice can be substituted for vinegar in many of these recipes.

We have not listed salt and pepper in our dressing recipes. Sea salt and freshly ground pepper or papaya pepper can be added according to your taste. Remember that mustard preparations tend to be rather salty. Most dressings prepared with mustard will not need additional salt. Culinary enthusiasts may wish to make their own mustard (page 96).

BASIC SALAD DRESSING

Makes about 3/4 cup

1 teaspoon Dijon type mustard
2 tablespoons plus 1 teaspoon raw wine vinegar
1/2 cup extra virgin olive oil
1 tablespoon unrefined flax seed oil

Dip a fork into the jar of mustard and transfer about 1 teaspoon to a small bowl. Add vinegar and mix around. Add olive oil in a thin stream, stirring all the while with the fork, until oil is well mixed or emulsified. Add flax seed oil and use immediately.

There are two kinds, or families, of EFAs [essential fatty acids]. The *omega-6* family is found mainly in seeds grown in temperate climates—safflower, sunflower and corn oils are all rich in omega-6 EFAs. . . Because of the long-term trend toward using vegetable oils in cooking and salad dressing, most American children today get plenty of omega-6 oils—but, as we shall see, many have problems in using them.

The EFA famine among American children mainly involves the other family: *omega-3* EFAs. Only one vegetable oil is really rich in omega-3s: food-grade flaxseed oil (also known as linseed oil). Leo Galland, MD *Superimmunity for Kids*

HERB DRESSING

Makes about 3/4 cup

3/4 cup basic dressing
1 teaspoon very finely chopped fresh herbs such as parsley, tarragon, thyme, basil or oregano

Prepare basic dressing and stir in herbs.

"There's only one fat that's safe to eat—olive oil," contends Dr. Harry Demopolous. . . When you eat rancid oils, he says, you infuse your body with destructive free radicals that create chain reactions, breeding more free radicals to attack your cells. Of all the oil, olive oil, because it is so concentrated in mono-unsaturated fatty acids, is least likely to turn rancid and destructive. On the other hand, most likely to become rancid are oils high in poly unsaturated fatty acids like corn, safflower and sunflower. Jean Carper *The Food Pharmacy Guide to Good Eating*

BALSAMIC DRESSING

Makes about 3/4 cup

1 teaspoon Dijon type dressing, smooth or grainy
2 tablespoons plus 1 teaspoon balsamic vinegar
1/2 cup extra virgin olive oil
1 tablespoon unrefined flax seed oil

Balsamic vinegar is a red wine vinegar that has been aged in wooden casks. It has a delicious, pungent flavor that goes well with dark greens such as watercress or mache.

Prepare as in basic dressing recipe.

GARLIC DRESSING

Makes about 3/4 cup

3/4 cup basic dressing
1 clove garlic

Prepare basic dressing. Peel garlic clove and mash in a garlic press. Stir into dressing. Let sit a few minutes to allow amalgamation of garlic flavor.

Know Your Ingredients

Name This Product #3

Soybean oil, high fructose corn syrup, water, pickle relish, vinegar, tomato paste, salt, dehydrated egg yolk, algin derivative and xanthan gum (for consistency), mustard flour, natural flavors, dehydrated onion, spice, calcium disodium EDTA (to preserve freshness).

See Appendix B for Answer

SUN DRIED TOMATO DRESSING

Makes about 3/4 cup

3/4 cup basic dressing
1 teaspoon sun dried tomato flakes (see Sources)
1 teaspoon finely chopped chives or green onion

Prepare basic dressing. Add tomato flakes and let stand a few minutes to allow dried tomatoes to soften. Just before serving add chopped chives or green onion.

In a six month double blind trial, 40 patients with rheumatoid arthritis receiving either 6 grams of primrose oil per day or 6 grams of olive oil, resulted in a reduction in the nonsteroidal anti-inflammatory dosage for 30 patients in each group. There was a significant reduction in morning stiffness with gamma-linolenic acid at 3 months and a reduction in pain and articular index at 6 months with olive oil. In this study, olive oil produced more improved clinical parameters than primrose oil. It has been noted in a major textbook that rheumatoid arthritis is less frequent in Italy. *PPNF Journal*

WALNUT DRESSING

Makes about 1/2 cup

2 tablespoon sherry vinegar
2 tablespoons unrefined walnut oil
6 tablespoons extra virgin olive oil

Like flax seed oil, walnut is rich in omega-3 fatty acids. Buy unrefined walnut oil in dark cans and store in the refrigerator.

Place all ingredients in a bowl and stir with a fork.

ROASTED TOMATO DRESSING

Makes about 2 cups

1 pound firm plum tomatoes
1 cup extra virgin olive oil
1/4 cup balsamic vinegar
1/4 cup finely minced shallot or green onion
1 teaspoon raw honey
2 tablespoons minced fresh basil (or 2 teaspoons dried basil)
1 teaspoon minced fresh oregano (or 1/4 teaspoon dried oregano)
1 tablespoon minced fresh parsley
2 tablespoons unrefined flax seed oil

This is a delicious dressing for salads in winter!

Wash and dry the tomatoes. Brush with olive oil and set in a shallow glass pan. Roast in a 400 degree oven about 30 minutes until skin begins to blister. Cool completely. Chop and set aside.

Whisk remaining ingredients except flax oil together in a bowl and season to taste with sea salt and freshly ground pepper. Stir in tomatoes. Let dressing sit an hour or so to amalgamate flavors. Just before serving, stir in flax seed oil. (Store leftover dressing in refrigerator.)

CREAMY DRESSING

Makes about 1 cup

3/4 cup basic dressing or herb dressing (page 118)
1/4 cup piima cream or creme fraiche

This is a traditional recipe of the Auvergne region of France.

Prepare basic dressing. Blend in cream with a fork.

When we take a factual look at the effect of the "fat syndrome" on brain and nerve function, on sense organs, on mucous secretion, on stomach and intestine function, on liver and gall bladder function, on lymph and blood vessels, on kidney function, on the skin, on respiration, on immunity, on sexuality and reproductive processes, on neuroses, on the "tired syndrome" or vital energy, or on the growth processes, it becomes indisputably obvious and scientifically established that all of these areas of human existence are solidly tied to the function of electron-rich, highly unsaturated fats as receiver, amplifier and transmitter of electromagnetic waves; as regulators of the vital life functions. . . Fats that have had their electron structure destroyed to make them keep longer—they normally attract oxygen—have a very detrimental effect of the future-directed, electron-rich human being. . . Fats that have had their electron structure destroyed promote the development of the "anti-human", within space and time. Fats that disturb the electron exchange within living tissue because they, like tar, act as insulator against electrical conductivity, plainly deaden the life functions at the respective operative locations, e.g. in organs and in growth centers in the body. Dr. Johanna Budwig *Flax Oil as a True Aid*

And I heard a voice in the midst of the four beasts say, A measure of wheat for a penny, and three measures of barley for a penny; and see thou hurt not the oil and the wine. *Rev 6:6*

CREAMY MAYONNAISE DRESSING

Makes about 1 1/4 cup

3/4 cup basic dressing (page 118)
1/4 cup piima cream or creme fraiche
1/4 cup homemade mayonnaise
1 tablespoon fresh herbs, finely chopped

Place all ingredients in a jar and shake vigorously, or blend in a bowl with a whisk.

CILANTRO LIME DRESSING

Makes about 3/4 cup

1/2 cup extra virgin olive oil
1 tablespoon unrefined flax seed oil
3 tablespoons fresh lime juice
1 tablespoon minced fresh cilantro
1/4 teaspoon dried oregano
dash cayenne pepper
pinch stevia powder

Place all ingredients in a bowl and stir vigorously with a fork.

MEXICAN DRESSING

Makes about 3/4 cup

1/2 cup extra virgin olive oil
1 tablespoon unrefined flax seed oil
3 tablespoons raw wine vinegar
pinch stevia powder
1 clove garlic, peeled and mashed
1/2 teaspoon dried oregano
1/4 teaspoon chile powder

Place all ingredients in a bowl and stir vigorously with a fork.

Unpasteurized milk and butter were used for thousands of years, with a history of conferring good health on their users. Since the time of Hippocrates, physicians used raw milk and raw butter as therapeutic agents to treat disease. Whole nations formerly depended upon dairy products as major sources of food. But when pasteurization was introduced, dairy products strangely and precipitously lost their health charms, almost as if somebody waved an evil wand and presto, dairy products were instantly cursed. For example, in the days before milk and butter lost their lipase due to the heat of pasteurization, millions of people lived on dairy products without getting atherosclerosis (clogged arteries due to cholesterol deposits) because lipase knows how to handle cholesterol.

We have lost our ability to tame this killer. Lipase was also a valued guest in olive oil and other oils when they were thick and opaque, but had to give up its residence when the factories made them clear. The commercial production of these oils coincides with the rise of cancer-related deaths in modern society. These strong indications of the value of lipase offer reasons why lipase should be given high priority in research to test its capacity to neutralize pathogenic effects. Edward Howell MD *Enzyme Nutrition*

BLUE CHEESE DRESSING

Makes about 1 cup

3/4 cup basic dressing (page 118)
2-4 tablespoons crumbled blue cheese

If possible, use genuine Roquefort cheese made from sheeps milk, which is rich in lauric acid. Place all ingredients in a food processor and pulse a few times until blended; or mash cheese into dressing with a fork.

The balance between fat and protein, between high quality fat and high quality protein, is exceedingly important for all vital life functions, for all life processes in this bipolar, biologically significant system that regulates all life functions. There you will find an easily influenced, easily directed, biological molecule that is prepared to store solar energy, to absorb or to release it, according to the person's need for energy and strength. It has been scientifically established that all brain functions require these very easily activated, threefold unsaturated fats. A Swede established that no brain function is possible without the threefold-unsaturated fats. The same applies to nerve function and to regeneration in the muscle following strenuous muscular activity, during the so-called oxidative-recovery phase of sleep. Dr. Johanna Budwig *Flax Oil as a True Aid*

ANCHOVY DRESSING

Makes about 1 1/4 cup

1 can anchovies packed in olive oil
3/4 cup extra virgin olive oil plus oil from anchovies
1 tablespoon unrefined flax seed oil
1 clove garlic, peeled and mashed
1 teaspoon Dijon style mustard
1/4 cup raw wine vinegar
1 tablespoon fresh lemon juice

Place all ingredients in food processor and blend until smooth.

CAESAR DRESSING

Makes about 3/4 cup

1/2 to 1 teaspoon Dijon style mustard
1 tablespoon raw wine vinegar
1 tablespoon fresh lemon juice
1/2 cup extra virgin olive oil
1 tablespoon unrefined flax seed oil
1 egg yolk
2 anchovy filets
1 clove garlic, peeled and mashed

Place all ingredients in food processor and blend until smooth.

Fats and oils have been used in food preparation for centuries. Olive oil is probably the most ancient cooking oil, used as far back as ancient Egyptian times. Olive oil has proven itself with the test of time. Yet, only in the last decade has modern medical science recognized its healthful benefits. Cass Igram MD *Eat Right to Live Longer*

LEMON PEPPER DRESSING

Makes about 3/4 cup

2 tablespoons fresh lemon juice
1 tablespoon raw wine vinegar
1/4 teaspoon sea salt
1/2 teaspoon cracked pepper
dash stevia powder
1 clove garlic, peeled and mashed
1/2 cup extra virgin olive oil
1 tablespoon unrefined flax seed oil

Place all ingredients in a bowl and stir vigorously with a fork.

ORANGE DRESSING

Makes about 3/4 cup

3 tablespoons fresh orange juice
1/2 teaspoon finely grated orange rind
1 tablespoon raw wine vinegar
1/2 cup extra virgin olive oil
1 tablespoon unrefined flax seed oil

It is best to use an organic orange, so there will be no pesticides on the rind. Wash the rind well before grating.

Place all ingredients in bowl and stir vigorously with a fork.

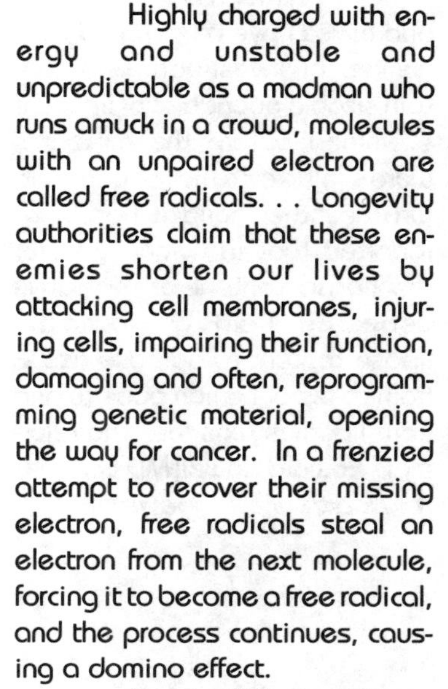

Highly charged with energy and unstable and unpredictable as a madman who runs amuck in a crowd, molecules with an unpaired electron are called free radicals. . . Longevity authorities claim that these enemies shorten our lives by attacking cell membranes, injuring cells, impairing their function, damaging and often, reprogramming genetic material, opening the way for cancer. In a frenzied attempt to recover their missing electron, free radicals steal an electron from the next molecule, forcing it to become a free radical, and the process continues, causing a domino effect.

Results differ in different parts of the body. In the skin, collagen is destroyed, causing wrinkling. There and in the body, fat becomes rancid and in time whole body organs or systems can be sabotaged. Synovial fluid (the natural lubrication in joints) thickens, making joint movement difficult and painful, a condition called arthritis.

More than 60 degenerative diseases common to aging can be caused by free radicals. The worst ones are atherosclerosis and the blocking of blood flow in arteries; Alzheimer's and Parkinson's disease, excessive loss of brain cells; cancer when genetic material is damaged and normal body materials are converted to carcinogens; cataracts caused by sunlight and oxidation; emphysema, inflammation and breaking down of lung tissue, heart disease, damage to heart muscle and stroke, attack of heart tissue when blood flow restarts. James F. Scheer *Health Freedom News*

Animal tissue fat, cream and olives have been found by a number of investigators to contain sizable quantities of lipase if examined before the materials were subjected to heat treatment. On the other hand it has been reported that in human obesity the lipase content of the fat is decreased. Dell'Acqua found the lipase content to adipose tissue from cases of human obesity and from lipomas was less than normal. Edward Howell MD *Enzymes for Health and Longevity*

ORIENTAL DRESSING

Makes about 1/2 cup

2 tablespoons rice vinegar
1 tablespoon soy sauce
1 teaspoon grated ginger
1 teaspoon toasted sesame oil
1 teaspoon finely chopped green onion or chives
1 clove garlic, peeled and mashed (optional)
1/2 teaspoon raw honey
1/3 cup extra virgin olive oil
1 teaspoon unrefined flax seed oil

Place all ingredients in a jar and shake vigorously.

TAHINI DRESSING

Makes about 2 cups

1 small onion, coarsely chopped
1 stalk celery, coarsely chopped
2 tablespoons soy sauce
fresh juice of 2 lemons
1/2 cup tahini
4 tablespoons extra virgin olive oil
1 tablespoon unrefined flax seed oil
1/8 to 1/4 cup water

Place celery and onion in food processor and pulse until finely chopped. Add remaining ingredients and process until well blended. Thin with a little water to achieve desired consistency.

Know Your Ingredients

Name This Product #4

Water, corn syrup, cultured lowfat buttermilk, vinegar, garlic juice, cellulose gel, sugar, salt, skim milk, sour cream (dried), onion (dried), xanthan gum, malto-dextrin, monosodium glutamate with potassium sorbate and calcium disodium EDTA as preservatives, lactic acid, natural flavor, propylene glycol alginate, cultured skim milk (dried), artificial color, phosphoric acid, lemon juice concentrate, green onion (dried), spice, Dl-alpha-tocopherol acetate (vitamin E)

See Appendix B for Answer

SAUCES, MARINADES & CONDIMENTS

Our collection of sauces and condiments can be divided into two categories: those composed of raw ingredients and therefore valuable as sources of enzymes; and those that have been heated. The first category includes various types of mayonnaise and marinades. Store-bought versions of these condiments have invariably been pasteurized and the vital enzyme component destroyed. But when you make these accompaniments yourself, taking care to use only raw, high-enzyme ingredients such as extra virgin olive oil, organic eggs, whey and cultured cream, your condiments will not only add taste to your meals, but will also serve as rich sources of vital nutrients. Whey added to mayonnaise promotes lacto-fermentation, thus augmenting enzyme content and increasing shelf life of this useful condiment.

Our heated sauces for meats, fish and enchiladas are made with homemade stocks so that, although the enzyme component may be lacking, the hydrophilic colloids of the gelatinous broth will contribute to digestibility, both of the sauce and the dish it accompanies.

Marinades that feature raw ingredients, particularly raw oils with their full complement of lipase, begin the digestive process of meats. Although the meats are usually cooked after several hours of steeping, their nutrients are nevertheless more available due to this pre-digestion; and of course, they are more tender and flavorful as well.

Politically correct nutrition eschews sauces, thereby implying that food that is good for us must necessarily be dry and bland. We submit that the right use of sauces, containing either rich stock or enzymes from whole raw ingredients, not only makes our food more appetizing, but also promotes easy digestion and assimilation.

MAYONNAISE

Makes 1 1/2 cups

1 whole egg, at room temperature
1 egg yolk, at room temperature
1 teaspoon Dijon-style mustard
1 1/2 tablespoons lemon juice
1 tablespoon whey (optional)
3/4-1 cup extra virgin olive oil
2 tablespoons unrefined flax seed oil
generous pinch sea salt

Homemade mayonnaise imparts valuable enzymes, particularly lipase, to sandwiches, tuna salad, chicken salads and many other dishes. It is so easy to make with a food processor, there is no need to buy commercial preparations. The addition of whey will help your mayonnaise last longer, adds enzymes, increases nutrient content and gives it an agreeable sour taste.

In your food processor, place egg, egg yolk, mustard, salt and lemon juice and optional whey. Process until well blended, about 30 seconds. Using the attachment that allows you to add liquids drop by drop, add the oils with the motor running. Taste and check seasoning. You may want to add more salt and lemon juice. If you have added whey, let the mayonnaise sit at room temperature, well covered, for 7 hours before refrigerating. With whey added, the mayonnaise will keep at least five weeks, refrigerated; without for about two weeks.

By adding extra bacteria to Waldorf-like salad and letting it ferment, its shelf life is extended to five weeks. Untreated such salads are soon contaminated by microorganisms and spoil. . . The new process, devised at the University of Wageningen, uses a naturally-occurring lactobacillus isolated from the water in which soy curd has been soaked. Often used to make yoghurt and salami, these bacteria grow well at 40-50 degrees C, producing lactic acid at the same time. Most organisms that spoil salads fail to grow at such high temperatures.

The bacteria are mixed into the salad dressing, inoculated for seven hours at 45 degrees C, and then refrigerated. The lactic acid produced by the bacteria during incubation prevent the growth of other bacteria at low temperatures. Fermentation delays the oxidation of saturated oils, which form the basis of the dressing, because the added bacteria consume all the oxygen. Fermentation also produces a pleasant, mildly sour taste many consumers prefer. *New Scientist*

HERBED MAYONNAISE

Makes 1 1/2 cup

1 1/2 cup homemade mayonnaise
1/2 cup fresh herbs, finely minced

We suggest dill as the best addition to mayonnaise but you may also add basil, tarragon or parsley. Chop or snip herbs finely and stir thoroughly into mayonnaise.

CURRIED MAYONNAISE

Makes 2 cups

1 cup homemade mayonnaise
1/2 cup piima cream or creme fraiche
3 tablespoons extra virgin olive oil
3 tablespoons raw vinegar
3 tablespoons curry powder

Blend all ingredients with a whisk. Use in curried chicken salad (page 392).

Water, soybean oil, sugar, vinegar, food starch-modified, salt, cellulose gel (microcrystaline cellulose), mustard flour, egg white, artificial color, sodium caseinate, xanthan gum, cellulose gum, spice, paprika, natural flavor, beta-carotene (color)

See Appendix B for Answer

SPICED MAYONNAISE

Makes 2 cups

1 small onion, coarsely chopped
2 tablespoons extra virgin olive oil
1 tablespoon curry powder
1/4 teaspoon ground cloves
1 teaspoon grated fresh ginger
2 tablespoons tomato paste
1 cup homemade chicken stock
1 teaspoon raw honey
1/2 teaspoon sea salt
1 cup homemade mayonnaise
1/2 cup piima cream or creme fraiche

This is an elegant sauce that goes well with cold chicken and rainbow rice salad (page 447).

Saute onion in olive oil. Add spices and cook gently. Add tomato puree and chicken stock. Blend well. Bring to a boil and allow the liquid to reduce to about 1/2 cup. Strain into a bowl. Let cool and whisk in honey until well blended. Blend in salt, mayonnaise and cream. The mayonnaise should be the consistency of thick cream.

Keeping up a high enzyme potential is the one way the body has to deal with tobacco smoke, short wave radiation, toxic chemicals and the prevention and cure of disease. There is no other mechanism in the body except enzyme action to protect the body from any hazard. It is ambiguous to say that nature cures, when we must know that the only machinery in the body to do anything is enzyme action. Hormones do not work. Vitamins cannot do any work. Minerals were not made to do any work. Proteins cannot work. Nature does not work. Only enzymes are made for work. So it is enzymes that cure. Therefore the ability of the body to make any of the numerous enzymes needed for good health and long life must be kept at a high level by the methods incorporated in The Food Enzyme Concept. Edward Howell MD *Enzymes for Health and Longevity*

The available evidence does not justify a placid continuance of a nihilistic attitude toward the vital forces operating in the living organism. It is a motif of science to reduce complex phenomena to simple integral units. Enzymes emerge as the true yardstick of vitality. Enzymes offer the only means of calculating the vital energy of an organism. That which has been referred to as "vitality", "vital force", "vital energy", "vital activity", "nerve energy", "vital resistance", "life energy", "life" and "life force" may be and probably is synonymous with that which has been known as "enzyme activity", "enzyme value", "enzyme energy", "enzyme vitality", and "enzyme content". The available evidence does not permit further procrastination but requires that what is known, vaguely and incomprehensibly, as life force or activity, be defined in terms of concrete and measurable enzyme units. In the face of the evidence which I present, it would be unscientific to continue fostering an unintelligible and uncertain attitude on matters having wide and intense bearing upon human conduct. Edward Howell MD *Enzymes for Health and Longevity*

Many of those biochemists and serious clinicians involved in the latest research on refined sugar have condensed their experience and research into one statement: "Consumption of refined sugar is the most pleasant means of gradual suicide." Only a handful of these researchers and serious clinicians realize that the above statement is only half true. The true part is that

CREOLE MAYONNAISE

Makes 1 1/2 cups

2 egg yolks, at room temperature
2 tablespoon fresh lemon juice
2 tablespoons whey (optional)
1 teaspoon Dijon-style mustard
1 clove garlic, peeled and crushed
1/2 teaspoon sea salt
1/2 teaspoon dried thyme
1/2 teaspoon dried basil
1/2 teaspoon dried oregano
1/4 teaspoon paprika
1/4 teaspoon tabasco sauce
1/8 teaspoon cayenne pepper
2/3 cup extra virgin olive oil
2 tablespoons unrefined flax seed oil

Place all ingredients except oils into food processor and blend thoroughly. With motor running, add oil drop by drop, using the oil-adding attachment. Check for seasonings. You may want to add more salt or lemon juice. If you have added whey, let the mayonnaise sit at room temperature, well covered, for 7 hours before refrigerating. With whey added, the mayonnaise will keep at least five weeks, refrigerated; without for about two weeks.

GREEN GELATIN MAYONNAISE

Makes 1 1/4 cups

1 bunch parsley, stems removed
1 whole egg, at room temperature
1 egg yolk, at room temperature
1 teaspoon Dijon-style mustard
1 1/2 tablespoons lemon juice
1 cup extra virgin olive oil
2 tablespoons unrefined flax seed oil
generous pinch sea salt
2 tablespoons unflavored gelatin
1/2 cup water

Place parsley in a large strainer and dip into boiling water. Drain and squeeze dry. Place parsley in food processor and pulse a few times. Add egg, egg yolk, mustard, salt and lemon juice. Process until well blended, about 30 seconds. Using the attachment that allows you to add liquids drop by drop, add the oils with the motor running. Melt gelatin in water over lowest heat. Stir into mayonnaise. Use for glazing poached salmon (page 256).

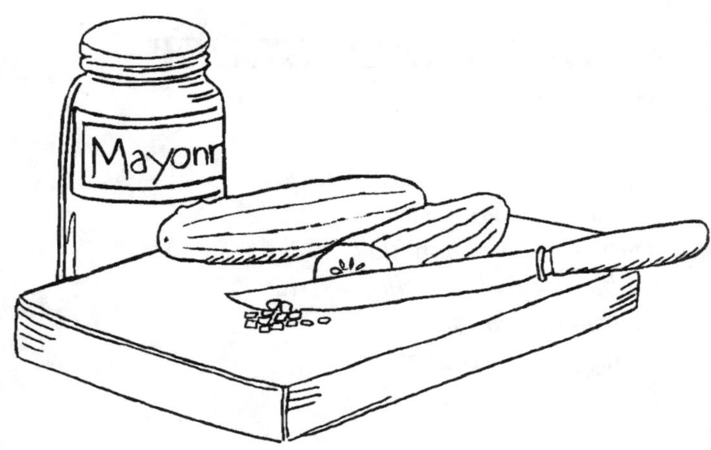

TARTAR SAUCE

Makes 1 1/2 cups

1 cup homemade mayonnaise
1/2 cup minced pickled cucumber (page 89)
2 tablespoons minced green onion
2 tablespoons finely chopped parsley
2 tablespoons small capers, rinsed in a strainer and dried with paper towels
1 tablespoon lemon juice
1/4 teaspoon sea salt
1/4 teaspoon freshly ground pepper
pinch cayenne pepper

This is wonderful with fish—and so much better than store-bought varieties. May be made up to two days in advance and stored in refrigerator, but serve at room temperature.

Blend all ingredients well. Check seasonings.

refined sugar consumption is gradual suicide. The untrue half is that it is pleasant. Anyone who has experienced the misery of constant tooth or gum problems, the financial ruin of constant illness, the frustration of low energy, the incapacitation of allergies, and the pain of arthritis, the crippling effects of a survived heart attack, or the terror of cancer is well aware that no matter how gradual the process, there is nothing pleasant about any of these afflictions. The latest research and serious clinical experience demonstrate that consumption of refined sugar is a major factor in all of the above conditions, plus many more. Bruce Pacetti DDS *PPNF Journal*

Know Your Ingredients

Name This Product #6

Enriched long grain rice, enriched vermicelli, dehydrated cream cheese, (sweet cream, dehydrated nonfat milk, cheese culture), dehydrated nonfat milk, salt, monosodium glutamate (natural flavor enhancer), dehydrated asparagus, dextrose, natural flavors, onion powder, partially hydrogenated soybean oil, dehydrated egg, dehydrated butter, dehydrated parsley, garlic powder, turmeric and paprika extractives (for color), sodium caseinate.

See Appendix B for Answer

HORSERADISH SAUCE

Makes 1/2 cup

1/4 cup fresh horseradish
1/4 cup piima cream or creme fraiche

Mix together with a fork. Serve with roast beef.

CREAMY DILL SAUCE

Makes 1 1/2 cups

1 egg
1 tablespoon grated onion
4 tablespoons lemon juice
4 tablespoons finely chopped dill
1 teaspoon sea salt
freshly ground pepper
1 cup piima cream

This is wonderful with cold poached salmon, salmon mousse or cold roast beef. Beat egg and combine with remaining ingredients. Check for seasonings. You may want to add more salt and lemon juice.

EGG MUSTARD SAUCE

Makes 1 cup

1/2 cup homemade mayonnaise
2-3 egg yolks
1 tablespoon Dijon-style mustard
2 tablespoons snipped dill
sea salt and freshly ground pepper

Blend all ingredients together and season to taste. Excellent with salmon.

Once upon a time there was a scientific debate. The debate was between the ideas put forth by Louis Pasteur and the ideas outlined by Antoine Bechamp. The scientific community adopted the ideas of Pasteur and completely rejected the ideas of Bechamp.

Because of that rejection, and the growth of dogma attached to the theories of Pasteur, our modern medical science may be digging a deep hole for all of us in our desires to overcome disease.

Medical and biological education today is based upon Pasteur's "germ theory of disease." Pasteur, who had immense political clout with Emperor Napoleon at the time, put forth the theory that germs, or microbial life, may be divided into "invariable" species and families. He proclaimed that each species caused a specific disease. Later Dr. Robert Koch put forth his famous "postulates" of microbial infections which solidified Pasteur's point of view. Thus, any germ shown to cause a disease is called a pathogen.

At the time of Pasteur, the greatest acknowledged biological scientist in France was Professor Bechamp, a physiologist who had no political clout despite enormous scientific prestige and credentials. Historians have shown that Pasteur plagiarized Bechamp in one important discovery about fermentation.

YOGHURT SAUCE

Makes 2 cups

1 1/2 cups yoghurt
1/4 cup lemon juice
1/4 cup water
3 cloves garlic, peeled and mashed
sea salt

Mix all ingredients together and season to taste with salt.

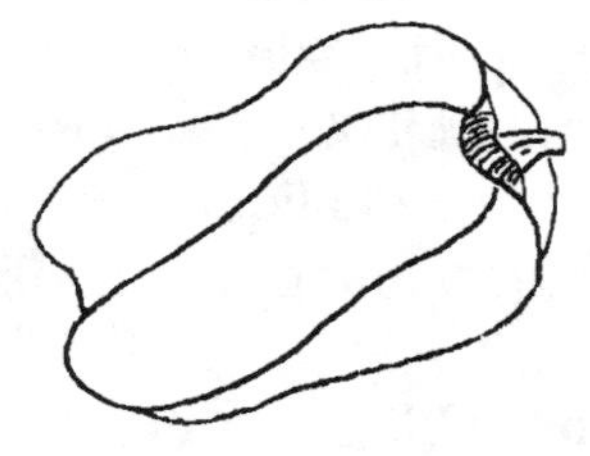

RED PEPPER SAUCE

Makes 4 cups

9 large red peppers, seeded and cut into quarters
3 cloves garlic, peeled and coarsely chopped
2 tablespoons extra virgin olive oil
3 tablespoons balsamic vinegar
1/3 cups sun dried tomatoes packed in olive oil
sea salt and freshly ground pepper to taste

Place pepper quarters in a 400 degree oven, skin side up, in an oiled pyrex dish. When peppers begin to soften, turn over and bake until skin loosens. Transfer to a plate and cover with a plastic bag for 10 minutes before removing skin.

Place skinned pepper pieces in food processor and process until smooth. Add remaining ingredients and process until smooth. Season to taste.

Variation: Creamy Red Pepper Sauce

Stir in *1/2 cup piima cream* or *creme fraiche*

Variation: Thin Red Pepper Sauce

Stir in *1/2 to 1 cup warm fish, chicken or beef stock.*

Bechamp's discovery about the nature of microbial life was exactly the opposite of what Pasteur proclaimed and science adopted. Briefly, Bechamp discovered a "symbiotic" relationship between microbes and larger animals. He also declared that all animal and plant cells contain extremely small granules which are not destroyed even when the organism or cell dies. He called them microzymas and demonstrated that these tiny specks could change form, and could result in changing the forms and the activity of other microbes.

Bechamp declared that Pasteur was wrong, that the nature of germs was not like higher animals. Microbial life is not firmly set into invariable species. Rather, microbial life is "pleomorphic"—capable of changing form and nature.

Despite his elegant presentations, the orthodoxy dominating scientific education ignored Bechamp and moved excitedly into what became the era of the pathogen hunters and "wonder drugs" that killed the pathogens.

In its ignorance of the forgotten Bechamp, medical science did not realize that the poisons they called drugs were opposed to nature's "symbiosis" and were perhaps encouraging pleomorphism to generate new and deadlier varieties of infections each generation. Tom Valentine *Search for Health*

About 25 years ago, doctors at Michael Reese Hospital in Chicago undertook some rather exhaustive investigations on the enzyme content of the saliva, pancreatic secretions and blood of human subjects including the very old. They found that most of the enzymes became weaker with advancing age. The doctors. . . found in older persons the enzyme lipase was low, with slow fat absorption from the intestine. They speculated that in hardening of the arteries, fat may be absorbed in the unhydrolyzed state. Lipase extracted from the animal pancreas was fed to both young and old subjects. Following use of the enzyme there was definite improvement in the character of fat utilization. There is evidence. . . that indicates that when fats, whether animal or vegetable, are eaten along with their associated enzymes, no harmful effect on the arteries or heart results. No atherosclerosis comes about. All fatty foods contain lipase in their natural state. Cooking or processing removes it. I have found there is no evidence of heart or blood vessel disease among wild animals consuming large quantities of fat. There is no evidence of these afflictions in whole nations of people eating foods containing fat when taken raw. Millions of wild creatures eat animal fats without suffering ill effects from cholesterol. Many different civilizations throughout history used large amounts of raw milk, cream, butter and cheese and maintained a high standard of health, comparatively free from cardiovascular impairment due to cholesterol deposits. Edward Howell MD *Enzyme Nutrition*

WATERCRESS SAUCE

Makes 1 1/2 cups

1 bunch watercress, stems removed
1 egg yolk
2 tablespoons lemon juice
1/2 cup extra virgin olive oil
1/2 cup piima cream or creme fraiche
sea salt

Place watercress in food processor and pulse until chopped. Add egg yolk and lemon juice and pulse until well blended. Using the attachment that allows you to add liquids drop by drop, add olive oil with motor running. Stir in piima cream and season to taste.

Variation: Cilantro Sauce

Use *1 large bunch cilantro, stems removed* instead of watercress and omit cultured cream.

ANCHOVY PASTE

(Anchoiade)

Makes 1/2 cup

2 cloves garlic
4 ounces canned anchovies with oil
1 tablespoon extra virgin olive oil
1/2 teaspoon raw vinegar

Place all ingredients in food processor and pulse to achieve a coarse paste. This is excellent spread on round croutons (page 491) or with Salade Variee for Grown-Ups (page 170).

CILANTRO MARINADE

Makes 1/2 cup

1 bunch cilantro, chopped
juice of one lemon
3 garlic cloves, mashed
1/2 cup extra virgin olive oil
freshly ground pepper

Mix all ingredients together.

TERIYAKI SAUCE

Makes 3/4 cup

1 tablespoon grated fresh ginger
3 garlic cloves, mashed
1 tablespoon toasted sesame oil
1 tablespoon rice vinegar
1 tablespoon raw honey
1/2 cup soy sauce

Use as a marinade for chicken or duck. Mix all ingredients together with a whisk.

BARBECUE SAUCE

Makes 1 1/2 cups

3/4 cup teriyaki sauce
3/4 cup naturally sweetened ketchup

Mix ketchup into teriyaki sauce with a whisk.

PEANUT SAUCE

Makes 2 cups

6 garlic cloves, peeled and coarsely chopped
2 inches fresh ginger, peeled and chopped
1 large bunch cilantro, chopped
1 tablespoon extra virgin olive oil
1 teaspoon Oriental hot chile oil
3/4 cup smooth natural peanut putter
3/8 cup soy sauce
3 tablespoons rice vinegar
1/2 - 1 cup chicken stock

Place garlic, ginger and cilantro in food processor and pulse until finely chopped. Add all ingredients but stock, pulse until well blended and transfer to a bowl. Bring stock to a boil and gradually blend into peanut mixture, whisking thoroughly. Keep warm by setting bowl in a pan of hot water over a very low flame.

At Baylor University, heart surgeon Michael DeBakey conducted a survey of 1,700 patients with such severe atherosclerosis that they had to be hospitalized, and only 20 percent—one out of five—had what is termed high blood serum cholesterol values. What does this indicate? That other factors than elevated cholesterol cause atherosclerosis.

Nicholas Sampsidis sums up the story neatly in *Homogenized*: "Heart disease doesn't start until something first induces cholesterol to come out of its liquid state and to solidify in the artery walls . Cholesterol has been implicated as the guilty party because of its presence at the scene of the crime. Cholesterol is very much like the school boy in a group caught throwing the last snowball after a window is broken. Although the whole group was involved in the crime, only the boy seen throwing the last snowball is blamed. . . cholesterol shares only a remote responsibility for heart disease. . . " James F. Scheer *Health Freedom News*

A member of the carrot family, cilantro is becoming increasingly easy to find in our markets. Although some people find the taste of cilantro unpleasant and "soapy", most are charmed by the pungent flavor of this staple of Mexican and Indian cuisines. Like all dark green vegetables, cilantro is a good source of carotenoids. The seed of cilantro is the spice coriander. SWF

In one fascinating experiment scientists deprived a group of test rats of taste sensation. Both this group and a control group were placed on normal rat diets, and in a short time the taste-deprived rats all died. When the rats were autopsied, scientists could find only one cause of death—clinical malnutrition. The scientists could come up with only one explanation—that there are important yet unknown physiological connections between taste and health. Similarly, hospital patients fed intravenously or through feeding tubes that bypass the mouth often report a nagging hunger for taste. Though the mechanisms that govern these phenomena are little understood, this much is certain: To be fully nourished by food, we must experience it through tasting and chewing. David Marc *Nourishing Wisdom*

BAGNAT SAUCE

Makes 2 cups

1 bunch Italian flat leaf parsley, coarsely chopped
4 cloves garlic, peeled and finely minced
1 small can anchovy filets, drained and minced
3/4 cup oil packed sun dried tomatoes, finely diced
1 cup extra virgin olive oil
3 tablespoons balsamic vinegar

This is an Italian sauce served with grilled chicken, duck, fish and meat. Don't let the anchovies deter you as their inclusion is essential to the character of this sauce. Do not use the food processor for this recipe. You will get a better texture by mincing all ingredients by hand.

Mix all ingredients except vinegar. May be kept refrigerated several days. Stir in vinegar just before serving.

Tahini is the paste of ground sesame seeds. Sesame seeds contain a high content of methionine and tryptophan, two amino acids usually lacking in vegetable foods. Sesame oil contains about 41 % stable oleic acid and an equal amount of omega-6 linoleic acid, with only trace amounts of omega-3. A small amount of flax seed oil added to tahini will correct this imbalance, and the combination of omega-3 fatty acids in flax oil with sulphur-containing methionine is a synergistic one. The high vitamin E content in sesame seed oil makes it resistant to rancidity. Buy tahini made from hulled seeds as the hulls contain oxalic acid, phytates and enzyme inhibitors—all anti-nutrients. SWF

TAHINI SAUCE

Makes 2 cups

2 cloves garlic, peeled and coarsely chopped
1 teaspoon sea salt
1/2 cup tahini
1 tablespoon unrefined flax seed oil
1 cup water
1/2 cup fresh lemon juice

This wonderful sauce is delicious with falafel (page 478). Place garlic in food processor with salt. Blend until minced. Add tahini and flax oil and blend. Using attachment that allows addition of liquids drop by drop and with motor running, add water. When completely blended, add lemon juice all at once and blend until smooth. Sauce should be the consistency of heavy cream. If too thick, add more water and lemon juice.

PESTO

Makes 1 cup

2 cups packed fresh basil leaves, washed and dried
2-4 cloves garlic, peeled
1/2 teaspoon sea salt
1/4 cup toasted pinenuts
1/4 cup good quality grated Parmesan cheese
1/4-1/2 cup extra virgin olive oil

Place basil leaves in food processor. Pulse until well chopped. Add garlic, salt, pinenuts and cheese and blend well. Using attachment for adding liquids drop by drop, and with motor running, add olive oil to form a thick paste. Pesto will keep several days, well sealed, in refrigerator; or it may be frozen.

Know Your Ingredients

Name This Product #7

Natural flavoring, modified corn starch, wheat flour, salt, maltodextrin, sweet cream, green peppercorns, monosodium glutamate (flavor enhancer), mustard flour, caramel color, onion, xanthan gum, sugar, spices, disodium inosinate and disodium guanylate (flavor enhancers), garlic, cream of tartar, lecithin (to prevent separation), and sulfating agents.

See Appendix B for Answer

PESTO SAUCE

Makes 1 1/2 to 2 cups

1 cup pesto
1/2 to 1 cup stock (fish, chicken or beef)

Use fish stock if you are serving this sauce with fish, chicken stock with chicken and beef stock with red meat.

Bring stock to a boil and pour in a thin stream into pesto, whisking constantly, until desired thickness is attained. Keep warm in a glass or ceramic container set in a pan of hot water over a very low flame.

The delicious taste and aroma of basil is the signature of Mediterranean cooking. The French call it *l'herbe royale* (the royal plant) for good reason. Tests have shown that the smell of basil has a salutary effect on peoples' outlook and disposition. It is valued for its ability to relieve intestinal gas and inhibit dysentery. The leaves may be brewed into a tea for these complaints. A relative of mint, Basil is easy to grow. It goes beautifully with tomato, fish and meat dishes. SWF

CURRY SAUCE

Makes 2 cups

2 tablespoons butter
2 tablespoons extra virgin olive oil
1 cup finely chopped onion
1 cup chopped yellow pepper
1 tablespoon red or green hot chile pepper, minced
3-4 tablespoons curry powder or curry paste
1 cup stock (fish, chicken or beef)
1 cup coconut milk and cream (page 144) or
7-8 oz creamed coconut (see Sources)
1/4 cup fresh lime juice
pinch sea salt
freshly ground pepper

Use fish stock if your sauce is for fish, chicken stock for chicken, beef stock for red meat.

Saute vegetables in butter and oil until tender. Add curry powder or paste and blend in. Add stock, bring to a boil and whisk smooth. Add coconut milk. Let mixture boil gently until reduced to about half. Off heat stir in lime juice and season to taste.

Strain sauce and serve with steamed fish, or with chicken or beef left from making stock.

Whenever we open a book on medicinal plants, we are surprised to find there almost all the herbs that play a part in good cooking. These "good herbs" are above all plants for our health. It is no accident that at the same time they are essential elements in food that we eat with pleasure. Here is the proof that for the cook, the food provider, good health and good taste go together. Claude Aubert *Dis-Moi Comment Tu Cuisines*

INDIAN CURRY BUFFET

Chicken with Curry Sauce

Basic Brown Rice

Fruit Chutney
Pineapple Chutney
Raisin Chutney
Chopped Crispy Peanuts
Chopped Green Onions
Chopped Cilantro

Dosas

Indian Salad

Cucumber Yoghurt Salad

Aristocratic Apples

CLARIFIED BUTTER

(Ghee)

Makes 3/4 cup

2 sticks butter

Those who are unable to tolerate milk protein in even the smallest amounts will want to clarify their butter, which is the process of removing the small amount of milk protein or casein contained in butter fat. Place butter in a small, heavy bottomed pan over lowest heat. Allow it to melt until foam has risen to the top. Carefully skim off foam. To remove every trace of milk solids, pour through a strainer lined with cheese cloth. Store in a tightly covered jar in the refrigerator. Use clarified butter for cooking and eating.

LEMON BUTTER SAUCE

Makes 3/4 cup

1/2 cup clarified butter, melted
juice of 1 lemon, strained

Mix butter and lemon juice. Excellent with artichokes.

HERB BUTTER

Makes 1 cup

1/2 cup parsley sprigs
2 tablespoons fresh tarragon leaves
1 teaspoon thyme leaves
2 sticks butter, softened

Place herbs in a strainer and plunge into boiling water for a few seconds. Rinse under cold water and pat very dry. Place in food processor and process until smooth. Add butter and pulse until well blended. Chill in a crock or in individual molds.

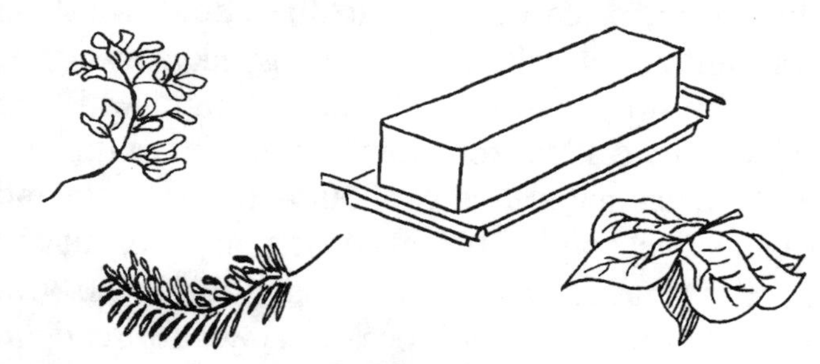

RED PEPPER BUTTER

Makes 1 cup

1/2 red pepper, cut into two pieces
2 sticks butter, softened

Place pepper pieces skin side up on an oiled pyrex pan and bake at 400 degrees until skin begins to buckle. Cover pepper pieces with plastic bag for about 10 minutes, then remove skin. Place pepper pieces in food processor and blend until smooth. Add butter and pulse until well blended.

Back in 1967 or so. . .a food technologist told me how he thought the term "plastic food" must have originated. Some biochemist, he speculated, must have observed that when looked at through a microscope, a hydrogenated fat molecule looks very much like a plastic molecule. . ."Lipid chemists," he explained, "actually talk about plasticizing oils.". . .I decided to discontinue selling margarine—as well as products containing vegetable shortening, margarine's cousin—and to perform a little experiment.

It was quite non-technical. . . I put a cube of margarine, the kind I had been selling, on a saucer and placed the saucer on the window sill in the back room of my store. I reasoned that if I made it readily available and if it was real food, insects and microorganisms would invite themselves to the feast. Flies and ants and mold would be all over it just as if it were butter. . . That cube of margarine became infamous. I left it sitting on the window sill for about two years. Nobody ever saw an insect of any description go near it. Not one speck of mold ever grew on it. All that ever happened was that it kind of half-puddled down from the heat of the sun beating through the windowpane, and it got dusty—very dusty, a cube of margarine doesn't clean up very well. Finally, it got to looking so revolting that I decided to terminate the experiment. For me, the experiment had not been foreshortened; I had reached the conclusion long ago that margarine basically is not food, whether or not it's like plastic. Fred Rohe
PPNF Journal

BERNAISE SAUCE

Makes 1 1/4 cup

2 tablespoons finely minced shallot or green onion
1 tablespoon finely minced fresh tarragon or
1 teaspoon dried tarragon
2 tablespoons white wine vinegar
2 tablespoons dry white wine or vermouth
5 egg yolks, at room temperature
1 stick butter, preferably raw, cut into pieces
fresh lemon juice
pinch sea salt and freshly ground pepper

Properly made, Bernaise sauce never attains more than a moderate heat, so that all the enzymes in the egg yolks are preserved. So delicious with meats and grilled fish, it is a sauce worth mastering—and not very hard to master at that.

In a small saucepan combine the shallots or onions, tarragon, wine and vinegar. Bring to a boil and reduce to about 1 tablespoon of liquid. Strain into a bowl.

Set the bowl in a pan of hot water over a low flame. Beat the egg yolks with a whisk. Add about half the butter, piece by piece, to the liquid, whisking constantly until melted. Add the egg yolks very slowly, drop by drop or in a very thin stream, whisking constantly. Add the remaining butter and whisk until well amalgamated. Sauce should now be warm and slightly thickened. Off heat add lemon juice, salt and pepper to taste. Sauce can be kept warm in the bowl set in hot water. Whisk occasionally until ready to serve.

[Many works] with humans and animals showed that margarine feeding had the effect of failing to bring out the secondary sex characteristics. . . not just a delay, but a complete failure to promote sex changes. Especially after two or three generations, males lose their heavy masculine frame and begin to become more effeminate. Females also begin losing their distinguishing build of femininity. Both sexes "approach a state of physical neutrality". . . The male no longer possesses the bodily strength and stamina that characterized men. . . The female no longer has the pelvic capacity needed for easy childbirth and other soft, rounded characteristics. Looking at photos of nude posterior views of such margarine and otherwise nutritionally castrated teenagers (aged 15 to 17), it is almost impossible to tell the boys from the girls. Judith A. DeCava *The Margarine Masquerade*

AUGUST DINNER

French Bean Salad

Marinated Grilled Swordfish

Bernaise Sauce

Onions Chardonnay

Berry Sherbert

BUTTER SAUCE

(Beurre Blanc)

Makes 1/2 cup

6 tablespoons minced shallots
6 tablespoons dry white wine
2 tablespoons fresh lemon juice
1 stick butter, preferably raw, cut into pieces
pinch sea salt and freshly ground pepper

This is the classic French sauce for fish. Properly made and not overheated, the butter will retain its enzyme content.

Place shallots, wine and lemon juice in a small pan. Bring to a boil and reduce to about two tablespoons. Strain into a small bowl.

Place the bowl in a pan of hot water over a low flame and add the butter piece by piece, whisking thoroughly after each addition. Sauce should become frothy and slightly thick. As soon as butter is amalgamated, remove from heat and season to taste. Serve immediately.

PARSLEY BUTTER SAUCE

Makes 1 cup

3 tablespoons shallots or green onions, finely chopped
2 tablespoons sherry vinegar
1/4 cup dry white wine
1 cup fish, chicken or beef stock
1/2 cup piima cream or creme fraiche
3 tablespoons butter, softened
1 tablespoon coarse mustard
2 tablespoons finely chopped parsley

Combine shallots or green onions, vinegar, wine, stock and cream in a pan, bring to a boil and reduce to about half, or until sauce thickens slightly. Reduce heat and stir in butter and mustard. Season to taste. Just before serving, stir in parsley.

I have referred to the importance of a high vitamin butter for providing the fat-soluble activators to make possible the utilization of the minerals in the foods. In this connection, it is of interest that butter constitutes the principal source of these essential factors for many primitive groups throughout the world. In the high mountain and plateau district in northern India, and in Tibet, the inhabitants depend largely upon butter made from the milk of the yak and the sheep for these activators. The butter is eaten mixed with roasted cereals, is used in tea and in a porridge made of tea, butter and roasted grains. In Sudan, Egypt, I found considerable traffic in high vitamin butter which came from the higher lands a few miles from the Nile Basin. This was being exchanged for and used with varieties of millet grown in other districts. This butter, at the temperature of that area, which ranges from 90 to 110 Fahrenheit, was, of course, always in liquid form. Its brilliant orange color testified to the splendid pasture for the dairy animals. The people in Sudan, including the Arabs, had exceptionally fine teeth with exceedingly little tooth decay. The most physically perfect people in northern India are probably the Pathans who live on dairy products largely in the form of soured curd, together with wheat and vegetables. The people are very tall and are free of tooth decay. Weston Price DDS *Nutrition and Physical Degeneration*

Know Your Ingredients

Name This Product #8

Tomatoes, sugar, corn sweetener, vinegar, salt, onion powder, natural flavorings, garlic powder, spices

See Appendix B for Answer

1923 was also the heyday of Prohibition. When booze became illegal here, sugar consumption zoomed. The whole country acted like a gathering of arrested alcoholics spending the evening at AA; they couldn't keep their mitts out of the candy jar. Teetotalers were often the biggest sugar fiends, vowing alcohol would never touch their lips while pouring in the sugar which produces alcohol in tummies instead of bathtubs. William Dufty *Sugar Blues*

If you just can't do without your coffee, you may have to do without some of the calcium in your bones, as various studies reveal. The more coffee you take in, the more calcium goes out. In one study, adult volunteers drank about four cups of coffee. . . Three hours later, they passed more calcium in their urine than individuals not drinking coffee. James F. Scheer *Health Freedom News*

SMOOTH TOMATO SAUCE

Makes 2 cups

2 ripe tomatoes
1 red pepper, seeded and chopped
1 onion, peeled and coarsely chopped
1/2 teaspoon sea salt
1/2 cup chicken or beef stock
8 tablespoons extra virgin olive oil

Blend tomatoes, pepper and onions in food processor. Place in a pan with remaining ingredients. Bring to a boil, cover and simmer 3 minutes. Remove top and cook, stirring constantly, for another 5 minutes or so.

CHUNKY TOMATO SAUCE

Makes 2 cups

2 tablespoons extra virgin olive oil
1/2 cup onion, finely chopped
3 cups fresh tomatoes, peeled, seeded and diced
2 tablespoons balsamic vinegar
2 cloves garlic, mashed
1/2 cup finely chopped basil
pinch sea salt
freshly ground pepper

This sauce is good with grilled tuna, sweetbreads and many other dishes.

Saute onions in olive oil until tender. Add tomatoes, vinegar and garlic. Bring to a boil and reduce until liquid is almost gone. Stir in basil and seasonings. Let sit off heat for about 1/2 hour to allow herb flavor to amalgamate into the sauce. Reheat before serving.

GRANDPA'S SALSA

Makes 2 cups

1 medium onion, peeled and finely chopped
1 cup green peppers, hot or mild, diced
2 ripe tomatoes, peeled, seeded and diced
extra virgin olive oil

Saute onions in olive oil until soft. Add tomatoes and peppers to onions and cook, stirring frequently, until most of the liquid has evaporated. Delicious with scrambled eggs.

GREEN ENCHILADA SAUCE

Makes 3 cups

2 onions, chopped
8 fresh tomatillos, husked and finely chopped
3 medium mild green Anaheim chiles, seeded and chopped
2 small jalapeno chiles, seeded and chopped
2 cloves garlic, peeled and chopped
3 tablespoons extra virgin olive oil
1 3/4 cups homemade chicken stock
pinch sea salt
1 bunch cilantro, chopped

This may be made in large batches and frozen. Be careful when preparing the chiles. It's best to wear rubber gloves when seeding and chopping jalapenos, and to avoid touching any part of your face.

In a heavy skillet, saute onions in olive oil. Add tomatillos and chopped chiles and saute gently several minutes. Add the stock, garlic and salt and bring to a boil. Simmer about 30 minutes, uncovered, until reduced and thickened. Off heat, add cilantro. Process in batches in your food processor until smooth. Reheat gently.

Would you believe that in all probability, you are "partially hydrogenated?" Over the years you have developed untold thousands of hardened (hydrogenated) cells. This is because these cells have inserted into their membranes trans fats from a dose of margarine or from some French fries cooked in a deep fryer, etc.

An example of this is what happens to white blood cells. These cells incorporate the hydrogenated fats you eat into their membranes. When this happens, the white cells become sluggish in function, and their membranes actually become stiff! Such white blood cells are poor defenders against infection. This leaves the body wide open to all sorts of derangements of the immune system. Cancer, or infections by yeasts, bacteria and viruses can more easily take a foothold.

Chemically altered and hydrogenated fats are no longer a food. They, in effect, become a poison, polluting the body's cells and organs. Once deposited within the tissues, these fats damage the cells and organs.

In fact, one of the quickest ways to paralyze your immune system is to eat, on a daily basis, significant quantities of deep fried foods, or fats such as margarine, partially hydrogenated cottonseed/palm/corn/ or sunflower oil, or lard. Cass Igram MD *Eat Right to Live Longer*

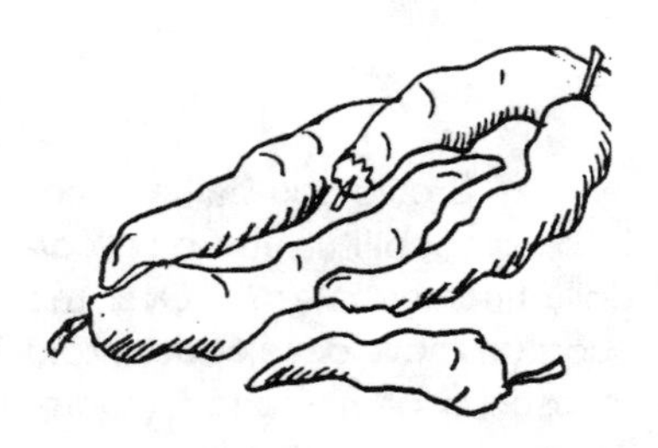

Hydrophilic colloids form the substratum of all living protoplasm. They possess the property of readily taking up and giving off the substances essential to cell life. . . Man's food in the raw state consists largely of hydrophilic colloids. The heat of cooking . . precipitates the colloids in our diet. This change in colloidal state alters the hydration capacity of our foods so as to interfere with their ability to absorb digestive juices. . . . Uncooked foods contain sufficient hydrophilic colloid to keep this gastric mucosa in excellent condition. On the other hand, man living largely on cooked foods presents a different problem. . . . The use of a hydrophilic colloid [such as gelatin] in the dietetic treatment of gastric complaint is frequently sufficient in itself to rectify what are apparently serious conditions. Gelatin may be used in conjunction with almost any diet. . . Its colloidal properties aid the digestion of many foods which cause the patient to suffer form "sour stomach". . . . In children who present problems of growth and development and those who show symptoms of allergy in the bowel, the hydrophilic colloid proves to be of great value. One usually prefers to use it in conjunction with a diet designed for the child's general upbuilding, although the addition of the colloid to the usual diet may be all that is necessary. Francis Pottenger MD *Hydrophilic Colloidal Diet*

RED ENCHILADA SAUCE

Makes 3 cups

2 ounces large whole dried red chiles
2 cups chicken or beef stock, warmed
2 cloves garlic, peeled and chopped
1/2 teaspoon sea salt
1/4 cup extra virgin olive oil
1 medium onion, finely chopped
1 teaspoon ground cumin
1 ripe tomato, peeled, seeded and chopped
1 tablespoon red wine vinegar

This sauce is far superior—both nutritionally and in terms of taste—to anything you can buy in a can. It can be made in large batches and frozen to have on hand when needed. Use either ancho or New Mexican chiles—both are available in Mexican or Latin American markets, in specialty stores and in supermarkets in the West. The New Mexican chiles are slightly milder.

Clean the dried chiles by removing the stem and seeds. Be sure to wear rubber gloves for this process and be careful not to touch any part of your face. Soak the pieces in the stock for about one hour.

Meanwhile, saute onion in the oil. Stir in cumin and cook, stirring, until well amalgamated into the oil. Add the tomato and cook a bit more. Add stock plus chiles, garlic and salt. Bring to a boil, skim and then reduce heat to a simmer. Cook, uncovered for about 10 minutes. Process in batches in your food processor until smooth. Correct seasoning.

PINEAPPLE VINEGAR

Makes 2 quarts

skin and core from 1 pineapple
2 quarts filtered water
2 teaspoons oregano
1/4 teaspoon red chile flakes
2 tablespoons whey (optional)

This is a tradition of the West Indies and is used to make cortido (page 85). Place all ingredients in a bowl, cover and let sit about 36 hours. Remove pineapple pieces and strain vinegar into clean jars. Cover tightly. This will keep in a cool place for several months.

PAPAYA PEPPER

seeds from 2 papayas

The papaya seed is rich in enzymes and can be used in place of pepper in any recipe. Place seeds with adhering pulp in warm water and work with hands to remove pulp. Let stand about 10 minutes. Pulp will rise to the surface where it can be skimmed off. Let seeds soak, covered, about 7 hours. Rinse seeds in a strainer and spread on a stainless steel baking pan. Bake at 150 degrees overnight or until completely dry. To use, grind in a pepper mill.

FERMENTED FISH SAUCE

Makes about 1 cup

1 1/2 pounds small fish, including heads, cut up
3 tablespoons sea salt
1 cup filtered water
2 cloves garlic, mashed
2 bay leaves, crumbled
1 teaspoon peppercorns
several pieces lemon rind
2 tablespoons whey

Toss fish pieces with salt and place into a wide mouth quart-sized mason jar. Press down with wooden pounder. Mix remaining ingredients and pour over fish. Add additional water until liquid comes to about 1 inch above the level of the fish. Cover tightly and leave at room temperature for 2 days. Transfer to refrigerator for several weeks. Drain off liquid through a strainer and store in refrigerator.

Certain things, like Gorgonzola cheese or hoppy ale, don't necessarily surrender their full charms on first taste. With repeated samplings, though, their complex multilayered flavors finally reveal themselves. Fermented fish definitely belongs on the same list. . . probably the most accessible of the many fermented-fish seasonings of Southeast Asia is fish sauce. This thin brown liquid is made by packing anchovies or other small fish in salt and allowing them to ferment for three months or more, drawing off the liquid as it seeps out.

While this may seem faintly repulsive, it is actually a part of the European culinary heritage. In classical Rome, one of the most popular condiments was a sauce called *garum*, made in an almost identical fashion, except that the innards of larger fish were added to ferment along with the anchovies.. . . Fish sauce serves much the same function in Southeast Asian cooking as salt does in Western cuisines, and the Vietnamese mode of cooking with it provides the best model for American tastes. It adds a depth of flavor and intensifies the tastes of other ingredients but does not stand out as an ingredient in itself. Once added to stew, condiment or salad, it ceases to taste of fish and instead serves to round out the many other bold flavors that are typical of the region's cuisine. John Willoughby and Chris Schlesinger *The New York Times*

COCONUT MILK AND CREAM

Makes 1 1/2 cups

2 coconuts

Using an ice pick, poke two holes in soft spots and allow to drain. Place in a 350 degree oven until coconuts crack. Use a hammer to split open. Separate coconut meat from shell using a sharp knife. Remove dark outer layer and dice white coconut meat into quarter-inch pieces. Place in food processor and process until well broken up. Add 1 cup warm water and process until fluffy.

Line a strainer with several layers of cheese cloth or a linen towel and place processed coconut meat in strainer. Allow to drain into a glass container, squeezing out all liquid with the back of a wooden spoon. Use immediately or refrigerate and use within 2 days.

"Creamed coconut", available in Indian and African food shops, can be used in place of homemade coconut milk and cream. This is a solid block of finely ground coconut with its oil, that melts when added to sauces. (See Sources)

DRIED SWEETENED COCONUT MEAT

Makes 3 cups

coconut meat remaining from above recipe
1/4 cup maple syrup

This makes an excellent topping for curry; we also call for coconut meat in several dessert and cookie recipes. Mix coconut meat with maple syrup, spread on an oiled pan and let dry in a 150 degree oven, about 12 hours.

Products of the coconut form a dietary staple in many nations, particularly Southeast Asia, the tropical regions of Latin America, and East Africa. Marco Polo referred to the coconut as the "Indian nut". Vasco de Gama used the word "coquos" in his *Rotiero* (1498-99) and Pigafetta, the official chronicler of the Magellan expedition to the Philippines, used the Italian form of "coche" (plural "coca") around 1522.

The coconut is relatively low in protein compared to other nuts and seeds. It provides calcium, iron, magnesium, phosphorus and potassium as well as small amounts of B vitamins.

The coconut contains up to 60 percent fat, and this fat is 92% saturated. But this is no reason to avoid coconut products. The principle fatty acid in coconut milk, lauric acid, is found in abundance in only one other source—butterfat, especially the butterfat in mother's milk. This medium chain fatty acid has potent anti-viral, anti-fungal and anti-microbial properties. In vitro it will inactivate the HIV virus as well as the measles virus, herpes simplex virus-1, vesicular stomatitis virus, visna virus and cytomegalovirus. Coconut oil is now being used to treat both AIDS and candida because of its antipathogenic effects in the gut; when absorbed the medium chain fatty acids in coconut oil give quick energy. Because coconut oil is so highly saturated, it is highly resistant to rancidity.

Coconut oil is a good substitute for hydrogenated oils. Is this why we hear so much adverse publicity about the coconut? SWF

GREAT BEGINNINGS

HORS D'OEUVRES & DIPS

Our recipes for hors d'oeurves and dips derive from a variety of ethnic traditions and feature fresh, unprocessed ingredients, with a special emphasis on fish eggs—roe and caviar. Fish eggs are valued by primitive peoples throughout the world for their ability to promote fertility, nourish pregnant women and children and prevent "big neck"—problems of the thyroid gland. Although they come under the category of "gourmet", such dishes make excellent snacks and lunchtime fare.

If you tolerate milk products, we also recommend our cream cheese-flax spreads (page 149) as a delicious combination of omega-3 fatty acids and sulphur-containing proteins.

TARAMOSALATA

Serves 12

1 pound smoked whole cod roe, casing removed
1/2 cup piima cream or creme fraiche
1 clove garlic, mashed
juice of 1/2 lemon
freshly ground black pepper
1/2 cup extra virgin olive oil

Use this delicious pink cream to spread on toasts, to fill celery, or serve in a crock with wholegrain crackers (page 489) or triangle croutons (page 491).

Place roe, cream, garlic, lemon juice and pepper in food processor and process until smooth. Using the attachment for adding oil, add the olive oil drop by drop to form a thick, mayonnaise-like emulsion. Chill several hours.

Variation: Budget Taramosalata

Use *raw fish roe, casing removed*, from any kind of fish, rather than smoked cod roe. High-nutrient roe can often be obtained at very low cost in season from a good fish monger.

SALMON EGG TOASTS

Serves 2-4

2 ounces fresh salmon eggs
2-4 slices wholegrain bread
butter
1 tablespoon fresh dill snippings

Toast bread and spread with butter. Spread salmon eggs on toast and sprinkle with dill snippings.

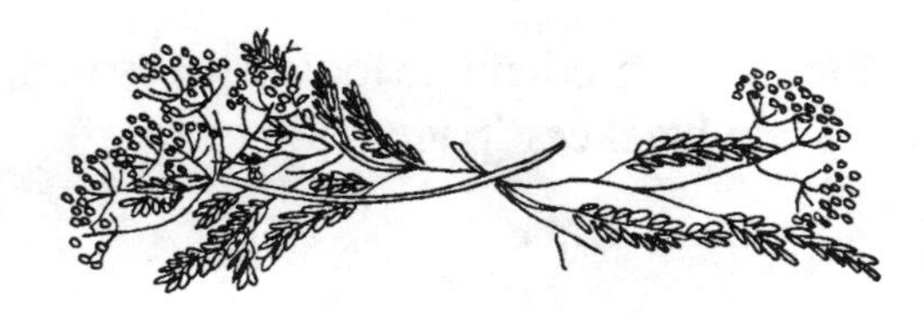

ANCHOVY TOASTS

Makes 1 dozen

12 triangle croutons (page 491)
1 cup anchovy paste (page 123)
2 tablespoons salmon roe (optional)

Spread croutons with anchovy paste and decorate each with 2 or 3 salmon eggs.

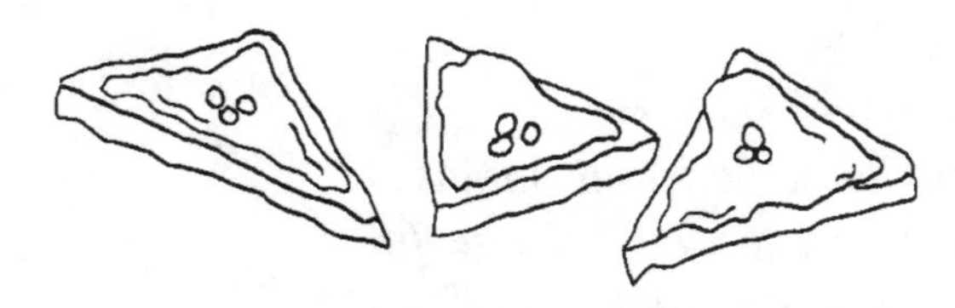

MACKEREL SPREAD

Makes 1 1/2 cups

1 cup pickled mackerel or herring (page 222)
1/2 cup piima cream or creme fraiche
squeeze of lemon juice
sea salt and pepper to taste

Blend all ingredients in food processor. Serve with wholegrain crackers (page 489) or triangle croutons (page 491). For adventurous eaters!

When it is recognized that in the Sierra the available water is largely that provided to the streams from the melting snows and from rains in the rainy season, it will be realized that these sources of fresh water could not provide the liberal quantity of iodine essential for human growth and development. It was, accordingly, a matter of great interest to discover that these Indians used regularly dried fish eggs from the sea. Commerce in these dried foods is carried on today as it no doubt has been for centuries. When I inquired of them why they used this material, they explained that it was necessary to maintain the fertility of their women. I was informed also that every exchange depot and market carried these dried fish eggs so that they were always available. Another sea product of very great importance, and one which was universally available was dried kelp. Upon inquiry I learned that the Indians used it so that they would not get 'big necks' like the whites. The kelp provided a very rich source of iodine as well as of copper which is very important to them in the utilization of iron for building an exceptionally efficient quality of blood for carrying oxygen liberally at those high altitudes. An important part of their dietary consists today as in the past of potatoes which are gathered and frozen, dried and powdered, and preserved in the powdered form. This powder is used in soups with llama meat and other products. Weston Price DDS *Nutrition and Physical Degeneration*

SALMON SPREAD

Makes 2 cups

1 cup fresh cooked salmon
1 small onion, grated
3/4 cup piima cream or creme fraiche
juice of 1 lemon
1 tablespoon capers, drained, rinsed and dried with paper towels
sea salt and pepper to taste

Blend all ingredients in food processor. Spread on wholegrain crackers (page 489) or toast.

SALMON STUFFED ENDIVE LEAVES

Makes about 30

30 endive leaves
1 cup cooked salmon
1/4 cup homemade mayonnaise
1/4 cup piima cream or creme fraiche
2 teaspoons unrefined flax oil
1 teaspoon grated ginger
1 tablespoon lime juice
1/2 teaspoon sea salt
dash cayenne pepper
fresh dill weed for garnish

Place salmon in food processor and pulse until well chopped. Add mayonnaise, piima cream, ginger, lime juice, sea salt and cayenne and process until smooth. Place a small spoonful in the hollow of each endive leaf, or use a pastry bag to make attractive rosettes. Garnish with snippets of fresh dill weed.

The hardy folk of the Northern Isles feasted on "made-dishes". They had strubba—coagulated milk whipped to consistency of cream. Klokks was new milk simmered until clotted, and flavored with cinnamon and sugar. Kirn mill was a curd of buttermilk with mill-gruel. Blaund was whey of bleddik or buttermilk. Hungmill was cream hung in a bag, like cream cheese. Klabba was junket set thick by action of "yearmin" (rennet). Eusteen was hot milk reduced by sherry to curd and whey. Pramm was cold milk mixed with meal, a dish for bairn or beggar. Eggaloorie was salt, eggs and milk boiled. Da pukkle was oats, called "bursteen" when ground. Virpa was a brew made of corn husks. A very popular dish was knocket corn, cracked wheat or groats boiled with kale and pork. At Christmas they had Yule-brunies or rye cakes. Ploy-skonn was a short-bread. The dairy and vegetable products were enhanced with slott, fish roe beaten to cream, with flour and salt added, or with stapp, a mixture of fish heads with liver. Special palates were pleased with kiossed heeds, fish heads which had become gamey. At Christmas and at embarking on perilous voyages they had whipkill, egg yolks with sugar beaten with cream and enforced with potent spirit. *Orkney and Shetland Miscellany*

CREAM CHEESE FLAX SPREAD

Makes 1 cup

1 cup homemade cream cheese (page 80)
2 tablespoons unrefined flax seed oil

Mix cheese with flax oil and place in a crock or serving container. Chill well. Serve with sour dough bread or wholegrain crackers (page 489).

Variation: Herbed Cheese Spread
Add *1 tablespoon fresh herbs, finely minced.*

Variation: Pepper Cheese Spread
Add *1 tablespoon cracked pepper.*

Variation: Garlic Cheese Spread
Add *two garlic cloves, peeled and mashed*

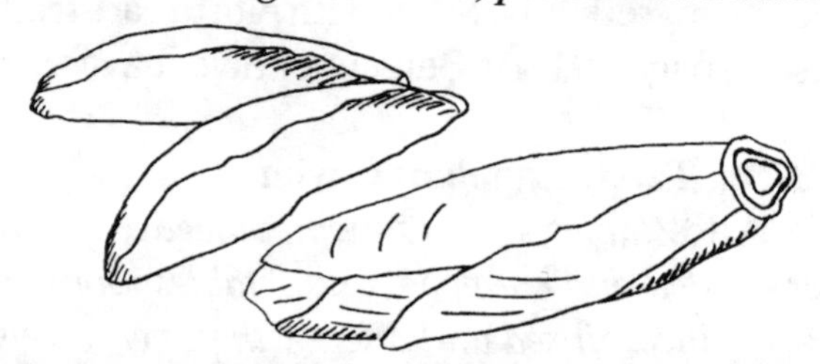

STUFFED ENDIVE LEAVES

Serves 15-30

30 Belgian endive leaves
3/4 cup radish, finely diced
3/4 cup celery, finely diced
2 tablespoons piima cream or creme fraiche
2 tablespoons homemade cream cheese (page 80), softened
1 teaspoon unrefined flax seed oil
1-2 teaspoons lemon juice
1/4 teaspoon freshly ground pepper
30 tiny watercress sprigs

Mix cream, cream cheese, flax oil, lemon juice and pepper. Stir in vegetables. Chill several hours. Place a spoonful in each endive leaf and garnish with watercress sprigs.

Our eating patterns have changed radically over the last hundred years—so much so that today we are in the midst of a famine. It's not the kind of famine that has, historically, decimated and immunity of whole nations. That kind of famine is easy to understand: it produces starvation and a critical lack of protein for the body. The famine we face today is more subtle, a product of highly developed, mainly Western, culture. It's hard to believe, because our supermarkets are packed with fresh produce and boxes and cans of everything, but we are literally starving for essential fatty acids or EFAs.

EFAs are found in many foods, but they are most richly concentrated in the oils of certain nuts, seeds and fish. Nuts, seeds and beans aren't important items in the diets of most Americans. Partly because of this, and partly because we eat much less fish than we used to—and overprocess most of what we do eat—one whole group of EFAs has been virtually eliminated from our diets. Leo Galland, MD *Superimmunity for Kids*

The cows are our friends, they give food, they give strength, they likewise give a good complexion and happiness.
Gautama Buddha

EGGPLANT CAVIAR

Serves 6-8

2 medium eggplants
sea salt
1 medium onion, finely chopped
2-4 cloves garlic, mashed
1/2 cup minced parsley or cilantro
1/4 cup toasted pine nuts (optional)
2 tablespoons lemon juice
1/4 cup extra virgin olive oil
dash cayenne pepper

Puncture the eggplants in a few spots and bake in a 375 degree oven for about one hour or until skin is wrinkled and eggplant is tender. Let cool. Peel and chop into a fine dice, sprinkle with salt, mix well and let sit about an hour in a colander. Rinse well with water and squeeze dry in a tea towel. Mix with remaining ingredients. Serve with pita bread, triangle croutons (page 491) or Belgian endive leaves.

Variation: Tangy Eggplant Caviar

Add *2 tablespoons raw wine vinegar*, *1 jalapeno pepper, seeded and chopped*, and *2 tablespoons small capers, drained, rinsed and dried with paper towels.*

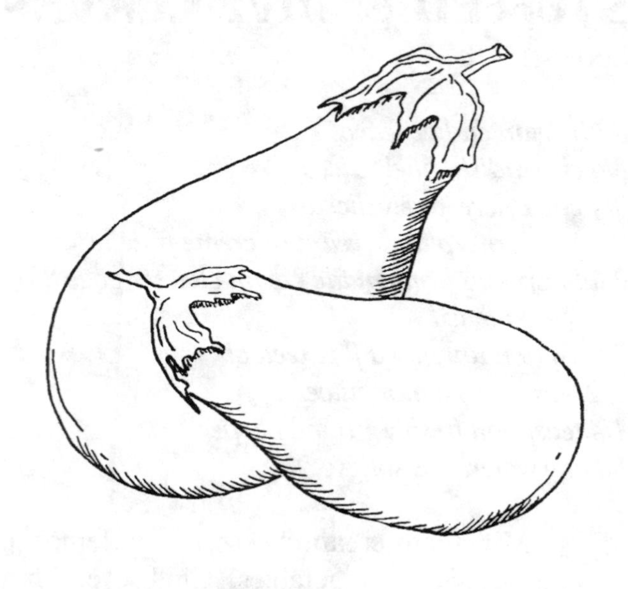

How many Americans would you guess eat french fries in fast food chain restaurants every year? After all, "billions of burgers sold" surely translates to an equal number of french fry orders consumed. Originally, the delicious fingers of deep-fried potato, which have been blamed on the famed French chefs, were cooked in, horror of horrors, old-fashioned lard. Over the past several years, the public relations conscious fast food giants were pressured mightily by well-meaning advocacy groups, especially the Center for Science in the Public Interest (CSPI), who obviously knew nothing about *trans* fats, to make their french fries "more healthy." This meant that the famous french fry had to be cooked in "partially hardened vegetable shortening" cooking oil rather than a saturated animal fat. Never mind that a potato deep-fried in . . . lard may be cooked in less time at a higher temperature—thereby leaving less total fat imbedded in the finished, more thoroughly cooked, less soggy, less rancid food product.

According to Dr. Mary Enig, Research Associate in the Lipids Research Group, Department of Chemistry and Biochemistry, University of Maryland, the nations' leading authority on the amounts of *trans* fats in foods, the new fast food french fries are loaded with the molecular misfits, the *trans* fatty acids. The fat in a fast food french fry cooked with partially hydrogenated vegetable shortening can have as high as 46% trans fat. Old fashioned lard had zero percent *trans* fat. This means that almost half the fat in the french fries is now the worst kind for human nutrition! Tom Valentine *Facts on Fats & Oils*

EGGPLANT RELISH

Makes 5 cups

4 medium eggplants
sea salt
4 medium tomatoes
1 medium onion, finely minced
1/2 cup finely chopped parsley
2 tablespoon small capers
2 tablespoons toasted pinenuts
1/4 teaspoon ground cumin
1/2 teaspoon sea salt
dash cayenne pepper
freshly ground pepper
2 cups tahini sauce (page 134)

Puncture the eggplants in a few spots and bake in a 375 degree oven for about one hour or until skin is wrinkled and eggplant in tender. Let cool. Peel and chop into a fine dice, sprinkle with salt, mix well and let sit about an hour in a colander. Rinse well with water and squeeze dry in a tea towel.

Meanwhile peel, seed and chop the tomatoes. Place capers in a strainer, rinse with water and dry with paper towels. Mix eggplant, onion, tomatoes, pinenuts and seasonings. Dress with tahini sauce. Cover and refrigerate at least one hour before serving. Serve with wholegrain bread, pita chips (page 489), or triangle croutons (page 491).

FINGER FOOD BUFFET

Eggplant Relish with Pita Bread

Salmon Egg Toasts

Assorted Canapes

Mushroom Crustades

Stuffed Belgian Endive

Stuffed Grape Leaves

Herbed Cheese Spread with Homemade Crackers

Red Pepper Quiche Squares

Chicken Brochettes

Hummus with Vegetable Sticks

Carob Dipped Strawberries

Punch

MUSHROOM CRUSTADES

Makes 3-4 dozen

1/2 recipe yoghurt dough (page 459)
butter and extra virgin olive oil
1/2 cup shallots, minced
1 pound mushrooms, washed, well dried and finely chopped
juice of 1/2 lemon
2 eggs, separated
1 cup piima cream or creme fraiche
sea salt and freshly ground pepper
freshly ground nutmeg

Roll out dough thinly and cut into rounds big enough to line miniature muffin tins. Oil muffin pans well and line muffin molds with dough rounds, removing excess. Bake at 350 about 30 minutes or until dough becomes slightly crusty.

Meanwhile, saute the shallots and mushrooms in butter and olive oil in a large skillet over a medium high flame. Add lemon juice and let pan juices evaporate. Process in food processor until smooth. Mix with beaten egg yolks, cream and seasonings. Beat egg whites with a pinch of salt until stiff and fold into mushroom mixture. Place a spoonful in each pastry cup and bake another 15 minutes at 350 degrees. These may be frozen and reheated.

I can't resist telling you . . . Senator George McGovern. McGovern is simply a trollop for the vegetable oil industry. In July, 1971, he announced that he would hold hearings on the "relation of diet to heart disease" and it was stated that he would only listen to the testimony of those who had already declared themselves on the side of vegetable oils. Other opinions were not welcome or asked for. William Campbell Douglass MD *Eat Your Cholesterol*

Because of the relentless propaganda of the cholesterol-fat school of nutrition and the unceasing efforts of the ersatz milk manufacturers, consumption of unadulterated milk, that is raw milk, is practically non-existent except in Georgia and California. Consumption of pasteurized, homogenized milk is also declining because of the cholesterol propaganda. While we do not lament the decline in pasteurized, homogenized milk consumption, it is a nutritional disaster that fresh raw milk is being thrown out along with the bad milk, and "filled milk" is gaining in popularity. It is guilt by association. Not enough people understand the problem. So milk substitutes have taken 30% of the dairy market. William Campbell Douglass MD *The Milk of Human Kindness*

CREAM CHEESE PASTRIES

Makes about 24

1/2 recipe yoghurt dough
1 cup homemade cream cheese (page 80)
1/2 cup melted butter
1 large or 2 small eggs
sea salt and freshly ground pepper
1 egg, lightly beaten

Roll out dough and cut into rounds big enough to line miniature muffin tins. Oil pan well and line muffin molds with dough rounds, removing excess. Mix cream cheese with eggs, melted butter and seasonings. Place a spoonful in each pastry shell. Bake at 350 degrees for 15 minutes. Brush tops with beaten egg and bake another 10 minutes.

Variation: Poi Pastries

Use *1 cup fermented taro (page 94)* in place of cream cheese.

CHICKEN BROCHETTES

Serves 6

6 skinless chicken breasts
1 teaspoon ground cardamom
1/2 teaspoon sea salt
1/2 teaspoon pepper
2 cloves garlic, peeled and mashed
1/4 teaspoon cayenne pepper
1/2 cup fresh lemon or lime juice
4 tablespoons clarified butter
2 cups peanut sauce (page 133)

Cut chicken into walnut sized pieces. Make a mixture of the spices and lime or lemon juice, mix with chicken pieces and marinate in refrigerator several hours or overnight. Pat pieces dry with paper towels. Skewer the meat and brush with butter. Grill under broiler for about 5 minutes per side or until cooked through. Arrange on a platter with peanut sauce in a bowl.

It is tempting to wonder . . . what role sugar played in the decline of the Arab Empire. . . the heirs of the Prophet are probably the first conquerors in history to have produced enough sugar to furnish both courts and troops with candy and sugared drinks. An early European observer credits the widespread use of sugar by Arab desert fighters as the reason for their loss of cutting edge. . . "The Turks and Moors cut off one piece [of sugar] after another and so chew and eat them openly everywhere in the street without shame". . . After the rise of Islam, sugar became potent political stuff. . . The same fate that had crippled Arab conquerors was now to afflict their Christian adversaries. En route to wrest the Holy Places from the grip of the Sultan, the Crusaders soon acquired a taste for the sauce of the Saracens. . . [An] early diplomatic position paper outlines a southern sugar strategy for bringing the wily Saracens to heel. "In the land of the Sultan, sugar grows in great quantities and from it the Sultans draw large incomes and taxes. If the Christians could seize these lands, great injury would be inflicted on the Sultan and at the same time Christendom would be wholly supplied from Cyprus. . . As regards Christendom, no harm would follow." . . . What followed was seven centuries in which the seven deadly sins flourished across the seven seas, leaving a trail of slavery, genocide and organized crime. British historian Noel Deerr says flatly: "It will be no exaggeration to put the tale and toll of the slave trade at 20 million Africans, of which two-thirds are to be charged against sugar."
William Dufty *Sugar Blues*

CANAPES

In many of the [South American] primitive tribes living by the sea we found emphasis on the value of fish eggs and on some animal forms for insuring a high physical development of growing children, particularly of girls, and a high perfection of offspring through a reinforcement of the mother's nutrition. It is also important to note that in several of the primitive tribes studied there has been a consciousness that not only the mothers should have special nutrition, but also the father. In this group very great value was placed upon a product obtained from a sea form know locally as the angelote or angel fish, which in classification is between a skate and a shark. . . [The eggs of the shark] are used as food by all, but the special food product for men is a pair of glands obtained from the male. These glands weigh up to a pound each, when they are dried. They have a recognized value among the natives for treating cases of tuberculosis, especially for controlling lung hemorrhages. The sea foods were used in conjunction with the land plants and fruits raised by means of irrigation in the river valleys. Together these foods provided adequate nutrition for maintaining high physical excellence. Weston Price DDS *Nutrition and Physical Degeneration*

Use thinly sliced sour dough bread (page 464), cut into rounds with a cookie cutter and spread with butter, homemade mayonnaise or cream cheese flax spread (page 149); or thinly sliced round croutons (page 491). Top with any of the following combinations. Chill well before serving.

Pickled salmon (page 221) with thinly sliced onion rings (use pearl onions) and 2-3 small capers, drained, rinsed and dried with paper towels, on cream cheese flax spread (page 149)
Salmon eggs with sprinkles of fresh dill on butter
Pickled mackerel or herring with sprigs of dill on mayonnaise
Thinly sliced rare beef with a few gratings of fermented daikon radish (page 91), dollop of horseradish or sprinkle of chives on round croutons
Thinly sliced red radish on thickly spread butter
Natural peanut butter with sprinkling of finely chopped duck cracklings (page 273), finely chopped crispy peanuts or dried sweetened coconut meat (page 144)
Chicken liver pate (page 192) on butter with small parsley leaf or sliver of pickled red pepper (page 92)
Black caviar with finely chopped onion on cream cheese flax spread (page 149) or fermented taro (page 94)
Tomato, peeled, seeded and finely diced mixed with squeeze of lemon juice and finely chopped basil on round croutons
Herbed cream cheese spread (page 149)
Salmon spread (page 148)
Finely diced cooked chicken mixed with finely chopped cashews, green onions and Oriental dressing (page 124)
Crabmeat mixed with homemade mayonnaise

There is more simplicity in the man who eats caviar on impulse than in the man who eats grapenuts on principle. G.K Chesterton

CHICKEN LIVER PATE

Serves 12-18

3 tablespoons butter
1 pound chicken or duck livers, or combination
1/2 pound mushrooms, washed, dried
and coarsely chopped
1 bunch green onions, chopped
2/3 cup dry white wine or vermouth
1 clove garlic, mashed
1/2 teaspoon dry mustard
dash dill weed
dash rosemary
1 tablespoon lemon juice
1/2 stick butter, softened
sea salt

Melt butter in a heavy skillet. Add livers, onions and mushrooms and cook, stirring occasionally, for about 10 minutes until livers are browned. Add wine, garlic, mustard and herbs. Bring to a boil and cook, uncovered, until liquid is gone. Allow to cool. Process in food processor with softened butter. Add sea salt to taste. Place in a crock or mold and chill 8 hours. Serve with wholegrain bread or triangle croutons (page 491).

While glucose [from refined sugar] is being absorbed into the blood, we feel "up." A quick pick-up. However, this surge of mortgaged energy is succeeded by the downs, when the bottom drops out of the blood glucose level. We are listless, tired; it requires effort to move or even think until the blood glucose level is brought up again. Our poor brain is vulnerable to suspicion, hallucinations. We can be irritable, all nerves, jumpy. The severity of the crisis on top of crisis depends on the glucose overload. If we continue taking sugar, a new double crisis is always beginning before the old one ends. The accumulative crisis at the end of the day can be a lulu. After years of such days, the end result is damaged adrenals. They are worn out not from overwork but from continued whiplash. Overall production of hormones is low, amounts don't dovetail. This disturbed function, out of balance, is reflected all around the endocrine circuit. The brain may soon have trouble telling the unreal from the real; we're likely to go off half cocked. When stress comes our way, we go to pieces because we no longer have a healthy endocrine system to cope with it. Day-to-day efficiency lags, we're always tired, never seem to get anything done. We've really got the sugar blues.

The late endocrinologist John W. Tintera was quite emphatic: "It is quite possible to improve your disposition, increase your efficiency, and change your personality for the better. The way to do it is to avoid cane and beet sugar in all forms and guises."
William Dufty *Sugar Blues*

GUACAMOLE

Makes 1 1/2 cups

2 ripe avocados
juice of 1 lemon
2 tablespoons cilantro, finely chopped (optional)
pinch sea salt

Peel avocados. Place flesh in a bowl and squeeze lemon juice over. Use a fork to mash—do not use a food processor. Guacamole should be slightly lumpy. Stir in the cilantro. Guacamole should be made just before serving as it will turn dark in an hour or two. Serve with vegetable sticks or baked tortillas (page 490), broken into chips.

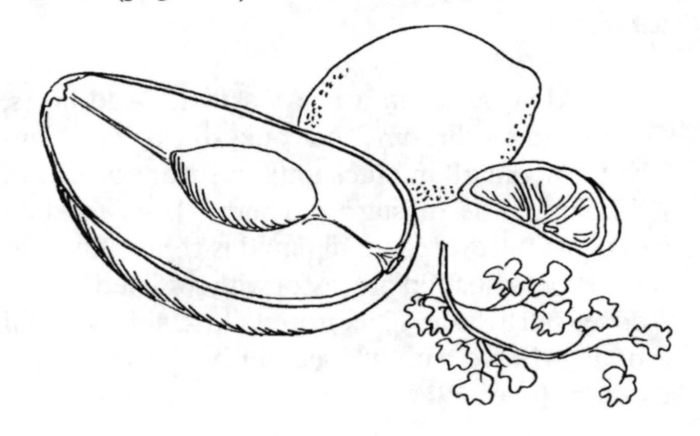

Shoppers err in refusing to buy avocados because of high fat content. Avocados contain from 5 to 22 percent fat, mostly mono-unsaturated oleic acid, in a form that is absolutely fresh, with its full complement of lipase and vitamin E. Oleic acid has been shown to reduce cholesterol, so go ahead, buy those avocados.

Avocados also contain carotenoids, B-complex and C vitamins and numerous minerals such as potassium, magnesium, iron, calcium and phosphorus.

The name avocado comes from an Aztec word meaning "testicle tree" because the rounded fruits grow in pairs. There are many varieties. The best from the point of view of flavor and ripening characteristics are the dark-skinned Haas avocados. They should be stored at room temperature (no colder than 55 degrees) until they turn soft. They can then be stored in the refrigerator for a week or so.

To prepare, cut in half, remove seed with the point of a knife, peel and slice. Immediately dribble on lemon or lime juice to prevent discoloration. SWF

CREAMY AVOCADO DIP

Makes 1 1/2 cups

1 ripe avocado, peeled and cut into pieces
3 anchovy filets
1/2 cup piima cream or creme fraiche
juice of 1 lemon
2 teaspoons unrefined flax seed oil
1 clove garlic, mashed

Place all ingredients in food processor and blend until smooth. Chill well before serving. Serve with vegetable sticks or baked tortillas (page 490), broken into chips.

CUCUMBER YOGHURT DIP

Makes 2 cups

1 large cucumber, peeled, seeded and finely chopped
sea salt
1 cup plain yoghurt
2 cloves garlic, crushed
1 tablespoon fresh mint, finely chopped
1 tablespoon fresh parsley, finely chopped
1 tablespoon lemon juice
freshly ground black pepper
pinch cayenne

Salt chopped cucumber and let stand in a colander about 1 hour. Mix other ingredients and stir in cucumber.

Know Your Ingredients

Name This Product #9

Skim Milk, partially hydrogenated soybean oil, onion, cellulose gel, citric acid, salt, sugar, mono- and diglycerides, hydrolyzed vegetable protein, romano cheese sodium hexametaphosphate, monosodium glutamate, cellulose gum, xanthan gum, natural and artificial flavoring, garlic, celery.

See Appendix B for Answer

EGGPLANT DIP

(Baba Ganouj)

Makes about 2 cups

3 large eggplants
2 cloves garlic, mashed
sea salt to taste
juice of 4-5 lemons
1 cup tahini
2 tablespoons extra virgin olive oil
cayenne pepper

Puncture the eggplants in a few spots and bake in a 375 degree oven for about one hour or until skin is wrinkled and eggplant is tender. Let cool. Peel and chop into a fine dice, sprinkle with salt, mix well and let sit about an hour in a colander. Rinse well with water and squeeze out juices with a tea towel. Puree in blender with remaining ingredients. Place in a bowl and decorate with a sprinkle of cayenne pepper. Serve with pita bread or pita chips (page 489).

Western medicine and science has only just begun to sound alarm signals over the fantastic increase in its per capita sugar consumption, in the United States especially. Their researches and warnings are, I fear, many decades too late. . . I am confident that Western medicine will one day admit what has been known in the Orient for years: Sugar is without question the number one murderer in the history of humanity—much more lethal than opium or radioactive fallout—especially to those people who eat rice as their principal food. Sugar is the greatest evil that modern industrial civilization has visited upon countries of the Far East and Africa. . . foolish people who give or sell candy to babies will one day discover, to their horror, that they have much to answer for. Sakurazawa Nyoiti *We are all Sanpaku*

Unpasteurized milk products and butter were used for thousands of years, with a history of conferring good health on their users. Since the time of Hippocrates, physicians used raw milk and raw butter as therapeutic agents to treat disease. Whole nations formerly depended upon diary products as major sources of food. But when pasteurization was introduced, dairy products strangely and precipitously lost their health charms, almost as if somebody waved an evil wand and presto, dairy products were instantly cursed. For example, in the days before milk and butter lost their lipase due to the heat of pasteurization, millions of people lived on dairy products without getting atherosclerosis (clogged arteries due to cholesterol deposits) because lipase knows how to handle cholesterol. Edward Howell MD *Enzyme Nutrition*

I used to spend my school vacation on a farm where the animals received no food except that which they could find in the pasture and woods. These were not heavy milk producers with enormous udders. The cows were never ill; the need for a veterinarian was negligible. Contrast this with championship milkers with their large udders which are usually afflicted with mastitis and its associated discharge of pus. This unsavory condition usually requires almost continuous use of penicillin to keep the milk flowing. These champions are fed objectionable concentrates and other materials at odds with enzyme nutrition. What will you have, less good milk, or an abundance of milk incriminated as a cause of heart and artery disease? Edward Howell MD *Enzyme Nutrition*

ROQUEFORT DIP

Makes 2 cups

1 cup crumbled Roquefort cheese
1/2 cup heavy cream
1/2 cup piima cream or creme fraiche
1 tablespoon unrefined flax seed oil
1 teaspoon worcestershire sauce
freshly ground pepper

Mix all ingredients together. Serve with raw sugar snap peas or vegetable sticks. Delicious!

CHEESE DIP

Makes 2 cups

1/4 pound raw cheddar, grated
3 ounces Roquefort cheese, crumbled
1 1/2 cup piima cream or creme fraiche
1 tablespoon unrefined flax seed oil
2 tablespoons chives, chopped
2 tablespoons parsley, finely chopped
1 teaspoon soy sauce
freshly ground pepper

Mix all ingredients together. Serve with raw vegetable sticks or sugar snap peas.

HUMMUS

Makes 2 cups

2 cups cooked chick peas (page 477)
3 cloves garlic, mashed
1/4 cup tahini
1 tablespoon unrefined flax seed oil
1/2 cup fresh lemon juice
cayenne pepper

Using a slotted spoon, place cooked chick peas in food processor. Add remaining ingredients and process until smooth. The hummus should be creamy and not too thick. Add some of the cooking liquid if it needs thinning. Serve with vegetable sticks and pita chips (page 489).

VEGETABLE SALADS

When we lament the problems of the modern machine age, we sometimes loose sight of the many benefits industrialization confers. One of those blessings is the availability of a variety of fresh vegetables at all seasons of the year. Take advantage of this wonderful state of affairs—as unique in the history of mankind as the ubiquitous availability of junk food.

The key to a good salad is vegetables at the peak of freshness, cut up into small pieces, then dressed with a high enzyme dressing composed of raw ingredients—high quality oils, vinegar, lemon juice, whey, avocado, and raw or cultured cream. Chopping or grating vegetables is the first step in the process of thorough digestion, leaving less for the teeth and digestive juices to do, and allowing more surface area of the vegetables to be coated with healthful dressing.

We encourage you to mix vegetables of several colors in your salads. Different colors in vegetables denote the presence of vitamins and minerals in different proportions. A salad that mixes green, white, orange, red and maroon colored vegetables ensures a full complement of nutrients.

Most vegetables in the salads we present here are raw, but we do include lightly blanched or steamed vegetables occasionally. Light cooking actually makes the nutrients in some vegetables such as asparagus and French beans, more available. And raw vegetables are not for everybody, especially those with delicate intestinal tracts. If salads give you problems, turn to soups as a way to consume a variety of fresh vegetables.

For those who tolerate cheese, we submit that the combination of raw cheese with salad dressing containing flax seed oil is a synergistic one. According to Dr. Johanna Budwig, the sulphur-containing proteins in cheese combined with the omega-3 fatty acids in flax seed oil result in a powerful tool for a host of metabolic processes. Many imported cheeses such as Roquefort and Parmesan are made from raw milk. We especially recommend Roquefort cheese, made of sheeps milk, for its high lauric acid content.

Your salad should be a delight to the eye as well as to the tastebuds. Take care to make an attractive presentation and use your imagination to create beautiful arrangements on the plate. Don't hesitate to use large plates for your salad course—the way the Europeans do—for a more elegant display. With the right presentation and the right ingredients, even inveterate salad haters will tuck in to your offerings of raw vegetables.

ITALIAN SALAD

Serves 6

1 head romaine
1 bunch watercress
1 red pepper, seeded and cut into a julienne
1 cucumber, peeled, seeded, quartered lengthwise and finely sliced
1 heart of celery with leaves, finely chopped
1 small red onion, finely sliced
1/2 cup small seed sprouts (page 106)
2 carrots, peeled and grated
1 cup red cabbage, finely shredded
1 cup cooked chick peas (page 477)
3/4 cup basic or garlic dressing (pages 118 & 119)

This is a good, basic salad. Children love it. The secret is to cut everything up small. Remove the outer leaves of the romaine, slice off the end and open up to rinse out any dirt or impurities, while keeping the head intact. Pat dry. Slice across at 1/2 inch intervals. Place romaine in your salad bowl, then the water cress, then add chopped vegetables in different piles. Finally strew the sprouts and garbanzo beans over the top for an attractive presentation. Bring to the table to show off your creation before tossing with dressing. May be served with grated Parmesan cheese.

Variation: Mexican Salad

Use *Mexican dressing* (page 121) rather than basic or garlic dressing. Omit chick peas. Top with a *sprinkle of pepitas (page 485)*, or *thin strips of sprouted wheat tortillas, sauted in olive oil until crisp.*

Chinese who eat about three ounces a day of garlic, onions, scallions, and leeks are only 40 percent as likely to develop stomach cancer as those who eat only an ounce of the allium vegetables daily. That's what a group of National Cancer Institute and Chinese scientists found in Shandong Province, a region of China known for its high stomach cancer rates. The researchers believe that regularly eating small mounts of the garlic and onion since childhood accounts for the protection. A medium onion or one half cup of raw chopped onions weighs about three ounces. Jean Carper *The Food Pharmacy Guide to Good Eating*

Some researchers believe a higher level of raw food in our diet is very advantageous. In one study, Douglass asked a group of persons with high blood pressure to add as much raw food to their diet as they conveniently could. After six and one half months, raw food was providing approximately 62% of their daily caloric intake. He reported a statistically significant reduction in both high blood pressure and weight in those consuming much of their food raw. Eighty percent of those persons on the raw food diet also gave up smoking and alcohol spontaneously. Douglass cautioned against trying to consume an exclusively raw food diet, because fruitarians have died from various disease conditions including destruction of the heart muscle, and total body edema. Chris Mudd *Cholesterol and Your Health*

CAESAR SALAD

Serves 6

2 large heads romaine lettuce
1 ounce good quality Parmesan cheese
1/2 cup salad croutons (page 491)
3/4 cup garlic, anchovy or Caesar dressing (pages 119 & 122)

The secret of this recipe is the quality of Parmesan cheese. Reggiano is best; Gran Padrino is also very good. For a much better taste than store-bought powdered Parmesan, buy it in block and grate it fresh when needed.

Remove outer leaves of the lettuce, slice off the end and open up to rinse out any dirt or impurities, while keeping the head intact. Pat dry and slice across at 1 inch intervals. Grate cheese using large holed side of the grater. Toss romaine and cheese with dressing of your choice. Add the croutons after tossing with the dressing—otherwise they absorb too much oil.

Lettuce comes from the plant family that includes daisies and thistles. Romaine lettuce or *Cos* is derived from the word Roman. One of the most popular of numerous varieties of lettuce, it has been grown for thousands of years and was popular during Roman times—so the designation "Caesar salad" for a salad composed of Romaine lettuce is apt. American per capita consumption of lettuce of all types doubled from the 1940's to the 1970's.

Unfortunately, the most popular variety of lettuce—iceberg—is not one that we can recommend. Iceberg lettuce accumulates cadmium, a toxic metal, and rates poorly in nutrient content. But other lettuces provide carotene, B-complex vitamins and potassium, phosphorus and calcium. Oriental medicine uses romaine lettuce in the treatment of alcoholism. SWF

SALADE D'AUVERGNE

Serves 4

1 large head romaine lettuce
1 ounce freshly grated Parmesan cheese
1/2 cup salad croutons (page 491)
1/4 cup warmed crumpled duck cracklings (page 273)
1 cup creamy dressing (page 120)

This is the traditional salad of the Auvergne region of France. It resembles a Caesar salad—and, in fact, it almost certainly is the precursor of the Caesar salad—differing in only the type of dressing used. Prepare as the Caesar salad in the preceding recipe.

Dr. V. G. Heiser in a recent talk to the National Association of Manufacturers told of experiments on 4,000 rats in which half were fed on a natural diet and the other half received the kind of food the average family uses. At the end of two years, the first group was essentially free from disease while the group partaking of human diet, was afflicted with a number of diseases including gout, gastric ulcer, arthritis and tuberculosis. Edward Howell MD *Enzymes for Health and Longevity*

ANY LETTUCE SALAD

Serves 4

1 large head or 2 small heads of any lettuce such as Boston, red, curly, etc., preferably organic
1/2 cup walnut dressing (page 119)
2 tablespoons freshly shelled walnuts, finely chopped
2 tablespoons freshly grated Parmesan cheese

Wash and dry lettuce. (See Kitchen Tips and Hints. page 65.) Toss with dressing and divide between four plates. Sprinkle on walnuts and cheese.

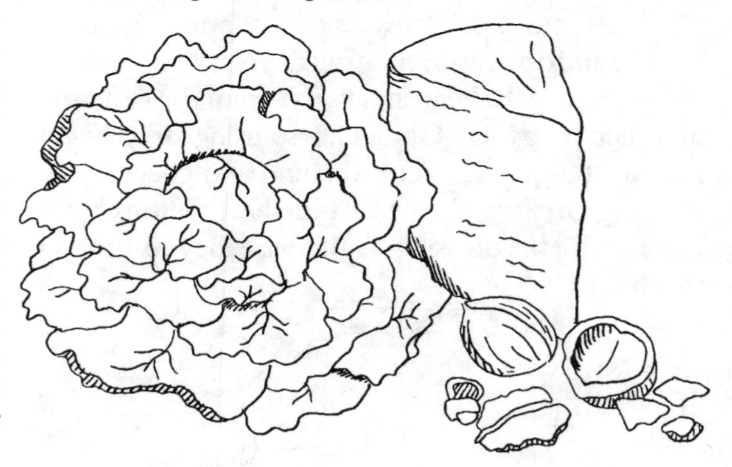

Many thousands of words have been written about the value of raw versus cooked vegetables in the diet. The simplest rules to remember are that man and herbivorous animals must cook their vegetables in order to break down the cellulose (wood) box in which the vegetable cell is stored. Man uses heat; herbivorous animals use fermentation, for which they have separate stomachs. But to man, raw vegetables are also of great value, mainly for bulk and roughage as well as to keep the intestinal content from becoming too dry. The human intestinal tract is so constructed that roughage is needed for rapid elimination of waste products and, equally important, for keeping the muscles strong. It must be remembered, of course, that when the intestinal lining is catarrhal or inflamed, rough textured food often irritates or may even cause bleeding; hence, great discretion must be used with raw vegetables and fruits. Henry Bieler MD *Food is Your Best Medicine*

BABY SPINACH SALAD

Serves 4

6 cups baby spinach leaves
1 medium red onion
1 teaspoon grated orange peel
3/4 cup basic dressing (page 118)
1/2 cup salad croutons (page 491)
freshly grated Parmesan cheese

Spinach leaves should be very small and fresh. Remove stems, wash and shake or pat dry. Slice onion very thinly. Mix orange peel with dressing. Toss spinach and onions with dressing. Add the croutons last, otherwise they will absorb too much oil. Divide salad between 4 plates and garnish with Parmesan cheese.

A team of researchers at Emory University School of Medicine is exploring the disease-fighting potential of glutathione, another antioxidant concentrated in green leafy vegetables namely broccoli, parsley and spinach. In laboratory tests glutathione can inactivate at least thirty cancer-causing agents that may damage cells, according to Dr. Dean P. Jones, associate professor of biochemistry at Emory. Jean Carper *The Food Pharmacy Guide to Good Eating*

WATERCRESS SALAD

Serves 4

2 bunches watercress
2 heads Belgium endive
1 head radicchio or 1/4 head red cabbage
1 small red onion
2 tablespoons toasted pine nuts
3/4 cup balsamic dressing (page 118)

Cut leaves off watercress, rinse and shake or pat dry. Remove outer leaves of endive and slice at 1/4 inch intervals. Finely shred the radicchio or red cabbage. Slice onion very thinly and cut slices into quarters. Mix all ingredients with dressing and divide between 4 plates.

One of the most delicious of the dark green leafy vegetables, with a peppery, mustard-like flavor, watercress grows in shallow streams of clear running water. Watercress is rich in essential fatty acids, chlorophyll, carotenoids and many beneficial minerals including iron, sulphur, calcium, iodine and vanadium. Folk medicine values watercress for a variety of ailments including anemia, poor circulation, edema and inflammation. Iodine and vanadium in watercress aid in the formation of red blood corpuscles. Watercress is 20 times richer in vanadium than mother's milk. Raw watercress juice is said to have the property of removing the brown coating which tobacco smoke leaves on the lungs. SWF

MESCLUN SALAD

Serves 4

6 cups mesclun greens
3/4 cup balsamic or walnut dressing (pages 118 & 119)
1 tablespoon pinenuts
Roquefort cheese (optional)
8 round croutons (page 491), optional

Mesclun is a mixture of tender baby lettuces and herbs. It is becoming available in many gourmet and health food stores across the country and it is almost always organic. Mesclun salad can be served at the beginning of the meal, as a side dish to fish or meat, or as a gourmet salad course, with cheese and croutons, coming after the main course and before dessert.

If salad is not pre-washed, rinse and shake or pat dry. Mix with pinenuts and dressing and divide between 4 large plates. Garnish each plate with slice of Roquefort cheese and two croutons.

Oils in the green parts of plants are EFA-rich. More than half. . . of the fatty acids of dark green leaves are the essential, triply-unsaturated w3, alpha-linolenic acid (LNA, 18:3w3) which is especially concentrated in the membranes of green, chlorophyll-containing, photosynthesizing organelles (chloroplasts). Here, LNA takes part in processes by which plants capture sunlight energy and store that energy in the bonds of the molecules they make—sugars, starches, proteins and fats. Udo Erasmus *Fats that Heal, Fats that Kill*

MACHE SALAD

Serves 4

Mache, or lamb's lettuce, is the queen of salad greens. Every vegetable merchant in France carries mache, but it is hard to find in America. If you live in a big city, you can buy mache from a wholesaler or restaurant supply merchant. A few specialty markets are now carrying mache in smaller containers. It comes in a box, with tender green leaves still attached to their dirt plugs so they stay fresh for up to two weeks. Like all dark green vegetables, mache is rich in carotenoids, essential fatty acids and minerals. SWF

3-4 cups mache leaves
2 heads Belgium endive
1 medium head radicchio
1 tablespoon pinenuts
3/4 cup balsamic dressing (page 118)

Cut mache leaves off stems. Remove outer leaves of endive and cut at 1/4 inch intervals. Shred the radicchio very finely. Mix mache, endive, radicchio and pinenuts with dressing. Divide between 4 plates. If you are serving this as a salad course between the main dish and dessert, you may wish to garnish the plates with a slice of Roquefort cheese and round croutons.

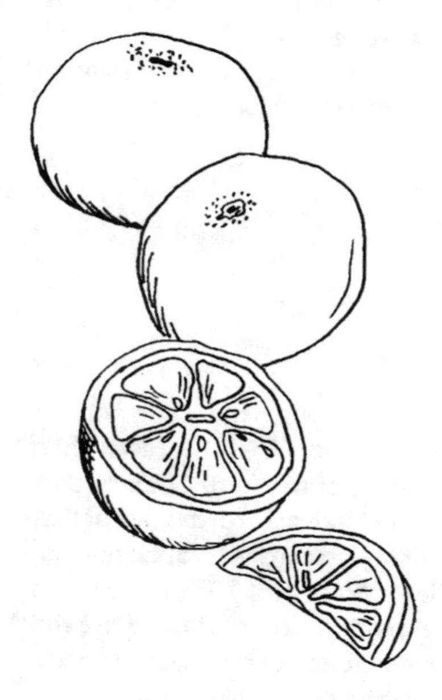

RADICCHIO AND ORANGE SALAD

Serves 4

Europeans have used radicchio for years, but this fine vegetable is only now making its way into American cuisine. A member of the chicory family, it is a good source of vitamin C and carotene; it is also high in calcium. The vegetable is now available year round. Select heads that are firm and fresh looking. Radicchio will keep for up to seven days in the refrigerator. SWF

3 large heads radicchio
2 oranges
2 red onions
extra virgin olive oil
3/4 cup orange dressing (page 123)

Cut onions into thin slices, brush both sides with olive oil, and bake at 300 degrees for several hours until dried out and browned. Meanwhile shred the radicchio thinly. Peel oranges and cut slices out from between membranes. Mix radicchio with dressing and divide between 4 plates. Top with orange wedges and grilled onion slices. Serve at once.

ENDIVE SALAD

Serves 4

6-8 large heads Belgium endive
l bunch cilantro, chopped
l bunch green onions, finely chopped
1/2 head radicchio (optional)
2 tablespoons finely chopped parsley
1 tablespoon pinenuts
3/4 cup balsamic dressing (page 118)
crumbled Roquefort cheese

Remove outer leaves of endive and discard. Remove several leaves from each head and arrange around the outside of the plates, tapered ends pointing outward. Slice remaining endive at 1/4 inch intervals. Shred radicchio finely. Mix vegetables and pinenuts with dressing and mound in the center of the endive leaves. Garnish with cheese. Serve immediately.

Variation: Endive Salad Platter

For parties, arrange endive leaves around outside of a platter. Mound salad in middle and serve crumbled blue cheese on the side.

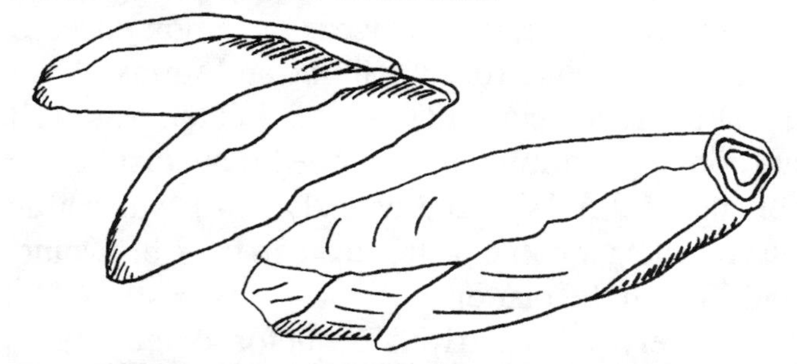

Belgium endive is also a member of the chicory family, bred to produce edible leaves, rather than edible roots. Whiteness of the leaves is achieved by etiolation—that is dirt is piled up around the plant as it grows upwards, to keep the leaves from turning green. With its distinctive crispness and wonderful bitter taste, characteristic of all members of the chicory family, Belgium endive is a versatile vegetable for the gourmet cook. SWF

TOMATO CROUTON SALAD

Serves 4

4 medium ripe tomatoes
sea salt
1 cup salad croutons (page 491)
1/4 cup basil, finely cut up
3/4 cup basic or garlic dressing (pages 118 & 119)

Peel tomatoes (See Kitchen Tips and Hints, page 65), remove seeds and chop. Toss with sea salt and let drain in a colander about 1 hour. Mix all ingredients and serve immediately.

Beta-carotene, the stuff in carrots and green leafy vegetables, can increase immune functioning. Tests show that in cell cultures beta-carotene boosted the ability of neutrophils (white blood cells) to kill bacteria and improved functioning of macrophages, immune system regulators of infection fighters such as interferon and tumor necrosis factor.

Scientists are particularly excited by animal research showing that feeding beta-carotene spurred the production of immune products that directly killed tumor cells; beta-carotene animals had tumors only one-seventh the size of those in animals not given beta-carotene. In men large doses of beta-carotene. . . increased the numbers of T helper cells that help produce antibodies. Jean Carper *The Food Pharmacy Guide to Good Eating*

TOMATO PLATTER

Serves 4-6

4 ripe tomatoes, preferably organic
2 cucumbers, peeled and thinly sliced
1 small red onion, finely sliced
1 head Belgian endive (optional)
fresh cilantro or basil
1 ripe avocado
1/2 cup black olives
6 tablespoons extra virgin olive oil
2 tablespoons raw wine vinegar
1 large lemon
freshly ground pepper
Roquefort cheese or feta cheese (optional)

Remove the outer leaves of endive, cut off end and separate into leaves. Make a fan of endive leaves at one end of a large, flat platter. Slice tomatoes very thinly and arrange around the outside edge the platter. Strew cucumbers in the center of the tomato ring. Arrange sliced onions over the tomatoes. Strew olives over salad. Dribble the olive oil over all, dribble on vinegar, then squeeze on lemon juice. If you are using cilantro, chop it fine and sprinkle over all. (Basil is best cut with scissors.) Let the platter sit at room temperature at least one hour. Just before serving, peel and slice the avocado, brush with a little oil and vinegar in the platter to keep from browning, and garnish the platter.

Serve this salad with Roquefort or feta cheese on a side plate. This is a delightful and refreshing first course during the summer months.

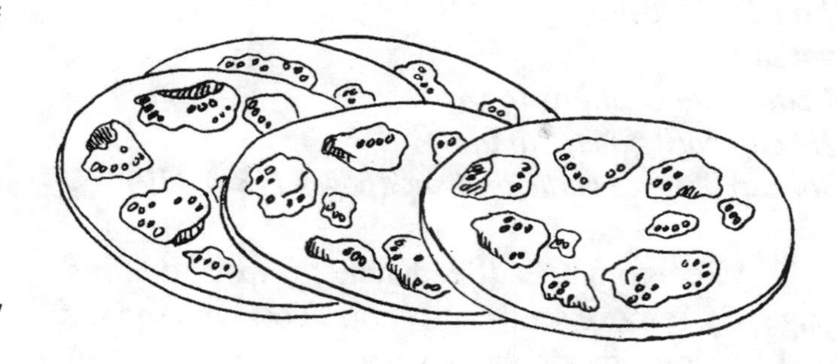

Eating tomatoes may help protect you from pancreatic cancer, a particularly virulent malignancy that kills 22,000 Americans yearly. So suggests a study at Johns Hopkins University. Investigators found that the blood of a group of such cancer victims was markedly low in levels of a vegetable compound called lycopene—a red pigment found in red vegetables and fruits, notably tomatoes and strawberries. In fact, those with the least lycopene in their bloodstreams were five times more likely to develop pancreatic cancer than those with the highest blood levels of lycopene. Jean Carper *The Food Pharmacy Guide to Good Eating*

Parenthetically speaking, cooking foods above 118 degrees Fahrenheit destroys digestive enzymes. When this happens, the pancreas, salivary glands, stomach and intestines must all come to the rescue and furnish digestive enzymes. . . to break down all these substances. To do this repeatedly, the body must rob, so to speak, enzymes from the other glands, muscles, nerves and the blood to help in its demanding digestive process. Eventually the glands—and this includes the pancreas—develop deficiencies of enzymes because they have been forced to work harder due to the low level of enzymes found in cooked food. . . . your chances, therefore, of not putting a burden on your pancreas are better if you eat as much raw food as possible. William H. Philpott MD *Victory Over Diabetes*

TOMATO AND CORN SALAD

Serves 4-6

4 ripe tomatoes
3 ears fresh corn, cut off cob
1 red onion, finely chopped
1 jalapeno pepper, seeded and chopped
1 small bunch basil leaves, snipped with scissors
3 tablespoons extra virgin olive oil
1 tablespoon balsamic vinegar
sea salt and freshly ground pepper
Romaine or Boston lettuce leaves

Peel tomatoes (See Kitchen Tips and Hints, page 65), remove seeds and chop. Combine tomato, corn, onion, pepper and basil with vinegar and olive oil. Season with salt and freshly ground pepper. Cover salad and refrigerate for several hours. Serve on large lettuce leaves.

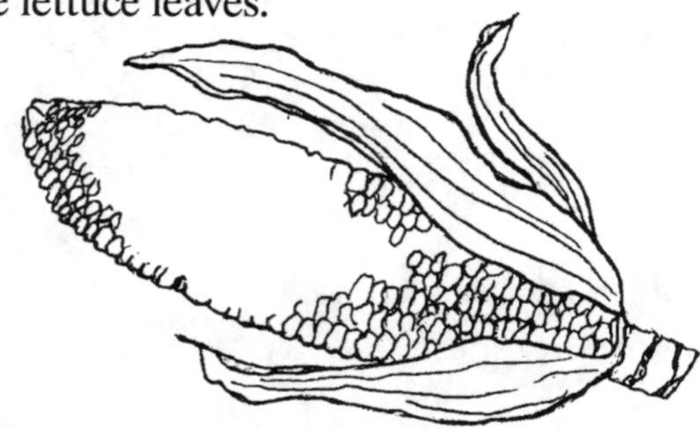

TOMATO CUCUMBER SALAD

Serves 6

3 ripe tomatoes
2 cucumbers, peeled, cut lengthwise into quarters, seeded and sliced
1 red pepper, seeded and cut into a julienne
1/2 red onion, thinly sliced
3/4 cup basic dressing or herb dressing (page 118)

Peel tomatoes (See Kitchen Tips and Hints, page 65), remove seeds and chop. Mix all ingredients. Chill well before serving.

The people of Hunza have lived in relative isolation high in the Himalaya mountains for over 2,000 years, following a way of eating and thinking that has lengthened their lives and reduced their susceptibility to the diseases of civilized man. In this tiny country many Hunzas live to be over 100 year of age, physically healthy and mentally alert. Men in their 90's play polo and volleyball and father children. These sturdy people often walk over a hundred miles a day, go barefoot in the snow or swim in icy water. The mortality rate of infants is very low and death usually comes to the very aged in their sleep with no specific cause. The whole body just finally wears out. The secret of their healthy life is found in their simple and natural diet, vigorous outdoor life and freedom from mental worry. These mountain dwellers eat little meat. They live mainly on vegetables, often eaten raw, fruits grown on their intricately terraced mountain sides, goat milk, wheat cakes (*chapattis*) and mineral rich, milky colored glacier water. They flavor their food with mint, salt, green pepper, ginger and curry. Herb tea, with salt, is enjoyed as well as grape wine. Apricots are very important in the Hunza diet. The fruit is dried and stored for winter use and the oil extracted from the pits is used in cooking and is a major source of fat in their diet. Food is scarce so everyone eats sparingly, however no one ever starves. There is no tooth decay, cancer or respiratory disease in Hunza. "Nutrition: The Appetite of Man" PPNF

[Calorie lists] in use make no distinction between raw calories and cooked calories. . . It makes good logic to remember that the vast multitudes of creation have been thriving on raw food, but not getting fat, for millions of years. Raw calories are relatively non-stimulating to glands and tend to stabilize weight. Cooked calories excite glands and tend to be fattening. I am not here referring to something like a dish of cooked spinach, which has few calories in the first place. But a slice of bread or a boiled potato stimulates glands and will put on the ounces which add up into many pounds. Let us learn something from animals. Technical men in the business of extracting the maximum profit from farm animals found it was not economical to feed hogs raw potatoes. The hogs would not get fat enough. Cooking the potatoes, however, produced the fat hogs that brought the farmer the kind of money required to make a profit. This in spite of the extra expense of labor and energy involved in cooking. Edward Howell MD *Enzyme Nutrition*

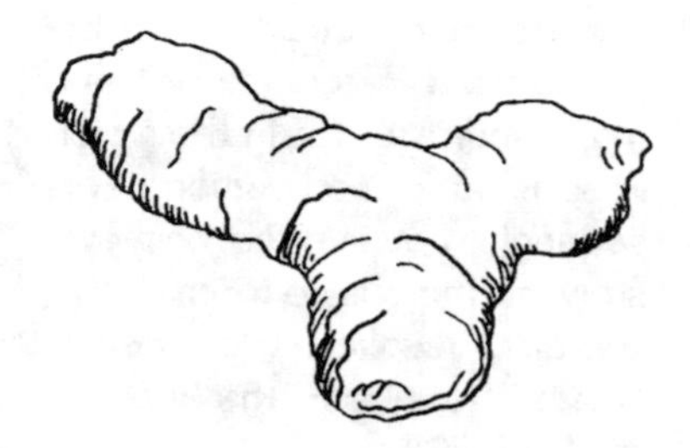

CHISMOLE

Serves 4-6

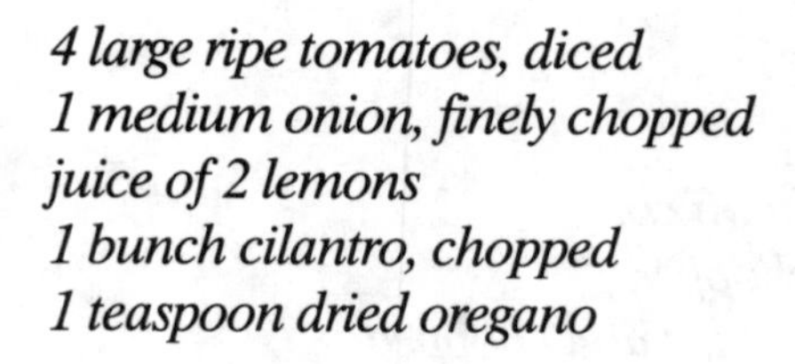

4 large ripe tomatoes, diced
1 medium onion, finely chopped
juice of 2 lemons
1 bunch cilantro, chopped
1 teaspoon dried oregano

This salad comes from Central America and is traditionally served with beans. We like to serve it with black bean tostados (page 402) or as a garnish to other South of the Border fare. But this refreshing mixture stands on its own, or goes well with such Yankee food as roast beef and potato salad.

Mix all ingredients. Cover and let stand at least one hour before serving.

INDIAN SALAD

Serves 4

3 large tomatoes
1 bunch green onions, finely chopped
1 cucumber, peeled, seeded and finely chopped
1 bunch cilantro, chopped
1 1-inch piece ginger, grated
1 jalapeno pepper, seeded and chopped
juice of 2 lemons

Peel tomatoes (See Kitchen Tips and Hints, page 65), remove seeds and chop. Mix all ingredients. Cover and refrigerate for several hours. Serve on lettuce leaves or as an accompaniment to Indian dishes.

INDIAN YOGHURT SALAD

(Raita)

Serves 6

2 cucumbers, peeled, seeded and finely chopped
sea salt
1 red or green pepper, seeded and finely chopped
1 small red onion, peeled and finely chopped
2 cups plain yoghurt
1/2 teaspoon cumin seeds

Place chopped cucumbers in a colander and mix with sea salt. Let stand for an hour or so. Pat dry and mix with other ingredients. This is traditionally served with curries and spicy food.

When the sugar in milk, lactose, is turned into lactic acid by bacterial action, it functions as a digestive antiseptic, and makes the calcium and phosphorus in milk products more available for absorption and use by the body. When the population of lactic bacteria in the intestine is increased . . . synthesis of vitamin B6 is improved, which promotes the production of niacin (vitamin B3) from the amino acid tryptophan. This nutrient enhancement supports the immune system and improves host resistance. William H. Lee PhD *The Friendly Bacteria*

SALADE VARIEE

Serves 4

4 medium carrots, peeled and grated
1 cucumber, peeled and finely sliced
1 red pepper, seeded and cut into a julienne
or 1 large tomato, peeled, seeded and chopped
1/4 head red cabbage, finely shredded
1 teaspoon finely chopped parsley
3/4 cup basic dressing (page 118)

This is a simple salad that makes an attractive presentation. The different vegetables are arranged in little piles on large plates. Children who are often picky about eating several foods mixed together like this salad because each vegetable is separate. And they like the different colors—white, orange, red and maroon and green.

Mix carrots, cucumber, pepper or tomato and red cabbage separately with a portion of dressing. Put four piles, one of each vegetable, on large plates. Sprinkle on parsley. Serve immediately.

To get the most beta-carotene from a carrot you need to break down its cellular structure. That releases more beta-carotene for absorption, says James Olson, a leading expert on carotenoids at Iowa State University. There are two ways to do it: by cooking carrots slightly or by chopping, grating, pureeing and liquefying carrots. This allows your digestive juices to come in better contact with the carrot's beta-carotene. "If you actually nibble on a raw carrot Bugs Bunny style, you absorb very little of the carotene—about 5 percent," says Olson. "Cooking it makes 25 to 30 percent of the beta-carotene available, and pureeing cooked carrots allows your body to absorb about 50 percent," he says. Jean Carper *The Food Pharmacy Guide to Good Eating*

SALAD VARIEE FOR GROWN-UPS

Serves 6

1/2 pound French beans, cut into 1-inch pieces
2 heads fennel, sliced very thin
2 red peppers, seeded and cut into a julienne
extra virgin olive oil
sea salt and freshly ground pepper
1 cup anchovy paste (page 132)

Blanch beans in boiling water for about 8 minutes or until tender. Rinse under cold water and let drain. In separate bowls toss vegetables with olive oil, salt and pepper. Chill well. Arrange a pile of beans, fennel and peppers on each plate and place a generous spoonful of anchovy paste in the center.

In 490 BC the Greeks defeated the Persians in a battle that was fought in a fennel field. Thus one of the most famous battles in history was named after a vegetable. A runner raced 26 miles to carry news of the victory to Athens. The word for fennel in Greek is *marathon*.

A member of the anise family, fennel is as common in Mediterranean markets as celery and carrots are in ours. The stalks form a kind of false bulb that has many of the properties of celery. In fact, fennel can be used in place of celery in many recipes. Fennel is a good source of carotene and is said to help in weight reduction. SWF

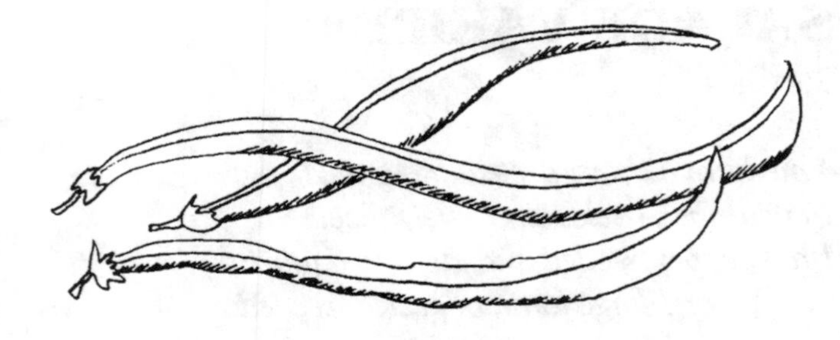

FENNEL SALAD

Serves 6

6-8 medium fennel bulbs plus leaves
3/4 cup lemon pepper dressing (page 123)
piece of good quality Parmesan cheese

Remove outer leaves of fennel and slice *very* thinly. Cut slices into quarters. Snip 1-2 tablespoons fennel leaves into a bowl. Mix with the fennel slices and dressing. Arrange on plates and top each salad with several shavings of Parmesan cheese, cut with a cheese slicer.

Some intriguing experiments were performed on normal people and diabetics . . . at George Washington University Hospital in 1929. The subjects ate almost two ounces of raw starch and then had blood tests for sugar. Eating cooked starch, as is well known, causes the blood sugar of diabetics to skyrocket, unless they use insulin. The diabetics in the study used no insulin and yet after raw starch ingestion, the blood sugar rose only 6 milligrams the first half hour. Then it decreased 9 milligrams after 1 hour, and 14 milligrams 2 1/2 hours after ingestion of the raw starch. In some diabetic individuals, the decrease in blood sugar was as much as 35 milligrams. In the normal persons, there was a slight increase followed by a slight decrease in blood sugar in 1 hour. This is convincing evidence that there is a difference between raw and cooked calories. Edward Howell MD *Enzyme Nutrition*

WINTER SALAD

Serves 6

2 fennel bulbs
1/4 head red cabbage
2 heads Belgium endive
2 large carrots
1 red pepper
1 cucumber
1 heart of celery with leaves
1 small red onion
1 bunch cilantro
1 avocado
1 tomato
1 tablespoon toasted pine nuts
3/4 cup balsamic dressing (page 118)
Roquefort cheese (optional)

The basis of this substantial salad is fennel and the secret to its success is to cut the vegetables up very small.

Remove outer leaves from fennel bulbs; slice very finely and cut slices into quarters. Thinly shred the cabbage. Remove outer leaves of endive and slice across at 1/4 inch intervals. Peel the cucumber, cut lengthwise into quarters, and slice thinly. Peel and grate the carrot. Chop the celery, onion and peppers finely. Chop the cilantro. Mix all together with the pinenuts and dressing. Arrange on plates and decorate with thin slices of avocado and tomato. May be served with crumpled roquefort cheese.

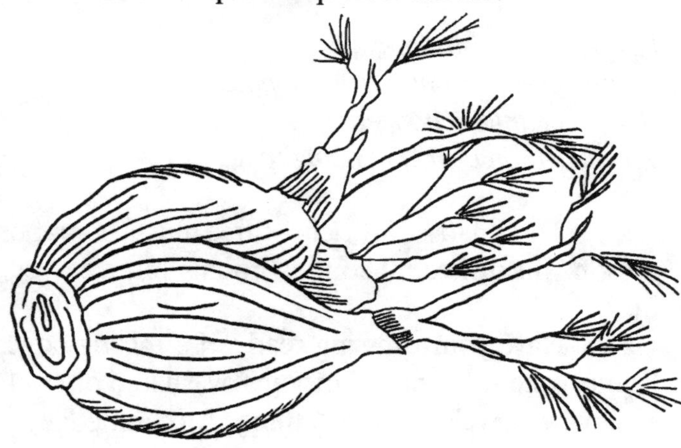

Most people do not seem to have a large variance of vitamins and minerals over the years. However, the enzyme levels drop significantly in aging; as the body gets weaker and the enzymes get fewer, old age symptoms manifest. At the world famous Michael Reese Hospital in Chicago, researchers found that old people have only one-thirtieth as much enzymes in the saliva as young folks. Also people with high enzyme diets have extensive longevity patterns. For example, people like Georgians, Equadorans, and Hunzas have diet rich in enzymes and have a high concentration of centenarians. They make extensive use of fermentation—soy, dairy, vegetables and fruits. Also, they utilize sprouting as well as soaking of seeds which increases the enzyme level up to twenty times, and raw or undercooked food. They also fast seasonally during periods of food scarcity. . . during fasting there is a halt in digestive enzyme production. The enzymes are used to digest the partially digested stored food of fatty tissue, scars, arthritis, tumor, hardening of the arteries, etc. Thus the enforced fast is another health and longevity promoting benefit. Victoras Kulvinskas *Introduction to Enzymes for Health and Longevity*

In order to evaluate the status of food enzymes in normal nutrition and metabolism, [it is important] to learn the condition of health of animals reared under aseptic condition, given sterile food with the usual sterile vitamin accessories, and allowed to drink only sterile water and breathe only sterile air. Just such an experiment has been in progress at the Laboratories of Bacteriology, University of Notre Dame, for the past 12 years, during which time more than 2,000 germ-free guinea pigs, as well as germ-free chicks, rats, mice, rabbits, cats and insects were born and reared under rigidly aseptic conditions. . . . Sterility of the intestinal tract during the lifetime of the animal is assured by frequent tests for bacteria... [the] sterile animals often grow to unusual size but very few of them are healthy. It is stated their digestive tracts are "delicate" and they apparently lack something which germs could furnish them. . . sterile animals are on the whole a little more susceptible to infectious diseases than animals raised normally, and a great many organic diseases show up in germ-free animals. Edward Howell MD *Enzymes for Health and Longevity*

SUMMER SALAD

Serves 6

3/4 cup lemon pepper dressing (page 123)
1 bunch celery, finely chopped
2 cucumbers, peeled, quartered lengthwise and finely chopped
2 bunches green onions, finely chopped
2 green peppers, seeded and finely chopped
1 bunch radishes, finely chopped
3 tomatoes
1 tablespoon finely chopped parsley or chives

This salad may be prepared several hours in advance of your meal. The secret to its success is, as always, to cut the vegetables into a fine dice.

Mix up the dressing in a large bowl. Add celery, cucumbers, green onions, peppers and radishes. Toss well with dressing, cover and refrigerate several hours.

Just before serving, slice the tomatoes thinly and cut the slices in half. Arrange the slices around the outer edge of your plates and make a mound of salad in the center of each. Sprinkle with chopped parsley or chives.

MUSHROOM SALAD

Serves 4

12 medium mushrooms
1 bunch green onions, finely chopped
1 bunch cilantro, chopped
3/4 cup lemon pepper dressing (page 123)

This salad is very rich—three mushrooms per person will suffice. The mushrooms must be very fresh.

Have your dressing ready in a mixing bowl. Remove stems from mushrooms, wash and dry well with paper towels. Slice very thinly. Mix immediately with dressing, green onions and cilantro. Divide between four plates and serve.

ASPARAGUS VINAIGRETTE

Serves 4

24 spears medium-sized asparagus
3/4 cup sun dried tomato dressing (page 119)

Wash asparagus and trim green skin off about one inch of the ends. Steam in a vegetable steamer until just tender. Let cool. Divide between four plates and spoon dressing over.

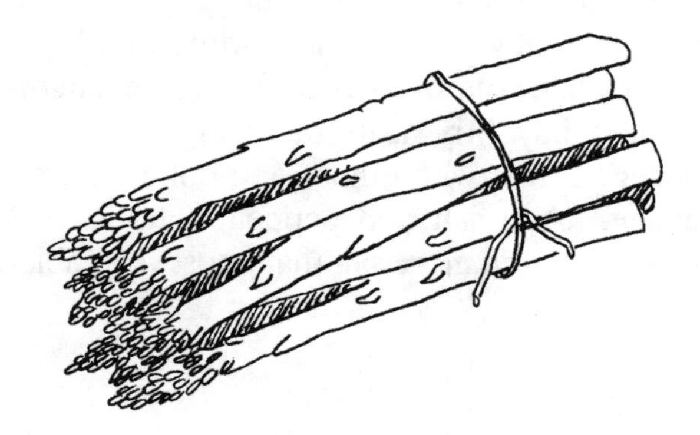

FRENCH BEAN SALAD

Serves 4

1 pound French beans
1 medium red onion, finely sliced
2 tomatoes
2 tablespoons chopped crispy pecans (page 485)
3/4 cup basic dressing

This elegant and unusual salad features tender french beans or *haricots verts*, not to be confused with string beans. Remove ends from beans. Meanwhile bring a pan of salted water to boil. Plunge beans into boiling water and cook for about 8 minutes until beans are tender. Pour into a colander and rinse immediately with cold water. Let drain and cool.

Slice tomatoes thinly and cut slices in half. Arrange the slices around the outer edge of 4 plates. Place beans in the center and strew onions on top, along with the chopped pecans. Spoon on dressing. Serve immediately.

In certain Eastern and European esoteric healing traditions, the body is characterized as cyclically passing through three distinct phases: cleansing, building and sustaining. . . Different nutritional systems enhance one particular phase more than others, sometimes in dramatic fashion. For example, a raw foods diet steers the body into a cleansing state, causing the breakdown of diseased tissues and the release of stored toxins. If you undertake a raw foods diet while the body is already in a cleansing state, or ready to move into one (for instance in the early spring when we naturally shed excess fatty tissue accumulated in the winter), the diet may have profound effects. Illness and pains may vanish, stores of energy by released, and a wonderful clarity of mind appear.

Those who have this experience correctly perceive the healing effect of the diet but often incorrectly conclude that the diet works all the time and for all bodies. . . What is more, many people who follow a year-round raw foods regimen meet with relative success because they live in hot weather or tropical locations like Hawaii, Florida, or Southern California—environments that naturally support the cleansing process. Try eating raw fruits and vegetables for twelve months in Montana and you will learn firsthand why it does not always work. David Marc *Nourishing Wisdom*

Excessive use of salt is generally held to be objectionable. It is demonstrable that various salts, including NaCl, stimulate enzyme activity in the test tube as well as the digestive flow, and it is not inconceivable that the propensity of the organism for salt on a heat-treated diet is actuated by a need for digestive enzymes. Cooked foods taste "flat" without addition of salt, and since digestive secretions do not flow properly in the absence of relish for food, it might be expected that digestion would be embarrassed. It has been shown, however, that on a raw food diet there is no need for table salt. Consequently the excretion of chlorides in the urine is very low, but the blood chlorides are higher than on a heat-treated diet containing added salt, an unexpected and surprising circumstance. As added incongruity relates to the fact that persons on salt-free raw diets have been shown to tolerate the sweating bath better than those on a heat-treated diet containing added salt. In view of this disturbing evidence, it seems reasonable to reexamine the propriety of exclusive reliance on extra NaCl intake in occupation entailing exposure to heat and to advise use of more raw foods for such workers. Edward Howell *Enzymes for Health and Longevity*

DILLED POTATO SALAD

Serves 8

16 small red potatoes
2 red onions, finely chopped
1 bunch fresh dill, snipped
raw wine vinegar
1 1/4 cups creamy mayonnaise dressing (page 121)

Wash potatoes but do not peel. Bring a large pot of water to boil. Plunge in the potatoes and cook until still slightly firm. Remove with slotted spoon.

While potatoes are still warm, cut lengthwise and slice thinly. Mix warm potatoes with a few dashes of vinegar. Mix with onions and dill and toss with dressing. Add salt and pepper to taste. (Note: Potatoes require more salt than most vegetables.)

FRENCH POTATO SALAD

Serves 8

16 small new potatoes
2 green peppers, seeded and cut into a julienne
2 red peppers, seeded and cut into a julienne
1 large red onion, chopped
raw red wine vinegar
3/4-1 1/4 cups basic dressing (page 118)

Wash potatoes but do not peel. Bring a large pot of water to the boil. Plunge in the potatoes and cook until still slightly firm. Remove with slotted spoon.

Cut potatoes into quarters lengthwise and then slice finely. Splash a bit of vinegar on the still warm potatoes. Mix with peppers and onions and toss with dressing. Add salt and pepper to taste. (Note: Potatoes require more salt than most vegetables.)

MAGGIE'S POTATO SALAD

Serves 8

8 yellow potatoes
1 small head celery, finely chopped
1 cucumber, peeled, seeded and finely chopped
1 red onion, finely chopped
1 bunch radishes, finely chopped
2 tablespoons celery seeds
1 1/4 cup creamy mayonnaise dressing (page 121)
1 tomato

In this recipe, celery seeds, rather than mustard and pickles, provide a pleasant tart taste that combines so well with starchy potatoes.

Peel potatoes and cook in boiling water until still slightly firm. (Save potato peels for potassium broth, page 566.) Cut into a 1/2 inch dice. Mix with vegetables, celery seeds and dressing. Season with salt and pepper. Garnish with tomato wedges.

CELERY ROOT SALAD

Serves 4

1 large celery root
1/4 cup lemon juice
1/2-3/4 cup creamy mayonnaise dressing (page 121)

The French enjoy this salad—called *celeriac roumelade*—with cold meats and charcuterie. It makes a nice accompaniment to cold roast beef.

Bring a pot of water to boil and add lemon juice. Meanwhile peel the celery root. With water ready, grate or julienne the celery root in your food processor and immediately plunge into boiling water. After about 10 seconds, pour into a colander and rinse with cold water. Shake or pat dry and mix with dressing. Refrigerate several hours before serving.

These facts suggest clearly that the enzymes present in raw, uncooked food relieve the pancreas and salivary glands of the necessity of enlarging from excess work. The considerable hypertrophy of the pancreas and salivary glands which has been found to occur in human races living upon large quantities of cooked carbohydrates indicates the nature of the intrepid but deplorable compensatory measure the organism is forced to adopt and is added proof of the profound influence for good of enzymes naturally supplied in raw foods.

That the pancreas and salivary glands of human beings living upon the customary heat-treated enzyme deficient diet are hypertrophied and overworked organs is not difficult to believe. Those races subsisting largely upon heat-treated carbohydrates appear to have the largest pancreatic and salivary glands. Thus, Stisen has shown that the pancreas of Malays of Java has an average weight of 105 grams, while the average weight of the American pancreas is about 20 grams less. And this in spite of the fact that Americans average some 20 or 30 pounds heavier in body weight than Javanese. Stisen observed that other organs are heavier in Occidental than in Malays, excepting the pancreas and salivary glands which alone are heavier in Malays. He attributes the large pancreas and salivary glands of Malays to a diet rich in carbohydrates. Edward Howell MD *Enzymes for Health and Longevity*

In a recent analysis parsley, along with broccoli and spinach, topped the list of 100 common foods analyzed for their content of a disease fighting compound glutathione. According to Dr. Dean Jones, associate professor of biochemistry at Emory University school of medicine, glutathione is a potent protector of bodily cells. At least thirty cancer-causing agents are deactivated when they encounter glutathione, he notes. Further, glutathione is an antioxidant. . .which means it may help throw off numerous disease processes. For example, glutathione in Dr. Jones' lab test has neutralized peroxidized fats that help clog arteries. . . To get the most glutathione, eat foods raw. From 30 to 60 percent is lost in cooking. Processed vegetables—as in canned green beans—have virtually no glutathione, says Dr. Jones. Jean Carper *The Food Pharmacy Guide to Good Eating*

Organic gardeners, in my opinion, are way ahead of pill-popping users of nutritional supplements—at least synergistically speaking. That's because eating carrots—an excellent source of beta-carotene—is probably superior to taking beta-carotene alone; eating collard greens—which contain lots of vitamin C—is probably better than taking vitamin C alone (yes, even natural vitamin C); and eating endive—a good source of vitamin E—is probably better than taking natural vitamin E in capsules. And the superiorities of which I speak are not due to non-related beneficial characteristics (like the fiber in carrots) of the

ORIENTAL CELERY ROOT SALAD

Serves 4

1 large celery root
2-3 carrots, peeled and grated
1 red pepper, seeded and cut into a julienne
1 bunch green onions, finely chopped
2 tablespoons chopped cilantro
1 cup Oriental dressing (page 124)

Peel and grate celery root and immediately mix with dressing. Stir in remaining ingredients. Chill well before serving.

TABOULI

Serves 8

1/2 cup bulgur (page 436)
3 bunches parsley
2 bunches green onions, finely chopped
3 tomatoes
1/2 cup fresh mint leaves, cup up finely with scissors (optional)
1/2 cup or more lemon juice
1/2 cup or more extra virgin olive oil

This middle eastern makes a wonderful buffet dish. Soak bulgur for about 10 minutes in warm—not hot—water. Pour into a strainer, rinse and squeeze dry with hands.

Meanwhile, wash and dry the parsley. (See Kitchen Tips and Hints, page 65) Use your food processor to chop the parsley as fine as possible. Peel tomatoes (See Kitchen Tips and Hints, page 65), remove seeds and chop. Mix all ingredients. Cover and refrigerate several hours before serving.

SPROUT SALAD

Serves 4

6 cups fresh mung bean sprouts (page 105)
1 bunch green onions, finely chopped
1 tablespoon sesame seeds, toasted in oven
1/2 cup Oriental dressing (page 124)

Steam sprouts for about 1 minute or until just tender. Let cool. Mix all ingredients. Divide between 4 plates.

whole food. Nope. I mean that eating a carrot that contains a fixed amount of the cancer-fighting nutrient beta-carotene will probably provide more cancer-fighting beta-carotene nutritional benefit than taking the same fixed amount of beta-carotene in the purest, most concentrated, most natural beta-carotene supplement you can find. Why? Synergy. Jim Duke, Ph D *Organic Gardening July/August 1995*

HIGH ENZYME SALAD

Serves 4

1 cup sprouted sunflower seeds (page 106)
4 carrots, peeled and grated
1 cucumber, peeled and finely chopped
1 red pepper, seeded and finely chopped
1 bunch green onions, finely chopped
2 ounces grated raw cheddar cheese (optional)
3/4 cup basic dressing (page 118)
1 avocado
radicchio or red lettuce leaves

This salad is a meal in itself. Mix sprouted sunflower seeds, carrots, cucumber, pepper, onions and cheese with dressing. Serve on radicchio or lettuce leaves and garnish with avocado slices.

Evidence is submitted indicating that a comprehensive test of the capacity of the animal organism to endure on an enzyme-free diet requires exclusion of exogenous enzymes gaining entrance through the agency of air borne bacteria, yeasts and fungi. The efficiency of these unicellular organisms as enzyme producers has been widely demonstrated in industrial processes. There are good grounds for believing that the enzyme-deficient animal organism reluctantly offers a culturing abode to bacteria, yeasts and fungi with the object of confiscating their enzymes. The evidence warrants a strong suspicion, that the unnatural appropriateness of enzyme-deficient organisms for exogenous enzymes may invoke bacterial activity of intractable magnitude and engender susceptibility to infections. Due consideration should be accorded these factors in accounting for the widespread incidence of bacterial diseases. Edward Howell MD *Enzymes for Health and Longevity*

CARROT SALAD

Serves 6

12 medium carrots, peeled and grated
1 cup chopped fresh pineapple, drained
1/2 cup raisins
1/2 cup chopped crispy pecans (page 485)
1 tablespoon finely chopped parsley (optional)
3/4 cup basic dressing (page 118)

Mix all ingredients together and chill well. Children love this salad.

Yogurt, one of the world's universal health foods, is more than just tangy, thickened milk. It has a venerable reputation, reaching back to biblical days, for settling the stomach and preventing and curing gastrointestinal maladies. Modern research decidedly proves that yogurt contains several natural antibiotics that can kill infection-causing bacteria, including salmonella (the cause of salmonella food poisoning) and E. coli, bacteria often responsible for traveler's diarrhea. And solid studies show that the acidophilus-type culture used to make some yogurt can help block the activation of cancer-causing agents in the human colon. . . The bacteria convert milk into yogurt by the process of fermentation. . . The organisms even continue to multiply in the warm environment of the stomach and intestines. During fermentation the bacteria create numerous chemical by-products such as lactic acid, that also fight disease. Jean Carper *The Food Pharmacy Guide to Good Eating*

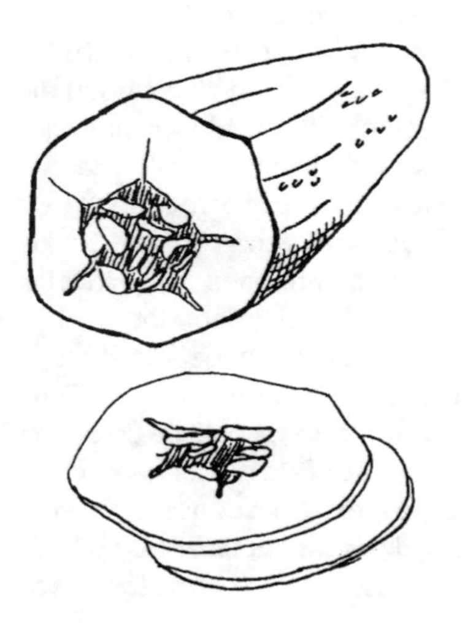

BALSAMIC CARROT SALAD

Serves 10-12

1 pound carrots, peeled and processed into a small julienne
1 heart celery, chopped very fine
2 red peppers, cut into small slices
2 bunches green onions, chopped
1 bunch cilantro, chopped
1 1/2 cups balsamic dressing (page 118)

This makes an excellent buffet salad. Mix all ingredients well.

JICAMA SALAD

Serves 4

1 large jicama (about 1 1/4 pounds)
seeds from 1 pomegranate
3/4 cup cilantro lime dressing or Mexican dressing (page 121)

Peel and grate jicama. Mix immediately with dressing. Chill well. Mix with pomegranate seeds and serve.

CUCUMBER YOGHURT SALAD

Serves 6

3 cucumbers
1 teaspoon sea salt
3/4 cup plain yoghurt
2 cloves garlic

Peel cucumbers and slice very thinly using the fine blade in your food processor. Place in a bowl and mix with salt. Cover and refrigerate for several hours.

Place cucumbers in a colander and let drain about 1/2 hour, turning occasionally. You may wish to pat or squeeze to remove remaining moisture.

Peel and crush garlic and mix with yoghurt. Add cucumbers to yoghurt mixture. Chill well. Serve with pita bread.

COLE SLAW

Serves 6

1 head cabbage, finely shredded
2 carrots, peeled and grated
1 small red onion, finely chopped
1 tablespoon celery seeds
1 cup creamy dressing (page 120)

Mix all ingredients. Chill well before serving.

ORIENTAL COLE SLAW

Serves 6

1 head oriental cabbage, finely shredded
1 bunch green onions, finely chopped
1/2 cup crispy almonds (page 487), slivered in food processor and toasted
4 ounces buckwheat or brown rice pasta, broken into 1-inch lengths, cooked and drained
1 teaspoon finely grated orange rind
1 cup Oriental dressing (page 124)

This is an excellent salad for pot luck style parties. Pat cooked noodles dry and saute in olive oil until crisp. Drain well. Mix all ingredients. May be refrigerated several hours before serving.

AVOCADO GRAPEFRUIT SALAD

Serves 4

2 ripe avocados, well chilled
2 grapefruit, well chilled
1 head Boston lettuce
2 tablespoons green onions, finely chopped
3/4 cup basic or Mexican dressing (pages 118 & 122)

Peel and slice avocados; peel grapefruit and remove sections. Arrange on Boston lettuce and pour dressing over. Serve immediately.

It is widely believed that obesity is a disease of civilization and is associated with adverse nutrition in which enzyme undernutrition is implicated. Thus it can be said that the brain becomes smaller both under the influence of civilization and obesity. The evidence creates strong suspicion that as a person puts on useless fat his brain gets smaller. It is a glorious thought that if you are overweight and take off 20 to 30 pounds through a diet containing 75 percent raw calories, you may add good weight to your brain for more brain power, and be in a better mental condition to deal with taxing business and personal problems. Edward Howell MD *Enzyme Nutrition*

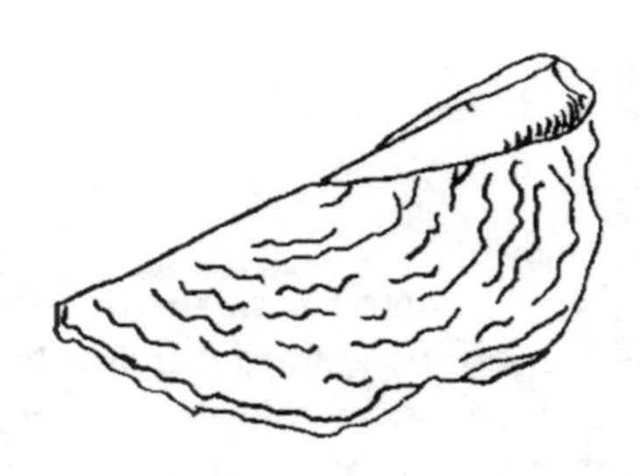

There is not a known remedy that will cure diabetes without a reformation along the lines that caused it. . . Plenty of whole grains, bran and oatmeal are very beneficial in diabetes. Raw vegetables of all kinds—red cabbage, cauliflower, watercress, Brussels sprouts, okra, cucumbers, onions, etc. A big emphasis needs to be placed on raw foods as they stimulate the pancreas and increase insulin production. Green beans and cucumber juice contain a hormone needed by the cells of the pancreas in order to produce insulin. Jerry Lee Hover ND *Health Freedom News*

BEET SALAD

Serves 4

I am frequently asked about the value of a vegetarian diet. I do not advocate it as a way of life. While one cannot live comfortably in our environment without vegetables and fruits, one cannot live entirely on them and still remain in a state of buoyant health. I do, however, advocate a vegetable diet when the patient is "over-proteinized" after eating too much meat over a long period of time. When this happens, I place him on a vegetable diet until his tissues are free of too much stored animal protein. And then I suggest a diet with not too high a percentage of flesh, eggs and dairy products. Henry Bieler MD *Food is Your Best Medicine*

6 medium beets
3 tablespoons raw apple cider vinegar or beet kvass (page 568)
4 tablespoons extra virgin olive oil
1 tablespoon orange juice
pinch salt
pinch cayenne pepper
1 teaspoon caraway seeds
pinch cloves
pinch cinnamon
1/2 teaspoon finely grated lemon peel
1/2 teaspoon finely grated orange peel
lettuce leaves for garnish

This is an adaptation of a Russian recipe. Bake beets about one hour or until tender. Peel and chop finely. Meanwhile mix together other ingredients. Mix with beets and refrigerate several hours. Serve on lettuce leaves.

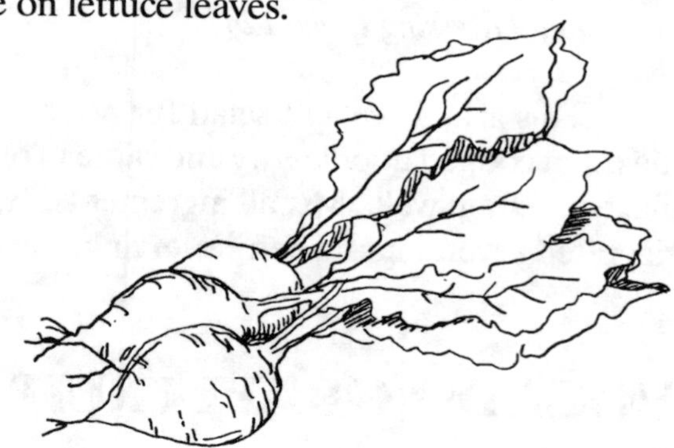

Personal observations have led many food faddists to conclude that certain food combinations are dangerous. For example, it is commonly said that starch and protein is a bad combination. What these faddists miss seeing is that starch and protein and *toxic bile* form a bad combination. As most diet books are based on personal idiosyncrasies and prejudices, the usual result is an amazing collection of good and bad combinations. Nature, in her wisdom, has never created a food which is entirely protein, starch or sugar. Even meat contains relatively large amounts of starch (as glycogen and muscle sugar). Henry Bieler MD *Food is Your Best Medicine*

ZUCCHINI SALAD

Serves 4

8 small zucchini, very fresh
1/2 cup lemon pepper dressing
2 teaspoons dried oregano
8 Boston lettuce leaves

Scrub zucchini and remove ends. Cut lengthwise into quarters and slice thinly. Mix with dressing and oregano. Refrigerate several hours. Serve on Boston lettuce leaves.

SOUPS

The preparation of soup is an undervalued, even a dying art, yet nothing is so satisfying as a bowl of homemade soup. The virtual absence of homemade soup in today's American diet is an unfortunate circumstance—soups form an integral part of every one of the world's great cuisines. For many cultures, soup is a breakfast food. The Japanese begin their day with a bowl of fish broth and rice. French children traditionally consumed leftover soup before they started off to school—the very unhealthy French breakfast of coffee and white bread was adopted on a wide scale only after the Second World War.

Our soups can be divided into two categories. Clear unblended soups featuring meat, vegetables or grains in a meat-based broth; and creamy blended soups. We have already discussed the health-promoting properties of meat broths in the diet; the addition of vegetables, legumes, grain and meat to such a broth, in which all the minerals of meat, bone and marrow are present in easily assimilable form, results in a soup that can serve as a meal in itself.

Blended soups may seem more trouble to make, but a small investment in a hand-held blender will enable you to prepare them with ease. The French, who traditionally eat blended soups with the evening meal, have made use of these nifty gadgets for decades. A hand-held blender allows you to blend your soup in its own cooking pot. The whole process takes less than a minute or two and leaves no other pans or equipment to clean up.

Most of our blended soups call for the addition of piima cream or *creme fraiche* as a final step. It is important to add the cream to your soup in the bowl, and not in the pot, for any heating the cream receives will destroy its valuable enzyme content. Most traditional soup recipes call for the addition of cultured cream in this way—to the slightly cooled soup in the bowl rather than in the pot. Here is another example of folk wisdom serving as a guide to healthy eating. Remember, if you can touch the soup with your finger and not be burned, the enzymes will survive.

Do not hesitate to add cultured cream to your soup for fear of eating too much fat. The cream not only supplies valuable enzymes, but also fat soluble vitamins in abundance. These fat soluble minerals are what your body needs to utilize the minerals in the soup. Furthermore, cultured cream imparts a smooth texture and delicious taste to soup, ensuring that it will be eaten with relish by young and old.

You may also, in the Russian tradition, add beet kvass (page 568) or cultured whey (page 80) to your soups. If your do not reheat them after doing so, they will, like fermented cream, provide valuable enzymes and lactic acid, along with an agreeable sour taste. Another excellent addition to soup is fish sauce. You can make this yourself (page 143), or buy a Thai or Vietnamese variety (called *nam pla* or *nuoc mam*). These clear brown fermented sauces, made from the whole fish including the head and organs, are rich in iodine and other substances beneficial to the thyroid gland. On heating the fishy taste disappears but the nutrients remain. You may add fish sauce to any heated soup instead of salt.

We urge you to make soups a standard of your repertoire. With a judicious choice of ingredients, they provide nourishing, easily-assimilated fare for young and old. Soup is the perfect way to get vegetables into those members of your family who normally turn up their noses at green things, or who may have trouble digesting raw salads. Lentil and bean soups, prepared with meat stocks and served with whole grain bread, make a complete meal that's quick to prepare and easy on the budget.

SPICY CHICKEN SOUP

Serves 4

1 quart chicken stock
1/4 teaspoon dried chile flakes
1/2 teaspoon freshly grated ginger
sea salt or fish sauce to taste
several green onions, very finely chopped
1 tablespoon finely chopped cilantro

This simple but flavorful soup is a good way to begin a rich meal like Thanksgiving dinner; served in a mug without the garnish, it is a powerful and comforting remedy for colds and sore throat

Bring the stock to a boil, skim any foam that rises to the top and add chile flakes and ginger. Simmer for about fifteen minutes. Season to taste. Ladle into soup bowls and garnish with onions and cilantro.

Variation: Spicy Turkey or Duck Soup

Use *turkey or duck stock.*

CHICKEN AND RICE SOUP

Serves 6

2 quarts chicken stock
1 cup brown rice
1 cup finely diced chicken meat and/or chicken liver and heart (leftover from making the stock)
1 1/2 cup finely diced vegetables such as carrot, celery, red pepper or string beans, or 1 box frozen chopped vegetables
sea salt or fish sauce and pepper to taste

Bring stock and rice to a boil and skim off any foam that may rise to the top. Reduce heat and cook, covered, about one hour until rice is tender. Add the vegetables, diced meats and seasonings and cook until just tender, about five to ten minutes. Children love this!

Variations: Chicken Noodle Soup

Substitute *1 cup buckwheat or brown rice pasta broken into bits* for the brown rice. Simmer ten minutes before adding vegetables.

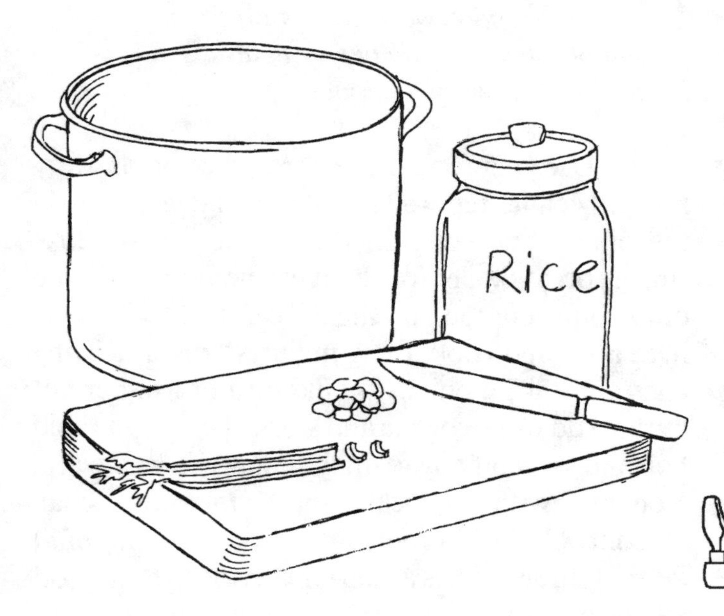

Know Your Ingredients

Name This Product #10

Enriched wheat flour (wheat flour, niacin, reduced iron, thiamine mononitrate, riboflavin), partially hydrogenated cottonseed oil, dehydrated vegetables (green pea, carrot, green bean), salt, freeze dried chicken, whey, buttermilk, non-dairy creamer (corn syrup solids, partially hydrogenated soybean oil, whey, sodium caseinate, sugar, dipotassium phosphate, mono and diglycerides), butter powder, hydrolyzed vegetable proteins, monosodium glutamate, xanthan gum, onion powder, cheddar cheese powder, chicken fat, natural flavors, soy sauce powder, garlic powder, chicken powder, spices, potassium carbonate, sodium carbonate, sugar, carrot and turmeric oleoresins as color, sodium alginate, disodium guanylate, disodium inosinate, sodium tripolyphosphate, citric acid, tocopherols, sodium citrate and sodium sulfite to preserve freshness. [!]

See Appendix B for Answer

SAFFRON SOUP

Serves 6

6 cups chicken or duck stock
1/8 teaspoon saffron threads
1 cup finely chopped spinach
2 green onions, very finely chopped
2 tablespoons lemon juice or whey
sea salt or fish sauce and pepper to taste

Bring stock to a boil and skim off any foam that may rise to the top. Add saffron and simmer for about 1/2 hour. Add spinach and onions and simmer a few minutes more. Off heat add lemon juice or whey and season to taste. Ladle into heated bowls.

FRENCH ONION SOUP

Serves 6

4 or 5 red onions
4 tablespoons butter
2 quarts beef stock
1/2 cup cognac
1/2 cup red wine
1 tablespoon arrow root mixed with
1 tablespoon water (optional)
sea salt or fish sauce and pepper to taste
2-3 tablespoons whey (optional)

Use your food processor to slice onions very thinly. Melt butter in a large stainless steel pot. Add the onions and cook on the lowest possible fire, stirring occasionally, for about two hours, or until the onions are very soft and slightly caramelized. Raise heat a bit and cook a few minutes longer, stirring constantly. The onions should turn brown but not burn. Add wine, cognac and stock. Bring to a rapid boil and skim off any foam that may rise to the top. You may wish to thicken the soup with a small amount of the arrow root mixture. Keep adding until desired consistency is achieved. Season to taste. Add a teaspoon so of whey to soup in the bowl for an agreeable tartness. Serve with round croutons (page 491) and a platter of raw cheeses.

Let's not forget that several years ago a study in the prestigious medical journal *Chest*, to the surprise of researchers, revealed that chicken soup really is "good for you, especially if you have an upper respiratory infection." As researcher Dr. Marvin Sackner, pulmonary specialist at Mount Sinai Medical Center in Miami Beach, concluded: "There's an aromatic substance in chicken soup, not yet identified, that helps clear your airways." He meticulously measured the effects of cold water, hot water, and hot chicken soup on the rate of flow of mucus and airflow through nasal passages. Hot water cleared congestion in airways better than cold water, but best of all was hot chicken soup. Even cold chicken soup worked to a lesser extent. Jean Carper *The Food Pharmacy Guide to Good Eating*

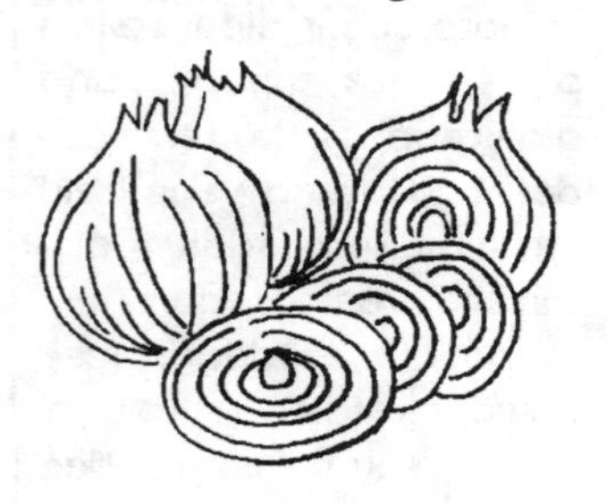

Cholesterol is especially important to our brains. That's right, the dietician of today's "most hated" substance is essential to the human brain function. In fact, infants need a constant supply of cholesterol during brain development, which is why mother's breast milk is so high in it. Modern science tripped over itself somehow when it named cholesterol the bugaboo of heart disease. Nature doesn't make that kind of mistake—but man does. [Some soy-based infant formulas contain no cholesterol.] Tom Valentine *Facts on Fats & Oils*

JAPANESE NOODLE SOUP

Serves 6-8

1 1/2 quarts fish stock, clarified
1/2 cup dry white wine
4 tablespoons soy sauce
1 cup brown rice or buckwheat noodles, broken up
1/2 cup chopped dried seaweed or
1 cup chopped spinach
2 tablespoons fish sauce (optional)

If using seaweed, combine all ingredients except noodles and simmer at least 1 hour; 10 minutes before serving add noodles. If using spinach, combine all ingredients and simmer 10 minutes.

MISO SOUP

Serves 6-8

1 1/2 quarts homemade fish stock
4 tablespoons soy sauce
3-4 tablespoons miso
1 onion, sliced
1/2 green or Chinese cabbage, coarsely shredded
2 tablespoons fish sauce (optional)

Bring stock to a boil, skim and whisk in miso. Add remaining ingredients and simmer gently until vegetables are soft.

COCONUT MILK SOUP

Serves 6-8

1 1/2 quarts homemade fish or chicken stock
1 1/2 cups coconut milk and cream (page 144)
or 7-8 oz creamed coconut (see Sources)
1 pound chicken or fish, cut into small cubes
3 jalapeno chiles, diced
1 tablespoon grated fresh ginger
2 tablespoons fish sauce
2-4 tablespoons lime juice
chopped cilantro for garnish

Simmer all ingredients until meat is cooked through. Garnish with cilantro.

Use of the soy bean dates back thousands of years in China. Analysis of ancient texts reveals that originally the soy bean was cultivated for its nitrogen-fixing qualities, and not as a food source. This is because soy beans contain potent enzyme inhibitors that cause intestinal problems, cancer and growth retardation. In addition, soy beans have a high phytate content—higher than any other legume. These substances block the absorption of essential minerals such as iron, calcium, magnesium and zinc. It was during the Chou Dynasty (1134-246 BC) that soy beans were first designated as the fifth sacred grain, along with barley, wheat, millet and rice. This is an indication that the Chinese had by that time learned to process soy beans to make them edible. The process of precipitation to make tofu and bean curd removes a portion of the enzyme inhibitors, but none of the phytates. Fermentation of cooked beans to make soy sauce, miso, natto and tempeh removes not only enzyme inhibitors but phytates as well. Miso is thus superior to tofu from a nutritional point of view. It is a salty paste—smooth or chunky—with a meatlike flavor. It is used as a seasoning and as a dietary staple in the daily preparation of miso soup in Japanese homes. It is rich in omega-3 fatty acids but has an incomplete protein profile, lacking methionine in particular. For a balanced diet, miso should be combined with fish stock and whole grains. SWF

THAI FISH SOUP

Serves 6-8

1 1/2 quarts Oriental fish stock
3/4 pound shelled shrimp
3/4 pound fish, skinned and cut into chunks
1 cup brown rice
2 cloves garlic, peeled and mashed
1 tablespoon freshly grated ginger
grated rind of 1 organic lemon
4 tablespoons fish sauce

Bring stock and rice to a boil and skim. Add seasonings. Simmer at least one hour. Add fish and shrimp and simmer about 10 minutes more.

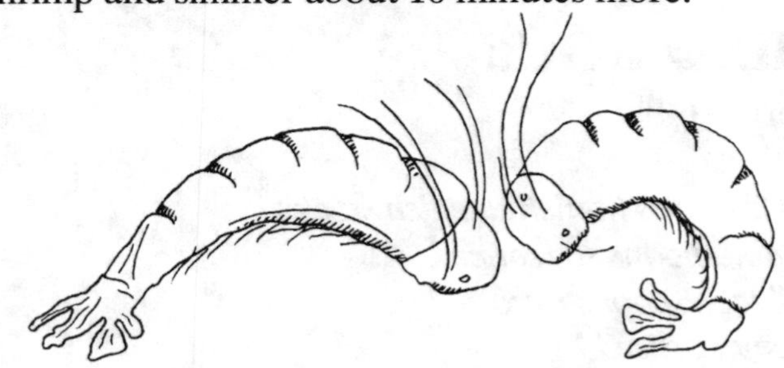

MEDITERRANEAN FISH SOUP

Serves 6-8

1 1/2 quarts fish stock
1 pound fish, skinned and cut into chunks
3/4 pound shelled shrimp or crab meat
2 onions, peeled and chopped
extra virgin olive oil
4 tablespoons tomato paste
3 cloves garlic, peeled and mashed
sea salt or fish sauce to taste
several sprigs fresh thyme and rosemary, tied together

In a large pot, saute onions in olive oil. Add tomato paste and stir around. Add fish stock, bring to a boil and skim. Add remaining ingredients and simmer about 1/2 hour. Remove thyme and rosemary before serving.

I see too many risks in the Spartan vegetarian diet. Most vegetarians are opposed to eating red meat, but I see no reason why they can't include poultry and fish in their diets, or at least dairy products and eggs. . . The great peril of the strict vegetarian diet is suppression of the protective and life-giving thyroid function by minimizing the intake of essential vitamins. Stephen E. Langer MD *Solved: The Riddle of Illness*

Chinese doctors 2,000 years before Christ rejuvenated aging patients with failing faculties by means of an animal thyroid soup, with the result that patients felt younger, had more energy, and often regained ability to think and remember. Many centuries later, during Queen Victoria's reign, London's most prominent Harley Street doctors took a cue from the Chinese and served elderly and failing patients special sandwiches whose main ingredient was raw animal thyroid gland. Stephen E. Langer MD *Solved: The Riddle of Illness*

Pickled fish-brine or sauce, made from fish heads, organs and bones, is called "ketsiap" in the Chinese Amoy dialect. This became the Malay "kechap", a condiment that Dutch traders imported from the Orient. It was a fish sauce similar to the Roman garum. It wasn't until American seamen added tomatoes from Mexico or the Spanish West Indies to the condiment that tomato ketchup was born. The original universal condiment was fish sauce, not tomato sauce! Fish sauce is rich in special substances that nourish the thyroid, and makes a most nutritious addition to soups and stews. SWF

CRAB SOUP

Serves 6

2 quarts homemade fish stock
1/4 teaspoon red chile flakes
generous pinch saffron threads
several sprigs fresh thyme, tied together
1 pound fresh lump crab meat
3 ripe tomatoes, peeled, seeded and chopped
3 ears white corn, cut off the cob
sea salt or fish sauce and pepper to taste
1/2 fresh chives, chopped, for garnish

Bring fish stock to a boil and skim any foam that rises to the top. Add red chile flakes, saffron and thyme. Reduce heat and simmer for about one hour, until the flavors have permeated the stock. Remove the thyme. Add crab, tomatoes and corn. Simmer about five minutes until corn is tender. Season to taste. Ladle into heated soup bowls and garnish with chives.

RICH BEEF AND RICE SOUP

Serves 6

2 onions, peeled and coarsely chopped
2 carrots peeled and coarsely chopped
2 quarts beef stock
8 to 10 cloves garlic, peeled and coarsely chopped
1 cup red wine
1 cup chopped parsley
1 cup brown rice
sea salt or fish sauce and pepper to taste
1/4 cup beet kvass (page 586) or whey (optional)

Saute onions and carrots gently in a little butter until soft. Add stock, garlic and wine, bring to a boil and skim. Simmer about 1/2 hour. Add parsley and simmer an additional 5 minutes. Strain. Add rice and simmer at least 1 hour. Season to taste. Off heat, stir in fermented vegetable juice or whey.

In their native state the natives of the Torres Strait Islands have exceedingly little disease. Dr. J.R. Nimmo, the government physician in charge of the supervision of this group, told me in his thirteen years with them he had not seen a single case of malignancy, and had seen only one that he had suspected might be malignancy among the entire four thousand native population. He stated that during this same period he had operated several dozen malignancies for the white population, which numbers about three hundred. He reported that among the primitive stock other affections requiting surgical interference were rare.

The environment of the Torres Strait Islanders provided a very liberal supply of sea foods and fertile islands on which an adequate quantity of tropical plants are readily grown. Toro, bananas, papaya, and plums are all grown abundantly. The sea foods include large and small fish in great abundance, dugong, and a great variety of shellfish. These foods have developed for them remarkable physiques with practically complete immunity to dental caries. Wherever they have adopted the white man's foods, however, they suffer the typical expressions of degeneration, such as loss of immunity to dental caries; and in the succeeding generations there is a marked change in facial and dental arch form with marked lowering of resistance to disease. Weston Price DDS *Nutrition and Physical Degeneration*

MEXICAN SOUP

Serves 6

2 quarts chicken stock
1 cup tomato paste, preferably organic
4 cloves garlic, mashed
1/4-1/2 teaspoon red chile flakes
fish sauce or sea salt and pepper to taste
1/2 cup fresh lime juice
strips of corn or sprouted whole wheat tortilla, fried until crisp in olive oil, for garnish
1 avocado, diced, for garnish
piima cream or creme fraiche for garnish

Bring stock to a boil with tomato paste, garlic and red chile flakes. Simmer about 1/2 hour. Just before serving, stir in seasonings and lime juice. Serve with garnishes.

Hawk reported in 1923 on feeding experiments which established the supplementary action of gelatin in connection with a cereal diet. Downey, in the same year, found gelatin to be an efficient supplement for the proteins of whole rye, pearl barley and whole barley. Based on the findings of McCollum, Downey was also led to the conclusion that white wheat bread and whole wheat bread would be increased in nutritive value by the inclusion of gelatin. He accordingly conducted feeding experiments with the addition of 5% of gelatin to white wheat bread (salts and vitamins A and B were added) and found that the food value was improved to such an extent that growth rate of the experimental animals was normal and they were able to reproduce and raise healthy, well-formed young. On the same ration, but without the gelatin, ratio of growth was about half normal and only two scrawny and poorly formed young were raised. . .while rats fed exclusively on chick peas exhibited retarded growth, normal growth resulted on the addition of gelatin. N.R Gotthoffer *Gelatin in Nutrition and Medicine*

KOREAN SOUP

(Sol Long Tang)

Serves 6

1 1/2 quarts beef stock
1/2 pound beef brisket, sliced very thin
1/2 cup brown rice
1/2 cup buckwheat or brown rice noodles, broken into pieces
2 tablespoons soy sauce
1 tablespoon fish sauce (optional)

Bring stock and rice to a boil and skim. Add brisket, soy sauce and fish sauce and simmer for 1 hour. 10 minutes before serving add noodles.

If there is one dish that is the Korean cuisine's soul food, it is sol long tang, a long-simmered beef broth served with paper-thin slices of beef brisket, rice and noodles. Koreans eat it morning, noon and night. Elaine Louie *The New York Times*

RUSSIAN BEET BROTH SOUP

Serves 6

2 quarts beef or chicken stock
2 large beets
juice of 1 lemon
1/2 cup beet kvass (page 586)
finely chopped chives

Use a rich stock made by simmering at least 24 hours. Bring stock to a boil and skim. Peel beets, chop coarsely and add to stock. Simmer very gently for about 1/2 hour or until beets are tender. Strain. Season to taste and add lemon juice and beet kvass. Ladle into heated soup bowls and garnish with chives. Serve with Cream Cheese Pastries (page 153).

ROMAN EGG SOUP

(Stracciatella)
Serves 6

2 quarts chicken stock
4 eggs
4 tablespoons finely powdered Parmesan cheese
2 tablespoons very finely chopped parsley
sea salt and freshly ground pepper to taste

The secret to this delicious soup is, once again, the quality of the stock. Use only a very rich, dark colored chicken stock that has been made by simmering at least 24 hours.

Bring stock to a boil and skim. Meanwhile whisk up the eggs with the cheese. While stock is boiling vigorously, add the egg-cheese mixture in a thin stream, all the while beating the soup with a whisk. Season with salt and plenty of fresh ground pepper to taste. Just before serving stir in the finely chopped parsley.

Wherever the typical American diet exists, there too exists a high incidence of heart disease, diabetes and cancer. Poor diet impairs the function of the human body. Poor nutrition alters immune function, impairs circulation, and disturbs hormonal balance, resulting in disorders ranging from heart disease and arthritis to cancer. . . The worse the diet, the more likely it is that heart disease, stroke, heart attack, hardening of the arteries, high blood pressure, cancer or arthritis will develop. The longer an individual is on a poor diet, the more rapidly will such diseases occur. A nutritionally depleted diet affects the gene pool as well. If your ancestors had a poor diet—a diet rich in refined sugars, white flour, processed food, and refined fats—your genes will be affected. Then you will be even more vulnerable than they were to the development of the diseases of civilization. Cass Igram MD *Eat Right to Live Longer*

CIOPPINO

Serves 8

1 or 2 onions, finely chopped
1/4 cup extra virgin olive oil
6 ounces tomato paste
1 cup dry white wine or vermouth
1 1/2 quarts fish stock
several sprigs fresh thyme
1/2 teaspoon oregano
1/4 teaspoon red chile flakes
pinch saffron threads
3 large garlic cloves, peeled and mashed
4 tomatoes, peeled, seeded and chopped
2-4 tablespoons fish sauce
sea salt and freshly ground pepper
1 pound fresh sea bass, cut into cubes
1 pound fresh crab meat
1 pound fresh scallops
1 pound bay shrimp
16 fresh clams (optional)
8 crab claws

Needless to say, all the seafood you use must be very fresh. You can substitute lobster for crab and mussels for clams, etc.

In a large stainless steel pot saute onion gently in olive oil. Stir in tomato paste and add wine, stock, spices and garlic. Bring to a rapid boil and cook vigorously, skimming occasionally, until the stock is reduced to the consistency of thin cream. Remove thyme and season with sea salt and pepper to taste. Add the seafood and tomatoes and cook gently for about ten minutes. Ladle into large heated bowls, making sure everyone has one crab claw and two clams.

Serve the cioppino with a Caesar salad and fresh sour dough whole grain bread with butter.

Since Viti Levu, one of the islands of this group, is one of the larger islands of the Pacific ocean, I had hoped to find on it a district far enough from the sea to make it necessary for the natives to have lived entirely on land foods. . . by using a recently opened government road, I was able to get well into the interior of the island by motor vehicle, and from this point to proceed father inland on foot with two guides. I was not able, however, to get beyond the piles of sea shells which had been carried into the interior. My guide told me that it had always been essential, as it is today, for the people of the interior to obtain some food from the sea, and that even during the times of most bitter warfare, between the inland or hill tribes and the coast tribes, those of the interior would bring down during the night choice plant foods from the mountain areas and place them in caches and return the following night to obtain the sea foods that had been placed in those depositories by the shore tribes. . . He told me further that they require food from the sea at least every three months, even to this day. This was a matter of keen interest and the same time disappointment since one of the purposes of the expedition to the South Seas was to find, if possible, plant or fruits which together, without the use of animal products, were capable of providing all of the requirements of the body for growth and for maintenance of good health and a high state of physical efficiency. .. no places were found where the native plant foods were not supplemented by sea foods. Weston Price DDS *Nutrition and Physical Degeneration*

LEFTOVER LEG OF LAMB SOUP

Serves 8

1 leftover leg of lamb with meat attached
leftover sauce from leg of lamb
1/4 cup vinegar
3 onions, peeled and coarsely chopped
3 carrots, peeled and coarsely chopped
1 red or green pepper, seeded and chopped
3 turnips, peeled and chopped
3 zucchini, chopped
4 cloves garlic, peeled and chopped
several sprigs fresh thyme, tied together
1/2 teaspoon crushed dried green peppercorns
1/4 teaspoon dried red chile threads
generous pinch saffron powder
1 cup brown rice
1/2 cup dried currents (optional)
sea salt or fish sauce and pepper to taste

This is a good way to stretch a leg of lamb into another meal. Leftover lamb meat, normally unappetizing when served a second time, becomes flavorful and tender. While not exactly gourmet fare, this soup always gets eaten to the last spoonful. It should be started in the early morning and allowed to simmer all day. This recipe uses all the vegetables and seasonings of couscous, but substitutes brown rice for the semolina, which is really just a version of white flour pasta.

Place vegetables in a large stainless steel pot with the lamb, vinegar and leftover sauce. Cover with filtered cold water and bring to a boil. Skim before adding thyme, chile flakes and saffron. Let this cook gently, covered, about twelve hours or longer. At least one hour before serving remove the lamb and strain the sauce into a another large pot. Add rice and optional currents to this broth and simmer an hour or more. Meanwhile discard the cooked vegetables and let the meat cool. Remove the meat from the bone and cut across the grain into small pieces. When the rice is tender, return the meat to the broth and season to taste.

A recent research report has de-demonized, at least a little, one of our most important nutrients—cholesterol. The experts who have been telling us not to eat high-cholesterol foods, such as eggs, butter and T-bone steak (all the good stuff that made America great), are now saying it's okay to eat these foods—*if* you're over 70. The Yale University study reported in the November 2, 1994 issue of the *Journal of the American Medical Association* claims that people over 70 with "high cholesterol" levels do not have any more heart attacks than those whose cholesterol is considered normal or even low. They are no more likely to die of any form of heart disease or from any cause.

Dr. Stephen B. Hulley, of the University of California at San Francisco, said he was "deeply concerned" about the number of elderly people who were taking cholesterol-lowering drugs when "we actually don't know whether you're better off with a high or low [cholesterol], so there is no point in measuring it." William Campbell Douglass MD *Second Opinion*

Whoever is failing in his whole body and whose veins are withered should often sip the juice of lamb and of the soup in which it was cooked. Also he should eat some of the meat and, when he improves, he can eat even more of the meat if he wants.

St. Hildegard of Bingen

OXTAIL AND BARLEY SOUP

Serves 8

4 pounds fresh oxtails
filtered water
1/2 cup dry white wine
1/4 cup vinegar
2 onions, peeled and chopped
2 carrots, peeled and chopped
2 celery stalks, chopped
fresh thyme sprigs, tied together
1-2 teaspoons crushed dried green peppercorns
pinch red pepper flakes
l cup barley, roasted in the oven, and soaked at least 7 hours
sea salt or fish sauce and pepper to taste
chopped cilantro or finely chopped parsley

Place oxtails in a stainless steel baking pan and bake in a 350 degree oven for about one hour or until well browned. Transfer oxtails to a stainless steel pot and pour out grease. Add wine and a little water to the baking pan and deglaze by bringing to a rapid boil, while stirring to loosen any coagulated beef juices in the pan. Pour this liquid into the pot and cover all the oxtails with cold water. Add vinegar and bring to a boil. After skimming, add thyme, onions, carrots, celery, red pepper flakes and peppercorns. Simmer, covered, for at least 24 hours.

Remove oxtails and allow to cool. Strain 3 quarts of stock into another pot and add soaked barley. (Reserve any remaining broth for other uses.) Bring to a boil and simmer for about one hour or until barley is tender. Meanwhile, remove meat from the bones (there's no other way to do this but with the fingers) and chop finely. When the barley is tender, add chopped meat. Season generously. Ladle into individual bowls and garnish with chopped parsley or cilantro.

Barley is one of the oldest cereal grains, used most frequently in the making of beer, but also traditionally made into bread and gruels. Barley water, a thin porridge made of barley, is said to be easy to digest and a tonic to the liver. In Britain it is fed to convalescents. Most barley is available to the consumer in "pearled form", with the thick outer layer, and hence most of the nutrients removed. Look for whole barley and be sure to soak it before using it or the results will be difficult to digest. SWF

The recent national meeting of the American Chemical Society reported new studies on the effects of soluble fiber. Barley reduced serum cholesterol levels by as much as 15% in hypercholesterolemic persons in two studies cited by Rosemary K. Newman of Montana State University. She cited three reasons for this effect of barley. First, it contains beta-glucans and other viscous soluble fiber components which reduce absorption of fats and cholesterol. Other soluble fibers, such as those of oat and guar gum, also contain beta-glucans. Also, the fiber tends to bind to bile acids, which are removed from the body rather than recycled, thus requiring the conversion of more cholesterol to bile acids. Finally, barley contains fat soluble antioxidants related to vitamin E called tocotrienols that reduce cholesterol synthesis in the liver. Newman says, "We have not seen any other grain that carries barley's double whammy"—that is, high beta glucan levels as well as tocotrienols. James F Scheer *Health Freedom News*

MINESTRONE

Serves 6

2 quarts beef stock
1 clove garlic, peeled and mashed
2 cups kidney beans, cooked (page 469) or sprouted (page 105)
1 cup buckwheat or brown rice pasta, broken in bits
2 carrots, peeled and chopped
2 tomatoes, peeled, seeded and chopped
1 cup fresh spinach or chard, finely chopped
sea salt or fish sauce and pepper to taste
freshly grated Parmesan cheese for garnish

This hearty soup is a meal in itself. Once again, the secret is the richness of the stock.

Bring stock to a boil and skim. Add remaining ingredients and simmer about 10 minutes. Season to taste and garnish with cheese.

Little is known of the part potassium plays in the human body, but certainly it must be important as small quantities of it are present in all parts of the body, particularly within the cells. Osmotic balance between the contents of the cells and their surrounding fluids depends greatly upon potassium. When meat is being cooked, a considerable portion of the potassium content passes into the broth. When this is eaten in the form of a soup, bouillon or consomme, it results in a stimulatory effect upon the digestive organism. This is given as one good reason for beginning a meal with a meat broth soup. H. Leon Abrams *Your Body is Your Best Doctor*

SAUERKRAUT AND BEAN SOUP

Serves 6

2 cups cooked small white beans, either cooked (page 469) or sprouted (page 105)
1 1/2 quarts chicken or beef stock
2 cloves garlic, peeled and mashed
pinch red pepper flakes
1 pound spicy chicken sausage, cooked and sliced into rounds
sea salt or fish sauce and pepper to taste
2 cups sauerkraut (page 84)

Bring broth to a boil and skim. Add other ingredients except sauerkraut and simmer for 15 minutes or until sausage is cooked. Off heat stir in sauerkraut and ladle into heated bowls.

When harvested with dedication and care, the oceans give us a natural sea salt with the most exquisite taste and physiologically vital mineral mix. Today, every common table salt is artificial and pales beside the real sea salt. Out of the richest spectrum of 92 essential minerals found in the ocean, the industrial refined variety retains only two! Debased white table salt deserves all of its bad name and all the misdeeds as charged. Jacques DeLangre *Seasalt's Hidden Powers*

PESTO SOUP

Serves 8

2 quarts beef stock
1 teaspoon sea salt
1/4 teaspoon saffron threads
freshly ground pepper
3 carrots, peeled and diced
1 leek, trimmed, washed and diced
2 cups small white beans, either cooked (page 469) or sprouted (page 105)
4 ounces brown rice or buckwheat pasta, broken into bits
1 cup green beans, french cut (page 348)
1/2 cup pesto (page 135)
2 tablespoons tomato puree

Bring stock to a boil, skim and add seasonings, carrots, leeks, and white or navy beans. Simmer gently until vegetables are soft. Add green beans and spaghetti pieces and simmer about 10 minutes more. Place pesto and tomato paste in a bowl. Blend with a little of the hot stock and then blend this mixture back into the soup. Check seasonings and serve.

An article in the January 1973 issue of the *National Geographic* points out that there are places in the world where people live much longer and remain more vigorous in old age than in most of our modern societies. Dr. Alexander Leaf, M.D.. . . visited three of the best known of these regions. They were all remote, mountainous, and over a mile high—the Andean village of Vilcabamba in Ecuador—the Land of the Hunzas in Kashmir—and Abakhazia in Russia on the border of the Black Sea. . . . Dr. Leaf commented that his confidence in the importance to health and longevity of low animal fat, low cholesterol, low caloric diet was somewhat shaken by the eating habits of the Caucasus. Dietary study of the habits of 1,000 persons above the age of 80, including more than 100 centenarians, showed that the old people consumed about 1,900 calories daily—considerably more than most people of such advanced age. 70 to 90 grams of protein were included in the diet—milk being the main source of protein. The daily fat intake was about 40 to 60 grams. Bread provided the major source of carbohydrates. . . [Dr. Leaf] does not discuss the fact that each of these communities is situated in a valley supplied with water which washes silt from a mountain behind them. He does not recognize that they drink the silted water, they fertilize the crops they eat with the silted water, they eat the flesh and drink the milk of the animals that were raised on this silted water, and they have a constant supply of trace elements throughout their lives that is as good or better than any other place on earth. Melvin Page DDS *Metabolic Aspects of Health*

KISHK SOUP

Serves 6

1 1/2 quarts chicken or beef stock
1 1/2 cups kishk (page 436)
sea salt or fish sauce and pepper to taste

This favorite Middle Eastern winter food incorporates all the elements found universally in traditional ethnic cuisines—sprouted grains, fermented grains, fermented milk products and meat broths.

Bring stock to a boil and skim. Add kishk and simmer about 1 hour. Season to taste.

CREAM OF VEGETABLE SOUP

(Potage Bonne Femme)
Serves 6-8

2 medium onions or 3 leeks, peeled and chopped
2 carrots, peeled and chopped
4 tablespoons butter
4 medium baking potatoes or 6 red potatoes, washed and cut up
2 quarts stock or combination of water and stock
several sprigs fresh thyme, tied together
1/2 teaspoon dried green peppercorns
4 zucchini, sliced
sea salt or fish sauce and pepper to taste
piima cream or creme fraiche

This basic vegetable soup recipe is a perennial favorite—and it's a great way to get your children to eat zucchini!

Melt butter in a large stainless steel pot and add onions or leeks and carrots. Cover and cook over lowest possible flame for at least 1/2 hour. The vegetables should soften but not burn. Add potatoes and stock to the pot. Bring to a rapid boil and skim off any impurities that may rise to the top. Reduce heat, add thyme sprigs and crushed peppercorns. Cover and cook until the potatoes are soft. Add zucchini and cook until they are just tender—about five to ten minutes. Remove the thyme sprigs. Puree the soup with a hand-held blender.

If soup is too thick, thin with water. Season with salt and pepper. Ladel into heated bowls and serve with cultured cream. Serve with round croutons (page 491).

Calcification of the arteries (arteriosclerosis), the joints (degenerative arthritis) and the [pineal] gland may be due to the excessive intake of fractionated milk, i.e., skim or low-fat milk. On the advice of physicians, millions of people have switched to low-fat milk under the mistaken belief that avoiding the milk fat will enable them to avoid hardening of the arteries. Drinking fractionated milk may cause exactly the opposite effect!

Many other millions are drinking low-fat milk to avoid weight gain. . . Do you know how a farmer fattens his hogs? *He feeds them skim milk.* William Campbell Douglass MD *The Milk of Human Kindness*

Know Your Ingredients

Name This Product #11

Beef stock, carrots, tomatoes, potatoes, celery, peas, zucchini, green beans, cabbage, water, modified food starch, spinach, salt, vegetable oil (corn, cottonseed or partially hydrogenated soybean oil), dehydrated onions, yeast extract and hydrolyzed vegetable protein, high fructose corn syrup, monosodium glutamate, beef fat, caramel color, natural flavoring, dehydrated garlic and oleoresin paprika.

See Appendix B for Answer

The food engineers seem determined to wipe out the entire dairy industry. . . and maybe the human race. Europeans are now producing margarine cheese. The price differential will be enormously in favor of fake cheese guaranteeing its popularity. It is so much like real cheese that "if a cheese made with vegetable oil was judged together with other cheese, it is doubtful, whether anyone would realize that a margarine cheese was among them."

Crest Foods of Ashton, Illinois now produces vegetable fat "sour cream". It is doubly pasteurized and homogenized *at least twice.* William Campbell Douglass MD *The Milk of Human Kindness*

Feeding tests were conducted to compare the feeding value of the following fats and oils for calves: butterfat, lard, tallow, coconut oil, peanut oil, corn oil, cottonseed oil, and soybean oil. . . In average daily gain in weight as well as in general well-being, the calves fed butterfat excelled those in all other groups; Following closely were those receiving lard and tallow. Corn oil, cottonseed oil and soybean oil were the least satisfactory. . . They appeared unthrifty, listless and emaciated. Some calves in these groups died and others were saved only by changing to whole milk. Weston Price DDS *Nutrition and Physical Degeneration*

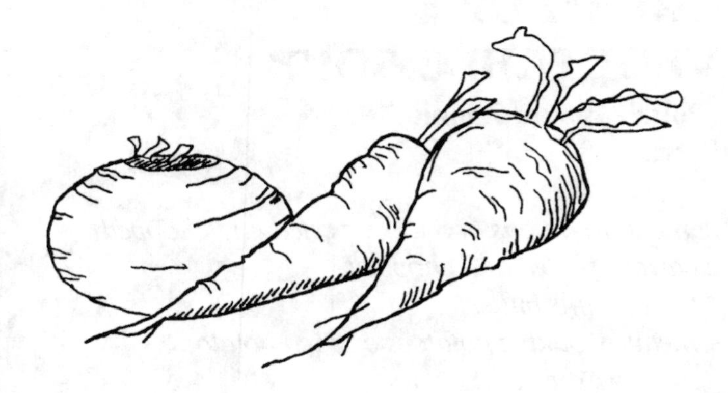

WINTER ROOT SOUP

Serves 6-8

4 tablespoons butter
3 medium onions, peeled and chopped
2 leeks, washed, trimmed and sliced
4 carrots, peeled and sliced
2 turnips peeled and sliced
3 parsnips, peeled and sliced
1 1/2 quarts chicken stock or combination water and stock
several thyme sprigs, tied together
4 cloves garlic, peeled and mashed
pinch cayenne pepper
2 medium potatoes, peeled and sliced
sea salt or fish sauce and pepper to taste
freshly ground nutmeg
piima cream or creme fraiche

Melt butter and cook onions, leeks, carrots, turnips and parsnips about 1/2 hour over low heat, stirring occasionally, until soft. Add stock and bring to a boil. Skim foam. Add potatoes, garlic, thyme and cayenne. Simmer, covered for about 1/2 hour until all vegetables are soft.

Remove thyme and blend soup with handheld blender. Season with salt, pepper and nutmeg. If soup is too thick, thin with a little water. Ladle into heated bowls and serve with cultured cream.

FENNEL SOUP

Serves 6

3 fennel bulbs, trimmed and sliced
2 leeks or medium onions, trimmed and sliced
4 tablespoons butter
1/2 teaspoon ground anise seed
1 teaspoon ground fennel seed
1/2 cup dry white wine (optional)
2 quarts chicken stock or
combination water and stock
3 cloves garlic, peeled and coarsely chopped
1 teaspoon green peppercorns, crushed
6 medium red potatoes, cut in quarters
sea salt or fish sauce and pepper to taste
3-4 tablespoons snipped fennel leaves
piima cream or creme fraiche

Cook fennel and onion gently butter until tender. Add anise and fennel seeds and stir around until amalgamated. Add stock and optional wine. Bring to a boil and skim off any foam that rises to the top. Add potatoes, peppercorns and garlic.

Cover and simmer until the potatoes are soft, about 1/2 hour. Blend with a hand-held blender. If the soup is too thick, thin with a little water. Season to taste and stir in fennel snippings. Ladle into heated bowls and serve with cultured cream.

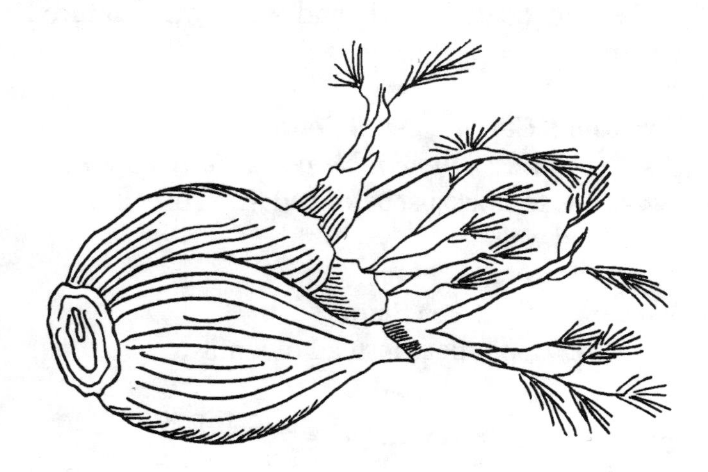

Raw foods enthusiasts point to scientific evidence which shows that when cooked foods are consumed, the white blood cell count immediately rises, while no such increase occurs when eating raw fruit or vegetables. The white blood cells function as immune system scavengers, removing foreign organisms and any chemical compounds the body considers invasive. The conclusion is drawn that therefore cooked foods are bad because the body considers them invasive and toxic, and raw foods are good because they evoke no immune system response. However, one can look at the same results and conclude that the cooked food is stimulating the immune function and causing the increase in white blood cells not because the food itself is toxic, but because a function of cooked food is to "exercise" the immune system in producing white blood cells for real emergencies, somewhat akin to a biological fire drill. Indeed, it is quite natural for the body to use the invasion of low doses of microorganisms or chemical poisons to immunize itself against greater danger. And on one level food *is* a foreign substance that the body must "overcome" through the process of digestion and assimilation. In this sense cooked food can be seen to strengthen the system while raw foods simply do not have the same white-blood-cell-stimulating effect. David Marc *Nourishing Wisdom*

ROMAN LENTIL SOUP

Serves 8

3 medium onions, peeled and sliced or
3 leeks, washed, trimmed and sliced
3 carrots, peeled and sliced
4 tablespoons extra virgin olive oil
2 quarts chicken or beef stock
or water plus stock
2 cups red or brown lentils,
soaked 7 or more hours
several sprigs fresh thyme, tied together
1/2 teaspoon dried green peppercorns
1/4 cup fresh lemon juice or whey
sea salt or fish sauce and pepper to taste
piima cream or creme fraiche

In a large stainless steal pot, cook vegetables gently for about one half hour in melted butter. When the vegetables are soft, add stock and lentils and bring to a boil. The lentils will produce a great deal of foam—be sure to skim this off. Reduce heat and add thyme and the crushed peppercorns. Simmer, covered, until the lentils are tender—about one half hour. Remove the thyme.

Puree soup with a hand-held blender. Thin with water to desired consistency. Off heat add lemon juice or whey and season with salt and pepper. Ladle into heated bowls and serve with cultured cream.

Variation: Curried Lentil Soup

Add *2 or more tablespoons curry powder or curry paste* to stock just before addition of vegetables and blend well.

Variation: Split Pea Soup

Use split peas instead of lentils.

The hearty Roman soldier carried 80 pounds plus his armor and walked 20 miles per day. His fare consisted of coarse bread and porridge of millet or lentils, supplemented with *garam* or *liquamem*, fermented fish sauce. This condiment supplied him with nutrients from the animal kingdom on a daily basis. Made from the heads and organs of fish, it is especially rich in iodine and vitamins A and D, and thus contributed to the robust strength of the Roman legions. SWF

No single substance will maintain vibrant health. Although specific nutrients are know to be more important in the functions of certain parts of the body, even these nutrients are totally dependent upon the presence of other nutrients for their best effects. Every effort should therefore be made to attain and maintain and adequate, balanced daily intake of all the necessary nutrients throughout life. Lavon J. Dunne *Nutrition Almanac*

. . . vegetable oils also cause premature aging in millions of Americans. A plastic surgeon did a study in which he examined the diets of his patients and correlated them with facial skin wrinkling. Those patients eating a high vegetable fat diet had 78% more facial wrinkles and many appeared 20 years older than they were. William Campbell Douglass MD *Eat Your Cholesterol*

CHESTNUT SOUP

Serves 6

2 onions, peeled and chopped
2 carrots, peeled and chopped
4 tablespoons butter
6 cups chicken stock
or water plus stock
1/2 cup sherry (optional)
1/4 teaspoon cayenne pepper
pinch nutmeg
several sprigs fresh thyme, tied together
13 ounces frozen peeled chestnuts or
about 4 cups unpeeled fresh chestnuts
sea salt or fish sauce and pepper to taste
piima cream or creme fraiche

You can make this delicious, sweetly flavored soup very easily with peeled, frozen chestnuts if you can find them. Its still worth doing if you have to start with the unpeeled variety. (See page 539 for preparation of chestnuts.)

Cook carrots and onions gently in the butter until soft. Add sherry, stock and chestnuts. Bring to a boil and skim. Add thyme and nutmeg and simmer, covered, for about fifteen minutes. Remove thyme.

Puree with a hand-held blender. Season to taste with sea salt and fresh ground pepper. Ladle into heated bowls and serve with cultured cream.

When animals are placed on skim milk with the vitamins lost from the cream replaced, the animals develop very poorly. But when four percent butter fat is fed to similar animals, they develop normally. The vegetable oils now being pushed on the American people, by organized medicine and self-styled nutrition experts will not work as a substitute for cream.

Skim milk-fed animals develop testicular atrophy with complete sterility. Male sterility is a major concern in our country today and the skim milk fad may be a major contributing factor.

The test animals also developed severe calcification of most large blood vessels, anemia, and high blood pressure. Another characteristic of the syndrome that may be of significance in human medicine is the development of calcium deposits around the bone openings in the spine that provide for the exit of nerves. Sciatica and other nerve compression syndromes may be caused by this nutritional deficiency. Also, a decrease in hearing, leading to complete deafness was consistently found. William Campbell Douglass MD *The Milk of Human Kindness*

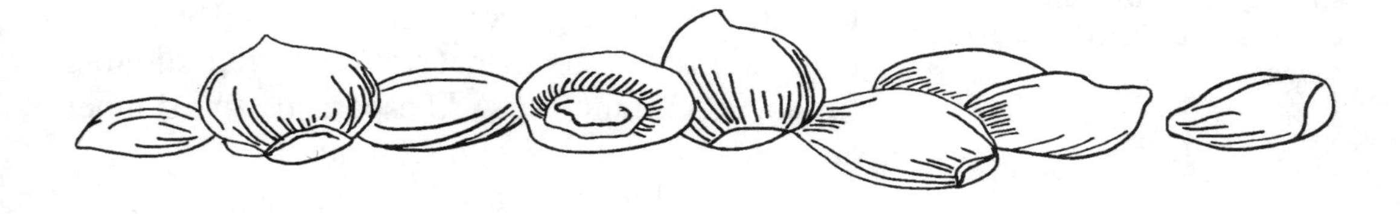

WATERCRESS SOUP

Serves 6

2 medium onions, peeled and chopped
3 tablespoons butter
1 1/2 quarts chicken stock
4 red potatoes, cut into quarters
2 large bunches watercress leaves, rinsed
sea salt or fish sauce and pepper to taste
piima cream or creme fraiche

Saute the onions gently in a little butter until soft. Add stock and potatoes. Bring to a boil and skim any foam that rises to the top. Simmer until potatoes are soft, about 1/2 hour. Add watercress and simmer another 5 minutes, no longer.

Blend soup with a hand-held blender. Season to taste. Ladle into heated bowls and serve with cultured cream.

ASPARAGUS SOUP

Serves 6

2 medium onions, peeled and chopped
3 tablespoons butter
1 1/2 quarts chicken stock
4 red potatoes, quartered
2 bunches tender asparagus, tough ends trimmed off and cut into 1/4 inch pieces
2 cloves garlic, peeled and coarsely chopped
sea salt or fish sauce and pepper to taste
piima cream or creme fraiche

Saute onions gently in a little butter until tender. Add stock, garlic and potatoes and bring to a boil. Skim off any foam that rises to the top. Simmer for about 15 minutes. Add asparagus and simmer another 10 minutes or so until tender.

Blend with a hand-held blender. Pass the soup through a strainer to remove any strings from the asparagus. Season to taste. Reheat, ladle into heated bowls and serve with cultured cream.

Dr. T. W. Gullickson, Professor of Dairy Chemistry, University of Minnesota, proved the nutritional superiority of butter fat over vegetable oils, which are the main ingredients of the vegetable margarines. Gullickson used skim milk and combined it with lard, tallow, coconut oil, corn oil, cottonseed oil or soybean oil in place of the cream and fed it to calves. The vegetable oil substitutes were mixed with skim milk in an attempt to imitate the 3.5 percent butterfat of milk. As often happens in research, they proved something entirely different from their original objective. They had set out to find a cheaper way to raise calves for veal production. What they found was that calves will only grow on God's own natural milk, and when fed vegetable oil substitutes instead of the cream, they sicken and die.

On the corn oil mix three out of eight died within one hundred-seventy days, some as soon as thirty-three days. On cottonseed oil three out of four died within one hundred-twenty-six days. Pick your favorite vegetable oil—the result was the same. The survivors quickly recovered when switched to whole raw milk. If vegetable oil products are so devastating to the health of calves, do you think maybe they are bad for you, too? William Campbell Douglass MD *The Milk of Human Kindness*

MUSHROOM SOUP

Serves 6

2 medium onions, peeled and chopped
3 tablespoons butter
2 pounds fresh mushrooms
butter and extra virgin olive oil
1 quart chicken stock
1/2 cup dry white wine
1 piece whole grain bread, broken into pieces
freshly ground nutmeg
sea salt or fish sauce and pepper to taste
piima cream or creme fraiche

The mushrooms must be very fresh! Saute the onions gently in butter until soft. Meanwhile, wash mushrooms (no need to remove stems) and dry well. Cut into quarters. In a heavy cast-iron skillet, saute the mushrooms in small batches in a mixture of butter and olive oil. Remove with slotted spoon and drain on paper towels. Add sauted mushrooms, wine, bread and chicken stock to onions, bring to a boil and skim. Reduce heat and simmer about 15 minutes.

Blend soup with a hand-held blender. Add nutmeg and season to taste. Ladle into heated soup bowls and serve with cultured cream.

RED PEPPER SOUP

Serves 6

6 red peppers, seeded and chopped
2 medium onions, peeled and chopped
extra virgin olive oil
1 1/2 quarts chicken stock
1 small bunch fresh basil, cut into small pieces
sea salt or fish sauce and pepper to taste
piima cream or creme fraiche

Saute peppers and onions in olive oil. Add stock, bring to a boil and skim. Reduce heat and simmer about 1/2 hour. Blend with a hand-held blender. Stir in basil and season to taste. Ladle into heated bowls and serve with cultured cream.

Know Your Ingredients

Name This Product #12

Water, mushrooms, modified food starch, cream, corn starch, vegetable oil (corn, cottonseed or partially hydrogenated soybean oil), wheat flour, sugar, salt, whey protein concentrate, potassium chloride, spice extracts, disodium inosinate, disodium-guanylate, maltodextrin, dehydrated garlic, mushroom powder, and calcium lactate.

See Appendix B for Answer

To me, true health is. . . achieved by following the laws of nature; when you break them, illness results. Health is not something bestowed on you by beneficent nature at birth; it is achieved and maintained only by active participation in well-defined rules of healthful living—rules which you may be disregarding every day. Henry Bieler MD *Food is Your Best Medicine*

Practically every culture in the temperate portions of the globe values garlic for its strong flavor as well as for its medicinal properties. It is used extensively in Mediterranean, North African, French and Korean cuisine.

Garlic contains an oil called allyl disulphate that acts as an anti-bacterial agent in the gut. Garlic is recommended for a variety of ailments including blood pressure disorders, infections, colds and flu, headaches and parasites. In recent decades, research has revealed that garlic lowers cholesterol, protects against cancer, prevents blood clotting, aids in the treatment of bronchitis and emphysema, and strengthens the immune system. It is a rich dietary source of sulphur and selenium. Garlic's therapeutic powers remain intact even after a light cooking. According to Oriental medicine, garlic increases body heat and may contribute to an angry or fiery temperament and hence should be avoided by the choleric.

To peel large amounts of garlic, place whole heads in a 300 degree oven until the skin loosens; cloves are then easily removed. SWF

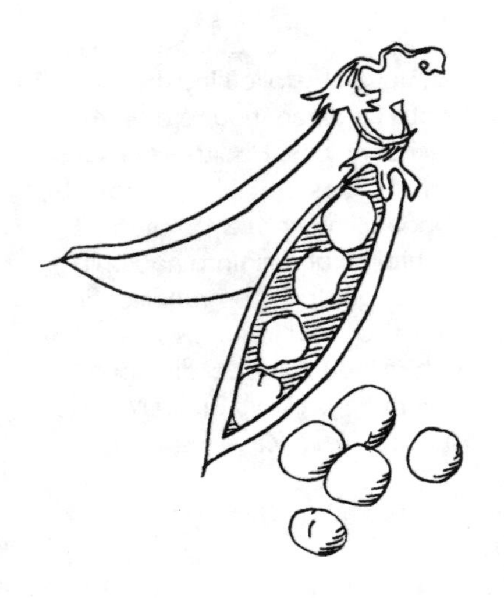

GARLIC SOUP

Serves 6

2 medium onions, peeled and chopped
16 cloves garlic, peeled and chopped coarsely
2 stalks celery, chopped
3 tablespoons butter
1 1/2 quarts chicken stock
2 potatoes, washed and cut up
several sprigs fresh thyme, tied together
1 teaspoon dried green pepper corns, crushed
3 yellow crookneck squash, washed, trimmed and sliced
sea salt or fish sauce and pepper to taste
piima cream or creme fraiche

Saute onions, garlic, leek and celery gently in butter until soft. Add chicken stock and potatoes. Bring to a boil and skim. Add thyme and crushed pepper corns. Simmer covered until potatoes are tender. Add squash and simmer about 10 minutes more or until squash is tender. Blend soup with a hand-held blender. If soup is too thick, thin with water. Season to taste. Ladle into heated bowls and serve with cultured cream.

FRESH PEA SOUP

Serves 6

2 medium onions, peeled and chopped
3 tablespoons butter
2 pounds freshly shelled or frozen peas
1 1/2 quarts chicken stock
1/2 teaspoon dried green peppercorns
sea salt and freshly ground pepper
piima cream or creme fraiche

This delicious soup can be made in less than 15 minutes, and will satisfy the most exacting gourmet. Saute onions gently in butter until tender. Add peas and stock, bring to a boil and skim. Simmer about 15 minutes. Blend with a hand-held blender. Season to taste. Ladle into heated bowls and serve with cultured cream.

TOMATO DILL SOUP

Serves 6

2 medium onions, peeled and coarsely chopped
3 celery stalks, coarsely chopped
3 tablespoons butter
8 ripe tomatoes, peeled, seeded and coarsely chopped or 2 large cans tomatoes
2 cups water (if using fresh tomatoes)
1/2 teaspoon dried green peppercorns, crushed
sea salt and freshly ground pepper
1/4 cup snipped fresh dill
piima cream or creme fraiche

Saute onions and celery gently in butter until tender. Add fresh tomatoes and water or canned tomatoes and their juice, bring to a boil and skim. Add crushed peppercorns. Simmer about 15 minutes.

Blend with a hand-held blender. Thin soup with a little water if necessary and season to taste. Stir in the dill. Ladle into heated bowls and serve with cultured cream.

BEET SOUP

Serves 6

6 medium beets
1/2 stick butter
1 quart water
piima cream or creme fraiche
sea salt and freshly ground pepper
2 tablespoons finely chopped chives

This easy soup brings out the exquisite sweet flavor of beets. Use water, not stock.

Peel beets, chop coarsely and saute very gently in butter for 1/2 hour or until tender. Add water, bring to a boil and skim. Simmer about 15 minutes. Blend with hand-held blender. Season to taste, ladle into heated bowls and serve with cultured cream and chives.

Primary prevention trials which have shown that the lowering of serum cholesterol concentrations in middle-aged subjects by diet, drugs, or both leads to a decrease in coronary heart disease have also reported an increase in deaths due to suicide or violence. . . published work [describes] a physiological mechanism that might account for this curious finding. One of the functions of serotonin in the central nervous system is the suppression of harmful behavioral impulses. When mouse brain synaptosomal membrane cholesterol is increased there is a pronounced increase in the number of serotonin receptors. Low membrane cholesterol decreases the number of serotonin receptors. Since membrane cholesterol exchanges freely with cholesterol in the surrounding medium, a lowered serum cholesterol concentration may contribute to a decrease in brain serotonin, with poorer suppression of aggressive behavior. Hyman Engelberg MD *The Lancet*

Some of the penalties for using "a synthetic, imitation, chemically-embalmed substitute for butter" include: 1. Sexual castration in the growing child, with oversized females fatter and taller than boys. 2. Loss of ability to maintain calcified structures like bones and teeth. Dental caries, pyorrhea, arthritic, osteoporosis and similar maladies result. 3. Degenerative diseases like multiple sclerosis, disorders of menopause, elevated cholesterol, heart muscle disorders, eczema, dermititis, and other skin disorders, nerve disorders and the list can go on. Judith A DeCava *The Margarine Masquerade*

CARROT SOUP

Serves 6

2 medium onions, peeled and chopped
1 pound carrots, peeled and sliced
1/2 stick butter
1/2 teaspoon freshly grated lemon rind
1/2 teaspoon freshly grated ginger
2 teaspoons curry powder
1 1/2 quarts chicken stock
sea salt or fish sauce and pepper to taste
piima cream or creme fraiche

Saute onions and carrots very gently in butter about 45 minutes or until tender. Add stock, bring to a boil and skim. Add lemon rind, ginger, and curry powder. Simmer, covered, about 15 minutes. Blend with a hand-held blender. Season to taste Ladle into heated bowls and serve with cultured cream.

SQUASH AND SUN-DRIED TOMATO SOUP

Serves 6

1 butternut squash
2 medium onions, peeled and chopped
2 tablespoons butter
1 cup sun-dried tomatoes, packed in oil
1 quart chicken stock
1/4 teaspoon red chile flakes
2 tablespoons finely chopped basil
sea salt or fish sauce and pepper to taste
piima cream or creme fraiche

Cut squash in half lengthwise and place, cut sides down, in a glass baking pan with about 1/2 inch of water. Bake at 350 degrees until tender, about one hour. Meanwhile, saute onions gently in butter until tender. Add tomatoes, stock and chile flakes. Bring to a boil and skim. Scoop cooked squash out of skin and add to soup. Simmer about 1/2 hour. Blend with a hand-held blender. Thin with water if necessary. Add basil and season to taste. Ladle into heated bowls and serve with cultured cream.

The traditional medical school teaches that alcoholism is primarily a mental disease, a personality disorder or a weakness from which the person is trying to escape. The medical community fully recognizes that an alcoholic is generally malnourished, but the idea that alcoholism might be caused by lack of nourishment to the brain cells has received very little consideration. Dr. Roger J. Williams, former Director of the Clayton Foundation Biochemical Institute and first elected President of American Chemical Society, claims that it is quite possible that malnutrition develops as a forerunner of alcoholism, and that it is only when malnutrition of the brain cells becomes severe that true alcoholism appears. "Furthermore," he states, "I will herewith positively assert that no one who follows good nutritional practices will ever become an alcoholic." Lynn Sorenson *Health Freedom News*

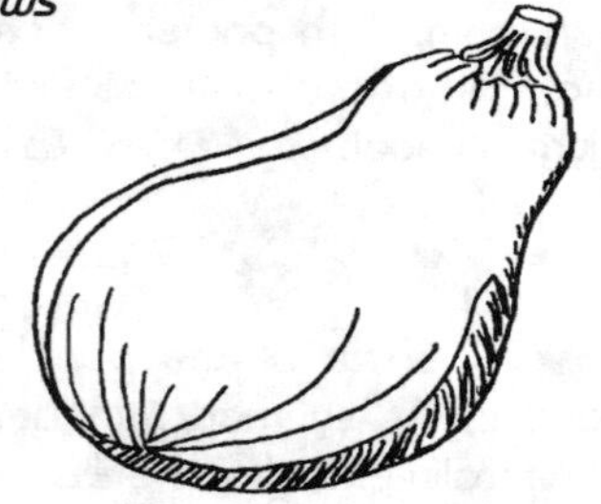

The black hat that butter has worn for the past generation may not be entirely warranted. Nor is the white hat worn by corn oil.

At least this is the indication from research conducted at Oregon Health Sciences University. Although butter does raise blood cholesterol in some individuals, the Oregon scientists found that rats given a diet rich in butterfat showed lower blood pressure than those given corn oil as their sole dietary fat. James F. Scheer *Health Freedom News*

PEANUT SOUP

Serves 6

2 medium onions, peeled and chopped
1 medium light green chile pepper or red pepper, seeded and chopped
1 teaspoon freshly grated ginger
2 tablespoons butter
1 cup freshly ground peanut butter
1 1/2 quarts chicken stock, heated
4 cloves garlic, peeled and coarsely chopped
1/4 cup soy sauce
1/4 cup finely chopped cilantro
piima cream or creme fraiche

Saute onion, pepper and ginger in butter until tender. Add peanut butter. Slowly add heated stock, beating constantly with a whisk. Bring to a simmer, not a boil. Add soy sauce and garlic and simmer about 10 minutes.

Blend with a hand-held blender. Ladle into heated bowls, garnish with cilantro and serve with cultured cream.

The peanut is a legume that is particularly rich in protein and fat. It is an excellent source of niacin, pantothenic acid and bioton as well as other B vitamins, vitamin E and iron, calcium and potassium. Peanuts are also rich in tryptophan, an amino acid that promotes a healthy nervous system. As peanuts are often grown as a rotation crop with cotton, a heavily sprayed commodity, it is important to buy only organic peanuts and peanut butter. The carcinogenic mold aflatoxin that sometimes develop in peanuts, especially those grown in moist climates, is virtually neutralized by cooking or soaking. Peanuts should never be eaten raw. Buy freshly ground peanut butter made from roasted organic peanuts. SWF

ALMOND SOUP

Serves 6

2 medium onions, peeled and coarsely chopped
3 tablespoons butter
3 cups finely ground crispy almonds (page 487)
1 quart chicken stock
1/2 teaspoon ground cardamom
sea salt or fish sauce and pepper to taste
piima cream or creme fraiche

Saute onions gently in butter until tender. Add almonds and stock, blend together with a whisk and heat gently. Add cardamom and simmer about 15 minutes.

Blend with a hand-held blender. Season to taste. Ladle into heated bowls and serve with cultured cream; or allow to cool, stir in cream and serve the soup chilled.

Nuts, particularly peanuts and almonds, . . . surprisingly may help prevent the crippling bone disease osteoporosis. These foods are high in trace mineral boron, now thought critical in producing hormones that help regulate calcium metabolism. Tests by Dr. Forrest H. Nielsen, at the US Department of Agriculture's Human Nutrition Research Center in Grand Forks, North Dakota, found that women on low-boron diets were more apt to lose calcium and magnesium, essential for keeping bones strong. But when given three milligrams of boron a day for three months, their calcium losses dropped by 40 percent. People who eat lots of fruits and nuts get an average three milligrams daily, says Nielsen. One of the richest sources: peanuts. Three-and-a half ounces contain two milligrams of boron. Jean Carper *The Food Pharmacy Guide to Good Eating*

BLACK BEAN SOUP

Serves 6

2 medium onions, peeled and coarsely chopped
extra virgin olive oil
4 cups cooked beans with bean juice (page 469), or 4 cups thick leftover bean liquid
1 quart beef or chicken stock
1/2 cup sherry
4 cloves garlic, peeled and mashed
1 teaspoon ground cumin
1 teaspoon dried oregano
1/4-1/2 teaspoon red chile flakes
1/4 cup fresh lime juice
sea salt or fish sauce and pepper to taste
piima cream or creme fraiche
chopped cilantro for garnish
finely chopped green onion for garnish

This is a good way to use leftover beans, or the thick bean juice that is left after all the beans have been eaten. Saute onions gently in olive oil until tender. Add beans or bean liquid, sherry and stock, bring to a boil and skim. Add cumin, oregano, garlic and chile flakes and simmer about 15 minutes. Blend with a hand-held blender. Reheat and add lime juice. Season to taste with sea salt and freshly ground pepper. Ladle into heated bowls and serve with cultured cream, cilantro and green onions.

I found Junkie dead this morning. She was cold and still and dark red-brown blood showed on her nose and paws.

What had I done? I killed her. For fourteen weeks I fed her "junk" food. She ate white flour products of white bread, saltines, doughnuts, sweet rolls, dinner rolls and cookies. Highly sweetened foods were candies, gum drops, malted milk balls, candy corn, marshmallows, sugar frosted cereals, chocolates and jelly on her bread.

Her death abruptly ended my experiment raising two young white rats. Junkie's food contrasted with Goodie's which were nutritious whole foods. She drank milk, had hard boiled eggs, shells and all, whole wheat bread, butter and peanut butter, oats, popcorn, dry beans and seeds, meat, fish, chicken, liver and a fresh dark green cabbage leaf or a piece of fruit.

I wanted to demonstrate the effects of these two diets so I could show off my rats at fairs, in nutrition classes and at day care centers, for both children and parents. The two rats showed a startling difference.

They began when about a month old, weighing almost the same at 128 and 129 grams.. . . I kept them in separate cages and fed them enough of their different diets so they always had more food than they could eat. . . Goodie drank milk but Junkie refused uncarbonated soft drinks so I stopped offering them. . . when both were about the ages of an eight year old child, Goodie weighed 469.1 grams and Junkie weighted 168.7 grams.

SAFFRON SHRIMP BISQUE

Serves 6

2 medium onions, peeled and chopped
2 carrots, peeled and chopped
2 stalks celery, chopped
4 tablespoons butter
shells and heads from 2 pounds fresh shrimp
(reserve shrimp for other uses)
extra virgin olive oil
3 quarts filtered water
2 tablespoons gelatin (see Sources)
2 tablespoons tomato paste
1/4 teaspoon saffron threads
1 clove garlic, peeled and mashed
1 teaspoon green peppercorns, crushed
several sprigs fresh thyme, tied together
1/3 cup armagnac or dry sherry (optional)
2 tablespoons arrowroot mixed with
2 tablespoons water
sea salt or fish sauce and pepper to taste
1 cup piima cream or creme fraiche

Saute onions, carrots and celery in butter about one hour or until slightly caramelized. In a heavy bottomed pot saute shrimp heads and shells in olive oil until they turn pink. Add water and sauted vegetables and bring to a rolling boil. Skim. Add gelatin, tomato paste, saffron, garlic, peppercorns and thyme. Boil, uncovered, for about 1 hour or until stock is reduced by half. Strain into another pot and add optional sherry or armagnac. Simmer another 10 minutes. Spoonful by spoonful add arrowroot mixture until desired consistency is obtained. Season to taste. Ladel into heated bowls and serve with cultured cream.

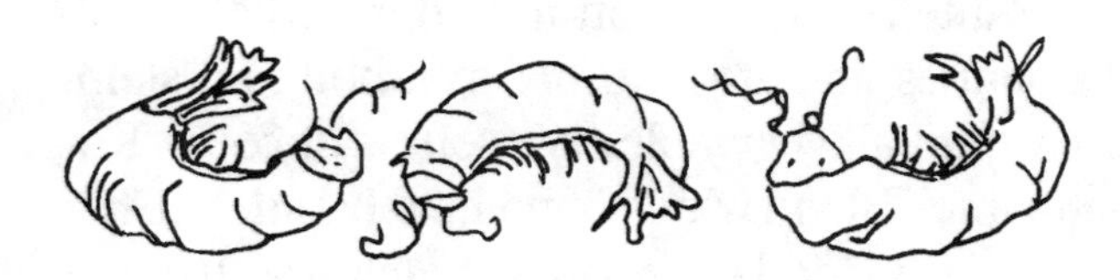

This contrast in weight showed. When I picked up Goodie she felt firm and solid, but Junkie was light and frail. Goodie's fur was full and thick, but Junkie's fur was so thin her skin showed through. . . There were contrasts in endurance. I noticed this when I took both out of their cages to let visitors examine them closely. This extra handling had no effect on Goodie, but Junkie tired quickly and curled up for sleep at every chance while Goodie was up and peering out at the excitement.

I had little warning that the end was near for Junkie. She was vigorous, though small and undersized, until the day before yesterday when I saw her lose her balance briefly. . . when she tried to walk she kept falling over. . . I endeavored to revive her with a little milk, whole wheat bread, peanut butter and a green cabbage leaf. . . She nibbled on the leaf but I was too late.

It was sobering to wheel a shopping cart later today in a supermarket past shelf after shelf of candies and sweet rolls from which I had selected Junkie's foods. If mothers and teachers could see my little Junkie cold and dead on these foods, they would think twice about letting their children have them, certainly not as a day to day diet.

It could be misleading to look at an undersized active child and think he's doing well. You often hear, "He's the wiry type." Beware. Junkie was active and outwardly healthy up to the day before she collapsed. Ruth Rosevear *PPNF Journal*

Many people are not aware that you can actually have a cholesterol deficiency, and that this deficiency can damage the heart! The heart cannot function adequately unless the nerves which control it are healthy—a state dependent on an adequate supply of cholesterol and other nerve-nourishing substances. . . very low levels of cholesterol. . . have been associated with increased cancer risk. Cholesterol is needed to protect cells from damage by radiation, toxins, viruses, and other substances which can initiate cancer. Cass Igram MD *Eat Right to Live Longer*

CURRIED APPLE SOUP

Serves 6

6 tart apples
butter and extra virgin olive oil
2 medium onions, peeled and chopped
1 teaspoon grated fresh ginger
1 teaspoon each dry mustard, turmeric, ground cumin, and ground coriander
1/4 teaspoon each cloves, cinnamon and cayenne
1 1/2 quarts chicken stock
juice of 1 lemon
sea salt to taste
piima cream or creme fraiche

Saute onions in butter and oil until soft. Stir in seasonings. Add stock and apples and simmer until apples are soft. Blend with hand-held blender. Season with lemon juice and salt. Ladel into heated bowls and serve with cultured cream.

VICHISSOISE

Serves 8

3 leeks, peeled, cleaned and chopped
4 potatoes, peeled and chopped
butter and extra virgin olive oil
6 cups chicken stock
several sprigs thyme, tied together
1 cup piima cream or creme fraiche
sea salt and freshly ground pepper to taste
finely chopped chives for garnish

We make a compromise for tradition in this recipe and use peeled potatoes, to achieve a creamy white vichissoise. (Use peels to make potassium broth, page 566.)

Saute leeks until soft in butter and olive oil. Add potatoes and stock, bring to a boil and skim. Simmer until all vegetables are soft. Let cool. Remove thyme. Blend with a hand held blender. Chill well. Process in food processor in batches with piima cream until frothy. Season to taste. Serve in chilled soup bowls and garnish with chives.

DR. CONNELLY'S VEGETABLE SOUP

Serves 6

4 cups chicken stock or water
4 tablespoons tomato paste
1 cup french beans, cut into 1-inch lengths
1 cup finely chopped celery with leaves
2-3 medium zucchinis, quartered lengthwise and thinly sliced
2 tablespoons parsley, finely chopped
1/2 teaspoon paprika
sea salt or fish sauce and freshly ground pepper

This is a tasty version of Bieler broth (page 567), recommended for increased energy and treatment of stress. In particular, zucchini with its high sodium content feeds the adrenal glands. Dr. Thomas Connelly, DC of Washington DC recommends this soup for back pain, ligament problems and other symptoms of depleted adrenal function.

Bring stock or water and tomato paste to a boil, blend with a wire whisk and skim. Reduce heat, add ingredients and simmer until they are just tender and still green, about 10 minutes. Stir in parsley and season to taste.

COLD CUCUMBER SOUP

Serves 4

2 medium cucumbers, peeled and sliced
1 cup chicken stock
1 cup piima cream, creme fraiche or plain yoghurt
2 mashed cloves garlic
1 tablespoon lemon juice
sea salt and freshly ground pepper
1 teaspoon finely chopped mint or dill (optional)

Place all ingredients except seasonings and mint or dill in food processor and blend until smooth. Season to taste. Stir in the mint or dill and season to taste. Serve well chilled.

These oils [in margarine] are as refined as the gasoline in your car. In the refinery they are treated with a caustic soda solution which removes the lecithin, an essential nutrient. Then the oil is steam-cleaned under a vacuum at tremendous temperature. This second step should destroy any remaining food value in the oil, but, just in case, the oil is then bleached at a high temperature to remove any color.

The liquid oil is then chemically treated by being bombarded with hydrogen under pressure in the presence of the metal nickel. This "hydrogenation" process is what makes the oil look like real butter. But now it's no longer a "polyunsaturate" which is supposed to be so good for you. The remaining step in the manufacture of plastic butter is to steam clean it *again* at high temperatures to deodorize it. Then the preservative and color are added, and it is ready for your table.

The liquid part of margarine, which is the second largest component, is usually *repasteurized*, that is reheated, skim milk. So the butter substitute on your toast has been steam-cleaned or superheated at least *four times*. William Campbell Douglass MD *The Milk of Human Kindness*

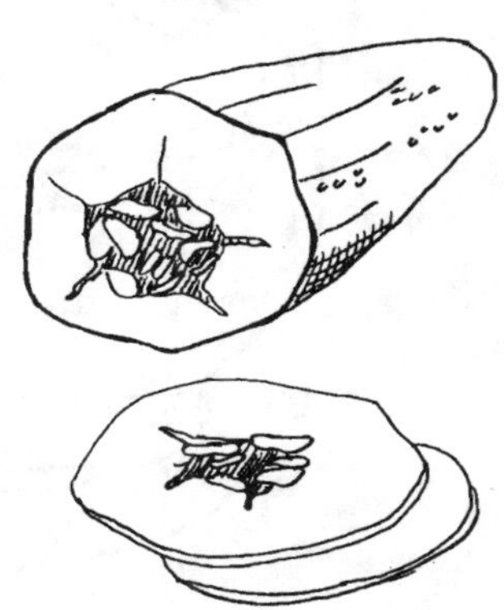

PINK GAZPACHO

Serves 6

NEW WORLD DINNER

Pink Gazpacho

Crab Cakes with Red Pepper Sauce

Gourmet Succatash

Strawberry Pecan Tart

6 ripe tomatoes, peeled, seeded and chopped
1 cucumber, peeled and chopped
2 green peppers, seeded and chopped
3 cloves garlic, peeled and chopped
1 cup whole grain bread crumbs
5 tablespoons raw vinegar
5 tablespoons extra virgin olive oil
2 tablespoons tomato paste
2-3 cups water
sea salt and pepper
salad croutons (page 491) for garnish
1 bunch green onion, finely chopped, for garnish
1 cucumber, peeled and finely chopped, for garnish

The combination of ingredients in this soup seems unlikely but this version of gazpacho is truly delicious, a wonderful starter for a summer meal. The accompaniments—croutons, green onions and cucumber—are a must.

Mix vegetables, vinegar, oil, bread crumbs and tomato paste in a bowl and let stand about 1 hour. Blend in batches in a food processor, adding water as needed to make a puree. Thin with water to desired consistency. Season to taste. Chill well before serving. Serve with croutons, finely chopped green onion and finely diced cucumber.

By slowing down stomach emptying time, fats promote more complete digestion and help ensure that no undigested food enters our colon to feed yeasts, fungi and strange bacteria. Fats and oils also inhibit the growth of fungi and yeasts.

Short-chain fatty acids such as butyric acid (4:0) found in butter serve as food for beneficial bacteria in our intestine. Others, like caprylic acid (8:0) slow down the growth of yeast cells. Udo Erasmus *Fats that Heal, Fats that Kill*

UNBLENDED GAZPACHO

Serves 6

1 cup lemon pepper dressing (page 123)
2 bunches green onions, finely chopped
2 green peppers, seeded and finely chopped
1 bunch celery, with leaves, finely chopped
3 cucumbers, peeled, seeded and finely chopped
1 bunch radishes, finely chopped
1 quart chicken stock
6 tomatoes, peeled, seeded and chopped
1/4 cup finely chopped chives
1 tablespoon finely chopped parsley

This unusual gazpacho will draw raves from your guests. The secret is to chop all the vegetables very small and use a very rich chicken stock.

Mix green onions, celery, peppers, cucumbers and radishes with dressing and marinate, refrigerated, for 12 to 24 hours. Stir in stock and tomatoes. Ladle into soup bowls and garnish with chives and parsley.

We now know that to replace saturated fats with unsaturated fats, while it *may* limit the risk of cardio-vascular disease, presents other less well known dangers. Although scientists are usually little inclined to base their arguments on tradition, they have nonetheless noticed that no peoples has consumed large quantities of polyunsaturated fats over long periods. The remarkable fact is that studies of non-industrialized peoples leads to the conclusion that the amount of polyunsaturated fats in the diet should be about 4% of the total caloric intake which is really very little—about 1 1/2 soup spoons per day of sunflower oil. . . On the other hand, the amount of saturated fat consumed varies considerably from one ethnic group to another. Claude Aubert *Dis-Moi Comment Tu Cuisines*

SPICED GAZPACHO

Serves 6

8 tomatoes, peeled, seeded and chopped
5 garlic cloves, peeled and chopped
5 stalks celery, chopped
2 medium red onions, peeled and chopped
5 tablespoons extra virgin olive oil
2 tablespoons lemon juice
1 tablespoon raw wine vinegar
2 1/2 teaspoons paprika
1 1/2 teaspoon ground cumin (optional)
1/4 teaspoon cayenne pepper
1/2 cup cilantro, coarsely chopped
1/2-1 cup water
sea salt and freshly ground pepper

Mix all ingredients except water together. Process in batches in food processor until not quite smooth. Thin to desired consistency with water. Season to taste. Serve well chilled.

RAW MEAT APPETIZERS

When Dr. Weston Price made his pioneering studies of primitive peoples around the world, he was struck by the fact that almost every group he visited ate a certain amount of their animal protein raw. The proportion of raw animal protein in the diet varied considerably. Among the Eskimos it verged on 100 percent; natives of the Polynesian islands consumed a good portion of the sea food they caught without cooking it; African tribes valued liver in its raw state as essential to good health and optimum growth and strength. Tribes whose eating habits were largely vegetarian nevertheless ingested raw animal protein in the form of grubs and insects adhering to plant leaves. The principal source of raw animal protein for European communities was unpasteurized milk products.

Today, unfortunately, raw dairy products are largely unavailable in America. We can and should, however, eat raw meat and fish on a regular basis. Almost every world cuisine offers recipes to satisfy what seems to be a universal requirement for raw animal protein—*steak tartare* from France, *carpaccio* from Italy, *kibbeh* from the Middle East and raw, marinated fish dishes from Scandinavian, Hawaii, Latin America and the Far East. The collection we offer here attests to the universality of this practice.

Many researchers have recommended that raw meat be included in the diet on a regular basis; but others, citing the problem of intestinal parasites, insist that meat should never be eaten raw. (No wonder most of us are confused about nutrition!) Parasite infection occurs frequently among the Japanese and Koreans, who habitually eat raw fish, so these warnings must be taken seriously. Fortunately we can eliminate parasites in meat without cooking it.

The problem of parasites in beef or lamb is easily solved. Simply freeze the meat for 14 days. According to the USDA, this will kill off all parasites. Needless to say, you should use only organic meat for your raw meat appetizers. The problem with fish is trickier as fish looses its firmness and texture when frozen. The solution—found universally among ethnic cuisines, especially in hot countries—is to marinate or ferment fish in an acid solution of lemon juice, lime juice or whey. This will effectively kill off all parasites and pathogens, and will serve to pre-digest the fish as well. We do not recommend *sushi*, which contains raw fish that has not been marinated.

If you are not used to eating meat raw but want to take that courageous first step, we suggest you begin with *kibbeh*, a mixture of raw lamb and bulgur (sprouted cracked wheat) from the Middle East. It is simply delicious, a meal in itself, as well as a dish that will please the most exacting gourmet. Then move on to the other recipes offered here, an eclectic sampling of raw meat dishes from around the world.

SIMPLE KIBBEH

Serves 6-12

1 pound ground lamb, frozen 14 days and thawed
1 cup bulgur (page 436)
1/4 cup pickled red pepper (page 93), processed to a paste in food processor (optional)
1 small onion, very finely chopped
sea salt and pepper
extra virgin olive oil
1 small onion, finely sliced
lemon wedges

Soak bulgur in warm water for 10 minutes. Pour into a strainer, rinse and squeeze out moisture. Mix with lamb, red pepper paste and onion. Add salt and pepper to taste. Form into a mound or loaf on a plate and brush with olive oil. Garnish with onion slices and lemon wedges. Serve with pita bread as an appetizer or on lettuce leaves as a first course.

SPICY KIBBEH

Serves 6-12

1 pound ground lamb, frozen 14 days and thawed
1 1/2 cup bulgur (page 436)
1 small onion, finely minced
2 tablespoons lemon juice
1 teaspoon each ground allspice and cinnamon
generous pinch nutmeg
1/4 teaspoon cayenne pepper
1/4 cup pine nuts, toasted in oven
extra virgin olive oil
2 small onions, thinly sliced
lemon wedges

Soak bulgur in warm water for 10 minutes. Pour into a strainer, rinse and squeeze out moisture. Mix with lamb, lemon juice, spices and onion. Add salt and pepper to taste. Form into a mound or loaf on a plate and brush with olive oil. Garnish with pine nuts, onion slices and lemon wedges. Serve with pita bread as an appetizer or on lettuce leaves as a first course.

In the *National Geographic* (1970), William S. Ellis described *kibbeh*, the national dish of Lebanon. It consists basically of raw lamb and crushed wheat. These foods are pounded together for about an hour in a large stone mortar, then kneaded, seasoned, and eaten raw—*kibbeh niebh*. The enzymes cathepsin and lipase of the lamb, and the protease, amylase and lipase of wheat, being liberated from their bondage by pulverization, cooperate to achieve predigestion and inactivation of enzyme inhibitors during the hour the food is being pulverized. Thereafter the predigestion continues both before and after the food is eaten, until the stomach acidity becomes very strong. People who eat this Lebanese dish save their own enzymes. Edward Howell MD *Enzyme Nutrition*

Pyridoxine or B6 deficiencies are widespread in America, in part because B1 and B2 added to white flour interfere with vitamin pathways involving B6, and also because our best source of this heat-sensitive vitamin—raw milk—is no longer sold commercially. This leaves raw meat and fish as the only sure source of B6 available to most Americans. Deficiencies of B6 have been linked with diabetes, heart disease, nervous disorders, carpel tunnel syndrome, PMS, morning sickness, toxemia of pregnancy, kidney failure, alcoholism, asthma, sickle cell anemia and cancer. B6 supplements have been shown to be highly effective in preventing blindness in diabetics. Americans would be wise to include raw meat or fish on a frequent basis to avoid these debilitating conditions. SWF

KEUFTAH

Serves 6

1/2 pound ground lamb, frozen 14 days and thawed
1 1/2 cups bulgur (page 436)
1 onion, minced
pinch cayenne pepper
1 tablespoon extra virgin olive oil
1 tablespoon lemon juice
2 tablespoons green pepper, minced
2 tablespoons green onions, minced
1/4 cup parsley, finely chopped
1 tablespoon fresh mint or basil, minced
extra virgin olive oil
1 lemon

Keuftah differs from *kibbeh* in that it contains a higher proportion of bulgur (cracked wheat). Soak bulgur in warm water for 10 minutes. Pour into a strainer, rinse and squeeze out moisture with hands. Mix with lamb, lemon juice, olive oil, spices, pepper, onion and herbs. Add salt and pepper to taste. Form a mound on a platter, brush with olive oil and decorate with lemon wedges. Serve with pita bread as an appetizer or on lettuce leaves as a first course.

CORNED BEEF

Makes 2 pounds

1 2-pound beef brisket, frozen 14 days and thawed
1/2 cup whey
1 cup filtered water
2 tablespoons sea salt
1 tablespoon mustard seeds
4-5 bay leaves, crumbled
1 tablespoon juniper berries, crushed
1 teaspoon red pepper flakes

Mix seasonings and rub into both sides of brisket. Place in a bowl that just contains it. Mix whey with water and pour over brisket. Cover and marinate at room temperature for about 2 days, turning frequently. Transfer to refrigerator. Use for sandwiches or corned beef hash (page 376).

Animal feeding experiments show that many changes besides bone growth take place when cooked foods are used. One of the most extensive of these studies, involving 900 cats over a period of 10 years, was done by F.M. Pottenger, Jr., M. D. Cats receiving raw meat and raw milk reproduced normally from one generation to the next. All kittens showed the same good bone structure, were able to nurse, were resistant to infections and parasites, and behaved in a predictable manner. From generation to generation they maintained regular broad faces with adequate nasal cavities, broad dental arches, and regular dentition with firm, pink membranes, and no evidence of infection.

Cats receiving cooked meat presented quite a different picture. Abortion was about 25 percent in the first generation and 70 percent in the second generation. Deliveries were difficult, many cats dying in labor. Mortality rates of the kittens were high, frequently due to the failure of the mother to lactate, or the kittens being too frail to nurse. The kittens did not have the homogeneity of those cats fed on raw foods. Instead, each kitten was different in skeletal pattern.

In the second generation the kittens had irregularities in the skull and longer, narrower faces; the teeth did not erupt at the regular time; and diseases of the gums developed. By the third generation the bones were very fine with scarcely enough struc-

STEAK TARTARE

Serves 20, as an appetizer

1 pound ground sirloin or filet, frozen 14 days and thawed
1 medium onion, finely minced
1/4 cup parsley, finely chopped
3 tablespoons Dijon style mustard
2 egg yolks, raw
sea salt, pepper and cayenne to taste
2 hard boiled eggs, chopped fine
1 red onion, finely chopped
1 cup small capers, drained, rinsed and dried with paper towels
sourdough bread or round croutons (page 491)
butter

Mix beef with egg yolks, onion, parsley and seasonings. Form as a mound on a platter. Surround meat with bread or croutons. Serve with chopped egg, chopped onion, capers and butter, each in a separate bowl.

STEAK TARTARE, MEXICAN STYLE

Serves 4

1/2 pound ground sirloin, frozen for 14 days and thawed
1/2 cup lime juice
1 small tomato, peeled, seeded and finely chopped
1 small onion, finely chopped
3 or 4 small green chiles, seeded and finely chopped
sea salt to taste

Mix beef with lime juice and marinate, covered, in the refrigerator for about four hours. Mix with remaining ingredients and let sit in refrigerator another 2 hours. Serve with baked or fried sprouted whole wheat tortillas (page 490).

ture to hold the skull together. The teeth were smaller and more irregular. Some mothers steadily declined in health, dying from some obscure tissue exhaustion about three months after delivery.

The cooked-meat-fed cats were irritable, the females dangerous to handle, and the males more docile, often to the point of being unaggressive. Sex interest was slack or perverted; and skin lesions, allergies and intestinal parasites become progressively worse from one generation to the next. Pneumonia, diarrhea, osteomyelitis, arthritis and many other degenerative conditions familiar in human medicine were observed. The kittens of the third generation were so degenerated that none lived beyond the sixth month, thus terminating the strain.

At autopsy the cooked-meat-fed females frequently were found to have ovarian atrophy and uterine congestion, and the males showed failure in the development of active sperm. Organs showed signs of degenerative disease. Bones were longer but smaller in diameter and had less calcium. In the third generation some had bones as soft as rubber—a true condition of osteogenesis. Emory W. Thurston PhD *Nutrition for Tots to Teens*

CARPACCIO

Serves 6

2 pounds filet of beef, frozen 14 days, partially thawed and sliced as thinly as possible
extra virgin olive oil
dried pink and/or green peppercorns, crushed
2 cups egg mustard sauce (page 130)

Arrange meat slices on individual plates leaving the center of the plate empty, cover with plastic wrap and place in freezer for about 1 hour or until meat is very cold.

To serve, sprinkle with olive oil and peppercorns. Place a ramekin of sauce in the middle of each plate. Serve with sourdough bread or round croutons (page 491).

Among the many items of information of great interest furnished by Dr. Romig [when I visited the Eskimos] were facts that fitted well into the modern picture of association of modern degenerative processes with modernization. He stated that in his thirty-six years of contact with these people he had never seen a case of malignant disease among the truly primitive Eskimos and Indians, although it frequently occurs when they become modernized. He found similarly that the acute surgical problems requiring operation on internal organs such as the gall bladder, kidney, stomach and appendix do not tend to occur among the primitives, but are very common problems among the modernized Eskimos and Indians. Growing out of his experience, in which he had seen large numbers of the modernized Eskimos and Indians attacked with tuberculosis, which tended to be progressive and ultimately fatal as long as the patients stayed under modernized living conditions, he now sends them back when possible to primitive conditions and to a primitive diet, under which the death rate is very much lower than under modernized conditions. Indeed, he reported that a great majority of the afflicted recover under the primitive type of living and nutrition. Weston Price DDS *Nutrition and Physical Degeneration*

VIETNAMESE RAW BEEF

Serves 4

1 pound sirloin roast, frozen 14 days, partially thawed and sliced very thin
1 tablespoon extra virgin olive oil
3 tablespoons fresh lime juice
1 small onion, thinly sliced
1 jalapeno pepper, seeded and thinly sliced
1 bunch green onions, finely chopped
1/2 cup crispy peanuts, (page 486), finely chopped
1/2 cup dried onion flakes, sauted in olive oil and drained on paper towels
1 bunch cilantro, chopped
lime wedges

Mix olive oil, lime juice, sliced onion and jalapeno pepper and brush on meat slices. Marinate meat in refrigerator for several hours.

Shake off excess marinade and vegetable slices from meat and arrange on a platter or individual plates. Sprinkle green onions, peanuts, fried onion flakes and cilantro over meat. Garnish with lime wedges and serve with basic brown rice (page 441).

RAW BEEF, KOREAN STYLE

Serves 4-6

1 pound sirloin or flank steak, frozen for 14 days and partially thawed
1 cup soy sauce
1/4 cup rice vinegar
1 teaspoon grated ginger
4 cloves garlic, mashed
1 teaspoon raw honey
3 tablespoons toasted sesame oil
1 bunch green onions, chopped
2 tablespoons toasted sesame seeds
dash cayenne pepper

Cut the flank steak on the bias at 1/8 inch intervals. Cut these strips into a julienne, and chop with a cleaver. Mix remaining ingredients and marinate beef in this mixture, refrigerated, for several hours. Serve with brown rice and kimchi (page 86).

Extemporaneous opinion as to the incidence of disease in wild animals is not consistent. Some will say that wild animals develop many diseases; others that wild animals in their natural habitat are singularly free from all diseases. I have been unable to find recorded evidence of any instance of a pathological condition in wild jungle animals. . . The incidence of disease in wild animals in captivity has been carefully studied by Dr. Fox, Pathologist to the Zoological Society of Philadelphia. [He found] at least 30 common pathological entities in zoo animals. . . Among those found were acute and chronic gastritis, duodenitis, enteritis, colitis, liver disease and nephritis, myrocardial degeneration, pernicious anemia, thyroid disease, arthritis, malignancy, tuberculosis, arterial disease and adrenal disease.

It seems to be the opinion, at least in some quarters, that such an imposing array of pathological conditions is not to be found in modern zoos since the dawn of the raw diet principle. It is interesting to note than when captive wild animals are fed a diet resembling human food in the sense of it being largely heat-treated, they develop diseases similar or identical to those found in human beings. Edward Howell MD *Enzymes for Health and Longevity*

CEVICHE

Serves 4-6

1 pound sea bass, white fish filets or mackerel
1/2 cup lime juice
2 tablespoons whey (optional)
2 medium tomatoes, peeled, seeded and diced
1 small red onion, finely chopped
1/4 cup extra virgin olive oil
2 small green chiles, seeded and finely chopped
sea salt to taste
2 tablespoons cilantro, finely chopped
2 avocados, cut into wedges
lemon wedges

Cut fish into 1/2-inch cubes. Mix with lime juice and optional whey in a bowl and marinate in the refrigerator for 12 to 36 hours, stirring occasionally, until fish becomes opaque or "cooked". Lift out of marinade with a slotted spoon. Mix with tomatoes, onion, peppers, olive oil, salt and cilantro and marinate another hour. Serve with avocado and lemon wedges.

MARINATED SALMON

(Gravlox)
Serves 10-12

2-3 pounds fresh salmon, center cut, cleaned, scaled, with skin left on, cut into 2 filets
1/4 cup sea salt
1/4 cup sucanat
2 tablespoons green peppercorns, crushed
1/8 cup whey
2 large bunches fresh dill, snipped

This gourmet delicacy is so easy to make yourself—why pay dozens of dollars per pound to purchase it from a delicatessen?

Using pliers, remove any small bones in the filets. Rinse well and pat dry. Mix sucanat, pepper and salt together and rub thoroughly into the flesh side of both filets. Sprinkle with whey and cover both filets with dill. Place the filets together, flesh side together, and wrap well in plastic wrap. Wrap all in aluminum foil. Place between two cookie sheets and set a heavy weight, such as a brick, on top. Refrigerate at least two days and as long as six days, turning every 12 hours or so.

To serve, remove foil and plastic wrap. Slice thinly on the diagonal. Serve as an hors d'oeuvre with sour dough bread or round croutons (page 491), and fresh chives or finely chopped onion; or on individual plates with a similar garnish and lemon wedges.

Variations:

Use *snapper or bass* instead of salmon and substitute *parsley, chervil or chives* for dill.

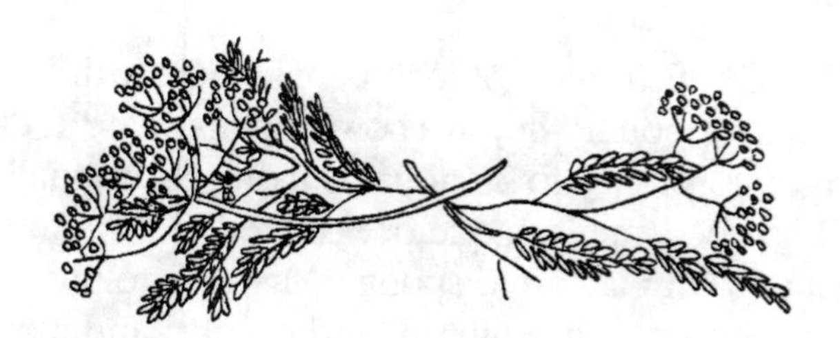

Health of the primitive Eskimo is stated by a number of qualified observers to be surpassed by no other race of people on this earth and equalled by few if any. . .The Eskimos showed no ketosis, having a remarkable power to oxidize fats completely, as evidence by the small amount of acetone bodies excreted in the urine during fasting. It is well known that in most human subjects ketosis appears when the material metabolized is restricted to protein and fat. . . It is not unlikely that freedom of the Eskimo from ketosis is related to ingestion of lipase with the food, causing better metabolism of fat than is the case with persons subsisting on the conventional heat-treated diet. . . Garber lived a number of years among Eskimos in northern Alaska and had occasion to observe their habits. Quotation: "Fish are put into a hole and covered with grass and earth and the mass is allowed to ferment and decay. I learned, to my utter astonishment, they would eat those rotten poisonous foods and thrive on them. Lest the reader might think that the cooking process would destroy the poisons in their vitiated foods, I wish to say that in only a few instances did they cook their food. The usual customary method was to devour it raw." Edward Howell MD *Enzymes for Health and Longevity*

TUNA TARTARE

Serves 4

3/4 pound fresh tuna, cut into 1/4 inch dice
1/4 cup lime juice
2 tablespoons whey (optional)
1 small red pepper
1/3 cup celery, diced
2 tablespoons red onion or scallions, finely diced
2 tablespoons small capers, rinsed, well drained and dried with paper towels
1 tablespoon fresh chives, chopped
1 tablespoon parsley, finely chopped
1 teaspoon fresh thyme leaves
1 tablespoon fresh basil, minced
1 tablespoon fresh lemon juice
3 tablespoon extra virgin olive oil
sea salt and pepper to taste
Boston lettuce leaves

Mix tuna with lime juice and whey, cover and marinate in refrigerator for 12 to 36 hours.

Cut pepper into quarters, remove seeds and place in a 450 degree oven, skin side up, for about 7 minutes or until the skin blisters. Cover with a plastic bag for 10 to 15 minutes and peel off skin. Cut into a fine dice.

Lift tuna out of marinade with slotted spoon and mix with vegetables and herbs. Mix lemon juice, olive oil and salt and pepper and toss with tuna mixture. Refrigerate, covered, for at least one hour. Serve on Boston lettuce leaves with round croutons (page 491).

As we have seen, the practice of eating autolyzed (predigested) meat and fish has been reported by a number of authorities as being common among diverse groups of Eskimos scattered over the northern regions and not related to each other. These groups are willing to overlook the objectionable odor because experience has taught them that the partially digested food gives them more endurance. Other groups of people around the world have likewise shared in finding unique values in partially digested protein food, such as aged cheese and hung, aged meat, In other words, autolyzed food, which has already been broken down into peptones and proteoses, uses less of our personal enzymes. This is what produces the feeling of well-being and surplus energy. Edward Howell MD *Enzyme Nutrition*

The food of these Eskimos in their native state includes caribou, ground nuts which are gathered by mice and stored in caches, kelp which is gathered in season and stored for winter use, berries including cranberries which are preserved by freezing, blossoms of flowers preserved in seal oil, sorrel grass preserved in seal oil, and quantities of frozen fish. Another important food factor consists of the organs of the large animals of the sea, including certain layers of the skin of one of the species of whale , which has been found to be very high in vitamin C. Weston Price DDS *Nutrition and Physical Degeneration*

When the first explorers visited the Marquesa Islands in the South Pacific, they described the inhabitants as the happiest, healthiest and most beautiful people in the world. . . Disease was unknown among these people. Their usual diet was steamed or fermented breadfruit, seafood and coconuts, supplemented by bananas, taro, and mangoes. Seafood was usually consumed raw and often alive. Small fish were eaten whole, while large fish were cut up and soaked in a mixture of sea water and lime juice. When food was cooked, it was wrapped in leaves and steamed in underground pits. This is the least destructive of all cooking methods, retaining the nutrients in the food. With the advent of trade ships, the natives eagerly exchanged their coconuts for refined flour, sugar, and opium. The Marquesan diet was seriously altered. By 1930 their population had dropped from 10,000 to less than 2,000. 37% of the people's teeth had been attacked by tooth decay and respiratory infection became common. Happily, the trade ships stopped visiting the Marquesans and most of the natives returned to their original simple (and highly nutritious) diet. They are regaining their health and their numbers are increasing. In 1973, natives in the inland villages showed little or no evidence of dental caries while those on the coast, where refined and canned foods were still available, had poor teeth. In our own United States 24 out of 25 children suffer dental disease before they are 6 years old. Over 98% of the population is afflicted with dental decay. *PPNF Journal*

SALMON CEVICHE

Serves 4

1 pound fresh salmon, skinned and cut into a 1/2 inch dice
1 small red onion, finely diced
2 teaspoons sea salt
dash Tabasco sauce
1 cup fresh lime juice
2 tablespoons whey (optional)
3 medium tomatoes, peeled, seeded and diced
1 bunch cilantro, chopped
Boston lettuce leaves
lime wedges

Mix lime juice with whey, onion, salt and tabasco sauce. Mix with salmon pieces. Cover and marinate in the refrigerator for at least 7 hours, and up to 24 hours, stirring occasionally. Before serving, mix with tomatoes and cilantro. Serve on Boston lettuce leaves and garnish with lime wedges.

MARINATED FISH IN COCONUT CREAM

Serves 4

1 pound whitefish, cut into 1/2 inch cubes
1 teaspoon sea salt
1/2 cup lime juice
1 tablespoon whey
3/4 cup coconut milk and cream (page 144)
1 bunch scallions, chopped
1 tomato, peeled, seeded and chopped (optional)
1 clove garlic, crushed (optional)
Boston lettuce leaves
1 tablespoon toasted sesame seeds

Mix salt with lime juice and whey. Toss with the fish and marinate at least 4 hours in the refrigerator. Drain the fish. Add coconut cream, scallions and optional tomato and garlic. Chill again about 1 hour. Serve on Boston lettuce leaves and garnish with sesame seeds.

PICKLED SALMON

Makes 1 quart

1 pound salmon, skinned and cut into 1/2 inch pieces
1 cup water
1/8 cup whey
1 tablespoon raw honey
1 tablespoon sea salt
1 cup pearl onions, peeled or 2 small onions, coarsely chopped
1 lemon, thinly sliced
1 tablespoon mustard seeds
1 teaspoon cracked pepper
2 bay leaves
1 bunch fresh dill, snipped

Mix water, whey, honey, and salt until salt and honey dissolve. Stir in lemon, onions, seasonings and fish. Place all in a quart-sized wide-mouth mason jar. Add more water if necessary to completely cover the fish. Cover tightly. Keep at room temperature for 24 hours before removing to refrigerator where the salmon will keep for several weeks.

To serve as an appetizer, arranges pieces of fish, onions and lemon in a bowl and serve with toothpicks. To serve as a first course, arrange on individual plates and garnish with tiny new potatoes, steamed and then tossed in a little of the marinade.

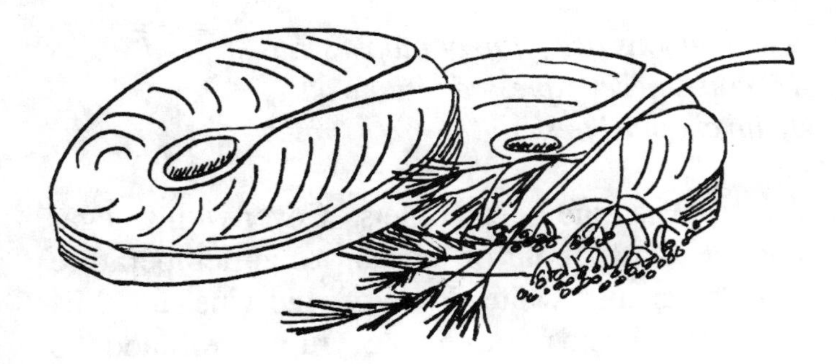

Dr. Crewe again reported on his work in 1930. . .[and] postulated, because of the remarkable effects seen in such a great variety of diseases, that raw milk may be supplying some hormonal elements to the patient. He repeatedly saw marked improvement in patients with toxic thyroid disease, a hormonal malady. Dr. Crewe was especially enthusiastic about raw milk in the treatment of disease of the prostate gland. . . Although Dr. Crewe's experiments were on the feeding of raw milk for disease, the key is not milk, but raw. The same results might be obtained, as Crewe implies, by eating fresh raw meat. He relates the story of the explorer Stefansson, who traveled the frozen Arctic with his colleagues living on fish, seal, polar bear, and caribou—nothing else for nine months. Most of this was eaten raw, and although undergoing the severest of hardships, they were never sick. On the return journey, they discovered a cache of civilized food, including flour, preserved fruits and vegetables, and salted, cooked meat. Against Stefansson's advice, the men ate this preserved food for several days. They quickly developed diarrhea, loose teeth, and sore mouths. Stefansson immediately placed them on raw caribou tongue, and in a few days they were well. William Campbell Douglass MD *The Milk of Human Kindness*

Herring and mackerel are two of the most abundant sea fishes; while they do not figure largely in gourmet cuisine, they form a staple of many ethnic cuisines, particularly in Holland and Scandinavian, where they are usually consumed pickled or smoked. Both are high protein and fatty fish, rich in fat soluble vitamins and omega-3 fatty acids. Herring is exceptionally rich in zinc, containing 110 milligrams per four ounce serving, almost ten times as much as the food next richest in zinc, sesame seeds. SWF

The greatest concentration of zinc in our body is in our eyes. . .The eyes alone use one-third as much oxygen as the heart, need ten to twenty times as much vitamin C as the joint capsules involved in the movement of our extremities, and require more zinc (our intelligence chemical) that any other organ system in the body. *PPNF Journal*

Pottenger proved there is a yet undiscovered deficiency disease, similar to Vitamin C deficiency (scurvy), that can be cured by giving an endocrine product *that contains no Vitamin C.* Raw milk has this unknown nutrient and pasteurized milk does not. Stefansson, a famous arctic explorer, demonstrated that a supposedly adequate intake of vitamin C in the form of tomato juice did not prevent scurvy in an arctic sea captain but just a few days on raw meat cured him completely. As shown by Pottenger, raw milk, if it had been available, would have accomplished the same thing. William Campbell Douglass MD *The Milk of Human Kindness*

PICKLED HERRING OR MACKEREL

1 1/2 pounds herring or mackerel
2 teaspoons sea salt
1 cup filtered water
1/8 cup whey
1 medium onion, peeled and coarsely chopped
1 teaspoon cracked pepper
1 teaspoon coriander seeds
2 bay leaves
1/4 teaspoon dried chile flakes

Scale, wash, skin and filet the fish (or have your fish monger do this for you.) Cut into small pieces. Mix with onions and spices and place in a quart-sized wide mouth mason jar. Mix salt, water and whey and pour over fish. Add more water if necessary to bring liquid to the top of the fish. Cover tightly. Leave at room temperature for 24 hours before transferring to refrigerator where it will keep for several weeks.

MUSTARD HERRING

Serves 6-8

2 pounds herring filets
1-2 cups raw vinegar
2 tablespoons Dijon type mustard
1 teaspoon sea salt
4 tablespoons rice syrup or maple syrup
1/2 cup expeller expressed sesame oil
1 cup chopped fresh dill

Wash the herring filets. Cover with vinegar and let stand 1 hour or more at room temperature until filets turn white. Pour off the vinegar. Mix mustard, salt and rice or maple syrup. Slowly add the oil to the mustard mixture, stirring constantly with a fork. If sauce is too thick, thin with a little water. Stir in the dill. Spread the filets in a glass dish and cover with sauce. Cover the dish and marinate for 2 days in the refrigerator. Serve with sour dough bread.

GOURMET APPETIZERS

A simple salad, a hearty soup, or a small serving of raw meat or fish —these best serve as starters for most evening meals. But sometimes the occasion calls for something grander. We offer this assortment of gourmet appetizers for your dinner parties and holiday feasts. Most feature nourishing traditional foods high in fat soluble vitamins such as sea food and organ meats. Start with the freshest and highest quality ingredients you can find and do pay attention to the presentation of your appetizers on the plate. The combination of good-tasting, nutritious food, attractively served, is sure to please your guests.

SAUTEED PRAWNS

Serves 4

12 large fresh prawns
4 tablespoons coriander seeds
1 tablespoon grated lemon peel
1 tablespoon cracked pepper
1 teaspoon sea salt
extra virgin olive oil
1 1/2 cup cilantro sauce (page 132)
cilantro sprigs for garnish

Peel the prawns carefully, leaving the tail. Using a marble mortar and pestle, or a mini grinder, crush or grind the coriander seeds until they are cracked. Mix cracked coriander seeds with lemon peel, pepper and salt. Press the mixture into the prawns, coating them completely. In a heavy skillet, saute the prawns in olive oil, a few at a time, until golden and cooked through. Spoon several tablespoons of cilantro sauce into each plate. Place three prawns on each plate and garnish with coriander sprigs.

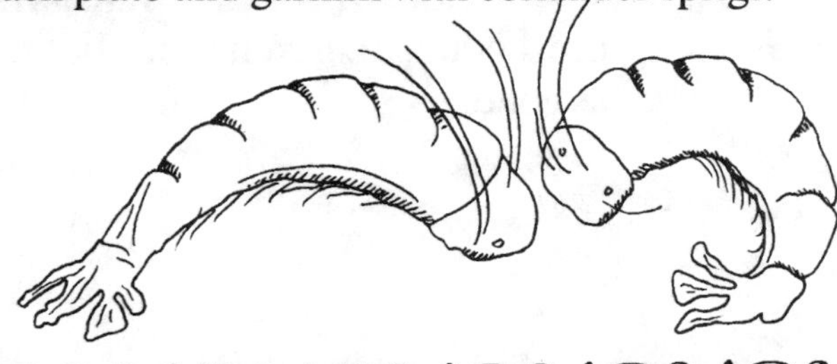

DUCK AND CHICKEN LIVER MOUSSE

Serves 8-10

Here in the land of the Three Musketeers, the Gascony region of southwest France, goose and duck fat are slathered on bread instead of butter, the people snack on fried duck skin and eat twice as much foie gras as other Frenchmen, and 50 times as much as Americans.

It was no surprise when Dr. Serge Renaud, in a 10-year epidemiological study that included surveys of eating habits, concluded that Gascons eat a diet higher in saturated fat than any other group of people in the industrialized world. . . But scientists crinkled a collective brow over Dr. Renaud's related findings about this region, which produces much of the world's foie gras, the fattened livers of ducks and geese. "The foie gras eaters of the Gers and Lot Departments in southwest France have the lowest rate of death from cardiovascular disease in the country," he said. . . . The basic Gascon in his blue beret would not be surprised. Standing in his barnyard Mr. Saint-Pe listened to Dr. Renaud's findings as though he were being told the obvious. "The people in my family live to be 90 years old," he said. "We cook everything in duck fat. We have foie gras on Sunday. Everybody knows this is the long-life diet." Elisabeth Rosenthal *New York Times*

1 1/2 pounds fresh duck livers
1 1/2 pounds fresh chicken livers
butter and extra virgin olive oil
1/2 cup dry white wine or cognac
1 cup beef or duck stock
2 eggs
1 cup piima cream or creme fraiche
sea salt and freshly ground black pepper
1-2 tablespoons truffle, very finely chopped (optional)
1 cup clarified beef or duck stock, cooled

Saute livers in butter and olive oil until all pink has gone. Pour in cognac or wine and 1 cup stock. Boil down until all liquid has almost completely evaporated. Let cool. Process half the livers with one egg and 1/2 cup cultured cream in food processor; repeat with other half. Transfer liver mixture to a bowl. Season generously and stir in optional truffles.

Line an oiled 1-quart loaf pan with oiled parchment paper. Pour pate into pan—it should be about two-thirds full. Spread top smooth. Cover with a piece of parchment paper and cover tightly with aluminum foil. Place in a pan of hot water and bake at 350 degrees for about 45 minutes. Let cool. Remove foil and top layer of parchment paper. Pour stock over, cover and chill well.

To serve, remove from loaf pan and slice. Serve with round or triangle croutons (page 491) or whole grain sour dough bread and thin slices of pickled cucumber (page 89).

Note: If duck livers are not available, you may use 4 pounds chicken livers, but the taste will not be as good.

DUCK TERRINE

Serves 10-12

1 5-pound domestic duck or 2 smaller wild ducks
livers from the duck(s)
1/4 pound calf's liver
3/4 pound ground veal
1 small onion, finely chopped
1 teaspoon sea salt
freshly ground black pepper
1 teaspoon canned green peppercorns, drained, rinsed and dried with paper towels
1/2 teaspoon ground all spice
1 teaspoon dried rosemary
1/4 cup dry white wine
grated rind and juice of 1 orange
about 1 cup clarified beef stock (page 115)

Terrines of all sorts form an important part of European cuisine. Most contain pork or pork fat. Here is an unusual recipe that does not. To prepare it you will need an oval, glazed 1-quart terrine, with a board cut to fit just inside the rim.

Remove skin and fat from the duck and cut away the duck meat. (Use skin and fat to make duck cracklings, page 273, and the carcass to make duck stock, page 115.) Cut duck meat and liver into small pieces. Mix the meats, onion, salt and peppers, allspice and rosemary in a bowl. Process this mixture in batches in your food processor. Stir in the wine, orange juice and rind.

Generously oil the mould and fill with the duck mixture. Wrap the board in parchment paper and set over the duck mixture. Weight down crosswise with a brick (so the brick pushes down the board but is not in danger of falling in the terrine.). Set in a pan of hot water and bake at 350 degrees for 1 1/2 hours. Refrigerate until cold. Pour the clarified bouillon (it should be cool) over the terrine and allow to refrigerate further.

To serve, slice the terrine and its layer of aspic into 1-inch slices. Arrange on individual plates with triangle croutons, finely sliced pickled cucumber and a few radishes for garnish.

Previously, food was considered to have no effects except for the production of heat and energy from fats and carbohydrates and the repair of tissues by proteins. Now it is known that food can change organs and tissues, including glands, for either better or worse. The fact that food can change the size and weight of these important glands (pituitary, testicle, ovary, pancreas, adrenal, thyroid) has been demonstrated over and over again by careful experimenters during past years. Professor Jackson and co-workers at the University of Minnesota fed white rats a diet containing 80 percent sugar (enzyme-free) and reported marked differences in the size and weight of all principal organs and glands. The importance of the pituitary in nature's scheme may be guessed by its being doubly shielded from physical injury, first by a substantial bony skull and then by being buried in the recesses of the brain. Since the pituitary gland has importance as a body regulator, the influence of food in modifying its size and function merits special attention. The pituitary has been credited with being a "master gland" of the body by virtue of exercising control and coordination of other endocrine glands. It has a degree of control out of proportion to its size. Edward Howell MD *Enzyme Nutrition*

BREADED BRAIN APPETIZER

Serves 8

2 pounds fresh calves brain
(See note on brains, page 288)
3 tablespoons soy sauce
1 medium onion, peeled and sliced
1 cup red wine
1 tablespoon green peppercorns, crushed
2 cups unbleached flour
1 teaspoon pepper
3 eggs lightly beaten
2 cups homemade whole grain bread crumbs
2 teaspoons fine herbs
1/2 teaspoon salt
butter and extra virgin olive oil
round croutons (page 491) for garnish
pickled cucumbers (page 89) for garnish
lime wedges for garnish

Marinate brains in mixture of soy sauce, wine, onions and pepper for several hours in the refrigerator. Mix flour with pepper and bread crumbs with fine herbs and salt. Carefully life brains out of marinade. Dredge first in flour, then in egg, then in bread crumb mixture. Saute in a mixture of butter and olive oil until golden and crispy on both sides. Arrange on individual plates with round croutons, thinly sliced pickles and lime wedges.

MARINATED SALMON PLATE

Serves 8

24 slices marinated salmon (page 218)
24 round croutons (page 491)
1/2 cup pickled daikon radish (page 91)
parsley sprigs

Arrange 4 slices marinated salmon and 4 croutons on each plate. Garnish each plate with a teaspoon of daikon radish and parsley sprigs.

The Samburu tribe of northern Kenya continues to baffle the cholesterol-fat alarmists. They drink nothing but milk for three days and then eat nothing but meat for one day. The sequence may vary, but in general, there are three milk days to one meat day. Pasteurization is unknown to them. The milk is cultured, similar to yoghurt.

They eat *four hundred grams* of fat per day. The average American, with his hardened arteries, eats a meager *eighty grams* of fat per day. The Samburu warrior, by tribal tradition, is bound from age fourteen to an *exclusive diet* of milk and meat for twenty years. No vegetable products are eaten except for some tree bark tea.

The Samburu's cousins to the south, the Masai, drink an average of seven quarts of very rich milk per day. Their diet is 60% saturated fat. When you consider that the average warrior weighs only one hundred thirty-five pounds, that's a *lot* of milk.

Mann and co-workers studied these tribes exhaustively. They found remarkably little heart disease, consistently normal blood pressure, no obesity, and a complete absence of rheumatoid arthritis, degenerative arthritis, and gout.

What about cholesterol? The average African child had a cholesterol value of 138. The average American child, 202. With increase in age, the native cholesterol values went *down* and the American values went *up*. Beyond the age of fifty-five, the mean cholesterol value of the African natives was 122. The American mean cholesterol for men was 234. William Campbell Douglass MD *The Milk of Human Kindness*

BRESAOLA AND MELON

Serves 4

4-6 ounces thinly sliced bresaola
1 ripe cantaloupe
freshly ground pepper
edible flowers for garnish (optional)

Bresaola is one of several air cured or fermented meats found throughout the Mediterranean region. It can be purchased at Italian delicatessens. Similar fermented meats include pemmican of the North American Indians (made from venison or fish, bear fat, maple syrup and berries), air dried mutton from the Faeroe Islands (valued by the natives for its strengthening properties) and cured dry sausages from France.

Slice melon and arrange artistically on four plates with slices of bresaola. Sprinkle with freshly ground black pepper and garnish with optional edible flowers.

COLD POACHED TROUT WITH MAYONNAISE

Serves 6

6 medium trout, scaled and cleaned
but heads left on
2-3 cups fish stock
1 cup herb or creole mayonnaise
(pages 126 & 128)
parsley sprigs for garnish

Place trout in a buttered pyrex dish. Bring stock to a boil and pour over fish. Bake at 350 degrees for about 15 minutes or until fish is tender.

Carefully remove fish and chill well. To serve, Arrange on individual plates with parsley sprig and ramekin of homemade mayonnaise.

Another link in the chain of evidence tracing effects to their causes is supplied by the illuminating behavior of the human and animal pancreas in response to extra work imposed by heat-treated, enzyme-deficient diet. The available evidence indicates that Orientals on a high carbohydrate cooked diet, essentially rice, display a pancreas approximately 50 per cent relatively heavier than that of Americans. The salivary glands of Orientals are also larger. Organ weight studies on experimental animals show that when a group of rats. . . is placed upon a heat-treated high carbohydrate diet and sacrificed after a period of feeding, the average weight of the pancreas and salivary glands shows a marked increase over a similar control group of animals on a mixed diet. This indicates that the pancreas and salivary glands are forced to undergo considerable hypertrophy to furnish the additional enzymes required, thus confirming experimentally in animals what has been observed in human beings. It is a singular circumstance that whereas cattle and sheep, ingesting a full quota of food enzymes, consummate the digestion of a comparatively high carbohydrate raw diet with only a small pancreas and without help from the salivary glands, human beings on a heat-treated mixed diet, lacking food enzymes, require a large pancreas and active salivary glands to digest a smaller amount of carbohydrate. And furthermore, a high carbohydrate, heat-treated diet engenders still greater enlargement of the pancreas and salivary glands in humans and animals. Edward Howell MD
Enzymes for Health and Longevity

FISH TERRINE WITH WATERCRESS SAUCE

Serves 8-10

1 1/2 pound filet of sole or flounder
3/4 pound salmon
1/2 cup dry white wine or vermouth
1/4 cup tarragon vinegar
1 small onion, finely chopped
several sprigs fresh tarragon
1 cup piima cream or creme fraiche
1 stick butter, melted
1 egg
2 egg whites
sea salt and freshly ground pepper
2 cups watercress sauce (page 132)

Cut the filets and the salmon into small pieces, keeping the two fish separate. Place wine, vinegar, onion and tarragon in a sauce pan and bring to a boil. Boil vigorously until reduced to about 3 tablespoons. Strain liquid and stir in the butter and the cream.

Butter a 1-quart terrine. Place half the white fish in the food processor along with 1/3 of the liquid and 1 egg white. Process until smooth. Season generously with sea salt and freshly ground pepper. Pour into the terrine and level with a knife. Process the salmon with another 1/3 of the liquid and the whole egg. Season to taste. Pour this over the first layer. Finally, process the remaining filets with the remaining liquid, 1 egg white and seasonings and pour this into the terrine. Cover with a piece of waxed paper or buttered parchment paper and a lid. Set in a pan of hot water and bake at 350 degrees for 50 minutes. Chill well before serving.

To serve, ladle several spoonfuls of sauce onto individual plates and place a slice of terrine on top of the sauce.

Variation:

Use *4 cups thin red pepper sauce* (page 131) in place of watercress sauce.

In nature fatty acids assume what is called the *cis* form. These *cis* fatty acids are naturally curved and biochemically suited for human nutrition because of the curvature of their shape and how electrons form around them. A *trans* fatty acid has the curve straightened out by placing a hydrogen atom (hydrogenation) in the wrong place—especially the wrong place for use by human metabolism.

The *trans* molecule simply doesn't fit in—it's the wrong shape and even more importantly, it has the wrong electrochemistry. However, and this is the dangerous part, *trans* fats do get taken up in the human metabolism and become part of the various functions required by fat in the human body, especially the making of cell membranes. Tom Valentine *Facts on Fats & Oils*

The biggest reason for the art of hydrogenation is firmly stated by Mr. Eckey in this book—hydrogenation provides an amazing shelf life and savings for consumers.

John Tobe remarked that "you save yourself a couple of pennies by buying a hydrogenated product, and will probably pay the doctor or the druggist or the hospital thousands of dollars through the years for the lousy few pennies these great benefactors of mankind, the processors, have saved you. They should be given citations and medals for the great work for humanity. You saved pennies but gained ill health." Tom Valentine *Facts on Fats & Oils*

SALMON MOUSSE WITH DILL SAUCE

Serves 12-18

1 tablespoon plus 2 teaspoons gelatin
1/2 cup cold water
1 cup boiling water
4 cups cooked salmon, flaked
2 tablespoons grated onion
1 cup homemade mayonnaise
2 tablespoons lemon juice
1/2 teaspoon tabasco sauce
1/2 teaspoon paprika
1 teaspoon sea salt
2 tablespoon small capers, rinsed, drained, dried with paper towels and chopped
2 tablespoons snipped dill
1 cup piima cream or creme fraiche
extra virgin olive oil
1 egg white, unbeaten
2 cups creamy dill sauce (page 130)

Soften gelatin in cold water, add boiling water and stir until well mixed. Add mayonnaise, lemon juice, onion, tabasco sauce, paprika, salt and dill. Mix well and chill to obtain a consistency of unbeaten egg white. Add salmon, capers and piima cream and mix well. Brush a 3 quart mold or individual molds with olive oil and then unbeaten egg white. Pour in mousse and chill well.

To unmold, dip mold or molds briefly into hot water and invert onto a plate. Serve with creamy dill sauce.

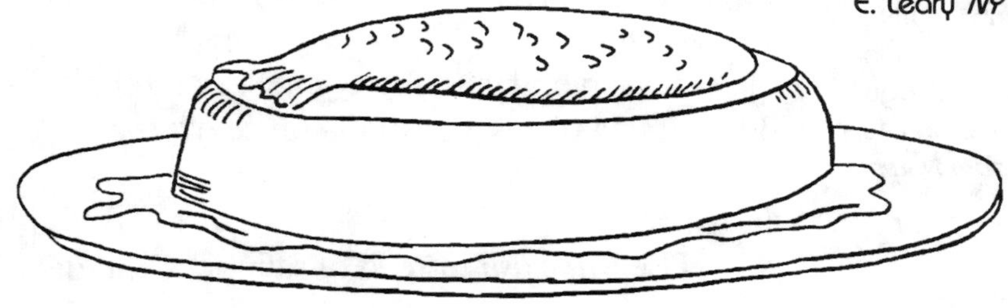

In the treatment of feverish and acute infectious diseases, it is evident that gelatin plays a double role. In the first place, the nutritive qualities of gelatin, its ready absorption and colloidal properties, make it ideally suited for inclusion in the diet both during the height of the fever and during convalescence. Bayley emphasized this factor from a nurse's viewpoint, observing that gelatin acts as a base for the preparation of many dainty, pleasing dishes which appeal to the patient with poor appetite, thus providing much needed nourishment. N.R Gotthoffer *Gelatin in Nutrition and Medicine*

Scientists say they have the first direct evidence that viruses can mutate and become deadly because of nutritional deficiencies in the hosts they infect. In their experiments, researchers found that a human virus normally harmless to mice mutated and became a heart-damaging agent in mice suffering from a nutritional deficiency. Once changed, they said, the virus was also able to infect and damage the hearts of nutritionally well-balanced mice.

This is the first time that a nutritional deficiency in host has been shown to alter viruses to make them permanently more virulent, the scientists said in a report published in today's issue of the journal *Nature Medicine*. Warren E. Leary *NY Times News Service*

SALMON QUENELLES WITH DILL SAUCE

Serves 6-8

1 1/2 pounds skinless salmon
1 1/2 tablespoons softened butter
5 slices whole grain bread, crusts removed, processed into crumbs
2/3 cup heavy cream
1 large egg, lightly beaten
2 tablespoons fresh lemon juice
1 teaspoon each sea salt and pepper
3 cups fish stock
1 cup piima cream or creme fraiche
1 tablespoon fresh dill, chopped

Quenelles are cylindrical concoctions of fish mousse, poached in stock and served with a sauce. They take time to make, but are greatly appreciated by gourmets.

In a food processor, puree salmon until smooth. Add the butter and puree until incorporated. Meanwhile soak the breadcrumbs in cream for several minutes. Add soaked breadcrumbs to food processor, along with egg, salt, pepper and lemon juice. Process until well blended.

Bring the stock to a boil, then reduce to a simmer. Shape fish mixture into cylinders using about 2 tablespoons of the mixture each. Place carefully in simmering stock and poach about 6-8 minutes. Remove with a slotted spoon to paper towels and keep warm in the oven while making sauce.

Strain the stock into another saucepan and bring to a rapid boil. Add the cream. Boil vigorously until reduced and thickened. Stir in the dill and check for seasonings.

To serve, divide the quenelles among individual serving plates and spoon sauce over.

Variation:

Use *white fish* instead of salmon. Omit dill.

Strict vegetarian women who breast-feed their infants may be subjecting them to possible long-term brain damage.

So indicate the findings of a research team made up of scientists from the University of Cincinnati, Harvard School of Public Health, Vanderbilt and Brandeis Universities.

Often these women eat sea vegetables, tempeh, miso and tamari that [theoretically] contain adequate amounts of vitamin B-12, believing that they fully supply the body's required vitamin B-12. However, . . .test reveal that individuals who ingested such products showed no increase in vitamin B-12 blood levels.

A similar study by Dutch bio-chemists demonstrated that ingested seaweed products did not correct vitamin B-12 deficiencies in infants. Neither did spirolina, a micro algae. And the researchers are still trying to understand why not.

Blood levels of vitamin B-12 in adult vegetarians were also found deficient by both research groups. Half the subjects tested were low in this vitamin and one-quarter of them were extremely low.

The Dutch researchers learned that infants of many vegetarian women have abnormal red blood cells, delayed motor skills and slow growth, compared with control group babies.

Best sources of vitamin B-12? Liver, sardines, mackerel, herring, salmon, lamb, Swiss cheese, eggs, haddock, beef, blue cheese, halibut, scallops, cottage cheese, chicken and milk. James F. Scheer *Health Freedom News*

CRAB CAKES WITH RED PEPPER SAUCE

Makes 8 patties

2 cups crab meat
2 small onions, finely minced
2 eggs, lightly beaten
2 tablespoons Dijon-type mustard
1/4-1/2 teaspoon cayenne
1 cup whole grain bread crumbs
1 bunch cilantro, chopped
1 teaspoon grated lemon rind
sea salt and pepper to taste
butter and extra virgin olive oil
2 cups red pepper sauce (page 131)
cilantro sprigs for garnish

Combine eggs with onions, breadcrumbs and seasonings. Mix in crab. Form into cakes. Saute until golden, a few at a time, in butter and olive oil. To serve, spread a few spoonfuls of sauce on individual plates. Place one or two crab cakes on top. Garnish with cilantro sprigs.

There are certain characteristics of the various dietaries of the primitive races, which are universally present when that dietary program is associated with a high immunity to disease and freedom from deformities. In general, these are the foods that provide adequate sources of body-building and body-repairing material. The use by primitives, of foods relatively low in calories has resulted in forcing them to eat large quantities of these foods. . . The primitives have obtained, often with great difficulty, foods that are scarce but rich in certain elements. In these rare foods were elements which the body requires in small quantities, including minerals such as iodine, copper, manganese and special vitamins. In connection with the vitamins it should be kept in mind that our knowledge of these unique organic catalysts is limited. The medical profession and the public at large think of vitamin D as consisting of just one chemical factor, whereas, investigations are revealing continually new and additional factors. A recent review describes in considerable detail eight distinct factors in vitamin D and refers to information indicating that there may be at least twelve. Clearly, it is not possible to undertake to provide an adequate nutrition simply by reinforcing the diet with a few synthetic products which are known to represent certain of these nutritional factors. By the mass of the people at large, as well as by members of the medical profession, activated ergosterol is considered to include all that is necessary to supply the vitamin D group of activators to human nutrition. Weston Price DDS *Nutrition and Physical Degeneration*

CRAB CREPES

Serves 8

16 buckwheat crepes (page 455)
2 tablespoons butter
1 cup shallots, finely chopped
1/4 cup dry white wine
1 cup fish stock
1 cup piima cream or creme fraiche
juice of 1/2 lemon
sea salt and freshly ground pepper
1 tablespoon arrow root mixed with 1 tablespoon water
1 pound fresh mushrooms, washed, well dried, sliced and sauteed in butter and olive oil
1 pound crab meat

Saute shallots in butter until soft. Add wine and stock and bring to a boil. Add cream and boil until sauce has reduced to about one half. Add lemon juice and seasonings to taste. Spoonful by spoonful, add the arrowroot mixture until desired thickness is obtained. Stir in mushrooms and crab meat and simmer until warmed through. Using a slotted spoon, place a spoonful or two in each crepe and roll up. Place two filled crepes each on heated plates and spoon a little of the remaining sauce over. Serve immediately.

Variation: Shrimp Crepes

Use *1 pound bay shrimp* in place of crab meat. Omit mushrooms.

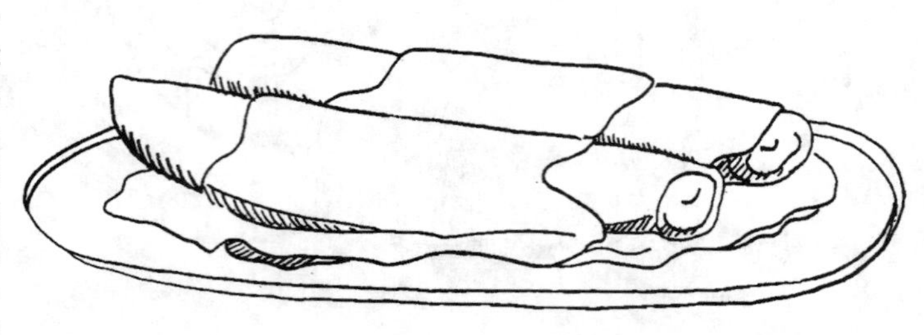

There's another phony milk you should know about. It's called UHT milk [and cream]. The dairy industry is producing this one in an attempt to regain business lost to filled milk and other junk beverages. UHT stands for ultra high temperature. What it means is that milk has been heated to such a high temperature that it is sterilized, just like surgical instruments. It can be shipped in unrefrigerated trucks—a tremendous savings to the dairymen. It will sit on a shelf, unrefrigerated, for months without spoiling. The reason it won't spoil is because no self-respecting bug will eat it. Bugs are smart. They like fresh food with nutrient value, not steam-cleaned pseudo food. William Campbell Douglass MD *The Milk of Human Kindness*

When a junkie dies, known or unknown, is it ever from "metabolic complications"? Of course not. Heroin is a killer. Junkies die of junk. Even when a drunk dies, he dies of his sins. But when a person dies of sugar blues, the mourners often serve sugar at the wake. Sugar-poisoning is a word wedding that rarely appears in print.

The same double standard is evident in the world of art and entertainment. Junkies die like flies every hour of every day on television. Many of these consoling sagas are brought to you by those wonderful people who push sugar and other products laced with sugar at every commercial break. William Dufty *Sugar Blues*

NEW POTATOES WITH CAVIAR

Serves 6

12 small new potatoes
melted butter
1/2 cup piima cream
4 ounces black caviar

Brush the potatoes with butter and bake at 400 degrees for about 3/4 hour or until soft. Cut off tops of potatoes and carefully scoop out flesh. Mash potato flesh, mix with piima cream and return to potatoes. Keep warm in oven until ready to serve.

To serve, place two potatoes on each plate and a generous spoonful of caviar on top of each.

SPINACH FETA PASTRIES

Serves 8-10

3 cups cooked chopped spinach, squeezed dry
1 large onion, finely chopped
1/2 cup pinenuts
sea salt and freshly ground pepper
freshly ground nutmeg
1 cup feta cheese, crumbled
1 recipe yoghurt dough (page 459)
unbleached flour

Mix spinach with onion, pinenuts, and seasonings. Form dough into 1 inch balls and coat balls in flour. Roll into rounds. Place a tablespoon of spinach filling on each and top with a teaspoon of crumbled cheese. Fold edges up to form a three sided pastry, leaving a small hole in the middle for air to escape. Place on well greased pans and brush with butter. Bake at 350 degrees for about 20 minutes or until golden.

Pasteurization began in 1895, and thus began the unfortunate habit of not worrying about cleanliness in the dairy because, with the heating of milk, cleanliness was no longer considered necessary. The bacteria in the milk would simply be boiled, killing the germs, and then the milk could be sold in this adulterated form. It has been sold that way ever since, and because of pasteurization, tuberculosis was not completely eliminated from cows in the United States until 1942. If the United States Public Health Service and the American Medical Association had done the responsible thing and backed the various medical milk commissions' efforts to keep milk clean, tuberculosis could have been eliminated from American cows many decades sooner.

Dr. Henry Coit, the father of certified milk, recognized clearly that top quality milk depended upon getting the milk fresh from the cow and not heating it as is done in the pasteurization process. He recognized that the best way to present the best and most nutritious product to the public was to deliver it as made by nature from a completely clean environment.
William Campbell Douglass MD
The Milk of Human Kindness

ROASTED VEGETABLE PLATTER

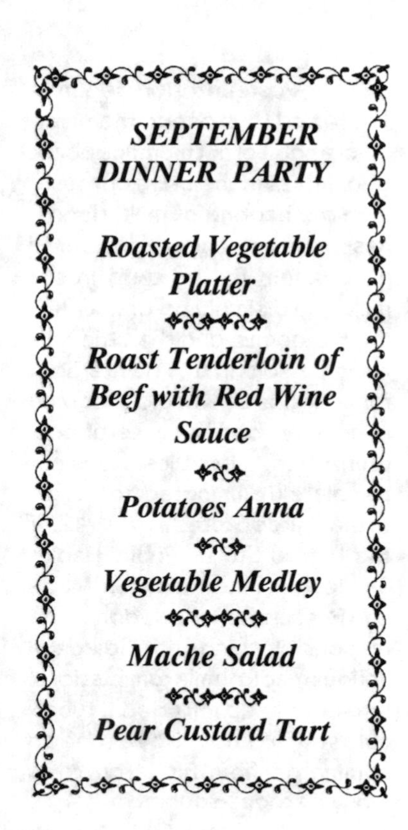

SEPTEMBER DINNER PARTY

Roasted Vegetable Platter

Roast Tenderloin of Beef with Red Wine Sauce

Potatoes Anna

Vegetable Medley

Mache Salad

Pear Custard Tart

Serves 8

8 red peppers, thick fleshed variety
12 Japanese eggplant
extra virgin olive oil
3 cloves garlic, finely chopped
freshly ground pepper
edible flowers for garnish or cilantro sprigs
round croutons (page 491)

Seed the peppers and cut into quarters. Place skin side up in an oiled pyrex dish and bake at 450 degrees about 20 minutes until skins become browned and begin to buckle. Remove pepper pieces to a plate and cover with a plastic bag. Let cool about 10 minutes and remove skins.

Meanwhile, wash eggplants and remove ends. Slice lengthwise and salt the slices. Let stand about one hour, rinse and pat dry. Place eggplant slices on well oiled cookie sheets and brush top side with oil. Broil under the grill until browned, turn, brush with olive and brown remaining side. Mix the chopped garlic with a little olive oil and brush cooked eggplant slices with the mixture.

Both the peppers and the eggplant may be made ahead of time and kept covered at room temperature for several hours. To serve, arrange four slices of pepper and several slices of eggplant on individual plates. Sprinkle with freshly ground black pepper. Garnish with edible flours or cilantro sprigs and serve with round croutons.

Throughout history, ocean salt has earned a hallowed reputation. Our ancestors saw it as an element that regenerates blood, a principle of equilibrium and life. To this day names of towns ending in "lick" still attest to the fact that our early ancestors were drawn to the seashores or the rock salt deposits of the earth. In England town names ending in "wich", in Germany "saal" as in Salzburg, remind us of its neolithic origins. Early settlements grew up around these salt beds and springs. Jacques DeLangre *Seasalt's Hidden Powers*

STUFFED MUSHROOMS

Serves 4

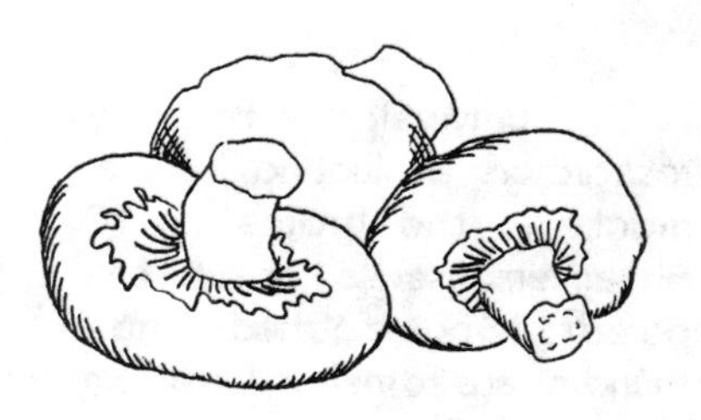

8 large or 12 medium mushrooms
1 1/2 cups whole grain bread crumbs
2 bunches green onions, chopped
1/2 cup freshly grated Parmesan cheese
sea salt and pepper
2-3 cloves garlic, crushed
butter and extra virgin olive oil

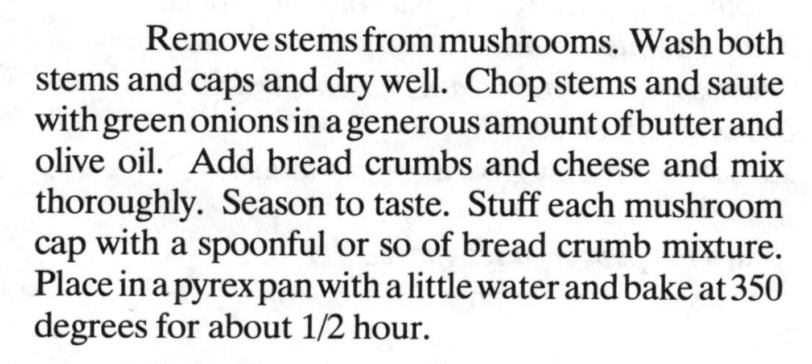

Remove stems from mushrooms. Wash both stems and caps and dry well. Chop stems and saute with green onions in a generous amount of butter and olive oil. Add bread crumbs and cheese and mix thoroughly. Season to taste. Stuff each mushroom cap with a spoonful or so of bread crumb mixture. Place in a pyrex pan with a little water and bake at 350 degrees for about 1/2 hour.

STUFFED GRAPE LEAVES

Serves 8

3 dozen grape leaves, home pickled (page 93)
or store bought preserved in brine
3 large onions, finely chopped
extra virgin olive oil
2 cups basic brown rice (page 441)
1 cup fresh dill, chopped
1/2 cup fresh parsley, chopped
1 bunch green onions, chopped
3 tablespoons toasted pine nuts
juice and grated rind of 2 lemons
sea salt and pepper
2 cups yoghurt sauce (page 131)

Rinse grape leaves and spread on paper towels to drain. Saute onions in olive oil until soft. Off heat, stir in remaining ingredients (except yoghurt sauce.) Place the grape leaves on a board, shiny sides down, and put 1-2 tablespoons of rice mixture in the center of each leaf. Fold the sides of the leaves to the center, then roll them up tightly, starting from the stem end. Chill well. Serve with lemon wedges and individual ramekins of yoghurt sauce.

[Food enzymes] work day and night to build up and later break down the millions of cells in both plants and animals. For centuries humans have put these enzymes to work at predigesting foods before eating them. Fermented foods and aged foods are predigested by their own inherent enzymes, or by starters such as those often used in the production of sourdough bread, yogurt and some cheeses. . . All uncooked foods contain an abundance of food enzymes which correspond to the nutritional highlights of the food. For example, dairy foods, oils, seeds and nuts, which are relatively high in fat content, also contain relatively higher concentrations of the enzyme lipase which aids in the digestion of their fats. Carbohydrates, such as grains, contain higher concentrations of amylase and lesser amounts of lipase and protease in the form of cathepsin and little amylase. Low-calorie fruits and vegetables contain lesser amounts of protein and starch digestants and sizable quantities of the enzyme cellulase, which is needed to break down plant fibers. Edward Howell MD *Enzyme Nutrition*

ROOT VEGETABLE TIMBALE WITH RED PEPPER SAUCE

Serves 8

1 pound carrots, peeled and coarsely chopped
1 pound rutabagas, peeled and coarsely chopped
1 pound parsnips, peeled and coarsely chopped
3 tablespoons softened butter
3 tablespoons piima cream or creme fraiche
6 eggs, lightly beaten
sea salt and freshly ground pepper to taste
freshly ground nutmeg to taste
2 cups red pepper sauce (page 131)
8 tablespoons pesto (page 135), optional

Cook carrots, rutabagas and parsnips in water until just tender—they shouldn't absorb too much water. Let cool and drain well on paper towels. Process in food processor with butter, cream, eggs and seasonings. Brush 8 individual conical timbale molds with melted butter and fill about three-fourths full with the vegetable mixture. Place in pan of hot water and bake at 350 degrees for about 45 minutes or until well set.

To serve, dip each mold briefly in hot water and invert on individual plates. Spoon red pepper sauce around the timbale and garnish each plate with a spoonful or two of pesto.

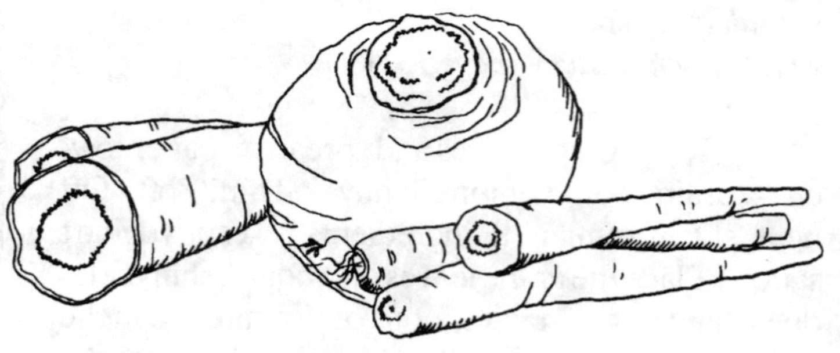

University of Kentucky researchers evaluating 18 elements in the brains of 10 Alzheimers disease patient, compared to 18 age-matched controls found increased mercury/selenium and mercury/zinc ratios in microsomal and nuclear fractions in the brains. Most significant was the increase in mercury in Alzheimers disease bulk brain samples, especially in the cerebral cortex, compared to controls. Alzheimers patients also had elevation of mercury in the nucleus basilis of Meynert, which is the major cholinergic projection to the cerebral cortex and is severely degenerated in Alzheimers disease patients. The elevated mercury/selenium and mercury/zinc ratios are of importance because selenium and zinc are used to protect against mercury toxicity. The release of mercury from dental amalgams is the main means of human exposure to inorganic mercury and vapor in the general population. There has been shown a direct correlation between the amount of inorganic mercury in the brain and the number of surfaces in Alzheimers fillings. Mercury from dental amalgam is passed rapidly and directly into body tissue and accumulates in patient bodies with time. This author feels that no exposure to mercury vapor can be considered harmless, since it has no known toxic threshold. Dental amalgams cannot be excluded as a primary potential source of Alzheimers disease. G. Bjorklund *PPNF Journal*

THE MAIN COURSE

FISH

For most Americans, fish is a restaurant food; few know how to prepare it at home and the average American child doesn't like it. This is a lamentable state of affairs, especially as nowadays fresh fish is so readily available in our markets.

Fish is *the* health food, *par excellence* (except, of course, for those who are allergic to it.) When Dr. Weston Price traveled throughout the world, studying primitive peoples on native diets, he discovered that those who ate fish had the best health, as revealed by their freedom from caries, width of palate and general state of well being. Fish eaters had thicker bones and better skeletal structure than groups that ate red meat. (Largely vegetarian groups placed third in all of Dr. Price's indicators of good health.)

Consumption of fish promotes excellent growth and bone structure; it also protects from the degenerative diseases so prevalent in this modern age. In a study conducted in the Netherlands, researchers found that just one serving of fish per week substantially reduced the incidence of coronary heart disease. All ocean fish are excellent sources of macro and trace minerals, particularly iodine and zinc. Our soils may be depleted of certain trace minerals, but every one we need exists in the boundless oceans; fish-eating is our only sure way to get our full complement of them all. Mackerel, anchovies and herring are especially rich in mineral nutrients. Deep sea oily fish such as salmon, tuna and swordfish are good sources of omega-3 and other long chain fatty acids. Most important, fish and all seafood are excellent sources of fat soluble vitamins—A and D. Remember that Dr. Price found the intake of these two essential nutrients to be ten times greater among primitive peoples than among Americans during the thirties. Today the disparity is almost certainly greater, as Westerners have cut back on their consumption of animal fats.

In recent years, many people have been persuaded to give up fish due to reports of mercury contamination. Mercury contamination *is* a danger when one eats fish from shoreline waters near industrial areas, or from contaminated fresh waters. For this reason we advise you to avoid fresh water fish unless you are sure of their origin, especially cat fish, carp and other scavengers; and to avoid over-consumption of shell fish. Shoreline feeders such as sole and flounder may be contaminated with PBC's. You needn't be concerned about mercury levels in deep sea fish such as salmon, tuna and swordfish. Small amounts of mercury occur naturally in these fish and they contain substances that bind with mercury to take it out of the body. Farm raised fish from relatively clean sub-Arctic waters are also safe, but their fatty acid profile will not be as good.

If you have not cultivated the art of preparing fish, but wish to begin, we advise you to start with simple preparations such as sauted filet of sole or grilled salmon, tuna or swordfish. These take little time to prepare and are most readily accepted by children and inveterate fish avoiders. They can be served plain or with any number of accompaniments listed in the sauces and condiments chapter. We allow unbleached white flour in small amounts for browning and breading.

From these simple recipes you can graduate to our parchment paper and leaf-wrapped recipes. Many traditional societies prepare fish by wrapping it in leaves and steaming it in the coals of a fire. This method preserves all nutrients and protects the fish from possible carcinogens.

Classic gourmet recipes call for poaching fish in stock, then reducing the stock to make a flavorful sauce. Butter or cream or both are then added. These sauces are easy to digest, and just loaded with minerals (from concentrated stock) and fat soluble vitamins (from cream and butter.) Poached fish may be kept warm in a heated oven, covered with a piece of parchment or waxed paper, for up to one-half hour while the sauce is being prepared and while you eat your first course.

Fish must be fresh to be good. Look carefully at the eyes and gills of the fish you buy—the eyes should be clear, not glazed, and the gills should be red. Always ask your fish merchant when his fish came in. If the fish has been sitting in his display case more than a day, don't buy it.

A good habit to initiate in your household is to serve fish at least once a week and we hope that the variety of recipes presented in this chapter, culled from many different cuisines, will make this easy for you to accomplish. You may want to prepare a special dessert for the same evening meal, if your children need coaxing to develop a taste for fish. No fish, no dessert is a good rule. Serve fish the day you buy it, to ensure that it is fresh.

SIMPLE BAKED FISH

Serves 4

1 1/2 pounds filet of white fish such as sole, whiting or turbot
juice of 1 lemon
1 tablespoon fish sauce (page 143), optional
dash cayenne pepper
1 tablespoon snipped fresh herbs

Place fish in a buttered baking dish. Sprinkle with lemon juice, cayenne, fish sauce, herbs and salt. Cover baking dish with foil (but don't let foil touch the fish) and bake at 300 degrees for about 15 minutes.

FILET OF SOLE MEUNIERE

Serves 6

1 1/2 pounds fresh filet of sole
2/3 cup unbleached flour
1/2 teaspoon pepper
sea salt
clarified butter (page 136)
extra virgin olive oil

This is the classic and simple recipe for sauted fish. Purists will object that we include recipes for pan-fried fish. Poached fish is probably preferable from a nutritional point of view, but some individuals, especially children, need an extra incentive to eat sea food, and a crisp, golden exterior is the best one we know of.

Wipe filets thoroughly and trim off any ends that are very thin in comparison to the rest of the filet. You may wish to cut the filets in half, cross wise. Dredge well in the flour mixed with sea salt and pepper.

Place equal parts of clarified butter and olive oil in a heavy bottomed frying pan and let them heat up. Saute the fish filets, a few at a time, over a moderately high flame, starting with the flatter side. Saute until golden, then turn. Cook 3 to 5 minutes per side, depending on the thickness of the fish. Transfer to a heated platter and keep warm in the oven while you prepare the other filets. You will need to replenish butter and oil between batches.

Serve with lemon wedges, cream of tartar sauce (page 129) or Creole mayonnaise (page 128).

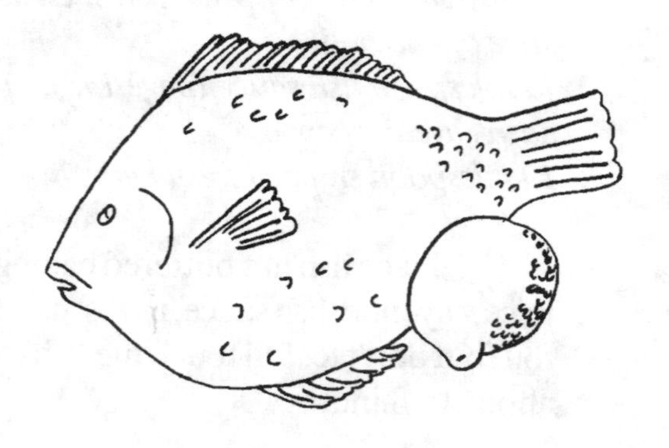

Communication is very difficult among many of the remote islands off the Irish coast. It would be difficult to find more complete isolation. . . We tried to get to the islands of Taransay and Scarpa on the west coast of the Isle of Harris, but were unable to obtain transportation since the trip can be made only in special, seaworthy crafts, which will undertake the passage only at certain phases of the tide and at certain directions of the winds. On one of these islands, we were told, the growing boys and girls had exceedingly high immunity to tooth decay. Their isolation was so great that a young woman of about twenty years of age who came to the Isle of Harris from Taransay Island had never seen milk. . . There are no dairy animals on that island. Their nutrition is provided by their oat products and fish, and by a very limited amount of vegetable foods. Lobsters and flat fish are a very important part of their foods. Fruits are practically unknown, yet the physiques of these people are remarkably fine. Weston Price DDS *Nutrition and Physical Degeneration*

BREADED WHITE FISH

Serves 6

1 1/2 pounds thick filets of white fish such as turbot or whiting
2/3 cup unbleached flour
1/2 teaspoon pepper
sea salt
3 eggs, lightly beaten
1 cup fine whole grain bread crumbs
1/4 teaspoon grated lemon peel
clarified butter (page 136)
extra virgin olive oil

Cut filets into pieces of approximately equal size. Mix sea salt and pepper with flour on a plate. Mix bread crumbs with lemon peel in a bowl. Dredge each piece of fish first in the flour mixture, next in egg, lastly in flour. Saute in batches in equal parts of butter and oil. Remove to a heated platter and keep warm while preparing the remaining pieces. You will need to replenish butter and oil after each batch.

Serve with lemon wedges, tartar sauce (page 129) or ginger carrots (page 87).

The Watusi is a very interesting tribe living on the east of Lake Kivu, one of the headwaters of the West Nile in Ruanda which is a Belgian Protectorate. They are tall and athletic. . . They have magnificent physiques. Many stand over six feet without shoes. Several of the tribes neighboring Ethiopia are agriculturists and grow corn, beans, millet, sweet potatoes, bananas, kafir corn and other grains as their chief articles of food. Physically they are not as well built as either the tribes using dairy products liberally or those using fish from the fresh water lakes and streams. They have been dominated because they possess less courage and resourcefulness. The government of Kenya has for several years sponsored an athletic contest among the various tribes, the test being one of strength for which they use a tug-of-war. One particular tribe has carried off the trophy repeatedly. This tribe resides on the east coast of Lake Victoria and lives very largely on fish. The members are powerful athletes and wonderful swimmers. Weston Price DDS *Nutrition and Physical Degeneration*

MARINATED GRILLED SWORDFISH OR TUNA

Serves 6

1 1/2 pounds swordfish or tuna steak
3/4 cup cilantro marinade (page 132)

Brush both sides of swordfish or tuna with the marinade and let stand, covered, in refrigerator for several hours. Grill under broiler or on barbecue for 5 to 10 minutes per side, depending on thickness of fish. Be careful not to let the fish burn.

A wonderful accompaniment to swordfish is Bernaise sauce (page138); tuna goes beautifully with chunky tomato sauce (page 140).

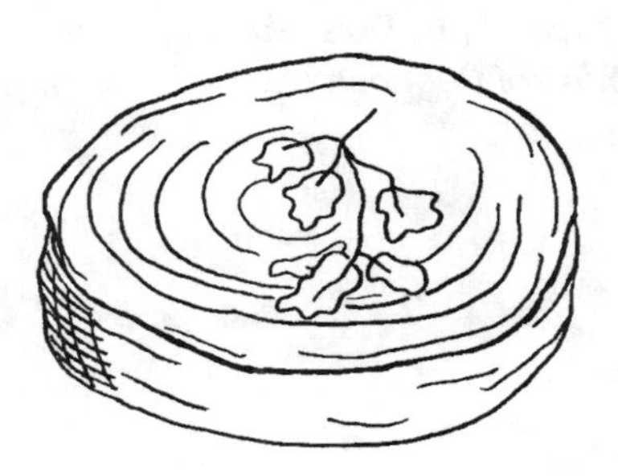

TROUT WITH ALMONDS

Serves 6

6 fresh whole trout
1 cup corn meal
1/2 teaspoon pepper
sea salt
clarified butter (page 136)
extra virgin olive oil
1 cup crispy almonds, slivered

Use trout that is farm-raised in unpolluted water, or trout you have caught yourself from an unpolluted stream. Clean well but do not remove heads. Pat dry. Dredge well in mixture of salt, pepper and cornmeal. Saute fish, one or two at a time, in equal amounts of butter and olive oil over a medium high flame, using a heavy skillet . They will need five to ten minutes on a side depending on thickness. Remove to a heated platter and keep warm in the oven while preparing remaining trout.

Pour out used oil and butter. Add 2 tablespoons each clarified butter and oil. Saute almonds until golden and pour over fish.

The purpose of these studies has included the obtaining of data which will throw light also on the etiology of deformities of the dental arches and face, including irregularity of position of the teeth [crowded, crooked teeth]. A marked variation of the incidence of irregularities was found in the different [African] tribes. This variation could be directly associated with the nutrition rather than with the tribal pattern. The lowest percentage of irregularity occurred in the tribes living very largely on dairy products and marine life. For example, among the Masai living on milk, blood and meat, only 3.4 per cent had irregularities, Among the Kikuyu and Wakamba, 18.2 and 18.9 per cent respectively had irregularities. These people were largely agriculturists living primarily on vegetable foods. In the native Arab school at Omdurman, among the pupils living almost entirely according to the native customs of selection and preparation of foods, 6.4 per cent had irregularities, while in the native school at modernized Khartoum, 70 per cent had irregularities. Weston Price DDS *Nutrition and Physical Degeneration*

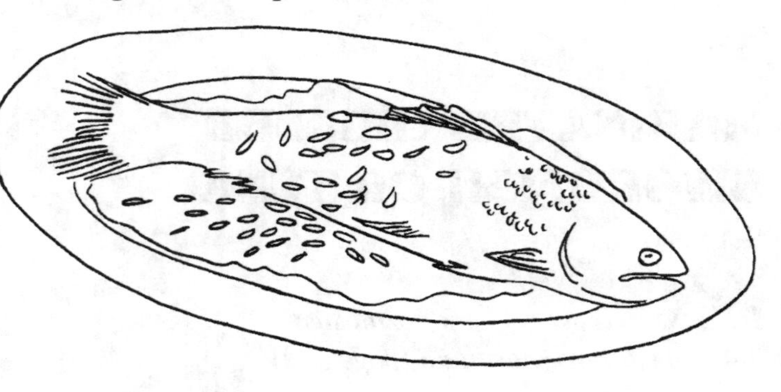

SIMPLE BAKED SALMON

Serves 6

1 1/2 pounds salmon filet
1/2 lemon
extra virgin olive oil
1 tablespoon unbleached flour
1/4 teaspoon paprika
sea salt

Set salmon, skin side down in a buttered pyrex baking dish. Squeeze on lemon juice, then brush generously with oil. Sprinkle on flour and spread with hands to make a thin, even coat. Sprinkle on paprika and sea salt. Bake at 350 degrees for 10 to 15 minutes or until salmon is almost, but not quite cooked through. Place under broiler for about one minute, until flour coating becomes browned.

Serve plain or with any one of a number of condiments and sauces including butter sauce (page 139), pesto sauce (page 135), or thin red pepper sauce (page 131).

RED SNAPPER, MEXICAN STYLE

Serves 4

4 red snapper filets
2 tablespoons lime juice
extra virgin olive oil
1 medium onion, thinly sliced
2 ripe tomatoes, peeled, seeded and chopped
1 bunch cilantro, chopped
1 teaspoon fresh chile pepper, diced
2 cloves garlic, peeled and mashed
pinch cinnamon
sea salt

Rub filets with lime juice, and let stand, covered, in refrigerator for several hours.

Using a heavy skillet, saute the filets in a little olive oil briefly, on both sides. Transfer to an oiled pyrex baking dish. Add more olive oil to the skillet. Saute onion until soft. Add remaining ingredients and simmer for about 30 minutes or more until most of liquid is absorbed. Season to taste with sea salt. Strew the sauce over fish and bake at 350 degrees until tender, about 25 minutes.

New evidence supports the theory that something in seafood—probably the oil—helps manipulate female hormones that in turn discourage breast cancer. Fish eaters around the world seem to have less breast cancer, according to investigators at the Ludwig Institute for Cancer Research in Toronto, who compared food consumption statistics with cancer rates in thirty-two countries. They noted that those countries where people ate the most calories from fish had the fewest cases of and deaths from breast cancer. For example, in Japan, where fish consumption is high, breast cancer is low. Numerous animal studies find that omega-3 fatty acids in the fat of fish may block the development of various cancers, in particular breast cancer. Jean Carper *The Food Pharmacy Guide to Good Eating*

Since the sea foods are, as a group, so valuable a source of the fat-soluble activators, they have been found to be efficient throughout the world not only for controlling tooth decay, but for producing a human stock of high vitality. Unfortunately the cost of transportation in the fresh state often constitutes a factor limiting distribution. Many of the primitive races preserved the food value, including vitamins, very efficiently by drying the fish. While our modern system of canning prevents decomposition, it does not efficiently preserve some of the fat soluble activators, particularly vitamin A. Weston Price DDS *Nutrition and Physical Degeneration*

A splendid illustration of the primitive Maori instinct or wisdom regarding the value of sea foods was shown in an experience we had while making examinations in a native school on the east coast of the North Islands. I was impressed with the fact that the children in the school gave very little evidence of having active dental caries. I asked the teacher what the children brought from their homes to eat at their midday lunch. . . I was told that they brought no lunch but that when school was dismissed at noon the children rushed for the beach where, while part of the group prepared bonfires, the others stripped and dived into the sea, and brought up a large species of lobster. The lobsters were promptly roasted on the coals and devoured with great relish. Weston Price DDS *Nutrition and Physical Degeneration*

As with men, insufficient intake of certain nutrients can often make women less prone to become pregnant. Research reveals that subnormal intake of vitamin B-6 (pyridoxine) can diminish the chances of conception . . . Sometimes birth control pills diminish the amount of available vitamin B-6 so that women who discontinue this oral contraceptive often cannot conceive until a year after cessation. Then, in one study, 98 percent of them taking vitamin B-6 regularly, resumed normal menstruation and became pregnant within 4 months. A painful complication that often comes with deficiency of vitamin B-6 is premenstrual syndrome, which could also serve to indicate why certain women are unable to conceive. James F Scheer *Health Freedom News*

SWORDFISH STEAKS, ORIENTAL STYLE

Serves 6

2 pounds swordfish steak, about 1 inch thick
extra virgin olive oil
sea salt and freshly ground pepper
3 cloves garlic, peeled
1/4 cup fresh ginger, peeled and coarsely chopped
2 tablespoons Dijon-type mustard
1/4 cup soy sauce
1 tablespoon raw honey
1/2 cup rice vinegar
2 tablespoons fish sauce (page 143), optional
1 tablespoon toasted sesame oil
1/3 cup extra virgin olive oil
1 bunch green onions, chopped
3 tablespoons sesame seeds, toasted in oven

Brush swordfish steaks with olive oil and sprinkle with salt and pepper. Grill about 5 minutes to a side on a barbecue or under a broiler. Transfer to a heated platter and keep warm until ready to serve. Meanwhile, place garlic, ginger, mustard, fish sauce and soy sauce in food processor and process until blended. Add honey and vinegar and process again. With motor running, add oil gradually so that sauce emulsifies and becomes thick.

Place swordfish servings on warmed plates. Spoon sauce over and garnish with green onions and sesame seeds. This dish goes well with spinach, chard, Chinese peas, or steamed Chinese cabbage.

SALMON FILET, ORIENTAL STYLE

Serves 6

2 pounds salmon filet
4 tablespoons sesame seeds
2 tablespoons rice vinegar
3 tablespoons soy sauce
2 tablespoons fish sauce (page 143), optional

2 tablespoons toasted sesame oil
1 tablespoon grated ginger
1 bunch finely chopped green onions
3 cloves garlic, minced
3 tablespoons fresh chives (optional)
grated rind of 1 lemon

Place salmon filet skin side down in an oiled pyrex baking dish. Combine all other ingredients and pour over fish. Cover pan with foil (but don't let foil touch the fish) and bake at 350 degrees about 15 minutes or until fish is just barely cooked through.

Slice the salmon into servings, transfer to individual plates and spoon sauce over each slice.

FISH WITH CURRY SAUCE

Serves 4

2 pounds firm-fleshed fish such as halibut or swordfish, cut into 1 inch steaks
extra virgin olive oil
2 medium onions, very thinly sliced
1 tablespoon fresh ginger, very finely minced
1 cup coconut milk and cream (page 144) or 7-8 ounces creamed coconut (see Sources)
1 cup fish stock
2 tablespoons lime juice
2 tablespoons curry powder or curry paste
1/4 cup fresh chile peppers, chopped

Remove skin and bone from fish steaks and cut into one inch cubes. Dry well and saute in batches in olive oil, using a heavy bottomed skillet. Remove to a heated platter, cover with parchment paper (see Sources) and keep warm while preparing remaining fish and sauce.

Add more olive oil to saute pan. Saute onions until soft. Add remaining ingredients, bring to a boil and simmer until sauce reduces and begins to thicken, stirring frequently. Season to taste with sea salt.

Return fish to pan and simmer for about 5 minutes or until fish is tender. Do not overcook. Transfer to a heated serving bowl and serve immediately.

While many of the primitive races studied have continued to thrive on the same soil through thousand of years, our American human stock has declined rapidly within a few centuries, and in some localities within a few decades. In the regions in which degeneration has taken place the animal stock has also declined. A decadent individual cannot regenerate himself, although he can reduce the progressive decadence in the next generation, or can vastly improve that generation, by using the demonstrated wisdom of the primitive races. No era in the long journey of mankind reveals in the skeletal remains such a terrible degeneration of teeth and bones as this brief modern period records. Must nature reject our vaunted culture and call back the more obedient primitives? The alternative seems to be a complete readjustment in accordance with the controlling forces of Nature. Weston Price DDS *Nutrition and Physical Degeneration*

FISH CAKES

Makes 8 patties

1-1 1/2 pounds white fish
1/2 pound fresh fish roe (optional)
2 small onions, finely minced
2 eggs, lightly beaten
2 tablespoons Dijon-type mustard
1/4-1/2 teaspoon cayenne
1 cup whole grain bread crumbs
1 bunch cilantro, chopped (optional)
1 teaspoon grated lemon rind
sea salt and pepper to taste
butter and extra virgin olive oil

This is a delicious way to eat inexpensive, coarsely grained fish. If your fish monger can supply you with roe from cod, whitefish, etc., don't hesitate to add this highly nutritious ingredient.

Place fish in a pan with water and simmer gently until fish is tender. Place in a bowl and break up with a fork. Meanwhile, place fish roe in its casing in a pan with water and a little vinegar or lemon juice and simmer for about 10 minutes. Rinse in a colander and remove roe from casing. Add to flaked fish and mix thoroughly.

Combine eggs with onions, breadcrumbs and seasonings. Add to fish and mix well. Form into cakes. Saute until golden, a few at a time, in butter and olive oil. Serve with parsley butter sauce (page 139), Creole mayonnaise (page 128) or red pepper sauce (page 131).

Cholesterol is an antioxidant and free radical scavenger which protects cell membranes. It is liberally disbursed in cell walls, protecting vital phospholipids from free radical damage. Cholesterol also acts as a precursor to the many steroid hormones and vitamin D. Vitamin D is normally produced in the skin by exposure of cholesterol to ultraviolet radiation from sunlight. Ultraviolet light is a form of ionizing radiation which produces free radicals in living tissues.

Total cholesterol (reflected by blood cholesterol) is determined primarily by cholesterol synthesis in response to ongoing oxidative stress from free radicals, not primarily by dietary cholesterol intake. Serum cholesterol levels are indicators of free radical damage and therefore correlate with the risk of atherosclerosis. Cholesterol is synthesized in the body as needed and with epidemic free radical diseases, blood cholesterol levels increase with age.... Dietary restriction of cholesterol and medications to reduce blood cholesterol have been counterproductive in the treatment of atherosclerosis because the antioxidant role of cholesterol has not been recognized. Unoxidized cholesterol is widely dispersed in cell membranes as a protective factor against atherosclerosis, cancer and other free radical induced diseases. E.M. Cranton, MD and J.P. Frackelton, MD *Journal of Holistic Medicine*

FISH FILETS IN PARCHMENT PAPER

Serves 6

2 pounds filet of sole, turbot or whiting
2 medium onions, very thinly sliced
1 cup piima cream or creme fraiche
2 tablespoons fish sauce, optional (page 143)
1 bunch cilantro, chopped

Cut six pieces of aluminum foil and line them with six pieces of parchment paper (see Sources) of slightly smaller size. Place a portion of fish on each. Top with onions, a teaspoon of optional fish sauce and a dollop of cream. Fold foil with parchment paper together at center, then at ends. Bake in a 350 degree oven, or on the barbecue for about 20 minutes.

To serve, place "packages" on individual plates. Open and sprinkle with cilantro. The foil and parchment paper will serve as bowls for the fish and its delicious creamy sauce.

TROUT IN PARCHMENT PAPER

Serves 4

4 trout
butter
8 shallots, peeled and finely chopped
1 cup dry white wine
1 tablespoon fresh herbs such as thyme, tarragon or rosemary

Wash trout well and pat dry. They should be whole but cleaned. You may remove the bones, but leave the skin on. Cut six pieces of aluminum foil and line them with six pieces of parchment paper of slightly smaller size. Place a trout on each one.

Saute shallots in butter, add wine and boil down until liquid is reduced to only a few tablespoons. Let cool. Stir in herbs and sea salt and pepper to taste. Spoon a little sauce over each fish. Fold foil together at center, then at ends. Bake in a 350 degree oven, or on the barbecue for about 30 minutes.

The Zutphen Study. . . was a study of the eating habits of inhabitants of one village in the Netherlands. In this study, the researchers found that even one serving of sea fish each week substantially reduced the incidence of CHD in the individuals who ate the fish.

Two interesting points were made in this study.

First, for those men who ate the fish, it did not matter how old they were, what their blood pressure or blood cholesterol level was, or, incredibly, how much they smoked. It also made no difference how active they were.

Secondly, the men who ate the fish not only had a lowered risk of heart disease, but they consumed significantly more animal protein, cholesterol and alcohol, and significantly less carbohydrate than the men who didn't eat fist and who suffered higher mortality rates. The men who had a lower risk of heart disease ate the very foods were are continually told not to eat, and they ate significantly less of the foods we are advised to eat!

The authors noted one other very astounding relationship. Those men who consume the most calories had the lowest blood cholesterol levels and those who consumed the least calories had the highest cholesterol levels. Chris Mudd *Cholesterol and Your Health*

LEAF WRAPPED SALMON

Serves 8

2 salmon filets, equal in size,
about 1 1/2 pounds each, skin removed
3 heads butter lettuce or other soft-leaf lettuce
1-2 cups stuffing (see below)

Prepare lettuce leaves by dipping whole heads into boiling water about 10 seconds. Remove immediately. Drain, remove leaves and spread out on kitchen towels. Meanwhile, prepare stuffing.

Butter an oblong pyrex dish and line it with one layer of overlapping lettuce leaves. Set in one filet, skin side down. Spread filet with stuffing and set other filet on top, skin side up. Fold lettuce leaves up to cover sides and a portion of the top of the fish. Cover top with one layer of overlapping leaves and tuck under. Bake about 45 minutes at 350 degrees. To serve, cut fish with lettuce wrapping crosswise into slices about 1 inch thick.

Lemon Almond Stuffing

1 cup whole grain bread crumbs
1 cup crispy almonds (page 487)
1 cup fresh parsley sprigs
1 tablespoon fresh tarragon or thyme leaves
1 tablespoon freshly grated lemon rind
1/4 cup fresh lemon juice
1/2 stick softened butter
pinch cayenne
sea salt

Place bread crumbs, almonds and parsley in food processor and pulse until coarsely chopped. Add herbs, lemon zest, lemon juice and butter. Process until well mixed. Add cayenne and sea salt and freshly ground pepper to taste.

A series of studies in Japan also showed that heavy seafood eaters were much less likely to die of strokes. Residents of fishing villages who eat about nine ounces of seafood daily have a 25 to 40 percent lower risk of stroke than farmers who eat only three ounces of fish a day. . . Researchers theorize that the omega-3 fatty acids in seafood may modify blood factors, helping protect against stroke. Seafood is also high in potassium. Jean Carper *The Food Pharmacy Guide to Good Eating*

Thinking is as biologic as is digestion, and brain embryonic defects are as biologic as are club feet. Since both are readily produced by lowered parental reproductive capacity, and since Nature in her large-scale human demonstration reveals that this is chiefly the result of inadequate nutrition of the parents and too frequent or too prolonged child bearing, the way back in indicated. Like the successful primitive racial stocks, we, too, can make, as a first requisite, provision for adequate nutrition both for generation and growth, and can make provision for the regulation of the overloads. We, like the successful primitives, can establish programs of instruction for growing youth and acquaint it with nature's requirements long before emergencies and stresses arise. Weston Price DDS *Nutrition and Physical Degeneration*

Cilantro Coconut Stuffing

1 bunch fresh cilantro
1/3 cup fresh mint leaves
1 cup dried unsweetened coconut
1/3 cup lemon juice
8 cloves garlic, peeled
8 small hot or 4 medium mild fresh green chiles
1 tablespoon grated fresh ginger
sea salt

Place all ingredients in food processor and process into a thick paste. Check seasonings.

Russian Style Stuffing

3 small bunches sorrel leaves or
1 large bunch spinach
butter and extra virgin olive oil
1/2 pound fresh mushrooms, washed and dried with paper towels
1 bunch green onions, finely chopped
1 tablespoon dried dill or 2 tablespoons fresh dill
1 cup cooked brown rice
sea salt and freshly ground pepper

Wash and chop spinach or sorrel. In a heavy skillet, saute in a mixture of butter and olive oil until soft. Set aside. Meanwhile chop mushrooms. Saute with onions in butter and olive oil until well browned. Mix sauted mushroom mixture with spinach, rice and seasonings.

Variation: Individual Leaf Wrapped Salmon

Use *8 salmon steaks*. Cut each in half at the spinebone, creating 16 pieces, and remove skin and bones. Place a spoonful of stuffing on one piece and another piece on top to form a "sandwich". Wrap each portion with 2 or 3 blanched lettuce leaves. Bake about 20 minutes.

You must have heard, "Go native!" as I have. It takes on a special new meaning for Hawaiian natives who lost weight dramatically, lowered their high blood pressure, cholesterol and dropped their alarming high blood sugar. How did they do it? By eating the foods their ancestors ate before Captain James Cook discovered the islands in 1788. Gradually under Western style living, they no longer have "Strong bodies and fine open countenances," as Cook described them in his journal, "with fine eyes and teeth. They have frank, cheerful dispositions with few native diseases". . . The irony is that in Hawaii, the healthiest state in the union from the standpoint of longevity, the natives have the shortest lifespan in the United States. The death rate in pure Hawaiians exceeds the national average by 278 per cent, cancer by 226 percent and diabetes an incredible 688 percent. Sixty-five percent are obese... .scientists decided to try the native Hawaiian diet for 21 days... Their foods included taro (a starchy root-like potato), poi (a mashed, slightly tart fermented form of taro) sweet potatoes, yams, breadfruit, greens (fern shoots and leaves of taro, sweet potato and yams), fruit, seaweed, fish and chicken. All foods were served either raw or steamed as in ancient cookery. . .The results caused [the scientists] to write eloquently. "Weight loss was dramatic," at an average of 17.5 pounds in three weeks. Cholesterol decreased an average of 14 percent. Triglycerides. . ."fell significantly," as did blood pressure. There was a "striking decrease in blood sugar."
Ruth Rosevear *PPNF Jurnal*

FILETS OF SOLE WITH CREAM SAUCE

(Filet de Sole Bonne Femme)
Serves 4

8 to 12 very fresh filet pieces (3 per person for small Dover sole, 2 per person for larger grey sole)
4 cups fish stock
1 onion, finely chopped
sea salt to taste
1 cup piima cream or creme fraiche
finely chopped parsley for garnish

Butter an oblong pyrex dish and strew the onions evenly on the bottom. Lay the sole pieces on the onions, being careful that they overlap as little as possible. Bring the stock to a boil and pour over the filets. Immediately transfer to a 300 degree oven.

Let the filets poach until just tender, from five to fifteen minutes depending on the thickness of the filets. Carefully lift the filets onto a heated platter, cover with a piece of parchment paper (see Sources), and keep warm in the oven while you are making the sauce. The filets will keep for a half an hour or more if properly covered, without loosing taste or moisture.

Strain the stock into a large skillet and bring to a rapid boil. Whisk in the cream. Continue boiling, skimming the froth occasionally, until the sauce has reduced to the consistency of thick cream. This will take from ten to fifteen minutes. As soon as the sauce reduces to the desired thickness, turn down to simmer. If the sauce gets too thick, thin with a little water or with the juices exuded by the filets on their heated platter. Taste before adding salt. It may not be necessary.

To serve, transfer the filets to heated plates and pat around with paper towels to mop up any juices. Pour the sauce over the filets and sprinkle on parsley. Garnish with lightly steamed small red potatoes or baby vegetables. Basic brown rice (page 441) is also an excellent accompaniment for this dish.

One of the earliest warnings about the rising tide of sugar in our diet came from that 1942 AMA report: "The consumption of sugar and of other relatively pure carbohydrates has become so great during recent years that it presents a serious obstacle to the improved nutrition of the general public." In the strongest terms possible, the report called for "all practical means to be taken to limit consumption of sugar in any form" in which significant nutrients are not present. . . It was a call unheeded. From the end of wartime rationing to the present, the food industry has known no limit, beyond the technical, in using sugar to cheaply enhance the appeal of its processed and fabricated foods. In these last 40 years industry has more than doubled the sugar it adds to our diet. But protests are no longer heard—the watchdogs of the public's welfare appear to have been pacified.

In the mid-1970s the blue-ribbon FASEB (Federation of American Societies for Experimental Biology), on contract to the FDA, wholeheartedly recommended the agency again approve sugar as a food additive, saying that with the possible exception of dental caries sucrose presents *no* risk to human health. Joseph D. Beasley MD and Jerry J. Swift MA *The Kellogg Report*

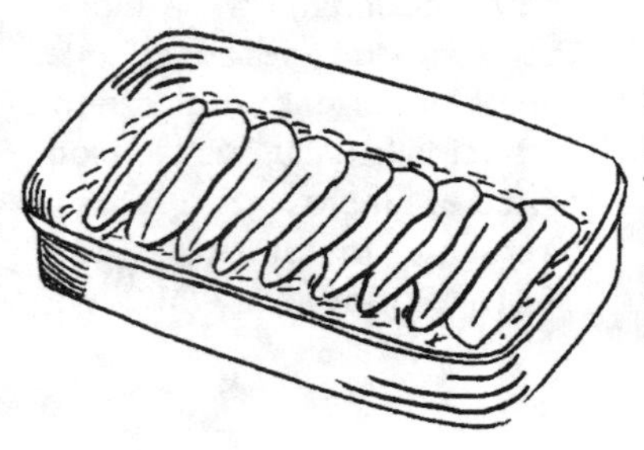

Variation: Filets of Sole with Portuguese Sauce

In addition to the basic ingredients, you will need *two ripe tomatoes*, peeled, seeded and chopped. Strew them in the pyrex pan with the onions. When you transfer the stock to a frying pan for reduction, do not strain out the onions and the tomatoes. Let them reduce with the sauce. Don't forget the chopped parsley—it looks so pretty with the tomatoes.

Variation: Filets of Sole with Julienne of Vegetables

Prepare the basic recipe. When the sauce has reduced to the desired thickness, stir in a julienne of vegetables made in the following manner:

Peel *one small carrot* and cut into thin strips, approximately 1/8 inch by 1/8 inch by one inch long; cut the skin off of *one zucchini* and cut this skin into similar strips. (Save the pulp for soups.) Trim the end and the green part off *one leek* and slit lengthwise half way through. Rinse clean under the tap. Cut rounds about 1/8 inch thick. (The rounds will open and separate when cooked, forming julienne strips.)

Bring a pan of salted filtered water to a boil. Put the carrots in a strainer, hold down in the boiling water for about one minute, then rinse with cold water. Strew onto a plate lined with several thicknesses of paper towels and pat dry. Repeat the process with the zucchini strips and the leeks. Mix vegetables together and add to sauce.

Variation: Filets of Sole with Pink Grapefruit Sauce

This is an easy variation with a beautiful presentation, yet worthy of the most elegant dinner party. Prepare the basic recipe, adding *1/2 cup fresh grapefruit juice* to the sauce.

Prepare individual plates with the following garnishes alternating around the outer edge of the plate: *sections of pink grapefruit*, *steamed Chinese peas*, and spoonfuls of *fresh tomato, peeled, seeded and finely chopped*. Place filets in center of plate, pour sauce over and sprinkle on a small amount of finely chopped parsley.

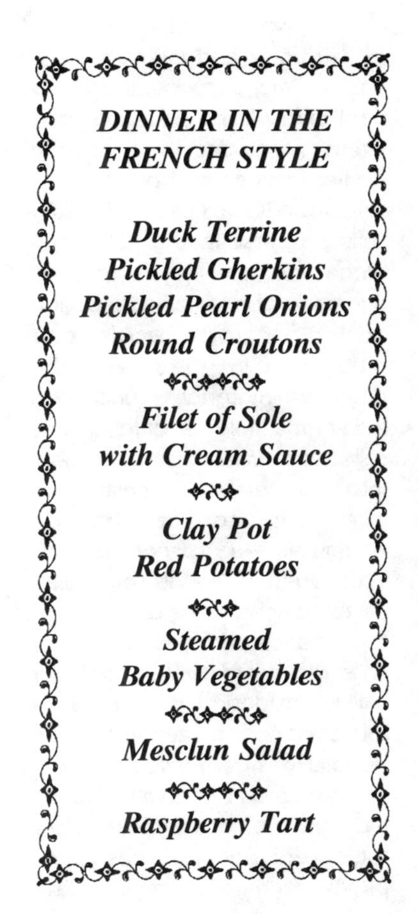

Organ weight studies have shown over and over again that poor nutrition profoundly disturbs the weight of most of the endocrine glands (such as the pituitary, thyroid and pancreas) as well as many organs. Obesity is accompanied by profound changes in endocrine and organ weights. Obesity *per se* is only the visible aspect of hidden and far more serious pathological conditions. In Dr. Marshall's mice, the liver became greatly enlarged, while the heart, kidneys, and pancreas also became enlarged. There is strong evidence recorded in the periodical literature that heavy use of refined sugar causes pituitary lesions and perhaps brain lesions. . . Edward Howell MD
Enzyme Nutrition

SALMON WITH BEURRE BLANC

Serves 6

2 pounds filet of salmon
4 cups fish stock
several sprigs fresh tarragon
1 stick softened butter
1 tablespoon fresh tarragon leaves, snipped
1 teaspoon vinegar

Butter or oil a small oblong pyrex dish, and set the filet, skin side down, in the dish. Strew with tarragon sprigs. Bring the stock to a boil and pour over the filet. If the liquid does not entirely cover the fish, add water. Set in a 325 degree oven and poach until just tender, from ten to fifteen minutes depending on the thickness of the filet. You can check for doneness with a fork. Be careful not to overcook. Remove from the oven when the inside is still a little rare. Set the filet on a heated platter, cover with a piece of parchment paper (see Sources) and keep in a heated oven while you prepare the sauce.

Pour stock into a heavy skillet and boil vigorously until it reduces to about 3/4 cup. Allow to cool slightly. Set cooled stock in a bowl set in barely simmering water. Using a wire whisk, add the butter to the stock, one tablespoon at a time, beating vigorously with each addition. Stir in vinegar and tarragon snippings. Do not let the sauce boil. When all the butter has been amalgamated, check for seasoning. Salt will probably be unnecessary. Divide the filet into servings and place on individual plates. Spoon a little sauce over each and serve immediately.

No wonder there is so much chronic and metabolic disease in America today. In order to deal with all the pollutions and stresses of modern living, healthy bodies must have strong healthy cells. The key to strong, healthy cells lies first in the cell membrane. Human cell membranes are made of a remarkable combination of fatty acids and proteins—with fatty acids the dominant material. When this man-made molecule of fatty acid, called the *trans* fatty acid, gets into cell membrane construction our cells cannot function optimumly—we cannot ward off viruses as well; the vital biochemical exchanges going on between the interior and exterior of our cells can be fouled up; and our cellular oxidation cannot be as robust as nature intended. Additionally, this degeneration of the cell membrane is cumulative as we continue to eat these *trans* fats every day—it doesn't improve over time, or simply vanish, it slowly gets worse and worse. And the rottenest thing about this entire story is that this molecular misfit, the *trans* fatty acid, is generally hyped by colorful and clever advertising to be "good for you." How in the world did this happen? How did a man-made molecule of very bad fat become a major part of everyday nutrition and get a reputation for being good? Encouraged by our mass media, we took ourselves off of butter and stopped cooking with lard and bought margarines and vegetable shortening because we were told it was the "healthy thing to do." And it's not true. It's the opposite—and the money power behind the promotional campaign knew it! They had to know it. Tom Valentine *Facts on Fats & Oils*

SALMON WITH SUN DRIED TOMATO SAUCE

Serves 4

1 filet of salmon, about 1 1/3 pounds
2 cups fish stock
3 tablespoons butter
8 shallots, finely chopped
4 tablespoons dried tomato bits (see Sources)
sea salt to taste

Butter or oil a small oblong pyrex dish, and set the filet, skin side down, in the dish. Bring stock to a boil and pour over the filet. If the liquid does not entirely cover the fish, add water. Set in a 325 degree oven and poach until just tender, from ten to fifteen minutes depending on the thickness of the filet. You can check for doneness with a fork. Be careful not to overcook. Remove from the oven when the inside is still a little rare. Set the filet on a heated platter, cover with a piece of parchment paper (see Sources) and keep in a heated oven while you are preparing the sauce.

While the filet is cooking, saute shallots a few minutes in butter, add the tomato bits and cook a few minutes more. After the fish has poached, transfer to strain stock into the shallot mixture, bring to a rapid boil and reduce the stock, skimming occasionally, until you have about a cup of liquid plus vegetables. Check for seasoning before you add salt. You may decide you don't need it.

To serve, portion the fish and lift off the skin. Set on heated plates and spoon on the sauce.

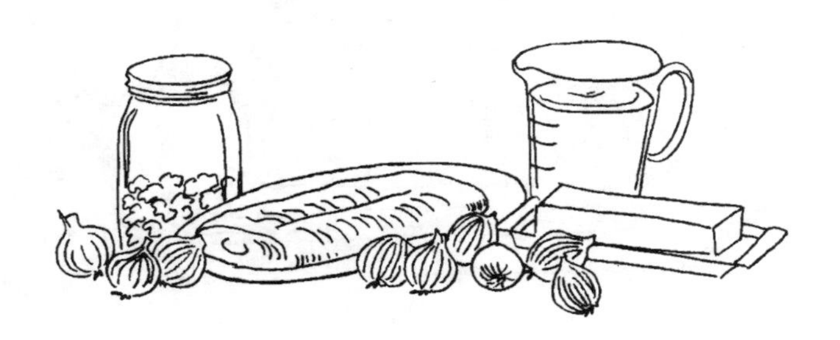

A major British study found that eating oily fish like salmon, tuna, mackerel and sardines cut the death rate by one third in middle-aged men who had already suffered a heart attack. In the study of 2,033 men under age seventy, researchers told one group of men to eat fish high in omega-3 type oil at least twice a week; another group was told to cut down on high-fat foods; another to eat more fiber; and a fourth was given no dietary advice. After two years the odds of dying of heart disease dropped by 29 percent among the fish eaters compared with the other men in the study. Jean Carper *The Food Pharmacy Guide to Good Eating*

SALMON WITH SORREL SAUCE

Serves 6

2 pounds filet of salmon
4 cups fish stock
1 cup piima cream or creme fraiche
about 4 cups packed fresh sorrel leaves
butter
sea salt

Butter or oil a small oblong pyrex dish, and set the filet, skin side down, in the dish. Bring the stock to a boil and pour over the filet. If the liquid does not entirely cover the fish, add water. Set in a 325 degree oven and poach until just tender, from ten to fifteen minutes depending on the thickness of the filet. You can check for doneness with a fork. Be careful not to overcook. Remove from the oven when the inside is still a little rare. Set the filet on a heated platter, cover with a piece of parchment paper (see Sources) and keep in a heated oven while you prepare the sauce.

Meanwhile, wash the sorrel leaves, shake dry and chop coarsely. Saute in a little butter until completely wilted. Set aside.

Pour poaching stock into a heavy skillet and bring to a rapid boil. Add cream, and boil vigorously until sauce has thickened and reduced to about 3/4 cup. Stir in the sorrel. Divide the filet into servings and place on individual plates. Spoon a little sauce over each and serve immediately.

Don't forget that your body needs some high quality saturated fat in your diet. The anti-fat craze that has swept America for the past 30 years is responsible for a lot of harm—a lot of misinformation. Here's another example: Researchers with the Department of Agriculture's Human Nutrition Research Center at Tufts University have learned that people who cut back on fat to the tune of eating only fish and vegetables appear to open themselves up to more infection. The low-fat diet, which called for eating fish every day, "significantly reduced the infection fighting power of certain white blood cells." This does not mean you can't eat fish every day if you want to, it means you need to eat some quality fat with it. Tom Valentine *Search for Health*

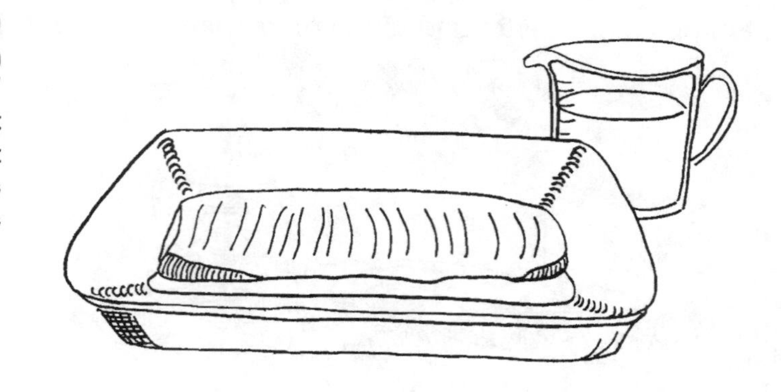

SALMON WITH FENNEL

Serves 6

6 salmon steaks
2-4 cups fish stock
1 fennel bulb, coarsely chopped
1/2 cup dry white wine
1 tablespoon fennel seeds
1 teaspoon dried green peppercorns
1 cup piima cream or creme fraiche
1/2 stick butter, softened
18 small sprigs fennel leaves (cut from bulb)
1 tomato, peeled, seeded and finely chopped
6 teaspoons salmon eggs (optional)

Remove bone and skin from steaks. They will form two pieces. Roll up each piece and tie with string, forming two small "medallions" per person. Set in a buttered pyrex dish, just large enough to hold the medallions and strew fennel bulb pieces around. Bring stock to a boil and pour over medallions. Add a little water if stock does not cover the fish. Bake about 8 minutes at 350 degrees or until just cooked. Strain stock into a heavy saucepan, cover medallions with parchment paper (see Sources) and keep warm in the oven while you prepare the sauce. (Discard the fennel.)

Bring stock to a rapid boil and reduce by half. Add wine, fennel seeds, peppercorns and cream and reduce to about 1 cup or until sauce has thickened. Strain into a bowl and beat in butter with a whisk, one tablespoon at a time. Set bowl in simmering water to keep warm.

Decorate plates with alternating fennel sprigs and spoonfuls of tomato around the outside edge. Remove strings from medallions and set two in the middle of each plate. Spoon sauce over each and decorate with salmon eggs.

For decades we've had dinned in our ears by research foundations and associations that we should follow a low fat-high polyunsaturated diet to prevent heart disease.

Then we learned that excess vegetable oils increase the need for vitamin E, bring on premature aging and cause facial skin to wrinkle far before it normally would.

Now the results of research by Gabriel Fernandes, associate professor of medicine in the division of Clinical Immunology at the University of Texas Health Center (San Antonio), point an accusing finger at this dietary change as a probable cause of the near epidemic proportions of malignant melanoma, a deadly skin cancer.

Experiments by Fernandes with mice on calorie-controlled diet with various amount of polyunsaturated and saturated fats show that heavy emphasis onpolyunsaturated fats could indeed by the culprit.

Mice on a diet of 20 percent polyunsaturated fat proved to be far more susceptible to transplanted melanoma and to the spread of it to their lungs than mice on a diet of 20 percent saturated fats. James F. Scheer *Health Freedom News*

WHOLE POACHED SALMON

Serves 20-30

NEW YEARS EVE BUFFET DINNER

Whole Poached Salmon
Egg Mustard Sauce
Red Pepper Sauce
Watercress Sauce

Steak Tartare
Round Croutons

Balsamic Carrot Salad

Asparagus Vinaigrette

Spinach Feta Pastries

Individual Lemon Mousse Tarts

Individual Walnut Tarts

1 whole salmon, cleaned, with head, tail and skin
cheesecloth and string
1/2 cup vinegar
3 bay leaves,
1 teaspoon juniper berries
1 lemon, sliced
1 teaspoon dried green peppercorns
1 1/4 cups green gelatin mayonnaise (page 128)
2 cucumbers

This is a great buffet dish and not very difficult to make. If you do not have a fish poaching pan, just use a turkey roaster with a rack at the bottom.

Remove the fins from the salmon. Wrap in cheesecloth and tie with string, leaving little handles of cheesecloth at each end. This will help you remove the fish without breaking it. Place in the pan on a rack and cover with boiling water. Add vinegar, bay leaves, juniper berries, lemon slices and peppercorns. Simmer—do not boil—until just tender. A good rule is to cook 10 minutes per inch of thickness at the thickest part of the salmon. (Use a ruler and measure across the back.)

Lift fish out with cheesecloth handles and place on a large platter. Remove cheesecloth. Remove skin but leave head and tail. Turn over carefully and remove skin from other side. Remove any liquid and debris from platter with paper towels. Cover and refrigerate.

When fish is cool, spread with green gelatin mayonnaise (page 128) and decorate with cucumber slices to resemble scales. Serve with a choice of sauces such as egg mustard sauce (page 130), Bernaise sauce (page 138), creamy dill sauce (page 130), red pepper sauce (page 131) or watercress sauce (page 132).

FOWL

As Americans have cut back on red meat, chicken has played an increasingly important role in our diet. Although chicken is a perfectly good source of animal protein, frequent chicken consumption requires a cautionary note. First of all, we must be careful of the source of chickens we buy. Battery or factory raised chickens are subjected to crowded living conditions and often substandard feed; they require frequent doses of antibiotics and growth hormones to reach adulthood. Many develop cancers and these cancerous chickens are not necessarily discarded. According to researcher Virginia Livingston Wheeler, these cancers can be transmitted to humans. We advise you to find a source of organic chicken, which is becoming more available in our markets and is worth the additional price.

Secondly, we warn you against eating chicken—even organically raised chicken—to excess. Any food eaten to the exclusion of others can lead to allergies, food addictions and adverse reactions. This is true of meats as well as vegetables, dairy products and grains. It is best to eat a variety of fowl—chicken, turkey, Cornish game hens and domesticated duck—and to vary your source of animal protein between fowl, fish, game and red meat.

In Europe, particularly France, chicken is eaten stewed or braised in liquid; in America chicken is traditionally eaten fried. Stewed chicken fails the test of taste appeal—it is often slimy and unappetizing—and fried chicken fails the test of good nutrition in that it is prepared with oils heated to high temperatures and these oils are absorbed into the batter or flour coating. We have chosen a middle ground and selected a variety of recipes for baked or pan-cooked chicken, turkey, game hen or duck. Baking or roasting fowl results in golden crispy skin, so appealing to children, and tender juicy meat. Most of our recipes call for the use of chicken stock in the sauce. Chicken stock provides a concentrated source of minerals and hydrophilic colloids that make your entire meal more digestible.

Don't neglect to eat the dark meat as well as the white. Not only is dark meat more flavorful and tender, it is superior nutritionally speaking, as it provides more minerals and fat soluble vitamins. And speaking of dark meat, do take advantage of domestic farm-raised duck now becoming more available in our markets. We suggest cutting ducks into pieces before preparing them, rather than cooking them whole. One duck will yield four generous servings; the carcass makes a rich stock for sauces and soups; the excess skin, when rendered of its fat, makes delicious cracklings for salads and is an excellent substitute for bacon; and the fat itself can be used in many ways. Duck fat is highly prized in France for cooking potatoes; and in Scandinavia where it is spread like butter on dark bread to make delicious sandwiches. It is high in stable oleic acid and rich in fat soluble vitamins.

ROAST CHICKEN

Serves 6

1 roasting chicken
1 medium onion, peeled and thinly sliced
2 whole heads garlic (optional)
butter and extra virgin olive oil
sea salt and freshly ground pepper
several sprigs fresh thyme, oregano or tarragon
1/2 cup dry white wine or vermouth
4 cups chicken stock

Strew onion slices in a stainless steel roasting pan. Cut optional heads of garlic in half and place, cut side down, in pan. Stuff fresh herbs into the cavity of the chicken and place on a rack in the roasting pan, underside up. Brush with a mixture of melted butter and olive oil and season with salt and pepper. Bake at 375 degrees for one hour. To turn chicken, insert a wooden spoon into the cavity. Lift chicken and rotate so that top side is up. Brush with more butter and oil, season with salt and pepper and return to oven. Bake another hour. Remove chicken to a carving board and cut into individual pieces. Reserve chicken pieces and garlic in a warm oven while making sauce. (Serve garlic heads to garlic lovers. Softened, individual cloves can be picked out with a fork. They are delicious.)

Remove rack from baking pan. You may pour off the fat if you wish but it is not necessary. Pour in wine and bring to a boil, stirring to loosen onion slices. Pour in stock and reduce to about half by vigorous boiling. Strain sauce into a small saucepan and keep warm over a low flame.

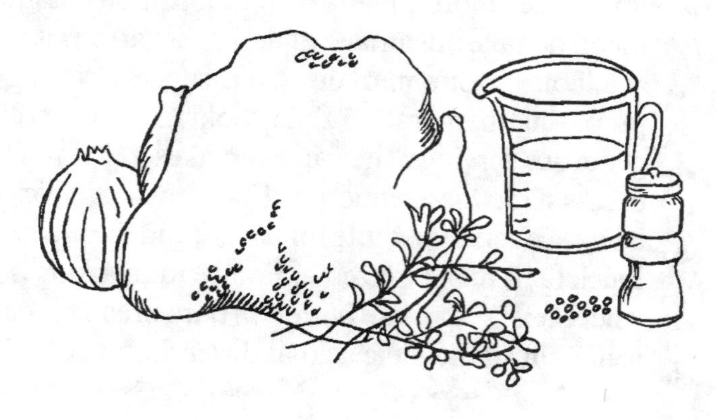

SUNDAY DINNER

Cream of Vegetable Soup with Round Croutons

Roast Chicken

Cottage Potatoes

Pickled Beets

Applesauce

A series of feeding experiments on rats showed differences in the nutritive value of common fats. The rats which received butter fat grew better than the rats fed vegetable oils, were better in appearance, and had better reproductive capacity. Apparently butter fat contains a substance not present in the other fats tested, which is essential for growth and health of young animals. This difference is not due to vitamins A, D, or E, but to a difference in the chemical constitution of the fats. These findings are significant to the knowledge of nutrition because they indicate additional reasons why milk fat has superior value for human diets. Weston Price DDS *Nutrition and Physical Degeneration*

BASIC BAKED CHICKEN

Serves 6

1 frying chicken, cut into pieces
2 tablespoons Dijon style mustard
2 tablespoons melted butter
1 tablespoon dried tarragon
1/2 cup dry white wine
2 cups chicken stock

Place chicken pieces skin side up in a stainless steal roasting pan. Mix mustard with butter and brush on chicken. Bake for about 2 hours at 350 degrees, or until pieces are golden. Remove to a heated platter and keep warm in the oven while making sauce.

Pour wine and stock into the pan and boil vigorously, stirring to loosen any accumulated drippings. Let sauce reduce to about one half. Check for seasonings and add sea salt if necessary. Strain into a small sauce pan or server.

Variation: Chicken with Cream Sauce

Strew *several sprigs fresh tarragon* over chicken in the pan. (Omit dried tarragon.) Add *1 cup piima cream or creme fraiche* to the stock and wine when you are reducing the sauce. Strain sauce into a small pan and add *2 tablespoons fresh tarragon leaves, chopped*.

Variation: Chicken with Red Pepper Sauce

Place *3 red peppers, cored, seeded and coarsely chopped in pan with chicken pieces.* After chicken has cooked, saute peppers in the fat in the roasting pan. Add wine and stock and reduce. Process in batches in food processor. Check seasonings and add sea salt if necessary.

Variation: Chicken with Peanut Sauce

Prepare chicken according to master recipe. When sauce has reduced, remove from heat and gradually add *1 1/2 cups peanut sauce* (page 133), using a wire whisk. Transfer sauce to a container set in hot water. Do not let the sauce boil or it will burn.

Actually the digestive mechanism of man is adapted to a mixed meat and vegetable diet. Human teeth consist of three types: canines or piercing teeth of the meat-eating animals, the incisors of plant-eating animals, and the molars or grinders of grain and nut eating animals. With respect to structure, human teeth are conclusive proof that the human body is adapted to a mixed animal and plant diet. Man has specific digestive ferments for meat proteins and other special digestive juices for carbohydrates. His stomach and intestinal tract is equipped to handle both. Man is naturally adapted to a mixed diet of animal and plant foods. H. Leon Abrams *Your Body is Your Best Doctor*

Know Your Ingredients
Name This Product #13

Water, corn syrup, partially hydrogenated soybean oil, mono and diglycerides, soy protein, sodium stearoyl lactylate, dipotassium phosphate, polysorbate 60, sodium acid pyrophosphate, salt, artificial flavor, colored with betacarotene.

See Appendix B for Answer

MOROCCAN STYLE CHICKEN

Serves 6

1 frying chicken cut into pieces
1/4 cup soy sauce
1/4 cup dry white wine
2 tablespoons honey
juice of 2 lemons
grated rind of 2 lemons or 3 tablespoons preserved lemon peel (page 96)
1 clove garlic, peeled and mashed
1 teaspoon curry powder
1/4 teaspoon ground ginger
1/2 teaspoon each dried oregano, thyme and green peppercorns, crushed
3 tablespoons melted butter
2 cups chicken stock
8 dried apricot halves, coarsely chopped and soaked in warm water

Mix soy sauce, wine, honey, lemon juice, lemon rind and all spices together. Marinate chicken pieces in this mixture for several hours or overnight. Remove pieces, pat dry and set skin side up in a stainless steel baking pan, reserving marinade. Brush with butter, season with sea salt and pepper and bake at 375 degrees for about 2 hours. Reduce heat if chicken begins to burn. Remove chicken to heated platter while making sauce.

Pour chicken stock into the pan, bring to a boil and stir well. Add marinade and drained apricot pieces. Let sauce reduce by about one half. Check seasoning and pour over chicken pieces.

It was the Miss America Pageant and after viewing it, I actually fell to prayer for the return of the American Beauty. This Pageant became for me a tragic testimonial to the physical degeneration that has occurred in the modern civilized world, especially during the last 40 years of advanced technology.

Deaf Smith County, Texas has sponsored an inordinate number of attractive pageant winners. It is not coincidence but the result of the water supply which is higher in zinc, iodine and magnesium, all of which contribute to the much denser and better proportioned bone structure of the men and women living there. It has become famous as an area without a toothache. What do teeth have to do with beauty? Decayed teeth, like crowded ones and under developed bones, also detract from our attractiveness.

Because of impoverished soils, poor water supplies, overprocessed foods and inadequate diets, that begin unwittingly as "high tech" baby formulas instead of human breast milk, we are seeing a rapid decline in beauty, intelligence and grace. The evidence is found in these pageants, lower SAT scores and in the growing consensus of distrust, inhumanity and immorality between men. Beauty is more than skin deep. The so-called "civilized" world is turning mean, and ugly to the very bone. R.M. Dell'Orfano *PPNF Journal*

SIMPLE CHICKEN BREASTS

Serves 6

6 skinless chicken breasts
juice of two lemons
extra virgin olive oil

Trim chicken breasts and pound lightly with small prong side of a meat hammer. Marinate several hours in lemon juice. Brush a heavy bottomed skilled with olive oil and allow it to heat up. Pat chicken pieces dry. Cook over moderate heat on both sides, two or three at a time, for about 5 minutes to a side, cooking skin side first. Transfer to a heated platter and keep warm in the oven. Serve plain or with an accompaniment such as corn relish (page 93), pineapple chutney (page 98), chismole (page 168), guacamole (page 156), curry sauce (page 136), or red enchilada sauce (page 142); or serve cold with Creole mayonnaise (page 128).

Variation: Mexican Chicken Breasts

Use *juice of 4 limes* in place of lemons. Add *1/2 teaspoon oregano* and *1/4 teaspoon chile flakes* to marinade. May be grilled or cooked on the barbecue.

Know Your Ingredients

Name This Product # 14

Tomatoes with tomato puree, cooked macaroni product, tomatoes, tomato puree, dry curd cottage cheese, onions, beef, mushrooms, low-moisture part-skim mozzarella cheese, corn syrup, modified cornstarch, garlic, tomato paste, enriched wheat flour, Parmesan cheese, salt, spices, romano cheese (made from cow's milk), hydrolyzed vegetable protein and autolyzed yeast extract, corn oil, sugar, xanthan gum, dehydrated onions, erthor-bic acid, caramel coloring, dried beef stock, natural flavorings.

See Appendix B for Answer

SPICED CHICKEN BREASTS

Serves 6

6 chicken breasts, skin on or off
4 tablespoons extra virgin olive oil
1 teaspoon turmeric
1 teaspoon cinnamon
1 teaspoon ground cumin
1 teaspoon paprika
1 teaspoon curry powder
1/2 teaspoon dried chile flakes
3 cloves garlic, peeled and mashed
1/2 teaspoon sea salt

Trim chicken breasts and pound lightly with small prong side of a meat hammer. Mix spices and garlic with oil and brush on. Marinate chicken breasts several hours or overnight. Brush a heavy skillet with olive oil and allow it to heat up. Pat chicken breasts dry and cook over medium high flame, two or three at a time, for about 5 minutes per side. Transfer to a heated platter and keep warm in the oven.

To serve, slice across the grain and arrange slices on individual plates. Dribble marinade over chicken.

Inquiry into the dietary history of patients diagnosed as schizophrenic reveals the diet of their choice is rich in sweets, candy, cakes, coffee, caffeinated beverages and foods prepared with sugar. These foods, which stimulate the adrenals, should be eliminated or severely restricted. A. Cott *Orthomolecular Approach to the Treatment of Learning Disabilities*

The teenage suicide rate has doubled since 1968, largely because mothers demonstrate their love by keeping the refrigerators stocked with sugary soda drinks and feed them cereals for breakfast and spaghetti for dinner. Their grandparents bring them candy and ice cream. Why do we insist upon rotting the brains of a whole generation of children, turning them into scholastic failures, delinquents, dropouts and welfare recipients? Whey do we drive more and more of them to suicide by feeding them ever more processed foods? I'll tell you why: Many people are getting rich at their expense. We look askance at African tribes when they cut faces and rub dyes into the wounds and when they circumcise women. That's child's play compared to what we do to our children. In our society, it's perfectly all right to maim and kill—so long as we do it in a socially acceptable way. H.L. Newbold MD *Type A Type B Weight Loss Book*

TAILGATE PICNIC

Breaded Chicken Breasts

Cole Slaw

Dilled Potato Salad

Corn Relish

Pecan Cookies

Grape Cooler

CHICKEN WITH SWEET AND SOUR SAUCE

Serves 6-10

12 chicken breasts, skin on
1 cup fresh orange juice
1 cup fresh lemon juice
1 cup vinegar
2 tablespoons fresh ginger, minced
2 tablespoons fresh garlic, minced
1/2 teaspoon red chile pepper flakes
3 tablespoons extra virgin olive oil
2 cups chicken stock

Trim chicken breasts and pound lightly with the small prong side of a meat hammer. Combine remaining ingredients except olive oil and chicken stock in a saucepan and bring to a boil. Reduce heat and simmer for several minutes. Allow to cool and stir in olive oil. Marinate the chicken breasts in this mixture for several hours or overnight. Remove from marinade and grill about 5 minutes per side under the broiler. Keep warm on a heated platter in the oven while making sauce.

Place marinade in a sauce pan with chicken stock and bring to a rapid boil. Allow to reduce to about one half. To serve, slice the chicken breasts across the grain, arrange on individual plates and spoon sauce over.

BREADED CHICKEN BREASTS

Serves 4-6

8 skinless chicken breasts
1 1/2 cups unbleached flour
1 teaspoon pepper
4 eggs, beaten
2 cups whole grain bread crumbs
1/2 cup grated Parmesan cheese
butter and extra virgin olive oil

This is a delicious substitute for fried chicken. It makes an excellent picnic dish. Leftover breaded chicken breasts can be warmed and sent to school in children's lunch boxes.

Trim chicken breasts and pound lightly with the small prong side of a meat hammer. Mix flour and pepper together on a plate; have beaten eggs ready in a bowl; mix bread crumbs and Parmesan cheese in another bowl.

Dip each piece, first in flour mixture, then in egg, then in bread crumb mixture. (Use tongs for this.) Saute a few at a time in butter and olive oil, about 7 minutes per side, being careful not to burn. Transfer to a heated platter and keep warm in the oven until ready to serve. Serve with lemon wedges, ginger carrots (page 87) or pineapple chutneyu (page 98).

The first phase of digestion begins in the mouth where the enzyme amylase becomes mixed with the food we are chewing and begins to digest starches. The production of saliva and the activity of amylase are considerably stimulated by . . several spices, notably pepper, ginger, hot pepper, curry and mustard. Research on the amount of saliva produced and the total activity of amylase shows that these spices and condiments can increase their activity by as much as 20 times. Claude Aubert *Dis-Moi Comment Tu Cuisines*

SESAME BUFFALO WINGS

Serves 8

24 buffalo wings
1/2 cup soy sauce
1/2 cup rice vinegar
2 tablespoons honey
juice of 2 lemons
grated rind of 2 lemons
1 clove garlic, peeled and mashed
1 teaspoon curry powder
1/4 teaspoon ground ginger
1/2 teaspoon dried oregano
1/2 teaspoon dried thyme
1/2 teaspoon dried green peppercorns, crushed
3 tablespoons melted butter
1/4 cup sesame seeds

Mix soy sauce, vinegar, honey, lemon juice, lemon rind and all seasonings. Marinate buffalo wings in mixture several hours or overnight. Remove from mixture and pat dry. Place in a stainless steel baking ban, brush with butter, sprinkle with sesame seeds and bake at 350 degrees about 1 1/4 hours. May be served with the marinade, gently heated, as a dip.

CHILD'S BIRTHDAY PARTY

Sesame Buffalo Wings

Carrot Salad

Apple Slices in Orange Juice

Crispy Cashews

Buttered Popcorn

Spice Layer Cake

Raspberry Drink

CHICKEN STIR FRY STEW

Serves 4-6

1 pound chicken breasts cut into small pieces
juice of 2 lemons
extra virgin olive oil
1 cup crispy peanuts (page 486)
1 bunch green onions, sliced on an angle
2 large carrots, peeled and cut into a julienne
1 cup broccoli cut into flowerets
2 cloves garlic, finely chopped
1 teaspoon grated ginger
1 tablespoon sucanat
1/4 teaspoon red pepper flakes
2 tablespoons soy sauce
1/8 cup rice vinegar
2-3 cups chicken stock
2 tablespoons arrowroot
mixed with 2 tablespoons water

This a delicious, low-cost family dish—always a favorite.

Marinate chicken pieces several hours in lemon juice. Remove and pat dry with paper towels. Mix chicken stock with vinegar, soy sauce, pepper flakes, ginger, sucanat and garlic and set aside. In a heavy skillet or wok, saute chicken in oil until cooked through. Using a slotted spoon, transfer chicken a bowl and reserve. Add more oil and saute peanuts a minute or two. Remove with slotted spoon. Add more oil and saute onions, carrots and peppers about 2 minutes. Add sauce mixture and bring to a boil. Return chicken and peanuts to pan and mix well. Add arrowroot mixture and simmer a minute or so until sauce thickens. Add broccoli and simmer until tender. Serve with basic brown rice (page 441).

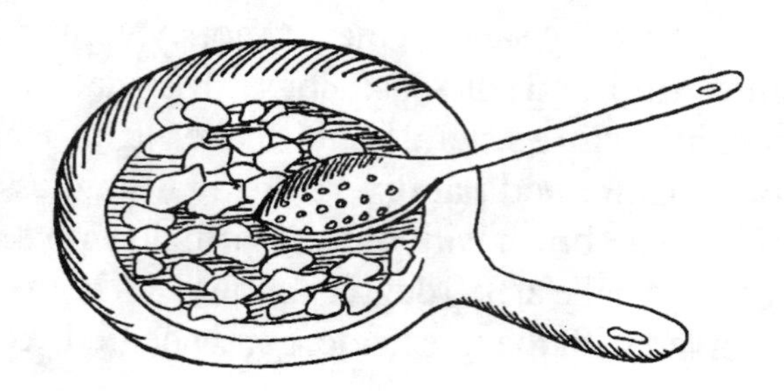

Other than the fact that margarine may kill you, what else is wrong with it? An English institution for boys ran a nutritional experiment in 1938. A group of boys were fed one and three-fourths ounces of New Zealand "grass-fed butter". Another group was fed margarine. The margarine proved "worthless for growth", but the butter group grew an extra .38 inches during the experimental period. The investigators had previously done a similar test on rats. They concluded, "There is something in butter that isn't in margarine and it works on boys the same as on rats." William Campbell Douglass MD *The Milk of Human Kindness*

Michael De Bakey, the world renowned heart surgeon from Houston who has devoted extensive research into the cholesterol coronary disease theory, states that out of every ten people in the United States who have atherosclerotic heart disease that only three or four of these ten have high cholesterol levels; this is approximately the identical rate of elevated cholesterol found in the general population. His comment: "If you say cholesterol is the cause, how do you explain the other 60 percent to 70 percent with heart disease who don't have a high cholesterol?" De Bakey made an analysis of cholesterol levels from usual hospital laboratory analyses of 1,700 patients with atherosclerotic disease and found that there was no positive or definitive relationship or correlation between serum cholesterol levels and the extent or nature of atherosclerotic disease. H. Leon Abrams *Vegetarianism: An Anthropological/Nutritional Evaluation*

CHICKEN CURRY

Serves 6

meat from 2 cooked chickens, cut up
(reserved from making stock, page 114)
butter and extra virgin olive oil
2 medium onions, finely chopped
2 tablespoons turmeric
1 tablespoon ground fenugreek seeds
1 teaspoon ground cumin
1/4 teaspoon cayenne pepper
1/2 teaspoon ground cloves
1 teaspoon ground coriander
1 teaspoon ground cardamom
2-3 cups chicken stock
juice of 1-2 lemons
2 cloves garlic, peeled and mashed
1 cup piima cream, creme fraiche,
coconut milk and cream (page 144) or
7-8 ounces creamed coconut (see Sources)
sea salt

Saute onions until soft. Add spices and saute, stirring, for several minutes. Add chicken stock and lemon juice and bring to a boil. Stir in garlic, chicken and cream. Simmer, uncovered, for about 15 minutes, stirring frequently, until sauce is reduced and thickened. Season to taste. Serve with traditional curry garnishes such as chopped green onions, chopped crispy peanuts (page 486), dried sweetened coconut meat (page 144), raisins, raisin chutney (page 100) and fruit chutney (page 98).

The theory that fats in the diet are the primary factor in causing heart disease is just that. This idea was started by a researcher named Ancel Keys. In 1953 he noted that certain cultures whose diets were high in fat also had a high incidence of heart disease. From then on, his theory became accepted as fact. No doubt, there is some truth to the theory but only on this basis—Americans and other people who have lots of heart disease eat massive quantities of REFINED FATS! That's right. It is not the fat itself, but how it is processed or refined that makes it damaging. That brings us back to the topic of sugar. It is proven that sugar intake is related to the increased incidence of all types of circulatory diseases.

Dr. Yudkin, a former professor of Nutrition and Dietetics at Queen Elizabeth College of London University and now Emeritus Dean of nutrition, first noticed that many of the same countries that had a high intake of fat had a higher intake of sugar! When looking at fat alone, Yudkin found no evidence that people who had high intakes of saturated fats from foods naturally high in fats such as milk, cheese, eggs, or meat had any greater incidence of heart disease than those who did not eat these foods. What he did find, however, was that high intakes of sugar had a clear-cut relationship to the occurrence of heart disease. Cass Igram MD *Eat Right to Live Longer*

Because table salt comes from the same batch as vacuum-refined industrial salt, it is treated with caustic soda or lime to remove all traces of magnesium salts. These vital magnesium salts are not taken out because they keep the salt from flowing out of the dispenser spout, it is because they bring in more profits on the chemical market. Yet these magnesium salts are a very necessary part of the food salt and fill important biological and therapeutic roles. Further, to prevent any moisture from being reabsorbed, salt refiners now add alumino-silicate of sodium or yellow prussiate of soda as desiccants plus different bleaches to the final salt formula. But since table salt, chemically treated in this way, will no longer combine with human body fluid, it invariably causes severe problems of edema, (water retention) and several other health disturbances. The fear of salt that we witness today and the virtual ban on consuming products with a high sodium content is a matter of serious concern to biologists. Salt-free diets can cause salt starvation, which is a stark reality of our modern world, but it is actually a starvation of macro- and trace minerals, a biological deficiency that refined sodium chloride alone cannot correct. Jacques DeLangre *Seasalt's Hidden Powers*

CHICKEN WITH WALNUTS

(Fesenjan)

Serves 6-8

meat from 2 cooked chickens, cut up
(reserved from making stock, page 114)
1 pound freshly shelled walnut meats
2-3 cups chicken stock
2-4 tablespoons sucanat
12 ounces concentrated pomegranate juice,
or 1/3 cup pomegranate "molasses"
(available at Middle Eastern markets)
sea salt to taste

This delicious recipe comes from Persia. Place walnuts in food processor and grind to a paste. Mix with stock, concentrated pomegranate juice and sucanat. (Note: Add the larger amount of stock if using pomegranate "molasses".) Heat up slowly and simmer for about 1/2 hour. Season to taste. Add chicken meat to sauce and simmer about 5 minutes or until chicken is warmed through. Serve with basic brown rice (page 441).

CHICKEN SUPREME

Serves 6

meat from 2 cooked chickens, cut up
(reserved from making stock, page 114)
1 pound fresh mushrooms, washed, dried
and sliced
4 tablespoons chopped shallots
butter and extra virgin olive oil
1/2 cup dry white wine
2 cups chicken stock
1 cup piima cream or creme fraiche
sea salt and freshly ground pepper

In a heavy skillet, saute mushrooms in 2 or 3 batches until golden. Reserve. Add more butter and olive oil and saute shallots until soft. Add wine and stock, bring to a boil and cook, uncovered, until stock has reduced to about one-third. Add cream and reduce further. Stir in chicken meat, mushrooms and seasonings and simmer five minutes. Serve with basic brown rice (page 441) or as a filling to buckwheat crepes (page 455).

The reason most people spread on the margarine instead of butter is that they think it will keep their hearts healthy, their arteries unclogged and their cholesterol down. Yet all the honest evidence proves just the opposite. High cholesterol levels are sometimes seen these days. Dr. Lee, after a barrage of scientific data, attributes this as "directly a consequence of the use of synthetic fats," like margarine. He continues: "Clinical tests on both man and animals show a constant rise in blood cholesterol if the test subject is fed with refined or synthetic fats, while when fed with natural [fresh, unrefined] vegetable oils, the blood cholesterol progressively returns to normal levels." Judith A. DeCava *The Margarine Masquerade*

CHICKEN GUMBO

Serves 8

cooked meat of two chickens,
(reserved from making stock, page 114)
butter and extra virgin olive oil
2 large onions, chopped
1 red pepper, seeded and chopped
1 green pepper, seeded and chopped
1/2 cup tomato paste
2-4 cups chicken stock
2 cloves garlic, crushed
1 teaspoon dried basil
1 teaspoon dried oregano
2 teaspoons sea salt
1/2 teaspoon green peppercorns, crushed
2-3 tomatoes, peeled, seeded and chopped
1 tablespoon file powder (available in gourmet markets and specialty shops)

Saute onions and peppers in butter and oil until soft. Add tomato paste and chicken broth and bring to a boil. Skim, reduce to a simmer, and add chicken meat and seasonings. Simmer about 1 hour, uncovered, stirring occasionally. 10 minutes before serving, stir in tomatoes and file powder. Serve with basic brown rice.

It is not true. . . that the absolute length of life has lengthened. Actually fewer persons alive at 70 today survive until 90 than 40 years ago. The lengthened life span of today is due to saving the lives of more babies and children. Edward Howell MD *Enzymes for Health and Longevity*

CORNISH GAME HENS WITH PINE NUT SAUCE

Serves 4

2 Cornish game hens,
2 cups chicken stock
1 teaspoon pepper
1 teaspoon lovage or celery seed
several sprigs parsley
pinch rosemary
1 tablespoon honey
1 tablespoon cider vinegar
1 teaspoon dry mustard
2 tablespoons extra virgin olive oil
1/4 cup pine nuts
1/4 cup dates, finely chopped

This recipe, from the third century manuscripts of Apicius, is a kind of Roman sweet and sour. Place birds in a small pot and cover with chicken stock. Bring to a boil and simmer for 15 minutes. Remove and split lengthwise. Pat dry with paper towels and set game hen halves, skin side up, in a stainless steel baking pan.

Place parsley in food processor fitted with a steel blade and chop with a few pulses. Add 1 1/2 cups stock, pepper, lovage or celery seed, rosemary, honey, vinegar, mustard and olive oil in processor and blend until smooth. Pour over game hens and sprinkle with pine nuts and dates. Bake in a 375 degree oven for 45 minutes or until golden.

Remove halves to a heated platter and keep warm while making sauce. Bring pan juices to a boil and reduce to about half. Spoon over game hens and serve.

If the best current knowledge were employed, enough food to feed the four billion people could be grown in the southern half of Sudan! It is only the western bias, the idea spread throughout the world that one must eat white grain and drink soda pop to be "civilized", that is responsible for the suffering of the millions of starving people in the world. It is a myth that there is not enough to go around, that there is no way the Earth can support its exploding population. The truth is that most of the world's food resources are controlled by a handful of greedy men, who deny people the right to grow food for themselves, but try to sell them western-produced junk instead. [Some experts] estimate that if all the arable land on earth were used properly and sowed with foods for human consumption, the Earth could support 60 billion people—almost fifteen times our current population! But it is true that there is no way we can feed the world population on Whoppers and Cheez-Wiz, let alone nourish it. Paul Stitt *Fighting the Food Giants*

CORNISH GAME HENS WITH GRAPES

Serves 4

2 Cornish game hens, split lengthwise
2 tablespoons extra virgin olive oil
2 tablespoons melted butter
sea salt and freshly ground pepper
1/2 cup dry white wine or vermouth
2 cups chicken stock
2 cups fresh grapes, red or green
2 tablespoons arrowroot mixed with
2 tablespoons water

Place game hen halves, skin side up, in a stainless steel baking pan. Brush with a mixture of butter and oil and season with salt and pepper. Bake at 375 degrees for about 1 1/2 hours. Remove to a heated platter and keep warm in the oven while making sauce.

Pour wine or vermouth into the pan and bring to a boil, stirring with a wooden spoon to scrape up any accumulated juices in the pan. Add chicken stock, bring to a rapid boil and let the sauce reduce for about 10 minutes until it thickens. Add the grapes and simmer about 5 minutes more. Spoonful by spoonful, add arrowroot mixture until desired thickness is obtained. Transfer game hens to individual plates and pour sauce over.

Cholesterol is a remarkable lipid. It is the central structure in the steroid group that includes the female and male hormones, the contraceptive pill, cortisone, vitamin D, and the steroid drugs that some athletes and older movie stars take. Cholesterol, despite all the bad press it has received, is a vital material in the human organism. It is part of the bile acids that digest fats, a major component of brain and nerve tissue, and a forerunner of many hormones, particularly the sex hormones. Cholesterol is found widely in animal foods (eggs, dairy products, poultry, shellfish), and our bodies manufacture significant amounts of it every day. "Without it the skin would dry up, the brain would not function, and there would be no vital hormones of sex and adrenal."

In the Big Fat Controversy, some researchers have reported statistical correlations between blood cholesterol levels and heart disease. Despite an enormous effort, however, scientists have not been able to establish, among normal healthy people on a good diet, understandable links between the cholesterol in one's food, the cholesterol in one's blood, and heart attacks or strokes. To the degree there are relationships—as there are among myriad factors and events in the body—no one knows what is causing what. Joseph D. Beasley MD and Jerry J. Swift MA *The Kellogg Report*

CORNISH GAME HENS, INDIAN STYLE

Serves 4

2 Cornish game hens, split lengthwise
1/2 cup plain yoghurt
1 teaspoon ground cumin
1 teaspoon turmeric
1 teaspoon ground fenugreek seeds
1 tablespoon lemon juice
2 cloves garlic, peeled and mashed
1/2 teaspoon grated ginger
1/2 teaspoon paprika
1/2 teaspoon salt
1 tablespoon extra virgin olive oil
2 tablespoons crispy almonds (page 487), slivered in a food processor

Combine yoghurt, spices, lemon juice, garlic, ginger, paprika, oil and salt in a large bowl. Brush on game hens and marinate in refrigerator for 4 to 6 hours. Place game hen halves, skin side up, in a stainless steel baking dish, spoon on any remaining marinade, and bake at 375 degrees for about 1 1/4 hours. Sprinkle almonds on and bake another 1/4 hour.

Now commonly used in Middle Eastern spice and curry mixtures, fenugreek seeds are an ancient medicinal herb, prescribed in ancient Egypt and India as a cure-all but in particular for tuberculosis, bronchitis, and sore throat. The seed is a carminative, relieving intestinal gas. It is used in the Mideast to treat diabetes, and there is increasing evidence showing that fenugreek seeds do lower blood sugar, as well as blood cholesterol. Jean Carper *The Food Pharmacy Guide to Good Eating*

The Medical Research Council of Great Britain in 1968 did a study in which the fate of patients put on a low-saturated fat diet after a heart attack was determined and compared to patients on a high saturated fat diet. They concluded that the unsaturated fat diet had no effect on the ultimate course of the patients. The number of second heart attacks and deaths were the same in both groups. Two other studies, one done in Oslo, Norway and one in England, came to the same conclusion. William Campbell Douglass MD *The Milk of Human Kindness*

TURKEY WITH CHESTNUT STUFFING

Serves 12-18

1 16-20 pound turkey
8 cups whole grain bread crumbs
2 teaspoons rubbed sage
2 teaspoons dried thyme
1 teaspoon sea salt
1 teaspoon pepper
4 medium onions, peeled and chopped
1 bunch celery, chopped
1 stick butter
2 cups coarsely chopped chestnuts (page)
(To peel, see page 359)
large needle and thick thread
2 onions, peeled and sliced
1 cup unbleached flour
4-6 cups turkey stock
cooked giblets, finely chopped (optional)

Remove neck and giblets from turkey and use for making stock (page 115). Saute onions and celery in butter in a large pan until softened. Mix with bread crumbs, seasonings and chopped chestnuts. The stuffing may be made ahead of time, but you should wait until you are ready to cook to stuff the turkey.

Stuff the neck cavity loosely and sew skin flaps to the body of the turkey with a large needle and thick thread. Stuff the main cavity loosely and fasten with skewers or merely bring the legs through a slit cut just behind the tail. Strew sliced onions in a large roasting pan. Set a rack over the onions and set turkey on the rack. Season with salt and pepper and bake at 350 degrees for about 5 hours, basting frequently.

Remove the turkey to a carving board. Sprinkle flour in the drippings and cook over a medium flame about five minutes, stirring constantly. Add stock and blend with a whisk. Bring to a boil and cook several minutes, stirring occasionally. Strain gravy into a sauce pan and allow to simmer for 1/2 hour or so until it reduces and thickens. Stir in optional giblets. If gravy gets too thick, thin with a little water.

THANKSGIVING DINNER

Spicy Turkey Soup

Turkey with Chestnut Stuffing

Onion Cranberry Compote

Sweet Potato Casserole

Celery Root Potato Puree

Peas

Sauerkraut

Pear Cranberry Pie

Pumpkin Pie

Apple Cider

TURKEY STIR FRY STEW

Serves 4-6

1 1/2 pounds turkey breast, cut into small pieces
extra virgin olive oil
2 bunch green onions, sliced on an angle
1 green or red pepper, seeded and chopped
1 cup chopped pineapple, drained
1 small can water chestnuts, drained and sliced
2 cloves garlic, finely chopped
1 teaspoon grated ginger
1/2 teaspoon red pepper flakes
2 tablespoon soy sauce
1 tablespoon sucanat
1/8 cup rice vinegar
2-3 cups chicken or turkey stock
2 tablespoons arrowroot
mixed with 2 tablespoon water

Mix stock with garlic, ginger, pepper flakes, soy sauce, sucanat, and vinegar and set aside. Pat turkey pieces dry. In a heavy skillet or wok, saute turkey in batches until cooked through. Using a slotted spoon, transfer to a heated bowl. Add more oil and saute onions and pepper about 2 minutes. Add sauce mixture and bring to a boil. Add cooked turkey, pineapple and water chestnuts to pan and mix well. Add arrowroot mixture and simmer a minute or so until sauce thickens. Serve with basic brown rice (page 441).

A product like Coca-Cola which contains known poisons and destroys teeth and stomach has one of the most stunning ad campaigns in the history of the Western world.

It is really fantastic: This unreal amount of money creating an illusion—the illusion that "coke is the real thing." Now coke executives have learned from extensive research that young America is searching for what is real, meaningful in this plastic world, and one bright ad executive comes up with the idea that it is Coke. Yep, Coke is the real thing and this is drilled into the minds of 97 percent of all young people between the ages of six and nineteen until their teeth are rotting just like their parents' did.

There is nothing truthful about advertising. Imagine a young pimply faced kid in front of a camera telling folks how clear his complexion was before he started drinking Coke; and even though he knows it's bumming his social life, he just can't seem to get off the stuff. That would be truth in advertising. Or how about a young girl holding up a can of orange drink made in New Jersey and saying the reason it's orange is because of the food coloring. The reason it is bad is because we use coal-tar artificial flavors and the reason we would like you to try it is because we want to make money. Truth in advertising would be the end of three major networks, 500 magazines, several thousand newspapers, and ten of thousands of businesses. So there will never be truth in advertising.
Paul Hawkin *The Magic of Findhorn*

PREPARATION OF WHOLE DUCK

Serves 8

2 whole ducks
fresh lemon juice

Whole ducks are worth doing if you are willing to take a little time in preparation. Two ducks will yield 8 good servings. The carcasses and wings can be used to make a rich duck stock (page 115) and meat picked from the carcasses will be sufficient to make a meal of burritos or enchiladas (page 404). The livers make a delicious pate (page 244) and the fat can be rendered and used for frying potatoes (page 375). The crispy pieces of fat produced by rendering are delicious on salads.

Using a very sharp, flexible fish filleting knife, trim off neck fat and skin, the tail, and fat at the back of the cavity. Carefully remove the wishbone in the front of the carcass. Make a slit along the backbone, cut down along the rib cage and remove the breasts on both sides. Remove the wings, and then the leg plus the thigh. Trim all the fat and skin off the carcass. Repeat the process with the second duck.

Trim excess fat off the four breasts and four thigh-leg pieces and marinate for several hours in fresh lemon juice; or marinate only the duck breasts and make preserved duck with legs and thighs (page 276). Proceed with the following recipes or any of your own invention.

Duck Fat and Cracklings: To render duck fat and make cracklings, cut pieces of fat and skin into small chunks and place in a heavy bottomed pan. Cook about 3/4 hour over medium heat until all fat has been rendered and skin pieces turn golden brown. Remove cracklings with a slotted spoon to paper towels and strain fat into a bowl. Cover and store in refrigerator.

The record indicates that the incidence of tooth decay has increased as humans have increased the refined plant carbohydrate of their diet and lowered their intake of animal protein. During the Paleolithic period, humans were largely meat-eaters and consumed most of their plant foods as they found them; however, as long as humans used whole grains, the incidence of tooth decay remained low. For example skeletal remains from Middle Age Denmark show about 6 percent of the total teeth with caries while other populations of Northern Europe approach a cavity rate of approximately 10%. As consumption of meat has decreased, and the consumption of grain foods and other carbohydrates (sugar and white flour) constitute a significant percentage of the diet, tooth decay has increased to epidemic proportions. H. Leon Abrams *Vegetarianism: An Anthropological/Nutritional Evaluation*

It would be extraordinary if sugar and white flour, known to wreak havoc on the teeth, did not also have profound repercussions elsewhere in the body.

Coronary disease has heretofore been regarded as a "complication" of diabetes. Both coronary disease and diabetes have a common cause: White sugar and white flour. William Dufty *Sugar Blues*

DUCK WITH GREEN PEPPER SAUCE

Serves 8

4 duck breasts and four thigh-leg pieces,
marinated in lemon juice (see page 273)
3 cups beef or duck stock
1/2 cup dry white wine or vermouth
1 small can green peppercorns, drained,
rinsed well and patted dry
1 cup piima cream or creme fraiche

Dry duck pieces with paper towels. Using a sharp knife, score the fat on the breasts and thighs. Cut the meat away from the underside of the thigh bone and open up a bit—this will facilitate browning. In a heavy bottomed skillet, saute the breasts, two at a time about five minutes per side. (Start by sauteing on the skin side, and the duck pieces will produce their own fat.) Remove to a heated platter. Pour out fat and saute the legs in the same manner. Pour out fat and add wine to the pan. Bring to a boil. Add stock and pepper corns and reduce to a simmer. Return the thigh pieces to the pan, cover and simmer about 15 minutes. (Keep breast pieces in oven—they should be medium rare or rare.) Remove leg pieces to heated platter, add cream to stock, bring liquid to a rapid boil and reduce to about 1 cup.

To serve, slice the breasts thinly and distribute to individual serving plates. Cut the leg from the thigh and place a leg or a thigh on each plate. Pour sauce over and serve immediately.

Variation: Duck Breasts with Green Pepper Sauce

Prepare recipe with duck breasts only.

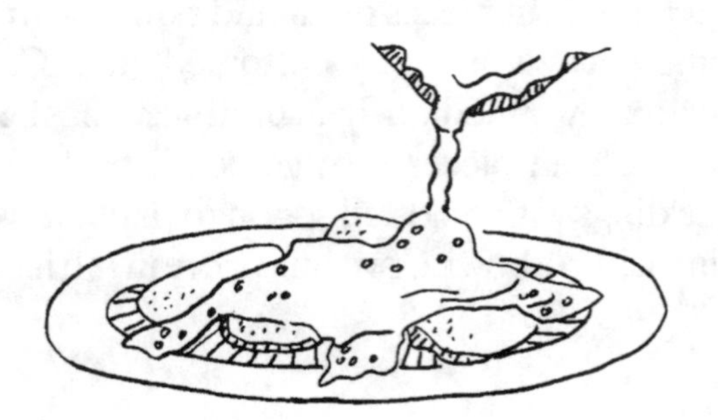

The current medical theory is that a high cholesterol diet causes high serum cholesterol which causes the atherosclerotic process. Although this theory appears to be correct, it isn't. . .In the 1970's I started looking at patients' cholesterol levels and saw many which didn't fit the theory. Many who were big cholesterol eaters and had a good lipid profile and many who were not cholesterol eaters who had a poor lipid profile. I knew then that something was wrong with the dietary cholesterol theory . . . I knew the real answer to the atherosclerotic process would be found by finding the cause of the initial injury to the intimal cells. I knew that all the theories of that injury had no scientific bases. In the early 1980's I suspected the oxidant free radical was the culprit. Finally in early 1987 I found the proof in the study of the exposure of guinea pigs to kerosene fumes. The liver increases the production of cholesterol in response to the injury to the intimal cells by oxidant free radicals. The cholesterol goes to the site of injury and itself becomes oxidized in an attempt to protect the cells. Roy W. Dowdell MD *Health Freedom News*

A high cholesterol diet is not the cause of atherosclerosis. In 50 men with a fourfold increase in dietary cholesterol, two-thirds failed to show an increase in serum cholesterol. Seven patients in another study, while consuming large amounts of beef fat and vitamin and mineral supplements showed a decrease in average cholesterol levels. Roy W. Dowdell MD *Health Freedom News*

DUCK WITH PLUM SAUCE

Serves 8

4 duck breasts and four thigh-leg pieces,
marinated in lemon juice (see page 273)
3 cups beef or duck stock
1/2 cup dry white wine
1 teaspoon freshly grated ginger
2 tablespoons plum jam,
honey or fruit-juice sweetened
2 tablespoons arrowroot mixed with
2 tablespoons water

Dry duck pieces with paper towels. Using a sharp knife, score the fat on the breasts and thighs. Cut the meat away from the underside of the thigh bone and open up a bit—this will facilitate browning. In a heavy bottomed skillet, saute the breasts, two at a time about five minutes per side. (Start by sauteing on the skin side, and the duck pieces will produce their own fat.) Remove to a heated platter. Pour out fat and saute the legs in the same manner. Pour out fat and add wine and stock to the pan. Bring to a boil, add ginger and jam and reduce to a simmer. Return the thigh pieces to the pan, cover and simmer about 15 minutes. (Keep breast pieces in oven—they should be medium rare or rare.) Remove leg pieces to heated platter, bring liquid to a rapid boil and reduce to about 2 cups. Spoonful by spoonful, add arrowroot mixture until desired thickness is obtained.

To serve, slice the breasts thinly and distribute to individual serving plates. Cut the leg from the thigh and place a leg or a thigh on each plate. Pour sauce over and serve immediately.

Variation: Duck Breast with Plum Sauce

Prepare recipe with duck breasts only.

That which is produced by Yin originates in the five flavors; the five organs which regulate the functions of the body are injured by the five flavors. Thus, if acidity exceeds the other flavors, then the liver will be caused to produce an excess of saliva and the force of the spleen will be cut short. If salt exceeds among the flavors, the great bones become weary, the muscles and the flesh become deficient and the mind becomes despondent. If sweetness exceeds the other flavors, the breath of the heart will be [asthmatic and] full, the appearance will be slack and the force of the kidneys will be unbalanced. If among the flavors bitterness exceeds the others, then the atmosphere of he spleen becomes dry and the atmosphere of the stomach becomes dense. If the pungent flavor exceeds the others, the muscles and the pulse become slack and the spirit will be injured.

Therefore if people pay attention to the five flavors and mix them well, their bones will remain straight, their muscles will remain tender and young, their breath and blood will circulate freely, their pores will be fine in texture, and consequently, their breath and bones will be filled with the essence of life. *The Yellow Emperor's Classic of Internal Medicine*

TERIYAKI DUCK BREASTS

Serves 4

4 duck breasts
3/4 cup teriyaki sauce (page 133)

Trim excess fat off the duck breasts, score the fat and marinate for several hours in teriyaki sauce.

Pat dry with paper towels and saute in a heavy skillet, two at a time, about five minutes per side, starting with the skin side down. Keep warm on a heated platter in the oven while doing the second batch. To serve, slice thinly across the grain, arrange on individual plates and dribble marinade over.

PRESERVED DUCK LEGS

(Confit de Canard)

2-4 duck thighs
2-4 duck legs (see page 273)
juice of 2 lemons
3 tablespoons coarse sea salt
6 cloves garlic, peeled and mashed
1 tablespoon dried thyme
1-2 cups rendered duck fat

You should be able to stuff the legs and thighs into 1 quart-sized wide-mouth mason jar. Mix lemon juice, sea salt, garlic and thyme together and rub this marinade thoroughly into duck pieces. Place in a bowl, cover and marinate in refrigerator for 24 hours. Stuff duck pieces into the jar. Melt fat and pour into jar. Duck pieces should be completely covered—if lacking sufficient duck fat, add melted butter. Cover tightly and store in refrigerator for 2 to 4 weeks.

To serve, place jar in pan of hot water and allow fat to melt. Remove duck pieces and pat dry. (Reserve fat for another batch of *confit* or use to saute potatoes.) Saute duck pieces gently in a heavy skillet, about 10 minutes per side.

Now researchers have designed rations for maneuvers and battlefield for US Army infantry men that almost guarantee to undermine their health, morale and weaken them for actual combat. Their rations contain nutritional Trojan Horses: junk foods and non-foods.

The army used to offer C-rations for eating on the battlefield. Then in 1980 they came out with Meals Ready to Eat (MRE), combat rations with 3,600 calories and, according to the surgeon general, the military daily allowance of minerals and synthetic vitamins.

Now the US Army's Natick Research Development and Engineering Center has "improved" these rations by offering more of the food that GI's ate at home, along with more choices on entrees.

These dietary delights include white bread, pound cake, M&M's, Tootsie Rolls, one-inch tall bottles of Tabasco sauce and drink mixes such as Kool-Aid and even pizza crusts baked with refined sugar to keep them from growing stale. The bread is wrapped in a small packet of preservative that absorbs oxygen and moisture.

That's not all. Coming up in the next few years are battlefield burritos, hamburgers and even hot dogs with buns. The hot dogs are smaller than the nitrate and nitrite-loaded kind sold in your supermarket, but—and get this—they taste "just like ballpark franks"—although, they're lower in cholesterol and sodium.

Goody! Goody! Perhaps this "Eat for Defeat" diet should be shared with the Soviet Union! James F. Scheer *Health Freedom News*

ORGAN MEATS

Almost all traditional cultures prize organ meats for their ability to build reserves of strength and vitality. Organ meats are extremely rich in fat soluble vitamins A and D, as well as essential fatty acids, rare very long chain superunsaturated fatty acids and the whole gamut of macro and trace minerals. Wild animals eat the organs of their kill first, thus showing a wisdom superior to our own. The first solid food that native African mothers give to their babies is raw liver, which they thoughtfully pre-chew. Folk wisdom throughout the world, including Europe, values brain as a food for babies and growing children.

American cookbooks of a century ago contained plenty of recipes for organ meats, and any authentic cookbook for ethnic cuisine—French, Italian, Greek, Middle Eastern or English—will feature several recipes for liver, kidney, sweetbreads and brains. What a pity these delicious and nutritious foods have disappeared from our tables.

Many of our grandparents will remember the days when liver was served once a week. Establishment nutritionists now recommend we discontinue this healthful practice in order to avoid cholesterol! Others have stopped eating liver fearing toxic substances, which can accumulate in the livers of all animals. As the function of the liver is to remove toxic substances from the blood, this is a legitimate concern. For this reason, it is best to buy organic liver, now becoming increasingly available in supermarkets and health food stores. Even organic liver may contain some toxic substances but its nutritive value outweighs the dangers of any toxins it contains. Not only does liver provide copper, zinc, iron and vitamins A and D in abundance, but it is also a rich source of antioxidants—substances that help your own liver remove toxic substances from the body.

If you are not used to eating organ meats, but wish to reinstate this healthful practice, start with sweetbreads (part of the thymus gland of the young calf), which do not have a strong flavor—breaded sweetbreads taste just like chicken. You can then graduate to liver, kidney and brains, all of which have stronger flavors or more exotic textures. All of these meats benefit from strongly flavored sauces that feature onions, wine, balsamic vinegar and that magic elixir, homemade beef or chicken stock.

If you cannot get your family to eat organ meats when served as such, there are plenty of ways to add them to their food without their knowledge. Poached brains can be chopped up and added to any ground meat dish, as can grated raw liver. A spoonful or two of grated liver added to brown rice as it cooks results in a flavorful casserole that is a complete meal. You can serve rice this way, without any other meat dish, and know that your family's requirements for high-quality animal products are being met.

PREPARATION OF SWEETBREADS

Sweetbreads need careful advance preparation before they can be cooked up for a final dish. Allow one pair of sweetbreads for two to four people, depending on appetites. They must be very fresh. Wash the sweetbreads, cover with cold water to which you have added a little vinegar and soak for about two hours, changing the water once or twice. This extracts the blood and helps remove any impurities. Remove, rinse and place in a saucepan. Cover with water or chicken stock, add 1 teaspoon of salt, bring to a boil and simmer for about 1/4 hour. Remove from poaching liquid (which can be reserved for another use), and allow to cool. Carefully remove all loose tissue, skin, fat and membranes, using a sharp knife. Place on a plate or platter, cover with parchment paper (see Sources) and place a board on top. Let the sweetbreads flatten in the refrigerator for several hours or overnight.

Until recent years it has been common knowledge among the superintendents of large zoos of America and Europe that members of the cat family did not reproduce efficiently in captivity, unless the mothers had been born in the jungle. Formerly, this made it necessary to replenish lions, tigers, leopards and other felines from wild stock as fast as the cages were emptied by death . . . The story is told of a trip to Africa made by a wild animal specialist from the London zoo for the purpose of obtaining additional lions and studying this problem. While in the lion country, he observed the lion kill a zebra. The lion proceeded then to tear open the abdomen of the zebra and eat the entrails at the right flank. This took him directly to the liver. After spending some time selecting different internal organs, the lion backed away and turned and pawed dirt over the carcass which he abandoned to the jackals. The scientist hurried to the carcass and drove away the jackals to study the dead zebra to note what tissues had been taken. This gave him the clue which when put into practice has entirely changed the history of the reproduction of the cat family in captivity. The addition of the organs to the foods of the captive animals born in the jungle supplied them with foods needed to make reproduction possible. Their young, too, could reproduce efficiently. As I studied this matter with the director of a large lion colony, he listed in detail the organs and tissues that were particularly selected by animals in the wilds and also those that were provided for animals reproducing in captivity. Weston Price DDS *Nutrition and Physical Degeneration*

SWEETBREADS IN TOMATO SAUCE

Serves 6

2 pair prepared sweetbreads
1 cup unbleached flour
1 teaspoon pepper
sea salt
butter and extra virgin olive oil
2 cups chunky tomato sauce (page 140)

Mix flour with salt and pepper. Pat sweetbreads dry and dredge in flour. (You may dredge them whole, or first slice them at 3/8 inch intervals, on the bias.) Saute in a mixture of butter and olive oil. Serve with tomato sauce.

BREADED SWEETBREADS

Serves 6

2 pair prepared sweetbreads
1 cup unbleached flour
1 teaspoon pepper
sea salt
2 eggs, lightly beaten
1 cup whole grain bread crumbs
1/2 teaspoon fine herbs
butter and extra virgin olive oil

Mix pepper with flour and fine herbs with breadcrumbs. Slice sweetbreads at 3/8 inch intervals on the bias. Dredge first in flour mixture, then in egg, then in breadcrumb mixture. Saute a few at a time in butter and olive oil. Keep warm in the oven while completing the saute process. Serve with a lacto-fermented condiment.

SWEETBREADS WITH MUSHROOMS AND CREAM

Serves 6

2 pair prepared sweetbreads
butter and extra virgin olive oil
1 pound fresh mushrooms, washed, well dried and sliced
1 cup dry white wine
2 cups beef or chicken stock
1 cup piima cream or creme fraiche

Slice sweetbreads at 3/8-inch intervals on the bias. In a heavy skillet, saute sweetbread slices in batches until golden. Transfer to a heated platter and keep warm in the oven. Add more butter and oil, if necessary, and saute the mushrooms. Strew over the sweetbreads. Pour out browning fat and add wine to the pan. Bring to a boil, stirring with a wooden spoon to scrape up any accumulated cooking juices. Add stock, bring to a boil and reduce to about half. Add cream and simmer until sauce thickens further. Check seasoning. Pour sauce over sweetbreads and serve.

Studies of Professor Fred Hale of Texas A. and M. College reveal he produces blind pigs at will by depriving healthy mothers of natural vitamin A before and after mating. Then by placing these blind pigs on a complete ration and mating them, these blind mothers farrow healthy pigs with good eyes. It is believed that much of the poor eyesight suffered by human beings today could be prevented by eating foods that provide complete nutrition for the whole body including the eyes. R. Dean Conrad *The Great American Tragedy*

Sherman, who has made many important contributions to our knowledge of vitamin A, has shown in a recent communication that an amount of vitamin A sufficient to support normal growth and maintain every appearance of good health in animals, may still be insufficient to meet the added nutritive demands of successful reproduction and lactation. With the failure to reproduce successfully, there usually appears in early adult life an increased susceptibility to infection, and particularly a tendency to lung disease at an age corresponding to that at which pulmonary tuberculosis so often develops in young men and women. He states, further, that vitamin A must be supplied in liberal proportions not only during the growth period but during the adult period as well, if a good condition of nutrition and a high degree of health and vigor are to be maintained.

Hughes, Aubel and Lienhardt have shown that a lack of vitamin A in the diets of pigs has resulted in extreme incoordination and spasms. They also emphasize that gilts bred prior to the onset of the nervous symptoms either aborted or farrowed dead pigs. Hart and Gilbert have shown that the symptoms most commonly seen in cattle having a vitamin A deficiency are the birth of dead or weak calves, with or without eye lesions. They report also a condition of newborn calves which simulates white scours, and the development of eye lesions in immature animals.

Hughes has shown that swine did not reproduce when fed barley and salt, but did so when cod liver oil was added to this food. Sure has shown that a lack of vitamin A produces in females a disturbance in oestrus

SWEETBREADS ON TOAST

Serves 6

2 pairs prepared sweetbreads, prepared as above
butter and extra virgin olive oil
1 cup shallots, chopped
1/2 cup red wine
1 1/2 cup beef stock
1 teaspoon green peppercorns, crushed
2 tablespoons arrowroot mixed with
2 tablespoons water
6 large round croutons (page 491)

Slice the sweetbreads at 3/8 inch intervals on the bias. Saute, a few slices at a time, in butter and olive oil, remove to a heated platter and keep warm in the oven. Pour off browning oil, add a bit of butter and saute shallots until golden. Add wine and bring to a boil, stirring with a wooden spoon to scrape up any accumulated juices. Add crushed peppercorns and stock, bring to a boil and reduce to about half. Spoonful by spoonful, add arrowroot mixture until desired thickness is obtained. Check for seasoning.

Place one crouton on each plate, place sweetbreads on the crouton and spoon sauce over. Serve immediately.

SWEETBREADS WITH PEARL ONIONS

Serves 6

2 pair prepared sweetbreads
butter and extra virgin olive oil
1/2 cup balsamic vinegar
2 cups beef stock
2 tablespoons arrowroot mixed with
2 tablespoons water
2 pounds pearl onions, peeled and sauted in butter

Slice the sweetbreads at 3/8 inch intervals on the bias. Saute, a few slices at a time, in butter and olive oil, remove to a heated platter and keep warm in the oven. Pour off browning oil, add balsamic vinegar and bring to a boil, stirring with a wooden spoon to scrape up any accumulated juices. Add stock, bring to a boil and reduce to about half. Spoonful by spoonful, add arrowroot mixture until desired thickness is obtained. Check for seasoning. Return sweetbreads to the sauce and stir in pearl onions. Simmer a minute or so before serving.

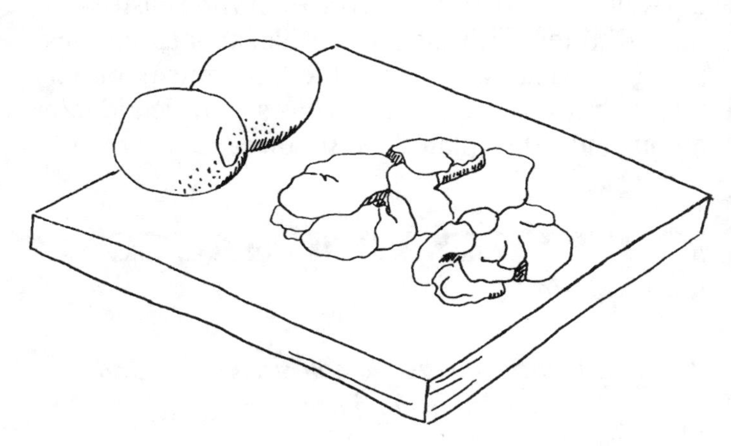

PREPARATION OF KIDNEYS

Both whole and sliced kidneys should be marinated in lemon juice for several hours before they are cooked. Remove from lemon juice and dry well with paper towels before browning. Whole kidneys should be cooked until they are just pink inside.

Most kidneys are sold with their layer of fat, and the thin filament surrounding the kidneys peeled off. There may be a button or knob of fat on the underside of the kidneys; retain this if possible—it is a very nourishing fat.

Both lamb and veal kidneys can be used in the following recipes. They should be very fresh with no unpleasant odor——check with your nose.

and ovulation, resulting in sterility. Further he states, that resorption of the fetus may be produced by lack of vitamin A, even on a diet containing an abundance of vitamin E, which is called the anti-sterility vitamin.

One of the most important contributions in this field has been made by Professor Fred Hale. He has shown that many physical deformities are readily produced by curtailing the amount of vitamin A in the ration of pigs. He produced fifty-nine pigs that were born blind, every pig in each of six litters, where the mothers were deprived of vitamin A for several months before mating and for thirty days thereafter. In pigs, the eyeballs are formed in the first thirty days. He found, as have several others, that depriving pigs of vitamin A for a sufficient period produced severe nerve involvements including paralysis and spasms, so that the animals could not rise to their feet. He reported that one of these vitamin A deficient pigs that had previously farrowed a litter of ten pigs, all born without eyeballs, was given a single dose of cod liver oil two week before mating. She farrowed fourteen pigs which showed various combinations of eye defects, some had no eyes, some had one eye, and some had one large eye and one small eye, but all were blind. . . One important result of Professor Hale's investigations has been the production of pigs with normal eyes, born to parents both of whom had no eyeballs due to lack of vitamin A in their mother's diet. The problem clearly was not heredity. Weston Price DDS *Nutrition and Physical Degeneration*

Many investigators have presented important data dealing with the role of vitamin A in prenatal as well as postnatal growth processes. It is known that the eye is one of the early tissues to develop injury from the absence of vitamin A, hence the original name for this vitamin was the xerophthalmic vitamin. The importance of vitamin A to the eye, and the fact that this vitamin is stored in eye tissue have been emphasized by several investigations. . . Edward Mellanby has presented important new data dealing with vitamin A deficiency and deafness. He states in an abstract of a paper read before the Biochemical Society, in London in November 1937, the following: In previous publications I have shown that a prominent lesion caused by vitamin A deficiency in young animals, especially when accompanied by a high cereal intake, is degeneration of the central and peripheral nervous systems. In the peripheral system it is the afferent nerves which are principally affected, including the eighth nerve. . . It has now been possible to show that vitamin A deficiency produced in young dogs degenerative changes in the ganglia, nerves and organs of both hearing and balance inside the temporal bone. All degrees of degeneration have been produced, from slight degeneration to complete disappearance of the hearing nerve. . .

The serious effects of deficiency in vitamin A on pregnant rats have been investigated and reported by Mason as follows: Abnormalities are described in the pregnancies of rats maintained on diets deficient in vitamin A in varying degree. Prolongation of the gestation period up to 26 days in severe cases

GRILLED KIDNEYS WITH HAZELNUT BUTTER SAUCE

Serves 4

1 pound kidneys, cut into walnut-sized pieces and marinated in lemon juice
1 tablespoon melted butter
3 tablespoons chopped hazelnuts
1/2 stick butter
1 tablespoon finely chopped chives

Remove kidney pieces from lemon juice and dry well. Thread on buttered skewers and baste with melted butter. Grill under the broiler about 5 minutes per side. Meanwhile, saute the hazelnuts in butter until lightly browned. Stir in chives. Divide kidneys among individual plates and spoon sauce over.

KIDNEYS IN WINE SAUCE

Serves 4 to 6

2 pounds kidneys, cut into lemon-sized pieces and marinated in lemon juice
butter and extra virgin olive oil
1/2 cup shallots, finely chopped
2 cups homemade beef stock
1/2 cup red wine
2 tablespoons arrowroot mixed with 2 tablespoons water

Remove kidney pieces from lemon juice and dry well. In a heavy skillet, saute in butter and olive oil over a medium flame, until browned all over. Transfer to a heated platter while making the sauce. Pour out browning fat and add a little butter to the pan. Saute shallots gently until soft. Add stock and wine, bring to a rapid boil and reduce to about half, or until stock begins to thicken. Add arrowroot mixture a spoonful at a time until desired thickness is obtained. Check seasoning and add sea salt and pepper as needed.

You may serve kidneys whole, with the sauce poured over; or slice the kidneys and warm the slices very briefly in the sauce.

KIDNEYS IN MUSHROOM SAUCE

Serves 4 - 6

2 pounds kidneys, cut into lemon-sized pieces and marinated in lemon juice
butter and extra virgin olive oil
1/2 pound fresh mushrooms, washed, well dried and sliced
1/2 cup red wine
2 cups homemade beef stock
1 cup piima cream or creme fraiche
2 teaspoons Dijon style mustard
2 tablespoons softened butter
1/2 teaspoon Worcestershire sauce (non-MSG variety)

Remove kidney pieces from lemon juice and dry well. In a heavy skillet, saute over medium high flame until browned all over. Do not overcook—they should be pink inside. Transfer to a heated platter and keep warm in the oven while making the sauce.

Pour out browning fat. Add more butter and oil to the pan and saute the mushrooms over medium high heat until browned. Transfer to a bowl and keep warm in the oven.

Pour out browning fat and pour wine and beef stock into the pan, bring to a boil and reduce to about half. Add the cream and reduce further. Meanwhile blend the mustard, softened butter and worcestershire sauce together with a fork.

When sauce has reduced to desired thickness, reduce to simmer and whisk in mustard mixture. Slice kidneys. Stir in kidney slices with their juice and mushrooms. Let heat just briefly. Serve immediately.

and a long and difficult labor which might last 2 days and often resulted in death of both mother and young were characteristic.

Defects due to deficiencies in vitamin A in the diet of dairy animals, . . . have been reported upon by Meigs and Converse as follows: In 1932 we reported from Beltsville that farm rations frequently fed to calves may be dangerously low in vitamin A. . . Of six calves born to these cows, two were dead, one was unable to stand and died shortly after birth, and three were both weak and blind. Weston Price DDS *Nutrition and Physical Degeneration*

. . . Americans are being saturated with anti-cholesterol propaganda. If you watch very much television, you're probably one of the millions of Americans who now has a terminal case of cholesterol phobia. The propaganda is relentless and is often designed to produce fear and loathing of this worst of all food contaminants. You never hear the food propagandists bragging about their product being fluoride-free or aluminum-free, two of our truly serious food-additive problems. But cholesterol, an essential nutrient, not proven to be harmful in any quantity, is constantly pilloried as a menace to your health. If you don't use corn oil, Fleishmann's margarine and Egg Beaters, you're going straight to atherosclerosis hell with stroke, heart attack and premature aging—and so are your kids. William Campbell Douglass MD *Eat Your Cholesterol*

KIDNEY RICE CASSEROLE

Serves 12

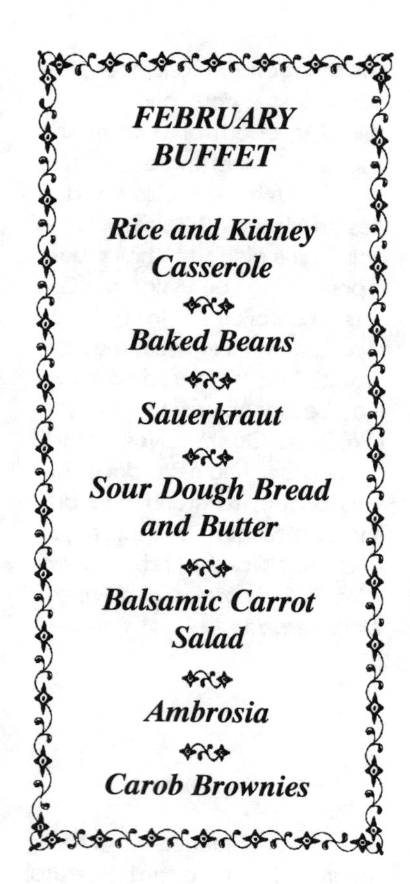

The numbers game is the biggest weapon used by the anti-cholesterol centurions to frighten the populace into a diet fit only for a zebra. These commanders have decreed that the magic number is 200 (mg per deciliter) for blood cholesterol, and the lower the reading the better. But recent exhaustive studies have shown that 250 is a level not associated with any increase in cardiovascular disease. Furthermore, the "lower-the better" rule is not only bad science but very dangerous advice. Extremely low cholesterol readings, those in the lower 10% of the population, have an increased mortality from all causes. "From all causes" means accidents, cancer, strokes, lung or kidney disease, etc.. William Campbell Douglass MD *Eat Your Cholesterol*

3 pounds kidneys
sea salt and freshly ground pepper
juice of 4 lemons
2 medium onions
butter and extra virgin olive oil
1/2 cup red wine
2 cups homemade beef stock
2 cloves garlic, peeled and mashed
3 cups brown rice
2 medium onions
butter and extra virgin olive oil
6 cups chicken stock or mixture of chicken stock and water
1/2 teaspoon sea salt
freshly ground pepper
1 cup raisins
1 cup crispy pecans (page 485), chopped
2 bunches green onion, finely chopped

Cut kidneys in small pieces and marinate for several hours in mixture of lemon juice, salt and pepper. Meanwhile prepare rice. Saute onion in butter and olive oil. Add rice and stir around until milky. Add liquid, salt, pepper, and raisins and bring to a rapid boil. Let liquid reduce to level of rice, then cover and place on lowest heat. Cook without removing top for at least 2 hours.

Drain kidneys and pat dry. Saute onion in butter and olive oil until golden. Reserve. Saute kidneys in batches until well browned. Reserve. Pour out cooking fat, add wine, stock and garlic to pan and bring to a boil. Return onions and kidneys to pan. Boil, uncovered, until liquid has reduced and thickened.

To serve, press rice into a mould and turn onto a large round platter. Place kidneys in the middle and garnish with pecans and chopped onions.

PREPARATION OF LIVER

Buy liver that is organic and very fresh. All liver recipes will be greatly improved if the liver slices are first soaked in lemon juice for several hours. This draws out impurities and gives a nicer texture. The butcher should remove the surrounding filament; otherwise the edges will curl when it is cooked. Liver should be sliced about 1/4 to 3/8 inches thick.

LIVER AND ONIONS

Serves 4

1 1/2 pounds sliced liver
juice of 2-3 lemons
1 cup unbleached flour
sea salt and pepper
butter and extra virgin olive oil
4 cups onions, finely sliced

Marinate liver slices in lemon juice for several hours. Pat slices dry and dredge in a mixture of flour, salt and pepper. In a heavy skillet and over a high flame, saute the slices, 2 at a time, in butter and olive oil. Transfer to a heated platter and keep warm in the oven. Meanwhile, in a separate pan, saute the onions in butter and olive oil over medium heat. Strew over liver and serve.

Variation: Liver and Mushrooms

Instead of onions, saute *1 pound of fresh mushrooms, washed, patted dry, and sliced.*

In the Anglo-Egyptian Sudan, there are several tribes living along the Nile. . . There are wonderful hunters and warriors among them. These tribes use milk, blood and meat from cattle and large quantities of animal life from the Nile River. Some of the tribes are very tall, particularly the Neurs. The women are often six feet or over, and the men seven feet, some of them reaching seven and a half feet in height. I was particularly interested in their food habits both because of their high immunity to dental caries which approximated one hundred per cent, and because of their physical development. I learned that they have a belief which to them is their religion, namely, that every man and woman has a soul which resides in the liver and that a man's character and physical growth depend upon how well he feeds that soul by eating the livers of animals. The liver is so sacred that it may not be touched by human hands. It is accordingly always handled with their spear or saber, or with specially prepared forked sticks. It is eaten both raw and cooked. Weston Price DDS *Nutrition and Physical Degeneration*

Since the organs, particularly the livers of animals, are storage depots of the vitamins, an important source of some of the fat soluble activators can be provided by extracting the fat of the livers and shipping it as liver oils. Modern methods of processing have greatly improved the quality of these oils. Weston Price DDS *Nutrition and Physical Degeneration*

BREADED LIVER

Serves 4

1 1/2 pounds liver, sliced 1/2 inch thick
juice of 2-3 lemons
unbleached flour
sea salt and pepper
butter and extra virgin olive oil
3 tablespoons Dijon style mustard
1 tablespoon shallots, finely chopped
1 tablespoon parsley, finely chopped
1 clove garlic, mashed
2 cups whole grain bread crumbs
4 tablespoons melted butter

This recipes requires that the liver be more thickly sliced than usual as it undergoes two cookings, once in the pan and once under the broiler. Marinate liver slices in lemon juice for several hours. Pat slices dry and dredge in a mixture of flour, salt and pepper. In a heavy skillet and over a high flame, saute the slices, 2 at a time, in butter and olive oil. Saute until liver becomes just slightly stiffened, but not cooked through.

Make a mixture of the mustard, herbs and garlic and brush it well on the liver slices. Dredge in bread crumbs. Arrange slices on an oiled broiler pan. Dribble half the butter over. Broil for a minute or so until well browned. Turn, dribble over remaining butter and broil the second side in the same manner.

George Bernard Shaw seems to have come into vegetarianism mainly because it was one of the trendy things to do among the English intellectuals he admired and envied. He had been drawn to the original Fabians—Sidney and Beatrice Webb, Sydney Olivier, the Rev Stewart Headlam, and Annie Besant—and through their interest in diet reform to Henry S. Salt, author of the book that had revolutionized Gandhi's ideas... While Shaw did not remove the image of peculiarity from the public view of the vegetarianism, he did a tremendous amount to convince the public that it was an eminently healthy regime. . . However, Mr. Shaw was forced to remind his correspondents "that vegetarianism does not mean living wholly on vegetables." Shaw ate cheese, butter, honey, eggs and on occasions cod liver oil. He also had to take extracts of liver for anemia, which began to affect him seriously in 1938, when he was 82. This is a common ailment with vegetarians who do not eat many eggs and is due to deficiency in vitamin B12... This vitamin is only found in animal foods, liver, kidneys and clams being rich sources, and unfortunately cannot yet be synthesized in the laboratory. Terence McLaughlin *A Diet of Tripe*

LIVER WITH BALSAMIC VINEGAR SAUCE

Serves 4

1 1/2 pounds sliced liver
juice of 2-3 lemons
1 cup unbleached flour
sea salt and pepper
butter and extra virgin olive oil
4 medium onions, thinly sliced
4 tablespoons balsamic vinegar
4 cups beef stock
2 tablespoons arrowroot mixed with
2 tablespoons water

Marinate liver slices in lemon juice for several hours. Using a heavy skillet, saute the onions in butter over medium heat until golden—about 1/2 hour. Remove with a slotted spoon and keep warm in the oven. Pat liver slices dry and dredge in a mixture of flour, salt and pepper. In a heavy skillet and over a high flame, saute the slices, 2 at a time, in butter and olive oil. Transfer to a heated platter and keep warm in the oven. Pour out browning fat. Add vinegar and stock to the pan, bring to a boil and reduce to about half. A spoonful at a time, add the arrowroot mixture until desired thickness is obtained.

Divide liver between individual serving plates, top with a spoonful of the onions, and pour sauce over.

However, journalists found out the situation [that George Bernard Shaw took liver extract for anemia] and naturally considered it a good story that the Grand Old Man of vegetarianism was 'cheating' on his diet. Alexander Woolcott spread the story in America and there was an immediate outbreak of fury in the American Vegetarian Party that their idol should have taken liver extract. Symon Gould of the Party wrote letters to Shaw in such a fierce vein that one can only imagine that he would have preferred the playwright to die unsullied than to go on living a useful life with the help of animal food. Shaw finally wrote a long open letter to Gould in 1948 telling him bluntly not to exaggerate the benefits of vegetarianism and to keep the moral and religious claims for the diet in some sensible proportion. He also made the point which is unfortunately still valid—that a strict vegetarian diet without dairy foods can cost a lot of money to keep up, because of the need for nuts and similar rather expensive sources of protein to replace the animal protein: "What you have to rub in," wrote Shaw testily, "Is that it is never cheap to live otherwise than as everybody else does, and that the so-called simple life is beyond the means of the poor." Terence McLaughlin *A Diet of Tripe*

PREPARATION OF BRAINS

The issue of the brain consumption has recently aroused controversy because of the scrapie problem, especially in Great Britain. The scrapie virus, which has been linked to Creutzfeldt-Jakob disease in humans, is a found in the brains of animals, especially sheep, that have been given feed containing animal parts. However, brains from US range-fed cattle do not pose any risk. Brains are highly valued in many ethnic cultures. Europeans formerly added a little chopped brain to baby food, to give their children good memories.

Brains have much the same texture as sweetbreads but they are more delicate. Like all organ meats, brains must be very fresh. Wash the brains, cover with cold water to which you have added a little vinegar and soak for about two hours, changing the water once or twice. This extracts the blood and helps remove any impurities. Remove, rinse and place in a saucepan. Cover with water or chicken stock, add 1 teaspoon of salt and juice of 1/2 lemon, bring to a boil and simmer for about 1/4 hour. Remove from poaching liquid, and allow to cool. Carefully remove all loose tissue, skin, fat and membranes, using a sharp knife. You may now place on a plate or platter, cover with parchment paper (see Sources) and place a weighted flat plate or cookie sheet on top. Let the brains flatten in the refrigerator for several hours or overnight.

It is significant that while these important factors are just coming to light in our modernized civilization, the evidence clearly indicates that several so-called primitive races have been conscious of the need for safeguarding motherhood from reproductive overloads which would reduce the capacity for efficient reproduction. For example, G. T. Gaden in his book *Among the Ibos of Nigeria* states: It is not only a matter of disgrace but an actual abomination, for an Ibo woman to bear children at shorter intervals than about three years. . . The idea of a fixed minimum period between births is based on several sound principles. The belief prevails strongly that it is necessary for this interval to elapse in order to ensure the mother being able to recuperate her strength completely, and thus be in a thoroughly fit condition to bear another child. Should a second child be born within the prescribed period the theory is held that it must inevitably be weak and sickly, and its chances jeopardized.

Similarly, the Indians of Peru, Ecuador and Columbia have been familiar with the necessity of preventing pregnancy overload of the mother. Whiffen in his book *North-West Amazona* states: The numbers (of pregnant women) are remarkable in view of the fact that husbands abstain from any intercourse with their wives, not only

SAUTEED BRAINS

Serves 6

1 1/2 pounds range-fed prepared calves brains
3 tablespoons lemon juice
2 tablespoons extra virgin olive oil
sea salt and pepper
1 cup unbleached flour
sea salt and pepper
butter and extra virgin olive oil

Cut the brains into 1-inch slices. Whisk the lemon juice, olive oil, salt and pepper together. Marinate the brains in the mixture for an hour or so. Remove from marinade, pat dry and dredge in a mixture of flour and salt and pepper. In a heavy skillet, saute the slices a few at a time in butter and olive oil. Transfer to a heated platter and keep warm in the oven until ready to serve. Serve with chunky tomato sauce (page 140) or a lacto-fermented condiment.

BRAINS IN WINE SAUCE

Serves 6

1 1/2 pounds range-fed prepared calves brains,
butter and extra virgin olive oil
1/2 pound fresh mushrooms, washed, well dried and sliced
1/2 cup shallots, finely chopped
1 cup red wine
2 cups homemade beef stock
2 tablespoons arrowroot mixed with 2 tablespoons water
6 round or triangle croutons (page 491)

Slice the brains into 3/8 inch slices and set aside. In a heavy skillet, saute the mushrooms until browned in butter and olive oil. Remove with a slotted spoon and set aside. Add a little more butter to the pan and saute the shallots. Pour in wine and stock and bring to a rapid boil. Allow sauce to reduce to about half. Spoonful by spoonful, add the arrowroot mixture until desired thickness is obtained. Strain the sauce into a sauce pan. Add the brain slices and mushrooms and allow to warm up.

To serve, place a crouton on each plate, carefully place brain slices on top and spoon sauce over.

during pregnancy but also throughout the period of lactation—far more prolonged with them than with Europeans. The result is that two and a half years between each child is the minimum difference of age, and in the majority of cases it is even greater

It may also be important to note that the Amazon Indians have been conscious of the fact that these matters are related to the nutrition of both parents. Whiffen states that: These Indians share the belief of many peoples of the lower cultures that the food eaten by the parents—to some degree of both parents—will have a definite influence upon the birth, appearance or character of the child.

This problem of the consciousness among primitives of the need for spacing children has been emphasized by George Brown in his studies among Melanesians and Polynesians in which he reports relative to the native on one of the Solomon Islands as follows: After the birth of a child the husband was not supposed to cohabit with his wife until the child could walk. If a child was weak or sickly, the people would say, speaking of the parents, "Ah, well, they have only themselves to blame." Weston Price DDS *Nutrition and Physical Degeneration*

BRAIN OMELET

Serves 4

1/3-1/2 cup range-fed prepared calves brains, finely chopped
4 eggs
1/2 cup parsley, finely chopped
1 small onion, finely chopped
sea salt and pepper
butter and extra virgin olive oil

This is a Lebanese dish designed for the squeamish, its virtue being that the brains are completely disguised.

Whisk eggs and stir in brains, seasonings, parsley and onions. Melt butter and olive oil in a large, well-seasoned skillet. When butter froths, pour in egg mixture. Cook several minutes, until omelet sets, then fold in half. Slide unto a heated platter and serve.

In most traditional cultures, the whole animal is used for food, including the brain and the endocrine glands. . . . People who eat fish heads (or other animal heads) generally consume the thyroid gland as well as the brain. The brain is the body's richest source of cholesterol, which, with adequate thyroid hormone and vitamin A, is converted into the steroid hormones pregnenolone, progesterone and DHEA, in proportion to the quantity circulating in blood in low density lipoproteins. The brain is also the richest source of these very water-insoluble steroid hormones. . . DHEA is know to be low in people in people who are susceptible to heart disease or cancer and all three steroids have a broad range of protective actions. Ray Peat PhD *Health Freedom News*

SAUTEED CHICKEN LIVERS

Serves 4

1 pound fresh chicken livers
1 cup unbleached flour
sea salt and pepper
butter and extra virgin olive oil
1/4 cup dry white wine
1 cup chicken stock
pinch powdered sage

Carefully remove veins from chicken livers and slice each one into about 3 slices. Dredge in flour mixed with salt and pepper. In a heavy skillet, saute slices, a few at a time, in butter and olive oil until golden. Remove and keep warm in oven. Pour out browning fat and add wine, stock and sage to the pan. Bring to a rapid boil and reduce to about half. Reduce heat to a simmer. Return livers to the sauce to warm through. Serve with basic brown rice (page 441) or round or triangle croutons (page 491).

They [the Indians] lived in a country in which grizzly bears were common. . . Their knowledge of the use of different organs and tissues of the animals for providing a defense against certain of the affections of the body which we speak of as degenerative diseases was surprising. When I asked an old Indian, through an interpreter, why the Indians did not get scurvy he replied promptly that that was a white man's disease. I asked whether it was possible for the Indians to get scurvy. He replied that it was, but said that the Indians know how to prevent it and the white man does not.

CHICKEN LIVERS WITH HAZELNUTS

Serves 4

1 pound fresh chicken livers
1 cup unbleached flour
sea salt and pepper
butter and extra virgin olive oil
2/3 cup hazelnuts, peeled and chopped
(To peel hazelnuts, see page 525)
1 bunch green onions, minced
4 cloves garlic, minced
2 cups chicken stock

Carefully remove veins from chicken livers and slice each one into about 3 slices. Dredge in flour mixed with salt and pepper. In a heavy skillet, saute slices, a few at a time, in butter and olive oil until golden. Remove and keep warm in oven. Pour out browning fat and add more butter. Saute hazelnuts until golden. Add scallions and garlic and saute very gently. Add chicken stock. Bring to a rapid boil and reduce until sauce thickens. Lower heat to a simmer. Return livers to the sauce to warm through. Serve with basic brown rice (page 441) or round or triangle croutons (page 491).

When asked why he did not tell the white man how, his reply was that the white man knew too much to ask the Indian anything. I then asked him if he would tell me. He said he would if the chief said he might. He went to see the chief and returned in about an hour, saying that the chief said he could tell me because I was a friend of the Indians and had come to tell the Indians not to eat the food in the white man's store. He took me by the hand and led me to a log where we both sat down. He then described how when the Indian kills a moose he opens it up and at the back of the moose just above the kidney there are what he described as two small balls in the fat. These he said the Indian would take and cut up into as many pieces as there were little and big Indians in the family and each one would eat his piece. They would eat also the wall of the second stomach. By eating these parts of the animal the Indians would keep free from scurvy, which is due to the lack of vitamin C. The Indians were getting vitamin C from the adrenal glands and organs. Modern science has very recently discovered that the adrenal glands are the richest source of vitamin C in all animal or plant tissues. Weston Price DDS *Nutrition and Physical Degeneration*

MAZALIKA

Serves 8

The British like kidneys in their meat pies. Peruvians enjoy *anticuchos*—marinated, grilled beef heart. Sicilians on the streets of Palermo can grab a quick spleen sandwich, Italians in general—and Egyptians—are partial to liver, while the Japanese go in for intestines. Chinese restaurants in New York serve pigs' ears. But in the US, where it is also known euphemistically as "variety meat", most offal is exported or processed into sausage and lunch meat or it ends up as pet food. . . Peter Gumbul *The Wall Street Journal*

1 pound beef heart
1 pound veal or lamb kidneys
1 pound sweetbreads
1 pound brains
juice of 4 lemons
sea salt and freshly ground pepper
3 medium onions, chopped fine
butter and extra virgin olive oil
1 cup red wine
2 cups beef stock
2 cloves garlic, peeled and mashed

This wonderful dish from Egypt is a testimony to the importance of organ meats in ethnic cuisines. It can be served with basic brown rice or in pita bread with tahini sauce and shredded lettuce.

Cut all organ meats into a small dice. (None need be pre-prepared.) Marinate heart and kidneys together for several hours in juice of 2 lemons plus salt and pepper; marinate sweetbreads and brains together for several hours in juice of 2 lemons and salt and pepper. Drain all meats and pat dry.

Saute onions in butter and olive oil until soft. Reserve. Saute heart and kidneys in batches until well browned. Reserve. Add wine, stock and garlic to pan and bring to a boil. Reduce to simmer. Add heart and kidneys to pan and simmer, uncovered, for about 15 minutes. Add onions, brains and sweetbreads and simmer, uncovered, for another 5 minutes or so or until most of liquid has evaporated. Serve with basic brown rice (page 441).

To serve with pita bread, let cook until liquid is almost completely gone. Serve with pita bread, tahini sauce (page 134), very thin slices of tomato and shredded romaine lettuce dressed with a little lemon juice.

Know Your Ingredients

Name This Product #15

Salt, hydrolyzed vegetable protein, sugar, monosodium glutamate, dehydrated onion, malto-dextrin, dextrin (with beef extract and partially hydrogenated soybean oil), caramel color, autolyzed yeast, corn oil, dry malt syrup, disodium inosinate, disodium guanylate, natural flavoring, not more that 2% silicon dioxide added as an anti-caking agent.

See Appendix B for Answer

SIMPLE SHAD ROE

Serves 4-6

1 shad roe (2 lobes)
sea salt
2 tablespoons raw vinegar
4 tablespoons butter
1-2 teaspoons paprika
freshly ground black pepper
1 lemon, cut into wedges

Place roe in a pan and cover with a mixture of filtered water, salt and vinegar. Bring to a boil, reduce heat and simmer about 10 minutes. Place roe in a colander and rinse with cold water. Using a sharp knife, peel off as much of the membrane as you can and cut out the vein.

Place roe in a baking dish and season with salt, paprika and pepper. Pour melted butter over. Broil until golden, turn and broil other side. Serve with lemon wedges.

SHAD ROE WITH WINE SAUCE

Serves 4-6

1 shad roe (2 lobes) prepared as in preceding recipe, omitting paprika
2 tablespoons butter
1 cup shallots, finely minced
1 cup white wine
2 cups chicken or fish stock
2 tablespoons arrowroot mixed with 2 tablespoons water
1 cup greens such as spinach or kale, finely chopped
sea salt and freshly ground pepper
fresh lemon juice

I have presumed in this discussion that the primitive races are able to provide us with valuable information. In the first place, the primitive peoples have carried out programs that will produce physically excellent babies. This they have achieved by a system of carefully planned nutritional programs for mothers-to-be. Those groups of primitive racial stocks who live by the sea and have access to animal life from the sea, have depended largely upon certain types of animal life and animal products. Specifically, the Eskimos, the people of the South Sea Islands, the residents of the islands north of Australia, the Gaelics in the Outer Hebrides, and the coastal Peruvian Indians have depended upon these products for their reinforcement. Fish eggs have been used as part of the program in all of these groups. The cattle tribes of Africa, the Swiss in isolated high Alpine valleys, and the tribes living in the higher altitudes of Asia, including northern India, have depended upon a very high quality of dairy products. Among the primitive Masai in certain districts of Africa, the girls were required to wait for marriage until the time of the year when the cows were on the rapidly growing young grass and to use the milk from these cows for a certain number of months before they could be married. In several agricultural tribes in Africa the girls were fed on special foods for six months before marriage. Weston Price DDS *Nutrition and Physical Degeneration*

"Fragile-X syndrome" describes a combination of traits that include long, narrow faces, large protruding ears, loose elbow and finger joints, flat feet, crowded teeth and mental retardation. Studies of mental institutions suggest that fragile-X syndrome is the most common form of retardation to "run in families". Politically correct science thus insists that fragile-X syndrome is an inherited condition. But the traits that define fragile-X syndrome are also those of vitamin A deficiency. The syndrome runs in families because bad eating habits run in families and because poor diet affects the quality of our genetic material. SWF

While preparing roe, saute shallots in butter until soft. Add wine and stock, bring to a boil and skim. Boil vigorously until sauce reduces and thickens. Spoonful by spoonful, add arrowroot mixture until desired consistency is obtained. Stir in greens and simmer until wilted. Season to taste with sea salt, freshly ground pepper and lemon juice. Slice roe, portion between individual plates and spoon sauce over.

ROE CAKES

Makes 8 patties

1 shad roe (2 lobes) or
3/4 pound roe from other fish
sea salt
2 tablespoons raw vinegar
1 medium onion, finely chopped
butter
1 1/2 cup whole grain bread crumbs
2 eggs, lightly beaten
sea salt and freshly ground pepper
1/2 teaspoon paprika
1 teaspoon dried thyme
butter and extra virgin olive oil

This recipe is for those who know they should eat fish eggs but don't like the taste. There is no fishy taste in these delicious patties.

Place roe in a pan and cover with a mixture of filtered water, salt and vinegar. Bring to a boil, reduce heat and simmer about 15 minutes. Remove roe to a colander and rinse with cold water. Using a sharp knife, remove all of the membrane and cut out the vein. Place roe eggs in a bowl. Meanwhile saute onion in butter until soft. Add onions, bread crumbs, eggs and seasonings to roe and mix well with hands. Form into patties. Saute until golden in butter and olive oil. Serve with a pickled condiment such as daikon radish (page 91) or ginger carrots (page 87); or serve for breakfast with scrambled eggs.

GAME

Game is not usually considered a health food but it should be. The meat of game animals such as deer, caribou, and elk, and of game birds like wild duck and goose, pheasant and quail is particularly rich in minerals. Game animals are an excellent source of balanced essential fatty acids, both omega-6 and omega-3. This may be why Edgar Cayce, America's "sleeping prophet", recommended game to so many people who came to him for readings.

Many people have difficulty getting used to the taste and texture of game, especially if they are accustomed to eating meat from domestic animals. Game meat has a tendency to be stringy and dry and the taste is very strong. These difficulties can be overcome with proper preparation and cooking. Game should "hang" or be aged for as long as possible in a cool, dry place to allow cathepsin, an enzyme naturally present in meat, to begin breaking down muscle fibers; and in most cases, game meat should be marinated for at least several hours, and as long as 48 hours, before it is cooked. If you take care in the preliminaries, the meat in your final dish will be flavorful and tender.

If you are lucky enough to have a hunter in your family, or if you have access to fresh game through a meat wholesaler or your local butcher, do take advantage of your good fortune and serve healthful game to your family as often as possible. We offer a selection of recipes that can be adopted to your tastes and to the kind of game you have on hand. (The recipes for venison can be used for any large game animal.) Most feature strongly-flavored sauces with a hint of sweetness that combine well with the strong taste of game meat.

A note to hunters; If it is possible to save the organ meats of your deer, elk, etc. by all means do so. (They must be chilled down quickly.) The liver and kidneys may be prepared according to the recipes in our chapter on organ meats. The thyroid gland, cooked in water to make a broth, makes in an excellent tonic. Antlers and feet, cut up and added to your stock pot, will give you a very rich broth.

VENISON MEDALLIONS IN TANGY SAUCE

Serves 6

12 venison pieces from the loin or back leg, about 2-3 inches by 1-1 1/2 inches
grated rind of 2 lemons
juice of two lemons
1 teaspoon dried thyme
butter and extra virgin olive oil
1/4 cup red wine vinegar
1 cup red wine
2 tablespoons blackberry or plum jam, honey or fruit juice sweetened
2 cups beef or venison stock
sea salt and freshly ground pepper

Make a mixture of the lemon rind, lemon juice and thyme. Pound the venison pieces lightly with the small prong side of a meat hammer and marinate in the mixture for several hours or overnight.

Pat the pieces very dry with paper towels. In a heavy skillet, cook the medallions quickly in the butter and oil, a few at a time, about 4 or 5 minutes per side. (The meat should be rare.) Transfer medallions to a heated platter and keep warm in the oven while making sauce.

Pour off the browning fat and add wine and vinegar to the pan. Bring to a boil, stirring with a wooden spoon to scrape off any accumulated juices in the pan. Add stock and jam, bring to a boil and skim. Let sauce reduce until it thickens. Season to taste.

Serve with any chestnut preparation (page 359) or with sauteed Asian pears (page 509).

Whoever eats of this meat [venison] frequently is cleansed of slime and filth. Whoever is plagued by precanerosis (vicht) should eat often from its liver and it will devour the vicht in him.

St. Hildegard of Bengin

VENISON WITH GINGER SAUCE

Serves 6

12 venison pieces from the loin or back leg,
about 2-3 inches by 1-1 1/2 inches
juice of 3 limes
2 bunches cilantro, chopped
1 tablespoon grated fresh ginger
1 teaspoon green peppercorns, crushed
butter and extra virgin olive oil
1/2 dry white wine
3 cups venison or beef stock
2 tablespoons plum jam,
honey or fruit-juice sweetened
1 tablespoon finely grated ginger
sea salt and freshly ground pepper
cilantro sprigs

Make a mixture of lime juice, chopped ginger, cilantro and peppercorns. Pound the venison pieces lightly with the small prong side of a meat hammer and marinate in the mixture 24 hours.

Pat the pieces very dry with paper towels. In a heavy skillet, cook the medallions very quickly in the butter and oil, a few at a time, about 4 or 5 minutes per side. (The meat should be rare.) Transfer medallions to a heated platter and keep warm in the oven while making sauce.

Pour off the browning fat and add wine and stock. Bring to a boil, stirring with a wooden spoon to scrape off any accumulated juices in the pan. Add ginger and jam, bring to a boil and skim. Let sauce reduce until it thickens. Season to taste. To serve, place two pieces of venison on each plate, spoon sauce over and decorate with cilantro sprigs.

Between 1910 and 1980, many changes took place in the kinds and amounts of fats and oils that people ate. . . Fats and oils (shortening, margarine, refined salad and cooking oils) account for 57%, dairy products account for 7%, and meat, poultry and fish account for 31% of the total increase in our fat consumption. The average intake of *trans*-fatty acids in hydrogenated products rose from zero in 1910 to close to 10% of all fats we consume today. . . . Our use of butter declined to 1/5 of its 1910 level, while our use of margarine increased 9 times. The use of lard went down to about 1/5 of its former level, while the use of vegetable shortenings almost doubled in the same time span. . . Consumption of whole milk is less than 1/2 of its level in 1910, consumption of cream is less than 1/3 of its 1910 level, but cheese consumption has almost tripled, ice cream and frozen desserts consumption has increased 5 times and low-fat milk consumption has increased by a factor of 3. Our annual consumption of sugar rose from 15 pounds per person in 1815 to about 90 pounds in 1910, about 120 pounds in 1980 and about 135 pounds today. Cholesterol intake from foods has remained essentially constant during the last 70 years. . . consumption if linoleic acid (18:2w6) increased by 170%. The consumption of w3s (LNA, EPA, DHA) decreased to 1/6 of its level in 1850, while w6 (LA, AA) consumption doubled during that time, resulting in widespread w3 deficiency and serious w3:w6 imbalance. Udo Erasmus *Fats that Heal, Fats that Kill*

VENISON STROGANOFF

Serves 6

12 venison pieces from the loin or back leg, about 2-3 inches by 1-1 1/2 inches
juice of 3 lemons
1 teaspoon green peppercorns, crushed
butter and extra virgin olive oil
1 cup red wine
3 cups venison or beef stock
2 tablespoons tomato paste
1 teaspoon paprika
1 cup piima cream or creme fraiche
sea salt and freshly ground pepper

Make a mixture of lemon juice and peppercorns. Pound the venison pieces lightly with the small prong side of a meat hammer and brush with lemon juice mixture. Marinate in refrigerator for 24 hours.

Pat the pieces very dry with paper towels. In a heavy skillet, cook the medallions very quickly in the butter and oil, a few at a time, about 4 or 5 minutes per side. (The meat should be rare.) Transfer medallions to a heated platter and keep warm in the oven while making sauce.

Pour off the browning fat and add wine and stock. Bring to a boil, stirring with a wooden spoon to scrape off any accumulated juices in the pan. Add tomato paste, paprika and cream, bring to a boil and skim. Let sauce reduce until it thickens. Season to taste with sea salt and freshly ground pepper. To serve, place two pieces of venison on each plate and spoon sauce over.

In the summer of 1933, [we made] contact with large bands of Indians who had come out of the Pelly mountain country to exchange their catch of furs at the last outpost of the Hudson Bay Company. . . they have remained as nomadic wandering tribes following the moose and caribou herds in the necessary search to obtain their foods.

The rigorous winters reach seventy degrees below zero. This precludes the possibility of maintaining dairy animals or growing seed cereals or fruits. The diet of these Indians is almost entirely limited to the wild animals of the chase. This made a study of them exceedingly important. The wisdom of these people regarding Nature's laws, and their skill in adapting themselves to the rigorous climate and very limited variety of foods, and these often very hard to obtain, have developed a skill in the art of living comfortably with rugged Nature that has been approached by few other tribes in the world. The sense of honor among these tribes is so strong that practically all cabins, temporarily unoccupied due to the absence of the Indians on their hunting trip, were entirely unprotected by locks; and the valuables belonging to the Indians were left in plain sight. . .

The condition of the teeth, and the shape of the dental arches and the facial form, were superb. Indeed, in several groups examined not a single tooth

VENISON STEW

Serves 6

3 pounds venison, cut into 1-inch cubes
2 cups red wine
butter and extra virgin olive oil
4 cups beef or venison stock
several sprigs fresh thyme, tied together
2 cloves garlic, peeled and mashed
8 juniper berries
1/2 teaspoon dried green peppercorns, crushed
several small pieces lemon zest
1 rutabaga, peeled and cut into 1/2 inch cubes
1 pound pearl onions, peeled and sauteed in butter
1 cup coarsely chopped kale or other dark green leafy vegetable
2 tablespoons arrowroot mixed with 2 tablespoons water
sea salt and freshly ground pepper

Marinate venison cubes in wine for 12-24 hours. Remove meat and dry well with paper towels. Reserve marinade.

In a heavy flame proof casserole, brown the venison cubes, a few at a time, in butter and olive oil. Transfer with a slotted spoon to a plate. Pour out browning fat and pour wine marinade into the pan. Bring to a boil, stirring with a wooden spoon to scrape up any accumulated juices. Add stock, bring to a boil and skim. Add thyme, garlic, peppercorns and lemon zest. Return meat to casserole, cover and bake in oven at 350 degrees for several hours. About 3/4 hour before serving, add the rutabaga.

When rutabaga is tender, transfer casserole to the stove. Spoonful by spoonful add the arrowroot mixture to the stew while it simmers, until sauce reaches desired thickness. Season to taste. Add the onions and kale and simmer a few minutes more.

was found that had ever been attacked by tooth decay . . . Careful inquiry regarding the presence of arthritis was made in the more isolated groups. We neither saw nor heard of a case in the isolated groups. However, at the point of contact with the foods of modern civilization many cases were found including ten bedridden cripples in a series of about twenty Indian homes. Some other affections made their appearance here, particularly tuberculosis which was taking a very severe toll of the children who had been born at this center. . . The suffering from tooth decay was tragic. There were no dentists, no doctors available within hundreds of miles to relieve suffering.

The physiques of the Indians of the far north who are still living in their isolate locations and in accordance with their accumulated wisdom were superb. There were practically no irregular teeth, including no impacted third molars, as evidenced by the fact that all individuals old enough to have the molars erupted had them standing in position and functioning normally for mastication. . .Where the Indians were using the white man's food tooth decay was very severe. . . In the new generation, after meeting the white civilization and using his foods, many developed crooked teeth, so-called, with deformed dental arches. . . Weston Price DDS *Nutrition and Physical Degeneration*

VENISON CHOPS

Serves 6

6 venison chops
2 cups red wine
1 teaspoon grated orange peel
1 teaspoon dried thyme
butter and extra virgin olive oil
2 cups venison or beef stock
juice of 1 orange
2 tablespoons arrowroot mixed with
2 tablespoons water
sea salt and freshly ground pepper

Marinate the chops in a mixture of the wine, orange peel and thyme for 12 to 24 hours. Dry cutlets well and reserve marinade.

In a heavy skillet, brown the chops, 2 at a time, about 5 minutes per side. Transfer to a plate while browning the remaining chops. Pour off browning fat and pour marinade into the pan. Bring to a boil, stirring with a wooden spoon to scrape up any accumulated juices in the pan. Add stock and orange juice, bring to a boil and skim.

Add the chops to the liquid, reduce heat, cover and cook about 1 hour. (If chops are from a young deer, and very tender, this step will not be necessary. They can be eaten medium rare.) Remove to a heated platter and keep warm in oven while finishing sauce. Bring to a rapid boil and reduce to about half. Add the arrowroot mixture spoonful by spoonful until desired thickness is obtained. Season to taste and serve.

Venison was a primary part of many of the Native Americans' diet. The deer meat was often roasted on spits, as was wild fowl. Venison was also used to make "pemmican", an early convenience food of the Indians. Pemmican was a mixture of thinly-sliced lean venison (or buffalo meat) dried in the sun, pulverized and mixed with melted animal fat and dried berries or cherries. This preparation was packed in sacks of hide, handy to carry. The high-protein mixture would purportedly keep indefinitely. The name comes from the Cree "pemmikkan" associated with their word "pimiy" meaning "grease" or "fat". Northwestern Indians utilized salmon to make a similar concoction. Patricia B. Mitchell *The Good Land*

The [Pima] Indians are especially fond of squirrels or any game. The old folks say that the reason the tribe is dying is because they are compelled to eat beef and flour instead of fish, game, acorns, buckeyes, wild bulbs and tubers, shell fish and seaweed, salt from the ocean and sugar from the pine tree.
Grace Hudson

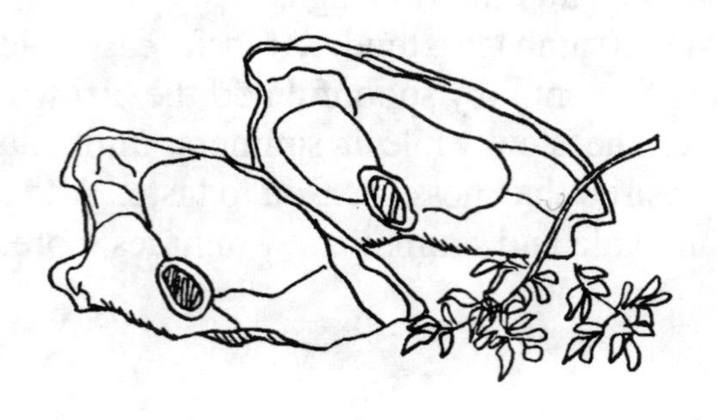

WILD DUCK STEW

Serves 6-10

4 wild ducks
2 cups dry white wine or vermouth
duck fat or butter
2 medium onions, peeled and finely chopped
2 carrots, peeled and finely chopped
1 red pepper, seeded and chopped
1/4 cup red wine
3-4 cups duck stock
several sprigs fresh thyme, tied together
1/2 teaspoon dried green peppercorns, crushed
2 tablespoons arrowroot mixed with
2 tablespoon water
1 pound pearl onions, sauteed in butter
sea salt and freshly ground pepper

Cut the ducks into parts. Use the backs and necks to make duck stock (page 115). Marinate the wing, leg, thigh and breast pieces in wine for 12-24 hours.

Dry pieces well with paper towels. Prick skin all over with a sharp needle—this will allow fat to drain out during the browning process. Place duck pieces skin side up in a stainless steel baking dish and brown in a 400 degree oven for about 1/2 hour until skin becomes golden. Meanwhile saute onions, carrots and pepper gently in a heavy flame proof casserole in a little butter or duck fat. Add wine marinade, stock and red wine. Bring to a boil and reduce liquid to about half. Add the duck pieces, thyme and seasonings. Cover and bake at 300 degrees for several hours.

Remove from oven and set casserole over a low flame. Add the arrowroot mixture, spoonful by spoonful until desired thickness is obtained. Season to taste. Add the onions and serve.

The Director of the National Museum in Iceland says that it is definitely established that during 600 years, 1200 to 1800 in Iceland, there were no dental cavities. The foods they ate were milk and milk products, mutton, beef and fish. They ate no carbohydrate. The only exception to this was a little moss soup in the summer, but this was a rare "fun food" of little nutritional importance.

Two Indian tribes reveal the same thing. The prehistoric Indians of California were vegetarians, unlike most folks of that period, and they had tooth decay. In contrast, the Sioux Indians lived on buffalo meat and were devoid of cavities. The Pueblos worshipped the Corn God, but he was not grateful. They have the most wretched teeth of all the American Indian tribes. They live on corn, squash and beans. The Laplanders, who ate mostly reindeer meat during the 18th century, rarely had cavities. Modern laps have a decay rate of 85% of their teeth. William Campbell Douglass MD *The Milk of Human Kindness*

To preserve health is a moral and religious duty, for health is the basis for all social virtues. We can no longer be useful when not well.

Samuel Johnson

DUCK STEW WITH DRIED CHERRIES

Serves 6-10

2 domestic ducks or 3 wild ducks
2 cups red wine
4 cups duck stock
several sprigs fresh thyme, tied together
1/2 teaspoon dried green peppercorns, crushed
several small pieces orange zest
8 ounces dried cherries
2 tablespoons arrowroot mixed with
2 tablespoons water

Cut the ducks into parts. Use the backs and necks to make duck stock (page 115). Marinate the wing, leg, thigh and breast pieces in wine for 12-24 hours.

Dry pieces well with paper towels. Prick skin all over with a sharp needle—this will allow fat to drain out during the browning process. Place duck pieces skin side up in a stainless steel baking dish and brown in a 400 degree oven for about 1/2 hour until skin becomes golden. Remove duck pieces to a flame proof casserole. Pour duck fat out of baking pan and pour in wine marinade. Bring to a boil, stirring with a wooden spoon to scrape up any accumulated juices in the pan. Add stock, bring to a boil and skim. Boil vigorously until liquid has reduced by about 1/2. Add the thyme, pepper corns and cherries. Pour sauce over duck pieces, cover casserole and bake at 300 for several hours.

Remove from oven and set casserole over a low flame. Add the arrowroot mixture, spoonful by spoonful until desired thickness is obtained. Season to taste with sea salt.

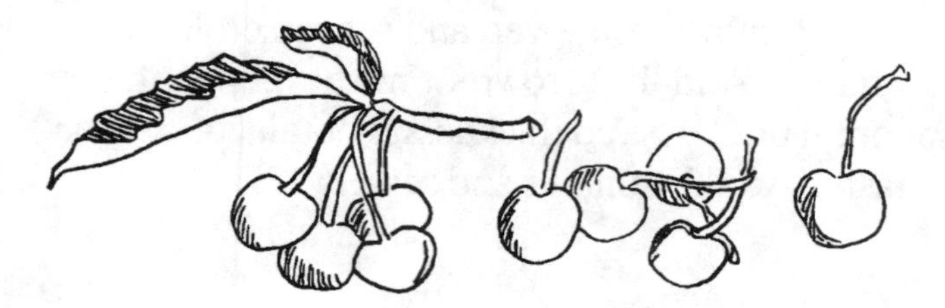

The flesh of bear hath a good relish, very savory and inclining nearest to that of Pork, The Fat of this Creature is least apt to rise in the Stomach of any other. The Men for the most part chose it rather than Venison. . . And now, for the good of mankind, and for the better Peopling an Infant colony, which has no want but that of Inhabitants, I will venture to publish a Secret of Importance, which our Indian . . . disclosed to me. I asked him the reason why few or none of his Country women were barren? To which curious Question he answered with a Broad grin upon his Face, they had an infallible SECRET for that. Upon my being importunate to know what the secret might be, he informed me that, if any Indian woman did not prove with child at a decent time after Marriage, the Husband, to save his Reputation with the women, forthwith entered into a Bear-dyet for Six Weeks, which in that time makes him so vigorous that he grows exceedingly impertinent to his poor wife and 'tis great odds but he makes her a Mother in Nine Months. Col. William Byrd II, 1728

In a short time a great number of people came to the spot. . . They stood around the lions and talked about them. . . Pooran Singh himself appeared . . . his melliferous Indian smile shone in the midst of his thick black beard, he stuttered with delight when he spoke. He was anxious to procure for himself the fat of the lions, that with his people is held in high esteem as a medicine,—from the pantomime by which he expressed himself to me, I believe against rheumatism and impotence. Isak Dinesen *Out of Africa*

DUCK CURRY

Serves 8-12

2 domestic ducks or 3 wild ducks
2 large onions, peeled and finely chopped
2 cups finely chopped celery
4-5 tablespoons curry powder or paste
1 teaspoon ground cardamom
1 teaspoon fennel seeds
1 teaspoon fenugreek seeds
1/4 teaspoon cayenne pepper
4 cups duck stock
1 tablespoon freshly grated ginger
4 cloves garlic, peeled and mashed
1 cup piima cream or creme fraiche
sea salt and freshly ground pepper

Remove the excess fat from the ducks and make duck stock from the whole birds (page115). (Make cracklings from the excess fat and skin, page 273.) Remove the meat from the ducks, chop coarsely and reserve in refrigerator. Strain stock into a bowl, refrigerate until it congeals and remove fat.

In a heavy skillet saute onions and celery until soft in a little butter or duck fat. Add curry powder or paste and other seasonings and cook about five minutes, stirring constantly. Add stock, bring to a boil and stir with a whisk to remove any lumps. Add garlic and ginger. Boil vigorously until sauce reduces to about 1/2. Add cream and simmer a few minutes more. Season to taste. Stir in reserved duck meat.

Serve with basic brown rice (page 441) and traditional curry accompaniments such as fruit chutney (page 98), raisins, dried sweetened coconut meat (page 144), chopped crispy cashews (page 487), duck cracklings (page 273) and chopped scallions.

The San Diego Indians of southern California changed their home sites with the supply of native foods. They fished from the ocean, hunted the plentiful game on the mountains and gathered acorns, seeds and wild greens when in season. They collected wild onion and sage for seasoning. Their staple meal was acorn mush, eaten from a common pot. The acorns were prepared by grinding on basaltic stones, leaching in sand, or pounding with rocks, which introduced much abrasive material to wear down the tooth enamel but at the same time prevented cavities. The acorn mush, supplemented with wild game, seafood and greens, supplied them with all the necessary nutrients. Early explorers and missionaries of the San Diego area reported that the local Indians were strong, hardy and seldom ill. But later studies indicate that when the Indians were deprived of their natural foods by living on reservations and eating modern foods, most of them suffered a sharp decrease in general health, and within a single generation became susceptible to eye diseases, a high tooth decay rate, bowed legs and tuberculosis.
"Nutrition: The Appetite of Man"
PPNF

DUCK WITH OLIVES

Serves 8-12

2 domestic ducks or 3 wild ducks
2 small onions, peeled and finely chopped
2 carrots, peeled and diced
3 cups duck stock
1 teaspoon fresh or dried tarragon leaves
1/2 teaspoon dried green peppercorns, crushed
juice of 1 lemon
1 cup piima cream or creme fraiche
1 1/2 cups sliced green olives
sea salt and freshly ground pepper

Remove the excess fat from the ducks and make duck stock from the whole birds (page 115). (Make cracklings from the excess fat and skin, page 273.) Remove the meat from the ducks, chop coarsely and reserve in refrigerator. Strain stock into a bowl, refrigerate until it congeals and remove fat.

In a heavy skillet saute onions and carrot until soft in a little butter or duck fat. Add stock, bring to a rapid boil and skim. Add tarragon and peppercorns. Boil, uncovered, for about 1/2 hour or more until stock is reduced to about 1 cup. Off heat, stir in lemon juice, cream, olives and duck meat. Season to taste. Transfer to a casserole and warm in a 200 degree oven for about 15 minutes. Serve on triangle or round croutons (page 491).

Anchorage. . . has an excellent government hospital which probably has been built around the life of one man whom many people told us was the most beloved man in all Alaska. He is Dr. Josef Romig, a surgeon of great skill and with an experience among the Eskimos and Indians, both the primitive and modernized, extending over thirty-six years. . . He took me, for example, to several typically modernized Indian homes in the city. In one, the grandmother, who had come from the northern shore of Cook Inlet to visit her daughter, was sixty-three years of age, and was entirely free from tooth decay and had lost only one of her teeth. Her son, who had accompanied her, was twenty-four years of age. He had only one tooth that had ever been attacked by tooth decay. Their diet had been principally moose and deer meat, fresh and dried fish, a few vegetables and at time some cranberries. Recently the son had been obtaining some modern foods. Her daughter, twenty-nine years of age, had married a white man and had had eight children. She and they were living on modern foods entirely. Twenty-one of her thirty-two teeth had been wrecked by dental caries. Their diet consisted largely of white bread, syrup and potatoes. Her children whom we examined ranged from five to twelve years of age, and in that family 37 percent of all teeth have already been attacked by dental decay. . . . not only was dental caries rampant, but that there were marked deformity of the dental arches and irregularity of teeth in the cases of the children. Weston Price DDS *Nutrition and Physical Degeneration*

PHEASANT WITH ORANGE SAUCE

Serves 4

2 pheasant, cut into quarters
2 cup dry white wine
grated zest from 2 oranges
melted butter
freshly ground pepper
3 cups chicken, turkey, duck or pheasant stock
juice from 2 oranges
2 tablespoons arrowroot mixed with
2 tablespoons water

Marinate pheasant pieces, turning occasionally, in a mixture of white wine and orange zest for 12 to 24 hours. Pat dry with paper towels and reserve marinade.

Place pheasant pieces, skin side up, in a stainless steel roasting pan. Brush with melted butter and sprinkle with pepper. Bake at 400 degrees for about 1 hour or until pieces are golden. Transfer pheasant pieces to a casserole. Add marinade to the roasting pan and bring to a rapid boil, stirring with a wooden spoon to scrape up any accumulated juices. Add stock and orange juice, bring to a boil and skim. Allow liquid to reduce slightly. Pour over pheasant pieces, cover casserole and bake at 300 degrees for at least 2 hours.

Remove pheasant pieces to a heated platter and keep warm in the oven. Strain the sauce into a saucepan and bring to a boil. Add the arrowroot spoonful by spoonful until desired thickness is obtained. Season to taste and serve.

HUNTERS FEAST

New Potatoes with Caviar

Pheasant in Orange Sauce

Steamed Spinach

Seasonal Lettuce with Blue Cheese Dressing

Pecan Tart

"Teeth superior on average to those of the presidents of our largest toothpaste companies are found in the world today, and have existed during past ages, among people who violate every precept of current dentifrice advertising. . . The best teeth and the healthiest mouths were found among people who never drank milk since they ceased to be suckling babes and who never in their lives tasted or tested any of the other things which we usually recommend for sound teeth. . . They never took any pains to cleanse their teeth or mouths. They did not visit their dentist twice a year or even once in a lifetime. . . so far as an extensive correspondence with authorities has yet been able to show, a complete absence of tooth decay from entire populations has never existed in the past, and does not exist now, except where meat is either exclusively or heavily predominant on the diet." Stephanson quoted in *The Milk of Human Kindness*

TERIYAKI QUAIL

Serves 6

12 quail, ribs removed and torso opened out
2 cups teriyaki sauce (page 133)

Marinate quail several hours or overnight in sauce. Grill under broiler about 10 minutes per side or cook on the barbecue. Eat with fingers—this is the only way to eat quail!

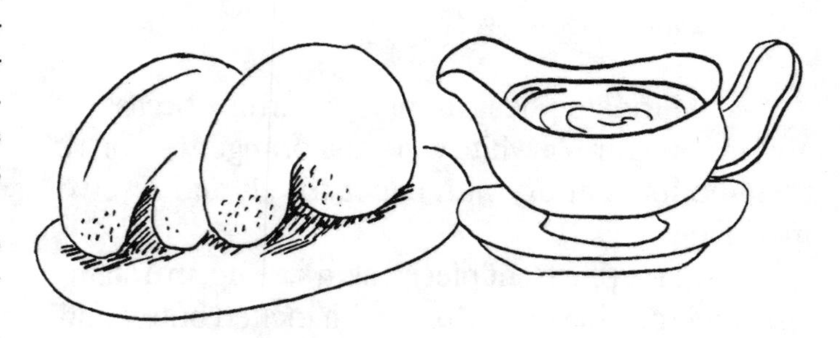

QUAIL MASALA

Serves 6

12 quail, ribs removed and torso opened out
1 cup yoghurt
1 medium onion, peeled and finely chopped
3 cloves garlic, peeled and crushed
1 teaspoon grated fresh ginger
1 teaspoon ground cumin
1/2 teaspoon turmeric
1/2 teaspoon ground cardamom
1/4 teaspoon ground cloves
1/4 teaspoon cinnamon
1/4 teaspoon cayenne pepper
1 teaspoon sea salt
1 bunch chopped cilantro

Mix yoghurt and remaining ingredients together. Marinate quail in yoghurt mixture several hours or overnight. Grill under broiler about 10 minutes per side or cook on the barbecue. Eat them with your fingers. . . no knives or forks allowed.

There are few if any problems connected with modern degeneration on which so much light is thrown as that supplied by recent investigations on the problems of paternal responsibility for defects in the offspring. There are several reasons for this. Because the mother has the sole responsibility for the nourishment of the fetus during the formative period and she alone provides the handicaps incident to the process of birth, it is very natural that defects are practically all interpreted as being associated with these [birth] processes. This unfortunately, has been embarrassed further by the fact hat since distortions in behavior do not appear until sometime after birth, normality was largely assumed to be present up to the time of the appearance and therefor of necessity would be contributions from the child's environment. As such they would be subject naturally to treatment by applying influences to change the mental environment. Hence the entire problem of the role of the sex cells through controlling the architecture of the body including the brain has been largely overlooked. Weston Price DDS *Nutrition and Physical Degeneration*

TRADITIONAL MEATS

Politically Correct Nutrition has singled out red meat—lamb, beef and veal—as a contributing factor, or even the main cause, of our two greatest plagues—cancer and heart disease. Consumption of these meats has dropped in recent years but heart disease remains our number one killer and the cancer rate continues to climb.

What light can the practices of traditional societies shed on the question of red meats? Surveys of ethnic diets show that red meat in the form of beef, goat and sheep is the second most preferred source of animal protein and fat in non-industrialized societies, second only to chicken (flesh and eggs) and more popular, or at least more available, than foods from the sea. These societies rarely suffer from cancer and heart disease. This fact alone should be enough to allay any fears about red meat.

The dangers inherent in red meat are due, we believe, to modern methods of raising calves, steers and lambs for the commercial market. Most commercially available red meat comes from animals that have been raised in huge feed lots on substandard feed, injected with steroids to make their meat tender and treated with antibiotics to stave off infections that inevitably result from poor diet and crowded conditions. The meat that such methods produce is not necessarily higher in fat content, as is generally believed, but has a higher water content than meat from free-range animals. Studies have shown that when meat has a high water content, it is also high in mutagens—substances that cause undesirable cell changes.

Fortunately, organically-raised free range beef and lamb are now becoming more available. If you eat red meat, we urge you to make every effort to obtain meat that has been raised under healthful conditions. Many markets in our larger cities now sell organically raised meats, and with a little searching a wholesale supply can always be found. Many farmers will sell sides or quarters of beef, lamb and veal directly to consumers. If you have freezer space, this is the most economical way to buy good quality beef and lamb. (Be sure to specify, when buying sides of meat directly from a farmer, that the meat be hung and allowed to age, like commercial meat, before it is packaged for your freezer. Otherwise it will be very tough.) When you purchase directly from the farm, you have the additional advantage of being able to obtain the organ meats, bones and hooves. Traditional societies do not let these valuable parts go to waste. The organ meats, extremely rich in fat soluble vitamins, are relished as delicacies in primitive societies; and the bones and hooves are used to make nutritious stocks which provide abundant minerals in a form that is particularly easy to assimilate.

Red meat is an excellent source of both macro and trace minerals, particularly zinc and magnesium. In meat, these minerals exist in a form that is much easier for the body to breakdown and utilize than the minerals in grains and pulses. Red meats are rich in vitamin B12, so important for healthy blood and nervous system; and in carnitine, which is essential to healthy functioning of the heart. Beef and lamb fat contain essential fatty acids and fat soluble vitamins, especially if these animals have been allowed to graze on green grass. These fat-soluble vitamins are what your body needs to utilize the minerals in all foods. In animal studies, beef fat has a cholesterol-lowering effect. Lamb fat is rich in conjugated linoleic acid, which has strong anti-cancer effects.

Our recipes for tender portions of beef and lamb—filet and rib cuts of beef, leg of lamb and lamb chops—allow these cuts to be eaten rare, with most of their enzyme content still in tact. Tougher cuts can be braised in stock to make flavorful stews. In braising, the temperature of the meat does not exceed 212 degrees so denaturing of proteins is minimized. The enzyme content is destroyed, but any minerals and amino acids that come out of the meat will be contained in the sauce. Many ethnic recipes call for marinating tougher cuts for 24 to 48 hours in wine, yoghurt or buttermilk. This process tenderizes and predigests the meat.

We do not recommend deep frying of red meats or any cooking methods that raise the internal temperature above 212 degrees. Research indicates that meats subjected to high heats are harder to digest, and may even foster the growth of pathogens and viruses in the colon. Here is yet another reason to consume meats with sauce or broth containing gelatin and hence hydrophilic colloids, to facilitate protein digestion.

We hate to be spoilsports but we must caution you against too frequent consumption of barbecued meats. Meat and meat fat that come in contact with open flames synthesize certain highly carcinogenic hydrocarbons. Interestingly, meat that is cooked *in front of* a fire (as on a spit) or meat that is cooked *under* an open flame (as under a broiler) develops far fewer of these carcinogens than meat cooked *over* an open flame. Meat that has been cooked in a pan or in liquid contains very few hydrocarbons in comparison with meat that has been barbecued. Your body can deal with these hydrocarbons if it is healthy and not overloaded. We urge you to eat barbecued meats only occasionally and when you do, be sure to eat them with one or more cruciferous vegetables such as cabbage, broccoli or Brussels sprouts. Even better, serve barbecued meats with fermented vegetables or relishes. The combination is synergistic, not only in terms of flavor, but also because the vegetables with their lactic-acid-producing bacteria and high enzyme content will help break down hydrocarbons in the intestinal tract.

PEPPER STEAK

Serves 4

4 small beef tenderloin steaks, cut at least 1 inch thick, or 2 rib eye or T-bone steaks
1 tablespoon dried green peppercorns
juice of one lemon
4 shallots or 1 bunch green onions, finely chopped
1/2 cup red wine
2 cups beef stock

Crush the peppercorns and mix them with lemon juice. Rub over steaks and marinate in refrigerator for several hours.

Brush a cast iron skillet with a little olive oil. Pat the steaks dry, leaving as much pepper adhering as possible. Heat the pan and cook steaks in two batches over medium high flame about 5 minutes to a side or until medium rare. Transfer to a heated platter and keep warm in the oven while making sauce.

Pour out any grease from pan. Add a little butter or olive oil and gently saute the shallots or green onions. Add wine and bring to a rapid boil. Add stock. Boil rapidly, until sauce is reduced to about 2/3 cup. Be sure to skim frequently any impurities that come to the top of the sauce. Transfer steaks to individual plates and spoon a little sauce over each.

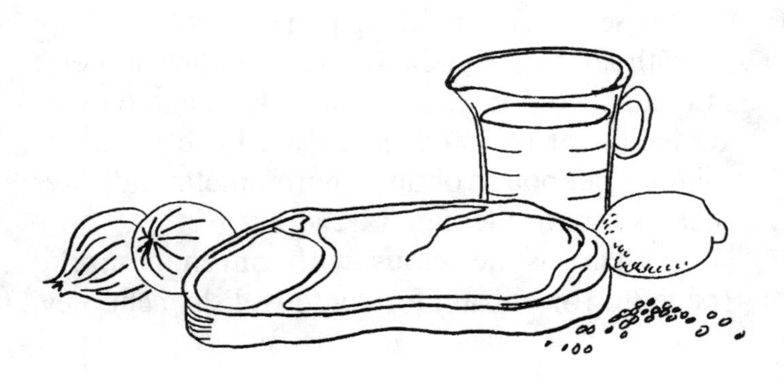

The Masai are tall and strong. . . For their food throughout the centuries they have depended very largely on milk, meat and blood, reinforced with vegetables and fruits. In the Masai tribe, a study of 2,516 teeth in eighty-eight individuals distributed through several widely separated manyatas showed only four individuals with caries. These had a total of ten carious teeth, or only 0.4 per cent of the teeth attacked by tooth decay. In contrast with the Masai, the Kikuyu tribe are characterized by being primarily an agricultural people. Their chief articles of diet are sweet potatoes, corn, beans, and some bananas, millet, and Kafir corn, a variety of Indian millet. The women use special diets during gestation and lactation. . .The Kikuyus are not as tall as the Masai and physically they are much less rugged. . . A study of 1,041 teeth in thirty-three individuals showed fifty-seven teeth with caries or 5.5 per cent. There were 36.4 per cent of the individuals affected. Weston Price DDS *Nutrition and Physical Degeneration*

There is no society in the world that is entirely vegetarian. The Hindus of India come closest. Dr. H. Leon Abrams reports on India, ". . . the greater percentage of the population, who subsist almost entirely on vegetable foods, suffer from kwashiorkor, other forms of malnutrition and have the shortest life span in the world." William Campbell Douglass MD *The Milk of Human Kindness*

QUICK STEAK

Serves 3-4

1 1/2-2 pounds steak such as rib eye or T-bone
1-2 tablespoons cracked pepper
butter and extra virgin olive oil
2-4 tablespoons worcestershire sauce (non-MSG variety) or fish sauce (page 143)
1 cup piima cream or creme fraiche

Sprinkle steaks with pepper and press in. Melt butter and olive oil in a heavy skillet. Saute steaks, a few minutes on a side, until rare or medium rare. Transfer to a heated platter and keep warm in the oven while making sauce.

Pour out browning fat and deglaze pan with worcestershire sauce or fish sauce. Add cream and bring to a boil. Skim. Simmer for several minutes until sauce thickens. Transfer to a heated sauce boat and serve with steaks.

RIB ROAST

Serves 6-8

a 3-rib standing roast, about 3 pounds
sea salt and pepper
a meat thermometer

Set roast in a baking pan on a rack and rub fat with salt and pepper. Insert meat thermometer into center of meat. Place in a 400 degree oven. Reduce heat to 350 degrees and bake for 15-20 minutes per pound or until thermometer indicates meat is rare or medium rare.

This is delicious with onion compote (page 367) or with any fermented relish or chutney.

No culture in the history of mankind has been based on a one-hundred percent vegetarian diet, and although one can theoretically, in the light of contemporary nutritional scientific knowledge, obtain all the nutrients needed to provide good health, the technology to insure such has not been developed and such a vegetarian diet is extremely risky. H Leon Abrams *Vegetarianism: An Anthropological/Nutritional Evaluation*

A tragic illustration of what a strict vegetarian, no-cholesterol diet may do to you is the case of famous basket ball star, Bill Walton. Walton was a fanatic about what he considered to be good nutrition. No animal food—dairy or otherwise—passed his lips. He developed severe osteoporosis and consequent foot and ankle fractures from the constant jumping on hard wood floors required of his sport. A brilliant career was finished. Walton, learning from his mistake, became a spokesman for the meat industry. William Campbell Douglass MD *Eat Your Cholesterol*

Besides containing heat units in the proportion of nine to four as compared to candy, natural fat furnishes normal heat and energy as intended by nature; whereas sugars do so by upsetting the body's chemistry. H. Leon Abrams *Your Body is Your Best Doctor*

FILET OF BEEF WITH RED WINE SAUCE

Serves 8

3 pounds filet of beef, trimmed of fat and tied
6-8 cups beef stock
1 cup red wine
2 tablespoons gelatin (see Sources)
sea salt to taste

The world's most renowned chefs do not cook filet of beef in the oven—they braise it in stock. The stock is then reduced to make the most delicious sauce imaginable.

The beef should be at room temperature. In a saucepan or skillet just large enough to hold the filet, bring the stock to a boil. Reduce to a simmer and add filet of beef. Simmer for 15 to 22 minutes. Beef should be rare or medium rare. Transfer to a heated platter and keep warm in the oven while making sauce.

Bring stock to a rolling boil and add wine and gelatin. Let boil until stock is reduced to about 1 cup, skimming frequently—this may take as long as 1/2 hour. The sauce should be thickened and shiny, about the consistency of maple syrup. Season to taste with sea salt—but you probably won't need it.

Slice beef thinly and arrange on individual plates. Spoon sauce over and serve immediately.

If it were not for beef, the United States could produce perhaps 25% of the small grain it does. . . The factors that would limit our production is winter kill and tillering.

First, winter kill happens when small grains such as wheat or oats get into what is called the joint stage. Grain planted in the fall sprouts and grows fairly rapidly. Once it sends up the stem that the grain head grows on, and it makes the first joint in that stem, if it gets about 10 degrees Fahrenheit, it will kill the plant.

To prevent this from happening, cattlemen and wheat farmers graze small grains with cattle. Without cattle grazing, the wheat, all wheat planted, as well as oats, would have to be planted in the spring. Usually moisture conditions remain too wet for this to work well.

Without beef you can kiss good-bye probably to 50% of the earth's population.

Another misconception is water supposedly taken up by cattle. Water weighs approximately eight pounds per gallon. A one thousand pound steer, if 100% water, would be 125 gallons of water. Where is the rest of the thousands of gallons of water? If handled properly, the waste water from cattle is a very valuable resource. It removes nitrate nitrogens and ammoniacal nitrogens. Nitrate nitrogens make forage, and ammoniacal nitrogens make seeds and flowers. Farmers pay big money for these in bag form, to apply to the land. Charles Hallmark *Health Freedom News*

STUFFED FLANK STEAK

Serves 4

1 flank steak
sea salt and freshly ground pepper
1/2 head bok choy
1 small onion, finely chopped
1 slice whole grain bread, crumbled
2 tablespoons raisins
butter and extra virgin olive oil
3/4 cup unbleached flour
1/2 teaspoon pepper
1/2 cup red wine
2 cups beef stock

When you buy the flank steak, have the butcher pass it through the tenderizer one time. Spread out flank steak and rub with pepper and a pinch of salt. Cut 4 lengths of string and set aside.

To make stuffing, cut the leaves off the fleshy part of the bok choy stalks. Wash them, chop coarsely and set aside. Chop the stalks and saute with onions in olive oil and butter until soft. Add bread slice, crumbled, and raisins and saute about 5 minutes more. Spread stuffing on flank steak. Roll up steak, tie with string and dredge in flour mixed with pepper.

In a heavy skillet, brown the flank steak on all sides in butter and olive oil. Remove and pour out fat. Add wine and stock to pan and bring to a boil. Skim. Reduce to a simmer, return flank steak to pan and simmer, covered, for 2 hours or until meat is tender.

Transfer flank steak roll to a heated platter and keep warm in oven while making sauce. Bring sauce to a boil and let it boil uncovered, skimming frequently, until sauce has reduced by about one half and has thickened slightly. Stir in chopped bok choy leaves and let simmer a minute or so.

To serve, slice crosswise and place slices on individual plates. Spoon sauce over.

Variation:

Use *celery* instead of bok choy for stuffing and add *2 cups chopped spinach or chard* to sauce instead of bok choy leaves.

For 12 years Russian researchers have been observing 180 men and women living in and around the town of Dageston, and ranging in age from 90 to 100 years. The men and women living in town were heavier in weight and had more disease of blood vessels than the people living in the nearby mountains. All of the people studied ate some meat, but the town dwellers ate more carbohydrate food than the mountain folk, whose diet was mainly dairy products and vegetable foods. Modern nutrition condemns butter as a source of cholesterol, but these Russians managed to reach ages past 90 while eating butter freely. . . In another study, Metchnikoff studied communities of Bulgarians who ate mainly raw dairy food—and lived past 100. Are we to close our eyes to this evidence? Perhaps there is a difference between the milk and butter of these simple people and ours. In fact, more than 90 percent of the enzymes in milk are destroyed by pasteurization. Chemists have identified 35 separate enzymes in raw milk, with lipase one of the chief enzyme actors. How much longer are we to ignore the value of food enzymes? Edward Howell MD *Enzyme Nutrition*

KOREAN BEEF

Serves 4

1 flank steak
1/2 cup soy sauce
2 tablespoons toasted sesame oil
1 bunch green onions, finely chopped
6 cloves garlic, peeled and mashed
2 tablespoons sesame seeds
1/4 teaspoon cayenne pepper
pinch stevia powder

KOREAN BEEF DINNER

Tuna Tartare

Korean Beef

Basic Brown Rice

Steamed Chinese Peas

Ginger Carrots

Using a very sharp and heavy knife, slice the flank steak as thinly as possible across the grain and on the diagonal. (This will be easier if the meat is partially frozen.) Mix other ingredients and marinate beef in the mixture, refrigerated, for several hours or overnight.

Fold or "ribbon" the strips and stick them on skewers, making 4 to 6 brochettes. Cook on barbecue or under grill, about 5 to 7 minutes per side. Meat should still be rare or medium rare inside. This is delicious with kimchi (page 86) or any of the fermented vegetables, especially ginger carrots (page 87). The lactic-acid-producing bacteria in the fermented vegetables are the perfect antidote to carcinogens which may have formed in the meat, especially if it has been barbecued.

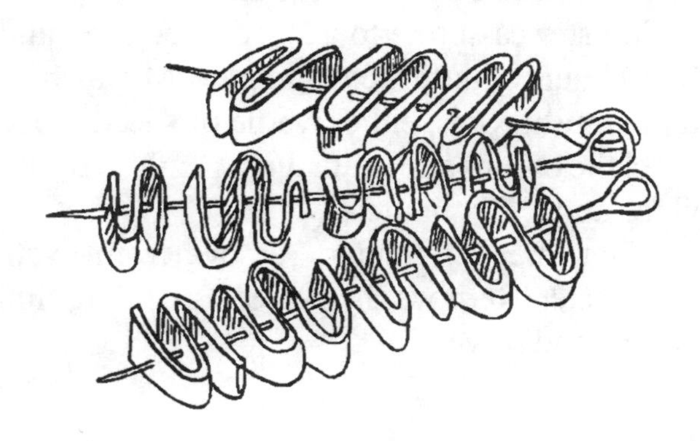

Fats have more than twice as many calories as carbohydrates, foods such as sugar, wheat, potatoes and fruits. Conventional wisdom says that reducing fats in the diet is essential for people who want to lose weight.

That *sounds* logical doesn't it? *But it's not true.*

In real life, eating fats helps you lose weight—but only if you make a deep cut in the carbohydrates you eat. Fats have more calories, but fats satisfy your hunger four or five times as much as carbohydrates. That's one of several reasons why eating fats helps people lose weight. H.L. Newbold MD *Type A Type B Weight Loss Book*

BEEF BOURGIGNON

Serves 6-8

3 pounds stew beef cut into 2 inch pieces
2 cups red wine
4 cups beef stock
butter and extra virgin olive oil
1/4 cup unbleached flour
several small slivers orange peel
several sprigs fresh thyme, tied together
1/2 teaspoon dried green peppercorns, crushed
1 pound fresh mushrooms
2 pounds medium boiling onions
sea salt and freshly ground pepper

Marinate the beef in wine for several hours or overnight. Remove and dry very well with paper towels. (This is important. If beef is too wet, it will not brown.)

Melt butter and oil in a heavy, flame proof casserole. Brown the cubes, a few at a time. Transfer to a plate with a slotted spoon. When all are browned, pour out cooking fat. Add a little butter to the casserole, let it melt, and add flour. Let it cook in the butter, stirring constantly. Add wine from the marinade and stock. Bring to a boil, stirring up scrapings from the bottom of the pan, and skim. Off heat return meat and juices that have accumulated in the plate, Add thyme, crushed peppercorns and orange peel.

Transfer casserole to a 300 degree oven and cook 3 or 4 hours or until meat is tender. Meanwhile, brown the mushrooms, either whole or sliced (page 367). Peel the onions and saute them gently in butter and oil for about 20 minutes.

When meat is tender, remove from oven. Season to taste. Remove thyme. Stir in onions and mushrooms and serve.

Know Your Ingredients

Name This Product #16

Wheat flour and starch, natural flavorings, beef fat, salt, onion, caramel color, corn syrup solids, monosodium glutamate (flavor enhancer), spices, sodium caseinate (milk protein), mono- and di-glycerides (for smoothness), garlic, disodium inosinate and disodium guanylate (flavor enhancers), BHA, propyl gallate and citric acid (as preservatives), and sulfating agents.

See Appendix B for Answer

ALL-DAY BEEF STEW

Serves 6-8

3 pounds stew beef, cut into 1-inch pieces
1 cup red wine
3-4 cups beef stock
4 tomatoes, peeled, seeded and chopped
or 1 can tomatoes
2 tablespoons tomato puree
6 whole cloves
1/2 teaspoon black peppercorns
several sprigs fresh thyme, tied together
2 cloves garlic, peeled and crushed
2-3 small pieces orange peel
8 small red potatoes
1 pound carrots, peeled and cut into sticks
sea salt and freshly ground pepper

When cooking is done well and with care, the good smells all go together to contribute, not only to the pleasure of the meal but also to its thorough digestion. The good smells coming from the kitchen activate the secretion of saliva and digestive juices. The stimulation of the taste buds by delicious tastes has the same beneficial effect.

A meal well presented, by the harmony of its forms and colors, evocative of a work of art, is not a simple esthetic exercise; it is also an aid to digestion as the sight of an appetizing dish stimulates the digestive juices, just as does its good smell and taste. Claude Aubert *Dis-Moi Comment Tu Cuisines*

This recipe and the two following are ideal for working mothers. The ingredients can be assembled in about fifteen minutes in the morning—or even the night before. The family will come home to wonderful smells permeating the house and a delicious dinner waiting.

Marinate meat in red wine overnight. (This step is optional.) Place all ingredients except for potatoes and carrots in an oven-proof casserole and cook at 250 degrees for 12 hours. Add carrots and potatoes during the last hour. Season to taste.

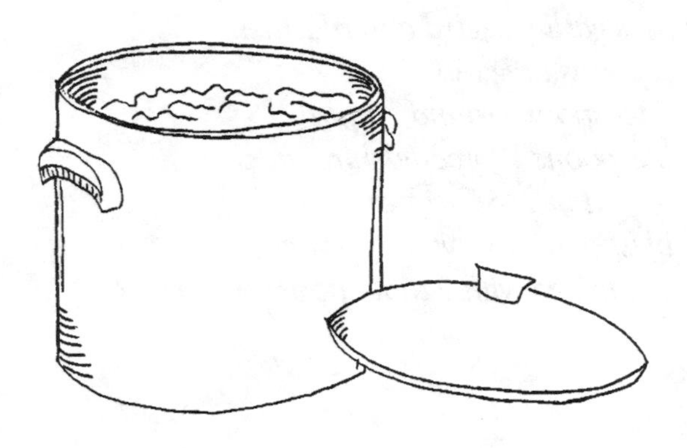

Under the stress of the industrial depression the family dietary of the children we studied was very deficient. They were brought to a mission where we fed them one reinforced meal at noon for six days a week. . . It is important to note that the home nutrition which had been responsible for the tooth decay was exceedingly low in body building and repairing material, while temporarily satisfying the appetite. It usually consisted of highly sweetened strong coffee and white bread, vegetable fat, pancakes made of white flour and eaten with syrup, and doughnuts fried in vegetable fat.. . The nutrition provided these children in this one meal included the following foods. About four ounces of tomato juice or orange juice and a teaspoonful of a mixture of equal parts of a very high vitamin natural cod liver oil and an especially high vitamin butter was given at the beginning of the meal. They then received a bowl containing approximately a pint of very rich vegetable and meat stew made largely from bone marrow and fine cuts of tender meat. The meat was usually broiled separately to retain its juice and then chopped very fine and added to

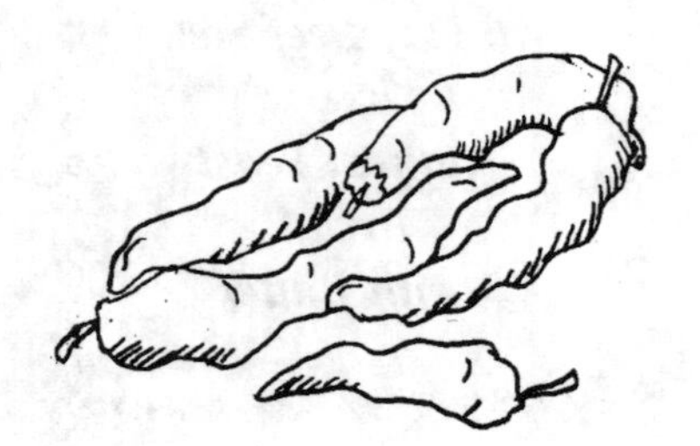

ALL-DAY SPICY STEW

Serves 6-8

3 pounds beef, cut into 1-inch cubes
juice of 2 lemons
4 tomatoes, peeled, seeded and chopped
or 1 can tomatoes
2 tablespoons tomato paste
2 medium onions, chopped
3 cups beef stock
1/4 teaspoon ground coriander
2 cloves garlic, peeled and chopped
1/2 teaspoon green peppercorns, crushed
1/2 teaspoon ground allspice
2 teaspoons chili powder
1/4 teaspoon cayenne pepper

Marinate beef overnight in lemon juice. Place all ingredients in an oven-proof casserole and bake at 250 degrees for about 12 hours. Serve with rice or corn tortillas. Season to taste.

ALL-DAY BEEF STEW WITH CHILES

Serves 6-8

3 pounds beef cut into 1-inch cubes
juice of 2 lemons
2-3 cups beef stock
2 onions, chopped
1 cup green chiles, chopped (can be mild or hot)
2 cloves garlic, peeled and mashed
2 teaspoons oregano
1 1/2 teaspoon ground cumin
2 tablespoons Worcestershire sauce
(non-MSG variety)
2 tablespoons arrowroot powder
mixed with 2 tablespoons water

Marinate beef overnight in lemon juice. Place all ingredients (except arrowroot mixture) in an oven proof casserole and bake at 250 degrees for about 12 hours. Remove to stove over a low flame. Spoonful by spoonful add arrowroot mixture until desired thickness is obtained. Season to taste.

BEEF STIR FRY STEW

Serves 6

1 pound stewing beef, cut into small pieces
juice of 2 oranges
extra virgin olive oil
1 cup crispy almonds (page 487), chopped
1 bunch green onions, sliced on an angle
2 large carrots, peeled and cut into a julienne
1 cup broccoli cut into flowerets
2 cloves garlic, finely chopped
1 teaspoon grated ginger
grated rind of 2 oranges
1 tablespoon sucanat
1/4 teaspoon red pepper flakes
2 tablespoon soy sauce
1/8 cup rice vinegar
2-3 cups beef stock
2 tablespoons arrowroot
mixed with 2 tablespoons water

Marinate beef pieces several hours in orange juice. Remove beef pieces and pat dry with paper towels. Mix stock with vinegar, soy sauce, pepper flakes, grated orange rind, ginger, sucanat and garlic and set aside. In a heavy skillet or wok, saute beef in oil until cooked through. Using a slotted spoon, transfer beef a bowl and reserve. Add more oil and saute almonds a minute or two. Remove with slotted spoon. Add more oil and saute onions, carrots and peppers about 2 minutes. Add sauce mixture and bring to a boil. Return beef and almonds to pan and mix well. Add arrowroot mixture and simmer a minute or so until sauce thickens. Add broccoli and simmer until tender. Serve with basic brown rice (page 441).

the bone marrow meat soup which always contained finely chopped vegetables and plenty of very yellow carrots; for the next course they had cooked fruit, with very little sweetening, and rolls make from freshly ground whole wheat, which were spread with the high-vitamin butter The wheat for the rolls was ground fresh every day in a motor driven coffee mill. Each child was also given two glasses of fresh whole milk. The menu was varied from day to day by substituting for the meat stew, fish chowder or organs of animals. . . Clinically this program completely controlled the dental caries of each member of the group. . . Several incidents of special interest occurred. Two different teachers came to me to inquire what had been done to make a particular child change from one of the poorest in the class in capacity to learn to one of the best. Dental caries is only one of the many expressions of our modern deficient nutrition. Weston Price DDS *Nutrition and Physical Degeneration*

TRADITIONAL POT ROAST

Serves 6-8

3 pounds rump roast
or other cut suitable for pot roast
1 quart buttermilk
butter and extra virgin olive oil
1 cup red wine
2 cups beef stock
several sprigs thyme, tied together
1/2 teaspoon green peppercorns, crushed
1 dozen small red potatoes
1 pound carrots, peeled and cut into sticks
2 tablespoons arrowroot
mixed with 2 tablespoons water
sea salt and freshly ground pepper

Traditionally in the German speaking areas of Europe, housewives marinated beef or game several days in buttermilk before cooking it. The results are extremely tender and flavorful.

Using a needle or skewer, stick the meat all over. Place in a bowl or glass loaf pan just large enough to contain the meat and pour butter milk over it. Allow to marinate in the refrigerator, turning occasionally, for several days.

Remove from buttermilk and dry off meat with paper towels. In a heavy, flame proof casserole, brown on all sides in butter and olive oil. Remove meat from casserole and pour out browning fat. Add liquids and seasonings. Bring to a boil and skim. Return pot roast to casserole and bake, covered for several hours or until tender. One hour before serving add potatoes and carrots.

Remove meat and vegetables and bring sauce to a boil on the stove. Add arrowroot mixture a spoonful at a time until desired thickness is obtained. Season to taste.

It has long been assumed that beef and eggs should be restricted in the diet because eggs and beef contain high levels of cholesterol.

The American Heart Association has recommended that cholesterol intake be reduced to 300 milligrams per day. The most current recommendations, however, call for dietary cholesterol levels to be reduced to even less that 300 milligrams per day, especially if one's blood cholesterol level is above 200 mg%.

To discover beef fat's effect on blood cholesterol levels, Reiser, a researcher, compared beef fat, coconut oil (another very saturated fat) and safflower oil (an unsaturated oil thought to be very desirable to one's health). It was found that when beef fat was added to the diet, blood cholesterol levels rose no more than when safflower oil was added.

Another researcher, according to Reiser, found that as beef fat was added to the diets of students with blood cholesterol levels of 140%, no increase in blood cholesterol could be measured. But in students with a blood cholesterol level of 190-195 mg%, beef fat consumption increased blood cholesterol levels to 210 mg%.

In another experiment, O'Brien tested the effect of red meat, fish, poultry, and three eggs daily on the blood cholesterol levels of test subjects. He found no difference in blood cholesterol levels in the test subjects regardless of which of the above foods they ate.

POT ROAST WITH CHILES

Serves 6-8

3 pounds rump roast
or other cut suitable for pot roast
1-2 cups red wine
butter and extra virgin olive oil
2 cups beef stock
2 ounces dried red chiles (hot or mild)
8 cloves garlic, peeled and chopped
3 tablespoons red wine vinegar
2 tablespoons tomato puree
1/4 teaspoon cinnamon
1/2 teaspoon dried green peppercorns, crushed
1/2 teaspoon dried oregano
several sprigs fresh thyme, tied together
sea salt and freshly ground pepper

Marinate meat in red wine for several hours or overnight. Remove from wine and dry off well with paper towels. In a heavy, flame proof casserole, brown the meat on all sides in butter and olive oil. Transfer meat to a plate and pour out browning fat.

Remove stems and seeds from chiles (Use rubber gloves for this.) Add all ingredients (except salt and pepper) to the casserole, bring to a boil, skim and return the roast to the pot. Bake in a 300 degree oven for several hours or until meat is tender.

Remove roast to a heated platter and keep warm in the oven. In a food processor, process the sauce in batches until smooth. Reheat the sauce in a sauce pan. If it is too thin, boil down for a bit. Season to taste. To serve, slice the beef and ladle sauce over each slice.

In one part of the trial, egg consumption increased blood cholesterol levels. However, in another part of the same trial eggs had no effect on blood cholesterol levels.

Another researcher compared beef tallow to corn oil in rats. He found liver fat (usually considered bad for health) was lower in the rats which were fed beef tallow compared to those which received corn oil.

Another recent investigator found that as men on a low fat, low cholesterol diet increased their stearic acid consumption, blood cholesterol levels dipped by 14%. LDL-cholesterol (the bad type) dipped by 21 % in subjects on the stearic acid.

According to this researcher, many scientific reports over the years have indicated that stearic acid does not raise blood cholesterol in man, "but the idea has not been widely accepted." Stearic acid is the major component of beef fat.

Many reports can be found indicating that egg consumption in a normal diet has no effect on long term blood cholesterol levels. In addition, egg consumption has never been shown to increase death rates in persons initially free of coronary heart disease. Some of the studies showing egg consumption to have no appreciable effect on blood cholesterol levels were with men who already suffered from cardiovascular disease.

In addition, it has now been discovered that eggs contain substantially less cholesterol than once thought (220mg/egg rather that the 300 mgs they were believed to have.) Chris Mudd *Cholesterol and Your Health*

LAMB CHOPS

Serves 4

8 lamb chops
freshly ground pepper
1/2 cup dry red wine
2 to 3 cups beef or lamb stock

You will need a very well-seasoned cast iron skillet for this recipe. Season the lamb chops with pepper and cut off any excess fat. Place the skillet over a moderately high fire. When it is hot, set four lamb chops in the pan. (No fat is required. The lamb chops will render their own fat, enough to keep the chops from sticking.) Cook about five minutes to a side, or until they are rare or medium rare. Keep in a warm oven while you are cooking the second batch, and preparing the sauce.

Pour the grease out of the pan and deglaze with the red wine and the beef stock. Boil rapidly, skimming off any dirty foam that rises to the top. Reduce to about 3/4 cup. The sauce should be the consistency of maple syrup.

Place the lamb chops on heated plates, with their accompanying vegetables, and spoon on the sauce.

The Congressional Record pointed out that Frederick Stare, professor of nutrition at Harvard, has accepted research funds from various food manufacturers. The Congressional Record said that food processing companies pay him a large personal salary for consulting with their boards of directors. Dr. Stare was at that time on the board of directors of food companies that put sugar in their canned beans. Which is Dr. Stare going to advocate, red meat or his company's sugar-laced canned beans? How do you think he will advise congressional committees asking his advice? H.L. Newbold MD *Type A Type B Weight Loss Book*

LEG OF LAMB WITH RED POTATOES

Serves 6

1 small leg of lamb
3 tablespoons butter
3 tablespoons Dijon mustard, smooth or grainy
1 onion, peeled and sliced
3 cloves garlic
several sprigs fresh thyme, rosemary or tarragon
a meat thermometer
12 new potatoes
1/2 cup dry white wine or vermouth
3-4 cups beef or lamb stock

Americans tend to overcook leg of lamb, so that it becomes tough and unpalatable. In France, the traditional Sunday *gigot* is served rare or medium rare. This is a much more nutritious and flavorful dish than the American version. The lamb is allowed to sit several days in the refrigerator before it is cooked—this allows the meat to partially autolyze, and contributes to tenderness and taste. The effect is the same as allowing game to hang until it becomes "ripe" and hence tender and flavorful.

Peal the garlic cloves but leave them whole. Place in the bottom of a stainless steal roasting pan along with the onion slices. Set the leg of lamb, fat side up, on a rack in the pan. Melt the butter and mix it thoroughly with the mustard. Brush this on the lamb and put sprigs of herbs on the top. Insert the meat thermometer. Set in an oven preheated to 400 degrees, and reduce heat immediately to 350. Cook until the thermometer registers rare or medium rare, about fifteen minutes to the pound. 1/2 hour before the roast finishes, strew the potatoes around the roast on the rack.

Remove the roast, set on a heater platter, and keep warm in the oven while finishing the potatoes and making the sauce. Remove the rack. Cut potatoes in half and place cut side down in the drippings. Bake another 1/2 hour or so until potatoes are soft. Transfer them to the heated latter. Pour wine into the pan and bring to a rapid boil. Add the stock. Stir well to deglaze the pan. Boil rapidly, skimming occasionally, until the sauce reduces to about 1 cup. Taste for seasoning. You probably won't need salt as the mustard contains salt that has made its way into the sauce. Strain into a heated sauce boat and spoon over thin slices of the lamb.

What to do with the leftovers? See Leg of Lamb Soup (page 191).

Variation: Leg of Lamb with Apricot Sauce

Using scissors, snip *1/2 cup dried unsulphured apricots* into strips. Soak in *1/2 cup red wine* for several hours. Add this to the sauce, omitting white wine. Serve with root vegetable medley (page 371).

From the strictly nutritional point of view, the macrobiotic diet has been reported to result in kwashiorkor (extreme protein deficiency) among strict adherents. A group of researchers at the University of Michigan made a study of babies who were maintained on the Zen macrobiotic diets and not only found that they were suffering from malnutrition, but further warned that mothers should not restrict their babies entirely to the macrobiotic diet. The Zen macrobiotic diet includes a special infant formula called Kokoh and the American Academy of Pediatrics Committee on Nutrition reported that infants fed on this baby formula from birth usually are underweight within a few months and below average in their total body length. Additional research and clinical observation found that babies who eat no animal protein fail to grow at a normal rate; this study found that infants on "vegan" diets, except for early breast feeding, did not grow nor develop as normally as babies on diets containing animal products or vegetarian diets supplemented with cow's milk. The American Academy of Pediatrics Committee on Nutrition stated that perhaps the most harmful diet for growing children is the Zen macrobiotic diet and reported that the results of such diet can be scurvy, anemia, hypoprotemenia, hypocalcemia, emaciation and even death. H. Leon Abrams *Vegetarianism: An Anthropological/Nutritional Evaluation*

STUFFED LEG OF LAMB

Serves 6-8

1 boned leg of lamb, butterfly cut
butter
1 medium onion, peeled and finely chopped
1 cup crispy pecans (page 485), chopped
6 cloves garlic, peeled and minced
1 cup cooked chopped spinach, well drained
1/2 cup mint leaves, chopped
zest of two oranges, finely grated
1 teaspoon dried thyme
1/4 teaspoon sea salt
freshly ground pepper
1/4 teaspoon cinnamon
1 egg, lightly beaten
2 tablespoons Dijon-type mustard
2 tablespoons butter
1 medium onion, peeled and sliced
1 cup dry white wine or vermouth
3-4 cups beef or lamb stock
juice of two oranges
sea salt

Open out the roast, cut several lengths of string and have them ready. To prepare stuffing, saute onion in butter. Add pecans, spinach, mint, garlic, zest, thyme, and cinnamon and blend well. Season to taste with salt and pepper. Allow to cool a minute and stir in the egg. Spread mixture on the roast, roll up and tie well at intervals.

Slice the second onion and spread it in a stainless steel roasting pan. Place the roast on a rack in the pan. Mix mustard with a little melted butter and brush the roast with the mixture. Bake about 1 1/2 to 2 hours at 350 degrees. Remove roast to a heated platter and keep warm while you make the sauce.

Remove rack from pan. Pour in wine and bring to a boil. Add stock and orange juice and boil vigorously, skimming occasionally, until sauce has reduced. Season to taste. Strain into a small saucepan and keep warm on lowest flame. To serve, slice the roast and arrange on individual serving plates. Ladle sauce over slices.

Did you know that your heart loves fat? The primary fuel used by the heart is fat. It specializes in the oxidation of fats into energy. Few people are aware of this fact, although it has been known by medical science for decades. No one is sure why the heart prefers fats above all other fuels. Possibly fats are a more efficient form of energy. The heart needs to be efficient in its energy production more so than any other organ. After all, our hearts never sleep—if your heart stopped to take a breather, you would be dead! The heart pumps 13,000 pints of fluid throughout the body each day. With this huge workload, it needs to have the most effective energy conservation mechanism possible. Fats are the most productive source, providing over twice the amount of energy per gram as do sugars, starches or proteins. Here again, the health of your heart depends upon a properly functioning liver—enter carnitine. Carnitine binds to the fatty acids and carries them into the heart's muscle cells. Once reaching the mitochondria, tiny factory-like organs located within the cells, carnitine releases the fatty acids. The mitochondria which are found within the heart cells in great number then burn the fats into energy. This energy is used to keep the heart pumping. Remember, the heart is the only organ in the body that never gets to rest.

RACK OF LAMB

Serves 4

1 rack of lamb
2 slices whole grain bread
2 tablespoons butter, softened
1 tablespoon finely chopped parsley
1/2 teaspoon sea salt
2 cloves garlic, peeled
1 medium onion, peeled and sliced
1/2 cup dry white wine or vermouth
3-4 cups beef or lamb stock
sea salt and freshly ground pepper

In the food processor, process the bread into bread crumbs. Add butter, sea salt and parsley and blend well. Spread this mixture on the top side of the rack of lamb. Place garlic cloves and sliced onion in a stainless steel roasting pan. Set the lamb on a rack in the pan and bake at 400 degrees for about 45 minutes. Lamb should be rare to medium rare.

Remove lamb to a heated platter and keep warm in the oven while making the sauce. Remove rack from the roasting pan. Pour in wine and bring to a boil. Add stock and boil rapidly, skimming occasionally, until liquid reduces and thickens. Strain into a saucepan and keep warm on a low flame. Season to taste. To serve, cut the rack of lamb between the ribs. Place two chops on each plate and spoon sauce over.

BUTTERFLY LEG OF LAMB

Serves 6-8

1 leg of lamb, bone removed and butterfly cut
1/2 cup fresh lemon juice
1/2 cup soy sauce

Score the lamb fat if it is very thick. Marinate several hours or all day in soy sauce and lemon juice. Broil or barbecue about 15-20 minutes per side. To serve, slice thinly across the grain. Lamb should be rare or medium rare. You may heat the marinade and serve as an accompaniment.

Those who promote a low fat, high-carbohydrate diet for heart disease never take the above mentioned facts into account. They neglect a most fundamental part of normal human physiology—that heart tissue prefers to utilize fat above all other dietary sources of caloric energy. Foods rich in fats such as meats, chicken, eggs, and nuts contain carnitine and other nutrients which help the body metabolize the fats which they naturally contain. This is another principle that the antinatural fat dieticians and nutritionists fail to grasp. Cass Igram MD *Eat Right to Live Longer*

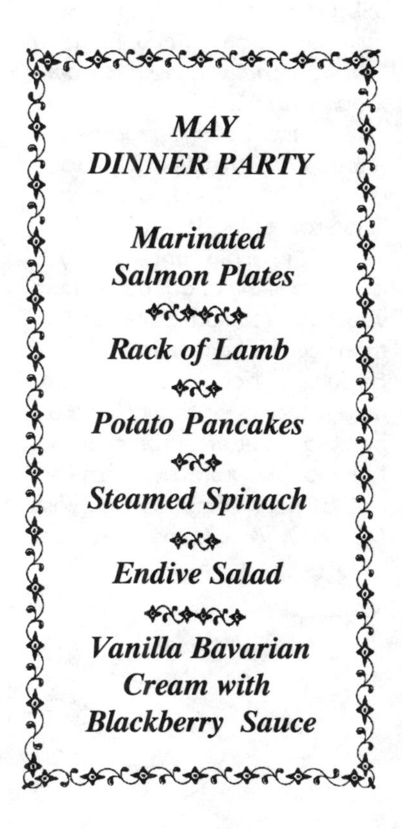

LAMB SHANKS

Serves 4

4 lamb shanks
1 cup red wine
butter and extra virgin olive oil
3 tablespoons vinegar
2 cups beef or lamb stock
2 tablespoons tomato paste
1/2 teaspoon dried oregano
1/2 teaspoon ground cumin
1/4 teaspoon cayenne pepper
3 cloves garlic, peeled and mashed
several sprigs thyme, tied together
sea salt and freshly ground pepper

Marinate lamb shanks in wine for several hours or overnight. Pat lamb shanks dry. In a heavy, flame proof casserole, brown the meat on all sides in butter and olive oil. Pour out browning fat. Add tomato paste, marinating wine and stock, bring to a boil, and skim. Add seasonings, except salt. Bake in a 300 degree oven for several hours or until lamb shanks are tender.

Remove lamb shanks to heated platter. Remove thyme. Bring sauce to a rapid boil, skimming occasionally, until it has reduced to about one-half and is thickened. Season to taste with sea salt.

The experts on the Senate Select Committee claim that countries with a high animal fat intake have higher rates of colon and breast cancer. This is simply not true. In fact, the opposite appears more likely.

Take Finland and the Netherlands for example. Their per capita daily animal fat consumption is the same. But the Dutch consume four times as much vegetable fat as the Finns, and they have twice the rate of colon and breast cancer. Many other examples could be cited.

Enig and co-workers at the University of Maryland did a statistical analysis of the same USDA data relied on by the Senate Committee. They found a "*strong significant positive correlation with*. . .vegetable fat, and *an essentially strong negative correlation*. . . with animal fat to total cancer deaths (and) breast and colon cancer incidence."

In plain language, you are more likely to get cancer from vegetable fat, such as margarine, than you are from animal fat such as butter. "Negative correlation" means that despite what the experts said, butter and other animal fats may be protective from cancer! William Campbell Douglass MD *The Milk of Human Kindness*

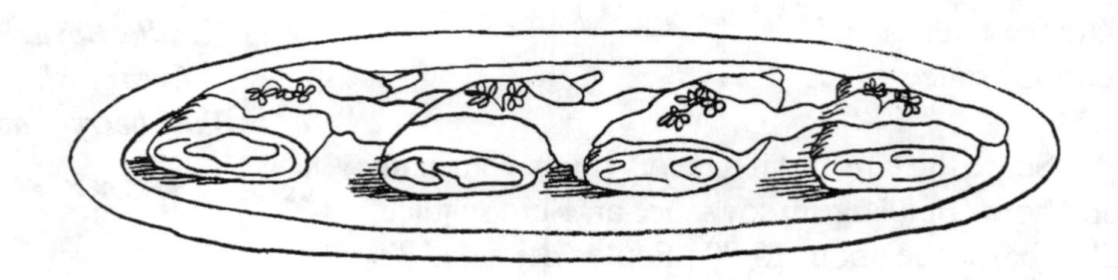

LAMB STEW

Serves 6-8

1 leg of lamb, cut into 2-inch pieces
1 cup red wine
butter and extra virgin olive oil
3-4 cups beef or lamb stock
several sprigs fresh thyme, tied together
1/2 teaspoon green peppercorns, dried
1/2 teaspoon whole cloves
several small pieces orange peel
4 cloves garlic, peeled and crushed
2 tablespoons tomato paste
2 tablespoon arrowroot mixed with 2 tablespoon water
sea salt and freshly ground pepper
1 pound turnips, scrubbed and quartered lengthwise
1 pound carrots, peeled and cut into sticks
1 pound small boiling onions, peeled
1/2 pound Chinese or sugar snap peas

Marinate lamb in wine for several hours or overnight. Remove from wine and dry off well with paper towels. (This is very important. If the meat is too damp, it will not brown.) In a heavy, flame-proof casserole, brown the meat in batches in butter and olive oil, removing to a plate. Pour out browning oil and add stock, wine used in the marinade and tomato paste. Bring to a boil and skim. Add seasonings. Return meat to casserole, along with the lamb bone, if you have it, cover and bake at 300 degrees for several hours or until meat is tender.

1/2 hour before serving, add turnips and carrots to the casserole. Saute the onions in butter and oil for about 20 minutes and add to stew.

Just before serving, add arrowroot mixture, 1 spoonful at a time, until desired thickness of sauce is obtained. Remove bone and thyme. Season to taste. Steam peas at the last minute and add to stew. Serve immediately.

Carnitine is an unusual amino acid that is biosynthesized in the liver of humans and is found highest in muscle and organ meats in the human diet. [The most abundant source of carnitine is lamb.] Carnitine is not found in vegetable sources. In human metabolism, it is utilized as a material which transfers fatty acids across the membranes of the mitochondria . . . where they can be used as a source of fuel to generate energy. In the absence of proper carnitine levels within the cell, the fatty acids are poorly metabolized and can build up within the cell or the surrounding medium, thereby leading to elevated blood fat and triglyceride levels. Carnitine has been found to have an important regulatory effect upon fat metabolism in heart and skeletal muscles. The administration of carnitine in tissue culture had been shown to stimulate fat metabolism and encourage the clearance of triglycerides and fatty acids.

Carnitine. . . is manufactured in the body from the amino acids lysine and methionine, but again not at levels adequate to meet the needs of all individuals, particularly if they are on a low lysine or methionine diet. . . The spermatozoa from lysine-depleted animals became infertile due to potential carnitine insufficiency. This is the first tissue to show deficiencies in animals that have been deprived of carnitine or lysine. . . There seem to be genetic limitations on the ability of some individuals to synthesize carnitine from lysine or methionine and therefor in these individuals carnitine may be an essential nutrient. Jeffrey Bland PhD *Octacosonal, Carnitine and other "Accessory" Nutrients*

INDIAN LAMB STEW

Serves 4-6

2 pounds lamb, cut into 3/4 inch pieces
1 cup yoghurt
1/2 teaspoon saffron threads
soaked in 2 tablespoons water
seeds of 5 cardamom pods
1 teaspoon cumin seeds
1 teaspoon coriander seeds
3 tablespoons butter
1 medium onion, finely chopped
2 cloves garlic, peeled and mashed
1 tablespoon grated ginger
3 tablespoons chopped green chile peppers
(hot or mild)
1/4 teaspoon ground turmeric
2-3 cups beef or lamb stock
juice of 3 limes or 1 large lemon
2 tablespoons arrowroot mixed with
2 tablespoons water
1/4 cup chopped fresh coriander
1 cup crispy almonds (page 487), chopped

Marinate the lamb in the yoghurt 12 to 24 hours in the refrigerator.

Spread the seeds on a plate and bake at 350 degrees for 10 to 15 minutes until browned. Set aside. Heat butter in a flame-proof casserole and saute the onions with cardamom, cumin and coriander seeds. Add lamb, marinade and stock, bring to a boil and skim. Add spices, garlic, ginger, chile peppers and lemon or lime juice. Cover the pot and simmer over low flame for about 1 1/2 hours, stirring occasionally. Add arrowroot mixture, a spoonful at a time, until desired thickness is obtained. Just before serving, stir in coriander leaves and almonds. Serve with basic brown rice (page 441) and fruit chutney (page 98).

The consequences of carnitine deficiency are many. In essence, fats can pile up throughout the arteries and within the cells, since without this key nutrient, they cannot be fully metabolized. The liver does make some carnitine on a daily basis. Vegetarians with high cholesterol and triglycerides are likely carnitine deficient, since few vegetables contain more than a trace of it. Meat products constitute the major sources. . . Carnitine-rich foods should be added freely to the diet despite their obvious fat content. Losses of carnitine from food due to cooking can be considerable. Meat, if cooked excessively, loses most of its carnitine. Broiled meats lose their carnitine in the juices; do pour the juice from the bottom of the pan over your meats. Make gravies with these juices and do not throw them out for fear of their fat content. Cass Igram MD *Eat Right to Live Longer*

Zinc is absorbed from the blood supply into the outer cortical areas of the brain where the highest levels of mental performance—memory, language, reason, insight—are controlled. If neurons in these cortical brain areas do not have access to zinc, their functions begin to deteriorate, and they cannot be activated or stimulated as easily with brain exercise. Several medical reports indicate the importance of dietary zinc for brain function. Herald Sandstead, one of the world's top experts on dietary zinc deprivation, reports that people who live in zinc-poor regions have deterioration of mental functions that can be alleviated with treatments of zinc. Michael D. Chafetz *Smart for Life*

MOROCCAN STYLE LAMB STEW

Serves 4-6

3 pounds lamb cut into 2-inch chunks
6 cloves garlic, peeled and mashed
1/2 cup extra virgin olive oil
4 teaspoons ground cumin
1 tablespoon freshly grated ginger
1 teaspoon sea salt
1 teaspoon ground turmeric
1 teaspoon paprika
1 teaspoon ground cinnamon
2 teaspoons dried green peppercorns, crushed
2-4 cups beef or lamb stock
1/4 teaspoon crumpled saffron threads
2 tablespoons arrowroot combined with 2 tablespoons water
15 black olives (optional)
1/4 cup chopped preserved lemons (page 96) or grated rind of one lemon
1 cup pitted prunes, chopped
1/4 cup chopped cilantro for garnish

Make a mixture of garlic, olive oil, cumin, ginger, salt, turmeric, paprika, cinnamon and pepper. Marinate lamb pieces in marinade for several hours or overnight.

Place marinated lamb and marinade in a heavy, flame-proof casserole along with stock. Bring to a boil and skim. Reduce heat to a simmer and add saffron. Bake in oven at 300 degrees for about 2 hours or until meat is tender. Stir in olives, lemons or lemon peel and prunes and simmer another 1/2 hour. Transfer casserole to medium flame on stove. Spoonful by spoonful add arrowroot mixture until desired thickness is obtained. Ladle into bowls and garnish with cilantro. Serve with brown rice and bulgur (page 441) or bulgur casserole (page 437).

Roger J. Williams Ph.D... . believes that since adults of widely different ethnic stock can physically thrive, without any cardiovascular symptom formation, on a high fat, high cholesterol, high caloric diet, "the evidence points strongly [contrary to popular medical thinking] toward the conclusion that the nutritional microenvironment of the body cells—involving minerals, amino acids, vitamins—is crucial, and that the amount of fat or cholesterol consumed is relatively inconsequential." William H. Philpott MD *Victory Over Diabetes*

Candida albicans resides in the lower bowel of the intestinal tract and consumes simple sugars and produces alcohol as one of its by products. While the yeast cells live off of sugar and carbohydrates, the HIV virus lives off of proteins that are not completely broken down in the stomach into their constituent amino acids. For harder to digest proteins like "glutens" in certain grains like wheat and "casein" in most dairy products and other proteins like eggs and meat cooked at high temperatures, the efficiency of protein digestion could drop to 60% or less. The higher the temperature the meat is cooked, the more coagulated the protein becomes and the harder it is for the digestive juices, like hydrochloric acid and pancreatic enzymes, to break down the proteins into simple amino acids. If 40% of the protein you ate passed into the colon undigested, the HIV virus could have a field day reproducing itself. Mark Konlee *Health Freedom News*

VEAL CHOPS

Serves 4

4 free-range veal chops
juice of one lemon
1/2 teaspoon dried thyme
butter and extra virgin olive oil
1/2 cup dry white wine or vermouth
2 cups beef stock

Trim any excess fat off the chops and marinate for several hours in the lemon juice and thyme. Wipe off thoroughly and brown in a heavy skillet, two at a time, on both sides in the butter and oil. Pour out browning oil and pour in the wine and stock. Bring to a rapid boil, skim and return the chops to the pan. Reduce heat to a simmer, cover and cook about 1/2 hour or until chops are tender. Remove chops to a heated platter and keep warm in the oven. Bring the liquid to a rapid boil, skimming occasionally, and let the sauce reduce to about 1/2 cup. Spoon over the chops and serve.

About the time we began exporting cokes and fast foods to the Soviet Union, we imported from the Russkies a book brimming over with secrets of long life. You judge who got the better deal.

Dr. G. Z. Pitskhelauri, famous Russian gerontologist, based his book *The Long Living of Soviet Georgia* on underlying reasons for the super longevity of residents of Georgia, supposedly the home of more 100-year-olds (and older) that any other area of the world. . .

Startling is the word for their typical diet, which contains two main items that are almost taboo in this country: fatty meats and whole milk products, as well as native sauces, herbs, various vegetable greens and a moderate amount of natural wines (non-sulphured.) James F. Scheer *Health Freedom News*

VEAL SCALLOPINI

Serves 6

1 1/2 pounds free-range veal scallopini
juice of 2 lemons
1 cup unbleached flour
1 teaspoon pepper
butter and extra virgin olive oil
1/2 cup cognac or dry white wine
2 cups beef stock
1 cup piima cream or creme fraiche (optional)

Trim the veal of any fat or gristle and pound on both sides with the small toothed side of a meat hammer. Marinate in lemon juice for several hours. Remove from marinade and dry meat very well with paper towels. (This is important. If the meat is too damp, it will not brown.) Dredge pieces well in mixture of flour and pepper. Using a heavy skillet brown scallopini in batches in butter and olive oil, transferring to a heated platter when done. Keepveal

A deficiency of vitamin B12 whatever its cause. . . leads to mental illness, often even more pronounced that the physical consequences. The mental illness associated with pernicious anemia. . . often is observed for several years. . . before any of the physical manifestations of the disease appear. . . Other investigators have also reported a higher incidence of low B12 concentrations in the serums of mental patients than in the population as a whole and have suggested that B12 deficiency, whatever its origin, may lead to mental illness. Linus Pauling PhD, *p11 Orthomolecular Psychiatry*

warm in the oven while making sauce. Pour out cooking oil and add cognac or wine to the pan. Bring to a rapid boil, add the stock and optional cream and let the liquid boil down, skimming occasionally, until you have about 1/2 cup. Season to taste. Pour sauce over veal and serve.

VEAL BIRDS

Serves 6

2 pounds free-range veal scallopini
1 cup basic brown rice (page 441)
1/2 cup dried apricots, chopped
grated rind of two lemons
1 bunch scallions, finely chopped
sea salt
butter and extra virgin olive oil
1 cup unbleached flour
1 teaspoon pepper
1/2 cup dry white wine
2-4 cups beef stock
juice of two lemons

Soak the apricot pieces in hot water for about one hour. Strain and mix them with rice, lemon rind and scallions. Season mixture to taste with sea salt. Trim the veal of any fat or gristle and pound on both sides with the small toothed side of a meat hammer. Place a spoonful of stuffing on each piece of veal, roll up and tie securely with string. Pat the birds dry with paper towel.

Dredge the veal birds in mixture of flour and pepper. In a heavy, flame proof casserole, brown the birds in batches in butter and olive oil, transferring to a plate for succeeding batches. Pour out browning oil and add wine to the pan. Bring to a rapid boil and add stock and lemon juice. Skim the sauce, return veal birds to the pan, cover and set in a 300 degree oven for about two hours.

When birds are tender, transfer to a heated platter. Bring the sauce to boil on the stove and reduce until it has thickened, skimming occasionally. Transfer the birds to individual plates and spoon sauce over them.

Taurine is an amino acid that is essential for the functioning of the heart muscle and the retina of the eye. Most of the taurine in your body is concentrated in your heart and eye; there is 100 to 400 times more taurine in these vital organs than in the bloodstream. Until recently, most nutritionists assumed that taurine (a nonessential amino acid) does not have to be absorbed from food, because it can be manufactured within the body through a chemical process involving the essential amino acids, methionine and cysteine.

However recent studies have shown that humans may have a critical nutritional need for dietary taurine. Scientists at the UCLA Medical Center in Los Angeles have found that lack of taurine in the diet leads to low blood taurine levels and retinal dysfunction. It was also found that a degenerative disease of the heart muscle in animals leading to heart failure can be completely reversed by the simple addition of taurine to their diet. Kurt W. Donsbach *Health Freedom News*

[For good vision] the first trait is adopting good habits of nutrition. Although the eyes and brain represent only 2% of our body weight, they require 25% of our nutritional intake. The eyes alone use one-third as much oxygen as the heart, need ten to twenty times as much vitamin C as the joint capsules involved in the movement of our extremities and require more zinc (our intelligence chemical) that any other organ system in the body. Claude A Valenti *PPNF Journal*

VEAL STEW

Serves 6

2 pound free-range veal stew meat
juice of two lemons
butter and extra virgin olive oil
1/2 cup white wine
4 cups beef stock
several small slices lemon rind
1/2 teaspoon green peppercorns, crushed
several sprigs fresh parsley, tied together
12 small red potatoes
1 pound carrots, peeled and cut into sticks
2 tablespoons arrowroot powder mixed with 2 tablespoons water
1/2 pound mushrooms
1/4 pound Chinese or sugar snap peas

Marinate the veal pieces in lemon juice for several hours. Dry thoroughly with paper towels. (Very important. If the meat is too damp it will not brown.) In a heavy, flame-proof casserole brown the meat in batches in the butter and olive oil. Transfer batches to a plate. Pour out browning oil and add the wine and stock. Bring to a rapid boil and skim. Add lemon peel, thyme and pepper. Add veal and any juices accumulated in the plate. Cover and cook for about 2 hours in a 300 degree oven. One hour before serving add potatoes and carrots.

Meanwhile wash, dry and saute the mushrooms, either sliced, quartered or whole (page 367). Prepare the peas and have ready for steaming at the last minute.

When meat and vegetables are tender, transfer the casserole to the stove and bring to a boil. Add arrowroot mixture, 1 spoonful at a time, until desired thickness is obtained. Just before serving, add the mushrooms and steamed peas. Ladle onto plates or soup bowls.

In deficiency of vitamin B12, slow and insidious brain, spinal cord, red and white blood cells abnormalities occur, some not reversible. Malabsorption, defective delivery, dietary absence or interference, bacterial overgrowth or parasites such as tapeworms are all important causes of deficiency. . . B12 seems to be synthesized only by microorganisms, wherever it is found in nature: on germs growing in the soil, sewerage and intestines. The main source appears to be the intestine of animals who chew their cud, thus the only real sources of B12 are essentially those of animal origin: liver, eggs, meat, milk and cheese. . . Vegetarians, particularly vegans, may experience a deficiency with insidious neurological damage occurring before it is noticed. This need to gain B12 from animal sources may explain why chimpanzees go on a rampage of killing and devouring other animals, as noted by the famous Jane Goodall. The very best form of cobalamin [B12] is only found in animal products. . . . Perhaps all the needs for vitamin B12 are not yet fully understood. It is also required for repairing and maintaining the spinal cord and perhaps other parts of the brain such as the myelin sheath. Kenneth Seaton *Health Freedom News*

VEAL MARROW BONES

(Osso Bucco)
Serves 6

6 1-inch slices free-range veal shanks
butter and extra virgin olive oil
1 large onion, coarsely chopped
2 carrots, peeled and coarsely chopped
1/2 cup dry white wine or vermouth
4 cups beef stock
4 tomatoes, peeled, seeded and chopped
or 1 can tomatoes
2 cloves garlic, peeled and mashed
several sprigs thyme, tied together
1/2 teaspoon dried green peppercorns, crushed
sea salt and freshly ground pepper

Tie the pieces of veal shank around the perimeter with string so that they hold together during cooking. Dry well with paper towels. In a heavy, flame proof casserole, brown the shanks, two at a time, in butter and olive oil, transferring to a plate. Pour out browning oil. Add wine and stock, bring to a boil and skim. Add tomatoes, garlic, and seasonings. Return veal to the casserole, cover and bake at 300 degrees for several hours or until tender.

Remove osso bucco to a platter, remove thyme and reduce the sauce by boiling, skimming occasionally. Spoon over the shanks and serve. This is excellent with polenta (page 461) or basic brown rice (page 441).

The overemphasis on unsaturated fats in the American diet, and vegetarians particularly, may lead to a brand new disease epidemic in the next 10-20 years. It is called Ceroid Storage Disease. Ceroid is a wax-like pigment that is formed from the heating of unsaturated fatty acids. It's called polymerization and you may polymerize yourself to an early grave if you get too fanatic about vegetarianism.

Let's look at a typical case of this new disease. A young man came to the emergency room complaining of bellyache. The operation revealed a spleen filled with ceroid. His history was interesting. He had been fed soy bean milk as an infant. As an adult he followed a strict vegetarian diet for religious reasons. This diet consisted of soy bean and wheat protein cooked in corn and Wesson oil. A perfect setup for ceroid storage disease. As pure vegetarianism becomes more popular, ceroid storage disease maybe come more common. William Campbell Douglass MD *The Milk of Human Kindness*

Whenever eating meat—chops, steaks, roast, etc.—one would be wise to eat part of the fat, as it is essential to good health. Too often we turn up our noses at the fat, and thus waste the part that is of prime importance for balanced nutrition. H. Leon Abrams *Your Body is Your Best Doctor*

GROUND MEATS

Ground meats are fine, as long as they are freshly ground and the meat is of good quality. The beauty of ground meat dishes is that almost any type of meat can be used in their preparation. Try substituting buffalo meat in dishes that traditionally call for beef or lamb. If you have hunters in your family, you can use ground venison or other game in any of these recipes. A small amount of chopped cooked liver or brain may also be added. If you prefer not to eat red meat, ground chicken or turkey can always be substituted, but be careful—as their fat contains a high content of polyunsaturates, ground turkey and chicken spoil more quickly than red meats. The results will also probably be more dry than the same dish prepared with red meat.

Speaking of fat, the question arises as to whether we should buy lean ground meats instead of regular. We suggest you buy regular ground for several reasons. The first is that while most of the fat cooks out of a dish made from regular ground meat, the result is still more tender, flavorful and juicy than the same recipe prepared with lean meat. Lean meat also looses moisture when it cooks, but the moisture it looses is in the form of water, so the end results can be quite dry. Remember that we need animal fats in our diet—fats are where animals store all the goodness of the grains and grasses that they eat. Finally, regular ground meats are less expensive; and the extra dollar per pound you pay for lean ground meat is essentially wasted during cooking. You should however, avoid preparing ground meats such as hamburgers and sausage on the barbecue, because this method of cooking results in the formation of many potent carcinogens. Cook hamburgers and similar meats in a heavy cast iron skillet to minimize their presence in the final product.

Our readers may have noticed that we do not have a chapter on pasta in our book, simply because pasta, even and especially whole grain pasta, is difficult to digest due to the fact that pasta flour in general has not been soaked, fermented or sprouted. Nevertheless, nobody expects today's mothers to raise children without preparing spaghetti for them once in a while. For this reason, we have included two spaghetti sauce recipes, one of which can be made without tomato products. Serve these with oriental pasta made from brown rice or buckwheat flour.

We have included many ethnic dishes that use ground meats including stuffed peppers, stuffed cabbage, moussaka, meat loaf, chile and lamb pastries. These are delicious and comforting preparations, flavorful alternatives to junk foods and good for parties, buffets and large family meals. Finally, we have included recipes for sausage made of chicken, turkey or lamb—all good alternatives to pork, delicious with grains and pulses, or with eggs or pancakes at the beginning of your day.

SPICY MEAT LOAF

Serves 8

2 pounds ground beef or other red meat
1 medium onion, peeled and finely chopped
1 carrot, peeled and finely chopped
1 stalk celery, finely chopped
3 tablespoons butter
1/2 teaspoon cayenne pepper
1 teaspoon dried thyme
1 teaspoon cracked pepper
1 teaspoon sea salt
1/1/2 cups whole grain bread crumbs
1 cup cream
1 egg
1 tablespoon Worcestershire sauce (non-MSG variety)
4 tablespoons tomato paste or naturally sweetened ketchup

Saute onions, carrots and celery in butter until soft. Add cayenne pepper, thyme, pepper and salt and stir around. Meanwhile, soak bread crumbs in cream.

Have a 9-by-13 pyrex pan ready. Using your hands, mix meat with sauteed vegetables, soaked bread, egg and worcestershire sauce. Form into a loaf and set in the pan. Ice with ketchup or tomato paste. Add about 1 cup water to the pan. Bake at 350 degrees for about 1 1/2 hours. Serve with sauerkraut (page 84) or ginger carrots (page 87).

Leftovers are great on sandwiches!

Know Your Ingredients

Name This Product # 17

Enriched macaroni, dried cheddar cheese, corn starch, partially hydrogenated soybean oil, dried tomato, salt, buttermilk, sugar, hydrolyzed vegetable protein and other natural flavorings, dried onion, dried corn syrup, disodium phosphate, dried garlic, sodium caseinate, citric acid, dipotassium phosphate, FD&C yellow No. 5 and other artificial color, sodium sulfite and BHA.

See Appendix B for Answer

According to the anthropologists, man was a meat-eater long before he took up Caesar salad. And if you think man ascended from the ape, then there is further proof that humans have always been carnivorous. It has always been assumed that primates were strictly vegetarians. Nothing could be further from the truth. Goodall studied apes in their natural habitat and discovered that they eat meat on a regular basis. . . the National Zoo in Washington attempted to breed Amazonian monkeys. They were fed a total fruit diet and nothing happened. Within weeks of feeding meat to the monkeys, normal mating took place and many healthy babies were born. William Campbell Douglass MD *The Milk of Human Kindness*

FOURTH OF JULY DINNER

Hamburgers with Spelt Buns

Homemade Mayonnaise
Corn Relish
Pickled Cucumber Slices
Sliced Tomato and Red Onion

Three Bean Salad

Corn on the Cob

Ginger Ale

Stars and Stripes Carrot Cake

John Ott, of time-lapse photography fame... tested three young athletes who ate hamburgers, with all the trimmings, that were prepared in a fast food restaurant. The first group of the hamburgers were cooked in the restaurant's microwave oven while another was prepared conventionally in an iron frying pan. This latter group and even the raw hamburgers held in hand resulted in strong muscle test results while the same athletes tested muscularly weak with the microwave cooked food. Ott also reported most food prepared in these appliances and especially meat, was less tasty. This opinion seems to be shared by most who use this form of cooking. George Meinig DDS *NewTrition*

HAMBURGERS

Serves 6

2 pounds ground beef or buffalo

Form meat into 6 patties about 1 inch thick. Heat a heavy cast iron skillet over a medium flame. When skillet is hot, add three patties. Cook about 7 or 8 minutes per side—hamburgers should be medium rare. Keep warm in oven while preparing the second batch.

Serve with whole grain hamburger buns (commercially available spelt buns are recommended), ketchup (page 95), mayonnaise (page 126), pickled cucumber slices (page 89), corn relish (page 93) and thinly sliced onions.

SPAGHETTI SAUCE

Serves 8

2 pounds ground beef or other red meat
2 onions, peeled and finely chopped
1 green pepper, seeded and finely chopped
3 tomatoes, peeled, seeded and chopped or 1 can tomatoes, drained and coarsely chopped
1 small can tomato paste
1 cup beef stock
1/2 cup red wine
1/2 pound chicken livers
2 tablespoons butter
1 teaspoon each dried thyme, rosemary, oregano and sage
sea salt and freshly ground pepper

Saute meat in a large pot until it becomes crumbly and all the pink is gone. You may pour out the melted fat, but it is not necessary. Meanwhile, saute the chicken livers in butter until cooked through. Cut into a fine dice. Add chopped livers and remaining ingredients to the beef, blend well, season to taste and simmer, covered, for about 1/2 hour. Serve with buckwheat or brown rice noodles.

TOMATO FREE SPAGHETTI SAUCE

Serves 8

2 pounds ground beef or other red meat
2 medium onions, peeled and finely chopped
3 cups beef stock
1 cup red wine
2 tablespoons snipped fresh rosemary leaves or 1 tablespoon dried rosemary
sea salt and freshly ground pepper

Saute ground meat in a heavy skillet until crumbly. Add onions, stock, wine and rosemary. Bring to a boil and cook uncovered for 15 to 30 minutes until liquid has reduced to almost nothing. Season to taste. Serve with buckwheat or brown rice noodles.

STUFFED PEPPERS

Serves 6

6 green peppers
1 pound ground beef or other red meat
1 medium onion, peeled and finely chopped
1 small can tomato paste
1 cup beef stock
1/2 teaspoon each thyme, rosemary and oregano, fresh or dried
2 cups basic brown rice (page 441)
1/4 cup toasted pine nuts
sea salt and freshly ground pepper
1 cup grated Parmesan or cheddar cheese

Carefully remove stems from peppers, slice in half lengthwise and remove seeds. Brown meat in a heavy skillet until crumbly. Add onion, tomato paste, stock and herbs. Bring to a boil and cook until liquid has reduced by about one half. Stir in rice and pinenuts and season to taste.

Set the pepper halves in a buttered pyrex dish, fill each with stuffing and top with cheese. Bake for about 1 hour at 350 degrees.

If you're buying extra-lean ground beef to lessen your intake of fat and cholesterol and think that the extra cost is worthwhile, think again!

That's the finding of nutritionists Kenneth Prusa and Karla Hughes, at the University of Missouri at Columbia who conducted an experiment to decide this very issue.

These researchers broiled hamburgers made from 100 grams of three grades of ground beef: regular, lean and extra-lean. And what did they fine? That the broiling process almost leveled out the cholesterol and fat content of the hamburger.

The remaining fat content varies by just five percent, despite a three-fold difference in the raw meat. (Regular hamburger has 28.5 percent fat content, compared with extra lean meat's nine percent.)

However, other surprising things happened during broiling. The higher-fat hamburger lost mainly fat and cholesterol, while leaner patties lost moisture. Is it logical that regular hamburger would cook down appreciably more in weight than lean and extra-lean? Actually, it cooked down only four percent more than the others.

Hughes stated that lean and extra-lean hamburger may not be worth the premium price compared with the regular grinds.

Then came the crusher to leaner grinds. A trained panel of hamburger tasters voted in favor of regular grinds because they were juicier and more tender! James F. Scheer *Health Freedom News*

SPICY STUFFED CABBAGE

Serves 6

1 large cabbage
1 pound ground red meat or turkey
2 medium onions, peeled and finely chopped
2 cups basic brown rice (page 441)
1/2 cup raisins
1/4 cup snipped fresh dill
2 cloves garlic, peeled and mashed
2 teaspoons ground cumin
1/2 teaspoon cinnamon
1/8 teaspoon ground cloves
sea salt and freshly ground pepper
1/4 cup pine nuts, toasted
1 egg, lightly beaten
4 cups beef or chicken stock
2 tomatoes, peeled, seeded and coarsely chopped
2 tablespoons arrowroot plus
2 tablespoons water (optional)

Remove core from the cabbage and set, core side down, in a large pot containing about 2 inches of water. Cover and steam about 15 minutes. Remove wilted outer leaves and steam a bit longer if necessary, to soften inner leaves. Strew leaves on a tea towel to drain and set aside.

Brown meat in a heavy skillet until crumbly and add onion, rice, raisins, pine nuts, herbs, spices salt and pepper to taste. Let cool slightly and stir in the egg. Place a spoonful of stuffing in each cabbage leaf, fold in sides and roll up. Arrange in several layers in a flame proof casserole, cover with stock, and tomato pieces. Bring to a boil and transfer to the oven. Bake at 300 degrees about 1 hour.

Remove cabbage rolls to a platter (use tongs for this) and keep warm in the oven. Return the casserole and its liquid to the stove. Bring to a boil and cook vigorously about 15 minutes, skimming occasionally, until stock has reduced and thickened. If sauce seems too thin, add arrowroot mixture, spoonful by spoonful, until desired thickness is obtained.

To serve, place two or three cabbage rolls on each plate and spoon sauce over them.

To distinguish the "strict" vegetarian diet from the easier regime allowing dairy products, it became the custom to call the strict dieters *vegans* and the others *lacto-vegetarians*. . . vegens run a serious risk of deficiency diseases owing to the difficulties of providing, with a vegetable diet, all the essential materials that the human body cannot synthesize for itself. Vitamin B12 is one of these, and vegans often get anemia. . . Other materials are the essential amino-acids, some of which are not included in very large amounts in the vegetable proteins in nuts and pulses, and vegans can suffer from a kind of kwashiorkor arising not from a gross shortage of protein, but from a lack of some of the essential building-blocks for it. Terence McLaughlin *A Diet of Tripe*

Most people are prone to think that eating fat makes fat, however fat does not make fat in the body. A healthy body must have fat to carry on its vital processes. Carbohydrates—the grains, bread, starches, and sugar—are the foods that make fat—and it is these foods that must be curtailed for the person who has great difficulty with obesity. People who wish to lose weight should give up grains, sugar and starches until their desired weight is attained, then they should eat grains and starches only moderately. H. Leon Abrams *Your Body is Your Best Doctor*

STUFFED CABBAGE, ORIENTAL STYLE

Serves 6

1 head cabbage
2 pounds ground turkey
1 cup basic brown rice (page 441)
2 bunches minced scallions
2 tablespoons toasted sesame oil
1 tablespoon freshly grated ginger
2 tablespoons soy sauce
1/4 teaspoon red chile flakes
1 bunch cilantro, minced
sea salt and freshly ground pepper
4 cups chicken or turkey stock
2 tablespoons arrowroot plus 2 tablespoons water (optional)

Remove the core from cabbage and set, core side down, in a large pot containing about 2 inches of water. Cover and steam about 15 minutes. Remove wilted outer leaves and steam a bit longer if necessary, to soften inner leaves. Strew leaves on a tea towel to drain and set aside.

Brown the meat in a heavy skillet until crumbly. Stir in scallions, rice and seasonings. Place a spoonful of stuffing in each cabbage leaf, fold in sides and roll up. Arrange in several layers in a flame proof casserole, and cover with stock. Bring to a boil and transfer to the oven. Bake at 300 degrees about 1 hour.

Remove cabbage rolls to a platter (use tongs for this) and keep warm in the oven. Return the casserole and its liquid to the stove. Bring to a boil and cook vigorously about 15 minutes, stirring occasionally, until stock has reduced and thickened. If sauce seems too thin, add arrowroot mixture, spoonful by spoonful, until desired thickness is obtained.

To serve, ladle sauce into individual plates and place two or three cabbage rolls on top.

Babies fed a strict vegetarian diet. . . do not grow at a normal rate. They get shortchanged on B12, folic acid, zinc, calories, proteins, calcium and riboflavin (B2). Even a *breast-fed* baby may become malnourished if the mother has been a true vegetarian for a number of years.

The Seventh Day Adventists are often cited as a good example of why you shouldn't eat meat. They have much less heart disease and cancer. But they eat plenty of dairy products and eggs, and they don't use tobacco, alcohol, coffee, tea, or cola beverages. William Campbell Douglass MD *The Milk of Human Kindness*

The propaganda blitz has been so awesome that even the New England Journal of Medicine. . . has abandoned science and swallowed the killer-cholesterol line. "The optimal intake of cholesterol," they editorialize, "is probably zero, meaning the avoidance of animal products."

After making this wrong-headed and unscientific statement, they temporize by admitting that "sound data are needed," "The lack of more direct human evidence remains frustrating," "In the absence of fully satisfactory data,. . . a reasonable policy would seem to admit uncertainty,. . . and we must 'hedge our bets.'" There is a certain wistfulness to this editorial as if they were saying, "Would someone please prove that our dietary recommendations have some scientific justification?" William Campbell Douglass MD *Eat Your Cholesterol*

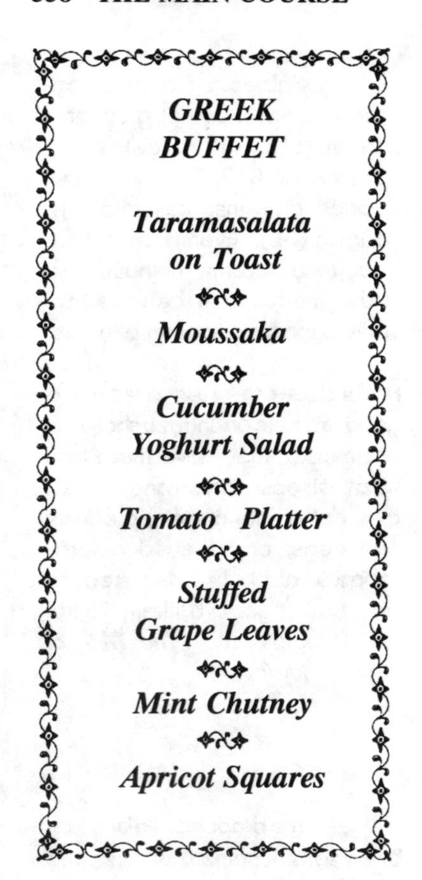

MOUSSAKA

Serves 12-18

8-10 large eggplants
extra virgin olive oil
4 pounds ground lamb
3 medium onions, minced
8 ripe tomatoes, peeled seeded and coarsely chopped or 2 cans tomatoes, drained and coarsely chopped
1 cup beef or lamb stock
1 teaspoon cinnamon
sea salt and freshly ground pepper
2 cups grated cheddar or Parmesan cheese

Moussaka makes a wonderful buffet dish and it is a welcome and healthier alternative to lasagna. You will need a rectangular pan that is at least 2 inches deep—a stainless steel baking pan will do nicely. Do not make the mistake of skimping on the eggplant—that is what gives this dish its distinctive character. Traditional recipes call for a layer of boiled-milk-based bechamel on top of the casserole. This makes for a rather indigestible combination. A scattering of grated cheese serves just as well to produce an appetizing crust.

Cut ends off eggplants and peel. Cut into 3/8 inch lengthwise slices. Salt and set aside, covered with a towel, for about 1 hour. Rinse slices well, dry off, and place on well oiled cookie sheets. Generously brush top sides with oil, grill under broiler until lightly browned.

Meanwhile, cook the lamb in a large pan until crumbly. Add onions, tomatoes, stock, cinnamon and salt and pepper to taste. Bring to boil, skim and let simmer, uncovered, until most of the liquid is evaporated.

Oil the baking pan. Arrange a layer of eggplant on the bottom, then a thin layer of meat, using a slotted spoon. Repeat for at least two more layers for at least three layers of eggplant, but four is better. Sprinkle cheese on top. Bake at 350 degrees for 1 hour.

Rat colonies maintained during their whole lives on conventional human-style diets, or even on diets supplemented artificially with minerals and vitamins, develop many pathological conditions not seen in rats during the abbreviated course of vitamin essaying. It is difficult to avoid the inference that the appearance of disease in long-term vitamin-supplemented diet experiments presages the need of the organism for all food constituents, including food enzymes, if optimal health and longevity are to be attained. Edward Howell MD *Enzymes for Health and Longevity*

LAMB MEATBALLS

Serves 6

2 pounds ground lamb
1 medium onion, finely diced
extra virgin olive oil
1 tablespoon dried rosemary or thyme
2 eggs
2 cups whole grain bread crumbs
1 cup cream
sea salt and freshly ground pepper
unbleached flour
1 cup red wine
2-3 cups beef or lamb stock
3-4 ripe tomatoes, peeled, seeded and chopped or 1 can whole tomatoes, drained and chopped
2 cups spinach, chard, kale or beet greens, coarsely chopped

Saute onion and rosemary in olive oil until soft. Meanwhile soak bread crumbs in cream. Mix onion mixture, eggs, bread crumbs and salt and pepper with ground lamb. Form into 1-inch balls. Dredge in flour and saute until golden in olive oil. Pour out browning oil and deglaze pan with red wine. Add stock and tomatoes and reduce by boiling until sauce thickens, skimming occasionally. Add meatballs and chopped greens to sauce and simmer for about 10 minutes or until cooked through. Serve with basic brown rice (page 441) or buckwheat or brown rice noodles.

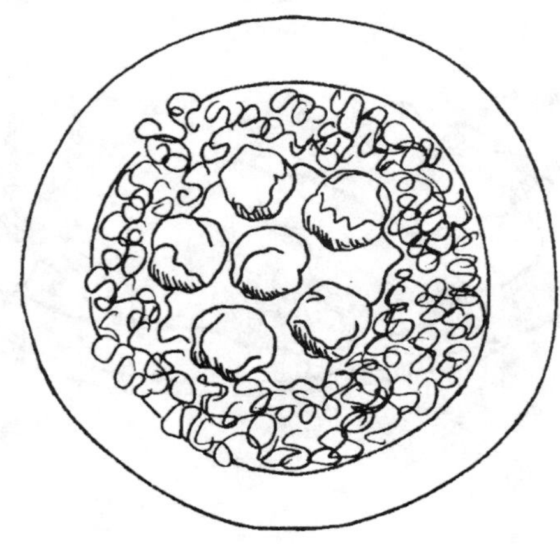

The American Heart Association . . . has gone way out on a limb concerning fat and cholesterol in our diet. They have recommended a shift to less milk, eggs, meat—what they mistakenly call "saturated" fats—to a diet containing more margarine, fish, and vegetable oils. They are *committed*. They must continue to support their completely untenable and nutritionally disastrous position or admit that they have made a terrible mistake.

The American Heart Association, the principle promoter of the fat-cholesterol theory of atherosclerosis, is now going after the children and recommending low-cholesterol diets for *3 year olds*. But the American Academy of Pediatrics is striking back. They point out that cholesterol is vital in growing children for the formation of bile salts, hormones and nerve tissue. *There is no population of children that has been raised on such a radical diet.* Yet the American Heart Association assures America's mothers that "there appear to be no demonstrated major hazards involved" if the kids follow the AHA's radical diet plan. But they go on to admit that ". . . several epidemiologic studies. . . have failed to observe significant correlations among dietary fat, serum cholesterol concentrations and coronary heart disease rates". . .In one study by Pearce and Dayton that the AHA did *not* mention, it was found that eight year olds on a low cholesterol, high unsaturated fat diet caused a twofold increase in *cancer*. . . But the AHA is recommending a drastic increase to *20% unsaturated fat.* William Campbell Douglass MD *The Milk of Human Kindness*

SAMOSAS

(Spicy Lamb Pastries)
Makes about 20

1 recipe basic yoghurt dough (page 459)
2 pounds ground lamb
2 medium onions, peeled and finely chopped
1/2 cup toasted pine nuts
1/2 teaspoon cinnamon
1/4 teaspoon cayenne pepper
sea salt
1 bunch cilantro, chopped
sea salt and freshly ground pepper
grated rind of 2 lemons
melted butter

In a heavy skillet, cook the lamb until crumbly. Remove with a slotted spoon. Add onions, pine nuts, and seasonings.

Roll dough out on a pastry cloth and cut into 3 to 4 inch rounds. Place a tablespoon of filling on each and spread to within 1/2 inch of edges. Fold edges up and pinch together to form a three sided pastry, leaving a small hole in the middle for air to escape. Place on well greased pans and brush with butter. Bake at 350 degrees for about 40 minutes or until golden. Serve with yoghurt sauce (page 131) or ginger carrots (page 87).

If you have a few spoonfuls of meat stuffing left over, use to make a sausage omelet (page 415).

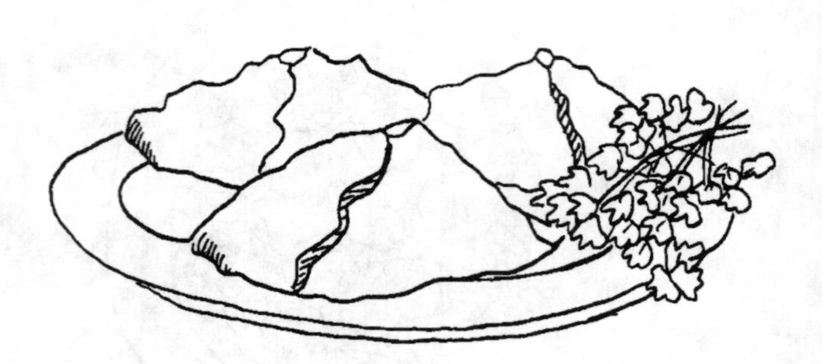

No two soils have exactly the same history, topography and climate, and soil-mineral differences may occur within the same fence lines. Albrecht [the soil specialist] visited a famous Hereford farm in Missouri and found an entire beef herd seriously afflicted with diseases that doctoring seemed unable to cure. On another farm nearby he found a similar herd in practically perfect health. Oddly, the herd on the second farm was started by animals born and brought up on the first farm. The health difference was a soil difference. The first man had been operating for fifty years on the same farm and had not maintained soil minerals. The second man, a newcomer, had taken sound advice and built up his soils. "Are We Starving to Death?" *The Saturday Evening Post* 1945

Man has been eating meat and fat for thousands of years, but hardening of the arteries is a new disease. My father, practicing medicine in Georgia fifty years ago, rarely saw a heart attack. Heart attacks have only become common since the advent of homogenized pasteurized milk, oleomargarine, and the increased consumption of polyunsaturated vegetable oils. William Campbell Douglass MD *The Milk of Human Kindness*

CHICKEN PATTIES

Makes 8-10 patties

2 pounds ground chicken
1 cup cooked spinach, chopped and well drained
1 medium onion, peeled and finely chopped
1/2 red pepper, finely chopped
2 cups whole grain bread crumbs
1 cup cream
2 eggs
1/4 teaspoon cayenne pepper
1 teaspoon sea salt
1/2 teaspoon dried thyme
extra virgin olive oil

Soak bread crumbs in cream. Mix all ingredients (except olive oil) and form into patties. Brush with olive oil and bake at 350 for about 25 minutes; or saute in a little butter.

BREAKFAST TURKEY SAUSAGE

Serves 6

1 pound ground turkey
1 small onion, peeled and finely chopped
1/4 teaspoon each cumin, marjoram, pepper, oregano, cayenne pepper, nutmeg and ginger
1/2 teaspoon each dried basil, thyme, sage
2 teaspoons sea salt
2 tablespoons whole grain bread crumbs
1 egg, lightly beaten
butter

Mix all ingredients, and chill well. Form into patties and saute in a little butter.

To store in freezer, form into a roll, wrap in plastic wrap and freeze. Thaw at room temperature several hours, or in the refrigerator overnight, remove plastic wrap, slice into patties and cook in a little butter.

A low fat, low cholesterol diet seems reasonable. Increased amounts of cholesterol and saturated fats in the diet will cause, on the average, an increase in the blood cholesterol level. The higher the levels of cholesterol in an individual, the greater his chances are of developing heart disease and of having a heart attack. Therefore, it seems obvious that a low fat, low cholesterol diet, with or without medicine, will cause a decrease in both heart disease mortality and in total mortality.

There is a problem with this simple deduction, however, that the medical community has chosen to overlook. The above supposition is incorrect. There is very little scientific evidence to directly indicate that reducing cholesterol and saturated fat in the diet will prolong an individual's life.

For years the medical profession has chosen to ignore scientific evidence from numerous studies that indicate such a diet may not increase an individual's life span and reduce total mortality. Now the medical community may be ready to back off a bit and at least partially replace the cholesterol theory with the idea that genetics may be the primary culprit in CHD [coronary heart disease]. The problem here is, obviously, that no one has control over his genetic makeup.

I would like to ask a simple question here. If genetics is a primary cause of CHD, why was there such a great increase in deaths from coronary heart disease between the mid 1920's and 1968? Did our genes change in a matter of just a few decades? Chris Mudd *Cholesterol and Your Health*

SPICY LAMB SAUSAGE

Makes about 20 small patties

2 1/4 pounds ground lamb or other red meat
1/2 cup sun dried tomato bits
1 medium onion, peeled and finely chopped
1/2 red bell pepper, finely chopped
extra virgin olive oil
2 tablespoons tomato paste
2 cloves garlic, peeled and mashed
1/4 cup toasted pine nuts
1/2 cup fresh cilantro, chopped
1 tablespoon fresh mint, chopped
1/2 teaspoon ground allspice
1 teaspoon cayenne pepper
1 teaspoon cumin
1 teaspoon ground coriander
2-3 teaspoons sea salt
1 teaspoon coarsely ground black pepper
1/4 cup fresh lemon juice
2 eggs, lightly beaten

Saute onions, peppers and tomato bits in olive oil until soft. Mix all ingredients together and form into patties. Saute about 7 minutes on a side in a heavy skillet brushed with olive oil.

The most dramatic failure to prove the cholesterol connection came when the Multiple Risk Factor Intervention Trial (MRFIT) collapsed in 1982. This long term study was meant to provide conclusive answers about the causes of heart disease. Five to six thousand men would be "put under intensive treatment. . . not only for reduction of cholesterol, by diet or drugs, but also for reduction of smoking and high blood pressure." The experimental group would then be compared to a control group who had received "usual care" from their own doctors. The results were resoundingly inconclusive. The difference in heart attack rates between the two groups was statistically insignificant. . . Most importantly "the cholesterol question. . . remains unresolved after two decades of controversy. . . The benefits of cholesterol reduction—and cholesterol's causal role in heart disease—remain uncertain." Joseph D. Beasley MD and Jerry J. Swift MA *The Kellogg Report*

Cutting out cholesterol to avoid heart attacks increases the risk of dying by violent means, according to a study published Friday in the British Medical Journal. . . researchers. . . found a low-cholesterol diet appeared to make people more aggressive. They said that in 1980, US average mortality rate from motor vehicle accidents, murders and suicides among middle-aged white males was 62 per 100,000 people, as against 107 per 100,000 among people trying to cut their cholesterol level. Attempts to cut cholesterol, the researchers said, "do not have a robust favorable effect on overall survival." *Reuters Wire Service*

A CATALOG OF VEGETABLES

A CATALOG OF VEGETABLES

The American love affair with fast food is almost incomprehensible considering the great variety of fresh vegetables now available year round in every American town. Only a few take advantage of this cornucopia. Most Americans eat vegetables rarely, and when they do their choices are confined to a few favorites—carrots, peas, tomatoes and potatoes. Yet fresh vegetables can be the highlight of every meal. Few of them require much time to prepare and most need very little time to cook. Furthermore, almost every vegetable that has been studied has been found to contain substances that benefit the heart and blood or counteract the formation of tumors. Fresh vegetables, eaten on a daily basis along with the right fats, are one of our best protections against coronary heart disease and cancer.

Steaming is the best way to cook most vegetables. This preserves most vitamins and minerals, and a good many enzymes as well, if the process is not allowed to continue too long. Light sauteing in butter or olive oil is also an acceptable cooking method. Some research indicates that cooking foods in oil actually makes nutrients more available. Other methods include blanching in boiling water and, for root vegetables, cooking in a clay pot.

While we recommend the inclusion of much raw food in the diet, some vegetables are best eaten cooked. For example, chemicals that block the production of thyroid hormone (known medically as goitrogens) occur in cabbage, broccoli, Brussels sprouts and kale. Substances that irritate the mouth and intestinal tract (called oxalate raphides) occur in beets, spinach and chard. Raw potatoes contain substances (called hemagglutinins) that disrupt the proper function of red blood cells. Cooking destroys or neutralizes these harmful substances (as does the fermentation process). Spinach and cabbage are popular salad foods, but should be eaten raw only occasionally.

It may sound like heresy, but we do not recommend saving vegetable cooking water. Adelle Davis was the first popular nutrition writer to suggest reusing cooking water, on the premise that vitamins and minerals lost from vegetables during cooking end up in the water. This may well be true, but unfortunately a lot of other things end up in the water as well—pesticides and nitrites from commercially grown produce along with many of the harmful compounds listed above. The solution is to steam lightly and not very long. Most of the vitamins and minerals will remain in the vegetables where they belong, and the small loss will be compensated by the fact that light cooking makes the nutrients in vegetables more readily available and assimilated.

There are several broad categories of vegetables. First are the dark green, leafy vegetables such as spinach, kale, chard and beet greens. These contain abundant vitamins and minerals, particularly B vitamins, calcium and trace minerals, and should be included in the diet on a regular basis—at least once or twice a week. A second category is the cruciferous vegetables—cabbage, Brussels sprouts, cauliflower and broccoli—that contain natural chemicals shown to block the formation of tumors in the digestive tract. Other categories are tubers (potatoes and sweet potatoes), root vegetables (carrots, turnips, parsnips and beets), the squash family (includes zucchini), the lily family (onions, leeks and garlic) and the nightshade family (tomatoes, eggplant and peppers).

While all vegetables contain good things, we must once again caution that our choice of vegetables must take into account individual food sensitivities. Vegetables from the nightshade family may cause arthritis and painful joints in sensitive individuals. The cruciferous vegetables have been in the spotlight recently but they are not for everybody—their high sulphur content may cause problems for some. Vegetables from the onion family tend to stimulate the glands, and should therefore be avoided by those suffering from fatigue or weak adrenal function. Almost any vegetable can cause adverse and allergic reactions if eaten to excess—that is why variety is so important.

The most important piece of equipment you will need for vegetable preparation is a two-part stainless steel steamer—like a double boiler, with holes in the bottom of the upper pan. A wooden cutting board, a heavy stainless steel or cast iron frying pan, and a collection of sharp knives complete the list of items necessary for successful vegetable preparation. A clay pot is also useful—potatoes are delicious cooked this way.

Frozen vegetables are acceptable on occasion but most of the vegetables you eat should be fresh, and organically grown if possible. All commercial vegetables should be washed in water with a little bleach, hydrogen peroxide or Dr. Bronner's Sal Suds (see Sources), and then thoroughly rinsed to remove chemical residues.

Dark green leafy vegetables tend to concentrate nitrites when commercially grown with high-nitrogen fertilizer. In the intestinal tract these nitrates may be transformed into potent carcinogens. Nitrates also tend to form in cooked vegetables during storage; for this reason we caution you against eating reheated vegetables, particularly green vegetables.

Don't hesitate to put butter on your steamed vegetables. The fat soluble vitamins and the X factor in butter are just what your body needs to fully utilize minerals in plant foods. Season vegetables lightly with sea salt.

ARTICHOKES

The artichoke is of Arabic origin—called *al-kharshuf* in Middle Eastern lands—that comes to us by way of Italy. Like all members of the thistle family, artichokes concentrate iodine when it is in the soil. Research indicates that the artichoke can benefit the intestinal tract and the heart; it has been shown to reduce blood clotting time and to neutralize certain toxic substances. Studies in Japan and Switzerland show that artichokes can lower blood cholesterol. In fact, a constituent of artichoke called cynarin has been formulated into a cholesterol-lowering drug. Folk wisdom values the artichoke as a stimulant to the bile. Artichokes are in season in the spring. Choose artichokes that seem heavy for their size and whose leaves are more or less free from dark streaks. SWF

Cut the stems off and place with leaves up in a vegetable steamer or, if you need more room, on a rack in a large pot containing about 1 inch of water. Steam, covered, until tender, about 1/2 hour. Remove with tongs and place artichokes, leaves down, in a colander to drain. Remove the outermost leaves and serve warm or cold with basic dressing (page 118), herbed mayonnaise (page 126), or lemon butter sauce (page 137).

Stuffed Artichokes
Serves 4

4 artichokes
1 cup extra virgin olive oil
4 cloves garlic, peeled and mashed
8 slices whole grain bread, processed into crumbs
sea salt and freshly ground pepper

Steam artichokes in a vegetable steamer according to the master recipe until just barely tender. Mix remaining ingredients including salt and pepper to taste. Pull artichoke leaves open a bit and use scissors to snip points off leaves. Press stuffing down between leaves. Return to steamer for another 5 to 10 minutes. These are messy to eat but delicious.

ASPARAGUS

Asparagus is an Italian vegetable that dates from the Renaissance. Much prized in Europe, asparagus dishes are featured in fine restaurants during the peak season—May and June. One restaurant in Germany lists 209 separate asparagus dishes on its menu!

Asparagus is a good source of rutin, a substance that prevents small blood vessels from breaking. Medieval medicine valued asparagus for the treatment of heart palpitations and as a diuretic. Asparagus is also high in carotenoids, B Complex, C and E as well as potassium, iodine and zinc.

Asparagus must be fresh to be good. Check the tips to see that the little buds are distinct; if the tips have gone mushy, the asparagus is not worth buying. SWF

Trim off the tough ends and rinse well. If asparagus is of large diameter, you may want to pare off about an inch of green from the ends. Place in a vegetable steamer and steam about five minutes until stalks turn bright green and can be pierced easily with a fork. Don't overcook! Transfer to a heated serving dish, place a generous pat of butter on top and finish with a squeeze of lemon juice. May be kept warm in the oven for about 1/2 hour.

Asparagus with Sesame Seeds
Serves 6

2 1/2 pound asparagus, trimmed
2 tablespoons extra virgin olive oil
2 tablespoons minced shallot
2 tablespoons sesame seeds, lightly toasted
juice of 1 lemon

Place oil and asparagus in a glass baking dish and toss so that the asparagus is completely coated with oil. Bake at 400 degrees for about 8 minutes, shaking the dish every two minutes or so. Sprinkle on the shallot and sesame seeds and bake, with one or two shakes, for one minute more. Transfer to heated serving bowl and squeeze on lemon juice. Season with sea salt to taste.

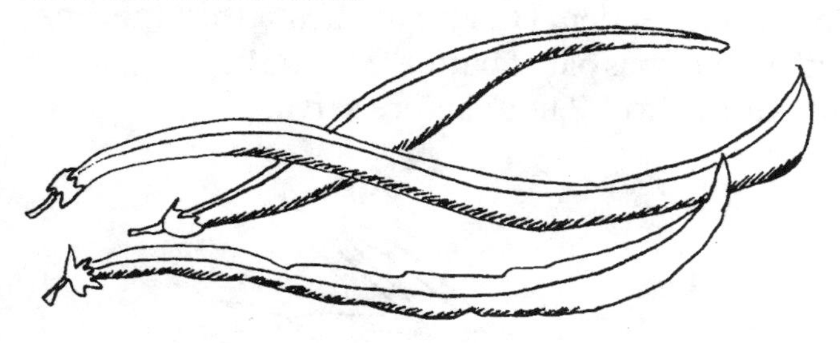

BEANS, FRENCH

These slender, tender beans are new in American markets, and still too expensive for everyday dinner fare; but they are worth buying for special meals, as they make a beautiful addition to the plate. Best time to buy is late summer, when they are in season locally, and have not been shipped long distances.

Snip off both ends. French beans can be steamed in a vegetable steamer but better results are obtained from blanching. Bring a pot of salted water to boil. Plunge in beans and cook rapidly for about 8 minutes, until they are tender. Pour beans into a colander and rinse with cold water. This will bring out an intense green color. Transfer to a heated serving dish and top with a generous pat of butter. Place in a warm oven to restore heat—they may be kept there for up to 1/2 hour before serving.

Want to stay young longer? Then eat your veggies and fruit—three vegetables and two fruits—every day. This is what Bruce Ames, Ph.D. University of California at Berkeley molecular biologist, told a recent meeting of the American Gerontological Society. If you do, you can help slash the incidence of cancer by about 25 percent. Why does this work?

Antioxidants in vegetables and fruits—vitamin C, E, and beta carotene—protect cells from damage caused by free radicals. These cell saboteurs have long been suspected of triggering various cancers.

In analyzing 99 studies probing for the connection between diet and cancer, UC nutrition researcher Gladys Block discovered that 89 reveal that vegetable and fruit antioxidants are a stout defense against numerous cancers. Thirty-three of these studies show that vitamin C in cantaloupes, citrus fruits and green leafy vegetables protect us from cancers of the cervix, the esophagus, and stomach.

Other research discloses that vitamin E in corn, greens and soy beans guards us against cancers of the breast, pancreas and stomach.

Beta carotene in carrots and apricots protect us from bladder and lung tumors

The Big Five—three fresh vegetables and two fresh fruits daily—are excellent guardians against cancer, assert Ames and Block, and yet, only nine percent of the population consumes them. James F. Scheer *Health Freedom News*

BEANS, GREEN

In France, our green or string beans are called *mange tous* and are considered inferior to the French beans or *haricots verts*. It is true that green beans are rather unappetizing eaten whole. They benefit enormously from being "French cut", which is quite easy with a food processor.

Cut each end from the bean with a knife, being careful to pull down at the same time so as to remove any strings. Break or cut the beans to fit sideways into your food processor. Fit the processor with the regular slicing blade and place the beans in sideways. The result will be beautifully French cut beans.

Place beans in a vegetable steamer and steam about 8 minutes until they have turned bright green and are just tender. Transfer to a heated bowl and toss with a generous pat of butter. May be kept in a warm oven for up to 1/2 hour before serving.

Green Beans with Almonds
Serves 6

1 1/2 pounds string beans, French cut
1/2 stick butter
1 cup crispy almonds (page 487), slivered

Steam beans as described above. Meanwhile sliver almonds using the fine slicer attachment in your food processor. Melt the butter in a frying pan, raise heat, add almonds and cook, stirring, until lightly browned. Be careful the almonds do not burn. Toss with the beans and keep warm in the oven until ready to serve.

Green beans and French beans are a variety of legume, and hence the relative of peas, peanuts, lentils and the many varieties of dried beans. Their pods are edible because of selective breeding to make them flavorful at an early or immature stage of growth. Like their cousins, the dried beans, they are high in calcium, potassium and B-complex vitamins. They have a higher carotenoid content than the dried variety and are often more digestible. String beans were particularly recommended by the late physician Henry Bieler for their alkaline content, and as a treatment for the pancreas and salivary glands. SWF

In movies with war themes, it is frequently the Marines who come to the rescue; in disease, it is just as frequently fresh and cooked vegetables which do the same thing. There is usually no need to rely on drugs. It must be remembered that all drugs are chemicals; the same chemicals in organic form are found in vegetables and other foodstuffs. Henry Bieler MD *Food is Your Best Medicine*

In the 1880's, the great majority of Americans ate at home: three family meals a day, home made, from whole foods.

In the 1980's, the great majority of Americans do *not* eat three family meals a day at home, meals are *not* normally homemade and the whole foods are *not* chosen to any great extent. Joseph D. Beasley MD and Jerry J. Swift MA *The Kellogg Report*

Green Beans with Onions
Serves 6

1 1/2 pounds string beans, French cut
1/2 stick butter
1/2 cup dehydrated onions

Steam the beans as described above. Meanwhile melt the butter in a frying pan, add onions and cook, stirring, until lightly browned. Be careful the onions do not burn. Toss with beans and keep warm in the oven until ready to serve.

Stir Fry Green Beans with Cashews
Serves 6

2 pounds string beans, French cut
1 cup crispy cashews (page 487), chopped
4 tablespoons extra virgin olive oil
1 teaspoon grated ginger
1/4 cup soy sauce
1 cup water, orange juice or chicken stock
2 tablespoons arrowroot mixed with
2 tablespoons water
1 teaspoon raw honey
2 teaspoons toasted sesame oil
2 cloves garlic, peeled and mashed (optional)
1/2 teaspoon dried rosemary

Combine mixture of the ginger, soy sauce, water or stock, honey, sesame oil, garlic and rosemary. Mix thoroughly with a wire whisk. Heat the oil in a skillet or wok. Stir fry the beans until just tender, about 5 minutes. Add cashews and the sauce mixture and bring to a boil. Add the arrowroot mixture and simmer until sauce thickens and all the beans are well coated.

Go ahead and eat those veggies!

They help prevent lung cancer, but it isn't just the beta-carotene in them that protects you.

This is the finding of Loic Le Marchand, whose group recently finished a study at the Cancer Research Center of Hawaii in Honolulu, reported in the Journal of the National Cancer Institute.

Over and above beta carotene, not-so-well-known vegetable constituents such as lutein, lycopene and indoles could be virtually anonymous soldiers who battle to protect our lungs.

Le Marchand and associates discovered that crucifers such a broccoli and cabbage, other green vegetables and tomatoes reduce the risk of lung cancer as much as beta carotene-rich vegetables. Cabbage and broccoli have previously been linked with reducing the risk of colon cancer, but not necessarily with lung cancer.

Indoles and related substances in vegetables have prevented various tumor formations in animals. In his human study, Le Marchand found that while a diet high in beta carotene reduced risk of lung cancer by three times in females and by two times in males, a diet of many different vegetables reduced the risk by seven times in females and by three times in males. Variety may be the spice of life, or, in the case of vegetables, it could be life itself. James F. Scheer *Health Freedom News*

BEAN SPROUTS

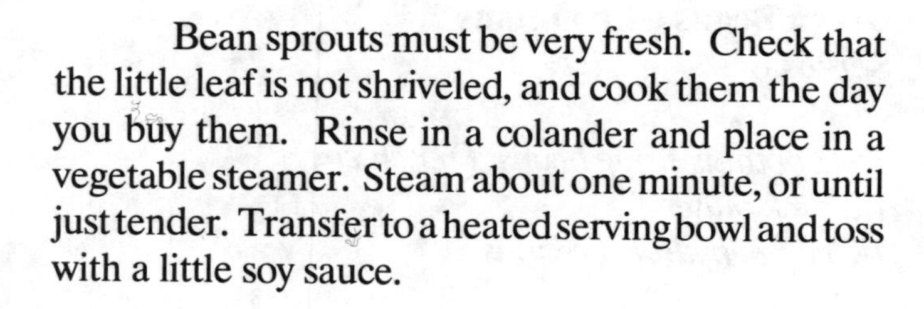

Bean sprouts must be very fresh. Check that the little leaf is not shriveled, and cook them the day you buy them. Rinse in a colander and place in a vegetable steamer. Steam about one minute, or until just tender. Transfer to a heated serving bowl and toss with a little soy sauce.

The bean from which the bean sprout grows is the mung bean, a small green bean used extensively in Asia. Mung bean sprouts are excellent sources of carotenoids, B-complex and vitamin C plus phosphorus, potassium, calcium and iron. Bean sprouts are exceptionally high in enzymes, and these magic substances will survive a light steaming. SWF

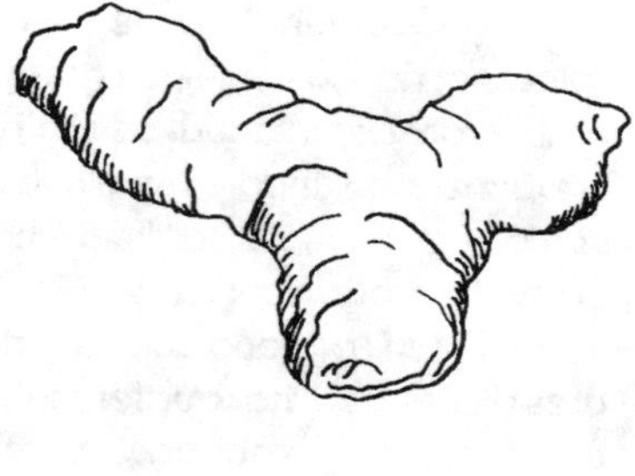

Stir Fry Bean Sprouts

Serves 6

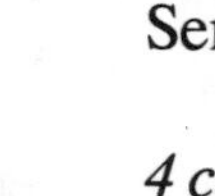

4 cups bean sprouts
1 red pepper, seeded and cut into strips
3 carrots, peeled and cut into a julienne
1/4 pound Chinese peas, ends removed
4 tablespoons extra virgin olive oil
1 teaspoon grated fresh ginger
1/4 cup soy sauce
1 cup water or stock
1 tablespoon arrowroot mixed with
1 tablespoon water
2 tablespoons toasted sesame seeds

Mix soy sauce, ginger and water or stock together and set aside. Heat oil in a frying pan or wok. Stir fry carrots a minute or two, add peppers and cook a minute more. Add Chinese peas and stir fry another minute. Add liquid mixture to vegetables and bring to a boil. Add arrowroot mixture along with sprouts and sesame seeds and cook a minute more, stirring constantly, until sauce thickens and vegetables become coated. Serve immediately.

The sprouting of seeds is one of the most fascinating natural phenomena. From this minuscule appendage, tiny part of a seed even tinier, is born the plant. That this sprout has exceptional nutritional value is thus not surprising. But even more remarkable is the ability of this sprout to produce a whole range of substances—principally vitamins and enzymes—that are completely absent, or present only in extremely small amounts, in the unsprouted seed. The seed becomes hardly recognizable and transforms itself into something new which is less energetic but richer in nutrients. Claude Aubert *Dis-Moi Comment Tu Cuisines*

Bean Sprout Curry
Serves 4

1 bunch green onions, finely chopped
2 stalks celery, finely chopped
1/4 green pepper, finely chopped
1 apple, peeled and chopped
1/2 stick butter
1 1/2 cup chicken stock
2 tablespoons arrowroot mixed with
2 tablespoons water
1 tablespoon curry powder
pinch cayenne pepper
1/2 cup currents
3-4 cups bean sprouts
finely chopped crispy peanuts (page 486) for garnish
finely chopped chives for garnish

Melt butter in a pan. Saute onion, celery, pepper and apple about one minute. Add stock, currents, seasonings and arrowroot mixture. Cook, stirring, until liquid begins to thicken. Add sprouts, mix well and cook until just tender, about one minute. Serve with basic brown rice (page 441) and garnish with peanuts and chives.

BEETS

Remove leaves, wash, and place in a heavy pan. Meanwhile, cut stems off the beets. There are two ways of cooking them. One is to cover with water and boil until tender; The other is to bake in a 250 degree oven for two hours or so or until tender. The later method is preferable from the nutritional point of view, but it takes longer. Peel the cooked beets, slice them and transfer to a heated serving bowl. Meanwhile cover the greens and simmer on lowest heat. (Do not add water as the moisture adhering to the leaves is sufficient to steam them.) As soon as greens are wilted, remove to a strainer or colander. Press out the juice, chop the leaves coarsely and mix with sliced beets. Toss with a pat of butter or with a little butter that has been melted with one mashed clove of garlic and a squeeze of lemon juice.

Beets were developed by German gardeners in the Middle Ages. Long valued as a blood tonic, they are rich in calcium, iron, magnesium, and phosphorus, as well as carotene, B-complex and vitamin C.

Beets are so concentrated, nutritionally speaking, that many natural vitamins are derived from them. Dr. Bruce West recommends eating a few spoonfuls of beets per day—either raw, fermented or cooked—as a sure method of ingesting adequate vitamins and minerals on a regular basis, and as a detoxicant as well. Beets and their tops contain special substances that protect the liver and stimulate the flow of bile. Beets and beet juice have been used successfully in cancer therapies.

Beet tops contain the same nutrients as the root with the added bonus of an exceptionally high carotenoid content. Always buy beets untrimmed as the leaves are a good indication of freshness; and always eat beet roots with their tops. The combination is excellent, nutritionally speaking, and the sweet beets are a good complement to their bitter greens. SWF

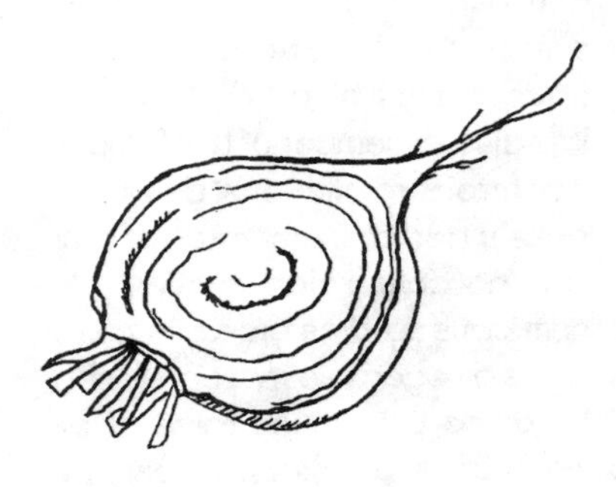

BROCCOLI

Broccoli tops the list of common vegetables for nutrient content. It is high in carotenoids and vitamin C and contains B-complex, calcium, phosphorus and potassium as well. New research reveals that broccoli is rich in chromium, a mineral that protects against diabetes. It contains some protein and is a good source of fiber. Like all vegetables of the crucifer family, broccoli is rich in indoles, a potent anti-cancer substance. Organic broccoli is now almost universally available—it is of course, superior in taste and nutrient content. SWF

Broccoli is one of the most amazing pharmaceutical packages in nature's food pharmacy. If it had a pharmacological label, it would read like this: Contains high concentrations of beta-carotene (suspected lung cancer antagonist); carotenoids (general anticancer agents); quercetin (antioxidant and anticancer agent); glutathione (antioxidant and anticancer agent); indoles (anticancer and detoxification compounds)... folate (anticancer agent); chromium (antidiabetic and anti-heart disease medication); readily absorbable calcium (needed to help prevent osteoporosis—also a suspected anticancer and high blood pressure medication); calcium pectate fiber (lowers blood cholesterol). It is also a member of the famous cruciferous family of vegetables, closely tied to lower rates of cancer, notably colon cancer. In numerous studies broccoli shows up as a vegetable most preferred by those with lower rates of all kinds of cancer. Jean Carper *The Food Pharmacy Guide to Good Eating*

Broccoli not only ranks number one in nutrient content, it is also the easiest vegetable of all to prepare. Cut into flowerets and steam about five minutes or until broccoli has turned bright green and is just tender. Transfer to a heated serving dish, top with a generous pat of butter and keep warm in the oven.

Broccoli Timbales
Serves 6

1 large bunch broccoli
4 tablespoons butter, softened
4 tablespoons piima cream or creme fraiche
4 eggs, lightly beaten
1 small onion, very finely chopped
sea salt and freshly ground pepper

Steam broccoli according to the master recipe. Place in food processor and pulse a few times until well chopped. Add remaining ingredients and blend well. Pour into 6 well-buttered conical timbale moulds. Place in a pan of hot water and bake at 350 degrees for 20 minutes. Loosen timbales with a knife and turn onto a warmed platter or individual plates.

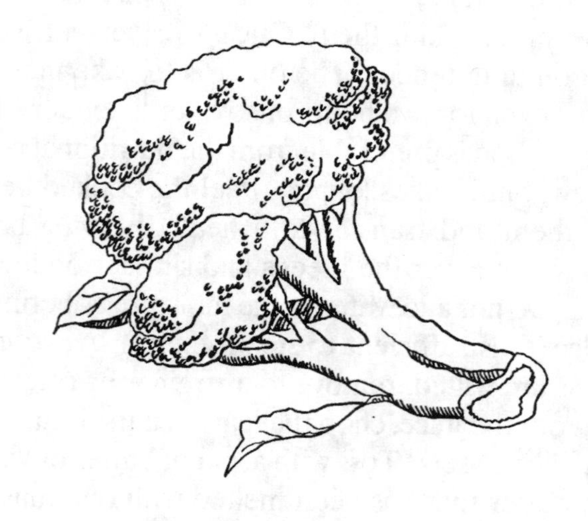

BRUSSELS SPROUTS

Cut tough ends off the sprouts and remove loose outer leaves. Make a little cross in the end. This will help the sprouts cook more evenly. Steam for 5 to 10 minutes until just tender—do not overcook! Transfer to a heated serving dish and top with a pat of butter. An alternate method is to cut the sprouts lengthwise into quarters and saute them gently in a little butter until tender. Top with a sprinkling of Parmesan cheese.

First planted in America by Thomas Jefferson, Brussels sprouts are a flavorful winter vegetable that can be ruined by overcooking. They contain a similar vitamin profile as other members of the cruciferous family, namely carotenoids and vitamin C and minerals phosphorus and calcium. Like cabbage and broccoli, Brussels sprouts contain a host of anti-cancer substances.

To remove insects from Brussels sprouts, cauliflower, artichokes, etc. soak thirty minutes in water to which 2 tablespoons of salt and vinegar have been added. Rinse well and proceed with cooking. SWF

BUTTERNUT SQUASH

Cut squash in half, remove seeds and set cut side down in a glass baking pan with about 1/2 inch of water. Bake at 350 degrees until tender, about one hour. Meanwhile, place equal parts of butter and raw honey in a little pitcher, set in hot water and let melt. (Don't let the mixture surpass 118 degrees or the valuable amylase enzymes in the honey will be destroyed.) To serve, place skin side up and pour a little honey-butter mixture into each cavity.

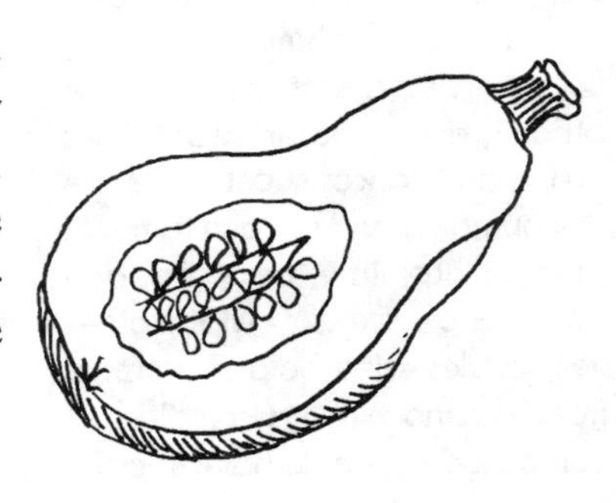

Butternut Squash Puree with Pecans
Serves 6

3 butternut squash
3 eggs, lightly beaten
1/4 teaspoon freshly grated nutmeg
1/2 teaspoon sea salt
freshly ground pepper
2 tablespoons butter
3/4 cup crispy pecans (page 485), chopped

Cook the squash as described above, scoop out into a food processor and blend until smooth. Add eggs, nutmeg and sea salt and pepper to taste. Transfer puree to an ovenproof serving dish. Melt butter and honey together and pour over the puree. Sprinkle on pecans. Bake at 350 degrees for about 30 minutes.

In tests at Cornell University, researchers fed one group of animals Brussels sprouts while a second group was fed ordinary rat chow. Both groups were injected with a powerful carcinogen. After fifteen weeks only 13 percent of the Brussels sprouts eaters had developed breast tumors compared with 77 percent of the chow-eaters. A possible reason: Brussels sprouts have high amounts of a compound called glucobardssicin that aids the liver in neutralizing and eliminating potential carcinogens. Jean Carper *The Food Pharmacy Guide to Good Eating*

CABBAGE, GREEN

Among vegetables, there's no question that the cabbage family gets the prize. It is rich in vitamin C, in protective indoles and in fiber, and contains as well lesser quantities of other protective substances. Broccoli and Brussels sprouts are the richest in cancer-inhibiting elements. A study done with two groups of volunteers confirmed the effectiveness of these crucifers. The first group ate what might be called a normal diet, while the second was given a diet rich in vegetables from the cabbage family, notably Brussels sprouts. Both groups ingested carcinogenic substances. The group eating a diet rich in crucifers eliminated these substances more quickly than the other group. Other vegetables rich in anti-cancer substances are the pumpkin and squash family. . . rich in vitamin C, carotene, and fiber, and carrots. Most other vegetables also help protect us from carcinogens. According to some studies, beets have specific anti-cancer properties. Claude Aubert *Dis-Moi Comment Tu Cuisines*

Cooked cabbage is delicious if prepared properly. The secret is to shred the cabbage very finely and to cook until just tender.

Remove outer leaves and shred cabbage with a sharp knife, or by cutting into quarters and feeding it through the food processor fitted with a fine slicing disk. Rinse cabbage and place in a heavy skillet. Do not shake water off—water adhering to cabbage will be sufficient to cook it. Top cabbage with a little salt, plenty of pepper and several generous pats of butter. Turn on heat and lower when cabbage starts to steam. Cook about five minutes, covered, or until cabbage is just wilted.

CABBAGE, RED

Unhappily, anxiety-ridden Americans, following the warning voices of televised drug commercials and newspaper ads, consider health something that can be purchased in a bottle at the drugstore; they forget, or never knew, that health can be found only by obeying the clear-cut laws of nature. Henry Bieler MD *Food is Your Best Medicine*

Red cabbage may be prepared as white cabbage but it takes a little longer to cook. It has a stronger flavor than white cabbage and is therefore more appetizing when dressed up according to the following recipes.

Red Cabbage, Dutch Style

Serves 6

1 red cabbage, shredded
1 bay leaf
1/2 teaspoon cloves
1/2 teaspoon sea salt
1 teaspoon raw honey
1 cup water
1/4 teaspoon cinnamon
2 apples, peeled and quartered
2 tablespoons butter
1 tablespoon raw wine vinegar

Rinse cabbage and place in a heavy pan. In a small pan, mix bay leaf, cloves, salt, honey and cinnamon with about 1 cup water and bring to a boil. Pour over cabbage. Cook cabbage gently about twenty minutes. Add the apple and cook another ten minutes. Remove cabbage with a slotted spoon to a heated serving dish and toss with the butter and vinegar.

Red Cabbage with Orange

Serves 6

1 red cabbage
1 small onion, peeled and chopped
rind of two oranges, finely grated
juice of two oranges, strained
1 teaspoon sea salt
1 clove garlic, peeled and finely chopped
1 tablespoon raw honey
3 tablespoons whey or raw wine vinegar
4 tablespoons butter

Shred cabbage. Combine orange rind, juice, onion, garlic, salt, honey and whey or vinegar. Pour over the cabbage and toss well. Marinate overnight, tossing occasionally.

Melt butter in a large saucepan or frying pan. Add cabbage mixture and bring to a simmer. Reduce heat, cover and cook gently for about 1 hour, uncovered, until cabbage is tender and liquid has evaporated.

Since ancient times, the cabbage has been a source of vitamin C during the winter months for peoples living in northern climes, from the Orient to the New World. It is a good source of fiber as well as of carotenoids, B-complex, vitamin C, potassium, magnesium and calcium. Raw cabbage has more vitamin C than cooked but cannot be recommended on a daily basis because of the presence of goitrogens, substances that block the formation of thyroid hormone. This in turn makes it difficult for the liver to convert the plant form of vitamin A (carotene or carotenoids) into the animal form which it can use. As a member of the cruciferous family, cabbage is rich in substances that block the formation and spread of tumors. Folk medicine values the cabbage for the stomach; Irish girls traditionally drank cabbage water for the complexion. Recent research has shown the juice of cabbage to be highly therapeutic for ulcers. SWF

Latest research on this subject indicates that sodium intake contributes less to hypertension that the ratio of sodium to potassium. In other words, it may be possible to prevent high blood pressure, by adding more potassium to the diet, rather than necessarily lessening the dietary sodium. . . [researchers] suggest that people take an extra helping of a potassium rich food—for instance a banana, some fresh broccoli, an avocado, Brussels sprouts, cauliflower, potatoes with skins, cantaloupe, dates, prunes and raisins. James F. Scheer
Health Freedom News

CARROTS

A native of Afghanistan, and related to celery, parsnips, caraway, cilantro, cumin and dill, the carrot is a most useful, versatile, nutritious and popular vegetable, revered not only as an accompaniment to other dishes, but as a base ingredient for soups, stocks, and stews. In hotels in the town of Vichy, France, carrots are eaten daily as part of a cure for overloaded digestions, and many cultures have valued them as an aphrodisiac. Research has shown that three raw carrots, eaten daily, lower blood cholesterol and that a single carrot per day cuts the risk of lung cancer among smokers in half. Carrots are rich sources of carotenoids, B vitamins, phosphorus, calcium, and all important iodine. SWF

Many people hate carrots because their only experience of this staple vegetable has been carrots boiled to death in water. A much more satisfactory way to prepare carrots is to saute them in butter. Don't be afraid to peel carrots. Unlike potatoes, which have nutrients concentrated just under the skin, the nutrients of carrots are more evenly distributed.

Peel carrots and cut into sticks about 3 inches long and 1/4 inch in width. Saute in butter about 20 minutes until golden, but still slightly firm. You may also cut carrots in a fine julienne (using a food processor) and saute in liberal amounts of butter and olive oil.

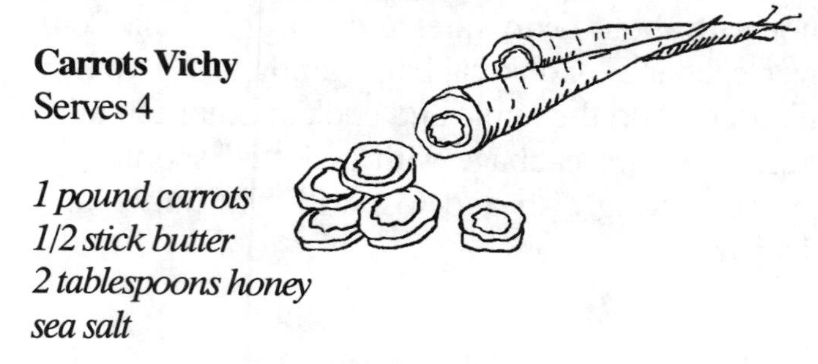

Carrots Vichy
Serves 4

1 pound carrots
1/2 stick butter
2 tablespoons honey
sea salt

Peel carrots and slice into rounds. Cover with filtered water and bring to a boil. Add butter and honey. Boil uncovered, skimming frequently, until liquid is reduced to almost nothing and carrots are well coated. You may want to add a tablespoon or two more of butter at the end. Season to taste with sea salt.

WEDNESDAY NIGHT DINNER

Any Lettuce Salad

Veal Chop

Steamed New Potatoes

Carrots Vichy

Carrots with Cream and Herbs
Serves 4

1 pound carrots, peeled and sliced on diagonal
3 tablespoons butter
1/2 cup piima cream or creme fraiche
1/4 cup chopped herbs such as basil, mint, dill or chives
sea salt and freshly ground pepper

Saute carrots in butter until tender. Add cream and boil down a minute or two until it thickens. Off heat, stir in the herbs and season to taste.

Carrot Curry

Serves 6-8

1 pound carrots, peeled and cut into sticks
butter and extra virgin olive oil
1 teaspoons mustard seeds
2 teaspoons ground cumin
2 teaspoons ground coriander
2 teaspoons turmeric
1 teaspoon fenugreek seeds
1 teaspoon dried dill
pinch cayenne
2 medium onions, sliced
2 red bell peppers, cut into a julienne
3-4 cups chicken stock
grated rind of 1 orange
1 tablespoon grated ginger
2 tablespoons arrowroot mixed with
2 tablespoons water
2 cups spinach leaves, finely cut up
sea salt
2 cups crispy cashews (page 487), chopped

Melt butter and olive oil in a large pot. Saute spices for several minutes, stirring constantly. Add onion and saute until soft. Add peppers and carrots and saute a few minutes more. Add stock, ginger, and orange rind and bring to a boil. Reduce to simmer and stir in cashews and salt to taste. Let simmer, uncovered until liquid is partially evaporated and carrots and peppers are soft. Spoonful by spoonful add arrowroot mixture until desired thickness is obtained. Stir in spinach and simmer another minute more. Serve with basic brown rice (page 441), fruit chutney (page 98) or raisin chutney (page 100).

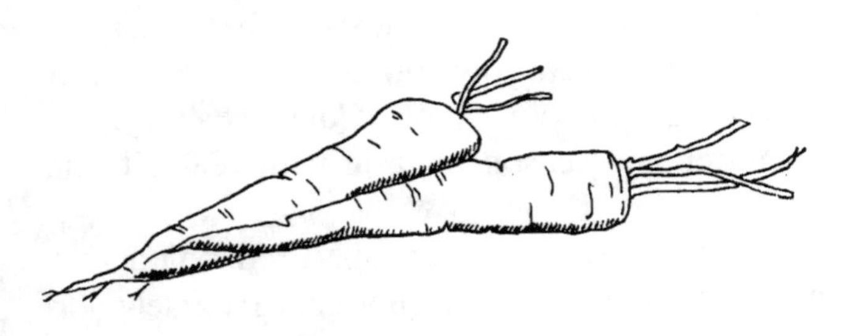

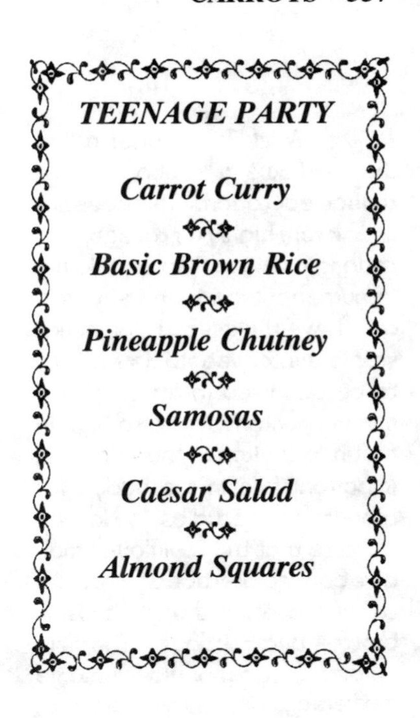

A sharp profile of how we Americans die, and what disables us in life, shows that chronic degenerative diseases are the enemy we all face. Heart attacks and heart disease, cancer, strokes, high blood pressure, diabetes, arthritic conditions, obesity, mental illnesses, addiction—and a host of other chronic conditions not reviewed; cirrhosis, kidney disease, back pain, chronic bronchitis, multiple sclerosis, migraine, ulcers, phlebitis, chronic impotence, asthma, allergies, lupus erythematosus, cataracts, ileitis and colitis, diverticulitis and diverticulosos, chronic constipation, gastritis, insomnia, anxiety, depression and chronic fatigue.

The superb accomplishments of modern medicine in managing accidents, infections and surgery will be of little help curing any of these. Before the "diseases of civilization", medicine is almost as powerless as we are. Joseph D. Beasley MD and Jerry R. Swift MA *The Kellogg Report*

CAULIFLOWER

Mark Twain once called the cauliflower a "cabbage with a college education." This does not speak very highly for college educations, as the cauliflower is lower in nutrients than its cousin broccoli. Nevertheless cauliflower is a staple winter vegetable and not to be despised for its fiber and mineral content. It is also high in biotin, a B vitamin that plays an important role in the body's fat production. Studies in Norway indicate that the cauliflower may give better protection against cancer of the colon that its cousins broccoli and cabbage. The new purple varieties now seen in some markets actually contain more carotenoids than white cauliflower. You needn't be put off by the color, they taste fine. SWF

Separate the cauliflower into flowerets. Steam about 10 minutes or until just tender. Transfer to a heated bowl and toss with a generous pat of butter, pepper, sea salt and a few grindings of nutmeg.

Breaded Cauliflower
Serves 6

1 head cauliflower
1/2 stick melted butter
2 cups fine wholegrain bread crumbs
4 tablespoons Parmesan cheese, finely powdered
sea salt and freshly ground pepper

Steam cauliflower flowerets until not quite tender. Let drain, pat dry and toss well with melted butter. Mix bread crumbs, cheese, sea salt and pepper to taste. Dip each floweret into bread crumb mixture. Place flat side down in a buttered glass baking dish. Bake at 350 degrees for about 15 minutes or until golden brown.

CHARD

Chard is a member of the beet family, selectively bred for its leaves rather than its root. Although chard is often referred to as Swiss chard, the champions of this versatile vegetable are the French who add it to soups, stuffings, pates, and pancakes.

Like all dark green leafy vegetables, chard is rich in iron, calcium, magnesium, vitamin C and carotenoids. Chard should always be eaten cooked as it contains oxalate raphides that may irritate the mouth and intestinal tract. These are neutralized during cooking.

Chard grown with high-nitrate commercial fertilizers may also be high in nitrates. Avoid buying chard that is not organically grown. SWF

Chard is one of many nutritious greens available year round. It is more bitter than spinach, but less expensive.

Remove stalks from leaves and tear into pieces. Wash well but do not shake off water. Place in a covered heavy pan over a medium flame. When chard begins to simmer, reduce heat and simmer until just wilted. Using a slotted spoon transfer to a serving dish. Use the back of your spoon to squeeze out any excess liquid, and pour this off. Cut up coarsely, toss with butter and season to taste with sea salt and pepper.

Alternately, saute chopped red onion in a generous amount of butter. Chop chard coarsely, add to onions, cover and steam a minute or so until wilted.

CHESTNUTS

To cook chestnuts, saute frozen or freshly shelled chestnuts in a little butter. Season to taste with sea salt, pepper and a little freshly grated nutmeg.

Chestnut Puree
Serves 6

6 1/2 ounces (1 package) frozen or freshly peeled chestnuts
1 cup chicken or beef stock
1/2 cup piima cream or creme fraiche
sea salt and freshly ground pepper

Cook chestnuts, uncovered, in stock until tender. Remove with a slotted spoon to food processor and process along with enough stock to achieve desired consistency. Stir in cream and season to taste with sea salt and freshly ground pepper. Transfer to a heated serving dish and keep warm in oven.

Chestnut-Zucchini Boats
Serves 6

2 cups chestnut puree
6 medium zucchini
sea salt

Trim ends off the zucchini and plunge into boiling salted water. Cook about 8 minutes or until just tender. Remove to a colander and rinse with water. Cut the zucchini lengthwise and scoop out center, leaving about 1/4 inch of outer flesh. Sprinkle insides with sea salt and place on paper towels, cut side down, for about 15 minutes to drain. Wipe insides with paper towel and fill with puree. Arrange in a buttered glass oven dish and warm at 200 degrees for about 1/2 hour.

Highly prized in Europe, the chestnut is a vegetable almost completely absent from American tables. This may be because a blight destroyed America's vast chestnut forests in the early 1900's.

As the flesh is soft at maturity, chestnuts are consumed as vegetables. The chestnut has the lowest fat content of any edible nut, and conversely a high carbohydrate content—hence the characteristic sweetness of the chestnut. They contain some protein and are rich in B vitamins, calcium, iron, phosphorus and potassium. Like the fruit of all trees whose roots extend far into the ground, chestnuts are a good source of trace minerals.

Chestnuts are in season in the fall. Select firm nuts with shiny skins. To peel, cut an X with a sharp knife on the flat side and roast or boil them for 10 to 15 minutes before removing the skin. Peeling chestnuts for purees, soups or stuffings is a chore but fortunately pre-peeled, frozen chestnuts are now available. These take all the work out of serving chestnuts and should set the stage for a comeback of this delicious vegetable. SWF

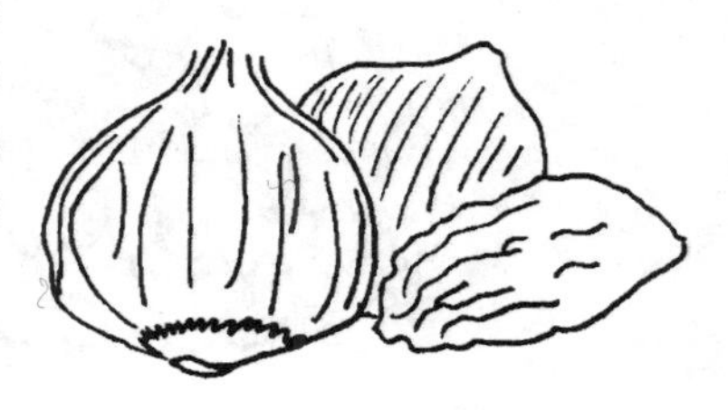

CORN

Corn is the only grain that we eat as a vegetable. It is also the only grain containing carotenoids. Surprisingly, the X factor or growth factor, identified by Dr. Price as a component of animal fats, has been detected in raw, unrefined corn oil. Corn also provides B-complex, potassium and phosphorus.

Corn has not been traditionally valued for its pharmacological powers but several studies link the consumption of sweet corn with low rates of colon, breast and prostate cancer, as well as heart disease.

The fresher the better is the rule for corn. For maximum sweetness, it is best to eat corn the day it is picked. It is easy to grow and forms a staple crop in American backyard gardens. Sweet corn needs no more than a few minutes steaming—never boil it! It is also delicious raw, cut off the cob and used in salads. Be sure to chew corn thoroughly or it will pass through undigested. SWF

Shuck and wash corn. Place sidewise in a frying pan with about 1/2 inch water. Cover and steam lightly for 5-10 minutes or until corn is just tender. Don't let corn get mushy—it should still have some crunch. Serve with butter or herb butter (page 137).

An alternate method is to leave the husks on corn and bake at 350 degrees until the green husks turn the color of straw. Remove and eat immediately. You may also place the ears, husks on, in the coals of a barbecue, turning from time to time until corn is tender.

Corn off the Cob, Mexican Style
Serves 6

6 ears corn, cut off cob
1 red pepper, seeded and chopped
1 green pepper, seeded and chopped
1 bunch green onions, chopped
1/2 stick butter
sea salt
cracked pepper

Saute peppers and onions gently in butter. Add corn, cover and let cook, stirring occasionally for 5 to 10 minutes or until corn is just tender. Season with sea salt to taste and lots of black pepper.

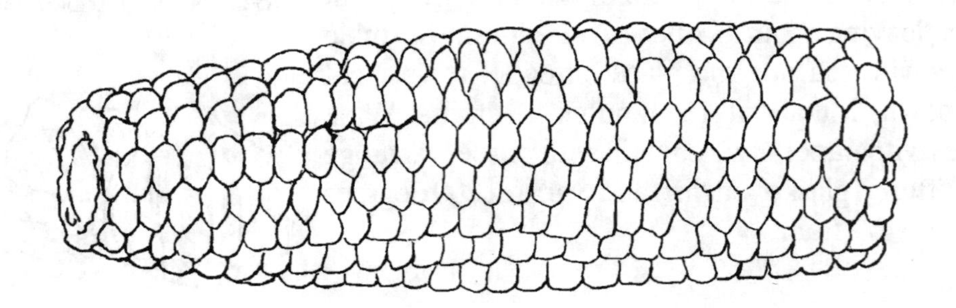

Corn off the Cob, Indian Style
Serves 6

6 ears of corn, cut off the cob
2 teaspoons yellow mustard seed
1/2 teaspoon fenugreek seeds
1/4 teaspoon red pepper flakes
1 teaspoon freshly grated ginger
1/2 stick butter
2 medium onions, peeled and chopped
1/2 teaspoon turmeric
2-4 jalapeno peppers, seeded and chopped
2 cloves garlic, peeled and minced
2 cups plain yoghurt
1/4 cup chopped cilantro

Saute mustard seeds, fenugreek seeds, red pepper flakes and ginger in butter. Add onion and jalapeno peppers and saute until tender. Add turmeric and stir around. Add corn and garlic and mix well. Simmer gently until corn is just tender. Stir in yoghurt. Season to taste with sea salt and garnish with chopped cilantro.

Were it not for corn, archeologists say, the Spaniards would have been mightily disappointed when they arrived in the Americas. . . Corn was what made the great civilizations of Central and South America possible. . .

Christopher Columbus first sampled corn in Cuba. . . declaring it "most tasty boiled, roasted, or ground into flour." When he returned to Spain, he took along a few specimen Indians, some handfuls of gold dust and a packet of corn kernels. These first seeds may not have made a big impression on Ferdinand and Isabella, but they quickly proved their value. Within a few years the Spaniards had introduced maize around the Mediterranean. By the mid-16th century corn was so familiar in the Southern European diet that it formed the basis of such national dishes as Italian *polenta* and the Romanian staple *mamaliga* (a sort of cornmeal mush). Corn also traveled to the Philippines and the rest of Asia; by 1560 it was a fixture in Chinese cooking, in everything from porridge to stir-fry. Portuguese traders, who used corn as slave-ship stores, carried the grain to Africa. It was an instant success there: corn grew more rapidly than other grains and it needed very little cultivation. . . But its advent in Africa was not an unmixed blessing. It produced something of a population boom, which may in turn have fed the slave trade. . . And it led to a serious imbalance in the African diet. By the late 18th century, many Africans ate almost nothing but corn and suffered from vitamin deficiency as a result. Africans today are still afflicted by pellagra or "mealie disease", a sickness related to malnutrition from over-reliance on corn. Mary Talbot *Newsweek*

EGGPLANT

Eggplant contains a bitter juice that must be removed by salting. Peel the eggplant and cut into 1/2 inch cubes. Place in a bowl and toss with a generous spoonful of fine sea salt. Let stand, covered, about 1 hour. Rinse in a colander and pat cubes dry with paper towels or a tea towel. Use prepared eggplant cubes in the following recipes.

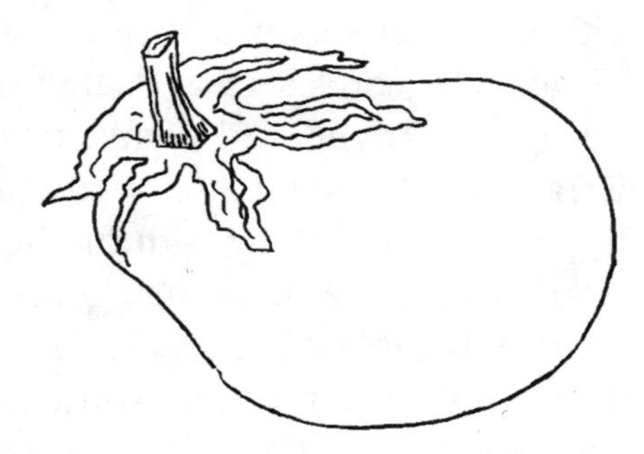

Although the eggplant is associated with Mediterranean cooking, its original home is tropical Asia. Primitive forms in this part of the world were very small and were invariable eaten pickled. The European name for eggplant—aubergine—is derived rather circuitously from the Sanskrit *vatin-ganah* which means anti-wind vegetable.

Until the potato reached Europe from the New World, the eggplant was the principle starchy vegetable, prepared in numerous ways, including fried like potatoes.

Eggplant contains carotenoids, B-complex, particularly folic acid, vitamin C, potassium, phosphorus and calcium. It contains some protein and is a good source of fiber. A study conducted at the University of Texas indicated that eggplant blocks cholesterol levels from rising when fatty foods have been eaten. Eggplant contains compounds called scopoletin and scoparone that block convulsions. African folk medicine values the eggplant to relieve nervous excitement and to counteract epilepsy, and as a contraceptive. In Korea, dried eggplant is used to treat a variety of illnesses, including measles, alcoholism and stomach cancer. SWF

Broiled Eggplant Slices
Serves 6

2 large eggplants
1 cup cilantro marinade (page 132)

Peel eggplants and slice lengthwise about 3/8 inch thick. Salt and let stand 1 hour. Rinse and pat dry. Place on a well-oiled cookie sheet and brush half the marinade on top of slices. Broil until golden, turn, brush other side with remaining marinade and broil again.

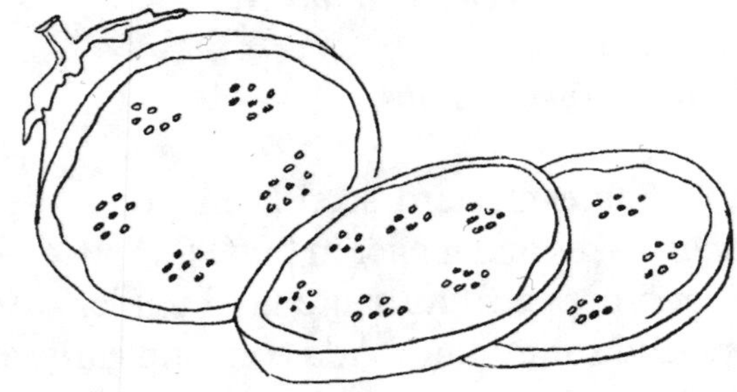

Eggplant with Tomatoes
Serves 6

2 eggplants
2 medium onions, peeled and chopped
3 tomatoes, peeled, seeded and chopped
2 cloves garlic, peeled
1 teaspoon dried thyme or 1/4 cup chopped fresh basil
extra virgin olive oil
freshly ground pepper

Peel and cube eggplant and prepare according to the master recipe (page 361). Saute the eggplant in small batches until golden in the olive oil, remove with a slotted spoon and drain on paper towels. (Eggplant absorbs a great deal of oil while cooking; add more oil as needed.) Saute onion in oil until tender, add tomatoes and cook about 5 minutes. Return eggplant to pan, along with mashed garlic cloves and the thyme or basil. Simmer gently for 5 to 10 minutes or until eggplant is tender and liquid from tomatoes has almost evaporated. Season to taste with freshly ground pepper.

Ratatouille
Serves 8

2 eggplants
1 zucchini, cut lengthwise and thinly sliced
1 green pepper, seeded and cut into strips
2 onions, peeled and sliced
4 tomatoes, peeled, seeded and chopped
4 cloves garlic, peeled and mashed
1 teaspoon dried thyme
extra virgin olive oil

There are two secrets to a good ratatouille: One is to saute all the vegetables separately; the second is to bake your casserole in an open shallow pan so that most of the liquid is absorbed. Peel and cube eggplant and prepare according to master recipe (page 361). Saute eggplant cubes in batches in olive oil. Remove with a slotted spoon to an oiled rectangular pyrex baking dish. Saute zucchini, pepper, onions and tomatoes in succession, adding more olive oil as necessary and removing to casserole. Add mashed garlic, and thyme to casserole. Mix well and bake, uncovered at 350 degrees for at least one hour. Ratatouille often tastes better reheated the next day.

Eggplant Curry
Serves 6

2 eggplants
2 medium onions, peeled and chopped
1 teaspoon fenugreek seeds
1 tablespoon ground coriander
1 tablespoon ground cumin
1 teaspoon turmeric
1/4 teaspoon cayenne pepper
1 teaspoon grated ginger
4 tomatoes, peeled, seeded and chopped
1/4 cup chopped coriander
extra virgin olive oil

It is important to keep in mind that, in general, the wild life has largely escaped many of the degenerative processes which affect modern white peoples. We ascribe this to animal instinct in the matter of food selection. It is possible that man has lost through disuse some of the normal faculty for consciously recognizing body requirements. In other words, the only hunger of which we now are conscious is a hunger for energy to keep us warm and to supply power. In general, we stop eating when an adequate amount of energy has been provided, whether or not the body building and repairing materials have been included in the food. The heat and energy factor in our foods is measured in calories. In planning an adequate diet, a proper ratio between body building and energy units must be maintained. It is important to keep in mind that while the amount of body-building and repairing material required is similar for different individuals of the same age and weight, it is markedly different for two individuals, one of whom is leading a sedentary, and the other an active life. Similarly, there is a great difference between the amount of body-building and repairing material required by a growing child or an expectant mother and an average adult. Weston Price DDS *Nutrition and Physical Degeneration*

Peel and cube eggplant and prepare according to the master recipe (page 361). Saute the eggplant cubes in batches in olive oil and transfer to a rectangular pyrex baking dish. Saute the onions in olive oil until tender along with spices. Add remaining ingredients except chopped coriander. Simmer a few minutes, stirring, until well mixed. Add to casserole and mix well. Bake, uncovered, at 350 degrees about 1 hour. Garnish with chopped coriander.

Kale is one of several dark green leafy greens of the cabbage family, related to collards and mustard greens. All of these greens provide calcium, iron and carotenoids in abundance, as well as many anti-cancer factors. Kale and related greens should always be eaten cooked—but not overcooked—so that the oxalate acids they contain are neutralized. Make an effort to buy organically grown kale. Dark leafy vegetables grown in nitrogen fertilized soils tend to concentrate nitrites, compounds which are transformed into carcinogenic nitrates and nitrosamines in the intestine. SWF

KALE

Remove stems, wash well, tear into pieces and place in a large covered pot. Place over a medium flame. When kale begins to simmer, reduce heat. Let simmer about 5 minutes until leaves are just wilted. Transfer to a strainer or colander and squeeze out liquid. Chop coarsely, place in a heated serving dish and toss with a generous pat of butter.

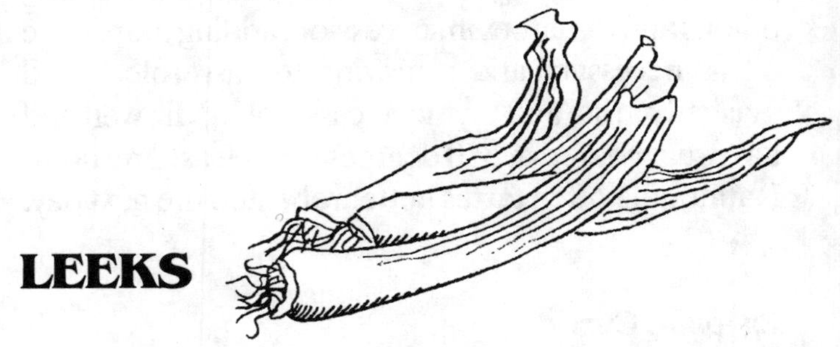

LEEKS

Leeks were once the stable vegetable of Europe. Unfortunately this fine root fell from favor in the 17th century, along with onions and garlic and any food that would "taint the breath". In recent years, leeks have made something of a comeback. They can always be used in place of onions although they have a slightly more pungent flavor than their bulbous cousins. Leeks are good sources of carotenoids, B-complex and vitamin C and are considered salutary for the liver.

Buy leeks that have not been trimmed as the leaves are your indication of freshness. Both the white part and the green should be used.

Leeks are often gritty and it is important to clean them well. To clean leaks, cut off end, remove outer leaf and slit lengthwise into the center. Open up and clean under running water. SWF

This cousin to the onion has been out of style for a number of years, but is poised for a comeback.

Braised Leeks
Serves 6

6 medium leeks
2 cups beef stock
1/2-1 cup grated Gruyere cheese

Trim ends off leeks and split lengthwise. Rinse well and set in a pyrex pan. Bring beef stock to a boil and pour over leeks. Bake at 350 degrees for about 1/2 hour or until stock has reduced and leeks are tender. Sprinkle on cheese and melt under broiler for a few minutes. Serve immediately.

Vegetable Leek Medley
Serves 6

3 leeks
2 zucchini
2 carrots
1 red pepper
1/2 stick butter
sea salt and freshly ground pepper

The secret to this attractive dish is proper cutting-up—the vegetables should be small and uniform. Cutting can be done in advance, and the dish prepared just before your meal.

Clean leeks, slice crosswise at 1/4-inch intervals and set side. Cut ends off zucchinis and make thick peelings of the skin. Cut the skin into a fine julienne and set aside. (Use the inner part for soups.) Peel the carrots and cut into a fine julienne. Seed the pepper and cut into thin, 1-inch strips.

Saute carrots and leeks in butter. When they are just tender, add the pepper and cook about one minute. Finally add zucchini and saute another minute. Season to taste with sea salt and freshly ground pepper.

Every new concept developed in medical science points the way to a new area awaiting further exploration. Discarding both the use of drugs and the germ theory of disease opened the way for me to explore new methods of eliminating the stagnating waste products from the body. Briefly stated, my position is: improper foods cause disease; proper foods cure disease. In upholding this theses, I have been in disagreement, at times sharp, with organized orthodox medicine. Henry Bieler MD *Food is Your Best Medicine*

LIMA BEANS

Plunge freshly hulled or frozen limas in boiling water and cook about 8 minutes or until tender. Drain in a colander and transfer to a heated serving dish. Toss with butter and season to taste with sea salt and pepper. You may want to first melt the butter and add to it one or two mashed garlic cloves.

Lima beans are one of the few beans that are eaten both dried, as a legume, and fresh, as a vegetable. They grow well in hot climates.

Lima beans contain B-complex vitamins, iron, potassium and phosphorus and a fair amount of protein. They contain more starch and less fat than most beans.

If you grow your own lima beans, you will be able to enjoy them freshly hulled. Avoid the hulled lima beans that sometimes appear in supermarkets and gourmet shops—these are usually dosed with preservatives. Your best bet is frozen limas, only slightly inferior, nutritionally speaking, to freshly hulled beans. SWF

Simple Succatash
Serves 6

2 cups shelled lima beans
6 ears corn, cut off cob
1/4 stick butter
1/2 cup piima cream or creme fraiche
1/2 cup chicken stock

Succatash comes from the Narragansett Indian word "misick-quatash", meaning ear of corn. Indian succatash consisted of beans, corn kernels, dog meat and bear grease. The succatash that finds its way to American tables has a slightly different list of ingredients.

Saute corn in butter until just tender. Add lima beans, cream and stock. Bring to a boil and skim. Simmer uncovered until the liquid has reduced and beans are tender. Season to taste with sea salt and freshly ground pepper. Succatash should be soupy, not too thick, and it is served in bowls.

Dr. William A. Albrecht, the famous soil specialist, reminds us that plants will make a lot of growth, just as you and I will, even when certain wanted minerals are missing. But the plants themselves will be different. Thus, cabbage is one thing if grown on one kind of soil, another if grown on another kind of soil. There are more minerals in it, or less, depending on the minerals in the soil, and apparently more or less proteins and vitamins in it. The same is true of carrots, beets, peas, oranges, apples potatoes, sweet corn or any other plant product we use as food. The calcium concentration of a lettuce leaf can be varied twofold and spinach threefold, according to the calcium in the soil. . . the same mineral variations occur in grasses and other plants eaten by domestic animals and what they eat, in turn, affects their products which we eat. Our beefsteaks, pork chops, lamb roasts and omelets can be mineral-shy, if the cows, hogs, lambs and chickens were shortchanged on their minerals.
The Saturday Evening Post 1945

Gourmet Succatash
Serves 8-12

2 cups shelled lima beans
6 ears of corn, cut off the cob
2 cups french beans, cut into 1 inch pieces
1/2 stick butter
1 bunch green onions, chopped
1 red pepper, chopped
1 cup piima cream or creme fraiche
1 cup chicken stock
sea salt and freshly ground pepper

Saute onion and pepper in butter. Add remaining ingredients, bring to a boil and skim. Simmer uncovered for about 10 minutes or until beans are tender. Season to taste and ladle into heated serving bowls.

MUSHROOMS

Mushrooms must be very fresh or they are not worth cooking. Remove stems, wash well and, most importantly, dry well. They can now be sauted in olive oil and butter either whole, quartered or in slices. To saute whole, melt butter and olive oil until it froths. Place mushrooms top side down in pan. When this side is golden, turn to other side. Saute another minute and transfer to heated platter or serving dish. Saute sliced or quartered mushrooms in small batches or they will not brown.

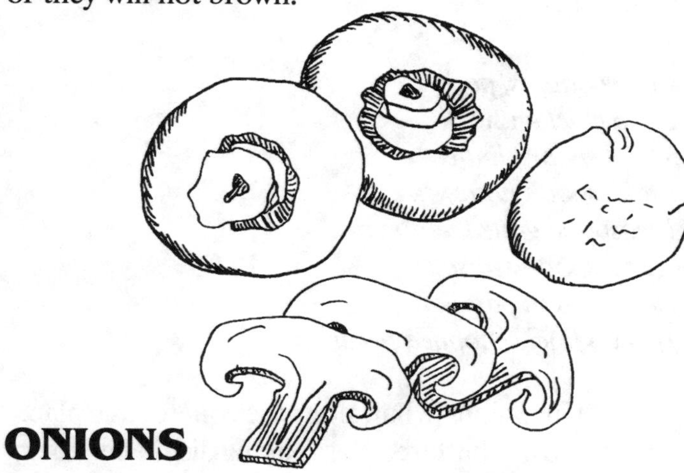

Mushrooms belong to the fungus family, one of the most primitive of all plant groups. Actually the mushroom is the fruit of the fungus, which grows underground. Mushrooms contain over 90% water and thus act as sponges, absorbing the flavors of other foods with which they are cooked. They contain protein, phosphorus, potassium, calcium, iron and B-complex vitamins, particularly biotin. Mushrooms are also rich in selenium, necessary for a healthy heart and circulatory system. Certain varieties of mushroom have long been valued for their medicinal properties in the Orient and in recent years the Japanese have done some interesting research in this area. A substance called adenosine has been isolated from the *mo-er* or tree ear mushroom; it has potent blood thinning and hence anticoagulating properties. Just a small amount of black tree ear mushroom can have a profound effect on reducing blood stickiness, clots and plaque buildup. Other commercially available mushrooms that seem to have these positive effects on the blood include the shiitake, enoki and oyster mushrooms. These mushrooms may also have salutary effects on cancer cells. Other commercially grown mushrooms seem to be devoid of specific pharmacological effects, but they are still valuable in the diet for their trace mineral and B-vitamin profile. SWF

ONIONS

This versatile vegetable is usually used in conjunction with other vegetables, but it also performs well on its own.

Onion Compote
Serves 6

6 large onions, peeled and thinly sliced
1/2 stick butter
2 tablespoons extra virgin olive oil

In a heavy skillet, cook onion in butter and olive oil on low heat for one hour or more, stirring occasionally. Onions will turn light brown and develop a caramel taste. This is delicious with roast beef.

The onion species—a subset of the lily family—is ubiquitous and no cuisine has developed that does not use the onion or one of its many cousins. They may have first been cultivated in Asia or India but wild onions are native in many localities including North America. The Great Lakes Indians called them *She-khe-ony*, and it is from this Indian word that the city of Chicago derives its name.

Onions are valued for their distinct flavor, which enhances the flavors of other ingredients in any dish, and they are a particularly good marriage with bland, starchy foods such as legumes or potatoes.

Onions contain carotenoids, B-complex vitamins—including all-important B6—and vitamin C, calcium, magnesium, potassium and sulphur compounds. They are universally valued for their medicinal properties which include the improvement of kidney function, lowering cholesterol and anti-bacterial qualities. According to some researchers, half a cup of raw onions per day is an excellent means of regulating cholesterol values and of protecting the blood from a tendency to coagulate and clot. Onions also have been shown to lower elevated blood sugar levels in test animals. Pasteur was the first to recognize that onions have strong anti-bacterial powers; onions are also helpful in breaking up mucus in the throat, lungs and nasal passages. Finally, recent research indicates that onions, with their concentrated sulphur com-

Onions Chardonnay
Serves 4

4-6 onions, peeled and very thinly sliced
1 cup dry Chardonnay

Place onions and wine in a pan. Bring to a boil, reduce and simmer, stirring occasionally, until most of the liquid has evaporated. This is a nice accompaniment to fish.

Baked Onions with Pecans
Serves 8

4 large onions, peeled
1 cup chicken stock
3 tablespoons butter
1 tablespoon honey
1 teaspoon grated lemon rind
1/2 teaspoon sea salt
1/4 teaspoon paprika
1/2 cup finely chopped pecans

Cut onions in half along the equator and place cut side up in a buttered glass baking dish. Mix stock, butter, honey, lemon rind, salt and paprika and heat gently until well blended. Pour over onions. Bake, covered, for about 50 minutes at 350 degrees, basting occasionally, until onions are just tender. Remove cover, sprinkle with pecans and bake another 10 or 15 minutes until lightly browned.

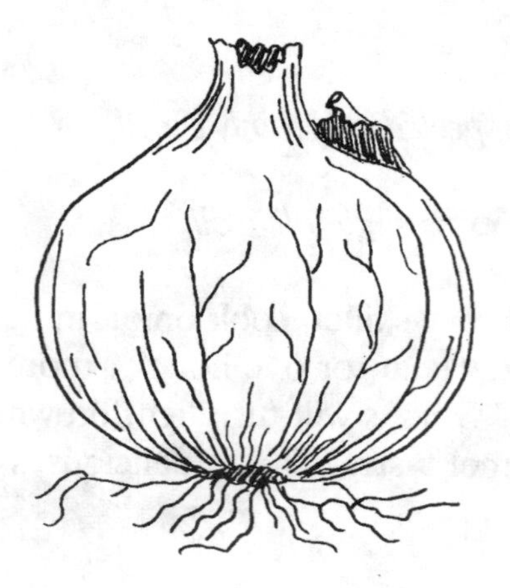

Stuffed Onions
Serves 8

4 large onions
extra virgin olive oil
1 1/2 cups fine wholegrain bread crumbs or basic brown rice (page 441)
1/4 cup pine nuts
1 teaspoon dried oregano
1/4 cup Parmesan cheese
2 teaspoons parsley, finely chopped
1 egg, lightly beaten

Cut onions in half along the equator and remove the inner part of the onion, leaving a shell two or three layers thick. Make a small slice on the bottom of each onion shell so that it will stand upright. Place shells in a buttered glass oven dish.

Chop the onions taken from the centers and saute in olive oil until tender. Add rice or bread crumbs, pine nuts, oregano, cheese and parsley and mix well. Off heat stir in the egg and season to taste with sea salt and pepper. Fill the onion shells. Put a little water in the baking pan and bake at 300 degrees for one hour.

Glazed Pearl Onions
Serves 6

30 pearl onions, peeled
1 tablespoon butter
1 tablespoon extra virgin olive oil
1 teaspoon honey
1/2 cup water or stock
1/2 cup red wine vinegar (optional)
pinch sea salt.

pounds, can be useful in treating cancer in some people. Onions also concentrate germanium when it is found in the soil. Germanium acts as an oxygen transporter and has been useful in cancer therapy.

On the other hand, certain yogic diets prohibit the onion because it is said to "increase body heat and the appetites". This may be because the onion acts as a stimulant to the adrenal glands. Those with weak adrenal glands should eat of the onion family sparingly as should individuals sensitive to sulphur-containing foods. SWF

Had your quercetin today? Maybe you have and didn't even know it.

Quercetin is one of the most powerful anti-cancer agents around, says Dr. Terence Leighton, a biochemistry professor at the University of California at Berkeley. Numerous experiments reveal that it blocks the first state of cell changes that permit cancer to develop.

OK. How can I protect myself with quercetin. Eat more broccoli, grapes, Italian squash and onions. Leighton says that people who eat a lot of broccoli and onions have a lower risk of certain cancers.

Red and yellow onions are rich in quercetin—about 10 percent of their dry weight. However, neither white onions nor garlic contains quercetin. So, if you want to keep cancer away, eat plenty of yellow and red onions. James F. Scheer *Health Freedom News*

A question arises at this point as to the efficiency of the human body in removing all of the minerals from the ingested foods. Extensive laboratory determinations have shown that most people cannot absorb more than half of the calcium and phosphorus from the foods eaten. The amounts utilized depend directly on the presence of other substances, particularly fat-soluble vitamins. It is at this point probably that the greatest breakdown in our modern diet takes place, namely, in the ingestion and utilization of adequate amount of the special activating substances, including the vitamins [A and D] needed for rendering the minerals in the food available to the human system. Weston Price DDS *Nutrition and Physical Degeneration*

Mix honey with stock or water and heat until honey is dissolved. Place onions, butter, oil, honey mixture and water and salt in a skillet large enough to accommodate the onions in one layer. Add the vinegar if you want a sour taste. Bring mixture to a boil, cover and cook a few minutes until the onions begin to soften. Remove lid from pan and continue cooking until water has evaporated and the onions become coated with glaze.

Onion Cranberry Compote
Makes 4 cups

2/3 cup yellow raisins
2/3 cup dark raisins
2 pounds small white onions, blanched in boiling water for 30 seconds and peeled
1/2 stick butter
3/4 cup white wine vinegar
1 cup dry white wine
3 cloves garlic, peeled and minced
1/2 teaspoon dried thyme
1 teaspoon sea salt
1 2/3 cups fresh cranberries, picked over

This is an excellent substitute for sugary cranberry relish at Thanksgiving.

Soak raisins in hot water for 10 minutes. Meanwhile, in a large saucepan, saute the onions in butter until well coated. Add wine and vinegar and boil down for several minutes. Add raisins with soaking liquid and remaining ingredients except cranberries. Liquid should just cover the onions—if not, add a little water. Simmer, covered, for about 1 hour, stirring occasionally. Remove cover, add cranberries and simmer uncovered for 15 to 30 minutes until liquid has thickened. Let cool. May be made up to 3 days in advance and kept in refrigerator. Serve at room temperature.

The cranberry grows wild in marshy places in New England and as far south as North Carolina. First called "fen berries" by the settlers, they were soon incorporated into their diets. Eventually the name changed to "craneberry" or "cranberry" because the slender stems of the fruit curve like the neck of a crane.

As early as 1860, medical science recognized the value of cranberries or their juice for the treatment of urinary tract infections and other kidney problems. Cranberries raise the level of acid in the urine and act as an antibiotic. SWF

PARSNIPS

The parsnip is a much maligned vegetable. When boiled in water, they are not very appetizing; but sauteed in butter they have a delicious taste and a nice texture. Remove ends, peel and cut into strips. Saute in butter until golden and just tender.

The parsnip was more popular in medieval times than it is today. Several centuries ago parsnips gave way to carrots at human tables and developed a reputation as an animal food. The Italians believe that pigs raised for *prochutto*—raw ham—give a more flavorful product if raised on parsnips. In Russia the word for parsnip is *pasternak*, a common last name and the moniker of one of Russia's most beloved writers, Boris Pasternak. The parsnip is sweeter than the carrot, especially if left in the ground until after the first frost. It contains carotenoids and vitamin C, calcium and potassium. The parsnip is rich in fiber. Medieval doctors prescribed the parsnip for toothache and stomachache, for impotence and dysentery. Modern researchers have not yet turned their attention to the parsnip. Who knows but that they wouldn't confirm these pharmacological properties of this flavorful and underrated vegetable. SWF

Parsnip Puree
Serves 6-8

1 1/2 pounds parsnips, peeled and cut into 1-inch pieces
2 potatoes, baked
1/2 cup piima cream or creme fraiche
1/2 stick butter, softened
1 teaspoon freshly grated ginger (optional)
pinch freshly ground nutmeg
sea salt and freshly ground pepper

Cook parsnips in boiling, salted water until tender, about 20 minutes. Drain and puree in a food processor along with scooped out potato flesh. (Save the skins for potato skins, page 495.) Add cream, butter and optional ginger and process until well blended. Season to taste. Transfer puree to a heated serving dish and keep warm in the oven.

Winter Root Medley
Serves 4

4 parsnips, peeled and cut into sticks
4 turnips, peeled and cut into quarters
1 rutabaga, peeled and cut into chunks
butter and extra virgin olive oil

In a heavy skillet, saute vegetables in butter and olive oil until golden.

In the summer of 1965, I met a wise man from the East, a Japanese philosopher who had just returned from several weeks in Saigon. "If you really expect to conquer the North Vietnamese," he told me, "you must drop Army PX's on them—sugar, candy and Coca-Cola. That will destroy them faster than bombs." William Dufty *Sugar Blues*

Peas belong to the legume family and the common garden green pea is a staple in many cuisines, usually eaten dried. But nothing can match fresh green peas for sweetness and flavor. Unfortunately few of us have time to shell fresh peas. Frozen peas are an acceptable alternative for soups and stews, and the Chinese pea or sugar snap pea brings all the flavor of fresh peas to your table without putting you to the trouble of shelling them.

Fresh peas provide carotenoids, B-complex, and vitamins C and E, as well as copper, iron, phosphorus and potassium. Studies have shown that peas can help prevent cancer in animals and that they act to lower blood cholesterol. A survey of diets in England and Wales indicates that peas may ward off appendicitis.

The surprising thing about peas is the fact that they contain anti-fertility agents. According to Indian scientist Dr. S. N. Sanyal, the population of Tibet has remained stable over the last 200 years because the pea forms a staple of the Tibetan diet. Dr. Sanyal isolated an anti-fertility compound in peas called m-xylohydroquinone which, when given to women in synthesized form, cut down the rate of conception by 50 to 60 percent. Unfortunately, the results are not as predictable as for other contraceptives and so this derivative of the pea has not been developed for the commercial market. Now that adverse side effects of the pill and other contraceptive methods are becoming known, it is time to renew research into natural anti-fertility agents like the pea. SWF

PEAS

Use freshly shelled peas or frozen peas. Plunge into boiling salted water for a few minutes, until just tender. Drain in a colander. Transfer to a heated serving dish, toss with butter and keep warm in the oven.

PEAS, CHINESE OR SUGAR SNAP

These are the delight of every serious cook. They take very little time to prepare and they add an elegant touch of bright green to the plate. Remove ends and strings and place in a vegetable steamer. Do not cook until just before serving your main course. Steam about one minute—no more—or until peas turn bright green. Arrange artistically on plates or transfer to a heated serving dish. This is one of the few vegetables that is not enhanced by butter; they are naturally buttery and can be eaten plain.

Stir Fry Chinese Peas with Sesame Seeds
Serves 6

1 pound Chinese peas, ends and strings removed
extra virgin olive oil
1 bunch green onions, cut into 1-inch pieces
2 tablespoons pine nuts
2 tablespoons sesame seeds, toasted in oven
1 tablespoon toasted sesame oil
sea salt and freshly ground pepper

Stir fry onions and Chinese peas in olive oil for about 3 minutes. Add pine nuts and sesame seeds and cook another minute. Off heat stir in the toasted sesame oil and season to taste. (Caution: Always add toasted sesame oil as a flavoring, never use it for frying or sauteing as it will quickly go rancid and develop a horrible taste.)

PEPPERS

Remove stems and seeds and cut into strips or chunks. Saute quickly in olive oil until tender. If you are using peppers of different colors, saute them separately and mix together at the end.

Peppers and Onions
Serves 4

2 medium onions, peeled and thinly sliced
2 red peppers, seeded and sliced into strips
butter and extra virgin olive oil
1/2 teaspoon fine herbs
2 cloves garlic peeled
1/2 cup finely shredded basil leaves
sea salt and freshly ground pepper

Saute onions and peppers gently in butter and olive oil for about 45 minutes until soft. Add herbs, crushed garlic and basil and cook another few minutes. The consistency should be like marmalade. Season to taste Remove with a slotted spoon to a heated serving dish. May be served as a side dish or as an appetizer on triangle croutons (page 491).

Peppers with Almonds
Serves 6

3 red peppers, seeded and cut into strips
2 green peppers, seeded and cut into strips
extra virgin olive oil
3/4 cup crispy almonds (page 487)
1/2 cup raisins
1 teaspoon honey
1/4 cup red wine vinegar
sea salt and freshly ground pepper

Saute peppers in olive oil until tender. Meanwhile dissolve honey in vinegar over a low flame. Add raisins and vinegar-honey mixture to peppers and boil down until most of liquid is evaporated. Meanwhile, slice almonds using the fine slicing blade of your food processor. Stir in almonds and season to taste. Can be served hot or at room temperature.

The pepper is one of those foods that came from the New World, but which is associated with many ethnic cuisines in Europe and Asia—the typical cuisines of India, Thailand, China, Hungary, Italy and Spain are almost inconceivable without the pepper.

Peppers can be divided into two main categories: the sweet peppers which are eaten as a vegetable; and the chile peppers or hot peppers, which are used as flavorings and spices. Both are members of the capsicum family, a subset of the nightshade category of plants. Thus the pepper is the cousin of eggplant, tomato and potato.

Peppers are rich in vitamin C and carotenoids and contain potassium and calcium. Red peppers are richer in these vitamins than green ones. The inner ribs of peppers are good sources of bioflavonoids, substances that protect blood capillaries from breakage. Chile peppers have numerous medicinal properties, most notably the ability to loosen phlegm. Consumption of chile peppers in moderate amounts is an effective remedy for chronic bronchitis and emphysema. Compounds found in chile peppers act as decongestants and also help dissolve blood clots. Extracts of pepper have been used to treat toothache and conjunctivitis. Like so many other vegetables, peppers have been shown to lower blood cholesterol. SWF

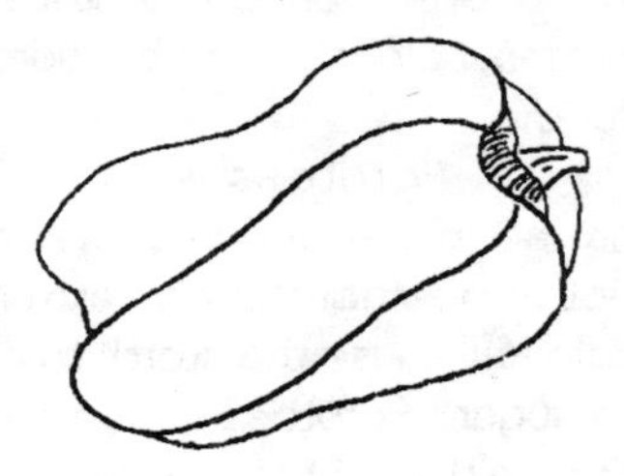

POTATOES

The potato ranks first among the many vegetables that came from the New World. European cuisine is not unthinkable without the potato. Yet the potato had difficulty winning acceptance. Starving German peasants at Kolberg could only be persuaded to eat potatoes at gunpoint; Antoine Parmentier succeeded in kindling an interest in the French by presenting a bouquet of potato flowers to Marie Antoinette; the English offered subsidies to grow potatoes. Only in Ireland did the potato catch on quickly. Since it grew underground, it was a crop that could survive the devastations of military skirmishes, all too frequent on the soil of poor Ireland at the time.

Potatoes provide vitamin C and B-complex as well as potassium, calcium and iron. Most of the nutrients are just under the skin, so don't peel them. The skin itself is full of fiber and can be kept in almost any potato preparation. In spite of the potato's popularity, there has been little research on the its pharmacological effects. Eating potatoes was formerly recommended by doctors in America for purifying the blood and curing indigestion. Potatoes contain chlorogenic acid, a chemical that prevents cell mutations leading to cancer. In some individuals, potatoes raise blood sugar levels quickly, so potatoes may not be a good choice for some diabetics. Yet the maverick physician Henry Bieler recommended potatoes as the most digestible carbohydrate food.

Potatoes should be stored in a cool dark place, but not in a refrigerator as extreme cold will cause the starch to turn to sugar. Potatoes will sprout if kept in the light too long—avoid

Nothing can match the versatility of the potato, and potatoes in their simplest form can be as satisfying as the most complicated dish. To bake, wash potatoes and cut a bit off each end. Bake in a preheated 350 degree oven for 1 to 1 1/2 hours or until tender. If you brush the skins with oil, they will get crispy. Serve with butter or cultured cream.

To cook red potatoes, wash well, dry and put them in a clay pot. Cover and set in a cold oven and turn on to 250 degrees. The potatoes will cook in 2 to 3 hours depending on their size. (They will cook faster if you raise the heat but the flavor will be less intense.) May be served plain or tossed with a little butter. Tiny red potatoes may be cooked in a clay pot for about 1/2 hour and then sauted whole in butter.

Stuffed Potatoes
Serves 6

6 baking potatoes
1/2 stick butter
1 cup piima cream or creme fraiche
1 bunch green onions, finely chopped
1/2 cup Parmesan cheese or grated raw cheddar
sea salt and freshly ground pepper

Bake potatoes as described above. Cut butter into pats and place in a large bowl. When potatoes are done, cut lengthwise and scoop out soft potato flesh into the bowl with the butter. Mash with a potato masher. Mix in cultured cream, cheese and onions. Season to taste. Spoon the potato mixture back into the shells and return them to a 150 degree oven to keep warm. If potatoes are not reheated to a high temperature, the enzymes in the cream will be preserved.

Rosemary Potatoes
Serves 6

2 pounds tiny red potatoes
butter and extra virgin olive oil
1 teaspoon dried rosemary
sea salt and freshly ground pepper

Cook potatoes until just tender in a clay pot. Saute in butter and oil with rosemary for a few minutes, until golden. Season to taste

Cottage Potatoes
Serves 6

6 large baking potatoes
1/2 stick butter
4 tablespoons extra virgin olive oil
sea salt

These are a nice alternative to deep fried potatoes. Wash potatoes but do not peel. Cut into 1/4 inch slices. Melt butter and oil together. Brush two cookie sheets with the oil mixture. Place slices on cookie sheets and brush top sides with remaining oil mixture. Sprinkle with a little sea salt. Bake in a 350 degree oven for about 45 minutes or until golden browned. Check the potatoes frequently for burning. If they are cooking unevenly, remove potatoes as they become done to a heated platter and keep warm.

Sauteed Potatoes with Onions
Serves 4

4 medium onions, peeled and thinly sliced
8 red potatoes
clarified butter or duck fat
extra virgin olive oil
sea salt and freshly ground pepper

eating these sprouts as they contain poisonous alkaloids. It is important to buy organic potatoes. Most commercial potatoes have been treated with sprout inhibitors that have mutagenic effects. However, there's nothing harmful about eating a potato that has small sprouts—just trim off the sprouts and discard them. SWF

You will probably be as surprised as I was to find practically nothing in a search of the literature on the effect of fried foods on the digestion. The one article on the subject refutes the old medical prejudice against fried foods.

Boggess and Ivy did their frying experiment with potatoes. They concluded that [pan-fried] potatoes were more easily digested that French fried [boiled in grease].

Dr. Frank Howard Richardson, commenting on the prejudice against frying, said, "There is a widely held belief, cherished by physicians and laity alike, to the effect that fried foods are harmful in general and that they are particularly harmful for children. An analysis. . . clearly demonstrates that it is not documented with scientific proof or with any proof at all for that matter. Rather, it is merely a repetition and reiteration in many different forms of this unproved old unscientific prejudice.

Food that is pan-fried in butter . . . is no worse than any other cooked food. In fact, Boggess in his experiment found that fried potatoes were more digestible than boiled potatoes.
William Campbell Douglass MD
The Milk of Human Kindness

Scattered across the earth are people of vastly different races, cultures, body types, and belief systems. They live near mountains, oceans, rivers, deserts, tundra, tropics, forests and flatlands. Some have only fish and a few varieties of plants available to eat, some an assortment of tropical fruits and vegetables, some have only yak milk, meat and a little grain, while others have enough fertile land and resources to raise crops, herd animals, and mass-produce every imaginable variety of food.

Is it sensible for any one people to tell another about the "true" ways to eat? Can a tribesman from West Africa whose staple food is cassava root tell an Eskimo he is wrong because his staple food is fish? Or can the Japanese tell the Mexicans of the absurdity of eating dairy, corn, hot peppers and food fried in lard, staple products completely unknown to native Japan? David Marc *Nourishing Wisdom*

Know Your Ingredients

Name This Product #18

Potatoes, cottonseed oil, sour cream and onion seasoning, salt. Sour cream and onion seasoning contains: dehydrated whey, dextrose, partially hydrogenated soybean oil, salt, dehydrated sour cream, onion and nonfat dry milk, monosodium glutamate, modified food starch, lactose, sodium caseinate, sugar, dehydrated parsley, garlic powder, citric acid, sodium citrate and imitation flavor.

See Appendix B for Answer

There are two secrets to this recipe. One is to parboil the potatoes first, before they are sliced and sauted; the other is to cook the onions separately.

Plunge potatoes in boiling water and cook about 10 minutes until just barely tender. Remove with a slotted spoon. Slice into 1/4 inch slices or cut into quarters. Saute in batches in butter or duck fat in a large frying pan. Meanwhile saute the onions in butter and oil in a separate frying pan. When both onions and potatoes are golden, transfer them to a heated serving dish and mix together. Season to taste.

The Best Hash Browns
Serves 4

4 medium potatoes
filtered water
1/2 cup whey
2 tablespoons sea salt
butter and extra virgin olive oil

These have a wonderful sour taste. Use the food processor to cut potatoes into a small julienne. Place in a bowl with water, whey and salt. Press potatoes down so that they are entirely covered with water, cover bowl and soak overnight. Pour out water, skim off top layer of potatoes (which will have turned brown), place potatoes in a tea towel and wring out thoroughly. Melt butter and olive oil in a large, heavy skillet. Place half the potatoes in the pan and press down firmly. Cover pan and saute over medium heat about 5 minutes. Turn potatoes and saute, covered, another 5 or so minutes or until potatoes are well browned. Repeat with second batch.

Variation: Corned Beef Hash

Mix *1 cup finely chopped corned beef (page 214), 1 medium onion, finely chopped and 1 red pepper, seeded and cut into a julienne* with potatoes after they have been squeezed dry and saute according to recipe for hash browns.

Potatoes Anna
Serves 4

4 medium potatoes
1/2 stick butter, clarified (page 136)
1/2 teaspoon dried thyme
1/2 teaspoon dried rosemary
sea salt and freshly ground pepper

Potatoes Anna is a traditional French dish, a sort of potato cake that is crisp on the outside and soft in the center. Its the kind of dish that draws raves from dinner guests, and it is not difficult to prepare successfully if the details are adhered to. You will need a 10-inch heavy, non-stick type skillet with sloping sides, such as an omelette pan. The "cake" also needs to be weighted on top. A 10-inch french tart pan bottom serves this purpose well. It should be buttered, placed on top of the potatoes and weighted down with a several cans.

Wash the potatoes but do not peel. Slice very thinly into a bowl of iced water. Put about 1/3 of the clarified butter in the pan and coat the bottom. Dry the potato slices well and arrange them in a swirling pattern to make one layer in the pan. Dribble butter on this layer and a sprinkle of the herbs, salt and pepper. Repeat process for two more layers. Don't be tempted to make a fourth layer if you have slices left over. The results will not be as good if the potato "cake" is too thick.

Place the tart pan bottom on top of the potatoes and weight it down. Cook the potatoes over medium heat for about 30 minutes or until bottom is golden. Check to see if anything is sticking and slide the potatoes onto a large plate. Place the pan over the potatoes, hold onto the plate and turn quickly. Reweight the "cake" and cook another 10 to 15 minutes more. Cut into wedges to serve.

The more defective this individual biochemical makeup is, by inheritance, enzyme deficiency, malnutrition, harbored infection or otherwise, the more likely the person is to develop maladaptive allergic-like symptoms on exposure to food and environmental contacts. Our peculiar cultural preferences for eating only a few types of food, for example, or our heavy consumption of refined carbohydrates. . . add materially to a developing state of nutritional deficiency with a corresponding multiple symptom production in our body tissue systems. Likewise, our nation's propensity to consume nutritionally deficient junk foods further increases the defective tissue states in the human body. These defective states undermine an individual's ability to handle without symptom formation the contacts he has with toxins, pollens, foods or chemical fumes. William H. Philpott MD *Victory Over Diabetes*

[Rosemary] has been shown to be a potent antioxidant by Japanese scientists. They have isolated at least four compounds in rosemary that act as antioxidants. In fact two of the rosemary compounds were about four times more active than. . . BHT and BHA, antioxidants used in the food industry to prevent rancidity. Jean Carper *The Food Pharmacy Guide to Good Eating*

Potatoes Gratin

Serves 8

6 large baking potatoes
4 cups beef stock
2 cups piima cream or creme fraiche
butter
sea salt and freshly ground pepper
1 clove garlic, peeled and minced

While Americans think that potatoes "au gratin" means potatoes in casserole with cheese, the dish is traditionally made only with milk and creme fraiche. Sliced potatoes are boiled the milk for about ten minutes until the starch has exuded into the milk. Then the milk is mixed with the cream, the potatoes put into an oven dish and the milk-cream mixture poured over. This process prevents the milk and the cream from separating. A golden brown crust forms during cooking. It has a delicious cheesy taste, hence the misapprehension.

We have substituted beef stock for milk and find that the recipe works just as well—with the added bonus that the hydrophilic colloids of the stock make this somewhat heavy dish more digestible. And the results are just as good.

Wash potatoes but do not peel. Slice into the stock and bring to a boil. Cook, stirring almost constantly, for about ten minutes. Meanwhile butter a 9-by-13 inch glass oblong pan and sprinkle bottom with salt, pepper and the minced garlic. Remove the potato slices with a slotted spoon and arrange them randomly in the casserole. Bring the cream to a boil, pour into the stock and boil the two together for a minute. Pour over potatoes. Bake at 350 degrees about 1 hour more until the liquid has evaporated and the top has turned golden. You may reduce heat to 250 degrees and cook another hour or so if the casserole seems too liquid.

An Establishment researcher has found that the best way to [combat colds and flu] is not through orthodox therapies, but through certain key nutrients, with an accent on vitamin C and potassium.

Joel Schwartz, a senior scientist with the Environmental Protection Agency, in a survey of 9,000 people, has discovered what many of us have known for years: that the higher the intake of vitamin C, the less likely people are to suffer from respiratory problems—allergies, colds and flu, and, among other things, bronchitis.

Schwartz believes that vitamin C's antioxidant powers probably help to repair sensitive lung tissues from day-to-day wear and tear and from damage caused by bacteria, viruses, pollens, dander, cigarette smoke and other environmental pollutants.

His second key finding is that people who go heavy on sodium and light on potassium—the later is plentiful in fresh vegetables and fruit—suffer more respiratory ills. It is important to take in less sodium and more potassium.

These are potassium and vitamin C-rich foods that could help: beans, parsley, peas, avocados, potatoes, bananas, oats, cantaloupe, cabbage, citrus fruits, cucumbers, berries, green grapes, broccoli, cauliflower and mangoes. James F. Scheer *Health Freedom News*

Potato and Celery Root Puree
Serves 8 to 10

6 baked potatoes
3 celery roots, peeled and cut up
2 cloves garlic, peeled and mashed
grated nutmeg, sea salt and pepper to taste
1 stick butter
1/2 to 1 cup piima cream or creme fraiche

This beats plain old mashed potatoes any day. Cover the celery root pieces with cold water, bring to a boil and cook until very tender, about 30 minutes. Cut up the butter and place in the bottom of a large bowl. Scoop out potato flesh into the bowl. (Save the skins for potato skins, page 495) Add the celery root and garlic, and mash all together. Add the cream to obtain desired consistency. If you want your puree really smooth, you may now mix with a handheld beater. Season to taste. Transfer to a buttered oven proof dish and keep warm in the oven.

Potato Pancakes
Serves 6

6 baking potatoes
1 tablespoon sea salt
3-4 tablespoons whey or lemon juice
2 medium onions
2 eggs, lightly beaten
3/4 cup spelt or unbleached white flour
sea salt and freshly ground pepper
butter and extra virgin olive oil

Wash potatoes and grate them in your food processor. Cover with water and stir in salt and whey or lemon juice. Cover and let stand several hours. Meanwhile grate the onions. Mix eggs with flour and onions. Season to taste. Dump the potatoes in a colander, rinse briefly, squeeze dry with a tea towel and stir into batter. Use a 1/4 cup measure to scoop batter for pancakes. Saute on both sides in a mixture of butter and oil until golden.

For centuries, uninformed and unskilled physicians would continue to relegate signs of sugar blues—the simple remedy for which they overlooked—to bewitchment. Three centuries of medical mischief would produce a veritable babel of Greek and Latin symptoma: Schizophrenia, paranoia, catatonia, dementia preacox, neuroses, psychoses, psychoneuroses, chronic urticaria, neurodermatitis, cephalaigia, hermicrania, paroxysmal tachycarida—all as scarifying as the devil himself. The wise people who understood what sugar blues were all about—the midwives, village herbalists and healers—had been driven underground. . . Physicians and priests condemned natural healers at home as witches and consigned them to damnation. William Dufty *Sugar Blues*

Atherosclerosis isn't the only disease the polyunsaturated oils can give you. Cancer can be induced in experimental animals with corn oil. Hypertension will occur in rats and chickens by feeding unsaturated oils whereas animal fats (lard, milk, butter) do not cause high blood pressure. Amyloidosis, a disease of protein degeneration, can also be induced by polyunsaturates. William Campbell Douglass MD *The Milk of Human Kindness*

SPAGHETTI SQUASH

This unusual vegetable is a good substitute for pasta. Cut in half lengthwise, remove seeds and place cut sides down in a baking pan filled with about 1/2 inch of water. Bake at 350 for about 1 hour or until tender. Turn the squash skin side down and remove the "strands" bit by bit with a fork. Garnish with butter and a little Parmesan cheese, or any one of a number of sauces such as pesto (page 135) or tomato sauce (pages 140 and 141). The strands may also be formed into patties and sauted in butter.

The body probably needs both animal and vegetable fats to maintain sound health. A study conducted among boys of Ruanda, Africa, a vegetarian population by necessity, found that carotene absorption by children was dependent upon the amount of fat in the diet, not the amount of carotene eaten. It was also established that a low fat intake results in poor absorption of both carotenoids and pre-formed vitamin A. When small amounts of [animal] fat were added to their vegetarian diet, improvement in the absorption of carotene resulted and Vitamin A levels increased. H. Leon Abrams *Journal of Applied Nutrition*

Spaghetti Squash Casserole
Serves 4

1 large spaghetti squash, prepared as above
2 medium onions
butter and extra virgin olive oil
2 ripe tomatoes, peeled , seeded and chopped
2 cloves garlic, peeled and chopped
1/2 teaspoon dried thyme
2 tablespoons fresh basil leaves, cut up
sea salt and freshly ground pepper
1/4 cup parsley, chopped
1 cup whole grain bread crumbs
1/2 cup freshly grated Parmesan cheese
2 tablespoons melted butter

Saute onion in butter and olive oil until soft. Add tomato, garlic, thyme and basil and cook gently until most liquid is absorbed. Mix with spaghetti squash, season to taste and pour into a well buttered pyrex dish. Mix parsley, bread crumbs and Parmesan and spread on top. Drizzle with melted butter. Bake uncovered at 350 degrees for about 1/2 hour or until most of the liquid is absorbed.

Even though calcium is present in spinach, children cannot utilize it. Data have been published showing that children absorb very little of the calcium or phosphorus in spinach before six years of age. Adult individuals vary in the efficiency with which they absorb minerals and other chemicals essential for mineral utilization. It is possible to starve for minerals that are abundant in the foods eaten because they cannot be utilized without an adequate quantity of the fat-soluble activators. Weston Price, DDS *Nutrition and Physical Degeneration*

SPINACH

In general, one bunch of spinach or one bag will serve 3 persons. Cut stems off leaves and wash well—even if prewashed, the leaves should be rinsed so that they are moist. Place in a large pot. Do not add more water to the pot. Water adhering to the leaves will be just enough to steam the spinach. Cover pot and place over a medium flame. When spinach begins to simmer, reduce heat. Cook several minutes or until leaves are just wilted. Using a slotted spoon, transfer to a heated serving bowl. Press with the back of the spoon to squeeze out any liquid and pour out. Make a few cuts through the spinach and top with a generous pat of butter.

Mary Jo's Spinach
Serves 6

2 bunches fresh spinach
3 tablespoons butter
1 clove garlic, peeled and mashed
1 tablespoon pine nuts, toasted
1 tablespoon sun dried tomato flakes (optional)

Steam spinach as described above. Melt butter with garlic, pine nuts and optional tomato flakes. Pour over spinach and mix slightly.

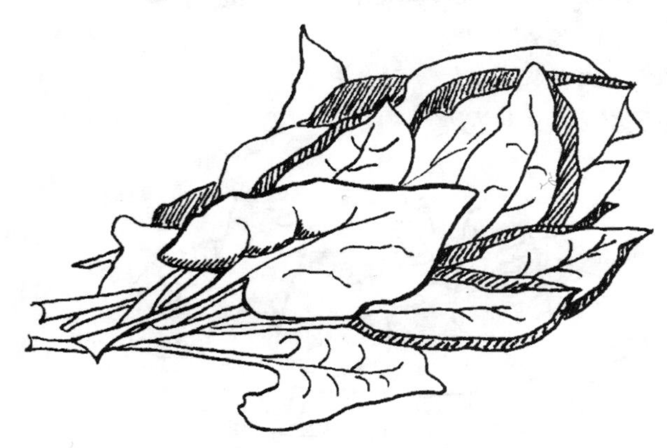

Spinach is the queen of the dark green leafy vegetables, the least bitter and most tender. The first record we have of spinach occurs in the year 647, when the king of Nepal sent a gift of spinach to the emperor of China. It was introduced into England in the middle of the 1500's.

Spinach is exceptionally high in carotenoids and vitamin C. It contains calcium and iron but scientists now believe that the form of iron contained in spinach is one that is not easily absorbed. Spinach also contains oxalic acid that can prevent calcium absorption. Oxalic acid is neutralized during cooking, so while cooked spinach can be eaten regularly, spinach salads should be eaten only on occasion.

Both the chlorophyll and carotenoids found so abundantly in spinach are potent cancer blockers. Japanese studies also indicate that spinach lowers blood cholesterol in laboratory animals. New research indicates that spinach is effective in preventing macular degeneration of the eye.

Spinach is now available at almost any time of the year. Many times you can buy it prewashed in sealed plastic bags. Do take advantage of the wonderful things that the modern age has made available to one and all and eat spinach regularly. SWF

Despite proof to the contrary, many doctors still cling to the germ theory of disease and to the necessity of drugs to combat germs. They point out that smallpox, diphtheria, typhoid fever and pneumonia have been conquered. That is true; no one can quarrel with them on that score. But such major chronic disorders as cancer, heart disease, diabetes, arteriosclerosis, nephrosis and hepatitis have increased eightfold,. Scientific medicine, while suppressing deadly infectious diseases by the use of modern drugs, antibiotics and immunizations, has not been able to reduce the killing power of another equally frightening set of diseases.

Instead of blindly following Pasteur (as so many medical men have done) I asked myself: Is invasion of the tissues from without-by bacteria and viruses—the only way by which human tissues are injured? Can disease come from other means? Shouldn't man's constitutional and environmental conditions also be considered? Hasn't the time come to expand our notions of illness and treatment beyond Pasteur's bacterial infection theory? Can it be possible that germs are merely a concomitant of disease, present in all of us but able to multiply in a sick individual because of disturbed function?

In seeking answers to these questions, I left Pasteur and his tiny organisms and went off on another road. . . I came to the conclusion that germs do not initiate a diseased state of the body but appear later after a person becomes ill. Henry Bieler MD *Food is Your Best Medicine*

Spinach Stuffed Mushrooms

Serves 8

1 cup cooked spinach
8 large mushrooms
1 bunch green onions, finely chopped
nutmeg, sea salt and freshly ground pepper
butter and extra virgin olive oil

Chop cooked spinach, place in a strainer and press out liquid. Meanwhile wash mushrooms and remove stems. Chop stems finely and saute with onions in butter and olive oil until tender. Add the spinach and cook another minute or so, mixing well, until all moisture is evaporated. Season to taste with nutmeg, sea salt and pepper. Place a spoonful or so in the hollow of each mushroom and place in a buttered glass pan. They may be prepared in advance to this point. To cook, add 1/4 inch water to the pan, place in a 350 degree oven and bake for about 20 minutes. This is a delicious and elegant accompaniment to beef.

Spinach Timbales

Serves 6

2 large bunches spinach
4 tablespoons butter, softened
4 tablespoons piima cream or creme fraiche
4 eggs, lightly beaten
1 medium onion, very finely chopped
freshly grated nutmeg
1/2 teaspoon sea salt
freshly ground pepper

Steam spinach as described above. Squeeze out liquid thoroughly and place in food processor. Pulse a few times until well chopped. Combine with other ingredients and season to taste with sea salt and pepper. Pour into 6 conical timbale moulds that have been well buttered or oiled. Place in a pan of hot water and bake at 350 degrees for 20 minutes. Loosen timbales with a knife and turn them onto a warmed platter or individual plates.

SWEET POTATOES

These can be baked like a regular potato. Serve with plenty of butter but there is no need to eat the skin. Sweet potatoes are just loaded with vitamins and fiber, through and through.

Sweet Potato Dollars
Serves 4

3 sweet potatoes
1/2 stick butter, melted
sea salt

Peel potatoes and slice crosswise at 1/4 inch intervals into "dollars". Brush two cookie sheets with butter. Arrange the dollars in one layer and brush with the remaining butter. Season lightly with sea salt. Bake about 45 minutes at 350 degrees.

There's probably no vegetable with a higher beta-carotene content than the sweet potato. This is the beta-carotene that protects us against cancer, colds, infections and other diseases. The carotene content of sweet potatoes actually increases as the vegetable is stored throughout the winter. But remember that our bodies can only convert carotene to vitamin A in the presence of bile salts. That's why it's so important to eat sweet potatoes with butter, egg yolks or cream. These fats stimulate the secretion of bile and help the body to convert carotenes to all- important vitamin A. These wonderful fats also make sweet potatoes taste delicious.

The sweet potato is a good source of iron, potassium, niacin and vitamin C. It contains fiber and is very rich in vitamin B6, a vitamin that is highly protective against heart disease. Last but not least, the sweet potato is rich in magnesium, another nutrient that protects against heart disease. SWF

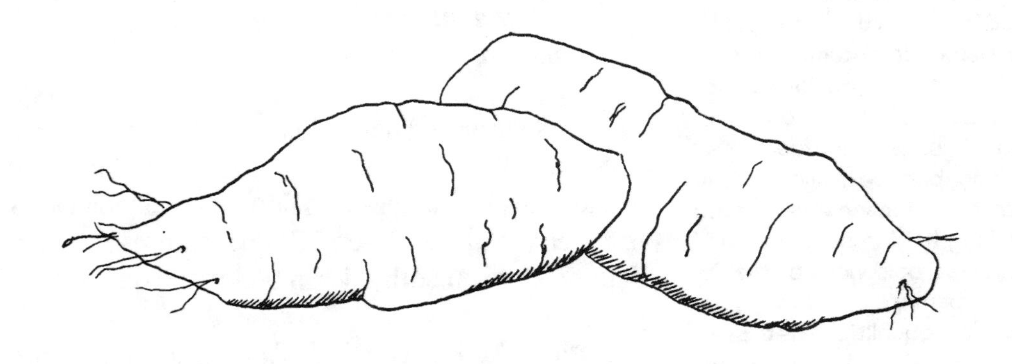

Peas, water, carrots, partially hydrogenated soybean oil, margarine (liquid corn oil, partially hydrogenated corn oil, water, salt, whey, mono- and diglycerides lecithin, artificially flavored and colored [carotene], vitamin A Palmitate and vitamin D added), maltodextrin, modified food starch, powdered sweet cream (cream cheese [sweet cream, nonfat dry milk, cheese culture], whey, sugar, modified food starch, citric acid, sodium citrate), salt, sugar, natural flavor, hydroxylated lecithin, disodium phosphate, onion powder, garlic powder, xanthan gum, spices.

See Appendix B for Answer

Can anyone imagine Italian or Greek cooking without the tomato? And yet the tomato is another newcomer to European cuisine, an import from the New World. When the tomato was first introduced to European tables, and before it became common fare, it was called the "love apple" and was reputed to be an aphrodisiac. This reputation faded after tomatoes became available to the masses. In America the tomato was long held in suspicion, and considered poisonous by the Puritans—perhaps out of fear of its aphrodisiac qualities. As this apprehension faded, the tomato became our most popular garden vegetable.

Sweet Potato Casserole
Serves 6

4 large sweet potatoes
grated rind of two lemons
juice of two lemons
1 stick butter, cut into pats
2 egg yolks
1/2 teaspoon sea salt

Tart lemon peel is a great foil for the sweetness of the potatoes. Boil potatoes in water until tender. Meanwhile place remaining ingredients in a large bowl. Peel potatoes while still hot (wear rubber gloves for this), place in the bowl, mash and mix with other ingredients. Transfer mixture to a buttered oven-proof casserole and bake in a 350 degree oven for about 1/2 hour.

Sweet Potato Pancakes
Serves 4-6

2 medium sweet potatoes, peeled and grated
1 large potato, grated
2 tablespoons whey or lemon juice
1 tablespoon sea salt
1 medium onion, minced
1 small carrot, grated
3 eggs, lightly beaten
4 tablespoons spelt or unbleached white flour
1 teaspoon sea salt
1/2 teaspoon pepper
freshly ground nutmeg
butter and extra virgin olive oil

Soak grated potato in water plus whey or lemon juice and salt for several hours or overnight. Squeeze dry in a tea towel. Mix eggs with flour and seasonings. Stir in grated vegetables. Use a 1/3 cup measure to scoop out batter. Saute on both sides in butter and olive oil.

Variation: Add *1/4 cup finely chopped cilantro* to batter. Omit nutmeg.

TOMATOES

Traditionally tomatoes have been boiled or stewed—a particularly nasty way to ruin a tomato. But they are very nice baked.

Baked Tomatoes
Serves 4

8 firm plum tomatoes
extra virgin olive oil
2 tablespoons honey

Brush tomatoes with olive oil and set in an oiled pie plate. Bake at a very low temperature (200 degrees) for at least 4 hours. Brush on honey, raise heat to 300 and bake another 20 or 30 minutes. The tomatoes will become browned and slightly caramelized. These are just delicious with red meats.

Stuffed Tomatoes
Serves 6

3 large tomatoes
sea salt and freshly ground pepper
2 slices whole grain bread
2 tablespoons butter, softened
2 tablespoons Parmesan cheese
1/2 teaspoon fine herbs

Slice tomatoes in half around the equator, remove seeds and place cut side up in a buttered baking dish. Sprinkle with a little sea salt and freshly ground pepper. Process bread in a food processor until it becomes fine crumbs. Add butter, cheese and herbs and pulse a few times until well blended. Spread a spoonful of the stuffing over each tomato half. Bake at 350 degrees for about 30 minutes.

Tomatoes are well known for their vitamin C content and also contain carotenoids, B-complex, potassium, magnesium, phosphorus and calcium. Unfortunately many tomatoes are picked green and then treated with ethylene gas which causes them to turn red without really ripening. These tomatoes have the flavor and texture of cardboard and are nutritionally inferior. Canned tomatoes, picked at the peak of ripeness surpass most store-bought tomatoes in nutritional qualities. Organic canned tomato products, with no salt added, are now sold in many stores. Even better, fresh organically grown and vine ripened tomatoes are now becoming more available. Hydroponically grown tomatoes, while perfect in appearance, are lacking in both nutrients and flavor.

To bring store bought tomatoes to the peak of ripeness, place them upside down in a sunny windowsill. When ripened they will keep about a week refrigerated.

As for the therapeutic benefits of the tomato, they are high in a carotenoid called lycopene that seems to be of great value in protecting us from cancer. Other studies have shown them to be helpful in preventing appendicitis. On the down side, some individuals are allergic to tomatoes. This is probably due to the fact that many people consume tomatoes in the form of tomato sauces and other tomato products to the exclusion of other vegetables. The answer to this is to eat a variety of vegetables, and keep the tomato in its proper place—as one of a great many vegetables that should be eaten on a regular basis but not to excess. SWF

TURNIPS

Turnips will not win any prizes for their vitamin and mineral content; but they excel in other non-nutrient substances, making them vegetables of importance.

Both the bulb and the greens are prime candidates as cancer preventers, because they, like cabbage and other cruciferous vegetables, contain compounds that thwart the development of cancer in laboratory animals. Rutabagas—large yellow turnips—are also chockful of anti-carcinogenic chemicals.

For example, formidable cancer fighters in the cruciferous family are compounds called glucosinolates. In laboratory animals these compounds block the development of cancer. Turnips have an exceptionally high range of glucosinolates compared even to other cruciferous vegetables, known to be high in glucosinolates. Jean Carper *The Food Pharmacy*

This European favorite, and its cousin the rutabaga, is rarely seen on American tables—and yet it was a stable in the early American farmers' diet, usually mashed up with plenty of butter and cream. The following recipes do justice to this neglected vegetable.

Turnip Puree
Serves 6

3 pounds turnips or rutabagas
2-3 baked potatoes
3/4 cup piima cream or creme fraiche
1 teaspoon dried thyme
sea salt and freshly ground pepper

Peel turnips and cook in salted water for about 45 minutes or until tender. Scoop flesh out of potatoes and add to turnips. (Reserve skins for potato skins, page 495.) Mix in the cream, thyme and seasonings to taste. Transfer to an buttered ovenproof casserole and reheat at about 200 degrees.

Why did the McGovern Committee ignore the scientific literature incriminating vegetable fats in atherosclerosis? Extensive studies with monkeys fed vegetable oils proved beyond a doubt that peanut oil. . . and other vegetable fats cause severe hardening of the arteries. With the current fixation on cholesterol in the nutritional establishment, it is important to note that on peanut oil the serum cholesterol remained low. The peanut oil may kill you but you can die with a normal cholesterol. William Campbell Douglass MD *The Milk of Human Kindness*

Glazed Turnips
Serves 6

2 pounds turnips, peeled and quartered
butter and extra virgin olive oil
1 cup beef stock
1 tablespoon parsley, finely minced

Blanch turnips in boiling salted water for 3 to 5 minutes. Drain and pat dry. Saute in butter and olive oil until lightly browned. Add stock and boil down until turnips are coated and liquid has almost completely evaporated. Sprinkle with parsley and serve.

YELLOW SQUASH

If you want your children to hate squash, just serve it to them boiled. Nothing could be slimier or more unappetizing. Instead, slice it lengthwise and saute the slices in butter and olive oil. Finish with sea salt, freshly ground pepper and a squeeze of lemon.

Yellow Squash Medley
Serves 4

4 small yellow squash
sea salt
1 medium onion, thinly sliced
2 medium tomatoes, peeled, seeded and chopped
2 tablespoons toasted pine nuts
1 tablespoon finely chopped parsley
cold pressed olive oil

Remove ends from squash and use food processor to cut them into a julienne. Sprinkle with sea salt and let sit about 1 hour. Rinse well and squeeze dry with a tea towel. Saute onion in olive oil until golden. Add squash and tomatoes and saute a few minutes more, over medium high heat, stirring constantly. Stir in pine nuts and parsley and serve immediately.

Yellow Squash Supreme
Serves 4

4 large yellow squash
extra virgin olive oil
3/4 cup grated Parmesan cheese

This gets gobbled up quickly. You may want to prepare a double recipe or eight squash for four people. Wash squash, remove ends and slice lengthwise at 1/4 inch intervals. Brush a cookie sheet with olive oil and arrange the slices in one layer. Brush top side with olive oil and broil under broiler until slices become lightly browned. Turn over, brush again with olive oil, and sprinkle on cheese and plenty of freshly ground pepper. Just before serving, place under broiler for a few minutes or until golden.

Squash is another vegetable that hails from the new world. The Massachusetts Indians called it *askut-asquash*. Squash is a member of the gourd family, and a relative of cucumbers and melons. The numerous varieties can be divided into two main categories: summer squash has soft skin and includes zucchini and crook necked or yellow squash; winter squash has a harder rind and includes butternut and spaghetti squash.

Both types provide carotenoids and vitamin C plus potassium, calcium and fiber. Winter squash is a better bet nutritionally but summer squash is more versatile from the cook's point of view.

The American Indians valued the seeds of both squash and pumpkin for various ailments but the pulp also has pharmacological properties, notably anti-cancer carotenoids. Winter squash and other deep orange vegetables are especially effective in preventing lung cancer. SWF

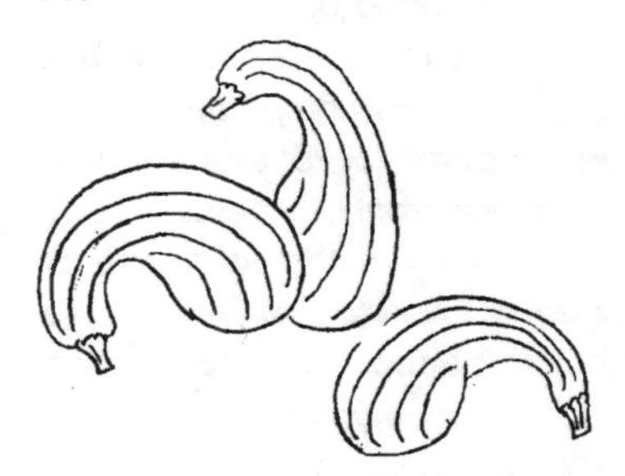

It is very wise, when one eats grilled fish or meats, to eat them with whole grains or vegetables, as these provide natural antidotes to carcinogenic substances formed during grilling. Claude Aubert *Dis-Moi Comment Tu Cuisines*

ZUCCHINI

Like all members of the squash family, zucchini is ruined by boiling. Even steaming gives results that are too watery. Instead, slice lengthwise and saute slices in butter and oil. Finish with a squeeze of lemon and sea salt and freshly ground pepper to taste. Another good method is to pass the zucchini through the small julienne slicer of your food processor. Mix with about 1 teaspoon sea salt and let stand 1 hour. Rinse in a colander and squeeze dry in a tea towel. Saute about 1 minute in a little butter and olive oil.

Zucchini, a member of the squash family, is a bland vegetable, especially rich in sodium. And since sodium, of all the alkaline elements of the body, is the most important, it follows that zucchini is a most healthful vegetable. The liver is the storehouse of sodium, an element necessary to maintain the acid-base equilibrium of the body. Without this acid-base balance, good health is impossible to maintain. The simple, bland zucchini, used as both food and medicine, is an ideal way to restore a sodium-exhausted liver. Henry Bieler MD *Food is Your Best Medicine*

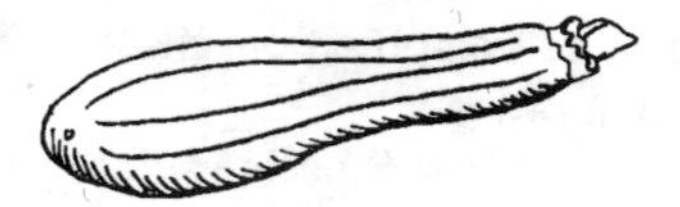

Germs, viruses and other microorganisms are usually present, but merely as scavengers that feed on toxic wastes. While we must thank Louis Pasteur for annihilating the belief that disease was caused by demons and evil, substituting in its place the germ theory, we must not forget that Bechamp, who was a contemporary of Pasteur, strongly maintained that the chemical background on which the germ fed was of equal importance. Man had to choose between the two causes of disease: either the toxic background, due to faulty living and eating habits, was responsible for disease; or a mysterious microorganism, hiding in dark corners, pounced upon the innocent and unsuspecting victim. The cure, according to this latter theory, depended upon the destruction of these microbes. Henry Bieler MD *Food is Your Best Medicine*

Zucchini with Tomatoes
Serves 4

2 medium zucchini
2 medium onions, peeled and chopped
2 medium tomatoes, peeled, seeded and chopped
1-2 cloves garlic, peeled and mashed
1/2 teaspoon dried thyme
extra virgin olive oil
freshly ground pepper

Cut ends off zucchini, cut into quarters lengthwise and slice thinly. Mix with sea salt and let stand about 1 hour. Rinse in a colander and pat dry. Saute zucchini in batches until golden. Set aside. Saute onion in butter and oil until tender. Add tomato, raise heat and saute a few minutes until liquid is almost all absorbed. Add zucchini, garlic, thyme pepper to taste. Saute about one minute more until flavors are amalgamated. Don't let zucchini overcook!

Zucchini Cakes
Makes 12-14

4 cups grated zucchini
sea salt
4 eggs, lightly beaten
1 small onion, finely chopped
2 cups whole grain bread crumbs
freshly ground black pepper

1/4 teaspoon cayenne pepper
1/2 cup Parmesan cheese
butter and extra virgin olive oil

Salt zucchini and let stand 1/2 hour. Rinse well and squeeze dry in a tea towel. Mix with eggs, onion, bread crumbs, cheese and seasonings. Form into cakes and saute in butter and olive oil.

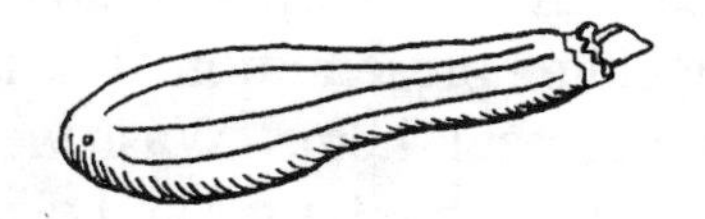

Stuffed Zucchini
Serves 8

8 small zucchini or 4 large zucchini
2 medium onions, finely minced
3/4 cup ground crispy almonds (page 487)
3/4 cup piima cream or creme fraiche
1 cup finely ground wholegrain bread crumbs
3/4 cup grated Swiss or Parmesan cheese
2 eggs
1/4 teaspoon powdered cloves
sea salt and freshly ground pepper

Remove the ends of the zucchini and blanch in boiling water about 8 to 10 minutes, depending on the size of the zucchini, or until flesh just becomes tender. Remove to a colander and rinse with cold water. Slice in half lengthwise and scoop out the flesh, reserving it in a bowl. Salt the inside of the zucchini shells and turn over to drain on paper towels. Meanwhile, saute the onion in a little olive oil. Chop the zucchini flesh, squeeze out water and add to onion. Saute several minutes more. Meanwhile beat the eggs and cream together. Stir in the onion and zucchini mixture, the almonds, about half the bread crumbs, half the cheese and the powdered cloves and season to taste. If mixture is too runny, add more bread crumbs.

Arrange zucchini shells in a buttered casserole and fill with the stuffing. Sprinkle remaining bread crumbs and cheese on top. You may prepare ahead of time to this point. Bake at 350 degrees for about 1/2 hour or until tops are golden.

Dr. Denham Harman, an authority on free radical chemistry and physiology, has stated that a reduction in these harmful reactions through dietary changes and/or the addition of protective elements in the diet would have a drastic effect. "This approach offers the prospect of an increase in the average life expectancy to beyond 85 years and a significant increase in the number of people who will live to well beyond 100 years."

Modern medicine, using a chemical approach , has failed to achieve this. The mean life span has remained virtually constant at 70 years since the mid-1950's. This life expectancy may well decrease in the future if we continue to be seduced by the false nutritional propaganda of the vegetable oil producers.

Harman studied the effect of various fats and oils on mice. He found that rats fed lard lived 9.2% longer than rats fed a polyunsaturate. In humans that translates to almost *7 years off your life* if you have been suckered into television nutrition and American Heart Association anti-cholesterol propaganda.

If unsaturated oil and lard are pushed to 20% of the total diet (well within the range of human consumption), the life span of the rats consuming the unsaturated oil was 17% less than those fed lard. Assuming a 70-year life span of man, this translates to almost *12 years less life* for the oil consumer as compared to lard users. William Campbell Douglass MD *The Milk of Human Kindness*

BABY VEGETABLES

Baby vegetables are becoming increasingly available in our markets. Unfortunately they often come from long distances and have therefore been treated with undesirable preservatives. They are rarely grown organically. However, if you can find locally grown baby vegetables, do use them for an appealing presentation. It is usually unnecessary to trim or peel them. Wash well and steam lightly or saute in a little butter and olive oil.

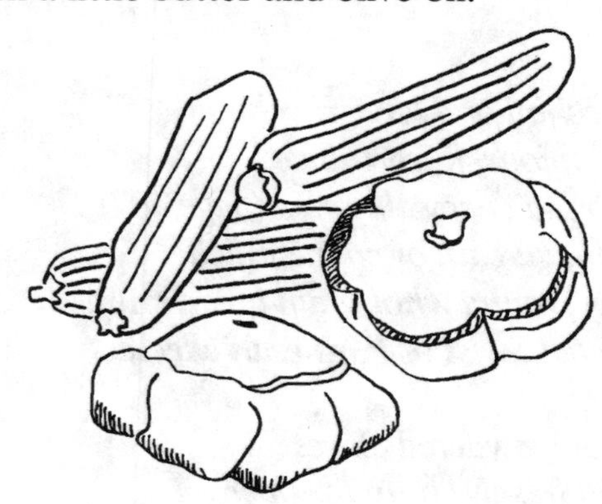

Researcher Richard Passwater states that of fourteen tests conducted, all showed a high correlation between eating high amounts of polyunsaturates and the occurrence of cancer in both humans and animals. He states that a large percentage of the population is consuming an excessive amount of polyunsaturates in the form of corn oil, peanut oil, margarines, soybean oil, etc., and notes that presently Americans eat two to three times the amount of vegetable oils than were consumed sixty years ago. Passwater stresses that only from two to four percent of one's diet should consist of vegetable fats. H. Leon Abrams *Vegetarianism: An Anthropological/Nutritional Evaluation*

VEGETABLE PUREE PANCAKES

Makes 4 pancakes

1 cup leftover vegetable puree such as parsnip puree, potato celery root puree or sweet potato puree
1 small onion, peeled and finely chopped
1 egg, lightly beaten
1/4 cup freshly ground spelt or unbleached white flour
sea salt and freshly ground pepper
butter and extra virgin olive oil

Mix leftover puree with chopped onion, egg, flour and seasonings. Melt butter and olive oil in a heavy skillet. Drop puree mixture in by spoonfuls and saute pancakes until golden. Turn and saute other side until golden. Remove to a heated platter and keep warm until ready to serve.

The deadly effect of the long-chain unsaturated fats on the immune system has led to the development of new products containing short and medium-chain saturated fats for intravenous feeding. . . Several aspects of the immune system are improved by short-chain saturated fats [found in butter]. Their antihistamine action is probably important, because of histamine's immunosuppressive effects. Unsaturated fats have been found to cause degranulation of mast cells. The short-chain fatty acids normally produced by bacteria in the bowel apparently have a local anti-inflammatory action. Ray Peat PhD *Health Freedom News*

LUNCHEON & SUPPER FOODS

MEAT SALADS

Our collection of luncheon and supper foods incorporates the principles of good nutrition that we have elaborated. They are based on whole, natural foods, especially favoring animal products high in fat soluble vitamins such as fish, organ meats and eggs; and a variety of vegetables to supply a wide range of vitamins, minerals and anti-carcinogenic agents. Dressings, sauces and condiments feature extra virgin olive oil with its full complement of lipase and anti-oxidants, as well as lacto-fermented dairy and vegetable products.

Many of our meat salads fall in the category of designer fare, and are suitable for the most elegant occasions. Others may be quickly assembled for family lunches. If you make chicken, turkey or duck stock regularly (as you should) you will have plenty of tender meat for the variety of meat salads presented here.

CURRIED CHICKEN SALAD

Serves 6

meat from 1 whole chicken,
used to prepare stock (page 114)
1 red pepper, diced
1 bunch green onions, finely chopped
3-4 celery stalks, diced
1/2 cup crispy almonds (page 487)
2 cups curried mayonnaise (page 127)

Slice almonds using the fine slicer in your food processor. Spread on a cookie sheet and toast in a 300 degree oven. Cut up cooked chicken finely, across the grain. Mix with chopped vegetables and almonds. Mix well with sauce. Serve with tomato slices and avocado wedges for garnish.

Note: Duck, goose or turkey meat may be substituted for chicken in this and the following three recipes.

ORIENTAL CHICKEN SALAD

Serves 6

meat from 1 whole chicken,
used to prepare stock (page 114)
1 red pepper, seeded and cut into a julienne
1 can water chestnuts, drained and sliced
1 bunch green onions, chopped
2 tablespoons toasted sesame seeds
1 cup Oriental dressing (page 124)
4 ounces brown rice or buckwheat noodles,
broken into 1-inch bits, cooked and drained
extra virgin olive oil
romaine leaves for garnish

Cut up meat coarsely and mix with vegetables. Toss with dressing and sesame seeds. Refrigerate an hour or so before serving. Meanwhile, saute noodle pieces in olive oil until crisp and drain on paper towels. Serve chicken on romaine leaves and garnish with sauted noodles.

A few decades ago, the late Gena Larson, nutritionist at Helix High School in La Mesa, California, shifted school lunches from junk foods to whole grain breads and rolls, raw certified milk and to fresh fruits and vegetables.

School marks shot up dramatically, and sports records that had stood for years were broken by athletes. Additionally, sports injuries declined sharply with far fewer broken bones than ever before. James F. Scheer *Health Freedom News*

COLD CURRIED CHICKEN PLATTER

Serves 12-15

Meat from two chickens,
used to prepare stock (page 114)
3 cups spiced mayonnaise (page 127)
8 cups rainbow rice salad (page 447)
cilantro sprigs for garnish

This is a delicious combination, and an attractive presentation for luncheons. You will need a large, flat oval platter.

Shape the rice salad into a ring around the outside edge of the platter. Separate the chicken breasts into several pieces but do not cut up any of the other chicken meat. Place in the center of the ring. Spoon a little of the sauce over the chicken to cover it and garnish with cilantro leaves. Serve with the remaining sauce on the side.

LADIES BUFFET LUNCHEON

Curried Chicken Platter

Rainbow Rice Salad

Spinach Feta Pastries

Broiled Eggplant Slices

Fruit Chutney

Lemon Tart

Raspberry Cooler

ORIENTAL CHICKEN PLATTER

Serves 8

meat from 1 whole chicken
used to prepare stock (page 114)
4 ounces brown rice or buckwheat noodles,
broken into 1-inch bits, cooked and drained
extra virgin olive oil
3 tablespoons expeller expressed peanut oil
2 teaspoons toasted sesame oil
1/4 pound snow peas, lightly steamed and cut into
quarters on an angle
1 red pepper, seeded and cut into a julienne
1/4 cup ginger carrot (page 87)
1 bunch scallions, chopped
2 cups bean sprouts, lightly steamed
1 can baby corn, drained and rinsed
cilantro sprigs for garnish
2 cups peanut sauce (page 133)

Cut up chicken meat coarsely. Meanwhile saute noodles in olive oil until crisp and drain on paper towels. Toss chicken with noodles and the sesame and peanut oil. Mix in snow peas, pepper, carrots and scallions. Place in a mound on a platter. Make a border with the bean sprouts and baby corn. Garnish with cilantro leaves. Serve with peanut sauce.

SIMPLE TUNA SALAD

Serves 4

1 large can water packed tuna, drained and flaked
1/4 red pepper, diced
1 celery stalk, diced
4 green onions, chopped
1/2 cup mayonnaise (page 126)

Mix all ingredients together thoroughly. Serve in sandwiches, or garnished with avocado and tomato wedges.

You're having a picnic at the beach or in the park; the typical American family arrives. The kids explode out of the station wagon before Dad has turned off the ignition. Mother starts unloading the car and informing Papa where to put the blanket. Before the soft drink cooler is sprung open, Mother attacks the air, sand, and greenery with lethal insecticide spray. Massive retaliation against the insect world that had beleaguered them on the last country jaunt. Mother has forgotten, if she ever knew, that just as spilled sugar in our kitchens attracts ants and insects, so does sugar in our bloodstreams attract mosquitoes, microbes and parasites.

One of the great joys of being sugarfree is to be able to lie on the beach or loll in the mountains without being bothered by mosquitoes or other creatures. Once off sugar for a year or so, try it an see if it isn't true for you too. If you take along a guest who's still addicted to sugar, lie side by side. See who the mosquitoes go for and who is left alone.

After all, its no accident that the first cases of mosquito-borne yellow fever—in the Western Hemisphere—occurred in the sugar island of Barbados in 1647. In the beginning it was called *nova pestis*. Yellow fever spread from one sugar center to another: Guadalupe, St. Kitts, Jamaica, Brazil, British Guinea, Spain, Portugal, New Orleans, and finally Cuba, where the US Army mounted a massive campaign at the turn of the twentieth century to make our sugar colony of Cuba safe from the mosquito. William Dufty *Sugar Blues*

TUNA TAHINI SALAD

Serves 6-8

2 large cans water packed tuna, drained and flaked
1/4 teaspoon cayenne pepper
2 cups tahini sauce (page 134)
4 medium onions, thinly sliced
melted butter and extra virgin olive oil
1/3 cup toasted pine nuts
cilantro sprigs for garnish
pita bread

Mix tuna with cayenne pepper and 1 cup sauce. Meanwhile, strew the onions on an oiled cookie sheet, brush with mixture of melted butter and olive oil and bake at 375 degrees until crispy. Mound the tuna on a platter. Scatter onions and pine nuts on top. Garnish with cilantro and serve with pita bread or whole grain crackers (page 489) and remaining sauce.

SALADE NICOISE

Serves 6

6 portions fresh tuna steak, about 4 ounces each
extra virgin olive oil
6 cups baby salad greens or frisee lettuce
6 small ripe tomatoes, cup into wedges
6 small red potatoes, cooked in a clay pot
1 pound french beans, blanched for 8 minutes and rinsed under cold water
2 dozen small black olives
2 cups herb dressing, made with finely chopped parsley (page 118)

Brush tuna steaks with olive oil and season with sea salt and pepper. Using a heavy skillet, cook rapidly, two at a time, for about 4 minutes per side. Set aside.

Divide salad greens between 6 large plates. Garnish with tomatoes, potatoes, beans and olives. Place steaks on top of greens and pour over dressing. This is delicious with sour dough bread or pizza toasts (page 495).

Dental researchers have proven that the teeth are subject to the same metabolic processes that affect other organs of the body. The entire body is one.

By adapting a technique originally developed to study movement of fluid within organs like the liver and kidneys, two researchers from the Loma Linda School of Dentistry have found that subtle changes in the internal activity of the teeth, *caused by sugar*, can be an early sign of later decay. . .

Resistance to tooth decay involves the health of the entire body. Complex physiological processes are involved in maintaining and protecting the health of the teeth. The two researchers found that:

—A high sugar diet can slow the rate of transport of hormonal chemicals by as much as two-thirds even in one week.

—Teeth with sluggish internal activity have a high incidence of decay.

—A hormone released by the hypothalamus stimulates the release by the salivary or parotid gland of a second hormone. This second hormone increases the rate of fluid flow in the teeth.

—A high sugar diet upsets the hormonal balance and reduces the flow in the internal system. This weakens the tooth and makes it more susceptible to decay.

—Healthy teeth are normally invulnerable to the microbes that are always present in the mouth.

Who wants to get rid of friendly germs in the mouth except those crazy people selling mouthwash? William Dufty *Sugar Blues*

SALMON AND MIXED GREENS

Serves 4

1 1/2 pounds fresh salmon filet
extra virgin olive oil
lemon juice
sea salt and freshly ground pepper
2 tablespoons unbleached flour
1/2 teaspoon paprika
6 cups baby lettuces or mixed greens such as watercress or mache
1 red pepper, seeded, cut into a julienne and sauteed in olive oil
1 pound brown mushrooms, washed, dried very well, sliced and sauteed in butter and olive oil
3/4 cup basic dressing

Brush salmon with olive oil. Squeeze on lemon juice and rub in pepper. Sprinkle on sifted flour and paprika. Bake at 350 degrees for about 10 minutes. Place under broiler for another 2 minutes until just lightly browned. Meanwhile mix greens with dressing and divide between four plates. Make a mound of peppers and mushrooms on each plate, place a portion of salmon on each mound of greens and pour pan juices over. Serve immediately.

"Eat more seafood!" is the clarion call from scientists around the world. And for good reason. Eating fish, especially deep-sea, cold-water fish high in omega-3 fatty acids, is one of the best bets for escaping numerous modern maladies, including heart disease, cancer, arthritis, psoriasis, high blood pressure, and strokes. Fish and fish oil may even slow down the spread of already existing cancer. . . What makes seafood so pharmacologically attractive is its unique type of fat or oil made up of long chains of molecules called omega-3 fatty acids. . . Rather quickly after you eat seafood, the omega-3s enter the membranes of your cells, rendering them less stiff and more pliable—more "normal," in evolutionary terms. . . . The evidence for the benefits of omega-3 and seafood is piling up in medical journals. Here are the new, compelling reasons to eat more seafood and get more omega-3s into your cells

Most dramatic is the connection between eating more seafood and having less heart disease. A recent study by Dr. Therese Colocek, . . . is a striking example. Her study of 6,000 middle aged men discovered that those who ate the amount of omega-3s in a single ounce bite of mackerel or a three-ounce portion of bass every day had a 36 percent lower chance of dying of heart disease over a six-year follow-up period.

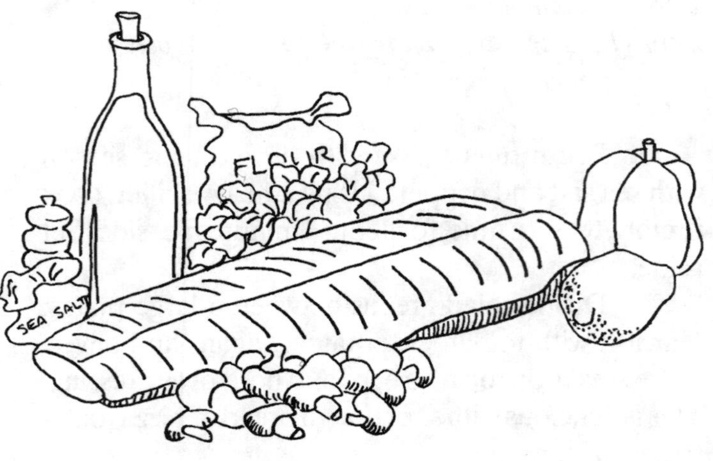

CRAB SALAD

Serves 6

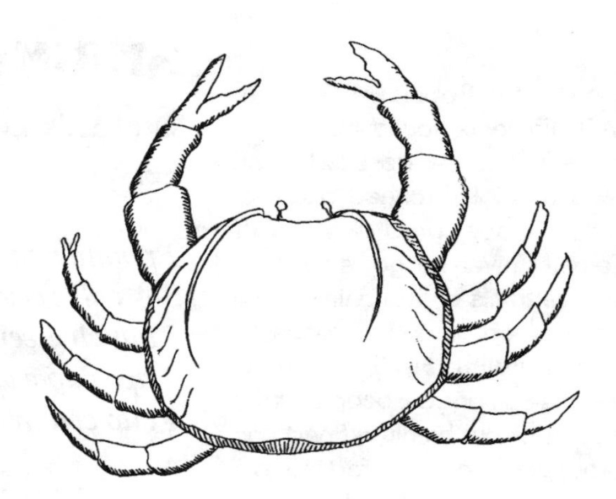

1 pound fresh crab meat, broken up
1 cup homemade mayonnaise
1 tablespoon green peppercorn mustard (available at gourmet shops)
12 asparagus spears, lightly steamed
2 tomatoes, cut into wedges
2 grapefruit, sections removed
6 small leaves romaine lettuce

Mix mustard with mayonnaise. Stir in crab meat and mix well. Divide among individual plates and garnish with tomato wedges, asparagus spears, grapefruit sections and lettuce leaf.

SWORDFISH SALAD

Serves 4

1 pound swordfish
1/2 cup soy sauce
2 teaspoons freshly grated ginger
2 bunches watercress, stems removed
4 ounces brown rice or buckwheat noodles, broken into 1-inch bits, cooked and drained
extra virgin olive oil
1 cup Oriental dressing (page 124)

Marinate swordfish in soy sauce and grated ginger for several hours in refrigerator. Broil 3-4 minutes to a side until just cooked through. Meanwhile, saute noodles in olive oil until crisp and drain on paper towels. Place a mound of watercress on each plate. Place a portion of swordfish on top. Pour dressing over and sprinkle with noodles.

A large-scale British study reported that eating more fish could intervene to save the lives of men who had already suffered heart attacks. Eating fatty fish but twice a week reduced their odds of a future fatal heart attack by about one third over a two-year period.

There's evidence that fish eaters have lower rates of cancer, notably breast cancer More dramatic, eating more fish and taking fish oil capsules may actually help halt the spread of cancer in those who already have the disease. . .

Unquestionably authorities term fish oil an anti-inflammatory agent. In some patients with rheumatoid arthritis, symptoms of join swelling, tenderness and fatigue have diminished after taking fish oil equal to that in a daily serving of seven ounces of salmon.

Psoriasis, an inflammatory skin disease, also improves in about 30 to 60 percent of people given varying doses of fish oil, according to the reports. Jean Carper *The Food Pharmacy Guide to Good Eating.*

SHRIMP AND PAPAYA SALAD

Serves 4

1 pound baby shrimp
3-4 stalks celery, finely diced
1 bunch green onions, finely diced
2 ripe papayas
1 cup creamy dressing (page 120)

Peel the papayas, halve and remove seeds. (Use seeds to make papaya pepper, page 143). Place hollow side up on individual plates. Mix shrimp with celery and dressing and spoon into papaya halves.

Sir Robert McCarrison, M.D. England, found his clinical animals became desexed when feed on highly refined and processed foods. Dr. Clive McCay of Cornell University got similar results with his clinical animals. All animals fed on natural foods retained vitality. Sterility is on the increase among our people. Is the eating of our highly refined and processed foods affecting our people as it does the clinical animals? R. Dean Conrad *The Great American Tragedy*

Know Your Ingredients

Name This Product #20

Strawberry filling (corn syrup, dextrose, strawberries, crackermeal, apples, wheat starch, partially hydrogenated soybean oil, citric acid, xanthan gum, red #40), enriched wheat flour, partially hydrogenated soybean oil, corn syrup, sugar, whey, dextrose, salt, baking powder, baking soda. Vitamins and minerals; niacinamide, iron, vitamin A (palmitate), vitamin B6 (pyridoxine hydrochloride), vitamin B2 (riboflavin), vitamin B1 (thiamin hydrochloride), and folic acid.

See Appendix B for Answer

SCALLOP SALAD

Serves 4

1/2 pound sea scallops sliced, rinsed, dried with paper towels and quartered
juice of 1 lemon
sea salt and freshly ground pepper
butter and extra virgin olive oil
6 cups baby greens
1/2 cup basic dressing (page 118)
1 1/2 cups red pepper sauce (page 131)

Saute the scallops quickly in butter and olive oil until opaque. Remove with a slotted spoon and toss with lemon juice and sea salt and pepper to taste. Toss the greens with the dressing. Place a portion of the red pepper sauce on each plate, make a mound of salad on top and arrange scallops on lettuce.

ORIENTAL RED MEAT SALAD

Serves 6

1 1/2 pounds beef flank steak, or similar cut from lamb or game
1/2 cup lemon juice
6 tablespoons soy sauce
2 tablespoons extra virgin olive oil or expeller expressed peanut oil
1 tablespoon toasted sesame oil
1 teaspoon grated fresh ginger
pinch red pepper flakes
2 tablespoons toasted sesame seeds
1/2 pound snow peas, steamed lightly and cut into quarters at an angle
1 pound bean sprouts, steamed lightly
1 red pepper, seeded and cut into a julienne

Using a sharp knife, score the flank steak or red meat pieces across the grain on both sides. Broil 3 or 4 minutes to a side, or until meat is medium rare. Transfer to a cutting board and let stand for 10 minutes. Meanwhile mix lemon juice, soy sauce, oils, ginger and red pepper flakes together. Cut the meat across the grain on an angle into very thin slices and cut these slices into a julienne. Marinate in soy sauce mixture for several hours in refrigerator. Mix with sesame seeds and vegetables just before serving.

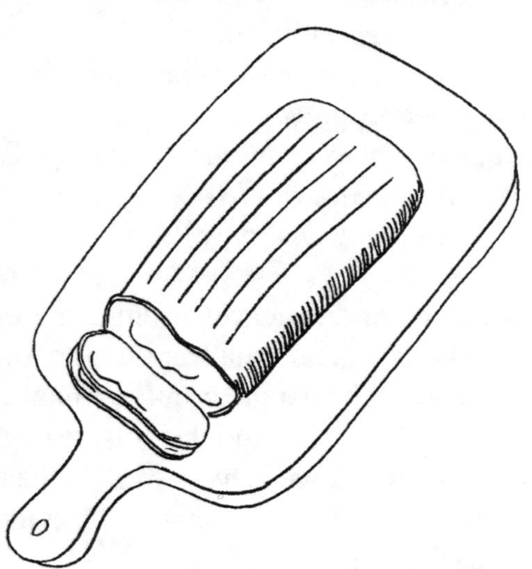

In early June, Indian Harchand Singh collapsed in the middle of a busy London intersection. He cracked his skull, but even worse, he awoke in the hospital to the news that he had suffered a serious heart attack. His cholesterol was normal and he ate a strict vegetarian diet. He was 38 years old.

This is not an unusual story for south Asians, most of whom are vegetarians. The south Asians of India, Pakistan and Bangladesh have a 40 percent higher rate of heart disease than the British, who eat a great deal of every conceivable type of animal meat and fat. In Singapore, the rate of heart disease is *400 percent* higher than the local Chinese—who eat a lot of pork. William Campbell Douglass *Second Opinion*

"There is extensive scientific literature concerning the hazardous effects of direct microwave radiation of living systems. . . It is astonishing, therefore, to realize how little effort has been taken to replace this detrimental technique of microwave [cooking] with technology more in accordance with nature. . .Of all the natural substances—which are polar—the oxygen of water molecules reacts most sensitively. This is how microwave cooking heat is generated—friction from this violence in water molecules. Structures of molecules are torn apart, molecules are forcefully deformed, called structural isomerism, and thus become impaired in quality. This is contrary to conventional heating of food where heat transfers convectionally from without to within. Cooking by microwaves begins within the cells and molecules where water is present and where the energy is transformed into frictional heat." Dr. Hans Hertel quoted in *Search for Health*

SWEETBREAD SALAD

Serves 6

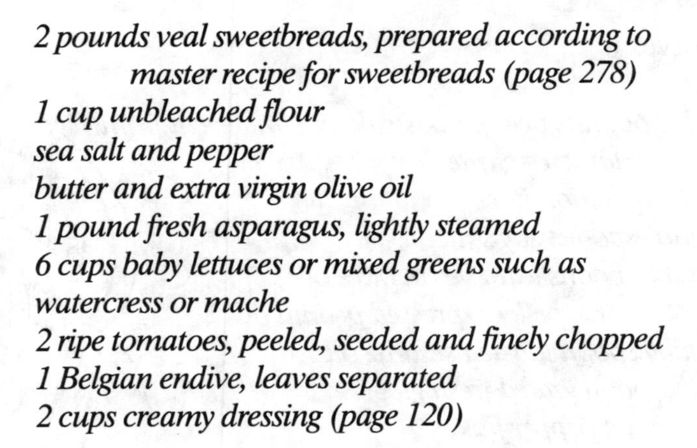

2 pounds veal sweetbreads, prepared according to master recipe for sweetbreads (page 278)
1 cup unbleached flour
sea salt and pepper
butter and extra virgin olive oil
1 pound fresh asparagus, lightly steamed
6 cups baby lettuces or mixed greens such as watercress or mache
2 ripe tomatoes, peeled, seeded and finely chopped
1 Belgian endive, leaves separated
2 cups creamy dressing (page 120)

Slice sweetbreads at 3/8 inch intervals. Dredge in a mixture of flour, salt and pepper and saute in butter and olive oil. Mound greens in the center of individual serving plates and decorate edges with asparagus, chopped tomato, and endive leaves. Place slices of warm sauted sweetbreads over greens and spoon dressing over.

DELUXE FRENCH BEAN SALAD

Serves 6

1 1/2 pounds French beans, cut in 1-inch lengths, blanched in boiling water for about 8 minutes and rinsed under cold water
3 Belgian endive, leaves separated
2 ripe tomatoes, peeled, seeded and finely chopped
12 triangle croutons (page 491)
6 slices duck and chicken liver mousse (page 224)
1 cup basic dressing (page 118) or walnut dressing (page 119)

Arrange endive leaves around the edges of individual plates. Place a small amount on tomato on each leaf. Cut each triangle crouton in half, spread with pate and arrange around the outside edge of the place, in between endive leaves. Mix the beans with basic dressing or walnut dressing and mound in the center of each plate.

DUCK BREAST SALAD WITH HAZELNUTS

Serves 4

2 duck breasts
1/4 cup lemon juice
1/4 cup extra virgin olive oil
6 cups baby lettuce or spinach
1 cup basic dressing
1 tablespoon hazelnut oil (see Sources)
1/2 cup hazelnuts, peeled and chopped

Trim excess fat off the duck breasts and score in a diamond pattern. Marinate several hours in mixture of lemon juice and olive oil. Pat dry and cook in a heavy skillet, several minutes to a side until medium rare. Transfer to a board and let stand 10 minutes. Slice thinly across the grain. Blend hazelnut oil with dressing and toss with salads and hazelnuts. Mound in the center of individual plates and place duck slices on top. Serve with round croutons (page 491).

. . . The same violent friction and athermic deformations that can occur in our bodies when we are subjected to radar or microwaves, happens to the molecules in the food cooked in a microwave oven. In fact when anyone microwaves food the oven exerts a power input of about 1000 watts or more. This radiation results in destruction and deformation of molecules of food and results in the formation of new compounds (called radiolytic compounds) unknown to man and nature. Today's established science and technology argues forcefully that microwaved food, and irradiated foods do not have any significantly high "radiolytic compounds" than do broiled, baked or other conventionally cooked foods—but microwaving does produce more of these critters. Curiously, neither established science nor our ever protective government has conducted any tests of the effects of eating the various kinds of cooked foods on the blood of eaters. [Dr. Hans Hertel] did test it, and the indication is clear that something is amiss and larger studies should be funded. Tom Valentine *Search for Health*

SOUTH of the BORDER

South of the Border foods—tostados, fajitas, enchiladas, tacos, chile, empanadas—can be made with nutritious ingredients and deserve a place in your repertoire. They are especially popular with children and offer a delicious alternative to the array of junk foods with which they are constantly tempted. As they tend to be rather heavy, they should always be served with a high enzyme condiment such as cortido, avocado or piima cream. (Cultured cream provides needed fat soluble vitamins to the largely vegetarian corn and bean combination of typical Mexican food.) Enchiladas, empanadas and burritos may be made ahead of time and frozen. Sprouted wholewheat tortillas for these recipes are made by Alvarado Bakery and are widely available in health food stores and gourmet markets.

BLACK BEAN TOSTADOS

Serves 8

4 cups black beans
2 tablespoons whey
1 teaspoon sea salt
4 cloves garlic, peeled and crushed
12 sprouted wholewheat tortillas
extra virgin olive oil
2 cups raw grated Monterey jack cheese
3 cups cortido (page 85)
4 cups chismole (page 168)
2 cups guacamole (page 156)

The combination of black beans on crispy tortillas with cortido (lacto-fermented spicy cabbage), chismole (tomatoes and cilantro) and guacamole always brings raves. If you object to frying the tortillas, simply warm them briefly in a skillet and brush with butter for a "soft" tostado.

Soak the beans in filtered water, whey and salt for 7 to 24 hours. Drain and rinse. Place in a large pot, cover with water and bring to a boil. Skim off scum before adding garlic. Cover and cook at least 4 hours. Meanwhile fry the tortillas, one at a time, in olive oil over medium high flame using a heavy skillet. Let drain on paper towels and keep warm in the oven.

To serve, place a tortilla on each plate, and spoon on the beans, using a slotted spoon. Sprinkle with cheese and serve with garnishes and remaining half tortilla per person.

CHICKEN TOSTADOS

Serves 6

meat from 1 whole chicken,
used to make stock (page 114)
2 medium onions, chopped
1 red pepper, seeded and diced
1 green pepper, seeded and diced
2-4 jalapeno peppers, seeded and diced
extra virgin olive oil
1/2 cup tomato paste
1 cup chicken stock
1 teaspoon dried oregano
1 teaspoon cumin
1/2 teaspoon red chile flakes
1 teaspoon sea salt
1 clove garlic, peeled and mashed
6 sprouted wheat tortillas
extra virgin olive oil
1 head romaine lettuce, finely shredded
3 cups chismole (page 168)
2 cups cortido (page 85)
grated raw Monterey jack cheese
piima cream or creme fraiche
avocado slices

Saute onions and peppers in olive oil until soft. Add tomato paste, stock and seasonings. Cut up meat and stir in. Check seasonings. Simmer for 15 minutes or so until most liquid has evaporated.

Meanwhile saute tortillas in oil until crisp. Drain on paper towels and keep warm in oven.

To serve, place a tortilla on each plate. Spoon chicken mixture on tortillas and serve with bowls of shredded lettuce, chismole, avocado, cheese, fermented cream and cortido.

Know Your Ingredients

Name This Product #21

Cultured sour cream, skim milk, whey protein concentrate, water, food starch-modified, lactic acid, maltodextrin, cellulose gum, potassium sorbate (a preservative), agar, vitamin A palmitate.

See Appendix B for Answer

All of us have been deceived. The refined and processed hydrogenated oils are more harmful than animal fat despite all the hype to the contrary. Tom Valentine *Facts on Fats & Oils*

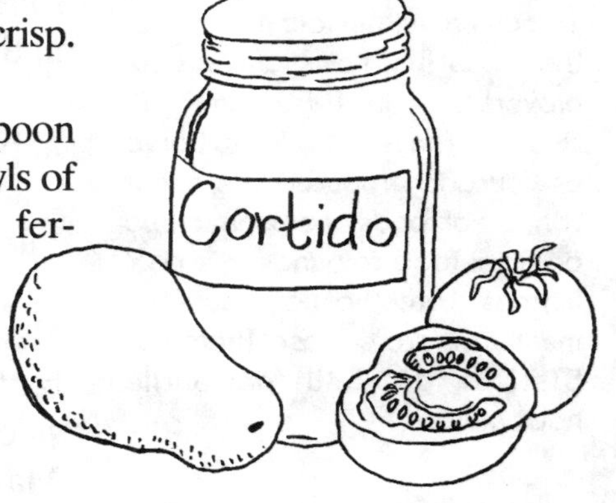

CHICKEN ENCHILADAS

Makes 18 enchiladas

meat from 2 whole chickens,
used to make chicken stock (page 114)
2 medium onions, finely chopped
2-4 small green peppers, hot or mild, seeded and
finely chopped
2 carrots, peeled and grated
1 cup sprouted small seeds such as sesame or
onion seeds
1/2 teaspoon cayenne pepper
2 teaspoons oregano
1 tablespoon ground cumin
18 corn tortillas
extra virgin olive oil
2 cups raw grated Monterey jack cheese
8 cups green or red enchilada sauce
(pages 141-142)
sliced avocados for garnish
creme fraiche or piima cream for garnish
salsa for garnish (page 95)

Finely dice chicken and mix with onion, pepper, carrot, sprouts and spices. Stir in 1 cup enchilada sauce. Meanwhile fry tortillas very briefly in olive oil so that they are softened, not crisp. Pat dry. Place about 2 tablespoons of chicken mixture in the center of each tortilla and roll up. Place in an oiled pyrex dish. (May be covered and frozen at this point.)

To serve, heat in 325 degree oven until steaming. Serve with red, green or pumpkin seed enchilada sauce, grated raw cheese, avocados, cultured cream and salsa.

Note: you may use *turkey*, *duck* or *goose* meat in place of chicken.

Variation: Chicken Burritos

Use *sprouted wheat tortillas* in place of corn. Heat briefly in a heavy skillet and brush with melted butter before filling with chicken mixture. Fold in sides before rolling up, and brush outside with butter. May be individually wrapped in aluminum foil and frozen. Remove foil before heating.

A nourishing diet brings more benefits than energy and endurance. . . Grades of a million New York city public elementary and junior high school students were tested before and after school lunches were improved. Soaring scores surprised school officials and researchers, too.

Average test grades of students in 803 schools rose by 16 percent within four years after the school lunch program was improved. . . . in 1980 came the change. The New York City Board of Education reduced the sugar content of foods and banned two artificial food colorings in school lunches. Later that year, achievement test scores rose [from the 51st] to the 57th percentile nationwide.

SWORDFISH ENCHILADAS

Makes 12 enchiladas

1 pound swordfish, brushed with olive oil, grilled and flaked
1 bunch green onions, chopped
4 cups green enchilada sauce
12 corn tortillas
extra virgin olive oil
1 cup raw grated Monterey jack cheese
1 bunch green onions, finely chopped for garnish
chopped cilantro for garnish
creme fraiche or piima cream for garnish

Mix 1 cup sauce and chopped green onions with the fish. Meanwhile fry tortillas very briefly in olive oil so that they are softened, not crisp. Pat dry. Place about 2 tablespoons of fish mixture in the center of each tortilla and roll up. Place in an oiled pyrex dish. (May be covered and frozen at this point.)

To serve, heat in 325 degree oven until steaming. Serve with remaining green sauce, raw cheese, green onions, cilantro and cultured cream.

Pleasantly surprised at this jump, the New York City public school officials outlawed foods with artificial coloring and flavorings. Again, test scores rose—this time to the 61st percentile.

Once more school officials acted, banning BHT and BHA, two common preservatives, from school lunches and substituting milk for carbonated beverages and candy. This time test scores rose to the 64th percentile.

Not only are school children benefiting. So are the schools, because of tremendous cost-savings brought about by the better noonday nutrition. Fewer special education teachers are now needed to offer individual instruction to children with reading problems, say the researchers. James F. Scheer *Health Freedom News*

Since the sea foods are, as a group, so valuable a source of the fat-soluble activators, they have been found to be efficient throughout the world not only for controlling tooth decay, but for the producing a human stock of high vitality. Unfortunately the cost of transportation in the fresh state often constitutes a factor limiting distribution. Many of the primitive races preserved the food value, including vitamins, very efficiently by drying the fish. While our modern system of canning prevents decomposition, it does not efficiently preserve some of the fat-soluble activators, particularly vitamin A. Weston Price DDS *Nutrition and Physical Degeneration*

OFFAL BURRITOS

Makes 24 burritos

1 brisket of beef or game
2 pounds sweetbreads or brains or combination
(See note on brains, page 288)
2 cups beef stock
1 small can tomato paste
2 onions finely chopped
1/4 -1/2 teaspoon cayenne pepper
1 tablespoon oregano
1 tablespoon cumin
4 cloves garlic, peeled and mashed
24 sprouted whole wheat tortillas
melted butter
red enchilada sauce (page 142) for garnish
cortido (page 85) for garnish
sliced avocados for garnish
creme fraiche or piima cream for garnish

They're not awful—they're good! This is a good way to get organ meats into your children without them knowing it. In this recipe, brains or sweetbreads need no special preparation. Place all ingredients (except garnishes, tortillas and butter) into a large pot. Bring to a boil and place in a 300 degree oven overnight or all day until meat is falling apart. Remove top for last hour or so of cooking so sauce thickens.

Remove meat and brains or sweetbreads and chop finely. Add sauce from the pan to moisten but the mixture should not be runny. Meanwhile, heat tortillas briefly in a heavy skillet and brush one side with melted butter. Place about 2 tablespoons of meat mixture in the center of each one. Fold in sides before rolling up, and brush outside with butter. May be individually wrapped in aluminum foil and frozen. (Remove foil before heating.) Heat at 325 degrees in an oiled pyrex dish until steaming. Serve with choice of garnishes.

Know Your Ingredients

Name This Product #22

Reconstituted nonfat dry milk, flour, water, chicken, green chiles, modified food starch, soybean oil, salt, chicken fat, chicken broth replacer (maltodextrin, salt, monosodium glutamate, chicken broth, hydrolyzed plant protein, disodium inosinate, disodium guanylate, autolyzed yeast extract), soy protein concentrate, dehydrated onions, jalapenos, whey, flavorings, sodium tripolyphosphate, spices, baking powder, cellulose gum.

See Appendix B for Answer

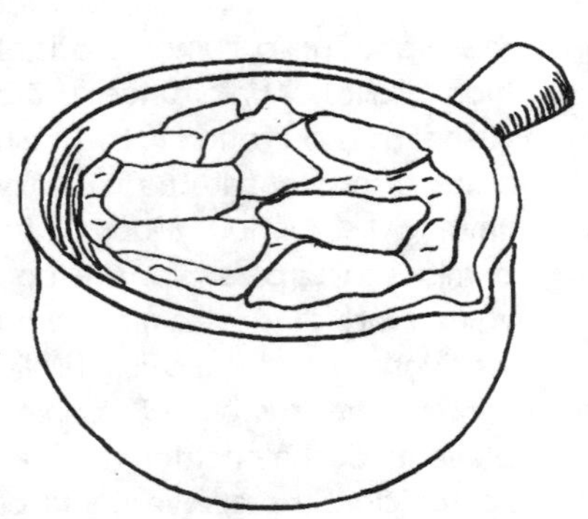

BLACK BEAN BURRITOS

Makes 18 burritos

2 cups cooked black beans (page 469)
2 cups basic brown rice (page 441)
1 medium onion, finely chopped
2 - 4 small green chiles, hot or mild, seeded and finely chopped
1/4 teaspoon cayenne pepper
1 teaspoon oregano
2 teaspoons ground cumin
18 sprouted wheat tortillas
melted butter
red enchilada sauce (page 142) for garnish
cortido (page 85) for garnish
sliced avocados for garnish
creme fraiche or piima cream for garnish

Mix together all ingredients (except garnishes, tortillas and butter). Meanwhile, heat tortillas briefly in a heavy skillet and brush one side with melted butter. Place about 2 tablespoons of bean mixture in the center of buttered side. Fold in sides before rolling up, and brush outside with butter. May be individually wrapped in aluminum foil and frozen. (Remove foil before heating.) Heat at 325 degrees in an oiled pyrex dish until steaming. Serve with choice of garnishes.

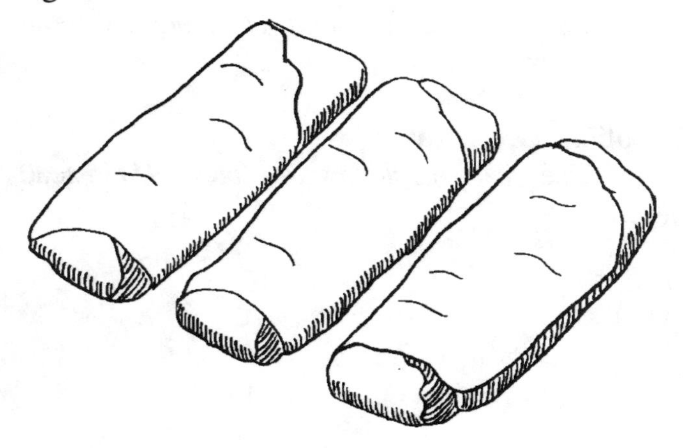

The relation of brain function to soil fertility is demonstrated in many sources of information. These include a percentage of grade school pupils in classes for mentally retarded and backward children. I have found the proportion in several districts to be above thirty percent, and progressively increasing in several states. In the group of southern states using the same examination, passing from grade schools to high schools, the data show a marked superiority in the proportion of children for the Panhandle area. The area is underlain with caliche subsoil which consists of calcium pebbles cemented together with calcium carbonate. . . I have shown that the milk and cream produced from wheat pasture in that area are very high in Vitamin A and Activator X. Many of the children are excellent. The average well above normal. The roots of the wheat plants in this district have been shown to penetrate down six feet, well into the subsoil. The district includes Hereford which has been highly publicized for its low incidence of dental caries. The cattle raised in that area are very superior, both for beef and for reproduction. The people can be also if they are as wise as the buffalo and cattle in the selection of their food. Weston Price DDS *Nutrition and Physical Degeneration*

CHICKEN TACOS

Makes about 1 dozen

Cooked meat from 1 chicken, reserved from making stock (page 114)
2 onions, peeled and chopped
2 green peppers, peeled and chopped
2 cups red enchilada sauce (page 142)
1 dozen corn tortillas
olive oil
grated raw Monterey jack cheese for garnish
cortido for garnish (page 85)

Saute onions and peppers in olive oil until tender and transfer to a bowl. Break chicken into small pieces. Mix chicken and sauce with sauteed peppers and onions.

Heat several tablespoons olive oil in a large heavy skillet. Add a tortilla and saute briefly on one side. Turn over and place a spoonful of chicken mixture just off center. Fold tortilla over and saute on both sides until crisp. Transfer to a platter lined with paper towels to drain. Repeat with other tortillas, adding more olive oil as necessary—you can have several tacos going at the same time in a large pan.

Serve with grated cheese and cortido.

Variation: Beef Tacos

Use *1 1/2 pounds ground beef, sauteed*, instead of chicken meat

Variation: Green Tacos

Use *green enchilada sauce (page 141)* instead of red.

The basic materials of food processing are the refined carbohydrates (mainly white flour and sugar) and processed oils. Given these three basics, processors can produce almost anything. The food industry has taken to sugar and hydrogenated fats not merely because of their taste appeal but because they are the cheapest constituents available for the manufacture of packaged foods. "One company can't sell a tomato, for example, for much more than another company. But process it into ketchup, add spices and a fraction of a cent of flavor, and bottle it; call it barbecue sauce; advertise it; tout its brand name; and higher and higher profits can be made because the product seems unique." We might begrudge the industry these manipulated profits if, in return, the purchaser got nutrients they need from the food product. Unfortunately, they don't. The profits are made at the consumers' twofold expense—in purchasing power and in nutrients needed. Joseph D. Beasley MD and Jerry J. Swift MA *The Kellogg Report*

FAJITAS

Serves 4-6

2 pounds beef, lamb, or chicken breast cut into strips, about 1/4 to 1/2 inch thick
6 tablespoons extra virgin olive oil
1/2 cup lemon or lime juice
1/4 cup pineapple juice (optional)
4 garlic cloves, peeled and mashed
1/2 teaspoon chile powder
1 teaspoon dried oregano
1/2 teaspoon dried thyme
1 red pepper, seeded and cut into julienne strips
1 green pepper, seeded and cut into julienne strips
2 medium onions, thinly sliced
extra virgin olive oil
12 sprouted wheat tortillas
melted butter
chismole (page 168) for garnish
guacamole (page 156) for garnish
creme fraiche or piima cream for garnish

Make a mixture of oil, lemon or lime juice, pineapple juice and spices and mix well with the meat. Marinate for several hours. Remove with a slotted spoon to paper towels and pat dry. Using a heavy skillet, saute the meat, a batch at a time, in olive oil, transferring to a heated platter and keeping warm in the oven. Meanwhile, mix vegetables in marinade. Saute vegetables in batches in olive oil and strew over meat. Heat tortillas briefly in a heavy cast iron skillet and brush with melted butter. Serve meat mixture with tortillas and garnishes.

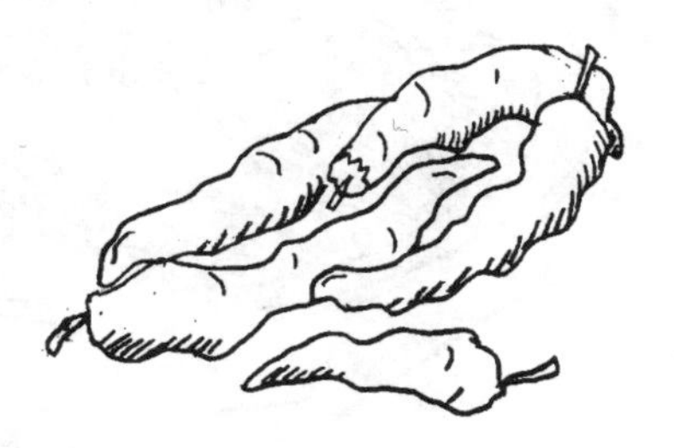

As Yudkin observed, for some adolescents the proportion of calories obtained from sweeteners may go as high as 50%. This means that youngsters who are at the peak of their growth period have to meet *all* their elevated nutrient needs with only half their diet. It is not surprising that obesity, hyperactivity, concentration problems, and behavior disorders have been spreading among students. Joseph D. Beasley MD and Jerry J. Swift MA *The Kellogg Report*

Know Your Ingredients

Name This Product #23

Skim milk, sugar, sodium caseinate, corn oil, cocoa, artificial flavors, magnesium sulfate, cellulose gel, salt, carboxmethyl cellulose, disodium phosphate, potassium citrate, sodium ascorbate, calcium carrageenan, ferric orthophosphate, vitamin E acetate, zinc sulfate, niacinamide, calcium pantothenate, copper sulfate, vitamin A palmitate, pyridoxine hydrochloride, thiamine hydrochloride, riboflavin, folic acid, biotin potassium iodide, vitamin B12, vitamin D.

See Appendix B for Answer

RED MEAT CHILE

Serves 8-12

Our ancestors knew nothing about vitamins, and they did fine. They didn't know about food additives, artificial coloring and flavoring, and above all about pasteurized, homogenized or skim milk. Medical researchers from other countries have attributed the high degree of heart disease and cancer in the US to our high consumption of milk—pasteurized, of course, and in recent years homogenized or skim. This, along with our national addiction to Coca-cola, ice cream, donuts, pizza, candy bars, gives us one of the highest rates of degenerative diseases in the world. For all these, other such popular favorites as powdered fruit drinks, sugar-coated cereals, hot dogs, potato chips, are susceptibility foods—foods, that is, which nibble away at, rather than build up, the body's immune system to disease. Bruce Pacetti DDS *PPNF Journal*

3 pounds coarsely ground beef, buffalo or game
extra virgin olive oil
1/4 cup red wine
2 cups homemade beef stock
2 onions, finely chopped
2 - 4 small green chiles, hot or mild, seeded and chopped
2 cans tomatoes, briefly chopped in food processor
3 cloves garlic, peeled and mashed
1 tablespoons ground cumin
2 tablespoons dried oregano
2 tablespoons dried basil
1/4 - 1/2 teaspoon red chile flakes
4 cups cooked kidney beans (page 469)
no-oil chips for garnish
chopped green onions for garnish
creme fraiche or piima cream for garnish
avocado slices for garnish
chopped cilantro for garnish.

Brown meat until crumbly in a little olive oil in a heavy pot. (Olive oil may not be necessary if the beef contains a lot of fat.) Add remaining ingredients and simmer about 1 hour. Serve with garnishes.

When a woman stays at home and cooks with good judgement and understanding, peace and happiness result. She thus control the family's health and destiny, also her husband's mood, disposition and feeling and assures the futures of her children

Jacques DeLangre

VEGETABLE CHILE

Serves 8

1 eggplant, peeled, cut into 1/2 inch cubes, salted and drained in a colander for 1 hour
2 zucchini, diced, salted and drained in a colander for 1 hour
extra virgin olive oil
2 onions, chopped
1 red pepper, seeded and diced
1 yellow or green pepper, seeded or diced
1 cup chicken stock
1 can tomatoes, chopped briefly in food processor
1 small bunch basil leaves, cut up
2 tablespoons chile powder
3 gloves garlic, peeled and mashed
1 tablespoon ground cumin
1 tablespoon oregano
2 cups cooked black beans (page 469)
2 cups corn kernels, fresh or frozen
chopped green onions for garnish
grated raw Monterey jack cheese for garnish
chopped cilantro for garnish
creme fraiche or piima cream for garnish

Rinse eggplant and pat dry. Saute in batches in olive oil and transfer, using a slotted spoon, to a large casserole. Rinse zucchini and pat dry. Saute in batches in olive oil and transfer, using a slotted spoon, to a casserole. Saute peppers and onions in batches and transfer to casserole. Add stock, tomatoes and seasonings to the pot, bring to a boil, skim and simmer for 1 hour. Add beans and corn kernels and simmer another 1/2 hour. Serve with garnishes.

We tried a starvation experiment with male rabbits, which are naturally great breeders. When we fed certain pens of rabbits a mineral-deficient hay in their diet, we reduced the males in a few weeks to the point where they wouldn't look at a woman rabbit. Other rabbits, kept on a similar but mineral-rich diet with hay from treated soil, were regular wolves. By reversing the diets, the wolves became woman-shy, and the tame cats became wolves. Lambs fed mineral-rich hay from treated soil made nearly three times as much gain in weight in a given time as other lambs from the same flock fed the same amount of hay from mineral-poor soil. Elephants in Burma and Ceylon, when fed on sugar cane, a mineral-poor diet, quickly become unable to do the heavy timber moving required of them. A properly mineral rich diet predisposes a man to health and normal functioning. And the healthier we are, the better we resist diseases that ought to lay us low. "Are We starving to Death?" *The Saturday Evening Post* 1945

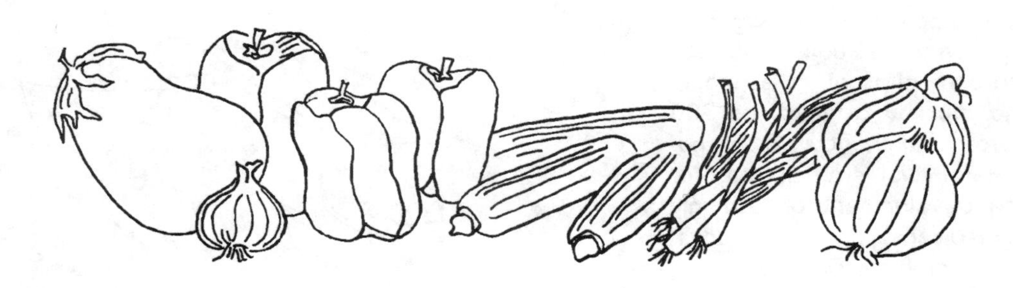

MARIA'S EMPANADAS

Makes about 2 dozen

2 pounds ground turkey
1 medium white onion, chopped
2 bunches green onions, chopped
1 red pepper, seeded and finely chopped
1 green pepper, seeded and finely chopped
4-5 cloves garlic, peeled and mashed
3 carrots, peeled and grated
2 tablespoons finely chopped parsley
1/4 cup chopped cilantro
1 cup cooked peas
1 cup cooked corn
1 1/2 cups basic brown rice (page 441)
1 teaspoon cumin seeds
freshly ground pepper
sea salt to taste
2 recipes yoghurt dough (page 459)

Saute turkey in a skillet with a little olive oil until cooked through, allowing some of it to become well browned. Season with 1/2 teaspoon cumin seeds, freshly ground pepper and salt to taste. In a separate skillet, saute onions and peppers in olive oil. Add carrots, garlic, 1/2 teaspoon cumin and salt to taste and saute a bit more. In a large bowl, mix cooked turkey, vegetable mixture, peas, corn and rice. Check seasonings.

Roll our pastry and cut into rounds, approximately 6 to 7 inches in diameter. Place several spoonfuls of filling off center (a scant 1/2 cup), fold pastry rounds and pinch edges. Bake at 350 degrees until lightly browned. May be individually wrapped in foil and frozen. Remove foil before reheating. Like all rich foods, these go well with lacto-fermented condiments.

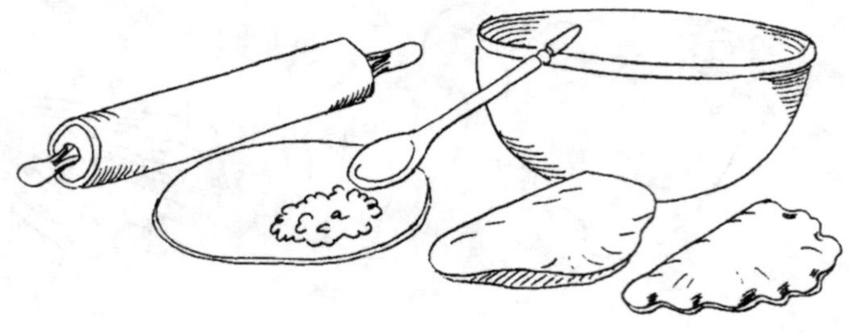

One will immediately ask about vegetarians. On close examination it will be found that vegetarians omit meat from their diet, but include milk, cheese, dairy products, and eggs—all animal protein. Milk is a form of modified blood, more specifically it may be termed white blood. The white of an egg, which is better for the body when cooked, is 100 per cent protein. It is necessary for a vegetarian to eat a relatively large amount of food in order to meet his basic needs because plant foods, due to their high cellulose content, are not easily assimilated and necessitate more work in chewing, flow of digestive juices, and intestinal movement. As far as the human body is concerned, vegetable protein is a poor substitute for animal protein. H. Leon Abrams *Your Body is Your Best Doctor*

Once again, more evidence is presented to demonstrate that there is no significant relationship between diets and cholesterol levels. An extensive analysis of data from a major six-year survey in Israel shows that average cholesterol levels is negatively correlated with consumption of eggs. In other words, there is no evidence for a relationship between eggs in the diet and your blood cholesterol level. . . This new and important study suggests that original studies overestimate the effect of cholesterol in the diet by as much as 300 percent. While your serum cholesterol level is a risk factor for the development of ischemic heart disease, eggs are not causing the problem. Dr. Betty Kamen *Health Freedom News*

EGGS

Shunned for several decades by the health conscious as a high-cholesterol food wrongly believed to cause coronary heart disease, the egg is making the comeback it deserves. The egg has provided high-quality protein and fat soluble vitamins to mankind for millennia. Properly produced eggs are rich in just about every nutrient we have yet discovered, especially in fat soluble vitamins A and D. Eggs also contain sulphur-containing proteins, necessary for the integrity of cell membranes; and tryptophan, an amino acid that promotes a healthy nervous system—no wonder the Japanese value eggs as a brain food. Egg yolk is the most concentrated source known of choline, a B vitamin found in lecithin that is necessary for keeping the cholesterol within the egg emulsified and thus keeps cholesterol moving in the blood stream.

It pays to buy the best quality eggs you can find—eggs from chickens fed flax or fish meal, or allowed to range free in areas where they can eat bugs and worms; their nutritionally qualities are far superior to those of battery raised eggs and even many so-called "free range" eggs. In particular, they contain a better fatty acid profile, one in which the omega-3 and omega-6 fatty acids exist in an almost one-to-one ratio; but in eggs from chickens fed only grains or soy meal, the omega-6 content can be as high as 19 times greater than all important triple unsaturated omega-3. Other very long chain and highly unsaturated fatty acids—necessary for the development of the brain—are found in properly produced eggs but are almost wholly absent in most commercial eggs. Look for eggs with the omega-3 content listed on the carton, such as Country Hen brand, available on the East Coast. High omega-3 eggs will become more available with consumer demand.

When broken into a bowl, the egg should have a dark yellow yolk that stands up clearly. The white should have two clearly defined sections—a more viscous part surrounding the yolk, and a thinner area on the perimeter.

Never eat powdered eggs, a source of harmful oxidized cholesterol.

Serve eggs often as a low cost alternative to meat and a priceless source of nutrients. One cautionary note: Raw egg whites contain a substance called avidin that may be harmful if consumed in excess as it interferes with the absorption of biotin, a B vitamin.

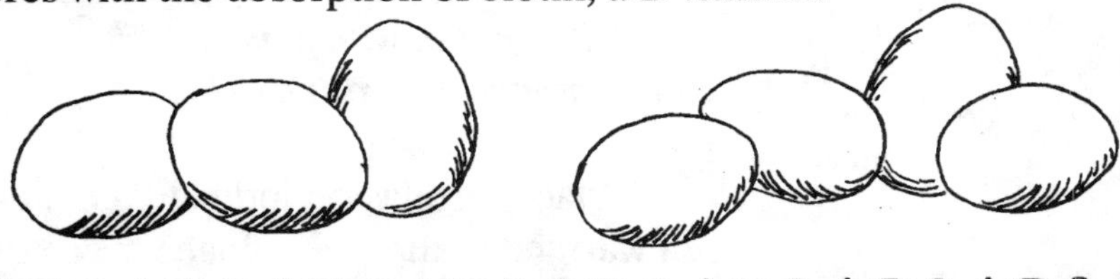

FRIED EGG

Some advocates of politically correct nutrition warn against eating fried eggs as if they were a veritable poison. However, many children—and adults as well—find a poached or boiled egg unpalatable but will eat an egg that has been fried or scrambled. There is absolutely nothing harmful in frying an egg gently in a little butter.

Melt the butter in a heavy skillet over a medium flame and crack an egg into the pan. Cover with a lid and cook gently for several minutes until the white becomes firm and the yolk somewhat thickened. Serve with toast or hash browns (page 376) or turkey sausage (page 341).

SCRAMBLED EGG

Serves 1

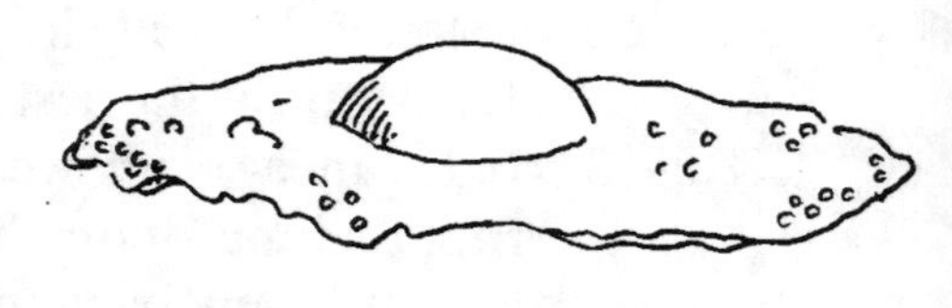

1 fresh egg
1 tablespoon cream
pinch sea salt
2 teaspoons butter

For results that have a more pleasant texture and superior taste, add cream rather than milk to eggs for scrambling.

Crack the egg into a bowl, add cream and salt and beat thoroughly with a wire whisk. Melt butter in a heavy skillet. Add beaten egg mixture and stir constantly with a wooden spoon until egg is scrambled. Eat immediately.

When you sit down to eat a meal it should be a time for pleasure and warmth, family and friends. Food should be enjoyed. Even more importantly, it should also be nourishment that meets all your body's needs. Nothing is more important for the good life than your food supply,

In these times our food supply is plentiful, but it lacks quality nourishment.

Chickens and eggs are near the top of the list of staple foods for our modern society. Problem is, most of the eggs and chickens available today are a

HUEVOS RANCHEROS

Serves 4

4 fresh eggs, scrambled or fried
4 corn tortillas, fried until crisp in olive oil, excess oil removed with paper towels
2 cups Grandpa's salsa (page 141)

Place tortillas on individual plates that have been warmed in the oven. Place fried or scrambled egg on each and top with salsa.

PLAIN OMELET

Serves 2-4

4 fresh eggs, at room temperature
3 tablespoons water
dash tabasco
pinch sea salt
2 tablespoons butter

Crack eggs into a bowl, add water, tabasco and salt and blend with a wire whisk. (Do not over-whisk or the omelet will be tough.) Melt butter in a well-seasoned cast iron skillet. When foam subsides, add egg mixture. Tip pan to allow egg to cover the entire pan. Cook several minutes over medium heat until underside is lightly browned. Lift up one side with a spatula and fold omelet in half. Reduce heat and cook another half minute or so—this will allow the egg on the inside to cook. Slide omelet onto a heated platter and serve.

Variation: Onion, Pepper and Parmesan Cheese Omelet

Saute *1 small onion, thinly sliced* and *1/2 red pepper, cut into julienne strips* in a little butter until tender. Strew this evenly over the egg mixture as it begins to cook, along with *2 tablespoons Parmesan cheese.*

Variation: Herb Omelet

Scatter *1 tablespoon parsley, finely chopped, 1 tablespoon chives, finely chopped* and *1 tablespoon thyme or other garden herb, finely chopped* over omelet as it begins to cook.

Variation: Mushroom Omelet

Saute *1/2 pounds fresh mushrooms, washed, well dried and thinly sliced* in a mixture of butter and olive oil. Scatter over the omelet as it begins to cook.

Variation: Sausage Omelet

Saute *1/4 cup turkey sausage mixture (page 341)* in a little butter until crumbly, or use *1/4 cup leftover samosa filling (page 340)*. Scatter over the omelet as it begins to cook.

far cry from the high quality natural nourishment they used to be—in fact, we consider today's mass-produced eggs and chickens such poor quality food that we have not consumed a supermarket chicken or egg since we can't remember when.

It is precisely because of mass production and chemicalized techniques that the chickens and eggs provided for mainstream America are not fit for human consumption.

Let's start with the egg. The egg from the chicken is considered to be the "most complete" protein source in a single food. In fact, the amino acid complex in eggs is so well proportioned that eggs are used as the reference point for judging the quality of protein in other foods. A good quality egg is particularly high in methionine, an amino acid largely missing from the source of the "staff of life"—grains.

Good quality eggs are an excellent source of carotene and vitamin A, thiamin (vitamin B1) and niacin. Eggs are also one of the few viable sources of vitamin D.

As for minerals, eggs are an outstanding source of "heme" iron, a most absorbable form, plus calcium and phosphorus and trace minerals. As the ads have stated so well—it's an "incredible, edible egg."

Eggs have been an important part of man's nutrition for a long, long time. No historian knows when people first began to eat eggs, but we do know that early Egyptian cakes were made with eggs because these delicacies have been found alongside the mummies in the tombs. Tom Valentine *Search for Health*

PARMESAN CUSTARD

Serves 6

4 egg yolks
1 1/2 cup whipping cream
1 cup freshly grated Parmesan cheese
pinch cayenne pepper

Beat yolks. Stir in cream, cheese and cayenne. Pour into individual ramekins and place in a pan of hot water. Bake at 350 degrees for 45 minutes. This makes a hearty first course during the winter months.

A pasteurized blend of egg whites, water, nonfat dry milk, modified food starch (corn), corn oil, sodium stearoyl lactylate, cellulose gum, magnesium chloride, beta carotene (for color), ferric orthophosphate, zinc sulfate, vitamin E acetate, calcium pantothenate, TBHQ (to maintain freshness), vitamins: cholecalciferol (D3), riboflavin (B2), pyridoxine hydrochloride (B6), thiamine (B1), cyanocobalamin (B12), folic acid.

See Appendix B for Answer

EGGPLANT KIKU

Serves 4-8

2 large eggplants, about 2 pounds, peeled and cut into 1/2 inch squares
2 medium onions, peeled and thinly sliced
extra virgin olive oil
6 eggs
2 cloves garlic, peeled and crushed
juice of 1 lemon
1/2 teaspoon sea salt
1/4 teaspoon freshly ground pepper
1/4 teaspoon saffron threads dissolved in 1 tablespoon hot water

Kiku is an Persian or Arabic dish that has many variations. It came to Spain during the Moorish invasions where it took the form of the Spanish tortilla or Spanish omelet, with potatoes as a filling.

Salt eggplant cubes and leave in a colander to drain for about one hour. Rinse well and pat dry. Using a heavy skillet, saute in batches until soft. Transfer to a bowl with a slotted spoon and mash up with a potato masher. Saute the onions until golden and add to the eggplant. Beat eggs with salt, pepper, lemon juice and saffron. Stir in the eggplant mixture. Pour into a well oiled 9-by-13 pyrex pan and bake about 30 minutes at 375 degrees or until top is browned. Cut into squares or diamonds and serve.

However, the Spirit expressly says that in latter times some will turn away from the faith, addicting themselves to seducing spirits, and to teachings of demons; teaching lies in hypocrisy; burning up their own conscience; hindering marriage; abstaining from foods which God created to be consumed with thankfulness by the faithful, and recognizers of the truth.

Tim 4:1-3

Variation: Zucchini Kiku

Omit the eggplant and use *3 medium zucchini, cut into a julienne*, using the julienne slicer of your food processor. Salt and drain in a colander for 1/2 hour. Rinse and pat dry. Saute about 1 minute in olive oil. Proceed with recipe. You may wish to sprinkle the top of the kiku with 1 *cup grated cheddar or Monterey jack cheese*.

Variation: Spinach Kiku

Omit eggplant and use *2 cups cooked chopped spinach, squeezed dry* mixed with *1 bunch chopped cilantro*, *1 tablespoon chopped dill* and *2 tablespoons chopped chives*. Mix with the sauted onions and proceed with recipe. Omit saffron and use *1/2 teaspoon ground fenugreek* and *1/2 teaspoon ground cumin*.

The prestigious *New England Journal of Medicine* had a report on eggs and cholesterol. A group of New Guinea natives, whose diet is exceedingly low in cholesterol, were fed eggs to measure the cholesterol-raising effect of eggs. They figured the serum cholesterol levels would be blown off the charts. The eggs had no significant effect on the blood cholesterol.

Another study done by the American Cancer Society revealed that non-egg users had a higher death rate from heart attacks and strokes than egg users. This was a very large (and so convincing) study involving over 800,000 people. William Campbell Douglass MD *The Milk of Human Kindness*

SPANISH OMELET

Serves 4

3 red potatoes, thinly sliced
1 medium onion, peeled and thinly sliced
extra virgin olive oil
6 eggs
1/2 teaspoon thyme
sea salt and freshly ground pepper

Saute the potatoes in olive oil in a cast iron skillet until golden. Transfer to a bowl with a slotted spoon. Saute the onions. Meanwhile, beat the eggs with seasonings. Return the potatoes to the pan, combine with onions, flatten to make an even layer and pour the egg mixture over the potatoes. Cook about 5 minutes over medium heat, lifting edges occasionally so uncooked top part can run under. Finish by placing under broiler for a minute or two. Cut into wedges and serve.

With all the publicity about eggs and cholesterol causing heart disease, the food industry quickly responded in making a preparation that looked and tasted like eggs... one such product was called EGG BEATERS. An experiment was conducted at the Brunsides Research Laboratory, University of Illinois by Meena Kasmau Navidi and Fred A. Kummerow in which one group of lactating rats were fed exclusively on fresh shell eggs and another on EGG BEATERS. The rats on fresh shell eggs thrived, were perfectly healthy and grew normally. Those on EGG BEATERS did not grow normally, were stunted, and all died long before reaching maturity. H. Leon Abrams *Vegetarianism: An Anthropological/Nutritional Evaluation*

VEGETABLE FRITATA

Serves 4

1 cup broccoli flowerets, steamed until tender and broken into small pieces
1 red pepper, seeded and cut into a julienne
1 medium onion, peeled and finely chopped
butter and extra virgin olive oil
6 eggs
1/3 cup piima cream or creme fraiche
1 teaspoon finely grated lemon rind
pinch dried oregano
pinch dried rosemary
sea salt and freshly ground pepper
1 cup grated raw Monterey jack cheese

In a cast iron skillet, saute the pepper and onion in butter and olive oil until soft. Remove with a slotted spoon. Beat eggs with cream and seasonings. Stir in broccoli, peppers and onion. Melt more butter and olive oil in the pan and pour in egg mixture. Cook over medium heat about 5 minutes until underside is golden. Sprinkle cheese on top and place under the broiler for a few minutes until the fritata puffs and browns. Cut into wedges and serve.

Variation: Leek Fritata

Omit broccoli, red pepper and onions and use *4 leeks, well rinsed, dried, sliced* and sauteed in butter and olive oil.

Variation: Zucchini Fritata

Omit broccoli, red pepper and onion and use *3 medium zucchini, cut into a julienne*, using the julienne slicer of your food processor. Salt and drain in a colander for 1/2 hour. Rinse and pat dry. Saute about 1 minute in olive oil. Proceed with recipe.

A number of studies reveal that the elimination of eggs from the diet does not lower the risk of coronary heart disease. One study, conducted by Cuyler Hammond and Lawrence Garfinkel of the American Cancer Society, involved 804,409 individuals who had no previous history of coronary heart disease. They were divided into two groups. One group was made up of those who ate five or more eggs each week in addition to eggs used in preparing other foods. The second group ate no eggs or less than four per week. The death rate from heart attacks and strokes was higher in the second group. H. Leon Abrams *Vegetarianism: An Anthropological/Nutritional Evaluation*

THIN HERB FRITATAS

Makes 6

3 eggs
1 tablespoon basil leaves, chopped or cut with scissors
1 tablespoon chives, chopped
1 teaspoon fresh thyme leaves
1 teaspoon finely chopped parsley
2 tablespoons freshly grated Parmesan cheese
2 tablespoons piima cream or creme fraiche
sea salt and freshly ground pepper
extra virgin olive oil

These delicious "egg pancakes" may be eaten in sandwiches.

Mix eggs with herbs, cheese, cream and seasonings. Heat olive oil in a small cast iron skillet. Pour 1/4 cup egg mixture into the pan and tilt the pan to spread the mixture. When the fritata has set, flip over to brown the other side. Transfer to a heated platter and keep warm in the oven while preparing the remaining fritatas.

EMBER DAY TART

Serves 4-6

1 flaky pie crust (page 524) or 1/2 recipe yoghurt dough (page 459)
2 large onions, chopped
4 eggs
2 tablespoons whole grain bread crumbs
1/2 teaspoon saffron threads dissolved in 1 tablespoon warm water
1/2 teaspoon sea salt
pinch nutmeg
2 tablespoons currents

This recipe is based on one taken from a 1390 Middle English cookbook. Ember Day was a meatless day that occurred each season.

Line a pie pan with pastry. Saute onions in a little butter until soft. Beat eggs and stir in onions, bread crumbs, seasonings and currents. Pour into pie shell and bake at 350 degrees for 30 to 40 minutes.

A number of patients were fed eggs—a high cholesterol food—fried in unrefined peanut oil. Blood cholesterol levels did not increase. But when the patients were fed the same food (eggs) fried in hydrogenated oil, there was a marked increase in blood cholesterol. The eggs did not produce any imbalance; neither did the natural, unrefined oil. Only the unnatural, hydrogenated fat produced imbalance. Another study. . . was performed on patients who had a significantly elevated cholesterol. These people were fed natural foods rich in cholesterol and natural oil components rich in phospholipids. . . Seventy-nine percent of these patients showed a marked decrease in blood cholesterol. Unrefined natural fats or oils and natural cholesterol-rich foods are not harmful—they are actually beneficial and keep cholesterol levels within normal limits. Judith de Cava *The Margarine Masquerade*

The public has not been well served by the recommendation that the long-standing custom of having one or two eggs for breakfast be discontinued and not more than two or three eggs per week be eaten—or worse, that the recently marketed "chemical egg" concoctions be substituted for the real thing! Eggs are a valuable food, providing excellent protein, vitamins, and minerals. The cholesterol in them is balanced with sufficient lecithin to keep the cholesterol circulating in the blood and prevent it from depositing in the arteries. This is another instance showing the balance in whole, natural foods. Emory W. Thurston PhD *Nutrition for Tots to Teens*

EGGPLANT TORTA

Serves 8

6 medium eggplants, peeled, sliced lengthwise, salted and allowed to drain in a colander for 1 hour
2 cups chunky tomato sauce (page 140)
1/2 cup freshly grated Parmesan cheese
1/2 cup freshly grated raw Monterey jack
3 large eggs, beaten

Rinse eggplant slices, pat dry, brush both sides with olive oil, place on baking sheets and bake at 375 for about 15 minutes or until lightly browned and soft. Line the bottom and sides of an oiled 9-inch by 2-inch springform pan with eggplant slices. Spread 1/3 of sauce over eggplant and sprinkle with 1/3 of the cheeses. Make another layer of eggplant, cutting edges so it fits neatly, followed by layer of sauce and cheese. Make a final layer of eggplant, sauce and Monterey jack cheese. Poke holes in the torta and pour the eggs over the top so that they soak in evenly. Sprinkle top with remaining Parmesan. Bake on a baking sheet at 350 degrees for about 1/2 hour. Let cool and run a knife around the inside of the pan before releasing spring. Cut into wedges with a serrated knife. May be served with additional tomato sauce.

For 15 years, an 88-year-old Denver man has been consuming 24 soft-boiled eggs a day. This particular story made it to the *New England Journal of Medicine* because a researcher from the University of Colorado wondered how this compulsive cholesterol cuisine might be affecting the man's health. To his surprise, the scientist found that despite a cholesterol intake close to 6,000 milligrams a day—well above the recommended maximum of 300 milligrams per day—the man had normal blood cholesterol and showed no signs of heart disease. . . Over the past 13 years, though, these's been a growing body of evidence that it might be something in our food that is causing . . . [blood] vessel damage. The suspected ingredient is a modified form of cholesterol called oxidized cholesterol. This is not the kind you find in eggs or other fresh foods. Oxidized cholesterol forms when cholesterol reacts with oxygen. This usually occurs when high-cholesterol foods are dried, such as in powdered eggs. Oxidized cholesterol also can be found in small amounts in powdered dairy products such as milk, cheese or butter. One soon-to-be-released study found significant amounts in fast food french fries that had been cooked in animal fat. Edward Blonz *PPNF Journal*

RED PEPPER QUICHE

Serves 4-8

1 recipe flaky pie crust (page 524)
or 1/2 recipe yoghurt dough (page 459)
2 red peppers, seeded and cut into a julienne
1 medium onion, finely sliced
3 egg yolks
1/2 cup creme fraiche or piima cream
sea salt and freshly ground pepper
1 cup freshly grated Parmesan or
Monterey jack cheese

Roll out dough and line a 10-inch French-style tart pan with a removable bottom. Half bake the crust for about 15 to 30 minutes (longer for yoghurt dough). Meanwhile, saute peppers and onion in a little olive oil and butter until soft. Beat yolks with cream, seasonings and half of the cheese. Strew the peppers over the crust and pour the egg mixture over. Top with remaining cheese and bake at 350 degrees for about 1/2 hour.

Variation: Mushroom Quiche

Substitute *1 pound fresh mushrooms, washed, well dried and sliced* for the peppers. Saute in a mixture of butter and olive oil and proceed with recipe.

Variation: Zucchini Quiche

Omit peppers and use *2 medium zucchini, cut into a julienne*, using the julienne slicer of your food processor. Salt and drain in a colander for 1/2 hour. Rinse and pat dry. Saute a minute or so in olive oil and proceed with recipe.

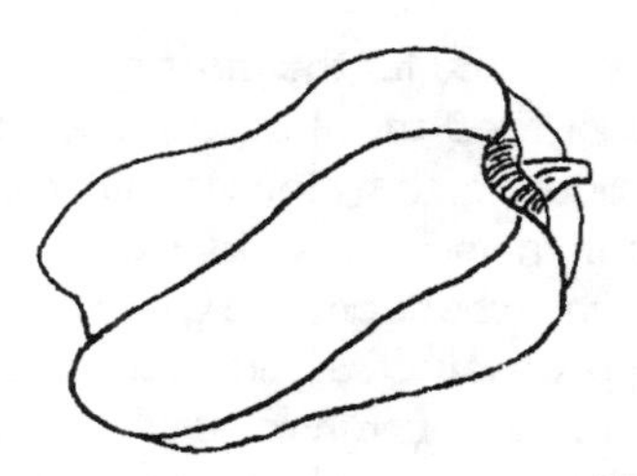

Since eggs have the highest amount of cholesterol per unit weight of all common foods (liver and brains have more), people began to fear them. Once called nature's most perfect food by nutritionists, eggs fell into disfavor and their consumption began to plummet after 1950. The average number of eggs consumed in the US per person per year dropped from a high of 389 in 1950 . . to only 234 in 1989. Americans are eating many fewer eggs today than at the turn of the century. . .Thousands of egg farmers have gone out of business over the last 30 years because of the false dietary cholesterol scare. And millions of Americans have given up or substantially reduced their consumption of one of the best and most economical foods available for no good scientific or common sense reasons. This nonsensical state-of-affairs will continue until the major media wake up and begin telling the public what is really going on. Russell L. Smith PhD *Health Freedom News*

CHEESE SOUFFLE

Serves 4

5-6 eggs separated, at room temperature
1/2 stick butter
1 cup unbleached flour
1 cup good quality cream
plus 1 cup water, warmed
6 ounces grated Swiss cheese
sea salt and pepper

Melt butter in a heavy saucepan. Add flour and stir with a wooden spoon for several minutes. Gradually add warm cream and water mixture, beating with a wire whisk. The white sauce should be very thick—the thicker the sauce, the lighter will be your souffle. Off heat, stir in cheese and seasonings, and then the egg yolks, one at a time. Place egg whites in a very clean glass or stainless steel bowl, add a pinch of sea salt and beat until stiff. Gently fold egg yolk mixture into egg whites and pour into a buttered 2-quart souffle dish. Place in a preheated 400 degree oven, lower heat to 350 degrees and bake for 40 to 45 minutes. Serve immediately.

By far the most efficient plant food that I have found for producing the high-vitamin content in milk is rapidly growing young wheat and rye grass. Oat and barley grass are also excellent. In my clinical work, small additions of this high-vitamin butter [from cows feeding on growing grass] to otherwise satisfactory diets regularly checks tooth decay when active and at the same time improves vitality and general health. . . Similarly the value of eggs for providing fat-soluble vitamins depends directly upon the food eaten by the fowl. The fertility of the eggs also is a direct measure of the vitamin content, including vitamin E. Weston Price DDS *Nutrition and Physical Degeneration*

The Anasazi Indians, builders of the famous cliff dwellings in Mesa Verde, Colorado, flourished from 650 to 1300 A.D. and then died out "mysteriously". In the early days of their civilization, they had plenty of game but archeologists find no animal bones in the trash heaps during the final century or so. Late human skeletal remains show bone deformities, rickets, rampant tooth decay and arthritis in individuals as young as 20 years old. The Anasazi ate corn, beans, pine nuts, yucca, herbs and berries. Their diet contained complete protein, essential fatty acids, minerals, and vitamins including lots of carotene. Their life-style gave them abundant exposure to sunlight. But in the final years, the Anasazi lacked animal products, particularly vitamins A and D. They died out and we will too if we eliminate animals fats from the diet. SWF

SANDWICH SUGGESTIONS

As sandwiches are a fixture on the American food scene, we should make every attempt to prepare them with nutritious ingredients. Basic to this effort is avoidance of the usual sandwich ingredients—preserved meats, condiments containing sugar and polyunsaturated oils, processed cheeses and unsuitable breads.

It is, in fact, modern bread that makes the sandwich possible and palatable. Old style, sourdough, slow-rise breads are too dense and hard for sandwich lovers; it was the advent of baker's yeast that allowed bakers to produce softly spongy and uniform bread for sandwiches. Baker's yeast produces a quick rise in bread in a very short period of time so that phytates in whole grains are not properly neutralized. Thus both whole grain and refined flour sandwich breads present health risks, especially when so many dough conditioners and preservatives are added, as is the custom.

However, there are compromise breads available that will serve for sandwiches. They are, unfortunately, all made with baker's yeast, but the grains are first allowed to sprout or sour. Look for sourdough or sprouted grain sandwich breads, preferably made with a variety of grains, in the freezer compartment of your health food store. Alvarado Bakery and Shiloh Farms both produce whole grain sprouted or sour dough sandwich breads of excellent quality. Pita bread has the opposite profile—it is not made with yeast, but unfortunately the dough is not allowed to sour. It should be avoided by those with grain allergies. It would be a shame, however, to prohibit pita bread altogether, as it makes such a great pocket for fillings.

Make an effort, then, to obtain nutritious bread and use it to produce sandwiches featuring fresh meats, marinated fish, nut butters, raw cheeses, sprouts, fresh and fermented vegetables, avocado, fresh butter, and homemade mayonnaise and other spreads with a high enzyme content.

Sandwiches in lunch boxes may be accompanied by fresh fruit, homemade cookies, crispy nuts (pages 485-487), trail mix (page 488), raw vegetables, and a thermos of homemade ginger ale (page 550), apple cider (page 551), or other refreshing lacto-fermented beverage. Samosas (page 340), empanadas (page 412) and breaded chicken breasts (page 262) also make nice lunch box fare.

NUT BUTTER SANDWICHES

Use peanut, cashew or almond butter made from organic, roasted nuts with fruit sweetened jam, apricot butter (page 101) or raw honey.

TUNA SANDWICHES

Use simple tuna salad (page 394) or tahini tuna salad (page 395). Spread bread with mayonnaise (page 126) or mashed avocado and fill with choice of small seed sprouts (page 106), thinly sliced tomato and lettuce.

TURKEY OR CHICKEN SANDWICHES

Used leftover turkey or chicken or buy a whole turkey breast and bake in the oven. Slice thinly. Spread bread with butter, mayonnaise (page 126) or Creole mayonnaise (page 128). Fill with choice of thinly sliced tomato, small seed sprouts (page 106), lettuce, thinly sliced red onions or sliced avocado.

CHICKEN SALAD SANDWICH

Spread bread with curried mayonnaise (page 127) and fill with curried chicken salad (page 392).

REUBEN SANDWICH

This delicious sandwich is composed of four fermented foods—five if you use cultured butter. Spread sour dough bread with butter and fill with thinly sliced corned beef (page 214), thinly sliced Swiss cheese and sauerkraut (page 84). Saute sandwich lightly in a dab of butter or extra virgin olive oil, on both sides, until lightly browned and interior is slightly warmed.

It seems that our contemporaries have little time to prepare nice meals—frozen foods, canned foods, fast foods have invaded our supermarkets and our restaurants.

We misunderstand our ancestors when we think that they could spend hours and hours preparing their meals. The old cook books may give this impression but these books were for the upper classes that could afford to hire cooks. Among the peasants, the women worked in the fields and there remained little time in the evenings to prepare dinner. At noon, the men often ate in the fields. For lunch they needed foods that were easily prepared—they needed "fast food"—and for dinner they ate one course meals, invariable something simple.

Many fermented foods can be eaten without any preparation—bread, cheese, sausage, lacto-fermented vegetables, olives, anchovies, fish and soy sauces, and many others.

After all, we didn't have to wait for the Americans to invent the cheese sandwich—a fermented fast food that is delicious as well as nutritious as long as the bread and the cheese are of good quality (increasingly rare these days because the fermentation process has been industrialized and therefore denatured.)

The Russians also invented fast food—long before the Americans. When Turgenov's hunter arrives without warning at the peasant's cottage, he is invariable offered rye bread, cheese, pickled cucumbers and kvass—three fermented foods and one fermented drink, always ready to be served to the passing guest. Claude Aubert *Les Aliments Fermentes Traditionnels*

ROAST BEEF SANDWICHES

Use thinly sliced roast beef with choice of thinly sliced red onions, small seed sprouts (page 106), avocado and lettuce. Spread bread with butter, Creole mayonnaise (page 128), horseradish sauce (page 130), or mustard.

VEGETABLE SANDWICHES

Spread bread thickly with butter and fill with thinly sliced radishes, thinly sliced red onion, or thinly sliced cucumber, or a combination. Cucumber also goes well with homemade cream cheese (page 80).

RAW CHEESE SANDWICHES

Spread bread with butter or mayonnaise (page 126). Fill with thinly sliced raw cheese. Raw cheddar cheese goes nicely with raisin chutney (page 100). Raw Monterey jack cheese goes well with cortido (page 85).

HERB FRITATA SANDWICH

Spread bread with butter or mayonnaise (page 126) and fill with thin herb fritatas (page 419).

MARINATED FISH SANDWICHES

Sliced marinated salmon (page 218) or drained and flaked marinated salmon (page 221) or mackerel (page 222), on toasted bread spread with homemade cream cheese (page 80), butter, mayonnaise (page 126) or Creole mayonnaise (page 128). A small amount of pickled vegetable such as sauerkraut (page 84) or daikon radish (page 91) may be added as fill.

MEATLOAF SANDWICH

Spread bread with mayonnaise (page 126) or homemade ketchup (page 95) and fill with sliced spicy meatloaf (page 333) and thinly shredded romaine lettuce.

Know Your Ingredients

Name This Product #25

Enriched flour (wheat flour, malted barley flour, iron, niacin, thiamine mononitrate, riboflavin), water, wheat bran, honey, high fructose corn syrup, soya bran, canola oil and/or soybean oil, rolled oats, rye flakes. Contains 2% or less of each of the following: molasses, raisin juice, crushed wheat, yeast, wheat gluten, salt, cultured whey, calcium sulfate, cough conditioners (may contain one or more of the following: calcium and sodium stearoyl, lactylate, ethoxylated mono- and di-glycerides, monocalcium phosphate, calcium carbonate), mono- and di-glycerides, yeast nutrient (ammonium sulfate). "No artificial preservatives added"

See Appendix B for Answer

"Doctor, is my baby all right?" is the first question of almost every woman when her child is born. I myself have heard the question thousands of times. If every mother's greatest wish is to have a truly healthy baby, why (in most cases) does she take such poor care of herself before the baby is born? And why does she feed her child from infancy to adulthood so improperly that illness inevitably results?

This century has been called "The Century of the Child" because of the tremendous interest in the physical and psychological growth of children. But as we look around us, where are these radiantly healthy children? Certainly their parents are anxious to rear healthy youngsters. Some eight thousand books on child care have been published in the last twenty-five years. Why then are the offices of the country's thousands of pediatricians and general practitioners filled with runny-nosed, tired, allergic, feverish, run-down, anemic, bespectacled, acne-ridden, too thin or obese children? The answer is simple:

(1) The mother's body was no fit environment for the child because her system was filled with waste products from improper food, drug residues, coffee acids, the poisons of cigarettes and alcohol.

(2) The growing child is improperly fed, spends too much time watching television, is driven everywhere instead of walking and devotes too little time to exercising in fresh air. Henry Bieler MD *Food is Your Best Medicine*

PITA BREAD SANDWICHES

Fill whole wheat pita bread with any of the following:

Falafal (page 478), tahini sauce (page 134) and thinly sliced cucumbers and tomato

Mazalika (page 292), tahini sauce (page 134) and thinly sliced cucumbers and tomato

Curried chicken salad (page 392)

Grated raw cheese, shredded lettuce, and salsa (page 95)

Sliced chicken or turkey, mayonnaise (page 126) or tahini (page 134), shredded lettuce and thinly sliced tomato

Simple tuna salad (page 394), mayonnaise (page 126), avocado, thinly sliced tomato and small seed sprouts (page 106)

Oriental red meat salad (page 399)

ROLL UPS

Use sprouted whole wheat tortillas and roll up with any of the following combinations:

Cream cheese flax spread (page 149), marinated salmon (page 218), dill sprigs and thinly sliced onion.

Creole mayonnaise (page 128), thinly sliced chicken or turkey, small seed sprouts (page 126) and thinly sliced tomatoes.

Mexican chicken breasts (page 261), sliced across the grain, guacamole (page 156) and chismole (page 168).

Thinly sliced roast beef, egg mustard sauce (page 130), and thinly sliced onion.

GRAINS & LEGUMES

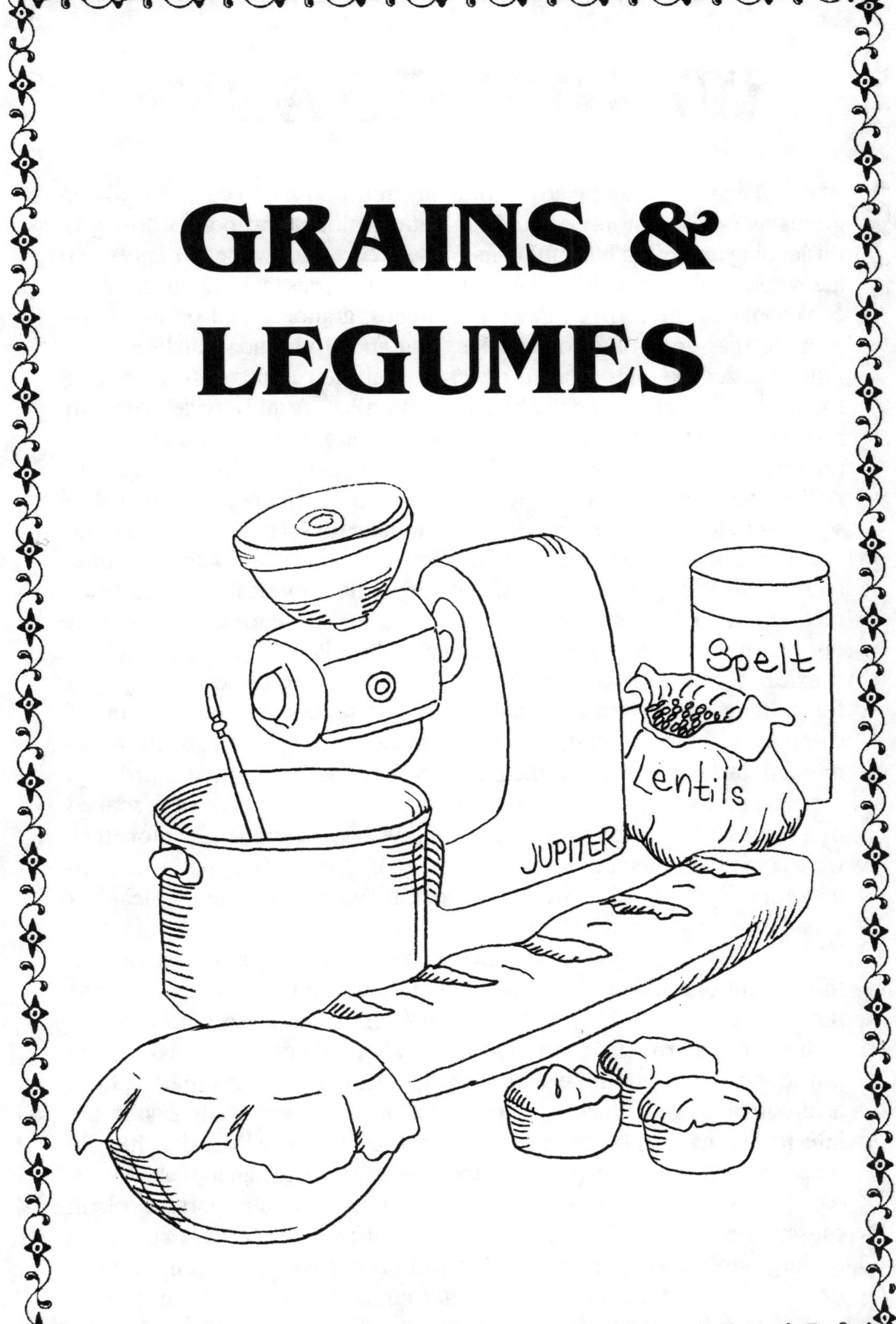

WHOLE GRAINS

The well-meaning advice of many nutritionists, to consume whole grains as our ancestors did, and not refined flours and polished rice, is misleading and often harmful in its consequences; for while our ancestors ate whole grains, they did not consume them as presented in our modern cookbooks in the form of quick-rise breads, granolas, and other hastily prepared casseroles and concoctions. Our ancestors, and virtually all pre-industrialized peoples, soaked or fermented their grains before making them into porridge, breads, cakes, and casseroles. A quick review of grain recipes from around the world will prove our point: In India, rice and lentils are fermented for at least 2 days before being made into *idli* and *dosas*; in Africa, the natives soak coarsely ground corn overnight before adding it to soups and stews and they ferment corn or millet for several days to produce a sour porridge called *ogi*; a similar dish made from oats was traditional among the Welsh; in some Oriental and Latin American countries rice receives a long fermentation before it is prepared; Ethiopians make their distinctive *injera* bread by fermenting a grain called teff for several days; Mexican corn bread cakes, called *pozol*, are fermented for several days and for as long as two weeks in banana leaves; before the introduction of commercial brewers yeast, Europeans made slow-rising breads from fermented starters; in America the pioneers were famous for their sourdough breads, pancakes and biscuits; and throughout Europe grains were soaked overnight, and for as long as several days, in water or soured milk before they were cooked and served as porridge or gruel. (Many of our senior citizens may remember that in earlier times, the instructions on the oatmeal box called for an overnight soaking.)

This is not the place to speculate on that mysterious instructive spirit that taught our ancestors to soak and ferment their grains before eating them; the important thing to realize is that these practices accord very well with what modern science has discovered about grains. All grains contain phytic acid (myoinositol-hexa) in the outer layer or bran. Untreated phytic acid combines with calcium, phosphorus, iron and especially zinc in the intestinal tract and blocks their absorption. This is why a diet high in unfermented whole grains may lead to bone loss and serious mineral deficiencies. Recent research indicates that phytic acid may play an important role in causing some forms of cancer. The modern misguided practice of consuming large amounts of unprocessed bran often improves colon transit time at first; but may lead to irritable bowel syndrome and, in the long term, mineral deficiencies and many other adverse effects. Soaking allows lactobacilli and other helpful organisms to break down and neutralize phytic acid. As little as seven hours of soaking in warm acidulated water will neutralize most phytic acid in grains. The simple practice of soaking cracked or rolled cereal grains overnight will vastly improve their nutritional benefits.

Soaking in warm water also neutralizes enzyme inhibitors, present in all grains, and encourages the production of numerous beneficial enzymes. The action of these enzymes also increases the amounts of many vitamins, especially B vitamins.

Scientists have learned that the proteins in grains, especially gluten, are very difficult to digest. A diet high in unfermented whole grains, particularly high-gluten grains like wheat, puts an enormous strain on the whole digestive mechanism. When this mechanism breaks down with age or overuse, the results take the form of allergies, celiac disease, mental illness, chronic indigestion and candida albicans overgrowth. Recent research links gluten intolerance with multiple sclerosis. During the process of soaking and fermenting, lactobacilli break down gluten and other difficult-to-digest proteins; in effect they predigest the grains, making their nutrients more readily available.

Animals that nourish themselves on grain and other vegetable matter have as many as four stomachs. Their intestines are longer as is the entire digestion transit time. Man on the other hand has but one stomach, and a much shorter intestine, relatively speaking, than herbivorous animals. These features of his anatomy allow him to pass animal products before they putrefy in the gut; but make him less well adapted to a diet high in grains—unless, of course, he lets the friendly bacteria of the microscopic world do some of his digesting for him in a container, just as these same lactobacilli do their work in the first and second stomachs of the herbivores.

Grains fall into two general categories. Those containing gluten such as oats, rye, barley, buckwheat and especially wheat should not be consumed unless they have been soaked or fermented; rice and millet do not contain gluten and are, on the whole, more easily digested. But whole rice and whole millet contain phytates. For optimum health benefits, they should be fully cooked for at least two hours in a high-mineral, gelatinous broth. This will neutralize a good portion of the phytates and provide additional minerals to compensate for those bound by the remaining phytates; while the gelatin in the broth will greatly facilitate digestion. We do not recommend the pressure cooker for grains because it cooks them too quickly.

We use several grains that are new to the Western vocabulary. One is spelt, an ancient grain praised by the medieval sage St. Hildegard as being particularly suited to the sick and those of a weak constitution. It is more soluble than wheat, oats, rye or barley and can be used in recipes where soaking is not possible or appropriate; nevertheless its nutritional benefits will be greatly enhanced by lacto-fermentation. With few exceptions, it can be substituted for wheat in all of our recipes. Another grain new to America is kamut, an ancient non-hybrid variety of wheat. Some people who are allergic to modern varieties of wheat report better results when they use kamoot instead. Teff is a grain from northern Africa, invariably fermented before being made into bread. Quinoa comes from the South American Andes and was first described in Western literature by Dr. Price. He noted that women in the Andes valued it for its ability to stimulate breast milk. Not technically a grain, but the fruit of the chenopodium family, it has superior nutritional properties. If you do not like the taste of all-quinoa products, you can substitute a portion of the flour in any of our recipes with a small amount of quinoa flour—but all quinoa products should be soaked. Andean Indians recognize that there are anti-nutrients in quinoa that are neutralized by soaking. Amaranth is another newly discovered grain, also from South America, that can be used in many of the following recipes. Buckwheat, another neglected grain, is valuable for its high content of cancer-preventing nitrilosides. Like quinoa, buckwheat is not technically a grain, but the seeds of an herb, a relative of rhubarb.

Our readers will notice that our recipes for breakfast cereals are all porridges that have been soaked overnight before they are cooked. You may also add a little ground flax seed to start your day with a ration of omega-3 fatty acids. These porridges marry very well with butter or cream, whose fat soluble activators provide the necessary catalyst for mineral absorption. Those with milk allergies can usually tolerate a little cream, thinned with water, on their breakfast cereal, or eat them with butter—a delicious combination. We do not recommend soy milk which has a high phytate content.

Nor do we recommend that popular "health" food granola, made from grains subjected only to dry heat and therefore extremely indigestible. Granola, like all processed breakfast cereals, should have no place on our cupboard shelves. A new generation of hardy children will only be achieved when we return to the breakfast cereals of our ancestors—soaked gruels and porridges.

A word about corn: Traditional recipes call for soaking corn or corn flour in lime water. This releases nicotinamide (vitamin B3) which otherwise remains bound up in the grain, and also improves the amino acid quality of proteins in the germ. Those who consume corn as their principle grain should take care to add dolomite (calcium carbonate) to cornmeal while it is soaking, in the proportion of about 1 teaspoon per cup of flour. (See Sources.) This simple precaution will help avoid the vitamin B3 deficiency disease pellagra, with its cruel symptoms of sore skin, fatigue and mental disorders.

BREAKFAST PORRIDGE

Serves 4

1 cup oats, steel cut or rolled, or coarsely ground in your own grinder
1 cup water plus 2 tablespoons whey, yoghurt or buttermilk
1/2 teaspoon sea salt
1 cup water
1 tablespoon flax seeds (optional)

For highest benefits and best assimilation, porridge should be soaked overnight or even longer. (Ancient recipes from Wales and Brittany called for a 24-hour soaking.) Once soaked, oatmeal cooks up in less than 5 minutes—truly a fast *food*.

Mix oats and salt with water mixture, cover and let stand at room temperature for at least 7 hours and as long as 24 hours. Bring additional 1 cup of water to boil. Add soaked oats, reduce heat, cover and simmer several minutes. Meanwhile, grind flax seeds in a mini grinder. Off heat, stir in flax seeds and let stand for a few minutes. Serve with butter or cream thinned with a little water, and a natural sweetener like sucanat, date sugar, maple syrup, maple sugar or raw honey.

The basic foods of these [isolated Gaelic] islanders are fish and oat products with a little barley. Oat grain is the one cereal which develops fairly readily, and it provides the porridge and oat cakes which in many homes are eaten in some form regularly with each meal. The fishing about the Outer Hebrides is specially favorable, and small sea foods, including lobsters, crabs, oysters and clams, are abundant. An important and highly relished article of diet has been baked cod's head stuffed with chopped cod's liver and oatmeal. . . [in the ports the] hardy fisherwomen often toil from six in the morning to ten at night. [We saw] fisher people with teeth of unusual perfection. . . It would be difficult to find examples of woman hood combining a higher degree of physical perfection and more exalted ideals than these weather-hardened toilers. Theirs is a land of frequent gales, often sleet-ridden or enshrouded in penetrating cold fogs. Life is full of meaning for characters that are developed to accept as everyday routine raging seas and piercing blizzards representing the accumulated fury of the treacherous north Atlantic. One marvels at their gentleness, refinement and sweetness of character. Weston Price DDS *Nutrition and Physical Degeneration*

Variation: Cream of Kamut

Use *1 cup coarsely ground kamut* instead of oats.

Samuel Johnson defined oats as "a grain used in England to feed horses and in Scotland to feed the populace." It has been observed that in these two regions, oats have produced magnificent examples of both species.

Although first discovered growing wild in barley fields in Russia, northern Africa and the Near East, oats thrive in colder climates of Scotland, Ireland and England. They were planted in Massachusetts in the 1600's and served as porridge for the growing nation. Oats are rich in B vitamins and in calcium, iron, magnesium, phosphorus and potassium. They contain more oil than most grains. Oats are low in gluten but contain more phytates than almost any other grain. Thus it is wise to soak oats if you eat them frequently. The phytates are contained in the bran of the oat and can have a chelating or detoxifying effect. This is why the oat bran fad gave beneficial results at first; but frequent ingestion of unsoaked oat bran can lead to mineral losses, allergies and irritation of the intestinal tract. SWF

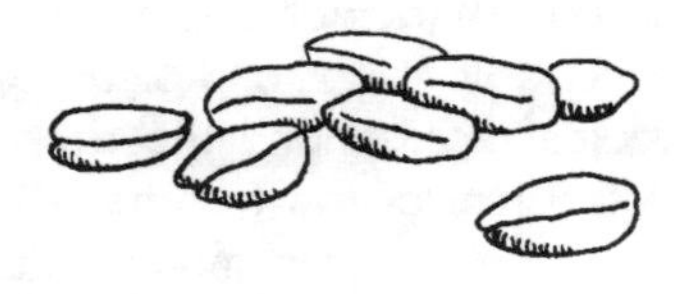

Variation: Cream of Rye

Use *1 cup coarsely ground rye or rye flakes* instead of oats. This has a wonderful texture and taste.

Variation: Cream of Teff

Use *1 cup teff grain*. May be soaked overnight but 24 hours is better. Delicious as a breakfast cereal.

Variation: Cream of Millet

Use *1 cup millet*. Soak 7 to 24 hours before preparing.

Variation: Grits

Use *1 cup coarsely ground corn* plus *1 teaspoon dolomite*. Soak overnight before preparing. Stir grits frequently while they cook.

GENUINE IRISH OATMEAL

Serves 4-6

1 cup whole oats, roasted until light brown in oven
3 cups filtered water
2 tablespoon whey, yoghurt or buttermilk
1 teaspoon sea salt
2 cups filtered water

Process roasted oats to a medium grind in a home grinder. (The resultant meal should be part flour, part small bits.) Soak overnight in salt, 3 cups water and whey, yoghurt or buttermilk. Bring additional 2 cups water and salt to a boil, add soaked oatmeal, and cook over very low heat, stirring frequently, for about 10 minutes.

In Scotland it was the custom to prepare oatmeal in large batches and pour the cooked meal into a drawer in the kitchen hutch or dresser! Squares of congealed oatmeal could then be cut out as needed and reheated by adding a little water. This process allowed the oatmeal to ferment a second time.

MEUSLI

Serves 4

1 cup oats or other grain, steel cut or rolled, or coarsely ground in your grinder
1/4 cup crispy almonds (page 487), slivered
1/4 cup dried sweetened coconut meat (page 144) or commercial dried unsweetened coconut
1/2 teaspoon cinnamon
1 1/2 cups water plus 2 tablespoon whey, yoghurt or buttermilk
1/2 teaspoon salt
1 cup water
1/4 cup raisins
1 tablespoon flax seeds (optional)

Mix oats with almonds, cinnamon and coconut. Combine oats mixture and salt with water mixture, cover and let stand at room temperature for at least 7 hours and as long as 24 hours. Bring additional 1 cup of water to boil. Add soaked oats and raisins, reduce heat, cover and simmer several minutes. Meanwhile, grind flax seeds in a mini grinder. Remove cereal from heat and stir in flax meal. Serve with butter or cream thinned with a little water, and a natural sweetener like sucanat, date sugar, maple syrup, maple sugar or raw honey.

FRIED MUSH

Makes 3 patties

1 cup leftover porridge
1 egg, lightly beaten
butter and extra virgin olive oil

This makes a excellent and economical after-school snack. Mix porridge with egg. Saute by spoonfuls in butter and olive oil. Serve with maple syrup or honey.

In the history of food, gruel and porridge came before bread. For cereals unsuitable to bread making, such as oats, corn or millet, this remains the principle way of consuming these grains. In northern Europe, oat and rye porridges were daily fare. "Porridge is the mother of us all" is a Russian proverb. Millet and buckwheat porridge were eaten in warmer regions. They were very popular in Germany as well as in Eastern Europe and in France. The Gaules were great consumers of millet porridge.

The term "gruel" and "porridge" covers preparations of differing consistencies, from rather liquid gruels that are drunk to *polenta*, which you can cut with a knife. In what measure were these preparations fermented? . . . *Braga*, one of the most ancient sour gruels that we know of is prepared with a thick porridge of cooked millet that is then diluted and fermented. Of a rather liquid consistency, it is drunk rather than eaten. Like other sour gruels of central and eastern Europe—*kiesiel, gieslitz, zu, brag*—can be compared to certain "beers" made from grains in Africa and South America—it is impossible to draw a precise line between these gruels and traditional beers. These are true liquid meals, like that of the Babylonians called "drinkable bread" and have played an important role in almost all civilizations. In Brittany *l'ar yod kierc'h*—oat porridge—was formerly eaten after one night of fermentation. This overnight fermentation gives this traditional dish its characteristic taste, slightly acid, that one seeks in vain in modern porridges. . . But who still eats oatmeal—even in Brittany? Claude Aubert *Les Aliments Fermentes Traditionnels*

FIVE GRAIN CEREAL MIX

Makes 10 cups

2 cups wheat or spelt
2 cups millet
2 cups short grain rice
2 cups barley or oats
2 cups split peas or lentils

This combination of grains conforms to the five grains recommended in the *Yellow Emperor's Classic of Internal Medicine*.

Mix together and grind coarsely. Store in refrigerator.

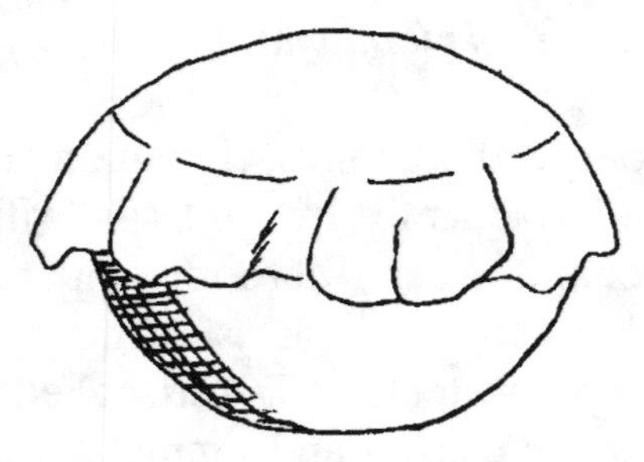

The poisons and medicines attack the evil influences. The five grains act as nourishment; the five fruits from the trees serve to augment; the five domestic animals provide additional benefit; the five vegetables serve to complete the nourishment. Their flavors, tastes and smells unite and conform to each other in order to supply the beneficial essence of life. Each of these five flavors—pungent, sour, sweet, bitter, and salt—provides a certain advantage and benefit. Their effect is either dispersing or binding and gathering, retarding or accelerating, strengthening or softening. *The Yellow Emperor's Classic of Internal Medicine*

FIVE GRAIN PORRIDGE

Serves 4

1 cup five grain cereal mix
1 cup water plus 2 tablespoon whey, buttermilk or yoghurt
1/2 teaspoon salt
1 cup water
1 tablespoon flax seeds (optional)

Mix five grain mixture and salt with water plus whey or yoghurt, cover and let stand at room temperature for at least 7 hours and as long as 24 hours. Bring additional 1 cup of water to boil. Add soaked cereal, reduce heat, cover and simmer several minutes. Meanwhile, grind flax seed in a mini grinder. Remove cereal from heat and stir in flax meal. Serve with butter or cream thinned with a little water, and a natural sweetener like sucanat, date sugar, maple syrup or raw honey.

Flax is an ancient plant found in northern climes whose seed oil is the richest known source of triple unsaturated omega-3 fatty acids. Before the advent of large commercial oil presses, flax "beaters" in European and Russian villages pressed oil out of flax seeds and sold it from door to door on a weekly basis, much as dairy products and eggs were also sold. Without knowing why, northern European peoples valued flax oil as a folk remedy. Flax oil has been used in natural programs for the treatment of heart disease, cancer, diabetes, PMS, arthritis and inflammatory and fibroid conditions.

Flax also contains protein, minerals and vitamins. It is an excellent source of mucilage and fiber. Flax is also the richest knows source of lignans, substances that have anti-viral, antifungal, anti-bacterial and anti-cancer properties. SWF

AFRICAN MILLET PORRIDGE

(Ogi)

4 cups millet
filtered water
1/4 cup whey

This is a recipe for the brave, the adventurous and the curious. Place millet in a large bowl. Cover with water. Place a clean towel over the bowl and let stand 24 hours. Pour off water and process until smooth in batches in food processor. Place ground millet in a bowl and mix with a generous amount of water. Strain through a strainer into another large bowl or pitcher, discarding the coarse slurry left in the strainer. Mix whey with strained liquid, cover and let sit at room temperature for 24 to 72 hours.

This liquid may now be cooked as porridge. Place 1 cup in a small pan and bring to a boil, stirring constantly with a wooden spoon. Cook, stirring, for several minutes. The resultant porridge will be very sour and may be eaten with a natural sweetener and a little cream thinned with water.

The *ogi* may be also be reduced to a paste, called *agidi*, by the following method: Line a large strainer with several layers of cheese cloth or a linen towel and pour fermented millet mixture through strainer. Tie up ends of cloth making a sack, and tie this sack to wooden spoon suspended over a pitcher or bowl. Let the *ogi* drain, just as you would drain cream cheese (see page 80). Store the strained *agidi* in the refrigerator in an air tight container. To prepare as porridge, bring salted water to boil, stir in *agidi* and simmer, covered, several minutes. Off heat, let stand several minutes. Eat as you would porridge, with a natural sweetener and butter or cream.

Variation: Welsh Oat Porridge (Llymru)

Use *oats* instead of millet. May be soaked in *buttermilk* instead of water.

Acid porridges prepared from cereals are still eaten . . . in different parts of the world, particularly in the developing countries, where they may represent the basic diet. *Ogi* (Nigeria), *Uji* (Kenya) and *Koko* (Ghana) are examples of these porridges prepared by the fermentation of maize, sorghum, millet or cassava followed by wet-milling, wet sieving and boiling. . . Ogi porridge has a smooth texture similar to a hot blancmange and a sour taste reminiscent of yogurt. . . . Ogi is consumed as a porridge (pap) with about 8% solids, or a gel-like product (agidi) by a very large number of Nigerians. Pap is by far the most important traditional food for weaning infants and the major breakfast cereal of adults. Infants 9 months old are introduced to ogi by feeding once per day as a supplement to breast milk. Keith H Steinkraus, ed.p189 *Handbook of Indigenous Fermented Foods,* Courtesy Marcel Dekker, Inc.

As an illustration of the remarkable wisdom of these primitive tribes, I found them using for the nursing period two cereals with unusual properties. One, was a red millet which was not only high in carotene but had a calcium content of five to ten times that of most other cereals. They used also for nursing mothers in several tribes in Africa, a cereal called by them linga-linga. This proved to be the same cereal under the name of quinoa that the Indians of Peru use liberally, particularly the nursing mothers. The botanical name is quinoa. This cereal had the remarkable property of being not only rich in minerals but a powerful stimulant of the flow of milk. Weston Price DDS *Nutrition and Physical Degeneration*

Know Your Ingredients

Name This Product #26

Corn, whole wheat, sugar, rolled oats, brown sugar, rice, partially hydrogenated sunflower oil, malted barley, salt, corn syrup, whey, malt syrup, honey, artificial flavor, and annatto extract (for color). BHT added to packaging material to preserve freshness.

See Appendix B for Answer

An example of this product differentiation and cost cutting in action is the process used for making cereals which are shaped like little O's, crowns, moons and the like. The machine used for making shaped cereals, called an extruder, is a huge pump with a die at one end. . . The slurry goes into the extruder, is heated to a very high temperature and pushed through the die at high pressure. A spinning blade slices off each little crown or elephant, which is carried on a stream of hot air past nozzles which spray a coating of oil and sugar on each piece, to seal off the cereal from the ravages of milk and give it crunch. This extrusion process. . . destroys much of the nutrient content of the ingredients, even the chemical vitamins. . . The amino acid lysine, a crucial nutrient, is especially ravaged by extrusion. Yet the only changes made in the dozens of variables in the extrusion process are those which will cut costs. . . regardless of how these changes will alter the nutritive value of the product. Paul Stitt *Fighting the Food Giants.*

BULGUR

Makes 4 cups

3 cups wheat berries

Bulgur or cracked wheat is a staple of Middle Eastern cuisine, used in tabouli, kibbeh, soups and casseroles. It is traditionally made from sprouted grain for a product infinitely more delicious and digestible than today's store-bought cracked wheat.

Sprout the berries in 2 jars according to instructions (page 105). Drain well, spread on a cookie sheet and set in a warm oven, no more than 150 degrees, overnight or until the berries are well dried. Grind coarsely in your grinder. Sift to separate flour from the cracked particles. (Use the flour for baking.) Store the bulgur in an air tight container in your refrigerator. As the bulgur has been sprouted, it does not require a long soaking before cooking.

KISHK

Makes 1 quart

4 cups cracked wheat or bulgur
4 cups yoghurt or 3 cups piima milk

This fermented dish comes from the Middle East. It is traditionally added to soups but can also be eaten with milk or dilute cream as a cold breakfast cereal. In fact, it is the only cold breakfast cereal that we can recommend.

Mix ingredients together in a bowl. Cover and let ferment 24 hours in a dark place. Spread as thinly as possible on oiled cookie sheets and bake overnight in a 150 degree oven or until kishk has dried. Place in batches in food processor and pulse until coarsely crumbled. Do not overprocess. Store in airtight containers in the refrigerator.

KISHK GRANOLA

Makes 6 cups

4 cups kishk
1 cup crispy pecans, almonds or cashews (pages 485 and 487), chopped
1 cup dried sweetened coconut (page 144)
1 cup dried fruit such as raisins or unsulphured apricots, cut into small pieces
1/2 cup sucanat

Mix all ingredients together. Store in zip lock bags or air tight containers in refrigerator. Eat like granola with milk or cream.

This cereal will actually keep well at room temperature and is a good provision to take when one is traveling and wants to avoid hotel breakfasts.

BULGUR CASSEROLE

(Fraykee)
Serves 4

1 cup bulgur (page 436)
2 cups cold water
pinch cinnamon
1/2 teaspoon sea salt
1/2 stick butter, softened
1/4 cup toasted pine nuts

This delicious grain preparation comes from Arabia. Heat a heavy cast iron skillet, add the bulgur and stir around a few minutes until it is toasted. Place toasted bulgur, water, cinnamon and salt in a pot, bring to a boil, reduce heat, cover and cook for 30 minutes. Turn off heat and allow to sit 5 minutes before removing lid. Turn into a casserole, toss with butter and top with toasted pine nuts.

Four sets of rats were given special diets. One group received plain whole wheat, water, vitamins and minerals. Another group received Puffed Wheat, water and the same nutrient solution. A third set was given water and white sugar, and a fourth given nothing but water and the chemical nutrients. The rats which received the whole wheat lived over a year on the diet. The rats who got nothing but water and vitamins lived for about eight weeks, and the animals on a white sugar and water diet lived for a month. But [the company's] own laboratory study showed that rats given vitamins, water and all the Puffed Wheat they wanted died in two weeks. It wasn't a matter of the rats dying of malnutrition; results like these suggested that there was something actually toxic about the Puffed Wheat itself. Proteins are very similar to certain toxins in molecular structure, and the puffing process of putting the grain under 1500 pounds per square inch of pressure and then releasing it may produce chemical changes which turn a nutritious grain into a poisonous substance. . . I was shocked, so I showed the report to Dr. Clark, who shared my concern. His predecessor, Dr. Graham, had published the report, and begged the company not to continue producing Puffed Wheat because of its poisonous effect on animals. Dr. Clark . . . went right to the president. . ." I know people should throw it on brides and grooms at weddings," [the president] cracked, "but if they insist on sticking it in their mouths, can I help it? Besides, we made $9 million on the stuff last year." Paul Stitt *Fighting the Food Giants*

CRACKED WHEAT SALAD

Serves 6

3 cups bulgur (page 436)
1 cup fresh lemon juice
2 cups water
1 green pepper, minced
1 red pepper, minced
2 bunches green onions, chopped
3/4 cup extra virgin olive oil
sea salt and freshly ground pepper
fresh pineapple rings, for garnish
orange slices, for garnish
1/2 cup crispy peanuts (page 486), chopped

Soak bulgur in lemon juice and water for 1/2 hour. Squeeze dry with hands and transfer to a bowl. Combine with peppers, onions, olive oil and salt and pepper. Garnish with pineapple rings, orange slices and sprinkle with peanuts.

In 1956, over 300 middle aged Englishmen, free of heart disease, were asked what they ate. The men were then studied for ten years. The researchers were astonished by what they found.

Men who consumed the most calories were found to have the least heart disease.

In addition, it was found that those men not prone to heart disease ate significantly more cereal fiber. However, it was found that fiber from other sources did not protect against heart disease. The author stated, "The composition of the diet (of the men on the high fiber cereal) does not impress (one) as being particularly 'health conscious'." Chris Mudd *Cholesterol and Your Health*

KASHA

Makes 4 cups

3 cups buckwheat groats

Kasha, or cracked buckwheat, is to Russia as bulgur is to the Middle East—the staple carbohydrate food used in numerous dishes, but chiefly as a simple casserole.

Sprout the groats in 2 jars according to instructions (page 105). Drain well, spread on a cookie sheet and set in a warm oven, no more than 150 degrees, overnight or until the berries are well dried. Store the kasha in an air tight container in your refrigerator. As the kasha has been sprouted, it does not require a long soaking before cooking.

Since World War II, the food industry in the US has gone a long way toward ensuring that their customers (just about all of America's children, as well as a good proportion of the adults) do not have to chew breakfast. The bleached, gassed, and colored remnants of the life-giving grains are roasted, toasted, frosted with sugar, embalmed with chemical preservatives, and stuffed into a box much larger than its contents. Fantastic amounts of energy are wasted by sales and advertising departments to sell these half-empty boxes of dead food—money back coupons, whistles and toy guns are needed to induce refined women to lift these half-empty boxes off supermarket shelves. William Dufty *Sugar Blues*

RUSSIAN KASHA

Makes 3 cups

1 cup kasha prepared according to preceding recipe
1 egg, beaten
2 cups homemade chicken stock
2 tablespoons butter
1 teaspoon salt
1/2 teaspoon freshly ground pepper
1/4 stick butter (optional)

The Russian method of preparing kasha, with egg, homemade chicken stock and butter, makes this casserole truly a meal in itself, nourishing fare for hardy peasants and modern sophisticates. Heat a heavy cast iron skillet, add kasha and cook, stirring, for about 5 minutes until kasha is toasted. Let cool. Mix toasted kasha with egg. Reheat the pan, pour in the kasha-egg mixture. Over medium high heat, flatten, stir and chop the kasha with wooden fork until the egg has cooked and the kernels are hot and mostly separated, about 2 to 4 minutes. Meanwhile bring chicken stock to a boil with butter and seasonings. Add kasha-egg mixture, bring to a boil, cover and turn heat to low. Cook about 30 minutes. Remove cover and fluff up with butter if desired.

Know Your Ingredients

Name This Product #27

Whole wheat, sugar, tricalcium and dicalcium (provides calcium), salt, malt extract, corn syrup, vitamin C (sodium ascorbate), zinc and iron (mineral nutrients), vitamin E (tocopherol acetate), trisodium phosphate, a B vitamin (niacinamide), a B vitamin (calcium pantothenate), annatto extract color, vitamin A (palmitate), vitamin B6 (pyridoxine hydrochloride), vitamin B2 (riboflavin), vitamin B1 (thiamin mononitrate), a B vitamin (folic acid), vitamin B12, and vitamin D. Freshness preserved with BHT.

See Appendix B for Answer

Buckwheat is not technically a grain, but the seeds of an herb, relative of rhubarb. The seeds, or groats, form a dietary staple in northern climates, especially in Siberian Russia, and in Brittany. Buckwheat is an important component of Jewish cuisine. It is high in lysine and calcium as well as vitamin E and the entire gamut of B complex. It is especially noted for its high nitriloside or B-17 content, a vitamin that plays an important role in the body's defense against cancer. SWF

KASHA NUT LOAF

Serves 8

3 cups cooked kasha (see preceding recipe)
butter and extra virgin olive oil
2 medium onions, finely chopped
1 cup celery, finely chopped
2 carrots, grated
2 cloves garlic, peeled and mashed
1 teaspoon dried thyme
1 teaspoon dried sage
1 teaspoon dried rosemary
6 eggs, beaten
3 cups crispy cashews (page 487), processed in food processor to a coarse meal
1 teaspoon cracked pepper
1 teaspoon sea salt
2-3 cups yoghurt sauce for garnish (page 131)

Saute onions, celery and carrots in butter and olive oil until soft. Stir in garlic and herbs and let cook another minute. Allow to cool slightly. In a large bowl mix kasha, eggs, cooked vegetables, salt and pepper and cashews. Press into a well buttered loaf pan. Cover and set in a pan of hot water. Bake at 350 for 1 hour. Cool and invert onto a serving dish, blotting up any liquid with a paper towel. To serve, slice and garnish with yoghurt sauce.

Variation: Sauteed Kasha Loaf Platter

Cut loaf into slices and saute in mixture of butter and olive oil. Arrange on a platter and keep warm in oven until ready to serve. Serve with side dishes of yoghurt sauce (page 131) and ginger carrots (page 87).

It's crystal clear that Americans. . . are paying for junk food addiction with their lives. The ones most devastated by the growth of the processed food industry are the populations of the underdeveloped nations. In their insatiable lust for sales, the food monsters are competing for overseas markets. They are pouring millions into Third World advertising campaigns, trying to convince the poor Brazilian farmer that "He Deserves a Break Today", and the starving child of Ghana that "Things Go Better with Coke" . . .The food giants are certainly racking up a lot of victories in the Third World. Two noted food researchers, Frances Moore Lappe and Joseph Collins, have visited the tiny, rotting stores in the rural areas of poor countries and have found chewing gum sold by the stick, Ritz crackers sold one-by-one, and two-packs of Twinkies split up so the awful things can be sold separately. This demand for this poison has been generated by food conglomerate advertising which is doing a great job of teaching people in poor lands "that their traditional diets of beans, corn, millet and rice are worthless as compared to what Americans eat." To the food conglomerates, poor people turning from native, whole foods to processed junk means profit; to the people themselves it means death. Paul Stitt *Fighting the Food Giants*

BASIC BROWN RICE

Serves 6-8

2 cups brown rice
butter and extra virgin olive oil
3 cardamom pods
4 cups chicken stock or combination of water and chicken stock
1 tablespoon gelatin (optional), see Sources
1/2 teaspoon sea salt

Many people are reluctant to switch from white to brown rice because they think that whole grain rice always cooks into a sticky mass. Not so! This method, used in India, followed to the letter will result in fluffy rice, every grain separate, every time.

In a heavy, flame proof casserole, melt butter and oil. Open cardamom pods and add seeds to the casserole. Stir rice into the butter and oil and saute about 5 minutes, stirring constantly, until rice begins to turn milky. Pour in liquid, add salt and optional gelatin and bring to a rolling boil. Boil, uncovered, for about 10 minutes, until water has reduced to the level of the rice. Reduce flame to lowest heat, cover tightly and cook for at least 1 hour, and as long as 3 hours. Do not remove lid during cooking.

Variation: Brown Rice and Bulgur

Use *1 cup brown rice* and *1 cup bulgur* (page 436).

Variation: Spelt Rice

Use *2 cups spelt* instead of rice.

Variation: Coconut Rice

Use *1-2 cups coconut milk and cream* (page 144), or *7-8 ounces creamed coconut* (see Sources), melted, as part of the 4 cups liquid.

Variation: Liver

Add *2-3 ounces liver, grated or finely chopped*, to rice as it cooks.

Rice is the staple food for peoples of the Orient. The Japanese and Chinese consume over 100 pounds of rice per person per year, while Americans eat less than 10 pounds of rice per year. Macrobiotic enthusiasts consider rice the most perfect grain, in which the yin and yang energies are in equilibrium. As rice contains no gluten, a difficult-to-digest protein found in wheat, oats, rye and barley, it is often well tolerated by those with grain allergies.

But the Westerner should not necessarily adapt Oriental rice-eating habits. The Oriental has a larger pancreas, larger saliva gland and longer intestine in proportion to body weight, than the Westerner, and these traits make him ideally suited to a grain-based diet. The Westerner who adopts the strict macrobiotic or Oriental diet, with rice at every meal, may develop serious health problems. Nevertheless, in moderation whole rice has a place in most diets, especially if it is prepared with a long steaming in mineral-rich broth.

Brown rice is highest of all grains in B vitamins, and also contains iron, vitamin E and some protein. These nutrients are almost completely missing in white rice.

Short grain rice is starchier and stickier than long grain rice. Basmati rice, grown in the Himalayas, wehini rice grown in California and texmati rice, grown in Texas, are noted for their rich flavor and aroma. SWF

SPICY RICE PEANUT LOAF

Serves 8

3 cups basic brown rice (page 441)
butter and extra virgin olive oil
1 bunch green onions, chopped
2 carrots, grated
2 cloves garlic, peeled and mashed
1/2 teaspoon turmeric
1/2 teaspoon ground cloves
1/2 teaspoon grated ginger
1/4 teaspoon red pepper flakes
2 tablespoons soy sauce
6 eggs beaten
3 cups crispy peanuts (page 486), processed to a fine meal

Saute onions, celery and carrots in butter and olive oil until soft. Stir in garlic and spices and let cook another minute. Allow to cool slightly. In a large bowl mix rice, eggs, soy sauce, peanuts and cooked vegetables. Press into a well buttered loaf pan. Cover and set in a pan of hot water. Bake at 350 degrees for 1 hour. Cool and invert onto a serving dish, blotting up any liquid with a paper towel.

Variation: Sauteed Rice Loaf Platter

Cut loaf into slices and saute in mixture of butter and olive oil. Arrange on a platter and keep warm in oven until ready to serve. Serve with side dishes of ginger carrots (page 87) and tsukemono (page 86).

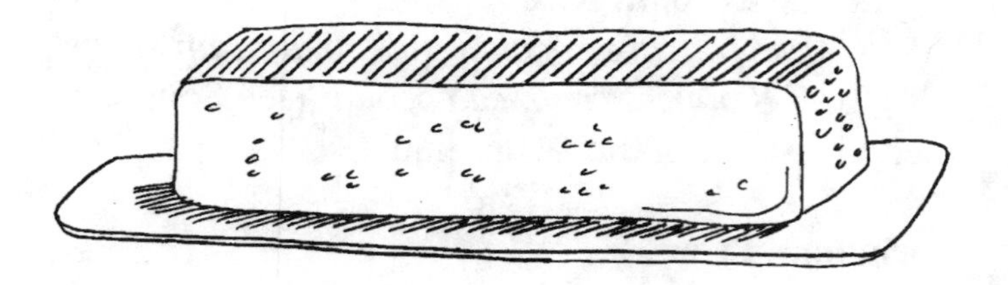

During the building of the great wall of China, coolies were fed salted [fermented] cabbage with their rice to keep them strong and healthy. Salting [fermenting] preserved the cabbage in season and out, and it was the only vegetable they had to supplement their complete, unrefined rice. When the Mongols overran China, knowing a good thing when they tried it, they adopted salted [fermented] cabbage as a very practical traveling rations. The Mongol armies got as far as Hungary in the thirteenth century, where they introduced salted cabbage to Europe. As sauerkraut, it became one of the principal foods of Germany and Eastern Europe.

Julius Caesar's legions, the most efficient fighting machine the world had ever known, ranged far from Rome. The sole provisions were sacks of grain—one for each man. Like the Viet Cong, Caesar's men did not have sugar or kitchens, nor did they have a medical corps, only surgeons for repairing wounds. They ate whole grains plain, on the march, or ground into Roman meal and supplemented with cabbage and any other vegetables they could scrounge. Pliny has said that cabbage kept Rome out of the hands of physicians for many centuries. It was the European armies traveling in the other direction that ran into trouble. In his history of the invasion of sugar-rich Egypt by the Crusaders of St. Louis in 1260, Sire Jean de Joinville described the funguous putrid bleeding gums, the hemorrhaging skin spots, and the swollen legs that plagued Christian armies and led to the ultimate defeat and capture of the holy knights and their commander. William Dufty *Sugar Blues*

BROWN RICE PILAF

Serves 6-8

1 1/2 cups brown rice
1 cup buckwheat or brown rice noodles, broken into 1-inch bits
1 medium onion, finely chopped
2 cardamom pods
1 teaspoon dried thyme or dill
grated zest of 1 lemon (optional)
butter and extra virgin olive oil
4 cups chicken stock or combination of chicken stock and water
1 tablespoon gelatin (optional), see Sources
1/2 teaspoon sea salt

In a heavy, flame-proof casserole, melt butter and oil. Open cardamom pods and add seeds to casserole. Add onion and thyme or dill and saute until onion is soft. Add noodles and saute, stirring, until they turn brown. Add rice and saute, stirring, until rice turns milky. Pour in liquid, add salt and optional gelatin and zest and bring to a rolling boil. Boil, uncovered, for about 10 to 15 minutes, until the water has reduced to the level of the rice. Reduce flame to lowest heat, cover tightly and cook for at least 1 hour and up to 3 hours. Do not remove lid during cooking.

At the beginning of World War II, the British crown colony of Singapore was threatened with a food crisis—the kind that faces many lands today. Malay and Singapore did not grow all the rice they needed; imports were about to be sharply reduced. The British medical officer of Singapore, Dr. Scharff, made the same kind of hard decision that had saved Denmark in World War I during the German blockade. Polished white rice was forbidden by military decree. Only unpolished brown rice could be sold. British military authorities were influenced by one factor only: Inadequate supplies. They were worried about quantity; quality was of no concern. They simply didn't want any food riots on their hands. . . the aftermath was startling, incredible. Dr. Scharff had originally gone to Singapore with the mission of reducing infant mortality from malaria. When he arrived, the mortality rate was 420 per 1,000 births. He used herculean but orthodox medical methods. In less than a decade, the program had reduced the death rate of infants to 160 per 1,000, almost on a par with the existing rate in Britain. However, after a year on the brown rice diet enforced by military decree, there was a dramatic shift in vital statistics. Instead of 160 infants dying in their first year of life, only 80 died. The figure was cut in half without medical efforts. William Dufty *Sugar Blues*

The US adventure in Viet Nam was, by world consensus, a folly on many levels. Perhaps, on the basic level of human nutrition, it was one of the sorriest stories of all. Viet Nam was one of the world's biggest rice bowls. For decades, Viet Nam exported rice to many parts of the world. Whole rice was the principal food of the Vietnamese. For years, the guerilla bands of the Viet Minh and Viet Cong sustained themselves with a food supply system as simple and primitive as that of the Roman legions of Julius Caesar. Each man carried a little sack of whole rice and some salt. They added manioc leaves, from the jungle, and fish when possible. For years they stymied the elaborately equipped and lavishly rationed armies of the West . . . When the victorious Viet Cong armies overran Saigon, they were exposed for the first time—like the Crusader arriving in the Holy Land centuries before—to the pause that refreshes, the Coke machine, the candy counter. It is their turn to accustom themselves to gluttony, and La Dolce Vita and to eat and drink sugar openly in the street without shame. William Dufty *Sugar Blues*

RICE AND CARROT CASSEROLE

Serves 6-8

2 cups brown rice
butter and extra virgin olive oil
1 medium onion, finely chopped
1 teaspoon thyme
4 whole cloves
3 cardamom pods
grated zest of 1 lemon (optional)
4 cups chicken stock or combination of chicken stock and water
1 tablespoon gelatin (optional) , see Sources
1/2 teaspoon sea salt
1 cup grated carrots
1/2 cup raisins

In a heavy, flame-proof casserole, melt butter and oil. Open cardamom pods and add seeds to casserole along with thyme, cloves and onion. Saute until onion is soft. Add rice and saute until milky. Pour in liquid, add salt and optional gelatin and bring to a rolling boil. Stir in carrots, raisins and optional lemon zest. Boil, uncovered, for about 10 to 15 minutes, until the water has reduced to the level of the rice. Reduce flame to lowest heat, cover tightly and cook for at least 1 hour and up to 3 hours.

PULAU RICE

Serves 6-8

2 cups brown basmati rice
1 medium onion, finely chopped
butter and extra virgin olive oil
1 teaspoon cumin seeds
1 teaspoon fenugreek seeds
2 teaspoons turmeric powder
4 cardamom pods
2 bay leaves
1 teaspoon salt
1 tablespoon gelatin (optional), see Sources
4 cups chicken stock or combination stock and water

In a heavy, flame-proof casserole, melt butter and oil. Open cardamom pods and add seeds to casserole along with onion, cumin and turmeric. Saute until onion is soft. Add rice and saute, stirring, until milky. Pour in liquid, add salt, optional gelatin and bay leaf and bring to a rolling boil. Boil, uncovered, for about 10 to 15 minutes, until the water has reduced to the level of the rice. Reduce flame to lowest heat, cover tightly and cook for at least 1 hour or for as long as 3 hours. Do not remove lid during cooking.

In *The Saccharine Disease (1975),* Cleave lays the blame for prevalence of diabetes on the doorstep of refined carbohydrates. He acknowledges the genetic basis of the disorder but "rejects unequivocally" the assumption that this is a "defect". "The hereditary features of the disease. . . do no more than reflect the inheritance of personal build, including that of the pancreas itself, rendering the persons concerned more vulnerable to the new environmental factor. . . These features in no sense indicate hereditary defect. . . the body is not built wrongly, but is being used wrongly." The more pronounced the genetic predisposition, according to Cleave, the earlier the onset of the disease, provided the triggering event occurs. In industrialized society, the triggering event appears to be the overload of sugar, white flour products, white rice and processed fruits and vegetables. "The consumption of refined carbohydrates. . . imposes unnatural strains upon the pancreas, either through overconsumption, or. . . rapidity of consumption and absorption, or. . . both." Joseph D. Beasley MD and Jerry J. Swift MA *The Kellogg Report*

MEXICAN RICE

Serves 6-8

2 cups brown rice
1 medium onion, finely chopped
butter and extra virgin olive oil
1 teaspoon achiote seeds (available in Latin American markets)
1 teaspoon cumin seeds
1/4 teaspoon red chile flakes
1 teaspoon dried oregano
1 teaspoon salt
4 cups chicken stock or combination stock and water
1 tablespoon gelatin (optional)
1 clove garlic, peeled and mashed
2 tablespoons green olives, chopped (optional)

In a heavy, flame-proof casserole, melt butter and oil. Saute achiote seeds in oil for about 5 minutes and remove. In the same oil, saute onion with red chile flakes and cumin seeds until onion is soft. Add rice and saute until milky. Pour in liquid, add salt, optional gelatin, oregano and garlic and bring to a rolling boil. Boil, uncovered, for about 10 to 15 minutes, until the water has reduced to the level of the rice. Reduce flame to lowest heat, cover tightly and cook for at least 1 hour and up to 3 hours. Do not remove lid during cooking. Off heat, remove lid and stir in optional olives.

MEXICAN RICE CASSEROLE

Serves 8

4 cups basic brown rice (page 441)
1 cup grated Monterey jack or cheddar cheese
2 bunches green onions, chopped
1/2 cup pitted black olives, chopped
1 cup pickled red peppers (page 93), chopped or 2 small cans green chile peppers, chopped
1 cup piima cream or creme fraiche
1/2 cup grated jack or cheddar cheese

This delicious dish is only for those with a high tolerance to milk products. Combine all ingredients except 1/2 cup grated cheese and pour into a buttered casserole. Top with cheese and bake at 350 for about 30 minutes.

GREEK RICE

Serves 6-8

2 cups basic brown rice (page 441)
2 onions, finely chopped
2 sticks celery, finely chopped
extra virgin olive oil
2 cloves garlic, peeled and mashed
2 tablespoons sesame seeds
2 tablespoons pepitas (page 485)
2 tablespoons pine nuts
1/4 cup freshly chopped mint
grated rind and juice of 1 lemon
1/2 teaspoon oregano
sea salt and freshly ground pepper

Saute onions, celery and garlic very gently in olive oil until soft. Meanwhile, spread seeds and pine nuts on a cookie sheet and toast in oven. Mix together all ingredients. Season to taste. Greek rice may be used as a stuffing in grape leaves, tomatoes, or eggplant, or served on its own.

Despite the efforts of ACT [Action for Children's Television], 600 million dollars is now spent yearly on children's advertising, 30 million of it by the cereal industry. This advertising, which necessarily glosses over such drawbacks as tooth decay in peddling candy to children, is adroit at deception. In 1982 "Sugar Smacks" was rechristened "Honey Smacks", presumably because honey is healthier. Of course, both versions of the cereal contain 57% refined sugars.

Although the motto of the market place, supposedly, is to "give the people what they want," the reality is more a matter of giving the people whatever increases one's market share. Most parents are trying to wean their children from excessive sweets, yet supermarkets and drug stores across the country always have candy prominently displayed at checkout counters—where parents are stuck on line with restless, candy-craving children. Kroger's, a Cincinnati grocery chain that conscientiously established a no-candy lane, prompted a representative of the national Candy Wholesalers Association to object: "Discipline begins with the parent, and our attitude is the product should be available." So much for giving the people what they want. Joseph D. Beasley MD and Jerry J. Swift MA *The Kellogg Report*

ALGERIAN WEDDING RICE

Serves 6-8

2 cups basic brown rice (page 441)
1 cup dried apricots, cut into bits, soaked in water about 1 hour and drained
1/2 cup crispy almonds (page 487), slivered and toasted
1/2 cup toasted pine nuts
2 bunches green onions, chopped
1/2 stick butter, softened
sea salt and freshly ground pepper

Toss the cooked rice with remaining ingredients. Season to taste. Place in a buttered casserole and bake at 250 for about 30 minutes.

RAINBOW RICE SALAD

Serves 8

4 cups basic brown rice (page 441)
1 red pepper, seeded and diced
1 green pepper, seeded and diced
1 bunch green onions, chopped
1 cup fresh pineapple, cut into small pieces
1/2 cup raisins
1 cup basic dressing (page 118)

Mix all ingredients together. May be pressed into a mold and inverted for serving.

ORIENTAL RICE SALAD

Serves 8

4 cups basic brown rice (page 441)
1 bunch green onions, chopped
1/2 cup crispy cashews (page 487), chopped
1 small can water chestnuts, drained and sliced
1 cup Oriental dressing (page 124)

Mix all ingredients together and let stand an hour or so before serving.

Wholesome foods are good for you, right? This is true as long as you are not allergic to them. In addition to the harmful foods. . . even some naturally good foods could be bad for you. . .you have been told that you couldn't go wrong with natural, unprocessed foods. However, this does not take into account the fact that you are probably allergic to several perfectly wholesome foods, which otherwise should be a part of your diet. . . In fact, the right diet cannot be designed for you without knowing just what your food allergies are, since each person's set of allergies are unique.

No one knows exactly why each individual has his own distinct set of allergies. Sometimes the reasons can be determined. A common cause is food cravings which lead to the overeating of a certain food for a prolonged period of time. Eventually, an allergy to the food develops. Other allergies may develop early in life and can persist to a degree into adulthood. Some food allergies can even be inherited. However, no one knows for sure why one person is allergic, say to wheat, while another is allergic to oats or rye. Regardless of the cause, many of the symptoms you may have are likely due to food allergies. Even if you do not have noticeable symptoms, it is likely that you are allergic to several foods. In addition, many diseases can be aggravated by continual exposure to allergic foods. Cass Igram MD *Eat Right to Live Longer*

WILD RICE

Serves 6-8

Not technically a cereal grain, but the seed of a marsh growing plant native to North America, wild rice is one of the few foods that comes to the consumer after it has been fermented. Wild rice is fermented for a week or two after harvesting to develop its flavor and to make hulling easier.

Wild rice is rich in protein, containing more lysine and methionine that most other cereals. It is high in B-complex vitamins and rich in minerals including magnesium, potassium, phosphorus and zinc. Wild rice in relatively low in fat—so eat it with plenty of butter! SWF

2 cups wild rice
butter and extra virgin olive oil
4 cups chicken stock or combination of chicken stock and water
1 tablespoon gelatin (optional)
1 teaspoon salt

In a heavy, flame proof casserole, melt butter and oil. Stir wild rice into the butter and oil and saute about 5 minutes, stirring constantly. Pour in liquid, add salt and optional gelatin and bring to a rolling boil. Boil, uncovered, for about 10 to 15 minutes, until the water has reduced to the level of the rice. Reduce flame to lowest heat, cover tightly and cook for at least 1 hour, and as long as 3 hours. Do not remove lid during cooking.

Know Your Ingredients
Name This Product #28

Enriched parboiled long grain rice (preserved with BHT), wild rice, hydrolyzed vegetable protein, monosodium glutamate, dried onion, salt, dextrose, beef extract, dried torula yeast, dried parsley, dried celery, dried garlic, partially hydrogenated vegetable oil, natural flavors, artificial flavor.

See Appendix B for Answer

WILD RICE CASSEROLE

Serves 6-8

2 cups wild rice, prepared according to preceding recipe
1/2 cup melted butter
1 bunch green onions, chopped
grated rind of 2 oranges
1/2 cup slivered crispy almonds (page 487) or pine nuts, toasted
1/4 cup finely chopped parsley or 1/2 cup coarsely chopped cilantro

Mix cooked rice with remaining ingredients. Place in a buttered casserole and bake at 250 for about 30 minutes.

Variation: Wahini Casserole

Use *wahini rice* instead of wild rice.

ECUADORIAN QUINOA CASSEROLE

Serves 6-8

2 cups quinoa
1 bunch green onions, chopped
2 tablespoons extra virgin olive oil
1 teaspoon achiote seeds
(available in Latin American markets)
4 cups homemade beef or chicken stock
1/2 teaspoon sea salt
3 cloves garlic, mashed
2 medium potatoes, washed and sliced
1 bunch cilantro, tied together
1/2 cup piima cream or creme fraiche
5 tablespoons homemade cream cheese

This authentic recipe from a chipper centenarian living in Equador, incorporates all the basic principles for easy digestion and thorough assimilation—use of rich stock made by boiling bones for a long time, pre-soaking of grain, and the addition of cultured cream and homemade cheese, rich in fat-soluble vitamins.

Soak quinoa overnight in a large amount of water. rinse and drain well. Saute achiote in oil for several minutes. Remove. Saute onions in the same oil, adding garlic at the last minute. Add quinoa and stock and bring to a boil. Skim, reduce heat, cover and simmer for 1 hour or more on very low heat. About 1/2 hour before serving, stir in the potatoes and salt. About 10 minutes before serving, add cilantro. To serve, remove cilantro and stir in cream and cheese.

Extensive laboratory determinations have shown that most people cannot absorb more than half of the calcium and phosphorus from the foods eaten. The amounts utilized depend directly on the presence of other substances, particularly fat-soluble vitamins. It is at this point probably that the greatest breakdown in our modern diet takes place, namely, in the ingestion and utilization of adequate amounts of the special activating substances, including the vitamins needed for rendering the minerals in the food available to the human system. Weston Price DDS *Nutrition and Physical Degeneration*

Quinoa is a staple food of the Incas and the Indians in Peru, Ecuador and Bolivia. During his pioneering investigations in the 1930's, Weston Price noted that the Indians of the Andes mountains valued gruel made of quinoa for nursing mothers. Quinoa contains 16 to 20 percent protein and is high in cystine, lysine and methionine—amino acids which tend to be low in other grains. It contains iron, calcium and phosphorus, B vitamins and vitamin E, and is relatively high in fat. Like all grains, quinoa contains anti-nutrients and therefore requires a long soaking as part of the preparation process. SWF

BREADS & FLOUR PRODUCTS

Most of our recipes for flour products, like those for whole and cracked grains, call for overnight soaking. Housewives of old knew that the most delicious pancakes, muffins and cakes could be made by soaking grains in buttermilk. Piima milk, or water plus the addition of whey or yoghurt, work less well for soaking purposes but the results are still satisfactory. Buttermilk, cultured milk, yoghurt and whey all provide both lactic acid and lactobacilli that begin the process of breaking down the phytates in bran, the proteins, especially gluten, as well as many other substances found in grain. All nutrients are more available in flour products that have been soaked or lacto-fermented. This method has the further advantage of so softening whole meal flour that the final product is often indistinguishable from one made with white flour. Breads, muffins and pancakes that have been made with soaked whole wheat or spelt flour need no baking powder to make them rise; and they are not characterized by that heaviness that can make whole grain products unpalatable.

If you do a lot of baking, a home grain grinder is a must. Grains quickly go rancid after grinding, and optimum health benefits are obtained from freshly ground grain. You may wish to keep unbleached white flour on hand for dusting pans, for browning and for use in rolling out doughs and kneading. We also allow unbleached flour for pie crust.

Pancakes, muffins and soda breads are easy to prepare. Please note that these soaked whole grain flour preparations take a bit longer to cook than those made with white flour. Sourdough breads take more dedication and time. They must be made with high-gluten flours, such as winter wheat or rye. While they have a delicious flavor, these breads may seem heavy to modern tastes. (For those who have neither the time nor the inclination for breadmaking, properly made sour dough breads are now commercially available. See Sources.)

Our readers will note that we avoid two stand-bys often associated with health foods—bran and wheat germ. Bran is high in phytates and should be consumed along with all the other portions of the whole grain, only after a long soaking. The danger of wheat germ is its extreme susceptibility to rancidity. Eating the bran and the germ separate from the starchy portion of grain presents as many problems as eating the starchy portion of grain separated from the germ and the bran. Traditional populations eat all parts of the grain together, freshly ground or milled, usually after a period of soaking or fermentation.

BAKING WITH ALTERNATE GRAINS

Allergies to grains are common, especially allergies to wheat. Individuals with grain allergies often tolerate wheat products that have first been soaked, sprouted or fermented; but many must avoid wheat altogether, even when it has been properly prepared. Spelt and kamut are the first choice for substitutes because they mimic the properties of modern hybrid wheat, and no special adjustments need be made when substituting them for wheat in most recipes.

Many alternate flours are also available—not only those that contain gluten such as corn, rye, barley or oat, but also non-gluten flours like rice, millet, buckwheat, amaranth, quinoa, potato, tapioca, bean and tuber flours. All of these may be used for baked goods such as muffins, pancakes, waffles and soda breads, but certain adjustments must be made to the recipes because these flours are heavier than wheat flour, and do not rise as well. Specific recipes for alternate flours are beyond the scope of this book. However, the following guidelines should suffice.

In addition to baking soda, homemade baking powder should be added to alternative grain recipes in the proportion of 2 level teaspoons per cup of flour. Prepare by mixing *1 part potassium bicarbonate* (available from your pharmacist), *2 parts cream of tartar* and *2 parts arrowroot*. Store in an airtight glass jar. In addition, you may wish to add guar gum to your batter if it seems too runny—often the case with alternate flours as they do not absorb water as well as wheat or spelt. Use 1/2 teaspoon per cup of flour.

All flour products should be soaked in an acidic medium such as buttermilk or water with whey or yoghurt added, for at least 7 hours. Baked goods made with alternate flours may take longer to cook that those made with whole wheat or spelt flours.

We must caution you against using soy flours. Soy contains not only a very high phytate content, but also potent enzyme inhibitors that are not inactivated by ordinary methods such as soaking, but only during a long, slow fermentation process that results in traditional fermented soy products such as *natto*, *miso* or *tempeh*. These anti-nutrients can inhibit growth and cause intestinal problems, swelling of the pancreas and even cancer. In addition, soy contains a high omega-3 content that quickly goes rancid when the bean is made into flour. Soy flour has a disagreeable taste that is difficult to mask—nature's way of telling us to avoid it.

PANCAKES

Makes 16-20

2 cups freshly ground spelt or whole wheat flour
2 cups cultured buttermilk, piima milk or
2 cups water mixed with 2 tablespoons whey or yoghurt
2 eggs, lightly beaten
1/2 teaspoon salt
1 teaspoon baking soda
1 tablespoon melted butter

Soak flour in milk or water with whey overnight. Stir in other ingredients and thin to desired consistency with water or more cultured milk. Cook on a hot, oiled griddle or in a cast iron skillet. These pancakes cook more slowly that either unsoaked whole grain flour or white flour pancakes. The texture will be chewy and the taste pleasantly sour. Serve with melted butter and maple syrup, raw honey, berry preserves (page 102) or apricot butter (page 101).

Variation: Corn Cakes

Use *1 cup stone ground corn flour* and *1 teaspoon dolomite* (see Sources) plus *1 cup spelt or wheat flour*.

Variation: Buckwheat Cakes

Use *1 cup buckwheat flour* plus *1 cup spelt or wheat flour*.

Variation: Crispy Pancakes

Let pancakes dry out in a warm oven. These make delicious snacks with raw honey, apple or apricot butter (page 101) or homemade cream cheese (page 80).

On every continent, mankind has fermented grains, pulses, vegetables, milk, meat and fish. Up until the beginning of the 20th century, the French peasant made his bread, his cheese, his sausage, his sauerkraut (in the east), his olives (in the Midi), his vinegar and often his wine, cider or beer. Each time he directed this fermentation process empirically and by himself. Sometimes it was of short duration, as for his bread; sometimes long and complicated, as for wine and aged cheeses. Fermented foods were prepared by each family—in Russia cucumbers, in Poland sour soups, in Japan *miso* and lacto-fermented vegetables, in Indonesia *tempeh*, in Mexico *pozol*, in Equador fermented rice, in West Africa *soumbala*, to give just a few examples. Without realizing it, everyone put millions of microorganisms to work on his behalf.

Almost everywhere in the world people ate fermented foods on a daily basis. They often ate them for breakfast, no doubt because after a night of sleep, the body needs something that is rapidly and easily digested.

The sour taste that characterizes so many fermented foods is found in every culinary tradition. Used in moderation, fermented foods satisfy the palate and fulfill a real physiological need, even if current nutritional practices fail to recognize this.

The practice of domestic fermentation still occurs in the Third World but is largely disappearing in industrialized countries, under the influence of western lifestyles and eating habits. Claude Aubert *Les Aliments Fermentes Traditionnels*

DUTCH BABY PANCAKES

Serves 4-6

1 cup freshly ground whole wheat or spelt flour
1 cup buttermilk or 1 cup water plus
1 tablespoon whey or yoghurt
4 eggs
1 teaspoon vanilla
1/2 teaspoon sea salt
1 cup filtered water
4 tablespoons butter

Soak flour in buttermilk for 7 hours or overnight. Place eggs in food processor and process several minutes. Add flour mixture, vanilla, water and salt and process another minute. Place 2 tablespoons butter in a large skillet and cook in a 400 degree oven until it melts and sizzles. Pour half the batter (about 1 1/2 cups) into pan. Bake at 350 degrees until puffed and browned. Repeat for second pancake. Dust with nutmeg if desired. Serve with butter and honey or maple syrup.

I know too that the body is affected differently by bread according to the manner in which it is prepared. It differs according as it is made from pure flour or meal with bran, whether it is prepared from winnowed or unwinnowed wheat, whether it is mixed with much water or little, whether well mixed or poorly mixed, overbaked or underbaked, and countless other points besides. The same is true of the preparation of barley meal. The influence of each process is considerable and each has a totally different effect from another. How can anyone who has not considered such matters and come to understand them possibly know anything of the diseases that afflict mankind? Each one of the substances of a man's diet acts upon his body and changes it in some way and upon these changes his whole life depends. Hippocrates

Celiac disease stems from grain allergies—or more precisely, allergies to the gluten and alpha gliadin components of grain. Those allergies cause malabsorption, and hence a massive deficiency, of Vitamins B1, B3, B12 and folic acid, and the mineral zinc. A serious deficiency in any one of those, if undiagnosed or untreated, can cause dementia. The allergies also cause malabsorption of essential minerals and trace elements such as calcium, magnesium, iron and manganese. In addition, they allow the absorption of toxic metals such as aluminum and higher than normal concentrations of aluminium in the brain is one of the dementia-causing features of Alzheimer's Disease. *PPNF Journal*

WAFFLES

Serves 6

2 1/2 cups freshly ground spelt or wheat flour
2 cups cultured buttermilk, piima milk or
2 cups water mixed with 2 tablespoons whey or yoghurt
2 egg yolks, lightly beaten
2-4 tablespoons maple syrup
2 tablespoons melted butter
1 teaspoon sea salt
4 egg whites
pinch sea salt

Mix flour with buttermilk or water mixture and let stand overnight. Stir in egg yolks, syrup, melted butter and salt. In a clean bowl, beat egg whites with pinch of salt until stiff. Fold into batter. Cook in a hot, well-oiled waffle iron. Serve with melted butter and maple syrup raw honey, berry preserves (page 102) or apricot butter (page 101).

Note: These waffles are softer that those made with white flour. However, they will become crisp if kept in a warm oven for several hours.

Modern commerce has deliberately robbed some of nature's foods of much of their body-building material while retaining the hunger satisfying energy factors. For example, in the production of refined white flour approximately eighty per cent or four-fifths of the phosphorus and calcium content are usually removed, together with the vitamins and minerals provided in the embryo or germ. The evidence indicates that a very important factor in the lowering of reproductive efficiency of woman hood is directly related to the removal of vitamin E in the processing of wheat. The germ of wheat is our most readily available source of that vitamin. Its role as a nutritive factor for the pituitary gland in the base of the brain, which largely controls growth and organ function, apparently is important in determining the production of mental types. Similarly the removal of vitamin B with the embryo of the wheat, together with its oxidation after processing, results in depletion of body-building activators. Weston Price DDS *Nutrition and Physical Degeneration*

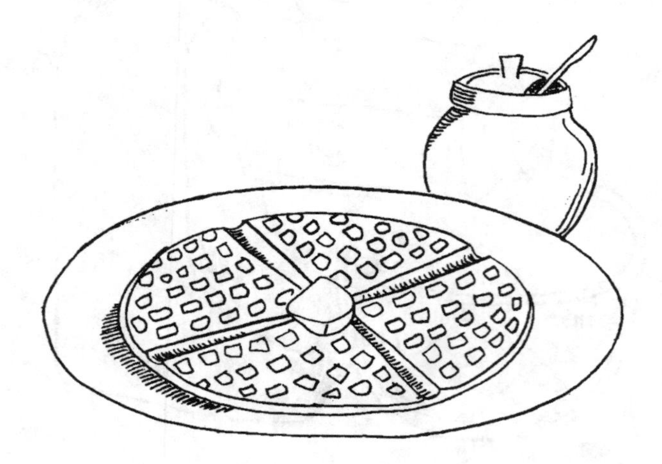

BUCKWHEAT CREPES

Makes about 18

1 cup freshly ground buckwheat
1 cup freshly ground spelt or wheat
2 cups cultured buttermilk, or
water mixed with 2 tablespoons
whey or yoghurt
3 eggs, lightly beaten
1/2 teaspoon salt
1/4 cup melted butter

Crepes make a wonderful snack; a big pile of crepes served with several choices of filling make an excellent luncheon or supper buffet.

Mix flour with buttermilk or water mixture and let sit overnight. Beat in remaining ingredients and thin with enough water to achieve the consistency of cream. Beat several minutes with an electric beater and chill well. Heat a heavy skillet. Brush with melted butter and use a 1/4 cup measure to ladle batter into pan. Tip pan to distribute batter. Turn after two minutes. Keep crepes warm in the oven while making the rest. Brush the pan with butter between each crepe. Fill with raw honey, apricot butter (page 101), grated raw cheese, ratatouille (page363), crab filling (page 232) or chicken supreme (page 266). Crepes may be made ahead of time and reheated.

Variation: Crispy Crepes

Pile crepes on a plate and leave in a 150 degree oven overnight. Crepes will dry out and become crispy. Delicious with raw honey.

Many people, especially women have been taking calcium supplements in their efforts to prevent osteoporosis and other disorders. Calcium is important, but so is magnesium. . . many patients who seek help for insomnia, tension and anxiety are magnesium deficient. . . Magnesium deficiency not only exists but is common. Although it is common, it is often undetected. Chronic deficiency can produce long-term damage and can be fatal. . .The richest sources of magnesium are also the richest sources of essential fatty acids. . . such as seed foods (including whole grains, nuts and beans). Other foods which are relatively rich in magnesium include buckwheat, baking chocolate, cottonseed, tea, whole wheat and leafy green vegetables including collard greens and parsley. The mineral is also plentiful in seafood, meats, nuts and fruit. What's more, you can protect your magnesium stores by avoiding . . soft drinks, especially those containing caffeine. Chronic Fatigue Syndrome patients are nearly always deficient in magnesium. . . they're frequently deficient in zinc and copper too. *PPNF Journal*

BASIC MUFFINS

Makes about 15

3 cups freshly ground spelt or whole wheat flour
2 cups cultured buttermilk, or water mixed with 2 tablespoon whey or yoghurt
2 eggs, lightly beaten
1 teaspoon sea salt
1/4 cup maple syrup
2 teaspoons baking soda
1 teaspoon vanilla
3 tablespoons melted butter

Mix flour with buttermilk or water mixture and let stand overnight. Mix in remaining ingredients. Pour into well buttered muffin pans, filling about three quarters full. Bake at 325 degrees for about 40 minutes or until a toothpick comes out clean. These muffins will puff up and then fall back a bit, to form flat tops. Note: 1 cup buckwheat flour or cornmeal may be used in place of 1 cup spelt or wheat flour.

Variation: Raisin Muffins

Add *1/2 cup raisins and 1/2 teaspoon cinnamon* to batter.

Variation: Blueberry Muffins

Pour batter into muffin tins. Place *5-7 blueberries, fresh or frozen* on each muffin. Berries will fall partway into the muffins. (If they are added to the batter, they sink to the bottom of the muffin.)

Variation: Dried Cherry Muffins

Add *4 ounces dried cherries* (available at health food stores and gourmet markets) and *1/2 cup chopped crispy pecans (page 486)* to batter.

Variation: Fruit Spice Muffins

Add *2 ripe pears or peaches, peeled and cut into small pieces* and *1/2 teaspoon cinnamon, 1/8 teaspoon cloves* and *1/8 teaspoon nutmeg* to batter.

Variation: Lemon Muffins

Add *grated rind of 2 lemons* and *1/2 cup chopped crispy pecans* to batter. Omit vanilla.

Variation: Ginger Muffins

Add *1 tablespoon freshly grated ginger* and *1 teaspoon ground ginger* to batter. Omit vanilla.

As one stands in profound admiration before the stalwart physical development and high moral character of these sturdy Alpine mountaineers, he is impressed by the superior types of manhood, womanhood and childhood that Nature has been able to produce from a suitable diet and a suitable environment. Surely, here is evidence enough to answer the question whether cereals should be avoided because they produce acids in the system. . . when one has contrasted these people with the pinched and sallow, and even deformed faces and distorted bodies that are produced by our modern civilization and its diets; and when one has contrasted the unsurpassed beauty of the faces of these children developed on nature's primitive foods with the varied assortment of modern civilization's children with their defective facial development, he finds himself filled with an earnest desire to see that this betterment is made available for modern civilization. Again and again we had the experience of examining a young man or young woman and finding that at some period of his life tooth decay had been rampant and had suddenly ceased; but, during the stress, some teeth had been lost. When we asked such people whether they had gone out of the mountain and at what age, they generally reported that at eighteen or twenty years of age they had gone to this or that city and had stayed a year or two. They stated that they had never had a decayed tooth before they went or after they returned, but that they had lost some teeth in the short period away from home. Weston Price DDS *Nutrition and Physical Degeneration*

BANANA BREAD

Makes 1 9-by-13 loaf

3 cups freshly ground spelt or wheat flour
2 cups cultured buttermilk, water mixed with
2 tablespoons whey or yoghurt
3 eggs, lightly beaten
1 teaspoon sea salt
1/2 to 1/4 cup maple syrup
2 teaspoons baking soda
1/4 cup melted butter
2 ripe bananas, mashed
1/2 cup chopped crispy pecans (page 485)

Mix flour with buttermilk or water mixture and let stand overnight. Beat in remaining ingredients. Pour into a well buttered and floured loaf pan. Bake at 350 degrees for 1 hour or more until a toothpick comes out clean

Variation: Zucchini Bread

Use *2 zucchinis* instead of 2 bananas and add *1 teaspoon vanilla extract*. Use the food processor to cut zucchinis into a julienne, toss with sea salt and let stand for 1 hour. Rinse and squeeze dry and stir into batter.

Variation: Banana or Zucchini Spice Bread

Add *1/4 teaspoon nutmeg, 1/2 teaspoon all spice, 1/2 teaspoon cinnamon* and *1/4 teaspoon ground ginger* to either of the above recipes.

Variation: Apricot Almond Bread

Omit bananas. Use *1 cup unsulphured dried apricots*, cut into pieces, soaked in warm water for 1 hour and drained, *1 cup chopped crispy almonds (page 487)* and *1 teaspoon vanilla*.

[Egyptian tomb scenes show] the processing of wheat grain into bread. One man we see pounding the grain with pestles in a solid cylindrical mortar. . . A woman passes the coarse flour through a sieve into a tray to remove husks and a companion grinds it still further. . . other scenes show the grinding operation repeated by successive teams until all the grain had attained the desired fineness, through thirteen sieving procedures. . . [but] many other accounts imply that the vast majority of peasants and workers ate a whole grain bread. This means that possibly only the pharaohs and nobles managed enough workers to produce a white flour bread. . . Mummy x-rays [show] curvature of the spine or scoliosis. . . This wife of a pharaoh suffered arthritis of the spine which would have been severely uncomfortable and marked scoliosis which would have made movement difficult and painful. This condition can be produced in rats born in laboratories today. While pregnant, the mother rats were fed a diet low in the trace mineral manganese. What does this have to do with ancient Egypt? When we remove the bran and germ from the whole grain as they were doing and as we do today, manganese diminishes greatly. . . Buck teeth, or malocclusion and impacted wisdom teeth appear. No doubt Dr. Price would spot this as the result of a deterioration of the diet of the parents. Ruth Rosevear *PPNF Journal*

YOGHURT HERB BREAD

Makes 1 9-by-13 loaf

3 cups freshly ground spelt or wheat flour
2 cups plain yoghurt
1/2 cup filtered water
3 large eggs, lightly beaten
1 teaspoon salt
2 teaspoons baking soda
1/4 stick melted butter
1/3 cup maple syrup
1 teaspoon dried dill
1/2 teaspoon oregano
1/2 teaspoon thyme
1/2 teaspoon basil
1/2 teaspoon tarragon

Mix flour with yoghurt and water and let stand overnight. Place flour mixture in food processor and process for several minutes to knead the dough. Add remaining ingredients and process until well blended. Pour into well-buttered loaf pan. Bake at 350 degrees for 50-60 minutes, or until a toothpick comes out clean.

Sir Robert McCarrison, M.D. of England, carried on elaborate experiments at Coonor, India, using over 2,000 clinical animals under controlled conditions.

Selecting out two of his experiments: The rats in one group were fed on the diet of the Hunzas of norther India. The Hunzas are large, strong and healthy, do physical work in their 80's and 90's and many live over 100 years. The diet of the Hunzas consists chiefly of whole grains, raw fruits and vegetables grown on organically fertilized soil, and milk products from goats. The groups of rats fed on the Hunza diet grew large, were healthy, long-lived, docile and affectionate.

The rats of the second group were fed on the diet of the Madrasi of southern India. The Madrasi are small, puny ailing people with a lifespan of less than 20 years.

The Madrasi live on such foods as polished rice, tapioca, pulses, condiments, very little milk and few vegetables (mostly refined foods). The rats fed on this Madrasi diet were sickly, nervous, vicious and short-lived and had the diseases common to the Madrasi. R. Dean Conrad *The Great American Tragedy*

BUTTERMILK BISCUITS

Makes about 12

3 cups freshly ground whole wheat flour
or mixture of whole wheat and spelt
2 cups buttermilk
4 tablespoons melted butter
1 1/2 teaspoons sea salt
1 tablespoon baking powder

Soak flour in buttermilk for 7 hours or overnight. Place in food processor and process several minutes to knead. Blend in remaining ingredients.

Cover hands in unbleached white flour to remove dough (which will be very sticky) from food processor and place on a well floured pastry cloth or board. Pat down with hands to about 3/4 inch thickness. Cut biscuits with a glass and place on a buttered baking sheet, reforming dough with hands as needed. Bake about 30 minutes at 350 degrees. Serve with butter and honey or mustard and cold meats.

Variation: Cheaters Biscuits

Use *1 cup unbleached white flour* and *2 cups whole wheat or spelt flour*. This makes a lighter biscuit.

YOGHURT DOUGH

1 cup plain yoghurt
2 sticks butter, softened
3 1/2 cups freshly ground spelt or wheat flour
2 teaspoons sea salt

This excellent all-purpose dough recipe makes enough for two 10-inch French style tart shells. This dough cooks rather slowly. For a pre-baked tart shell, allow 20 to 30 minutes at 350 degrees.

Cream yoghurt with butter. Blend in flour and salt. Let stand, covered, overnight. Roll on a pastry cloth using unbleached white flour to prevent sticking.

Know Your Ingredients
Name This Product # 29

Enriched flour (wheat flour, malted barley flour, iron, niacin, thiamine mononitrate, riboflavin), water, corn bran, high fructose corn syrup, wheat gluten, whole wheat flour, wheat bran. Contains 2% or less of each of the following: Molasses, yeast, canola oil and/or soybean oil, salt, soya flour, guar gum, calcium sulfate, dough conditioners (may contain one or more of the following: calcium and sodium stearoyl, lactylate, ethozylater mono- and diglycerides monocalcium phosphate, calcium carbonate, dicalcium phosphate), mono- and di-glycerides, yeast nutrients (diammonium phosphate and/or ammonium sulfate), calcium propionate (added to retard spoilage).

See Appendix B for Answer

CORNBREAD

Serves 6-8

2 cups stone ground corn meal
2 teaspoons dolomite (see Sources)
1 cup freshly ground spelt or wheat flour
3 cups cultured buttermilk, or water plus
2 tablespoons whey or yoghurt
3 eggs, lightly beaten
1/4 cup maple syrup
1 teaspoon salt
2 teaspoons baking soda
1/4 cup melted butter

Soak flour, dolomite powder and buttermilk or water mixture for 7 to 24 hours. Stir in remaining ingredients. Thin with a little water if necessary. Pour into a buttered and floured 9-by-9 baking pan. Bake at 350 degrees for about 3/4 hour or until a toothpick comes out clean.

Variations: Chile and Cheese Cornbread

Add *1 cup grated Monterey jack or cheddar cheese* and *1 small can diced green chiles* to batter.

CORNMEAL SPOON BREAD

Serves 12

2 cups whole grain cornmeal
2 teaspoons dolomite (see Sources)
4 cups cultured buttermilk, water plus
2 tablespoons whey or yoghurt
1/2 stick butter
1 medium onion, finely chopped
1 teaspoon sea salt
1/8 teaspoon cayenne pepper
2 teaspoons baking powder
5 large eggs, separated
pinch sea salt

While pellagra was being investigated as an interesting curiosity in Europe, it was becoming a way of life in the southern United States. . . The general diet consisted of corn meal and grits, soda biscuits, corn syrup and fat salt pork, and even when they had enough bulk of food, the Southerners developed sore skin and mouths, became thin and listless, and suffered from depression, hallucinations, irritability and other mental disorders. The clinical description of the typical poor Southerner, any time between about 1900 and 1940, comes alive in the novels of William Faulkner—the brooding sullenness suddenly shattered by outbursts of irrational anger, persecution mania, the feeling of people living in a cruel and demented world of their own. . . Doctors knew very well that diet was at the bottom of all the misery they saw around them, and that the disease could be kept at bay by a balanced food supply. . . The Red Cross distributed dried yeast, already noted as a cure for the disease, or could sometimes lend a rural family a cow until the general health and earning power had improved, but it was not until 1937 that it was finally proved that pellagra was due to a shortage in the diet of the very simple compound nicotinamide [vitamin B3]. . . The discovery that such a simple material could have such profound effects not only on the body but on the mind set off a great wave of nutritional research. One mystery was soon solved: doctors had known for years that poor Mexicans who also lived mainly on maize might suffer from many other diseases but very rarely from pellagra. It emerged that there was in fact some nicoti-

Mix cornmeal with buttermilk or water mixture and let stand at least 7 hours. Saute onions in butter. Beat egg yolks and blend into cornmeal mixture along with seasonings, sauteed onions and baking powder.

In a clean bowl, beat egg whites with pinch of salt until softly stiff. Fold into cornmeal mixture and pour into a buttered 9-by-13 inch pyrex pan. Bake about 35 minutes at 375 degrees, or until puffed and golden.

POLENTA

Serves 8

2 cups whole grain corn meal
2 teaspoons dolomite (see Sources)
2 cups filtered water
2 tablespoons whey or yoghurt
3 cups homemade chicken broth
1-2 teaspoons sea salt
1 medium onion, finely chopped, and sauteed in a little butter (optional)
2 tablespoon dried tomato bits, sauteed with the onions (optional)
1 teaspoon dried thyme (optional)
1/2-1 cup grated Parmesan or Monterey jack cheese (optional)

Soak cornmeal and dolomite powder in water and whey or yoghurt at least 7 hours. Bring chicken stock and salt to a boil. Slowly add soaked cornmeal, stirring constantly with a whisk. Lower heat and continue stirring for another 10 minutes or so until polenta is very thick. Stir in optional ingredients and pour into a buttered 9-by-13 pyrex dish. Bake about 1 hour at 350 degrees. You may brush with melted butter after about 30 minutes of baking. To serve, cut into squares.

Variation: Polenta Triangles

Cut *chilled leftover polenta* into triangles and saute in a mixture of *butter and extra virgin olive oil.*

namide in maize, but in a form that could not easily be absorbed. The Mexican women had a custom taken from traditional Indian food preparation of soaking the corncobs in lime water before they made their tortillas. This apparently released the vitamin. It is an ironic thought, that the adoption of one simple "primitive" custom might have saved the tens of thousands of ruined lives in the Southern states. Soon it was discovered that less of the vitamin was needed if there was plenty of protein in the diet, particularly protein containing the essential amino-acid tryptophan. This knowledge might not have helped much in the worst periods of pellagra, because the people were too poor to buy much protein, and tryptophan is one of the rarest of the amino-acids. However, it did explain why foods like milk and eggs, low in actual nicotinamide but rich in tryptophan, could keep pellagra away. Terence McLaughlin *A Diet of Tripe*

COUNTRY ITALIAN DINNER

Artichokes with Lemon Butter Sauce

Grilled Swordfish with Bagnat Sauce

Polenta

Steamed Broccoli

Baked Pears

CREAM CHEESE BREAKFAST PASTRIES

(Rugelach)

Makes 18-24

1 stick butter, softened
1 cup homemade cream cheese, softened (page 80)
2 cups freshly ground wheat or spelt flour
1/2 cup sucanat
1 tablespoon vanilla
1 teaspoon salt
1/4 cup melted butter
2 teaspoons cinnamon
1/4 cup finely chopped crispy pecans (page 485)

Mix butter, cream cheese and flour using an electric beater and let stand overnight. Mix in sucanat, vanilla and salt. Using unbleached white flour to keep from sticking, roll out dough on a pastry cloth to 1/4 inch thickness. Brush with mixture of melted butter and cinnamon and sprinkle with nuts. Roll up 1 1/2 turns and cut dough lengthwise. Roll another 1 1/2 turns and cut lengthwise. Repeat once more. You should now have three long rolls. Cut the rolls crosswise into 1 or 1 1/2 inch lengths. Place individual pastries on buttered cookie sheet and bake at 300 degrees for about 45 minutes. These store well in freezer or refrigerator and the flavor improves with time. Reheat before serving.

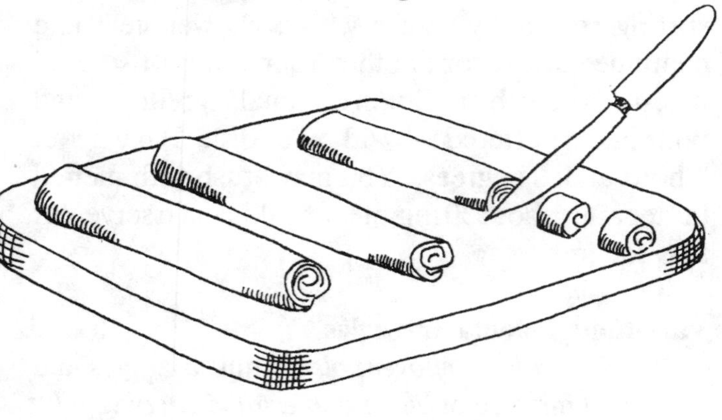

The fermentation of vegetables (sauerkraut, kimchi, pickles); grains (sourdough bread, kvass, kiesiel, kisra, koji); beans (miso, natto, tempeh) and fish are experiencing renewed interest. The savings in refrigeration cost alone would warrant the return to a safer, saner and more savory taste. As the world's fastest and best quality foods, these are always ready to be consumed, cold or warmed. Ancient standard cookbooks never mentioned fermented fast foods for the simple reason that those cookbooks were written for the rich and famous. Reading these ancient texts, one gets the idea that our ancestors spent a great amount of time preparing those fancy and elaborate meals. The truth is, simple folks toiled in the fields long hours, had to be in good health and had little time for preparing moveable-feast style lunches to be quickly consumed in the furrows. These foods often had to stand all morning long in the heat of harvest without the benefit of refrigeration. . . . Sour dough breads, pickled olives, herrings and anchovies, lacto-fermented vegetables and beans and sometimes yoghurt or cheese were the everyday fare. . . . A properly elaborated sourdough loaf acquires an unsurpassed taste and an aroma that no cracker or porridge can ever match. Sauerkraut achieves a succulent gourmet savor that cole-slaw never reaches. If you taste Normandy country farm butter, churned from aged fermented sour cream, you will never again eat creamery butter. Jacques DeLangre *Seasalt's Hidden Powers*

SOUR DOUGH STARTER

Makes about 3 quarts

2 cups freshly ground rye flour
2 cups cold filtered water
6 cups freshly ground rye flour
cold filtered water

Best results for sour dough starter are obtained from rye rather than wheat flour, perhaps because rye contains a much lower phytate content than wheat. You will need two gallon-sized bowls. Total time to make the starter is one week.

Grind 2 cups flour and let it sit for a bit to cool. In one large bowl, mix flour with 2 cups of cold water. The mixture should be quite soupy. Cover with a clean damp linen towel and place in a cool dark place. You may set the bowl outside in the shade if you live in an unpolluted area, and no pesticides have been used in your garden.

The next day and every day for a total of 7 days, transfer the starter to the other clean bowl and add 1 cup freshly ground rye flour plus enough cold water to make a soupy mixture. Cover and let stand.

After a few days the starter will begin to bubble and develop a wine-like aroma. In 7 days it is ready. Use 2 quarts for a batch of sour dough bread but save a one quart for your next batch of starter. If not using remaining starter immediately, you may store in an air tight jar in the refrigerator.

Do not be tempted to add honey to your starter, as some recipes require. Honey encourages the proliferation of yeasts at the expense of lactic-acid producing bacteria, and may give you an alcoholic fermentation.

To start a new batch of starter, place the quart of leftover starter in a clean bowl. Add 1 cup freshly ground rye flour plus water each day, changing bowls, until 3 quarts are obtained.

"But how do you make the sour dough?" Mrs. Boast asked.

"You start it," said Ma, "by putting some flour and warm water in a jar and letting it stand till it sours."

"Then when you use it, always leave a little," said Laura, "And put in the scraps of biscuit dough, like this, and more warm water," Laura put in the warm water, "and cover it," she put the clean cloth and the plate on the jar, "and just set it in a warm place, " she set it in its place on the shelf by the stove. "And it's always ready to use, whenever you want it." Laura Ingalls Wilder *By the Shores of Silver Lake*

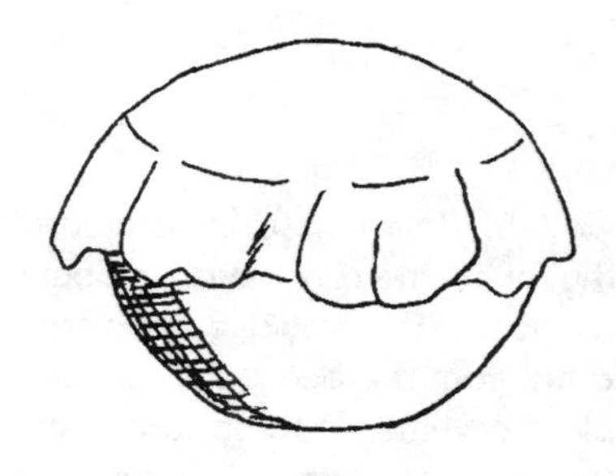

The history of bread making is a good example of the industrialization and standardization of a technique that was formerly empiric. . . It was simpler to replace natural leaven with brewers yeast. There are numerous practical advantages: the fermentation is more regular, more rapid and the bread rises better. But the fermentation becomes mainly an alcoholic fermentation and the acidification is greatly lessened. The bread is less digestible, less tasty and spoils more easily. Claude Aubert *Les Aliments Fermentes Traditionnels*

SOUR DOUGH WHOLE WHEAT BREAD

Makes 3 large loaves or 4 smaller loaves

2 quarts sour dough starter
13 cups freshly ground wheat or rye flour
or a combination
2 1/2 tablespoons sea salt crystals (not ground)
about 1 1/2 cups cold water

Traditional sour dough bread, prepared with a starter rather than with yeast, has a delicious flavor but tends to be heavy for modern tastes. Wheat gives a more satisfactory loaf than rye.

Place starter, salt and 1 cup water in a large bowl and mix with a wooden spoon until the salt crystals have dissolved. Slowly mix in the flour. Towards the end you will find it easier to mix with your hands. You may add the other 1/2 cup of water if the dough becomes too thick. It should be rather soft and easy to work. Kneed by pulling and folding over, right in the bowl, for 10 to 15 minutes; or knead in batches in your food processor.

Without pressing down the dough, cut or shape loaves into the desired shapes, or place into 3 well-buttered loaf pans. Cut a few slits in the top of the dough, cover and let rise at least 7 hours or overnight. Bake at 350 degrees for about an hour. Let cool well before slicing.

The bread will keep for up to a week without refrigeration.

Variation: Sour Dough Herb and Nut Bread

To each loaf, add *1 tablespoon rosemary* or *1 tablespoon dill* during kneading and *1/4 cup chopped crispy pecans (page 485) or freshly shelled walnuts* at the end of the kneading process.

Variation: Sour Dough Cheaters Bread

Use *3 cups unbleached white flour* and *10 cups whole wheat flour* for a lighter loaf.

Where do we find these lactic acid producing bacteria that cause milk to sour, that gives bread its aroma and that conserves vegetables? They are in the living soil and on healthy plants, in particular those that grow close to the soil. A protective coat of acid, truly an acid sheath, envelopes all higher organisms. In the mouth, the stomach, the intestine and in the reproductive organs, one finds a flora that produces lactic acid. Annelies Schoneck *Des Crudites Toute L'Annee*

Raw honey is noteworthy for having considerable plant amylase. The amylase does not come from the bee but is a true plant enzyme, concentrated from the pollen of flowers. . . If you wish to predigest a starchy food such as bread, spread some raw honey on it. The moment the honey and bread come into contact, the honey enzyme starts predigestion, and as you chew, more digestion takes place. If the bread with its honey-enzyme coating is allowed to stand at room temperature for 15 minutes before you eat it, there will be less work for salivary amylase. Edward Howell MD *Enzyme Nutrition*

SPICE BREAD

(Pain d'Epices)

Makes 2 9-inch rounds

4 cups sifted rye flour
1 cup raw honey
2 cups filtered water
2 teaspoons ground cinnamon
1 teaspoon ground coriander
1 teaspoon ground fennel
1 teaspoon ground cumin
1 teaspoon sea salt
grated rind of two oranges
1/2 cup sour dough starter

Mix spices, orange rind and salt with flour in a large bowl. Meanwhile gently heat the honey with the water until honey is dissolved. Let cool. Make a well in the flour and place the starter in it. Gradually add the liquid, stirring with a wooden spoon. The dough should be more liquid than bread dough. Line two well-oiled 9-inch cake pans oiled parchment paper and divide the batter between the two pans. Cover with a damp towel and let rise overnight. Bake at 350 degrees for 1 hour. Let cool slightly and remove from pan. Let sit for a day or two before eating.

In books on baking and even in nutritional/medical writings, the two techniques [for making bread], natural leaven (sourdough) and baker's yeast, are often mingled and confounded. . . Baking with natural leaven is in harmony with nature and maintains the integrity and nutrition of the cereal grains used. . . The process helps to increase and reinforce our body's absorption of the cereal's nutrients. Unlike yeasted bread that diminishes, even destroys much of the grain's nutritional value, naturally leavened bread does not stale and, as it ages, maintains its original moisture much longer. A lot of that information was known pragmatically for centuries and thus, when yeast was first introduced in France, at the court of Louis XIV in March 1668, because at that time the scientists already knew that the use of yeast would imperil the people's health, it was strongly rejected. Today, yeast is used almost universally, without any testing, and the recent scientific evidence and clinical findings are confirming the ancient taboos with biochemical and bio-electronic valid proofs that wholly support that age-old common sense decision.

Jacques DeLangre

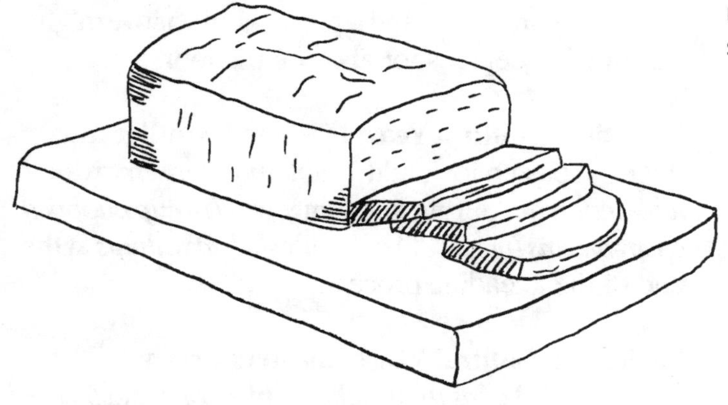

NATURAL YEAST BREAD

Makes 2 loaves

2 cups grapes, preferably organic, well washed and processed into a pulp
4 cups freshly ground whole wheat or rye flour or a combination
1 tablespoon sea salt
7 cups freshly ground wheat flour
1 tablespoon sea salt
filtered water

This makes a slightly lighter sourdough loaf than the preceding sourdough recipe, but the bread is still too heavy for traditional sandwiches. The starter can be prepared in 3 days rather than 7.

Place 2 cups grape pulp and 2 cups freshly ground whole wheat or rye flour in a clean bowl. Mix well, cover with a clean towel and let stand in a warm place. On day two transfer to a clean bowl and add 1 cup rye or wheat flour and 1 cup filtered water. Mix well, cover and let stand in a warm place. On day three transfer to a clean bowl and add the final cup of rye or wheat flour, and 1 cup water. Mix well, cover and let stand in a warm place for 24 hours. Starter is now ready. You should have about 5 cups. Use 4 cups for making bread and save 1 cup in a jar in the refrigerator for a new batch of starter.

To make bread, combine 7 cups flour with 4 cups starter, 1 tablespoon sea salt and about 1 1/2 cups water. Mix well with a wooden spoon or with your hands. To knead, process in two different batches in food processor and place each batch in a well-buttered loaf pan. Cover and let rise 7 hours or overnight. Bake at 300 degrees for about 1 1/2 hours.

Variation: Natural Yeast Herb and Nut Bread

To each loaf, add *1 tablespoon rosemary* or *1 tablespoon dill* during kneading and *1/4 cup chopped crispy pecans (page 485) or freshly shelled walnuts* at the end of the kneading process.

Variation: Natural Yeast Cheaters Bread

Use *2 cups unbleached white flour* and *5 cups whole wheat flour* for a lighter loaf

The nutrition of the people of the Loetschental Valley, particularly that of the growing boys and girls, consists largely of a slice of whole rye bread and a piece of the summer-made cheese (about as large as the slice of bread), which are eaten with fresh milk of goats or cows. Meat is eaten about once a week. In the light of our newer knowledge of activating substances, including vitamins, and the relative values of food for supplying minerals for body building, it is clear why they have healthy bodies and sound teeth. The average total fat-soluble activator and mineral intake of calcium, and phosphorus of these children would far exceed that of the daily intake of the average American child. The sturdiness of the child life permits children to play and frolic bareheaded and barefooted even in water running down from the glacier in the late evening's chilly breezes, in weather that made us wear our overcoats and gloves and button our collars. Of all the children in the valley still using the primitive diet of whole rye bread and dairy products the average number of cavities per person was 0.3. On an average it was necessary to examine three persons to find one defective deciduous or permanent tooth. The children examined were between seven and sixteen years of age. Weston Price DDS *Nutrition and Physical Degeneration*

ZARATHUSTRA BREAD

Makes 10 small loaves

3 cups red wheat berries
1/4 cup sesame seeds or caraway seeds (optional)
filtered water
1 teaspoon sea salt
1/2 cup currants or raisins (optional)

This chewy, sour bread is for purists!

Place wheat berries and optional seeds in a bowl, cover with water and let sit in a dark place for 24 hours. Pour out water, replenish and let sit another 24 hours. Test berries to see if they are soft. If the are still hard when pinched, replace water and let sit another 24 hours. Pour off excess water, transfer berries with a slotted spoon to a food processor and process with sea salt until smooth in food processor. Add optional currants or raisins and pulse a few times. Form into balls and flatten slightly. Place on an oiled cookie sheet and bake about 12 hours in a 150 degree oven, turning after about 6 hours If you live in a hot, dry climate, you can bake these in the sun—thus baked Zarathustra.

Variation: Essene Bread

Flatten the balls into flat rounds, about 1/4 inch thick. Bake on lowest oven heat, in a dehydrator, or, in hot dry climates, in the sun, turning once.

Variation: Essene Crackers

Oil 2 stainless steel baking pans and flatten dough into pans. Bake on lowest oven heat or in a dehydrator until crisp. Break up into crackers.

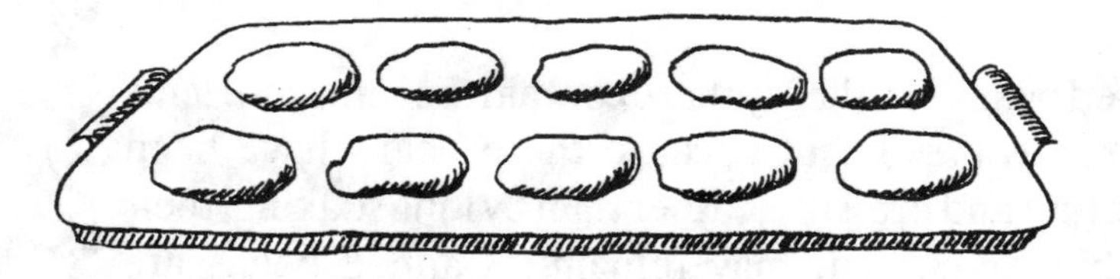

"How could we cook our daily bread without fire, Master?" asked some with great astonishment.

"Let the angels of God prepare your bread. Moisten your wheat, that the angel of water may enter it. Then set it in the air, that the angel of air also may embrace it. And leave it from morning to evening beneath the sun, that the angel of sunshine may descend upon it. And the blessing of the three angels will soon make the germ of life to sprout in your wheat. Then crush your grain, and make thin wafers, as did your forefathers when they departed out of Egypt, the house of bondage. Put them back again beneath the sun from its appearing, and when it is risen to its highest in the heavens, turn them over on the other side that they be embraced there also by the angel of sunshine, and leave them there until the sun be set. . ." *The Essene Gospel of Peace*

Many of our refined foods have additions of B-1 and B-2. The *British Medical Journal* in an article entitled "Imbalance of vitamin B Factors" reported "Recent experiments have produced clear cut evidence of the adverse effects that may be caused by the disturbance of the balance of the vitamin B factors in the diet." They have shown that the overloading of B1, for instance, can produce a definite deficiency of vitamin B6. It is becoming increasingly recognized that there is a need for caution in addition of a supplement of a single synthetic vitamin to food preparations National Health Federation *Seven Myths Exploded*

LEGUMES

Legumes or pulses such as beans, chick peas, lentils, peas, peanuts and cashews have nourished mankind for centuries. They are the poor man's meat throughout the world, providing complete protein when combined with grains. The combination of pulses, whole grains and a small amount of animal protein and good quality animal fat is the ideal low-cost diet. Legumes are rich in minerals and B vitamins. Recent research indicates that legumes contain several anti-cancer agents. All contain both omega-3 and omega-6 fatty acids. Kidney and pinto beans are high in omega-3's; chick peas are high in omega-6's.

Traditional societies whose cuisines are based on legumes prepare them with great care. Beans are well soaked before they are cooked to neutralize the phytic acid and enzyme inhibitors they contain, and to break down difficult-to-digest complex sugars. The soaking water is poured off, the beans are rinsed, and in the case of chick peas and fava beans, the skins picked off. As the legumes cook, all foam that rises to the top of the cooking water is carefully skimmed off. Sometimes water is replaced, midway during the cooking process. Such care in preparation ensures that legumes will be thoroughly digestible, and all the nutrients they provide well assimilated.

The Orientals have developed methods of inoculating soaked and cooked legumes, particularly soybeans, to produce products like *miso*, *tempeh* and *natto*. In fact soybeans should *only* be eaten after they have been fermented. They contain an enzyme inhibiting substance which can produce serious gastric distress, reduced protein digestion, and chronic deficiencies in amino acid uptake. These enzyme inhibitors are not deactivated by ordinary cooking. We also do not recommend soy milk because of its high phytate and enzyme inhibitor content.

Bland tasting legumes marry very well with many sorts of spices and they are particularly synergistic with sour foods. Always add lemon juice, or the liquid from fermented vegetables, to bean and lentil soups. Bean and lentil dishes go very well with sauerkraut and other lacto-fermented vegetables. In salads, beans and lentils are enhanced by copious amounts of onions.

What about canned beans? In theory these contain the same nutrients as beans you have cooked yourself; but because these beans have been softened by high temperature and pressure, rather than by long soaking, their phytate and enzyme inhibitor content may remain. Canned beans are therefore best eaten sparingly. When using canned garbanzo beans, rinse well and pick off the phytate-containing skins.

SIMPLE BEANS

Serves 8

2 cups black beans, kidney beans, pinto beans, black-eyes beans or white beans
filtered water
2 tablespoons whey
1 teaspoon sea salt
4 cloves garlic, peeled and mashed (optional)

Soak beans in filtered water, salt and whey for 12-24 hours, depending on the size of the bean. Drain, rinse, place in a large pot and add water to cover beans. Bring to a boil and skim off foam. Reduce heat and add optional garlic. Simmer, covered, for 4-8 hours. Check occasionally and add more water as necessary.

SIMPLE MASHED BEANS

Serves 6

2 cups dried Northern beans
filtered water
2 tablespoons whey
1 teaspoon sea salt
1 medium onion, coarsely chopped
1 medium carrot, peeled and chopped
1 medium parsnip, peeled and chopped
3 cloves garlic, peeled and crushed
1 medium onion, peeled and finely chopped
butter and extra virgin olive oil
1 teaspoon paprika

Soak beans in water, whey and salt for about 24 hours. Drain, rinse and place in a pot with onion, carrot and parsnip. Add water to cover beans and bring to a boil. Skim off foam that rises to top. Reduce to simmer and add garlic. Cover and cook at least 4 hours. Remove in batches with a slotted spoon to food processor and puree, adding enough cooking liquid to achieve desired consistency. Saute remaining onion until soft in butter and oil. Stir in paprika. Stir onion-paprika mixture into beans. Transfer to a heated serving dish.

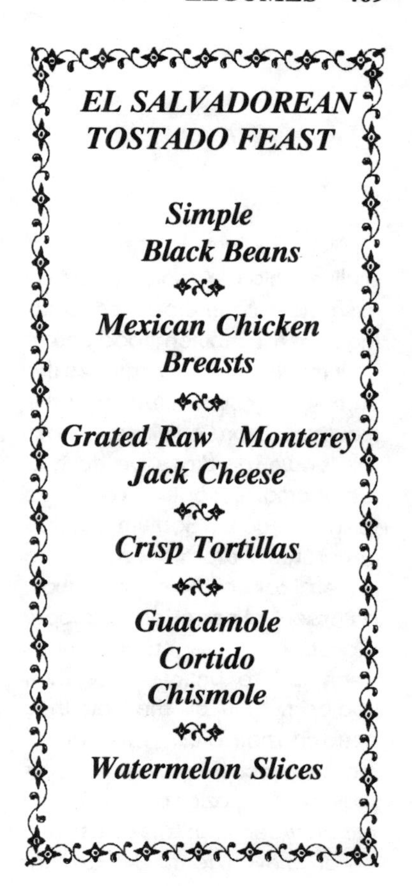

Vegetable protein is also important and is found in largest quantities in whole grains, seeds, beans, legumes, peas, nuts, etc. Vegetable protein alone cannot sustain healthy life because it does not contain enough of all of the amino acids that are essential. There is only one plant that can be classed as a complete protein—the soybean, but it is so low in two of the essential amino acids that it cannot serve as a complete protein for human consumption. In fact, most all plants lack methionine, one of the essential amino acids. Vegetable protein, when supplemented properly by animal protein, makes an excellent combination. Health cannot be maintained on a diet that omits animal protein. H. Leon Abrams *Your Body is Your Best Doctor.*

BAKED BEANS

Serves 6-8

4 cups white or brown beans
filtered water
2 tablespoons whey
1 teaspoon sea salt
2 medium onions
butter and extra virgin olive oil
1 small can tomato paste
3 tablespoons soy sauce
3 tablespoons vinegar
1/4 cup maple syrup
1/4 cup molasses
3 cloves garlic, peeled and crushed
pinch red chile flakes

Soak beans in filtered water, whey and salt for 24 hours. In a flame-proof casserole, saute onion in butter and oil. Drain beans, rinse and add to casserole, with enough water to cover them. Bring to a boil and skim. Add remaining ingredients, cover and bake in a 350 degree oven for about 6 hours. Serve with sauerkraut, whole grain bread and chicken or lamb sausage (pages 341 and 342).

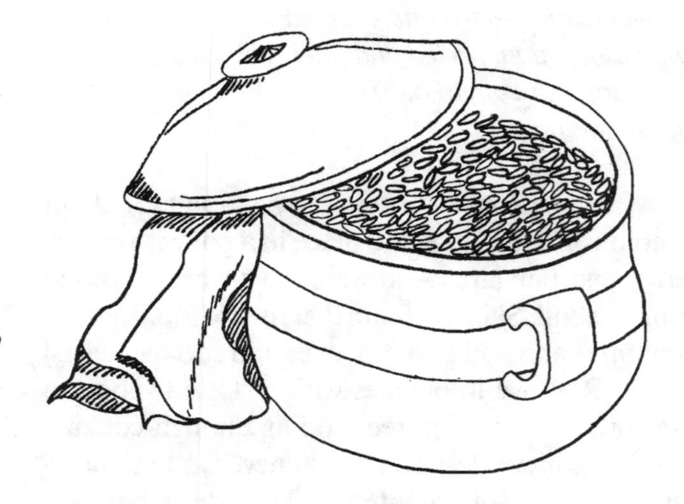

Sodium, in the form of sodium chloride (salt), plays an essential role in digestion, starting from the moment food enters your mouth. Salt. . . activates the primary digestive enzyme in the mouth, salivary amylase. . . Further down the digestive tract, in the stomach, sodium continues its good work. Sodium chloride generates hydrochloric acid in the parietal cells of the stomach wall, an essential secretion for proper digestion. . . Vegetarians have been led to believe that their vegies supply all the salt they need in their diet. This is completely false. Why are salt blocks provided for grazing animals? They are provided with this salt source because every farmer knows that without it, his vegetarian animals will get sick. . . Salt is the single element required for the proper breakdown of plant carbohydrates into usable and assimilable human food. A salt-free, vegetarian diet is a sure ticket to the hospital and a premature old age. Vegetarians are also prone to sugar addiction. The physiological explanation for this: Glucosides in grains are not digested without the presence of salt. As the body is denied these natural sugars, a deficiency develops and there is an insatiable desire to eat sweets. William Campbell Douglass *Second Opinion*

BAKED BEANS, FRENCH STYLE

Serves 6-8

4 cups dried northern beans
filtered water
4 tablespoons whey
2 teaspoons sea salt
1 cup extra virgin olive oil
1 small can tomato paste
4 cloves garlic, peeled and mashed
several sprigs fresh thyme, tied together
2 medium red onions, finely chopped
juice of 2 lemons

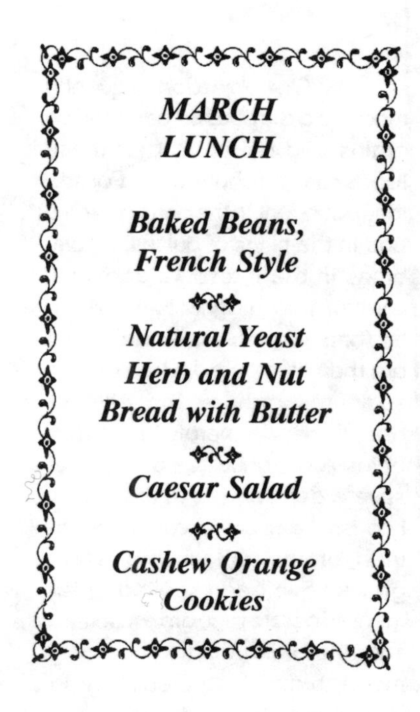

This unusual and delicious recipe calls for cooking the beans in oil rather than in liquid. A long soaking is therefore essential or the beans will be too hard. May be served warm or cold, as a bean salad.

Bring a pot of water to the boil and pour over beans. Add 2 tablespoons whey and 1 teaspoon salt and let sit 12 hours. Pour out excess water, repeat process and let stand another 12 hours. Pour beans into a colander, drain and rinse.

Heat olive oil in a pot and add beans, tomato paste, salt, thyme and garlic. Blend well. Bake at 300 degrees for about 6 hours. Check occasionally. If beans seem too dry, add more olive oil. Beans are done when they are soft but they will not be mushy like beans cooked in liquid. Remove thyme, fold in onions and lemon juice and serve.

Eating dried beans—legumes—can depress blood cholesterol whether you are on a low-fat or high-fat diet. Dr. James Anderson at the University of Kentucky College of Medicine found that eating a cup of cooked beans, such as navy or pinto beans or even canned baked beans, every day decreased blood cholesterol an average of 19 percent. And the beans worked on people eating moderately high fat diet—36 percent of calories from fat. Dr. David Jenkins at the University of Toronto found that daily regimen of beans (kidney beans, pinto beans, chickpeas, or red or green lentils) depressed cholesterol an average of 7 percent in men with high cholesterol who were already on a low-fat diet. Jean Carper *The Food Pharmacy Guide to Good Eating*

CASSOULET

Serves 12-16

6 cups great Northern beans
filtered water
3 tablespoons whey
1 teaspoon salt
preserved duck legs (page 276), 4 legs & 4 thighs, or 4 legs & 4 thighs of fresh duckling
2 medium onions, finely chopped
1 cup dry white wine
1/2 cup fresh lemon juice
several sprigs fresh thyme and 2 bay leaves, tied together
1/2 teaspoon ground cloves
6 cups homemade beef or chicken stock
4 cloves garlic, peeled and mashed
2 teaspoons sea salt
1 teaspoon dried green peppercorns, crushed
1 pound lamb stew pieces
1 large can tomatoes
2 cloves garlic, peeled and mashed
3 pounds garlicky lamb or chicken sausage
2 cups whole grain bread crumbs
1 cup grated Parmesan cheese (optional)
1/4 stick butter
1/4 cup finely chopped parsley

One objection frequently made to a diet based primarily on grains and pulses is that these foods contain phytic acid. Particularly abundant in the germ of grains and in the skins of pulses, it combines in the intestinal tract with calcium, iron, magnesium and zinc to form insoluble phytates that are then eliminated. According to some researchers, the elimination of these minerals in the form of insoluble phytates can lead to severe deficiencies in those who nourish themselves predominantly with grains, unless the whole grains have been soaked or fermented before they are consumed. The role of phytic acid has been most thoroughly studied in bread. In sour dough bread, with a long fermentation that is partially a lacto-fermentation, the phytic acid is almost completely destroyed. On the other hand, bread made with brewers yeast undergoes a rapid fermentation that is in large measure an alcoholic fermentation, and its phytic acid content remains largely intact. The phytase (enzyme needed to break down phytic acid) present in grains cannot do its work unless the pH becomes sufficiently low and the period of fermentation lasts a sufficiently long time. Claude Aubert *Les Aliments Fermentes Traditionnels*

This French version of baked beans and various meats makes a wonderful party dish. It is traditionally made with *confit* of duck or goose, but you may also use fresh duck pieces.

Soak beans in filtered water, salt and whey for 24 hours. In a flame proof casserole that is wide and shallow rather than deep, saute the*confit de canard* or the duck pieces in their own fat until nicely browned on all sides. Remove and reserve. Saute onion in duck fat. Add wine and boil down. Drain beans, rinse and add to the pot along with stock. Bring to a boil and skim. Stir in lemon juice, salt and pepper, garlic and thyme and bayleaf. Return the duck pieces to the casserole, cover and bake at 350 degrees for about 3 hours, stirring occasionally. Meanwhile, brown lamb pieces in olive oil in a heavy pan. Place canned tomatoes in food processor, pulse a couple of times and add to lamb. Add garlic and season with salt and pepper. Cover and simmer for about 3 hours, or until lamb is tender. 1/2 hour before casserole is finished, add sliced sausage to beans.

When beans are tender, remove thyme and bay leaf and stir in lamb. Saute bread crumbs in butter until browned. Mix with parsley and optional cheese and strew over casserole. Bake another 20 minutes, uncovered, at 350 degrees or until bread crumbs are crusty.

One of the outstanding changes which I have found takes place in the primitive races at their point of contact with our modern civilization is a decrease in the ease and efficiency of the birth process. When I visited the Six Nation Reservation at Brantford, Ontario, I was told by the physician in charge that a change of this kind had occurred during the period of his administration, which had covered twenty-eight years and that the hospital was now used largely to care for young Indian women during abnormal childbirth. . . A similar impressive comment was made to me by Dr. Romig, the superintendent of the government hospital for Eskimos and Indians at Anchorage, Alaska. He stated that in his thirty-six years among the Eskimos, he had never been able to arrive in time to see a normal birth by a primitive Eskimo woman. But conditions have changed materially with the new generation of Eskimo girls, born after their parents began to use foods of modern civilization. Many of them are carried to his hospital after they had been in labor for several days. Weston Price DDS *Nutrition and Physical Degeneration*

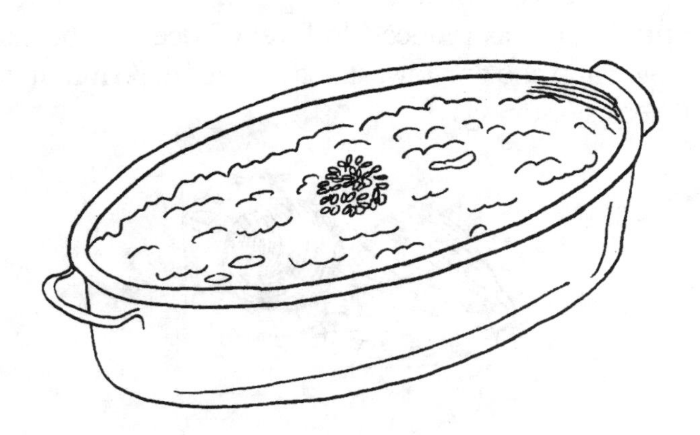

Primitive cultures showing a high immunity to dental disease and freedom from other degenerative processes had diets containing at least 10 times the vitamin A and D and at least 4 times the other vitamins and minerals found in a good modern diet. When the only foods available are unrefined and unprocessed, man must eat a wide variety and a large amount to meet his body's energy requirements. This usually supplies his body with the proper nutrients for good health and growth. Refining and processing of foods removes or destroys essential elements. It can make food a concentrated source of energy with little nutritional value. Modern man can easily fill his body's energy requirements without obtaining the nutrients for good health. When primitive man adopts the foods of modern society, his carbohydrate intake remains the same, but the form changes from whole grains and beans to sugar and other refined products. When primitive man adopts the foods of modern society, tooth decay and degenerative diseases follow. "Nutrition: The Appetite of Man" *PPNF*

BEANS AND RICE, JAMAICAN STYLE

Serves 6

1 cup red kidney beans
filtered water
1 tablespoon whey
1 teaspoon sea salt
1 cup coconut milk and cream, (page 144) or
7-8 ounces creamed coconut (see Sources)
1 bunch green onions, chopped
3 jalapeno peppers, seeded and chopped
3 cloves garlic, mashed
2 teaspoons dried thyme
1 teaspoon sea salt
1 teaspoon dried green peppercorns, crushed
2 cups brown rice, soaked for at least 7 hours

Cover beans with filtered water, add salt and whey and soak for 24 hours. Drain, rinse and place in a pot with coconut milk or creamed coconut and enough water to cover beans. Bring to a boil. (If using creamed coconut, boil, stirring, until it is melted.) Skim. Add all other ingredients except rice. Cover and simmer for about 2 hours or until beans are tender. Add rice and more water so that rice and beans are well covered. Bring to a boil and let boil until liquid has reduced to level of rice and beans. Cover and cook on lowest heat for about 30 minutes. Check seasonings.

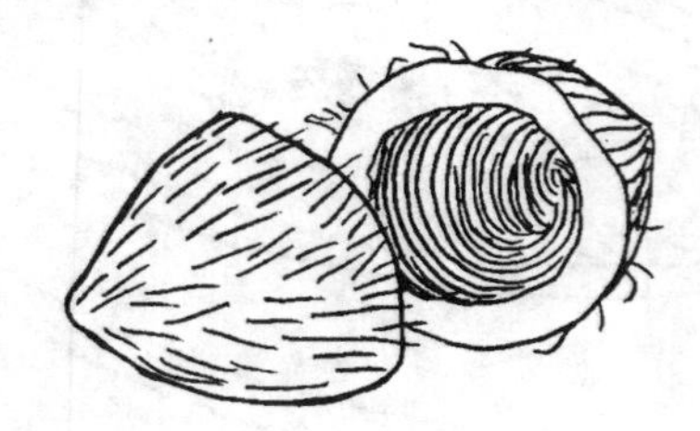

BLACK-EYED BEANS, PERSIAN STYLE

Serves 6

4 ounces dry black-eyed beans, prepared according to master recipe (page 469)
4-5 bunches chard, washed and chopped
2 bunches green onions, finely chopped
1 bunch parsley, finely chopped
1 bunch cilantro, finely chopped
1 medium onion, chopped
4-5 dried limes (available at Middle Eastern markets) or grated zest and juice of 3 fresh limes
butter and extra virgin olive oil

Saute green onions, parsley and cilantro in butter and olive oil, stirring constantly. Remove to a casserole. Saute onion and add to parsley mixture. If you are using dried limes, open up and remove seeds and membranes. Add dried limes (including skins) or lime juice and zest, cooked beans and chopped chard to casserole. Cover and simmer about 20 minutes. Serve with basic brown rice (page 441).

Yearbook of Agriculture has warned of subclinical deficiencies for over 35 years. In 1929 the first chapter appeared and they have continued since. The University of Minnesota published results of a test that caused nutritionists to take notice. In this test, cattle were fed grain that had been degerminated . . . and the cattle gained in weight and appeared in good health. They soon began to drop dead with heart failure while, at the end of 18 months the whole herd was dead, a control group of animals that were fed natural grains were thriving (and they didn't have irritation in their digestive tracts). Is this degermination process responsible for our extremely high rate of heart disease? Please note that the cattle did appear to be in good health and then suddenly developed fatal heart disease. Is this not as a result of subclinical deficiency? Very few, if any, of our populace have clinical symptom of heart disease until that moment when they have heart attacks . . . National Health Federation *The Seven Myths Exploded*

Whatever the father of illness, the mother is wrong food.
Chinese Proverb

Animal proteins (meat, fish, milk products, eggs) seem to present many drawbacks. . . Why not, then, replace animal protein with vegetable protein? These are found in grains, vegetables, oily fruits and above all pulses. But they are less well balanced than animal proteins. By proper combining of grains and pulses, one can improve the overall quality of protein from vegetable sources. But many people assimilate vegetable proteins less well than animal proteins. This leads to the common sense conclusion, found widely in books on diet and health, that half of our protein should be of animal origin, and half of vegetable origin. This rule really has no scientific foundation, as it is only necessary to eat a small amount of animal protein to aid the assimilation of vegetable proteins. Tradition and science confirm each other in this for once. The tradition: the French *pot au feu* (beef bouillon with bread), Italian pasta with Parmesan cheese, Spanish *paella*, Moroccan *couscous*, Indian *thali*, Japanese fish with rice—always the animal products, whether meat, fish or dairy product, were traditionally eaten in very small quantities.

By economic necessity? Perhaps. . . But also perhaps due to an ancestral intuition. For research done with animals has confirmed the wisdom of these practices. In one of these studies, conducted in Latin America, rats were give mixtures of corn and beans in various proportions, the two foods that form the basis of the diet of a large part of the population. In whatever proportions these foods were given, the growth of the rats was insufficient, even if theoretically the amount of protein was adequate. In contrast, it was sufficient to add just 2% of fish to the bean-

BLACK BEAN AND CORN SALAD

Serves 6

2 cups cooked black beans (page 469), drained
2 cups fresh corn kernels
2 jalapeno peppers, seeded and diced
1 red onion, finely chopped
1 cup basic dressing (page 118)
or 1 cup lemon pepper dressing (page 123)

Mix all ingredients together. Chill well before serving.

THREE BEAN SALAD

Serves 12

2 cups cooked kidney beans (page 469), drained
2 cups cooked chick peas (page 477), drained
2 pounds French beans, cut into 1-inch lengths, blanched in boiling water for 8 minutes, drained and rinsed
2 medium red onions, finely chopped
1/4 cup finely chopped parsley
1 red pepper, cut into a julienne
1 green pepper, cut into a julienne
juice of 1 lemon
1 cup garlic dressing (page 119)

Mix all ingredients together. Let stand an hour or so before serving.

SIMPLE CHICK PEAS

Makes 3 cups

1 cup dried chick peas
filtered water
2 tablespoons whey
1 teaspoon sea salt

Soak chick peas in water, salt and whey for 24 hours. Drain, rinse and pick off skins. Transfer to a pot, add water to cover and bring to a boil. Skim. Cover and simmer for about 6 hours or until chick peas are very tender. Drain and use in salads.

CHICK PEA STEW

Serves 8

4 cups cooked chick peas
1 cup millet, soaked at least 7 hours
butter and extra virgin olive oil
2 medium onions, finely chopped
8 cups chicken or beef stock
1/4 teaspoon cayenne pepper
1/2 cup currents
1 head broccoli, cut into flowerets
1 1/2 cups crispy cashews (page 487), chopped
3-5 tablespoons lemon juice
sea salt

Saute onions in butter and olive oil until soft. Add stock, bring to a boil and skim. Add millet and stir with a whisk to keep from clumping. Add chick peas, cayenne and currents, cover and simmer about 10 minutes. Add remaining ingredients and simmer a few minutes more until broccoli is tender. Season to taste.

corn mixture to considerably raise the growth rate of the animals (from 70 to 120% greater, according to the proportions of the two main ingredients.)

The small supplement of fish cannot in itself explain these spectacular results. Undoubtedly the added animal protein has a synergistic effect on the assimilation of the vegetable protein. The amount of fish given to the rats was the equivalent of 30 grams for a man—just one sardine!—as the only animal protein for the whole day. Another interesting observation: The combination of corn and fish (without beans) never gave as good results, whatever the amount of fish, as the trilogy of beans, corn and fish.

Why not follow these wise practices—that are moreover very economical—by preparing meals predominantly vegetarian with a small complement of fish, meat, cheese or egg? Claude Aubert *Dis-Moi Comment Tu Cuisines*

Chick peas or garbanzo beans are so old a food that they are unknown in their wild state. They form a staple of the diet in the Middle East and in Mediterranean countries. They are one of the most nutritious of all the legumes, high in calcium, phosphorus and potassium. They have an exceptionally high iron and vitamin C content and contain B complex as well. Like all pulses, they are rich in essential fatty acids. However, as chick peas are high in omega-6 fatty acids, they should not be consumed to excess. Their bland taste marries well with onions, spices and sour foods. SWF

FALAFEL

Serves 8

2 cups chick peas
filtered water
4 tablespoons whey
1 teaspoon salt
4 cups loosely packed parsley leaves
4 medium onions, coarsely chopped
4 large cloves garlic
1 teaspoon ground cumin
1 teaspoon ground coriander
1 teaspoon pepper
1 teaspoon salt
1 teaspoon cayenne pepper
1 teaspoon baking powder
extra virgin olive oil

Here is yet another delicious ethnic dish in which the main ingredient is fermented—in this case the base is chick peas. Falafel is a popular food throughout the Middle East

Bring filtered water to a boil and pour over chick peas. Add salt and whey and soak for 12 hours. Pour off excess water and pour in more boiling water. Let sit another 12 hours. Place 1 cup parsley in food processor and pulse until chopped. Add 1/4 of the chick peas, 1 onion, 1 garlic clove, and 1/4 teaspoon each of the remaining ingredients (except olive oil) and pulse until reduced to a coarse paste. The mixture should be finely enough ground to hold together, but not entirely smooth. Repeat process three more times. Mix all together, cover and refrigerate for at least 1 hour. Form into patties and saute in olive oil. Serve with tahini sauce (page 134), sliced tomatoes, sliced cucumbers and pita bread.

Know Your Ingredients

Name This Product #30

Rolled oats (with oat bran), rolled whole wheat, brown sugar, partially hydrogenated vegetable oil (soy-bean and/or cottonseed oil), nonfat dry milk, dried unsweetened coconut, oat bran, honey, corn syrup, raisins, crisp rice (rice, sugar, salt, malt), brown sugar, partially hydrogenated vegetable oil (soybean and/or cottonseed), corn syrup solids, glycerin, high fructose corn syrup, almonds, raisin juice concentrate, sorbitol, salt, cinnamon and cinnamon extractives, BHA (a preservative), citric acid (a stabilizing agent).

See Appendix B for Answer

SIMPLE LENTILS

Serves 6-8

2 cups lentils, preferably green lentils
filtered water
2 tablespoons whey
1 teaspoon sea salt
2 cups beef or chicken stock
2 cloves garlic, peeled and mashed
several sprigs fresh thyme, tied together
1 teaspoon dried pepper corns, crushed
pinch dried chile flakes (optional)
juice of 1-2 lemons or
3 tablespoons sauerkraut juice (page 84)

Soak lentils in filtered water, salt and whey for several hours. Drain, rinse, place in a pot and add stock to cover. Bring to a boil and skim. Add remaining ingredients except lemon or sauerkraut juice and simmer, uncovered, for about 1 hour, or until liquid has completely reduced. Add lemon juice or sauerkraut juice and season to taste. Serve with a slotted spoon. Excellent with sauerkraut and strongly flavored meats such as duck, game or lamb.

Since the beginning of civilization, the lowly lentil has nourished healthy peoples across a wide portion of the globe. Like all legumes, they are rich in calcium, phosphorus, potassium, zinc and iron as well as vitamin B complex. Lentils have a high molybdenum content, a mineral that plays a role in protein assimilation, iron absorption, fat oxidation and normal cell function. They have a low phytate content as well and thus need only be soaked a few hours, rather than overnight.

American markets usually carry brown lentils. Some markets carry the pretty red lentil, which is best used only for soups, as it disintegrates during cooking. The French prefer the tiny green lentil, available in gourmet and specialty shops. These make the most satisfactory cooked lentils as they hold their shape very well. SWF

Know Your Ingredients

Name This Product # 31

Cooked beans, water, tomato puree, light brown sugar, sugar, invert sugar, molasses, cottonseed oil, high fructose corn syrup, salt, modified food starch, pork, onion powder, spice and apple concentrate

See Appendix B for Answer

LENTIL SALAD

Serves 4

2 cups cooked green lentils
1 cup grated carrots
1 bunch green onions, chopped
2 tablespoons finely chopped parsley
3/4 cup basic dressing (page 118)

Mix all ingredients. Serve at room temperature.

LENTIL PECAN PATTIES

Makes 12 patties

3 cups cooked lentils, well drained
grated rind of 1 lemon
2 medium onions, finely chopped, sauteed in butter
2 cloves garlic, peeled and mashed
1 cup crispy pecans (page 485), ground to a powder in food processor
2 cups whole grain bread crumbs
2 eggs, lightly beaten
1 teaspoon sea salt
1/4 teaspoon cayenne pepper
1 teaspoon dry mustard
butter and extra virgin olive oil

Drain lentils very well in a colander. Place in a bowl and mash. Mix with remaining ingredients (except butter and olive oil.) Saute by spoonfuls in butter and olive oil, turning when well browned. Keep warm in oven until ready to serve. Serve with pickled vegetables such as cortido (page 85), sauerkraut (page 84) or ginger carrots (page 87).

Few people who have not been in contact with experimental data on metabolism can appreciate how little of the minerals in the food are retained in the body by large numbers of individuals who are in need of these very chemicals. If we are to provide nutrition that will include an adequate excess as a factor of safety for overloads, and for such periods as those of rapid growth (for children), pregnancy, lactation and sickness, we must provide the excess to the extent of about twice the requirements of normal adults. It will therefore, be necessary for an adequate nutrition to contain approximately four times the minimum requirements of the average adult if all stress periods are to be passed safely.

It is of interest that the diets of the primitive groups which have shown a very high immunity to dental caries and freedom from other degenerative processes have all provided a nutrition containing at least four times these minimum requirements; whereas the displacing nutrition of commerce, consisting largely of white-flour products, sugar, polished rice, jams, canned goods, and vegetable fats have invariably failed to provide even the minimum requirements. Weston Price DDS *Nutrition and Physical Degeneration*

INDIAN STYLE LENTILS

(Dal)

Serves 8

1 1/2 cups brown lentils
filtered water
2 tablespoons whey
1 teaspoon sea salt
1 teaspoon turmeric
freshly ground pepper
2 cloves garlic, peeled and mashed
1/2 stick clarified butter
1 1/2 teaspoons cumin seeds
2 small hot red or green peppers, seeded and chopped
1/3 cup chopped cilantro

Cover lentils with filtered water, add salt and whey and soak several hours. Drain, rinse and place in a pot, add water to cover and bring to a boil. Skim. Add turmeric, pepper and garlic. Simmer, covered, for about an hour or until lentils are very soft. Off heat, beat with a wire whisk until lentils are creamy. Meanwhile saute cumin seeds and chiles in butter until chiles are soft. Fold chile-cumin seed mixture and chopped cilantro into lentils and serve.

INDIAN STYLE DUMPLINGS

(Idli)

Serves 6-8

1 cup lentils, mung beans or chick peas
2 cups brown rice
filtered water
2 tablespoons whey
2 teaspoons sea salt
an egg poacher

These vegetarian "meatballs" may be served with a variety of sauces. Wash lentils and rice well and place in separate bowls. Cover each with filtered water, add 1 tablespoon whey to each and let soak overnight. Drain each in a colander and process separately in food processor with a little water until smooth. Blend lentil and rice dough together with salt—the dough should be rather firm. Cover and let stand in a warm place for 24 hours. Fill well-oiled egg poaching cups with batter, cover and steam for 15 minute or until a needle comes out clean. Serve hot with curry sauce (page 136), yoghurt sauce (page 131) or fruit chutney (page 98).

Variation: Indian Style Spicy Dumplings

Just before cooking, add *1/2 teaspoon pepper, 1/2 teaspoon ground cumin, 1/4 teaspoon nutmeg* and *1 teaspoon grated ginger* to dough and mix well.

Variation: Indian Style Picant Dumplings

Just before cooking, add *1 teaspoon fried mustard seed* and *2 tablespoons chopped cilantro* to dough and mix well.

In many countries around the world, lacto-fermented foods, or at least certain lacto-fermented foods, are valued for their medicinal properties. . . . In Europe during the 19th century, doctors prescribed sauerkraut for numerous diseases—for enlarged liver and spleen, hemorrhoids, constipation, nervous troubles and hysteria. In Germany and Poland, sauerkraut juice and juice of fermented cucumbers are still used to treat enteritis.

The therapeutic value of yoghurt is well known, notably for the reestablishment of intestinal flora. . . In India *idli* (lacto-fermented rice and lentils) is particularly recommended for children and people in a weakened condition; *dahi* (a fermented milk product similar to yoghurt) is recommended for dyspepsia, dysentery and various intestinal disorders. It is also recommended to stimulate the appetite and to increase vitality. In Mexico, *pozol* (fermented corn) is used to counter diarrhea; it is also made into poultices to dress wounds. Mixed with water and honey, it is given to the sick to bring down fevers.

Pulque, a fermented drink inherited from the Aztecs and made with cactus juice, is used to treat kidney infections and to stimulate lactation. In Nigeria *ogi* (lacto-fermented corn) is given to babies, to the sick and to convalescents; it also is valued for stimulating lactation. In Greece and Turkey *tarhanas* (mixture of wheat and fermented milk) is consumed in large quantities by nursing mothers, by infants when they are weaned, by the sick and the very old. Claude Aubert *Les Aliments Fermentes Traditionnels*

INDIAN STYLE PANCAKES

(Dosas)

Makes about 20

1 cup lentils, mung beans or chick peas
2 cups brown rice
filtered water
2 tablespoons whey (optional)
1 teaspoon salt

Wash lentils and rice well and place in separate bowls. Cover each with filtered water, add 1 tablespoon whey to each and let soak overnight. Drain each and process separately in food processor with a little water until smooth. Mix lentils and rice together with salt and enough water to make a batter about the consistency of cream. Cover and let stand 24 hours.

To cook, heat a cast iron skillet and brush with clarified butter. Ladle about 1/4 cup into pan and tip pan to spread batter. Cook about 5 minutes per side. (You may further thin batter with water to make a paper thin dosa, but it takes some practice to turn these without tearing.) Keep warm in oven while preparing remaining dosas. Brush pan with butter between each pancake. Serve hot or warm with curry sauce (page 136), yoghurt sauce (page 131) or fruit chutney (page 98).

Variation: Indian Style Coconut Pancakes

Place *2 cups finely grated fresh or dried coconut, 2 tablespoon coarsely chopped ginger, 2 small green chiles, coarsely chopped, 2 small onions, coarsely chopped, 1/2 teaspoon salt* and *1 bunch cilantro* in food processor and process to a paste. Blend into batter along with additional water if necessary to achieve desired consistency and proceed with recipe.

Variation: Indian Style Onion Pancakes

Saute *2 onions, very finely chopped* and *2 teaspoons mustard seeds in butter.* Stir into batter, along with additional water if necessary to achieve desired consistency and proceed with recipe.

Food of the Indian *idli* type, acidified and leavened through fermentation by heterofermentative lactic acid bacteria, constitutes a very interesting group of cereal-based foods of considerable potential importance in the developing and also the developed world where it is largely unknown. Idli is closely related to sourdough bread of the Western world, but it does not depend upon wheat or rye as a source of protein to retain the carbon dioxide gas during leavening. Leavening is produced by bacterial rather than by yeast activity.

The importance of idli lies in (1) its high degree of acceptability as a food in South India, (2) its protection against food poisoning and transmission of pathogenic organisms, because of its acidity, and (3) the fact that the idli fermentation can be used in many parts of the world using various combinations of cereal grains and legumes to produce acid, leavened bread or a pancakelike product. No wheat or rye flour is needed.. . .

Idli and dosa . . . can be consume directly "out-of-hand" following steaming or the cakes may be deliciously flavored with fried mustard seeds and chopped coriander leaves. The unflavored cakes are eaten with chutney and or sambar, a thin spiced soup of dhal and vegetables. . . These foods are an important source of protein and calories in the diet and nutrition of South Indians. Idli and dosa . . . constitute the breakfast of many South Indians, regardless of economic or social status. Because they are easily digested, they are often used as food for infants and invalids. Keith H. Steinkraus ed.p131 *Handbook of Indigenous Fermented Foods*
Courtesy Marcel Dekker, Inc.

SNACKS & FINGER FOODS

SNACKS & FINGER FOODS

In an ideal world we would consume all our food at sit-down meals; nevertheless snacks have their place in today's diet, especially for growing children and for those whose metabolisms require small frequent feedings. The wise parents will keep a variety of nutritious snacks on hand, but at the same time will see to it that they do not replace proper meals.

Many of our snacks call for nuts—almonds, pecans, cashews and peanuts—either plain, in mixes, or as a basis for several cookie recipes. Nuts are an extremely nutritious food if properly prepared. Once again, the habits of traditional societies should serve as a guide. They understood instinctively that nuts are best soaked or partially sprouted before eaten. This is because nuts contain numerous enzyme inhibitors that can put a real strain on the digestive mechanism if consumed in excess. Nuts are easier to digest, and their nutrients more readily available, if they are first soaked overnight, then dried in a warm oven. This method imitates the Aztec practice of soaking pumpkin or squash seeds and then letting them dry in the sun before eating them whole, or grinding them into meal.

Our cookie recipes feature nuts, butter or coconut oil, natural sweeteners and arrowroot. These recipes offer you the opportunity to discover the merits of coconut oil. Like butter, coconut oil is rich in short and medium chain fatty acids that the body absorbs directly from the small intestine for quick energy. Research has shown that coconut oil, like butter, promotes normal brain development, is less likely to cause weight gain than polyunsaturated oils, contributes to strong bones and has anti-carcinogenic and anti-fungal effects. (For arrowroot and unrefined coconut oil, see Sources.)

We have included a recipe for pizza—the perennial favorite—made with a yoghurt crust and fresh tomato sauce. All snacks feature whole natural ingredients in contrast to the empty calories—in the form of refined sweeteners, white flour and rancid and hydrogenated vegetable oils—that make up the vast majority of commercially produced snack foods. These empty snack foods, consumed in great quantities by our youth, have resulted in a generation of teenagers imbued with the vague feeling that they have been cheated—as indeed they have.

A popular "health food" snack we must warn you about is rice cakes, made from puffed or extruded rice. Although theoretically nutritious, because made from whole grains, they are grains that have been subjected to high heat and pressure to cause them to puff. Animal tests have shown that puffed grains are quite toxic, and therefore should be avoided.

PEPITAS

Makes 4 cups

4 cups raw, hulled pumpkin seeds
1 tablespoon sea salt
1 teaspoon cayenne pepper (optional)
filtered water

This recipe imitates Aztec practices of soaking seeds in brine, then letting them dry in the hot sun. They ate pepitas whole, or ground into meal.

Dissolve salt in water and add pumpkin seeds and optional cayenne. Soak for at least 7 hours or overnight. Drain in a colander and spread on 2 stainless steel baking pans. Place in a warm oven (no more than 150 degrees) for about 12 hours or overnight, stirring occasionally, until thoroughly dry and crisp. Store in an airtight container.

Variations: Tamari Pepitas

Use *2 tablespoons tamari sauce* in place of sea salt and cayenne.

CRISPY PECANS

Makes 4 cups

4 cups pecan halves
1 teaspoon sea salt
filtered water

The buttery flavor of pecans is enhanced by soaking and slow oven drying.

Soak pecans in salt and filtered water for at least 7 hours or overnight. Drain in a colander. Spread pecans on two stainless steel baking pans and place in a warm oven (no more than 150 degrees) for 12 to 24 hours, stirring occasionally, until completely dry and crisp. Store in an airtight container. Great for school lunches!

Variation: Tamari Pecans

In place of salt, add *1/4 cup tamari sauce* to soaking water.

If you eat substantial quantities of raw pecans, walnuts, Brazil nuts, filberts or others, you have a choice of swallowing enzyme capsules with them to neutralize their enzyme inhibitors or first germinating the nuts and letting nature do the job through increased enzyme activity resulting from germination. . . In the year 1918 or thereabouts, I was imbued with the idea of trying to avoid cooked food because of the potential destructiveness of heat. . . I thought that raw meat was unsuited for the human diet and that the protein and fat of palatable raw tree nuts would take its place. . . after a period of about two months during which I consumed liberal quantities of raw tree nuts of several kinds, I began experiencing an unpleasant heavy sensation in the abdomen, and a feeling of extreme fullness, and some nausea. The symptoms were pronounced enough to force my giving up this tasty diet. Almost anyone can eat several nuts without feeling any effect. But it is common knowledge that nuts "are heavy on the stomach" if consumed in substantial quantity. The enzyme inhibitors in seeds explain the mystery, but they were not identified until 1944. Edward Howell MD *Enzymes for Health and Longevity*

HOLIDAY PECANS

Makes 4 cups

Pecans are the pride of the South. They grow on huge trees throughout the Mississippi River Valley, especially in Georgia, New Mexico and Texas. Pecan trees grow to 150 feet with trunks of 7 feet in diameter. Mature trees can produce up to 200 pounds of nuts.

Like all nuts, pecans contain sprout inhibitors that can irritate the mouth and cause digestive problems. Native Americans understood instinctively that pecans had to be treated in some way before being consumed. They ground the nuts and soaked them in water, to make a nutritious milky drink, much as European farmers made a kind of milk with walnuts.

Pecans contain about 70 percent fat, most of it monounsaturated oleic acid. This stable oil protects pecans from rancidity so that they keep better than many other kinds of nuts. Pecans contain calcium, iron, magnesium, phosphorus, potassium and selenium. They are an exceptionally rich source of manganese. Like all nuts from large trees whose roots extend far down into the earth, pecans are good sources of trace minerals. They contain B-complex vitamins, carotenoids and vitamin C in small amounts.

Pecans will last about 4 months at room temperature. To keep them longer, store in refrigerator. SWF

4 cups crispy pecan halves
3 egg whites
pinch sea salt
1/2 cup maple syrup
1 tablespoon vanilla extract

Beat egg whites with salt in a clean bowl until stiff. Slowly beat in maple syrup and vanilla. Fold in pecans until well coated. Spread on two buttered stainless steel baking pans and place in a warm oven (no more than 150 degrees) for several hours until the egg white coating hardens. Store in an air tight container in the refrigerator.

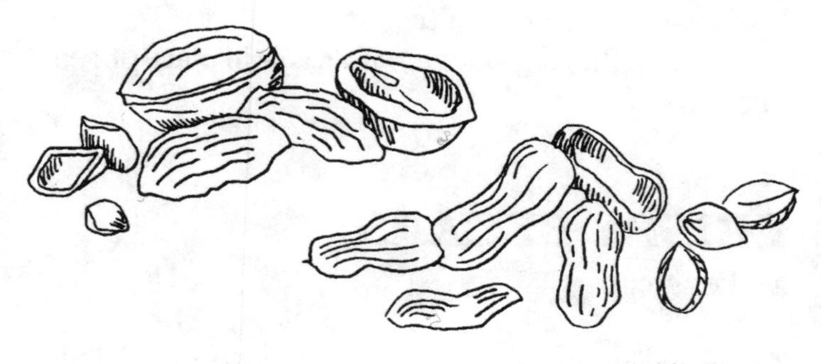

CRISPY PEANUTS

4 cups "blanched" raw peanuts
1 tablespoon sea salt
filtered water

Soak peanuts in salt and filtered water for at least 7 hours or overnight. Drain in a colander. Spread on two stainless steel baking pans and place in a warm oven (no more than 150 degrees) for 12 to 24 hours, stirring occasionally, until completely dry and crisp. Store in an airtight container.

CRISPY ALMONDS

4 cups "blanched" almonds
2 teaspoons sea salt
filtered water

Blanched or skinless almonds will still sprout, an indication that the "blanching" process has not destroyed the enzymes. (The skins are probably removed by a machine process.) Many people find that almond skins are irritating to the mouth, even when they have been soaked or sprouted. There is still plenty of goodness in skinless almonds. We use crispy almonds in numerous dessert recipes.

Soak almonds in salt and filtered water for at least 7 hours or overnight. Drain in a colander. Spread on two stainless steel baking pans and place in a warm oven (no more than 150 degrees) for 12 to 24 hours, stirring occasionally, until completely dry and crisp. Store in an airtight container.

CRISPY CASHEWS

4 cups "raw" cashews
1 tablespoon sea salt
filtered water

Some care must be taken in preparing cashews. They will develop a disagreeable taste if allowed to soak too long or dry out too slowly, perhaps because they come to us not raw, but having already undergone two separate heatings. You may dry them in a 200 to 250 degree oven—the enzymes have already been destroyed during processing.

Soak cashews in salt and filtered water for 6 hours (no longer). Drain in a colander. Spread on two stainless steel baking pans and place in a warm oven (about 200 degrees) for 12 to 24 hours, stirring occasionally, until completely dry and crisp. Store in an airtight container. Great for school lunches!

The cashew nut comes from a pear-shaped fruit called a cashew apple. Curiously, the nut grows outside of the apple and hangs down so that it can be easily harvested. A native of Brazil, where natives make the apples into preserves or liqueur, the cashew also grows in India. About 90% of our domestic supply of cashews comes from India.

Cashews are rich in protein as well as magnesium, phosphorus and potassium. They contain less fat that most other nuts. Cashews contain a toxic oil called cardol between the inner and outer shell. This is released by cracking the nuts and roasting them at 350 degrees. They are then cracked and roasted once again. These are then marketed as "raw" cashews. We recommend that you soak "raw" cashews and then lightly toast them to neutralize any phytates and to allow exogenous enzymes to begin the digestive process.

Always buy whole cashew pieces as they are less likely to be stale. SWF

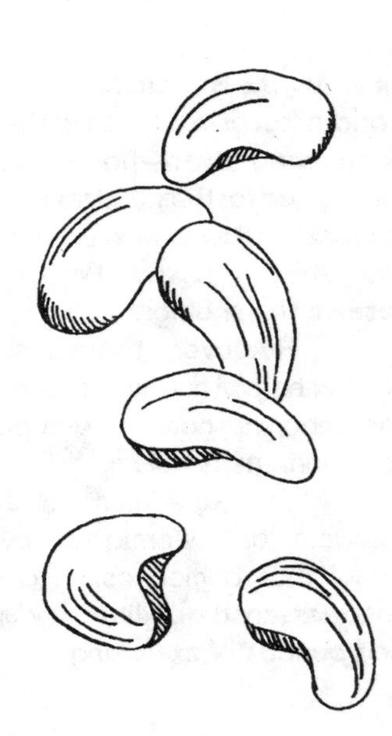

Corn syrup, enriched flour (niacin, iron, thiamine mononitrate, riboflavin, sugar, water, partially hydrogenated vegetable and/or animal shortening (contains one or more of: canola oil, corn oil, cottonseed oil, soybean oil, beef fat), eggs, skim milk, contains 2% or less of: whey, modified food starch, salt, leavening (baking soda, monocalcium phosphate, sodium acid pyrophosphate), mono- and di-glycerides, lecithin, sodium stearoyl lactylate, and artificial flavors, artificial colors (red 40 and yellow 5), sorbic acid (to retard spoilage).

See Appendix B for Answer

TAMARI NUT MIXTURE

Makes 3 cups

1 cup crispy almonds
1 cup crispy pecans
1 cup crispy cashews
2 eggs, lightly beaten
3 tablespoons tamari sauce

Mix tamari sauce with eggs and stir in nuts until well coated. Spread on a buttered stainless steel baking pan. Bake at 150 degrees, stirring occasionally, until completely dry and crisp. Store in an airtight container in the refrigerator.

TRAIL MIX

Makes 5-6 cups

1 cup crispy pecans
1 cup crispy cashews
1 cup raisins
1 cup unsulphured dried apricots, cut into pieces
1 cup dried sweetened coconut meat (page 144)
1 cup carob chips (optional)

Mix all ingredients together. Store in an airtight container.

CAROB CHIPS

Makes 1 cup

3/4 cup carob powder
1/4 cup sucanat
1 cup coconut oil
1 tablespoon vanilla

Place all ingredients in a glass container and set in simmering water until melted. Mix together well. Spread mixture on a piece of buttered parchment paper (see Sources) and allow to cool in refrigerator. When hardened, remove parchment paper. Place in food processor and pulse a time or two. Store chips in an airtight container in the refrigerator.

For years, the B vitamins, vitamin E and octocosonal—as well as desiccated liver—have been spotlighted for their contributions to greater endurance in exercises and athletic games. And they deserve the spotlight.

However, there's still another helpful nutrient for endurance that, until now, has escaped attention: magnesium.

Two experiments at the University of California at Davis reveal that a magnesium deficiency lessens the ability to endure long periods of exercising

WHOLEGRAIN CRACKERS

2 1/2 cups freshly ground whole wheat or spelt flour, or a mixture
1 cup plain yoghurt
1 teaspoon sea salt
1 1/2 teaspoon baking powder
2 tablespoons sesame seeds
4 tablespoons butter

Mix flour with yoghurt and let stand at least 7 hours or overnight. Melt butter in a small pan and cook sesame seeds in butter until golden. Place soaked flours with salt and baking powder in food processor and process until well blended. Add sesame seeds with butter and pulse once or twice to blend. Roll out thinly on a pastry cloth (use unbleached white flour to keep from sticking) and cut into desired shape with a cookie cutter or glass. Place on a greased cookie sheet and let dry in a 150 degree oven (or a dehydrator) for several hours or overnight.

PITA CHIPS

Makes 48

6 whole wheat pita breads
1 stick butter, melted
4 tablespoons extra virgin olive oil
grated rind of 1 lemon (optional)
1 mashed garlic clove (optional)

Cut pita breads across center into quarters. Open up and place pieces, inside part up, on cookie sheets. Mix optional garlic and lemon rind with melted butter and olive oil and brush on pita pieces. Place under broiler for a few minutes until lightly browned, or bake in a slow oven (250 degrees) for several hours until crisp.

Foods richest in this mineral are blackstrap molasses, sunflower seeds, wheat germ, almonds, soybeans, Brazil nuts, pistachios, soy lecithin, hazelnuts, pecans, oats and walnuts, brown rice, chard, spinach, barley, salmon, corn, avocados and bananas.

Roughly 50 percent of magnesium in foods is absorbed.

It is well to remember that magnesium and calcium are removed from soft water, a good reason to drink bottled water with a high mineral content. James F Scheer *Health Freedom News*

Know Your Ingredients

Name This Product #33

Enriched wheat flour (contains niacin, reduced iron, thiamine mononitrate [vitamin B1], riboflavin [vitamin B2]), whole wheat, bleached wheat flour, vegetable shortening (partially hydrogenated soybean oil), rice, rolled oats, brown sugar, yellow corn meal, sugar, oat bran, barley flakes, salt, high fructose corn syrup, leavening (baking soda, yeast, calcium phosphate), modified cornstarch, malted barely flour, whey, onion powder, soy lecithin (emulsifier).

See Appendix B for Answer

Corn, Vegetable Oil (Contains one or more of the following: Corn Oil, Canola Oil, Sunflower Oil, Cottonseed Oil, Partially Hydrogenated Canola Oil, Partially Hydrogenated Sunflower Oil, and/or Partially Hydrogenated Soybean Oil) and Salt

See Appendix B for Answer

SOFT TORTILLAS

sprouted whole wheat tortillas (Alvarado brand)
melted butter

Heat a heavy, well-seasoned skillet over a medium flame. Place one tortilla on skillet for about one minute. Turn for another few seconds. Remove to a platter and brush with melted butter. Repeat with other tortillas. Keep warm in oven. May be eaten with fajitas (page 409), filled with various fillings or simply rolled up with a little grated raw cheese.

BAKED TORTILLAS

sprouted whole wheat tortillas (Alvarado brand)
butter and extra virgin olive oil

Melt butter with oil. Brush tortillas with this mixture, arrange on cookie sheets and place in a 250 degree oven. Bake several hours until crisp. May be broken into "chips".

A diet high in unsaturated fatty acids, especially the polyunsaturated ones, can destroy the body's supply of vitamin E and cause muscular lesions, brain lesions, and degeneration of blood vessels. Care must be taken not to include a large amount of polyunsaturated oil in the diet without a corresponding increase in the intake of vitamin E. Linus Pauling PhD, p155 *How to Live Longer and Feel Better*

FRIED TORTILLAS

sprouted whole wheat tortillas (Alvarado brand)
extra virgin olive oil

Using a heavy cast iron skillet, fry tortillas one at a time on both sides until crisp. Drain on paper towels and keep warm in oven.

ROUND CROUTONS

1/2 loaf commercial sour dough whole grain baguette
3/4 stick melted butter

Slice loaf at 1/4 inch intervals and brush with butter. Bake at 250 degrees for about 1 hour or until they turn crisp.

Recent, preliminary evidence . . . suggests that partially rancid fats, rather than animal fat per se, may be one of the real villains responsible for atherosclerosis. Sources of stale fats include products such as bread, crackers, pastries and commercial cereals made from stored processed flour. Granville Knight *Introduction to Nutrition and Physical Degeneration*

TRIANGLE CROUTONS

6 slices sprouted or sourdough whole grain sandwich bread
3/4 stick melted butter

Trim crusts off bread (save for bread crumbs) and cut slices in half on diagonal to form two triangles. Brush with melted butter and bake at 250 degrees for about 1 hour until crisp.

SALAD CROUTONS

3 slices sprouted or sourdough whole grain sandwich bread
3/4 stick melted butter or mixture of melted butter and extra virgin olive oil
1 clove garlic, mashed (optional)
1 teaspoon fine herbs (optional)

Trim crusts off bread. Mix optional garlic and herbs with melted butter. Brush on both sides of bread. Bake at 250 degrees for about 1 hour, turning once, until toasts are crisp. Allow to cool slightly and cut into small cubes.

Know Your Ingredients

Name This Product # 35

Enriched corn meal, (corn meal, ferrous sulfate, niacin, thiamine, mononitrate and riboflavin), vegetable oil (Contains one or more of the following: canola, corn, cottonseed, or partially hydrogenated [canola, cottonseed, soybean or sunflower] oil), whey, cheddar cheese (milk, cheese culture, salt, enzymes and calcium chloride), salt, sour cream, artificial flavor, monosodium glutamate, lactic acid, artificial colors (yellow #6, turmeric and annatto), and citric acid. No preservatives.

See Appendix B for Answer

POPCORN

Makes 8 cups

1/4 cup popcorn
2 tablespoons extra virgin olive oil
sea salt
1/4-1/2 cup melted butter or coconut oil, or a mixture

Popcorn is a nutritious snack enjoyed by young and old; but remember that popcorn is prepared without the all important soaking or fermenting process, so don't overdo.

Place oil and corn in a large, heavy skillet. Cover tightly and cook over a medium flame, shaking constantly until popping starts. Lower heat slightly and cook, shaking, until popping dies away. Transfer to a large bowl. Dribble on melted butter and coconut oil and shake on sea salt. Mix well and serve.

Note: A home popper is a good investment that makes popcorn-making fun and easy for children.

Variation: Cheese Popcorn

Add *1/4-1/2 cup finely powdered Parmesan cheese* to melted butter and oil and proceed with recipe.

Variation: Sweet Popcorn

Add *1/2 cup maple syrup* to melted butter and oil and proceed with recipe. Omit salt.

There are still those diehards who insist that a candy bar or a couple teaspoons of sugar in the tea will charge you up with more energy than anything else.

Well, 'tain't so!

That's the word from Robert E. Thayer, Ph.D., psychologist at California State University, Long Beach, who ought to know, because he conducted an experiment, comparing energy generated from a candy bar fix with ten minutes of brisk walking.

His finding? That rushing to the vending machine on a ten-minute break gives you a greater boost for sagging energy than a chocolate bar.

Thayer's test involving 18 students over 12 days, compared energy levels from the exercise and from the candy bar without the exercise. Invariably the students felt greater energy at intervals of 20 minutes, one hour and two hours from the exercise than from the candy.

The energy boost from the candy bar lasted little more than 20 minutes and dropped off fast within two hours. Tension and stress usually mounted after the candy and decreased after the 10 minute walk.

So the next time you're tempted to reach for a sweet to beat fatigue, don't. Instead, go take a hike! James F. Scheer *Health Freedom News*

CELERY WITH PEANUT BUTTER

several large stalks celery
1/2 cup freshly ground peanut butter
1/4 cup dried sweetened coconut (page 144), optional

Wash celery well and cut into 3-inch lengths. Fill hollow with peanut butter. Sprinkle with optional coconut.

Not eating enough fruit and nuts high in the trace mineral boron can make your brain sluggish, according to research at the US Department of Agriculture. In tests James G. Penland, Ph.D. put fifteen people over age forty-five alternately on a low-boron and a high-boron diet for about four months. In both cases he monitored the electrical activity of the brains. When they ate scant boron, their brain waves produced more beta and delta waves, signs of drowsiness and reduced mental activity. On high-boron diets their brain waves picked up.

"It's an exciting finding," he says, "because it confirms that good diet enhances brain functioning." Foods high in boron are nuts, legumes, leafy vegetables like broccoli, and fruits, especially apples, pears, peaches and grapes. Jean Carper *The Food Pharmacy Guide to Good Eating*

APPLE SLICES

Serves 4

2 apples, peeled, cored and cut into slices
juice of 1 orange

Dip each slice of apple in the orange juice and arrange on a serving plate. The orange juice keeps the apple from turning brown, and marries well with the flavor of apple.

Bananas have some mysterious substances that prevent ulcers in animals. A recent study by researchers at the University of New England in Australia noted that rats fed bananas and then fed high amounts of acid to induce ulcers had very little stomach damage. The bananas prevented 75 percent of the expected ulcers. Researchers believe the bananas somehow helped create a barrier between the stomach lining and the acid.

In other studies Indian physicians have successfully treated ulcers with powder made of unripe plantains, a large member of the banana family. Jean Carper *The Food Pharmacy Guide to Good Eating*

CAROB BANANA DELIGHTS

Serves 8

4 bananas
toothpicks
1 cup warm carob sauce (page 518)
1/2 cup finely chopped crispy pecans (page 485)

Slice bananas and stick a toothpick in each. Line a cookie sheet with waxed paper, place slices on it and freeze. Remove from freezer. Holding toothpick, dip each slice in carob sauce and then into the nuts. Place again on waxed paper, cover and freeze.

PIZZA

Makes 2 10-inch pizzas

1 recipe yoghurt dough (page 459)
2 cups chunky tomato sauce (page 140)
2 teaspoons dried Italian herbs
3 cups grated mozzarella cheese

Roll out yoghurt dough and line two 10-inch French style tart pans. Partially bake at 350 degrees for 20-30 minutes. Meanwhile, process tomato sauce in food processor until smooth. Stir in Italian herbs. Spread tomato sauce thinly on pizzas and top with grated cheese. Bake at 350 degrees for about 1/2 hour until crust fully cooks and cheese is melted.

Variations:

Add any of the following toppings to basic pizza:

sliced green peppers
sliced onion
anchovy pieces
crumbled or sliced cooked turkey or lamb sausage
blanched broccoli pieces
fresh tomato slices
sauteed mushrooms

It is recognized that sugar present in chocolate milk, juice, soda, kool-aid, etc. as well as in solid forms such as candies and cakes, can all interact with gastrointestinal yeasts to form fermentation products.

These fermentation products include alcohol such as ethanol, as well as mold products. A combination of direct drug effect, as well as chemical intolerance in hypersensitization to mold products have long been associated with mood changes including what appears to be a mild drunken state, hyperactivity, dyslexia and chemical imbalances that may refer to depression, hyperactivity, mania, etc. Gaynelle D'Arco *Health Freedom News*

The second reason I dislike microwave ovens is the more serious situation. What about the quality of the food that comes out of the oven and is immediately consumed—free radicals and all. With the depressed immune system of the average affluent American, the last thing we need is another increase in our free radicals. It is well documented that microwaves are powerful enough to rupture cell walls of the food matrix and this is undoubtedly why protein molecules are altered from microwave cooking. Warren Clough *PPNF Journal*

PIZZA TOASTS

Makes 8

8 slices whole grain sour dough bread
extra virgin olive oil
4 ripe tomatoes
1 teaspoon Italian seasonings
1/2 cup grated mozzarella cheese

Slice tomatoes about 1/2 inch thick. Spread on paper towels placed on cookie sheets. Bake at 200 degrees for several hours until most moisture is evaporated or absorbed. Meanwhile brush bread slices with olive oil, spread on a cookie sheet and bake at 200 for an hour or so until just barely crisp. Arrange tomato slices on bread, sprinkle with seasonings and grated cheese and place under broiler for a minute until cheese just begins to melt.

POTATO SKINS

Serves 4

4 large baking potatoes
melted butter
1 cup grated raw cheddar or Monterey jack cheese
1 bunch green onions, finely chopped, for garnish
duck cracklings (page 273) for garnish
chismole (page 168) for garnish
guacamole (page 156) for garnish
piima cream or creme fraiche for garnish

Bake potatoes according to master recipe (page 374) until soft. Split lengthwise and scoop out flesh. (Use flesh for potato celery root puree, page 379, parsnip puree, page 371 or turnip puree, page 386.) Brush skins with butter, inside and out and bake at 350 degrees for about 1/2 hour or until skins become crisp. Serve with cheese and garnishes.

Patricia Hardman, Ph.D., Director of Woodland Hall Academy, a school for children with hyperactivity and learning disabilities in Maitland, Florida, says, "We can change a child's behavior dramatically by lowering his or her intake of sugar. If a child comes to school extremely depressed or complains that nothing is going right, or if he flies off the handle and can't be controlled, we ask him what he's been eating. It's almost always the case that the night before he had ice cream or soda or some other food with a lot of sugar."

"We had one child who was tested for his I.Q. and scored 140. Three days later he was tested and scored 100! It turned out that grandma had come for a visit and, that morning, had made the child pancakes for breakfast. Of course, they were smothered in store-bought sugary syrup. We waited another three days without sugar and tested him again. Sure enough, he scored 140. There's no doubt about it. Sugar makes children poor learners. At Woodland Hall, sugar is eliminated from the diet of every child." Gaynelle D'Arco *Health Freedom News*

SUNFLOWER SEED BROWNIES

Makes about 18

4 cups freshly ground hulled sunflower seeds
1/2 cup carob powder
1/2 cup sucanat
1/2 to 1 cup chopped crispy pecans
1 tablespoon vanilla
3/4 cup water

This unusual brownie recipe contains no flour, but is based on ground sunflower seed. It is baked very slowly in the oven so that all the enzymes and anti-oxidants are preserved. The long period of baking, in which the sunflower meal is warm and moist, also neutralizes all enzyme inhibitors. Use your grain mill, fitted with the stainless steel grinder, to make the sunflower meal.

Mix sunflower meal with carob powder, sucanat and nuts. Mix vanilla with water. Pour liquid into sunflower seed mixture and blend well. Dough should be very thick. Line a 9-by-13 pyrex pan with parchment paper (see Sources) and pat dough to a thickness of 1/2 inch. Bake at 150 degrees for about 12 hours, turn and bake another 12 hours. Allow to cool and cut into squares. Store in an airtight container in the refrigerator. Should be eaten as soon as possible after preparation.

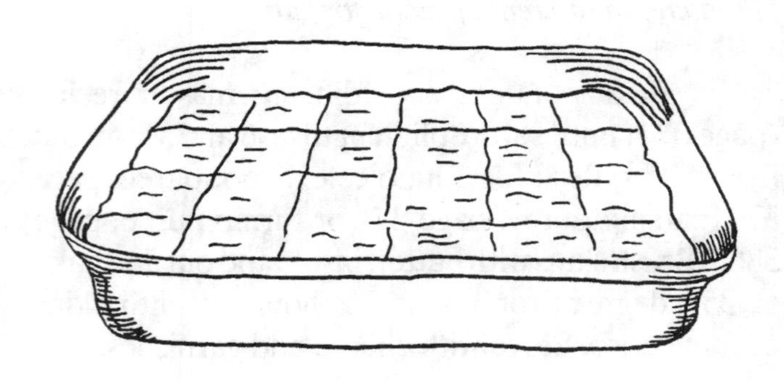

Native to North America, the sunflower was first grown and used by American Indians. It was introduced to Europe in the 1500's where cultivation became widespread, principally for sunflower oil. Sunflower seeds are loaded with nutrients, containing calcium, iron, magnesium, phosphorus and potassium. They are good sources of B vitamins and carotenoids. They contain 27 percent protein, but it is an incomplete protein so sunflower seeds and their meal should be eaten with grains, legumes or dairy products. They contain about 50 percent fat, most of which is linolenic acid, so they should not be consumed in excess. For reasons unknown, sunflower oil is more stable than other high omega-6 oils. SWF

Know Your Ingredients

Name This Product #36

Whole grain oats and wheat, brown sugar, raisins, corn syrup, rice, dried coconut, almonds, glycerin, partially hydrogenated cottonseed and/or soybean oil, modified corn starch, salt, cinnamon, nonfat dry milk, polyglycerol esters, malt flavoring. Vitamins and Minerals: Vitamin E (alpha tocopherol acetate), niacinamide, zinc (oxide), iron, vitamin B6 (pyridoxine hydrochloride), vitamin B2 (riboflavin) vitamin A (palmitate; protected with BHT), vitamin B1, (thiamin hydrochloride), folic acid, and vitamin D

See Appendix B for Answer

APRICOT TOASTS

Makes 4

4 thick slices sour dough whole grain bread
softened butter
6 apricots
12 teaspoons sucanat

Plunge apricots about 10 seconds in boiling water, remove and peel. Cut in half and remove stones. Generously butter the bread and place 3 apricot halves, cavity side up, on each slice and press in. Sprinkle each half with 1 teaspoon sucanat. Bake about 40 minutes at 300 degrees.

The current practice, encouraged by doctors and the American Heart Association, of increasing the consumption of vegetable oils in the diet is a nutritional disaster. Unsaturated fatty acids are needed only in small amounts in the diet. They are in adequate supply in vegetables, nuts and meat. It would be difficult, even in the average American diet, not to get adequate amounts of unsaturated fats.

Unsaturated fats found in vegetable oils increase the production of "free radicals," which are by-products of cellular chemistry. They are like tiny hand grenades that devastate body tissues, leading to degeneration and early aging. These little free radical killers lead to hardening of the arteries and cancer.

In fact, the major cause of aging is probably "free radical" formation. William Campbell Douglass MD *The Milk of Human Kindness*

CAROB CHEWS

Makes 2 dozen

1 cup crispy almonds (page 487)
1 cup crispy cashews (page 487)
1/2 cup carob powder
1/2 cup raw honey
1 tablespoon vanilla
1 teaspoon sea salt
1 cup dried sweetened coconut meat (page 144)
or commercial unsweetened coconut meat

Place almonds and cashews in food processor and pulse until finely chopped but not pulverized. Meanwhile place honey, carob powder, vanilla and salt in a glass container set in simmering water until melted. Blend well. Add honey mixture and coconut to nuts in food processor and pulse a few times more. Line a large loaf pan with parchment paper and spread mixture about 1/2 inch thick. Wrap up in parchment paper and refrigerate several hours. Cut into small squares and store in an air tight container in the refrigerator.

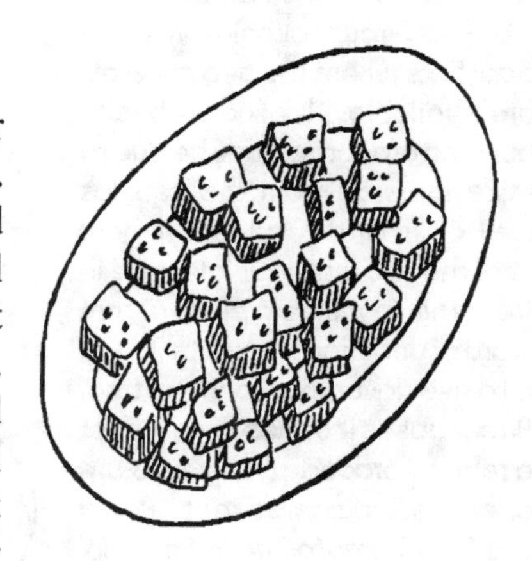

ALMOND COOKIES

Makes 18

1 1/2 cups crispy almonds (page 487)
1 stick softened butter or 1/2 cup coconut oil
1 cup arrowroot
1/2 cup sucanat
1/2 teaspoon sea salt
1 teaspoon vanilla extract
1 teaspoon almond extract
18 crispy almonds (page 487)

Place almonds in food processor and process to a fine meal. Add remaining ingredients except 18 almonds and process until well blended. Form dough into walnut-sized balls and place on an oiled cookie sheet. Press an almond into each. Bake at 300 degrees for about 20 minutes. After 5 minutes in the oven, press cookies down lightly with a fork. Let cool completely before removing to an air tight container. Store in refrigerator.

Arrowroot flour, the only starch with a calcium ash, is a nutritious food, obtained from the fleshy root stock of a tropical American plant. It is an easily digested food well fitted for infants and the convalescent.

It resembles cornstarch in being white, fine and powdery. When heated in water in certain portions, it thickens to form a jelly, an excellent thickening agent. It is also considered more desirable for gravies, sauces and pastries than some of the more common starches and flours. It is used primarily for food in dietetic use, where it enjoys a reputation for smoothness and palatability.

Arrowroot was once widely used in baby formulas as a superior carbohydrate, experience having shown it agreed with babies better than any other starch or sugar. We now find the reason. It is the only starch product with a calcium ash. In this regard, the calcium chloride, in the form of calcium found in arrowroot starch, is very important for the maintenance of proper acid and alkali balances in the human body.

Arrowroot only thrives on tidal flats where the sea minerals are available. Its known health building properties may be due to trace minerals from the sea, as well as from the calcium it gets from the sea water. If it is used in ice cream formulas in place of corn starch, arrowroot imparts a vanilla like flavor, a smooth texture. Arrowroot as it comes to you is not a refined product, it is simply the dried and powdered root. Royal Lee DDS *Journal of the Royal Academy of Research Biochemists*

RASPBERRY JAM COOKIES

Makes 16

1 cup crispy almonds (page 487)
1 stick softened butter or 1/2 cup coconut oil
1 cup arrowroot
1/2 cup sucanat
1/2 teaspoon sea salt
1 tablespoon vanilla
1/4 cup fruit juice or honey sweetened raspberry jam

Place almonds in food processor and process to a fine meal. Add remaining ingredients except jam and process until well blended. Form dough into walnut-sized balls and place on an oiled cookie sheet. Press each down slightly, make an indentation and fill with raspberry jam. Bake at 300 degrees for about 20 minutes. Let cool completely before removing to an air tight container. Store in refrigerator.

PEANUT COOKIES

Makes 16

1 1/2 cups crispy peanuts (page 486)
1 stick butter, softened, or 1/2 cup coconut oil
1 cup arrowroot
1/2 teaspoon sea salt
1/2 cup sucanat
1-2 teaspoons vanilla

Place all ingredients in food processor and blend well. Form into balls and place on buttered cookie sheet. Bake at 300 degrees for about 20 minutes. After 5 minutes in the oven, press cookies down lightly with a fork. Let cool completely before removing to an air tight container. Store in refrigerator.

Variation: Peanut Coconut Cookies

Add *1/2 cup dried sweetened coconut meat (page 144)* or *1/2 cup dried unsweetened commercial coconut* to dough along with an additional *1 tablespoon butter or coconut oil.*

Almonds, though high in fat, still may help fight heart disease, according to Dr. Gene A. Spiller, a noted researcher and director of the Health Research and Studies Center in California.

In an experiment Dr. Spiller asked a group of men and women with moderately high cholesterol (average around 240) to eat three-and-a half ounces of almonds a day for three to nine weeks. Other groups in the study ate the same amount of fat from cheese or olive oil. Everybody ate equal amount of grains, vegetables and fruits.

Surprise! The almond-eaters' cholesterol dropped from 10 to 15 percent compared with the cheese eaters' cholesterol. Olive oil also reduced cholesterol, but almonds were slightly better.

Dr. Spiller explains it this way: most of the fat in almonds is the same type as that in olive oil—monounsaturated, which is linked to healthier blood and less heart disease. . . . Other nuts exceptionally high in monounsaturated fat are filberts (hazelnuts) and pistachios. Jean Carper *The Food Pharmacy Guide to Good Eating*

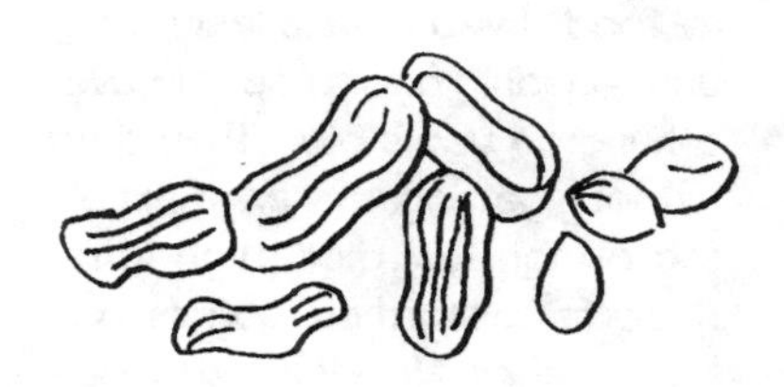

PECAN COOKIES

Makes 18

1 1/2 cups pecan crispy pecans (page 485)
3/4 stick butter, softened, or 3/8 cup coconut oil
1/2 cup sucanat
1 cup arrowroot
1 teaspoon vanilla
1/2 teaspoon sea salt
18 crispy pecan halves (page 485)

Place pecans in food processor and process until finely ground. Add remaining ingredients (except pecan halves) and process several minutes until smooth. Form into walnut-sized balls and place on a well-oiled cookie sheet. Press a pecan half in each. Bake at 300 degrees for about 20 minutes. Let cool completely before removing to an air tight container. Store in refrigerator.

In 1927, it was observed that diet lacking unsaturated fats prevented the development of spontaneous tumors. Many subsequent investigators have observed that the unsaturated fats are essential for the development of tumors. . . Saturated fats—coconut oil and butter, for example—do not promote tumor growth. . . When pregnant mice were fed either coconut oil or unsaturated seed oil, the mice that got coconut oil had babies with normal brains and intelligence, but the mice exposed to the unsaturated oil had smaller brains and had inferior intelligence. . . . For many years studies have been demonstrating that dietary coconut oil causes decreased fat synthesis and storage, when compared with diets containing unsaturated fats. . . the absence of osteoporosis in some tropical populations might relate to their consumption of coconut oil and other saturated tropical oils. Ray Peat PhD *Health Freedom News*

GINGER SNAPS

Makes 18

1 1/2 cups crispy almonds (page 487)
1 stick butter, softened, or 1/2 cup coconut oil
1 cup arrowroot
1/2 cup sucanat
1 tablespoon water
1 1/2 teaspoons ground ginger
1 teaspoon cinnamon
1/4 teaspoon nutmeg
1/4 teaspoon ground cloves
1/2 teaspoon sea salt

Place almonds in food processor and process until finely ground. Add remaining ingredients and blend well. Form into balls and place on a well-oiled cookie sheet. Bake at 300 degrees for about 20 minutes. After 5 minutes in the oven, press cookies down lightly with a fork. Let cool completely before removing to an air tight container for storage. Store in refrigerator.

Dr. Clive McCay. . . found in his long-time experiments at Cornell University that "animals fed very modest amounts of natural foods lived in excellent health until equal in age to people over a hundred years old. They died without getting cancer. Animals fed a high fuel diet [high in refined fats, starches, sugars and highly refined foods] lived a normal or shortened span of life and had the usual diseases of old age such as cancer." Dean Conrad *The Great American Tragedy*

CASHEW ORANGE COOKIES

Makes 18

1 1/2 cups crispy cashews (page 487)
1 stick butter, softened, or 1/2 cup coconut oil
1 cup arrowroot
1/2 cup sucanat
1/2 teaspoon sea salt
grated rind of 1 orange
1/2 teaspoon orange extract
1/2 teaspoon vanilla

Place cashews in food processor and process until finely ground. Add remaining ingredients and blend well. Form into balls and place on a buttered cookie sheet. Bake at 300 degrees for about 20 minutes. After 5 minutes in the oven, press cookies down lightly with a fork. Let cool completely before removing to an air tight container for storage. Store in refrigerator.

Suspected as a migraine causative for decades, chocolate has been cleared on the basis of insufficient evidence Now things may be changing, thanks to new findings from a study by biochemist Vivette Glover. . . Twenty heavy migraine sufferers volunteered for the study—12 eating real chocolate and eight eating a carob placebo made to taste identical to the chocolate.

Twenty-four hours after volunteers ate their test samples, five chocolate eaters experienced pounding migraines, while the placebo eaters showed no symptoms. Asked what chemical in chocolate brought on the migraines, Glover said that they had not as yet been isolated. Yet two of the strongest suspects are catechin, also present in red wine, and theobromine, a biochemical cousin to caffeine in coffee. James F. Scheer *Health Freedom News*

CAROB COOKIES

Makes 18

1 1/2 cups crispy almonds (page 487)
1 1/4 stick butter, softened, or 5/8 cup coconut oil
1 cup arrowroot
1/2 cup sucanat
1/2 teaspoon sea salt
1/2 cup carob powder
1 tablespoon vanilla

Place almonds in food processor and process until finely ground. Add remaining ingredients and blend well. Form into balls and place on buttered cookie sheet. Bake at 300 degrees for about 20 minutes. After 5 minutes in the oven, press cookies down lightly with a fork. Let cool completely before removing to an air tight container. Store in refrigerator.

Know Your Ingredients

Name This Product #37

Sugar, enriched flour (contains niacin, reduced iron, thiamine mononitrate {vitamin B1}, riboflavin {vitamin B2}), vegetable shortening (partially hydrogenated soybean oil), cocoa, (processed with alkali), high fructose corn syrup, corn flour, baking soda, chocolate, whey, soy lecithin (emulsifier), and vanillin, an artificial flavor.

See Appendix B for Answer

Know Your Ingredients

Name This Product #38

Unbleached wheat flour, partially hydrogenated vegetable shortening (soybean and cottonseed oils), brown sugar, invert syrup, cranberries, raisins, honey, sugar, egg whites, leavening (ammonium bicarbonate, baking soda, cream of tartar), soy lecithin, vanilla extract, salt and orange oil.

See Appendix B for Answer

It can be seen from a simple inspection [of the statistics] that cholesterol levels [are] apparently more closely related to sugar consumption than to fat consumption. For instance, in can be seen that two countries with the highest fat consumption, Spain and Ethiopia, had two of the lowest national blood cholesterol levels. However, these two countries with high fat consumption levels both had very low sugar consumption levels. On the other hand, two countries, Chile and Venezuela, with high sugar consumption levels, but with relatively low national fat consumption levels, had two of the highest national blood cholesterol levels. Chris Mudd *Cholesterol and Your Health*

MACAROONS

Makes 2 dozen

4 egg whites
pinch salt
2 tablespoons arrowroot
1/2 cup maple syrup
1 tablespoon vanilla
2 cups dried unsweetened coconut meat, finely cut

Line a baking sheet with buttered parchment paper (see Sources). Beat eggwhites with salt in a clean bowl until they form stiff peaks. Beat in the arrowroot and slowly beat in syrup and vanilla. Fold in coconut. Drop by spoonfuls on parchment paper. Bake at 300 degrees for about 1/2 hour or until lightly browned. Reduce oven to 200 degrees and bake another hour or so until macaroons are completely dry and crisp. Let cool completely before removing from parchment paper. Store in an air tight container.

DESSERTS

DESSERTS

Sugary sweets are the bane of the civilized world, wreaking havoc with the health of young and old. Commercial varieties contain not only refined sweeteners—usually sugar or corn syrup—but also refined flour along with highly processed and hydrogenated oils. And most contain little in the way of whole foods to compensate for these empty calories.

Yet it is perfectly possible to satisfy our inborn taste for sweet things with desserts that are nutritious. We offer here a selection of recipes featuring eggs, butter, cream, fruit, nuts and whole grains that have been soaked or fermented, along with moderate amounts of natural sweeteners. Natural sweeteners contain high amounts of minerals and other nutrients. Acceptable processed natural sweeteners are those in which the nutrients have been concentrated through boiling or dehydration, rather than stripped away as in white and brown table sugar, corn syrup or fructose.

Individual reactions to sweeteners, even and especially natural sweeteners, vary widely. Reseacher William H. Philpott found that many individuals experience a rapid rise in blood sugar when they consume one sweetener, but not another. He cites the example of a patient whose blood sugar skyrocketed when she ate any corn product; but who could eat ordinary white sugar with no rise in blood sugar levels. (This does not mean that white sugar was good for her.) It is wise to test your pulse before and after eating various sweeteners to see if any provoke a reaction. Some physicians have found that fructose in corn syrup provokes more consistently severe reactions than sucrose in table sugar.

With sugar so cheap and plentiful, we have lost sight of the fact that desserts are something that you should "deserve", and are not suitable for everyday fare. Even naturally sweetened desserts should be eaten only occasionally. We recommend you limit your dessert making to holidays and special occasion, and perhaps one or two evening meals per week. A good idea is to make dessert on nights when you are serving fish or liver or some dish your children might be reluctant to eat, and offer dessert as the prize for clean plates.

Most authorities recommend that sweets be eaten after a meal and never on an empty stomach when the sudden infusion of sweetness can send the blood sugar racing upwards; however, a minority opinion asserts that sweet things, especially those containing milk products like ice cream, should only be eaten between meals, so that they have less time to ferment in the stomach. The best advice we can give in the face of these conflicting opinions is to limit your intake of sweets and never eat anything that is too highly sweetened.

Avoiding sugar and keeping it away from your children is one of the most difficult things that parents are called upon to do in this life. It is a challenge that requires discipline, planning, creative alternatives and cunning strategy. The following tips may help you in the never-ending battle:

- Don't keep sweets around the house, even if you yourself have the willpower to resist temptation. Children will find their way to candies, cookies and other sweet snacks if they are available.

- Never shop when you are hungry.

- If you crave sweets after meals, try a handful of crispy pecans or cashews (pages 485 and 487), both of which have a sweet taste. Author Nancy Appleton suggests brushing your teeth immediately after meals as the sweetness of toothpaste may be just enough to conquer cravings. L. Glutamine, an amino acid available in capsule form, often helps dispel cravings for sweets (and alcohol too!) A lacto-fermented beverage taken with meals also helps eliminate post-prandial cravings.

- Don't forget to enlist the power of prayer in your battle against the sweet tooth.

- Make your children's school lunches. Unless their school policy is very enlightened, their school lunches will be loaded with sweet things.

- Never send a child to a birthday party or a sleep-over on an empty stomach; but fortify him beforehand with a large and nutritious sandwich or snack.

- Be resigned to that fact that you cannot keep sugar away from your children entirely. Don't make a fuss when they eat sweets and junk foods occasionally with friends or you might push them to eat sugar out of rebelliousness. You can protect them from occasional use of sugar by a diet that is consistently nutritious. When they are old enough, be sure to explain to them just why sugar is so bad for them. Remember that your example must serve as a guide to his adult eating habits.

GUIDE TO NATURAL SWEETENERS

Raw Honey: Honey that has not been heated over 117 degrees is loaded with amylases, enzymes that digest carbohydrates, as well as all the nutrients found in plant pollens. This makes it an ideal sweetener for porridge and toast, as the amylases in honey help digest grains. Glucose tolerance tests indicate that for most people, honey does not upset blood sugar levels as severely as does refined sugar. Buy honey labeled "raw" and use it in desserts that do not require heating.

Maple Syrup: The concentrated sap of huge deciduous trees, maple syrup is rich in trace minerals, brought up from below ground by the tree's deep roots. It imparts a wonderful flavor to cream-based desserts and may be used in baked goods such as muffins and pancakes.

Sucanat: Sucanat is dehydrated cane sugar juice, the sugar that the people of India have used for thousands of years. It is rich in chromium, magnesium, silica and other minerals. Sucanat has a wonderful flavor and closely mimics sugar in chemical properties. It gives the best results for cookies and cakes, but be careful not to overdo—in large amounts sucanat can upset the body chemistry just as much as sugar.

Date Sugar: Made from dehydrated dates, this is a very nutritious sweetener but it does not dissolve easily and is therefore unsuitable for many desserts. Its high tryptophan content makes it a good sweetener for hyperactive children, as this amino acid has a calming effect. Date sugar is delicious on porridge.

Stevia Powder: A sweet powder made from a South American herb, it can be used by those who are sensitive even to natural sweeteners. A little goes a very long way. As it does not add bulk to your preparations, ingredient proportions must be changed when it is used. A good sweetener for salad dressings, whipped cream and pie crusts.

Molasses: A "waste" product from the production of refined sugar, molasses has a strong taste and moderate sweetness. It is rich in minerals, especially chromium, potassium and iron.

Concentrated Fruit Juice: The least acceptable natural sweetener. It is the fructose, not the glucose, moiety of sucrose that causes deleterious effects, especially in growing children. Pure crystalline fructose and high fructose corn syrup should be strictly avoided.

SWEETS for KIDS of ALL AGES

APRICOT COMPOTE

Serves 6-8

3 cups dried unsulphured apricots
1/2 cup maple syrup
1 cup water
1/4 teaspoon sea salt
2 cups piima cream or creme fraiche
1/2 cup crispy almonds (page 487), toasted and slivered

Place apricots, maple syrup, water and salt in a sauce pan. Simmer, uncovered, for about 1 hour or until soft and most of liquid is absorbed or evaporated. Process in food processor until smooth and let cool. Fold piima cream into the apricot mixture and place in a serving dish, individual bowls or parfait glasses. Top with almonds. Serve well chilled.

Variation: Pear Compote

Use *dried pears* instead of apricots.

AMBROSIA

Serves 6-8

8 navel oranges
1/8 cup sucanat
1 cup unsweetened date pieces
3/4 cup dried sweetened coconut meat (page 144)
1 cup crispy pecans (page 485), chopped

Peel and slice oranges. Place in a serving bowl and mix well with sucanat. Sprinkle date pieces, coconut and pecans on top. Serve well chilled.

The desire for sweet is inborn and instinctual. Research reveals that as increasing amounts of sugar are added to a newborn's bottle, the rate of sucking increases. Small children offered a choice between a healthy food and a heavily sweetened one will overwhelmingly choose the sweet. Our first food, mother's milk, is naturally sweet, and some say it is very sweet when considering the highly sensitive taste buds of an infant. From an evolutionary standpoint, our preference for sweets is highly advantageous for survival. Not only did it direct early hominids toward easily available ripe fruits and vegetables, it kept them away from poisonous plants, which are usually bitter in taste. No sweet foods are known to exist in nature that are poisonous. But the longing for sweets goes far beyond biology. It goes beyond the pleasure of taste and beyond the instincts of the body.

In the spiritual tradition of India, it is said that if you could taste the soul, it would be sweet. Indeed, the human condition in some of its most precious moments is perceived as "sweet": "the sweet life", our "sweetheart", "sweet dreams", or "the sweet smell of success". Sweetness is an *experience*, and food is just one doorway that leads us there.

The Sufis believe that every object and sensation on the physical plane has a corresponding mirror image on higher planes. In their view the sweetness of food (on the physical level) is reflected in the sweetness of love (emotional), which is reflected in the sweetness of divine ecstasy (spiritual). Even though the sweetness of a chocolate truffle differs radically from the sweetness shared between lovers, the metaphoric connections still exist.

In fact, scientists have recently discovered a chemical compound in chocolate—phenylethylamine—believed to mimic the physiological sensations of love. Even more fascinating, in the religious traditions of the Hindus, Taoists, and Tibetan Buddhists, mystics have referred to ecstatic state where a sensation of indescribable sweetness spontaneously arises in the mouth. Contemporary accounts of this phenomenon are widespread among meditators and practitioners of religious traditions of the East and the West. Furthermore, the Austrian philosopher-scientist Rudolf Steiner pointed out the role various foods have played in evolution of consciousness in different historical epochs. Sugar is seen as a food that has had a powerful effect in helping to expand personality force, creativity, and self-consciousness. Even today historians are at a loss to understand why so many wars have been fought over sugar and different spices. I offer this reason: Sugar and spices were the drugs of earlier cultures. When these foods were first introduced, their effect was even more powerfully narcotic and mind-expanding than they are today.

CAROB DIPPED STRAWBERRIES

Serves 8

24 large strawberries with stems
2/3 cup carob powder
1 stick butter
1/3 cup maple syrup
1 tablespoon vanilla
pinch sea salt
1 1/4 cups heavy cream

Wash strawberries and set on paper towels to drain. Meanwhile, place other ingredients in the top half of a double boiler. Cook gently, stirring occasionally with a wooden spoon, until all ingredients are melted and amalgamated. Let cool slightly. Dip each strawberry in sauce and place on waxed paper. Chill well before serving.

FRIED PLATANOS

Serves 8

8 very ripe large platanos or 16 small red bananas
extra virgin olive oil
1 cup fresh orange juice
1/3 cup honey
1 teaspoon cinnamon
piima cream or creme fraiche for garnish

Peel platanos and cut lengthwise. Saute in batches in olive oil, transferring with a slotted spoon to an oblong pyrex dish. Make a mixture of the orange juice, honey and cinnamon. Pour over platanos and bake at 300 degrees for about 15 minutes. Serve in bowls with a dollop of cultured cream.

SAUTEED APPLES

Serves 4

4 apples, peeled and cut into chunks
1/2 stick butter

In a heavy skillet, saute the apples in butter until golden. Serve with whipped cream or cultured cream sweetened with a little stevia powder.

Variation: Sauteed Asian Pears

Use *4 Asian pears, peeled and cut into chunks*, instead of apples. This is a delicious accompaniment to game!

APPLESAUCE

Makes 4 quarts

1/2 case organic tart apples
juice of 2 lemons
1 cup maple syrup
2 teaspoons cinnamon
freshly grated nutmeg

This recipe yields a large quantity of applesauce that can be frozen. Be sure to use organic apples as they are not peeled before cooking.

Cut apples in quarters and fill a very large enamel or stainless steel pot. Squeeze lemon juice over top and add about 2 cups of water to the pot. Bring to a boil and simmer, covered, for several hours until apples are very tender. Push down with a potato masher occasionally, and check that the apples are not burning. Allow to cool and pass in batches through a Foley Food Mill or *moulin a legumes*. Stir in syrup and spices. Store in refrigerator or freezer. Serve with whipped cream or cultured cream sweetened with a little stevia powder; and crispy almonds (page 487) that have been sliced and toasted.

When we eat sweets, our desire is not just for food. Our longing is for the *experience* of *sweetness*, something we can taste on the tongue, in the heart, or in our most sacred thoughts. However, because it is more difficult to find a sweetheart or sweet Jesus, the mind often considers sweet foods an acceptable substitute. Food happens to be the most available form of the sweet experience. Can you see how we instinctively crave sweetness on several different levels? Do you understand why it is a perfectly natural biological phenomenon?

Sugary food is one of the most popular forms of substitute love. Its effect is even more potent when combined with the love-inducing chemicals in chocolate. The downside of repeated substitution is the same for sugar as it is for drugs, alcohol, or cigarettes: dependency. We become mechanically bound to sugar because it fulfills an immediate need and exerts a powerful narcotic effect.

It is important to note that the need for the sweet experience is inborn, but as every nutritional scientist knows, there is no physiological requirement for refined sugar in the diet. Quite the contrary. Excess sugar in the diet promotes tooth decay and obesity and has been implicated in heart disease, diabetes, hypoglycemia, immune deficiency diseases, digestive disorders, and allergies. Perhaps the most fascinating and best kept medical secret about sugar is that excessive consumption causes calcium loss, which leads to a much publicized disease of our day—osteoporosis. David Marc *Nourishing Wisdom*

ARISTOCRATIC APPLES

Serves 4

4 large tart apples
juice of 1 lemon
1/2 cup raisins
1/4 teaspoon saffron threads dissolved in
1 tablespoon water
1/2 stick butter
1/2 cup piima cream or creme fraiche
3 tablespoons maple syrup
1/2 cup crispy almonds (page 487),
slivered and toasted
1/4 teaspoon ground cardamom

Soak raisins in water with dissolved saffron threads. Peel, quarter and seed the apples and place in water mixed with juice of 1 lemon. Heat butter in a heavy skillet. Remove apple quarters from lemon water, pat dry and grate into the melted butter. Cook gently until excess moisture is evaporated. Drain raisins and add to the pan with remaining ingredients. Cook, stirring, until mixture is the consistency of thick applesauce.

For twenty years Japanese researcher Naosuke Sasaki, professor emeritus at the Hirosaki University School of Medicine in Hirosaki, Japan has tracked the blood pressure in more than 2,400 villagers in two adjoining prefectures in northeast Japan. In the prefecture of Aomori farmers eat lots of apples. In Akita prefecture they do not, preferring rice instead. Dr. Sasaki has found that those eating less than one apple a day tend to develop typical high blood pressure as they age. But villagers eating one to two apples a day had only modest increases in blood pressure. And those eating three or more apples a day did not have the expected high blood pressure. Furthermore, apple eaters of Aomori had a much lower stroke rate. Dr. Sasaki theorizes that something in the apples—perhaps potassium—helped counteract the blood-pressure-raising effects of a high-sodium, liberal-soy-sauce diet. Jean Carper *The Food Pharmacy Guide to Good Eating*

BAKED APPLES

Serves 6

6 large baking apples
6 tablespoons butter, softened
1/2 cup sucanat
grated rind of 2 lemons
juice of 2 lemons
1 teaspoon ground ginger
1/2 teaspoon ground cinnamon
1/4 teaspoon ground cloves
1/4 teaspoon ground cardamom
1/4 cup currents or raisins
1/4 cup coarsely chopped crispy almonds (page 487), or crispy pecans (page 485)

Core apples from stem side through the center (but not entirely through) and peel from top to about 1/3 the way down. Cream butter and sucanat. Stir in remaining ingredients and place a spoonful of stuffing in each apple. Place in a buttered baking pan with a little water. Bake about 2 hours at 325 degrees or until apples are tender.

Variation: Baked Quinces:

Use *6 quinces* instead of apples. Core from the bottom side and bake with the stem side down. These may need more time to cook.

Refined white sugar carries only negligible traces of body-building and repairing material. It satisfies hunger by providing heat and energy besides having a pleasant flavor. The heat and energy producing factors in our food that are not burned up are usually stored as fat. . . we have seen that approximately half of the foods provided in our modern dietaries furnish little or no body-building or repairing material and supply no vitamins. Approximately 25 per cent of the heat and energy of the American people is supplied by sugar alone which goes far in thwarting nature's orderly processes of life. Weston Price DDS *Nutrition and Physical Degeneration*

Yudkin analyzed the sugar consumption habits of men with atherosclerosis. . . . the men who had heart attacks reported a sugar intake nearly twice as high as those not having the heart attacks, and moreover, in patients with artery disease, the degree of atherosclerosis was proportional to the amount of sugar consumed. . . . The statistical figures indicate the relationship between sugar consumption and heart attack, and between sugar consumption and artery disease, was extremely strong in this study. Chris Mudd *Cholesterol and Your Health*

In Greek mythology, apples tasted like honey and healed all ailments. In American folk medicine, the apple is called "the king of fruits," a neutralizer of all the body's excess acids, and thus, according to a 1927 article in *American Medicine*, "therapeutically effective in all conditions of acidosis, gout, rheumatism, jaundice, all liver and gall bladder troubles, and nervous and skin diseases caused by sluggish liver, hyperacidity, and states of autointoxication." No doubt about it. Modern scientific investigations find apples a versatile and potent package of natural drugs that deserve their reputation for keeping doctors away. [The apple] helps keep the cardiovascular system healthy. First Italian, then Irish researchers, and now the French have all confirmed that eating apples puts a dent in blood cholesterol . . . Unquestionably, apples tend to be good for diabetics and other who want to avoid steep rises in blood sugar. Apples rank near the bottom of the "glycemic index" (a measurement of how fast blood sugar rises after eating). . . . This means that despite an apple's natural sugar content, it does not spur a rapid rise in blood sugar. The fruit keeps the throttle on insulin, and foods that do this invariably also lower blood cholesterol and blood pressure.

In fact, researchers at prestigious Yale University have found that you may have only to smell apples to get your blood pressure down. Dr. Gary Schwartz, director of Yale's Psychophysiology Center, reported that the aroma of spiced apples has a calming effect on many people that tends to lower blood pressure. Jean Carper *The Food Pharmacy*

APPLE COBBLER

Serves 6

8 tart apples
juice of 1-2 lemons
grated rind of 1 lemon
1 tablespoon arrowroot
2 tablespoons sucanat
1/2 teaspoon cinnamon
3/4 cup crispy almonds (page 487)
3/4 cup arrowroot
3/4 stick butter, softened
1/4 cup sucanat
1/4 teaspoon sea salt
1 teaspoon vanilla

Peel and core apples and cut into slices. Toss with lemon juice. Mix sucanat, lemon rind, arrowroot and cinnamon together and toss with apples. Place in a buttered baking or souffle dish. Place almonds in food processor and process to a powder. Add butter, arrowroot, sucanat, vanilla and salt and process until smooth. Crumble this mixture on top of the apples. Bake at 350 degrees for 1 hour. Serve with whipped cream or cultured cream sweetened with a little stevia powder.

Variation: Peach Cobbler

Use *8 ripe peaches* in place of apples and omit cinnamon.

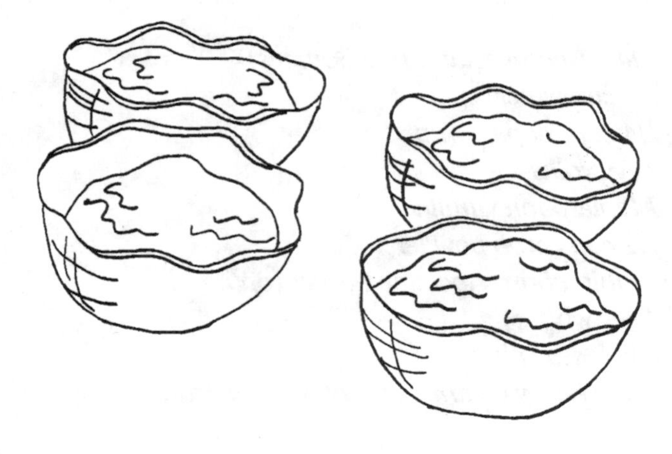

We can summarize from the preceding data that the present enzyme-deficient diet may be responsible for the reduction in brain weight and size, unfavorable enlargement of the pancreas, wasting of the precursors of metabolic enzymes, and many degenerative trends. Added to the modern catastrophe called the stove are hundreds of food factories whose job it is to "refine" or denature foods. In almost every case, refining eliminates much of the enzymes in foods, and in many cases also adds potential carcinogens to them. Edward Howell MD *Enzyme Nutrition*

ALMOND FOOL

Serves 4

2 cups crispy almonds (page 487)
2 teaspoons gelatin, (see Sources) dissolved in
1/2 cup warm water
1/4 cup sucanat
2 teaspoons vanilla
1/2 cup water
2 cups cream, whipped
1 package frozen berries
1/2 cup water
1/4 cup maple syrup

Pulverize almonds in food processor. Process with sucanat, vanilla, water and gelatin mixture until smooth and fluffy. Fold in whipped cream. Place in serving dish and chill well. In a food processor, puree berries with water and maple syrup and chill in a separate bowl. To serve, spoon almond mixture into serving dishes and top with a generous spoonful of pureed berries.

Variation: Almond Fool Parfait

Place layers of almond mixture and fruit puree in individual serving cups. Chill well.

Know Your Ingredients

Name This Product #39

Skim milk, water, sugar, partially hydrogenated soybean oil, modified food starch, salt, sodium stearoyl lactylate, artificial flavor, color added (including FD&C yellow #5)

See Appendix B for Answer

CAROB BAVARIAN CREAM

Serves 8

1 tablespoon gelatin (see Sources)
1/2 cup water
1/4 cup maple syrup
4 egg yolks
1 tablespoon vanilla
1/2 cup carob powder
1 tablespoon chocolate extract (optional)
4 egg whites
pinch sea salt
2 cup heavy cream, preferably unpasteurized

Warm gelatin in water over very low heat until melted. Place egg yolks, carob, maple syrup, optional chocolate extract and vanilla in food processor. Blend about 1 minute. Add gelatin mixture while motor is running. Remove bowl to refrigerator while beating cream and whites. In a clean bowl beat egg whites with salt until stiff. In another bowl beat cream until softly stiff. Process egg yolk mixture once more and fold into cream. Fold cream mixture into egg whites. Place in a serving dish, cover and chill for several hours before serving.

Table sugar (sucrose) has been condemned by dentists, nutritionists, and physicians for scores of years. It is the greatest scourge that has ever been visited on man in the name of food. Endocrinologists agree that the endocrine system of glands and the nervous system cooperate to regulate the appetite so that the right amount of the right kind of food is taken in. Sugar spoils this fine balance. Being almost 100 percent "pure", this high-calorie dynamite bombs the pancreas and pituitary gland into gushing forth a hyper-secretion of hormones comparable in intensity to that artificially produced in laboratory animals with drugs and hormones. Sugar is the culprit the endocrinologists have been looking for that has been throwing the finely regulated endocrine balance completely out of kilter. Edward Howell DDS *Enzyme Nutrition*

CAROB BROWNIES

Makes 24

3 cups freshly ground whole wheat or spelt flour
2 cups buttermilk, or water mixed with
2 tablespoons whey or yoghurt
1 1/2 sticks butter, softened
1 1/2 cups sucanat
4 eggs
1 tablespoon vanilla
1 tablespoon chocolate extract (optional)
1 teaspoon sea salt
3/4 cup carob powder
1 tablespoon baking powder
1 cup chopped crispy pecans (page 485)

It is easy—and much less costly—to produce a sugar rich in vitamins and minerals—and delicious as well—as they have done in India for thousands of years, by a simple evaporation of sugar cane juice. It is true that this "poorman's sugar", as they call it in the Third World, is not immaculately white and that it is not "modern". Because of its color, white sugar is a perfect symbol of "progress" and of western civilization, to which in these modern times all peoples unfortunately aspire. Claude Aubert *Dis-Moi Comment Tu Cuisines*

Mix flour with liquid and let stand at least 7 hours or overnight. Cream butter with sucanat. Add eggs, extracts, salt, carob powder and baking powder. Blend in soaked flour and fold in nuts. Pour into a buttered and floured 9-by-13 inch pyrex pan. Bake at 350 degrees for about 40 minutes. Allow to cool thoroughly and cut into squares.

GINGERBREAD

Makes 16

2 2/3 cups freshly ground spelt or wheat flour
2 cups cultured buttermilk, or water mixed with 2 tablespoons whey or yoghurt
1 1/2 sticks butter, softened
3 tablespoons freshly grated ginger
2/3 cup sucanat
1/3 cup molasses
2 eggs
1/2 teaspoon cinnamon
1/2 teaspoon ground nutmeg
1/4 teaspoon ground cloves
1 teaspoon dry mustard
1/2 teaspoon sea salt
2 teaspoons baking powder

Mix flour with liquid and let stand at least 7 hours or overnight. Cream sucanat with butter, molasses and eggs. Blend in remaining ingredients and blend this mixture with the soaked flour mixture. Pour into a buttered and floured 9-by-9 pyrex pan. Bake at 350 degrees for about 45 minutes. Serve with whipped cream sweetened with stevia powder.

With normal food that carries all needed nutritional factors, the glands know just when the body has had enough and will shut off the appetite just as abruptly as one would shut off a water faucet. But when sugar gets into the mouth and begins its evil machinations, it throws the endocrine switchboard into helter-skelter. The glands know the organism has been loaded up with a lot of calories but in spite of searching, the nutrients that normally go along with the calories cannot be found in the body. So an order to take in more food, in the expectation of getting the important vitamins, minerals, and enzymes, is issued in the form of increased appetite. Don't let it fool you, the increased appetite sugar induces is not a call for more sugar or the foods that it contaminates, but for the missing nutrient factors that your body craves. Eating added sugar in various foods and drinks every day is a way of perpetuating chronic overstimulation of the pituitary and pancreas glands. The thyroid and adrenals also feel the brunt of the affront. The false craving and feeling of well-being sugar induces is on a par with the ecstasy experienced when dope takes command in a victim's body. Therefore, far overshadowing the damage resulting from sugar as a carrier of empty calories, is its capacity to destroy the delicate endocrine balance and inaugurate a train of pernicious consequences. Edward Howell MD *Enzyme Nutrition*

Sugared cereal products and hundreds of other items are made by sugarization, accounting for an average consumption of 100 pounds each year for every man, woman, and child in the USA. If the government outlawed sugar, it would shake the foundations of American business. It remains to be seen whether the ultimate damage to twenty-first century man will accrue more from today's sugar eating or from the consumption of artificial sweeteners such as saccharine. Edward Howell MD *Enzyme Nutrition*

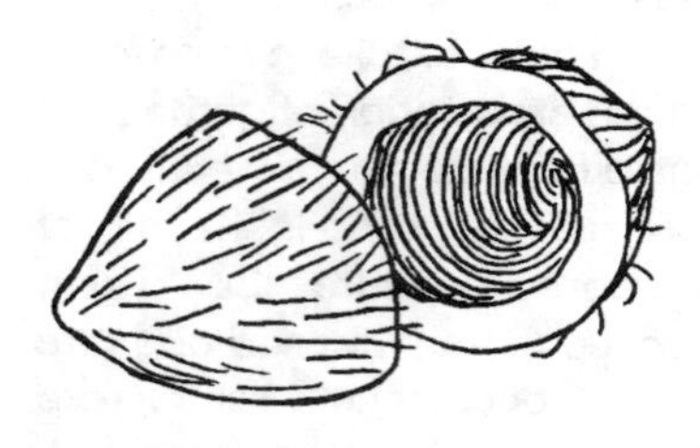

The latest explosive evidence incriminating table sugar as the chief architect of heart disease comes from the University of Hawaii (1972). C.C. Brooks and his associates fed pigs high-sugar diets. Sixty-eight of the eighty pigs developed heart disease in the left half of the heart. This backs up the contention that Dr. Yudkin and others have been making for many years. A remarkable added finding was that in pigs in which 10 percent of the sugar was replaced by coconut oil or beef tallow, the heart remained free from the endocarditis that afflicted the [other] animals. This may confound those who have been apprehensive about fat in the diet. Edward Howell MD *Enzyme Nutrition*

COCONUT BARS

Makes 16

3/4 cup crispy almonds (page 487)
1/2 stick butter, softened or 1/4 cup coconut oil
1/2 cup arrowroot
1/4 cup sucanat
1 teaspoon vanilla
pinch sea salt
1 egg
1/4 cup plain yoghurt,
piima cream or creme fraiche
1/2 cup maple syrup
1 tablespoon vanilla
grated rind of 1 lemon
2 tablespoons arrowroot
pinch sea salt
1 1/2 cups dried unsweetened coconut meat

Place almonds in food processor and process to a fine powder. Add butter, arrowroot, vanilla, sucanat and salt and process until smooth. Press into a well oiled 9-by-9 inch or 7-by-11 inch pyrex pan. Bake at 300 degrees for 20 minutes. Let cool. Beat egg with yoghurt or cultured cream, maple syrup, vanilla, lemon peel, arrowroot and sea salt. Stir in coconut and spread over almond pastry. Bake at 325 degrees for about 25 minutes. Let cool slightly before cutting into bars. Let cool completely before removing bars.

APRICOT BARS

Serves 12

3 cups dried apricots
1/2 cup sucanat
2 cups crispy almonds (page 487)
1 1/4 stick butter, softened
1 1/2 cups arrowroot
1/2-3/4 cup sucanat
1/2 teaspoon sea salt
1 teaspoon almond extract

Cook apricots in water until tender. Remove with a slotted spoon to food processor and process with 1/2 cup sucanat. Set aside and let cool.

Meanwhile, process almonds to a powder in food processor. Add remaining ingredients and process until smooth. Press 2/3 of the almond mixture into a buttered 9-by-13 pyrex pan, making a thin crust. Bake about 15 minutes at 350 degrees. Spread apricot mixture over crust and distribute the remaining 1/3 almond mixture, crumbled, over top. Bake at 325 degrees for about 45 minutes. Let cool slightly before cutting into bars. Let cool thoroughly before removing bars.

Dextrose, which is made by boiling corn starch with acid, should be reserved for occasional use as temporary intravenous medicine in hospitals. The indictment against both table sugar and dextrose is strong enough to demand that both be placed off-limits to people. Let them be available only by prescription issued by a doctor. The chemists in the large food processing plants are very efficient people. They know their subjects from A to Z. But the last thing they can afford to be concerned about is the consumer's health. Oh yes, they will protect the public health from immediate poisoning and the like. But they do not worry about what goes on in a consumer's body after 20 years of eating their products. If the result is a killing disease, it is given a name on a death certificate as an established disease entity and no one suspects that food had anything to do with it. Edward Howell MD *Enzyme Nutrition*

ALMOND BARS

Serves 12

1 recipe flaky pie crust (page 524)
1 cup honey or fruit juice sweetened raspberry jam
3 cups crispy almonds (page 487), sliced in food processor
1 cup maple syrup
1 tablespoon arrowroot

Line a buttered 9-by-13 pyrex pan with pastry and bake at 300 for about 15 minutes. Let cool and spread with jam. Bring syrup to a boil with arrowroot. Stir in almonds and spread mixture over jam. Bake at 325 degrees for about 30 minutes or until almonds become nicely browned. Let cool slightly before cutting into bars. Let cool completely before removing bars.

Sometimes the eastern Iroquois squaws seasoned the cornmeal foods with berries, mushrooms or maple sugar. Maple syrup and maple sugar were, in fact, Indian favorites. The granulated sugar could be dissolved in water as a refreshing beverage; other uses of maple syrup and sugar were to season fruits, vegetables, cereals and fish. . . Even when salt was available, Indians used it sparingly. . . because they believed that an excess of salt caused illness and an unnatural thirst. Patricia B. Mitchell *The Good Land*

VANILLA ICE CREAM

Makes 8 cups

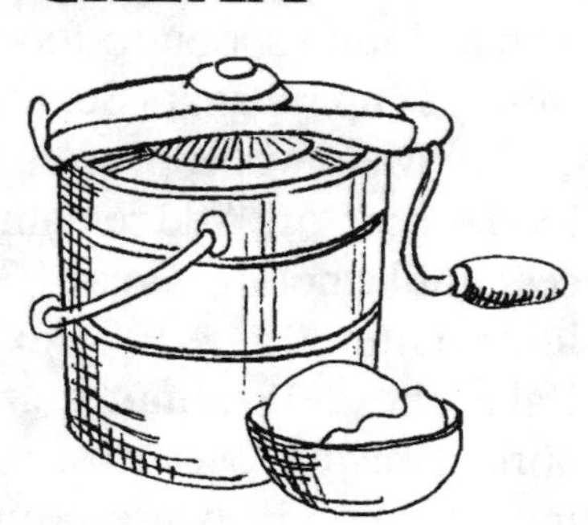

3 eggs
1/2 cup maple syrup or sucanat
1 tablespoon vanilla
2 teaspoons arrowroot
4 cups heavy cream

Ice cream should be made with the best quality cream you can find, preferably unpasteurized. Never use ultrapasteurized cream. You can use an ice cream maker if you like, but good results can be obtained by pouring the ice cream mixture into a shallow, rectangular plastic container and placing it directly into the freezer. To serve, cut the ice cream into squares and allow to soften a few minutes at room temperature.

Process eggs, maple syrup, vanilla and arrowroot in food processor for several minutes. In a clean bowl, beat cream stiff. Fold in the egg mixture and pour into a shallow container, cover and freeze for several hours before serving; or freeze in a commercial ice cream maker. Serve with Carob Sauce or Raspberry Sauce.

Each isolated Swiss valley or village has its own special feast days of which athletic contests are the principal events. The feasting in the past has been largely on dairy products. The athletes were provided with large bowls of cream as constituting one of the most popular and healthful beverages, and special cheese was always available. . . their cream products took the place of our modern ice cream. . . it is reported that practically all skulls that are exhumed in the Rhone valley, and indeed, practically throughout all of Switzerland where graves have existed for more than a hundred years, are found with relatively perfect teeth; whereas the teeth of people recently buried have been riddled with caries or lost through this disease. Weston Price DDS *Nutrition and Physical Degeneration*

The Prodigal Son, at his lowest ebb, ate "the husks that the swine did eat". His food was the carob pod, for millennia a staple of the Middle Eastern diet. In recent decades the carob's standing has risen considerably as people have discovered in the powder made from this hard, dark brown pod, an acceptable substitute for chocolate. Carob is an excellent source of calcium—containing three times more calcium than mother's milk! It also contains carotenoids, B vitamins, phosphorus and iron. It is naturally sweet, containing about 50% sugars. Unlike chocolate, carob contains no stimulants; it does however contain tannin, a substance that reduces the absorption of protein through the intestinal wall. It is therefore recommended that carob be used in moderation, especially in children's diets. SWF

CAROB SAUCE

Makes 2 1/2 cups

2/3 cup carob powder
1 stick butter
1/3 cup maple syrup
1 tablespoon vanilla
1 tablespoon chocolate extract (optional)
pinch salt
1 cup cream

Place all ingredients in the top half of a double boiler. Cook gently, stirring occasionally with a wooden spoon, until well amalgamated.

RASPBERRY SAUCE

Makes 4 cups

1 12-ounce package frozen raspberries,
1/2 cup maple syrup
1-2 cups water

Place partially thawed raspberries in food processor with maple syrup and process to make a thick paste. Gradually add water until desired consistency is obtained.

BERRY ICE CREAM

Makes 8 cups

2 cups berries, such as raspberries, blueberries, strawberries or blackberries, fresh or frozen
2 eggs
1/2 to 3/4 cup maple syrup, depending on sweetness of fruit
2 teaspoons arrowroot
4 cups heavy cream, preferably unpasteurized

Process eggs, maple syrup and arrowroot in food processor for several minutes. Add berries and process to desired consistency—either smooth or chunky. Beat cream in a clean bowl until softly stiff. Fold into berry mixture and pour into a shallow container, cover and freeze for several hours before serving; or process in an ice cream maker.

In the old days when ice cream was made of whole eggs, milk and sugar and laboriously cranked out in the old home freezer, a serving of ice cream was only an occasional family treat which didn't do much harm. Today in this mass producing, synthetic age, it is another matter entirely. Today you may be treating your family to poison! Ice cream manufacturers are not required by law to list the additives used in the manufacturing of their product. Consequently, today most ice creams are synthetic from start to finish. Analysis has shown the following:

DIETHYLGLYCOL: A cheap chemical used as an emulsifier instead of eggs is the same chemical used in anti-freeze and in paint removers.

PIPERONAL: Used in place of vanilla. This chemical is used to kill lice.

ALDEHYDE C-17: Used to flavor cherry ice cream. It is an inflammable liquid also used in aniline dyes, plastic and rubber.

ETHYL ACETATE: Used to give ice cream a pineapple flavor—and as a cleaner for leather and textiles; its vapors have been known to cause chronic lung, liver and heart damage.

BUTYRALDEHYDE: Used in nut flavored ice cream It is one of the ingredients of rubber cement.

AMYL ACETATE: Used for its banana flavor. It is also used as an oil point solvent.

BENZYL ACETATE: Used for its strawberry flavor, It is a nitrate solvent.

The next time you are tempted by a luscious looking banana split sundae think of it as a mixture of anti-freeze, oil paint, nitrate solvent, and lice killer and you won't find it so appetizing.

PPNF Journal

FRUIT ICE CREAM

Makes 8 cups

4 cups fruit such as peaches, pears or plums, peeled and sliced
2 tablespoons lemon juice
4 tablespoons maple syrup
1 teaspoon unflavored gelatin
4 cups heavy cream, preferably unpasteurized

Mix maple syrup with lemon juice and toss with fruit. Cover and let stand for 2 hours. Drain the fruit and combine 3/4 cup of juice with the gelatin. Heat gently until the gelatin is dissolved. Place fruit in food processor with gelatin mixture and process until desired texture is obtained—either smooth or chunky. Beat cream in a clean bowl until softly stiff. Fold in fruit mixture and pour into a shallow container, cover and freeze for several hours before serving; or process in an ice cream maker.

It's almost as if the devil sat down and listed all the criteria of a substance man could use to destroy himself. It would have to be pleasing to the eye and taste. It would have to be pure white and easily available. It would have to appeal to all the people of this world. The destroying effects would have to be subtle and take such a long time that very few would realize what was happening until it was too late. The cruelest criteria of all is it would have to be supported and distributed by the kindest, well meaning people to the most innocent people.

So far the devil is winning. Did you ever go to a church cake sale conducted in a grade school? Bruce Pacetti DDS *PPNF Journal*

LEMON SHERBERT

Makes 5 cups

grated peel of 2 lemons
juice of 2 lemons
1 egg yolk
2 cups piima milk (page 77) or cultured buttermilk
1/2 cup maple syrup
2 egg whites
pinch salt

Place lemon peel, lemon juice, egg yolk, piima milk or buttermilk and maple syrup in food processor and process several minutes. In a clean bowl, beat egg whites with sea salt until stiff. Fold in lemon juice mixture and pour into a shallow container. Cover and freeze for about 1 hour. Remove cover and beat with a fork. Cover again and freeze for several hours more. (Sherbert may also be processed in an ice cream maker.)

Sprawsen. . . observed that raw milk had specific effect on teeth of man, conferring considerable immunity to dental caries. It excelled pasteurized and sterilized milk in body-building properties. No incidence of dental caries showed in 40 children, brought up on raw milk from the age of 4 1/2 months to an average age of 4 years, although they had been on diets rich in refined carbohydrates. Edward Howell MD *Enzymes for Health and Longevity*

Lasby and Palmer. . . found the bones of rats fed on raw milk had a slightly higher percentage of ash and a slightly higher content in calcium and phosphorus than the bones of rats fed on pasteurized milk. Edward Howell MD *Enzymes for Health and Longevity*

BERRY SHERBERT

Makes 5 cups

3 cups berries such as raspberries, strawberries or blackberries, fresh or frozen
1/4 to 1/2 cup maple syrup depending on sweetness of berries
1/2 cup orange juice
1 cup piima milk (page 77) or cultured buttermilk
3 egg whites
pinch sea salt

Place fresh berries or partially thawed frozen berries in food processor with maple syrup, orange juice and piima milk or buttermilk. Process until smooth. In a clean bowl, beat egg whites with sea salt until stiff. Fold in berry mixture and pour into a shallow container. Cover and freeze for about 1 hour. Remove cover and beat with a fork. Cover and freeze again for several hours. (Sherbert may also be processed in an ice cream maker.)

It seems, therefore that we Americans are bent on "refining" ourselves into a chromium deficiency, the ultimate result of which is a significant glucose intolerance in the human body. This rather unhappy distinction of the United States is not shared by other countries that do not refine their foods. In a series of tests on men between the ages of twenty and fifty-nine, the amount of chromium found in the heart artery was 1.9 parts per million (ppm) in American men, 5.5 ppm in African men, 11 ppm in men from the Near East, and 15 ppm in men in the Far East. This evidence is one source of speculation which proves that there is indeed a definite link between the over-consumption of refined foods and a chromium deficiency. William H. Philpott MD *Victory Over Diabetes*

PLUM SHERBERT

Makes 2 quarts

5 pounds plums
2 cups filtered water
1 cup maple syrup

This delicious sherbert is best made in an ice cream maker. It is an excellent dessert for those who cannot tolerate milk products in any form.

Cut plums in half, remove seeds and cook with a small amount of water until soft. Blend with a hand held blender. Bring 2 cups water to a boil, add syrup and mix with a wooden spoon. Simmer for a few minutes. Let cool and add to plum mixture. Chill well, pour into an ice cream maker and freeze according to instructions.

Many people with sugar dependencies report that their need for sugar drops significantly when they cut down on meat.

Interestingly enough, we crave sugar also when there is not enough protein in the diet. The reason for this is that opposites, in their extremes, change into one another. Extreme pleasure becomes painful. Extreme light is blinding (darkness). And lack of protein or meat, an extremely expansive function, will cause us to crave the food we need least, an extremely expansive food like sugar. It is not unusual for people who switch to a vegetarian diet and have a lower protein intake to begin craving sweet foods. And vegetarians who eat too much refined sugar often have strong cravings for meat and fish. David Marc *Nourishing Wisdom*

Know Your Ingredients

Name This Product #40

Water, Corn syrup, hydrogenated coconut and palm kernel oils, sugar, sodium caseinate, polysorbate 60 and sorbitan monostrearate (for uniform dispersion of oil), natural and artificial flavors, xanthan gum and guar gum (thickeners), artificial color

See Appendix B for Answer

It used to be an apple a day that keeps the doctor away. Today, it's a banana. But who cares what healthful fruits or vegetable are used so long as you can keep illnesses and the doctor away?

Lewis Tobian, M.D., a professor of medicine at the University of Minnesota and a nutrition authority, really wants to keep other doctors away. He eats two bananas daily and indicates that, due to their high potassium content—about 400 mg. of potassium per unit—they may lower blood pressure and keep cholesterol from building up in the arteries. . .

However, bananas aren't the only potassium-rich foods. There are also apricots, avocados, dates, Brussels sprouts, lima beans, orange and grapefruit juice, carrots, tomatoes, potatoes, spinach and yoghurt. James F. Scheer *Health Freedom News*

CLAFOUTIS

Serves 8

3 cups fresh fruit such as pitted cherries, sliced nectarines or peaches, or pineapple cut into chunks
1/4 cup sucanat
3 eggs
1/2 cup sucanat
1/4 cup unbleached flour or 3 tablespoons arrowroot
1 1/3 cup piima cream or creme fraiche

This is a traditional French dessert, something between cake and custard. Sprinkle fruit with sucanat and set aside for about 1/2 hour. Remove with a slotted spoon to a buttered baking pan and bake at low temperature for an hour or more or until fruit is rather dry. Butter an easy-remove 10-inch cake pan. Beat eggs with 1/2 cup sucanat until smooth. Beat in flour or arrowroot and cream. Stir in fruit and pour batter into pan. Bake about 1 hour at 350 degrees. Let cool slightly before removing from pan.

TROPICAL DELIGHT

Serves 8

1 cup crispy peanuts (page 486)
3/4 stick butter, softened or 3/8 cup coconut oil
1 cup arrowroot
3/8 cup sucanat
1/2 teaspoon salt
1 teaspoon vanilla
3/4 cup dried unsweetened coconut meat
fresh bananas
whipped cream

Place peanuts, butter, flour, sucanat, vanilla and salt in food processor and process until smooth. Add coconut and pulse until well blended. Butter and flour a 10- or 12-inch French style tart pan. Press dough into pan, making an even layer. Bake at 300 for about 3/4 hour. Let cool. Cut into wedges and top with sliced fresh bananas and whipped cream.

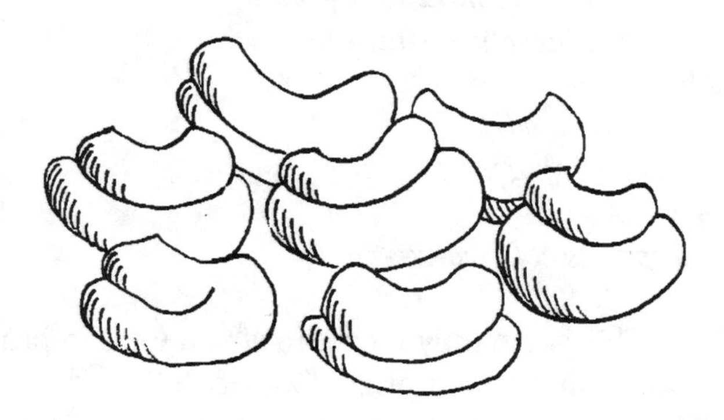

MERENGUES

Makes 6

6 egg whites
pinch sea salt
3 tablespoons arrowroot
1/4 cup maple syrup
1 tablespoon vanilla

These are delicious filled with fresh fruit and topped with whipped cream, and a good way to use up leftover egg whites. They should cook overnight in a warm oven—about 150 degrees. Be sure to use a very clean bowl to beat your egg whites.

Line a baking sheet with buttered parchment paper (see Sources). Beat egg whites with salt until they form stiff peaks. Beat in arrowroot. Slowly add maple syrup and vanilla, beating constantly. Place six blobs of egg white mixture on parchment paper and form a little hollow in each one. Cook overnight in a warm oven, about 150 degrees. Let cool before removing parchment paper. Store merengues in an airtight container until ready to use.

Most dentists and physicians sincerely believe the destructive action on tooth enamel is only a local one that is caused by bacterial action upon carbohydrates, primarily sugar, sweets and refined grains.

It is agreed that this is the outward inciting cause but the reason the bacteria and refined foods are able to attack the hard tooth enamel is due to changes that have taken place in the body and subsequently in the inside of teeth. . . Though hard to imagine, this very hard tooth enamel of ours is porous. Two percent of its volume is water and it, too, can flow in either direction. However, the normal flow is from the pulp and the odontoblast cells outwardly through the dentin and then through the enamel.

Not only is this fluid movement measurable but when laboratory rats are fed a high sugar cariogenic diet, the fluid movement is reversed and herein lies the reason teeth become susceptible to decay. . .

In addition to the changes good and bad nutrition have on dentin tubule flow and function, dietary habit have numbers of other actions that are involved in the cause of tooth decay. One of these is how the food we eat affects the acid base balance of the saliva. Under ideal dietary conditions the saliva is slightly alkaline. Like the blood, it has a 7.4 pH. When it falls below a pH of 7.0, as it does to a considerable extent after sugar and refined grains are eaten, the saliva becomes more acid and environmental factors in the mouth are more conducive to the development of tooth decay and dental erosion. *PPNF Journal*

PIES & CAKES

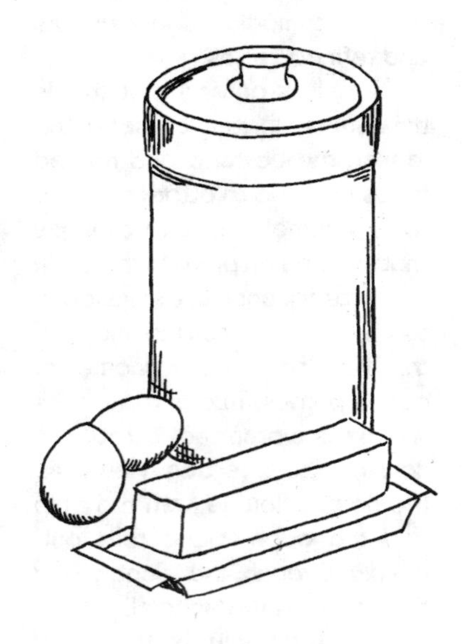

FLAKY PIE CRUST

1 1/3 cup freshly ground spelt flour
or unbleached white flour
pinch sea salt
pinch stevia powder
1 stick butter, frozen
2 egg yolks
3 tablespoons cold water

This is the only recipe in which we compromise somewhat on our principles. Spelt flour can be used for pie crust, but the exacting gourmet will prefer to use unbleached white flour. This recipe will make a 9-inch pie shell with enough left over for lattice work; or 2 8-inch French style tart shells; or 7 individual 4-inch tart shells.

Sift flour, sea salt and stevia powder into food processor. Place butter on a board and cut into small pieces using a sharp knife. Distribute butter over flour. Pulse processor several times until butter is broken into pea-sized pieces and is well distributed. Beat egg yolks briefly with a fork and dribble over flour mixture. Have water ready. Turn on processor and immediately pour water in. Stop processor at once. (Butter should still be visible as pea-sized pieces.) Turn crust unto waxed paper, wrap up and squeeze together, forming a ball. Refrigerate several hours. Roll on a pastry cloth using unbleached white flour to keep from sticking. When lining French style tart pans (with removable bottoms) press dough firmly into sides and drape over the top. Roll a rolling pin over the top to trim.

For a partially baked or fully baked tart shell, prick dough several times with a fork. Place in a cool oven and turn on heat. (Gradual warming will prevent the dough from excessive shrinking.) Bake at 300 for 15 minutes for partially baked pastry and 25 minutes for a fully baked pastry—longer if using spelt flour.

Enriched wheat flour containing niacin, reduced iron, thiamine mononitrate (vitamin B1) and riboflavin (vitamin B2), vegetable shortening (partially hydrogenated soybean oil), sugar, graham flour, brown sugar, corn syrup, salt, leavening (sodium bicarbonate, sodium acid pyrophosphate, mono-calcium phosphate), malt, cornstarch, soy lecithin and artificial flavor.

See Appendix B for Answer

HAZELNUT PIE CRUST

1 cup skinless hazelnuts
3/4 cup arrowroot
3/4 stick butter, softened or 3/8 cup coconut oil
1/4 cup sucanat
1/2 teaspoon sea salt

This makes a delicious press-in type of pie crust, enough for one deep 9-inch pie crust.

Place hazelnuts in food processor and process to a meal. Add remaining ingredients and process until smooth. Press into a well-buttered and floured pie pan. For a fully baked pie crust, bake at 325 degrees for about 1/2 hour.

Note: To peel hazelnuts, place on a cookie sheet and bake at 350 degrees until skins turn dark and begin to crack. Place in a kitchen towel and wrap up tightly. Hold towel-wrapped nuts in your hands and rub and squeeze for several minutes. Open up towel—most of the skins should have come off. Lift hazelnuts and shake off. Transfer to food processor.

Variation: Pecan Pie Crust

Use *1 cup crispy pecans (page 485)* instead of hazelnuts.

Variation: Almond Pie Crust

Use *1 cup crispy almonds (page 487)* instead of hazelnuts

No other product has so profoundly influenced the political history of the Western world as has sugar. It was the nickel under the foot of much of the early history of the New World. The Portuguese and Spanish empires rose swiftly in opulence and power. As the Arabs before them had crumbled, so they too fell rapidly into decline. To what extent that decline was biological—occasioned by sugar bingeing at the royal level—we can only guess. However the British empire stood by waiting to pick up the pieces. In the beginning, Queen Elizabeth I shrank from institutionalizing slavery in the British colonies as "detestable," something which might "call down the vengeance of heaven" on her realm. By 1588, her sentimental scruples had been overcome. The queen granted a royal charter extending recognition to the Company of Royal Adventurers of England into Africa, which gave them a state monopoly on the African slave trade. William Dufty *Sugar Blues*

Her majesty's government, with its vested interest in both slavery and sugar, spoke loftily of the empire. Britain was the center of the sugar industry of the entire world. "The pleasure, glory and grandeur of England has been advanced more by sugar than by any other commodity, wool not excepted," said Sir Dalby Thomas. "The impossibility of doing without slaves in the West Indies will always prevent the traffic being dropped." William Dufty *Sugar Blues*

RASPBERRY TART

Serves 6-8

1 recipe flaky pie crust (page 524),
fully baked as a 12-inch French style tart
or as individual tarts
2 cups honey or fruit juice sweetened
raspberry jam
1/2 cup pear or raspberry liqueur
3-4 cups fresh raspberries

Heat raspberry jam with liqueur and boil gently about 10 minutes. Brush tart shell or shells with melted jam. Arrange berries on top and drizzle remaining jam mixture over berries.

Variation: Raspberry Carob Tart

Use *1 1/2 cups carob sauce (page 518)* instead of raspberry jam. Brush tart shell or shells with warm carob sauce and arrange berries on top. A raspberry jam glaze is optional—not really necessary.

Variation: Blueberry Tart

Use *3-4 cups fresh blueberries* instead of raspberries.

US Department of Agriculture researchers are investigating ellagic acid, found primarily in strawberries, blackberries, raspberries, blueberries, cranberries, grapes, apples and various nuts, including Brazil nuts and cashews. Dr. Gary Stoner, director of experimental pathology, at the Medical College of Ohio in Toledo, says ellagic acid helps block four different types of cancer-causing agents, including the mold aflatoxin and nitrosamines, a class of virulent cancer-producing compounds. Jean Carper *The Food Pharmacy Guide to Good Eating*

Add blueberries to the list of foods that might help your heart by lowering blood cholesterol. A study at Ohio State University found that blueberries have about the same amount of pectin as apples, pears, and peaches (but not as much as citrus fruits). Several studies find that pectin—a soluble fiber—in foods significantly lowers blood cholesterol.

New research also shows that blueberries, like cranberries, may help prevent urinary tract infections. Israeli scientists noted that blueberries contain unknown compounds that combat bacteria known to cause such infections. Blueberries work the same way cranberries do, said the scientists. Jean Carper *The Food Pharmacy Guide to Good Eating*

STRAWBERRY PECAN TART

Serves 8

1 fully-baked pecan pie crust
in a 9-inch pie plate (page 525)
2-3 pints strawberries
2 tablespoons sucanat

Wash strawberries, trim off tops and quarter lengthwise. Toss with sucanat and chill several hours. Just before serving, fill pie crust with strawberries. Serve with whipped cream sweetened with a little stevia powder.

BERRY PIE

Serves 8

1 recipe fully-baked hazelnut pie crust in a 9-inch pie plate (page 525)
2 12-ounce packages frozen berries or 1 1/4 pounds fresh berries
1/2 cup water
1/4 cup maple syrup
2 tablespoons lemon juice
1 tablespoon gelatin (see Sources) dissolved in 3 tablespoons water over lowest heat

Place half the berries in food processor with water and maple syrup. Process until berries are liquefied. Add lemon juice and gelatin mixture while motor is running. Place remaining berries in cooled pie crust and pour gelatin mixture over them. Refrigerate several hours before serving.

In mice with surgically or chemically induced brain lesions, as in the Marshall, et. al. study, the liver, heart, kidneys and pancreas become enlarged. In a piece of research work done by a team long before the Marshal work, continuous intravenous injection of large amounts of dextrose (glucose) into 20 dogs caused death in all of them in 1 to 7 days. It also caused severe hemorrhage and destruction in the pituitary gland and pancreas, and marked liver enlargement. This and other experiments create a compelling reason to believe that the habitual use of refined sugars and other carbohydrates over long periods can create brain lesions similar to the brain lesions produced in the laboratory. Edward Howell MD *Enzyme Nutrition*

CRANBERRY PEAR PIE

Serves 8

1 recipe flaky pie crust (page 524)
12 ounces fresh cranberries
1 cup maple syrup
4 large pears
4 1/2 teaspoons arrowroot dissolved in 2 tablespoons cold water

Line a 9-inch pie plate with flaky pie crust dough and reserve the rest for making lattice work. Place cranberries and maple syrup in a saucepan. Peal and core the pears and cut into 1/2 inch pieces, adding to maple syrup as you cut. Bring to a boil and cook, stirring, for several minutes until cranberries begin to pop. Add the arrowroot mixture and cook another minute more, stirring constantly. Let cool slightly. Pour into pie shell. Make a lattice work to cover the pear mixture and bake at 350 degrees for about 45 minutes.

The US has consumed one-fifth of the world's production of sugar every year but one since the Civil War. By 1893, America was consuming more sugar that the whole world had produced in 1865. By 1920, at the time of the noble experiment in the prohibition of alcohol in the US, that figure for sugar consumption had doubled. Through war and peace, depression and prosperity, drought and flood, sugar consumption in America has risen steadily. It is doubtful there has ever been a more drastic challenge to the human body in the entire history of man. William Dufty *Sugar Blues*

PUMPKIN PIE

Serves 8

1 recipe flaky pastry crust (page 524)
1 can pumpkin puree
3 eggs
3/4 cup sucanat
1 tablespoon freshly grated ginger
1 teaspoon cinnamon
1/4 teaspoon sea salt
1/4 teaspoon powdered cloves
1/4 teaspoon nutmeg
grated rind of 1 lemon
1 cup piima cream or creme fraiche
2 tablespoons brandy (optional)

Line a 9-inch pie pan with flaky pie crust dough and pinch edge to make a border. Cream eggs with sucanat. Gradually blend in other ingredients. Pour into pie shell and bake at 350 degrees for 35 to 45 minutes.

Pumpkin and squash, notably the deep-orange winter types. . . are full of anti-cancer carotenoids, including beta-carotene. The secret, think most scientists, is that the carotenes are antioxidants that do battle against oxygen-free radicals, rendering them harmless. Thus, these orange vegetables may help save you from all kinds of ravages due to cancer and other chronic diseases as well as from aging. On the rampage, the oxygen-free radicals can destroy blood vessel walls, accelerate aging, aggravate inflammation, and latch on to parts of cells such as DNA, causing cell alterations leading to cancer.. . . Everybody, but in particular smokers, former smokers, and people who are around smokers, should make it a point to eat more deep-orange vegetables like winter squash and pumpkin. Jean Carper *The Food Pharmacy*

LEMON TART

Serves 8

1 recipe flaky pie crust (page 525)
3/4 cup crispy almonds (page 487)
3 eggs
3/4 cup sucanat
grated zest of 3 lemons
3/4 cup lemon juice
1/2 stick melted butter

Line a 10-inch French style tart pan with flaky pie crust dough. In a food processor, process almonds into a fine powder. Add eggs and sucanat and blend well. Blend in remaining ingredients. Pour into tart shell and bake at 350 degrees for 35 minutes.

Variation: Orange Tart

Use *orange zest* and *orange juice* instead of lemons.

Dr. Richard Anderson, US Department of Agriculture, is an expert on the metabolism of sugar. He suspected that certain foods might stimulate the activity of insulin and help the body process sugar more efficiently—with less insulin. . . When he measured insulin activity in test tubes in the presence of many foods, most had slight or no effect. But three spices and one herb actually tripled insulin activity: cinnamon, cloves, turmeric, and bay leaves. Cinnamon was the most powerful. Dr. Anderson says eating cinnamon, even in small amounts sprinkled on toast, can boost insulin activity. Thus there is pharmacological wisdom behind using cinnamon and cloves in sweets like pumpkin pie. Jean Carper *The Food Pharmacy Guide to Good Eating*

WALNUT TART

Serves 8

1 recipe flaky pie crust (page 524)
1 1/3 cup freshly shelled walnut meats
1/2 stick butter, melted
3/4 cup sucanat
2 eggs
1 teaspoon coffee extract
2 tablespoons brandy (optional)
1 teaspoon vanilla
1/2 teaspoon salt

Line a 10-inch French style tart pan with flaky pie crust dough. Process nuts in food processor to a fine powder. Add remaining ingredients and process until smooth. Pour into pie shell and bake at 350 for about 40 minutes.

Variation:

Use *1 1/3 cups crispy pecans* (page 485) in place of walnuts.

PECAN TART

Serves 8

1 recipe flaky pie crust (page 524)
1/2 stick butter, softened
3 eggs
1/2 cup sucanat
2 tablespoons piima cream or creme fraiche
grated rind from 1 lemon
1 tablespoon vanilla
1 tablespoon arrowroot
2 cups crispy pecans (page 485)

Line a 10-inch French style tart pan with flaky pie crust dough. Cream butter with eggs and sucanat. Beat in piima cream, vanilla, lemon rind and arrowroot. Fold in pecan halves. Pour into pie shell and bake at 350 degrees for about 35-45 minutes.

The walnut is a versatile and nutritious nut containing notable levels of minerals such as iron, magnesium, phosphorus, potassium and zinc. In earlier times, walnut "milk" made from pulverized walnuts soaked in water, served in European households that had no cow. Walnuts also contain about 60 percent fat, including a high proportion of omega-3 linolenic acid. This essential fatty acid is often deficient in the American diet, but its three double carbon bonds make it extremely susceptible to rancidity. You should therefore only use walnuts that you have shelled yourself. Fresh walnut oil, properly extracted and stored, is delicious and nutritious on salads but should never be used in cooking. SWF

Western medicine and science has only just begun to sound alarm signals over the fantastic increase in its per capita sugar consumption, in the United States especially. Their researches and warnings are, I fear, many decades too late. . . I am confident that Western medicine will one day admit what has been known in the Orient for years: sugar is without question the number one murderer in the history of humanity—much more lethal than opium or radioactive fallout—especially to those people who eat rice as their principal food. Sugar is the greatest evil that modern industrial civilization has visited upon countries of the Far East and Africa. . . foolish people who give or sell candy to babies will one day discover, to their horror, that they have much to answer for. Sakurazawa Nyoiti *We are all Sanpaku*

LEMON CHIFFON PIE

Serves 8

1 fully-baked hazelnut or almond pie crust in a 9-inch pie plate (page 525)
1 tablespoon gelatin (see Sources)
1/4 cup cold water
4 egg yolks
1/2 cup maple syrup
grated rind of 2 lemons
1/2 cup lemon juice
1/2 teaspoon sea salt
4 egg whites
pinch sea salt

Soak gelatin in water. In the top of a double boiler, beat egg yolks with a whisk until pale yellow. Add syrup, lemon juice, lemon rind, gelatin mixture and salt. Place over hot water and cook, stirring constantly with a wooden spoon, until thickened. Let cool. In a clean bowl, beat egg whites with a pinch of salt until they form stiff peaks. Fold in yolk mixture and pour into pie shell. Chill several hours before serving.

In the 1940's, Dr. John Tintera rediscovered the vital importance of the endocrine system (especially the adrenal glands) in "pathological mentation"—or brain boggling. . . Tintera published several epochal medical papers. Over and over, he emphasized that improvement, alleviation, palliation or cure was "dependent upon the restoration of the normal function of the total organism." His first prescribed item of treatment was diet. Over and over again he said: "The importance of diet cannot be overemphasized." He laid out a sweeping permanent injunction against sugar in all forms and guises.

While Egas Moniz of Portugal was receiving a Nobel prize for devising the lobotomy operation for the treatment of schizophrenia, Tintera's reward was the be harassment and hounding by the pundits of organized medicine. William Dufty *Sugar Blues*

APPLE TART

Serves 8

1 recipe flaky pie crust in a 12-inch French-style tart pan, fully baked (page 524)
8 tart apples
1 stick butter
1/2 cup sucanat

Peel and core apples and cut into chunks. In a heavy skillet, saute apples in butter until golden. Add sucanat and saute a few minutes more. Pour into baked pie shell. Served with whipped cream or piima cream sweetened with a little stevia powder.

The mind truly boggles when one glances over what passes for medical history. Through the centuries, troubled souls have been barbecued for bewitchment, exorcised for possession, locked up for insanity, tortured for masturbatory madness, psychiatrized for psychoses, lobotomized for schizophrenia.

How many patients would have listened if the local healer had told them that the only thing ailing them was sugar blues? William Dufty *Sugar Blues*

PEAR CUSTARD TART

Serves 8

1 recipe flaky pie crust (page 524) in a 12-inch French-style tart pan, fully baked
4 ripe pears, cored, cut in half and poached (page 543)
3 egg yolks
1/4 cup maple syrup
2 teaspoons vanilla extract
1 cup heavy cream
3/4 cup piima cream
1 cup seedless honey or fruit juice sweetened blackberry jam

This is a complicated recipe but the results are wonderful. The pie crust, pastry cream, poached pears and jam should all be prepared in advance and the tart assembled just before serving.

Combine cream, syrup and vanilla in a sauce pan and bring to a boil. Remove from heat and allow to cool slightly. Place egg yolks in the top of a double boiler and beat for several minutes until pale. Over a low flame, add the cream mixture very gradually, stirring constantly until the mixture thickens and becomes almost too hot to touch. Remove from heat and chill well.

To assemble, melt jam in a saucepan. Drain and pat dry pear halves and arrange in a ring on tart shell, cored side down. Spread pastry cream over pears and place a spoonful of jam on each. Serve at once.

Variation: Individual Pear Custard Tarts

For six individual tarts, use *3 poached pears*, keeping other ingredient amounts the same. Use one pear half per tart.

Man-refined sugar was introduced to Japan when the Christian missionaries arrived after the US Civil War. At first, the Japanese used refined sugar in the way the Arabs and Persians had used it centuries before: as a medicine. Sugar was taxed as severely as imported patented medicines. By 1906, 45,000 acres of sugar cane were cultivated in Japan, compared with 7 million acres devoted to the cultivation of rice. Interestingly enough , in its war with Russia in 1905, the Japanese armed forces carried their own food in much the same way as the Viet Cong in the 1970's. Each man had enough dried rice to keep him going for three days. This was supplemented with salt fish, dried seaweed and pickled umeboshi plums. William Dufty *Sugar Blues*

The difference between sugar addiction and narcotic addiction is largely one of degree. Small quantities of narcotics can change body-brain behavior quickly. Sugars take a little longer, from a matter of minutes in the case of a liquid, simple sugar alcohol to a matter of years in sugars of other kinds.

The enduring American fantasy of the dope pusher—imbedded in law and myth— is a slimy degenerate hanging around school playgrounds passing out free samples of expensive addictive substances to innocent kids. This fantasy devil was created at the turn of the century by and for a country of booze and sugar addicts with an enduring nostalgia for the friendly country store where so many of them got *their* habit. William Dufty *Sugar Blues*

APPLE PIE

Serves 8

1 recipe flaky pie crust (page 524)
8-10 tart apples
2 tablespoons arrowroot powder
2 tablespoons sucanat
grated rind of 1 lemon

Line a pie pan with flaky pie crust dough, reserving remaining pastry for the top of the pie. Core and peel apples and cut into chunks. Mix arrowroot, sucanat and lemon peel. Fill pie with apples, sprinkling arrowroot mixture on each layer. Cover pie with remaining pastry and pinch edges. Poke a few holes in the top and bake for about 45 minutes at 375 degrees.

Refined sugar is lethal when ingested by humans because it provides only that which nutritionists describe as empty or naked calories. In addition, sugar is worse than nothing because it drains and leeches the body of precious vitamins and minerals through the demands its digestion, detoxification, and elimination make upon one's entire system.

So essential is balance to our bodies, that we have many ways to provide against the sudden shock of a heavy intake of sugar. Minerals such as sodium (from salt), potassium and magnesium (from vegetables), and calcium (from the bones) are mobilized and used in chemical transmutation; neutral acids are produced which attempt to return the acid-alkaline balance factor of the blood to a more normal state.

Sugar taken every day produces a continuously overacid condition, and more and more minerals are required from deep in the body in the attempt to rectify the imbalance. Finally, in order to protect the blood, so much calcium is taken from the bones and teeth that decay and general weakening begin. William Dufty *Sugar Blues*

CHEESE CAKE

Serves 8

1 recipe almond pie crust (page 525) pressed into bottom and sides of a well-buttered and floured 9-inch springform pan
3 eggs
1/2 cup sucanat
3/4 cup yoghurt
1 cup homemade cream cheese (page 80)
2 tablespoons arrowroot
1 teaspoon vanilla
grated rind of 1 lemon

This rich dessert is only for those with a high tolerance to milk products. Beat eggs with sucanat for several minutes. Beat in remaining ingredients and pour into springform pan lined with crust. Bake at 350 degrees for about 40 minutes. Chill well before serving.

ORANGE CAKE

Serves 12-18

2 1/2 cups freshly ground whole wheat or spelt flour
2 cups cultured buttermilk, or water mixed with
2 tablespoons whey or yoghurt
2 sticks butter, softened
1 cup sucanat
2 eggs
1 teaspoon baking soda
1/2 teaspoon sea salt
grated rind of 2 oranges and 2 lemons
1/4 cup water (optional)
1 cup crispy pecans, finely chopped (page 485)
juice of 2 oranges and 2 lemons
1/4 cup whey
1/2 cup raw honey

This wonderful cake, suitable for festive holiday dinners, incorporates all the principles of enzyme nutrition and lacto-fermentation. The flour is soaked overnight in buttermilk, or water mixed with whey or yoghurt. This breaks down phytates and gluten in the flour and softens it so that the heaviness usually associated with whole grain products is avoided. After cooking, the cake is soaked for another day or so in a mixture of orange juice, lemon juice, raw honey and whey. This imparts enzymes to the cake along with a delicious flavor and moistness.

Soak flour in liquid for at least 7 hours or overnight. Cream butter with sucanat and eggs. Beat in soda, salt and grated rind. Little by little incorporate the soaked flour. Beat in 1/4 cup water to thin batter if necessary and fold in nuts. Pour batter into a well buttered and floured, fluted bundt pan or angel food cake pan. Bake at 300 degrees for an hour or more, or until a toothpick comes out clean. Let cool slightly. Place juices, honey and whey in a container and set in simmering water until honey is dissolved. Slowly pour this mixture over the cake until all is absorbed. Cover with plastic wrap and let stand at room temperature for 1 or 2 days. To serve, loosen sides with a knife. Turn over onto a serving place and tap pan until cake falls out.

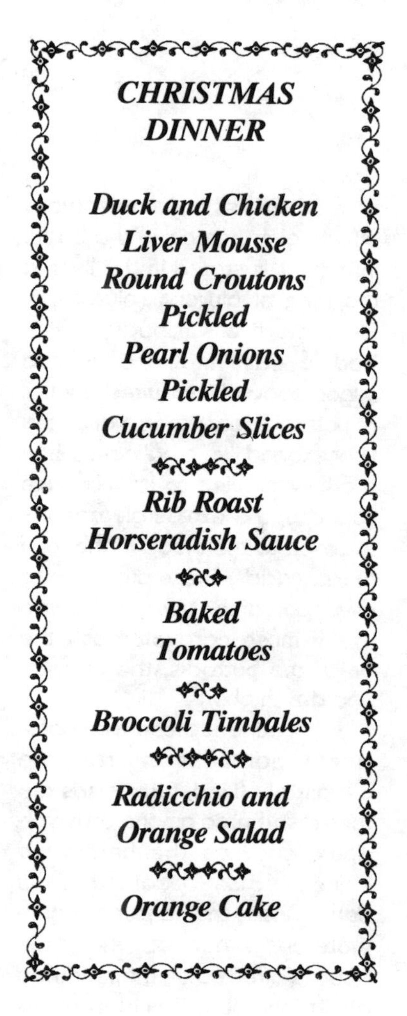

It would be extraordinary if sugar and white flour, known to wreak havoc on the teeth, did not also have profound repercussions elsewhere in the body.

Coronary disease has heretofore been regarded as a "complication" of diabetes. Both coronary disease and diabetes have a common cause: White sugar and white flour. William Dufty *Sugar Blues*

CARROT CAKE

Serves 16-20

2 1/2 cups freshly ground spelt or wheat flour
2 cups buttermilk, or water plus
2 tablespoons whey or yoghurt
2 sticks butter, softened
1 to 1 1/2 cups sucanat
4 eggs
2 teaspoons vanilla
2 teaspoons baking soda
1 teaspoon cinnamon
1 teaspoon sea salt
1 8-ounce can crushed pineapple, water packed
2 cups finely grated carrots
1 cup dried sweetened coconut meat (page 144)
or commercial unsweetened coconut meat
1/2 cup crispy pecans, chopped (page 485)
2 cups homemade cream cheese (page 80),
softened
1 stick butter, softened
1 tablespoon vanilla
1/2 - 3/4 cup raw honey

Soak flour in liquid for 7 hours or overnight. Line a buttered and floured 9-by-13 inch pyrex pan with buttered parchment paper (see Sources). Cream butter with sucanat. Beat in eggs, soda, cinnamon, and salt. Gradually add flour mixture. Fold in pineapple (with juice), carrots, coconut and nuts. Pour into pan and bake at 300 degrees for about 1 1/4 hours. Let cool slightly and turn onto a platter or tray.

To make icing, place cream cheese, butter, vanilla and honey in food processor and blend until smooth. Generously ice the top and sides of the cake. Decorate with flowers.

Variation: Stars and Stripes Cake

Use *blueberries* and *raspberries* to make an American flag on top of the cake.

Excess sugar eventually affects every organ in the body. Initially it is stored in the liver in the form of glucose (glycogen). Since the liver's capacity is limited, a daily intake of refined sugar (above the required amount of natural sugar) soon makes the liver expand like a balloon. When the liver is filled to its maximum capacity, the excess glycogen is returned to the blood in the form of fatty acids. These are taken to every part of the body and stored in the most inactive areas: the belly, the buttocks, the breasts, and the thighs.

When these comparatively harmless places are completely filled, fatty acids are then distributed among active organs, such as the heart and kidneys, these begin to slow down; finally their tissues degenerate and turn to fat. The whole body is affected by their reduced ability and abnormal blood pressure is created. . . . the circulatory and lymphatic systems are invaded and the quality of the red corpuscles starts to change. An overabundance of white cells occurs, and the creation of tissue becomes slower. . . Our body's tolerance and immunizing power becomes more limited, so we cannot respond properly to extreme attacks, whether they be cold, heat, mosquitoes or microbes. William Dufty *Sugar Blues*

POPPY SEED CAKE

1/4-1/3 cup poppyseeds
2 1/2 cups freshly ground wheat or spelt flour
2 cups cultured buttermilk, or water mixed with
2 tablespoons whey or yoghurt
2 sticks butter, softened
1 cup sucanat
2 eggs
1 teaspoon baking soda
1/2 teaspoon sea salt
grated rind of 1 lemon
1 tablespoon vanilla
1/4 cup water (optional)
juice of 1 lemon
1/4 cup whey
1/2 cup raw honey

Soak flour and poppyseeds in liquid for at least 7 hours or overnight. Cream butter with sucanat and eggs. Beat in soda, salt, vanilla and grated rind. Little by little incorporate the soaked flour. Beat in 1/4 cup water to thin batter if necessary. Pour batter into a well buttered and floured, fluted bundt pan or angel food cake pan. Bake at 300 degrees for an hour or more. Let cool slightly. Place lemon juice, honey and whey in a container and set in simmering water until honey is dissolved. Slowly pour this mixture over the cake until all is absorbed. Cover with plastic wrap and let stand for 1 or 2 days.

To serve, loosen sides with a knife. Turn over onto a serving place and tap pan until cake falls out.

Variation: Irish Seed Cake

Use *1/4 cup caraway seeds* instead of poppy seeds and *rind and juice of 2 oranges* instead of 1 lemon. Omit vanilla.

In his comprehensive study, published in 1971, that entailed years of research, Dr. Roberts concluded that a "significant source" of many unexplainable [automobile] accidents is that "millions of American drivers are subject to pathological drowsiness and hypoglycemia due to functional hyperinsulinism." He estimates that there may be as many as ten million drivers like that on the roads of America today.

In other words, low glucose levels in the blood gum up brain functioning, perceptions and reactions. What causes this condition? The doctor's answer: "The apparent increased incidence of hyperinsulinism and of narcolepsy [abnormal attacks of drowsiness] during recent decades can be large attributed to the consequences of an enormous rise in sugar consumption by a vulnerable population." William Dufty *Sugar Blues*

SPICE LAYER CAKE

Dr. Yudkin reports another recent experiment which pointed the other way. He persuaded seven young men each to swallow a tube first thing in the morning so that samples could be obtained of their gastric juices at rest; then, at fifteen minute intervals—after they had swallowed a bland test meal consisting mainly of pectin—further samples were taken. Samples were analyzed in the usual way, measuring the degree of acidity and digestive activity. Then the patients were put on a high-sugar diet for two weeks and tested again. Results showed that two weeks of a sugar-rich diet was enough to increase both stomach acidity and digestive activity of the gastric juices, of the kind one finds in people with gastric or duodenal ulcers. The rich diet of sugar increased stomach acidity by 20 percent or so and the enzyme activity was increased almost three times. William Dufty *Sugar Blues*

3 cups freshly ground spelt or wheat flour
2 1/2 cups buttermilk, or water mixed with
2 tablespoons whey or yoghurt
2 sticks butter, softened
3 eggs
1 1/2 cups sucanat
1 tablespoon baking soda
1/2 teaspoon sea salt
1 teaspoon cinnamon
1 teaspoon ground ginger
1/2 teaspoon nutmeg
1/8 teaspoon cloves
1/4 teaspoon ground white pepper
1 cup honey or fruit juice sweetened raspberry jam
2 cups homemade cream cheese (page 80)
1 stick butter, softened
1 tablespoon vanilla
1/2 cup raw honey

Soak flour in liquid for 7 hours or overnight. Cream butter with sucanat. Blend in eggs, soda, salt and spices. Gradually blend in flour mixture. Pour into 2 buttered and floured easy-remove 10-inch cake pans. Bake at 300 degrees for about 45 minutes. Let cool before removing.

To make icing, blend cream cheese, butter, honey and vanilla in food processor. To assemble cake, use raspberry jam between layers and ice top and sides of cake with cream cheese icing. Chill well.

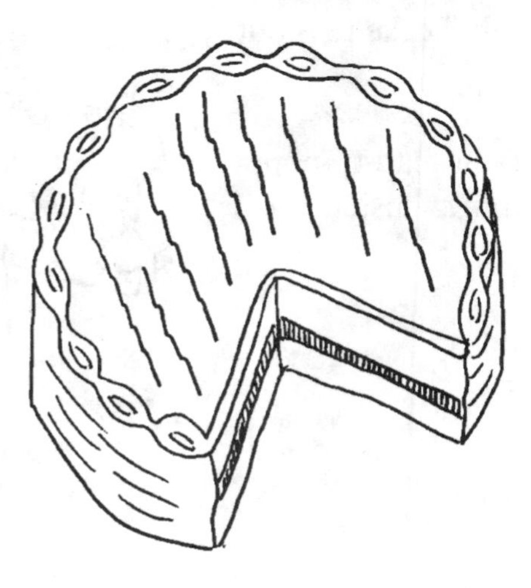

BREAD & RICE CAKE

Serves 8

3/4 cup basic brown rice (page 441)
3 slices whole grain bread, crumbled by hand
1 cup piima cream or creme fraiche
1/2 cup raisins
1/2 stick butter, melted
1/2 cup chopped crispy pecans (page 485)
3 eggs
3/4 cup sucanat
grated rind of 1 orange

Soak crumbled bread with cream. Using a wooden spoon, mix all ingredients. Pour into a buttered 9-inch easy-remove cake pan. Bake at 350 degrees for 1 hour or more. Let cool before removing from pan.

FLOURLESS ALMOND CAKE

Serves 8-12

4 egg yolks
1/2 cup sucanat
grated rind of 1 lemon
1 teaspoon almond extract
1 cup finely grated carrots
1 cup crispy almonds (page 487), processed into a coarse meal
1 tablespoon arrowroot
1/2 teaspoon sea salt
4 egg whites
pinch sea salt
2 tablespoons pine nuts (optional)

Butter and flour an 8-inch easy-remove cake pan. Beat egg yolks with sucanat for about 5 minutes with an electric beater. Blend in lemon rind, almond extract, carrots, almonds, arrowroot, and sea salt. In a clean bowl, beat egg whites with pinch of sea salt until stiff. Fold egg yolk mixture into egg whites and pour into cake pan. Sprinkle pine nuts on top. Bake at 350 degrees for about 45 minutes. Let cool before removing from pan.

[Throughout the Azores and the West Indies] enormous quantities of wood were consumed in building the many sugar mills and converting the cane into sugar. Mills failed if their owners did not have access to large amounts of timber because, as Gonzalo Fernandez de Oviedo, who spent many years on Espanola observed, "You cannot believe the quantities of wood they burn without seeing it yourself." Experts in West Indian sugar production estimated that from six to eight slaves had to be constantly employed in carrying fuel in the forest and transporting it to the mill for optimum efficiency. To provide fuel for one mill stripped about ninety acres of forest land each year. John Perlin *A Forest Journey*

Know Your Ingredients

Name This Product #42

Sugar, bleached flour, egg whites, pineapple, nonfat milk, water, wheat fiber, modified cornstarch, baking powder (sodium acid pyrophosphate, baking soda, monocalcium phosphate), mono-and diglycerides, dextrin, natural & artificial flavors, oat fiber, maltodextrin, corn syrup, salt, dextrose, lemon puree, potassium sorbate (apreservative), beta carotene, sodium stearoyl lactylate, xanthan gum, guar gum, citric acid.

See Appendix B for Answer

FLOURLESS CAROB CAKE

Serves 8

3/4 cup carob powder
1 stick plus 1 tablespoon butter
3 tablespoons water
1 tablespoon vanilla
1 tablespoon chocolate extract (optional)
6 egg yolks
1/2 cup sucanat
5 egg whites
pinch salt
1 cup carob sauce (page 518)

This is a delicious, moist and rich cake—indistinguishable from chocolate. (Well, almost.)

Butter and flour two easy-remove 9-inch cake pans. Place butter, carob powder, water and extracts in a glass container set in a pan of water over a low flame. Melt and blend well. Beat egg yolks with sucanat for about 5 minutes with electric beater. In a clean bowl beat egg whites with pinch of salt until stiff. Mix carob mixture with egg yolk mixture and then fold into egg whites. Divide batter between two pans. Bake at 350 for about 25 minutes. Let cool slightly. Remove one layer to a serving dish and place other layer on top. Frost top with carob sauce and let it dribble over the sides.

"No cask of sugar arrives in Europe to which blood is not sticking. In view of the misery of these slaves anyone with feelings should renounce these wares and refuse the enjoyment of what is only to be bought with tears and death of countless unhappy creatures."

Thus wrote French philosopher Claude Adrien Helvetius in the middle of the eighteenth century when France had moved into the front ranks of the sugar trade. The Sorbonne condemned him. Priests persuaded the court he was full of dangerous ideas; he recanted—in part to save his skin—and his book was burned by hangmen. The virulence of his attacks on slavery brought his ideas to the attention of all Europe. He said in public what many people thought in secret.

The stigma of slavery was on sugar everywhere, but most particularly in Britain. Everywhere sugar had become a source of public wealth and national importance. Through taxes and tariffs on sugar, government had remained a partner in organized crime. Fabulous fortunes were being amassed by plantation owners, planters, traders and shippers; and the sole concern of European royalty was how they were to take their cut. William Dufty *Sugar Blues*

GOURMET DESSERTS

VANILLA BAVARIAN CREAM WITH BLACK-BERRY SAUCE

Serves 12

1 tablespoon gelatin
1/2 cup water
4 egg yolks
1/2 cup maple syrup
1 tablespoon vanilla
4 egg whites
pinch sea salt
2 cups heavy cream, preferably unpasteurized
1 12-ounce package frozen blackberries
1/2 cup maple syrup
1-2 cups water
fresh blackberries for garnish

Mix gelatin with water and dissolve over lowest heat. Place egg yolks, syrup and vanilla in food processor and process until smooth. With motor running, pour in gelatin mixture and process briefly. Place food processor bowl and its contents in refrigerator while completing next steps. In a clean bowl beat the egg whites with pinch of sea salt until they form stiff peaks. In a separate bowl, beat the cream until softly stiff. Return food processor bowl with gelatin mixture to machine, scrape down sides and pulse briefly. Fold egg yolk mixture into cream and this mixture into egg whites. Pour into individual molds and chill for several hours.

Meanwhile place partially thawed berries and syrup in food processor and process until smooth. Add water to achieve desired consistency. (Sauce should not be too thick.)

To serve, dip molds briefly in boiling water and invert onto soup places. Spoon sauce around molded Bavarian cream and decorate with blackberries.

Downey considered that gelatin was recognized as a valuable addition to the dietary because of its easy digestion, ready absorption, protein sparing ability and supplementary protein value, He also noted that gelatin aided in the digestion of other foods, especially milk and milk products, and served as a base for many attractive and appealing dishes. N.R Gotthoffer
Gelatin in Nutrition and Medicine

Sugar, which had up to about 1600 been extremely expensive, and only used for making luxury confectionery for the very rich, had fallen in price dramatically when the seventeenth century trade with the East opened up, and was freely available for such dishes as fruit tarts and puddings. One immediate result of this was that the teeth of the well-to-do, who could afford to eat large quantities of the new sugary dishes, began to show rapid signs of decay, especially as the custom of cleaning the teeth was not very common. The courtiers, always the first with new fashions, were inevitably also the first to display the stigmata of excessive sweet-eating: a visitor to England in 1598, Paul Hentzner, who saw Queen Elizabeth arriving at the royal Palace of Greenwich, remarked on her black teeth, "a defect the English seem subject to, from their too great use of sugar." Terence McLaughlin
A Diet of Tripe

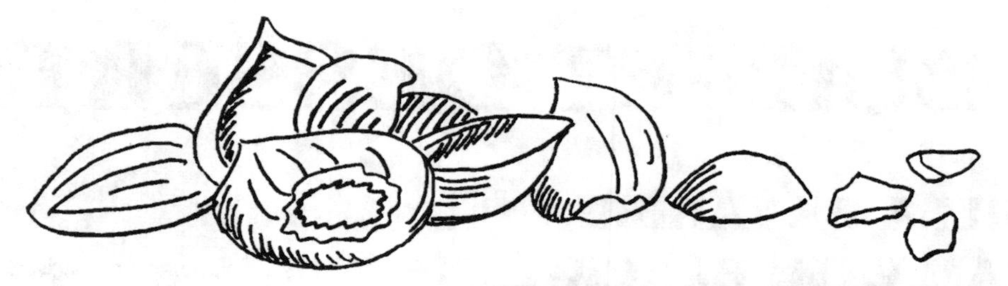

HAZELNUT SHORTCAKE

Serves 8

Some people shun nuts because they are high in fat. True, they are, but nuts are a terrific pharmacological package. Nuts are definitely not just a high-fat, empty calorie food. If you do not eat nuts, you may cheat yourself of vitamin E, an antioxidant linked to lower rates of cancer. Walnuts also are extremely high in the marvelous omega-3 fatty acids, as well as antioxidants such as ellagic acid. Almonds, hazelnuts and pistachios are rich sources of monounsaturated fat, in particular oleic acid, which has recently been revealed as an antioxidant. Eating almonds has lowered blood cholesterol in human tests. One major study decidedly linked low rates of heart disease with consumption of nuts. People who eat nuts seem to have a lower risk of Parkinson's disease.

As Dr. David Jenkins, University of Toronto, points out, the almond is full of the right stuff; most of its fat is monounsaturated; it is exceptionally low in saturated fat (even lower than olive oil); it is full of vegetable protein and fiber. It also helps keep blood sugar and insulin levels steady and this may help fight high blood pressure, diabetes, obesity, and general atherosclerotic damage to arteries. Nuts also have anticancer compounds. Jean Carper *The Food Pharmacy Guide to Good Eating*

1 1/2 cups hazelnuts, peeled
1 cup arrowroot
1/2 teaspoon sea salt
1 stick butter, softened
1/2 cup sucanat
3 cups fresh berries such as strawberries, blueberries, blackberries or raspberries
2 cups heavy cream
pinch stevia powder
1 teaspoon vanilla

To peel hazelnuts, place on a cookie sheet and bake at 350 degrees until skins turn dark and begin to crack. Place in a kitchen towel and wrap up tightly. Hold towel-wrapped nuts in your hands and rub and squeeze for several minutes. Open up towel—most of the skins should have come off. Lift hazelnuts and shake off. Transfer to food processor.

Process nuts to a fine meal. Add arrowroot, butter, salt and sucanat and process until well blended. Butter and flour a 12-inch French style tart pan and press dough into the pan to make an even layer. Bake at 300 for about 1/2 hour. Let cool. Meanwhile whip cream, adding stevia powder and vanilla when cream begins to stiffen. Cut shortcake into wedges and top with fresh berries and whipped cream.

BERRY CREAM CHEESE DELIGHT

Serves 8

2 cups homemade cream cheese (page 80)
1/2 cup raisins, soaked for 1 hour in water
grated rind of 2 lemons
1/2 cup cognac
1/4 cup raw honey
1 teaspoon cinnamon
3-4 cups fresh berries

Using a slotted spoon, transfer the soaked raisins to a pan. Add cognac and lemon zest and simmer for about 10 minutes, so that all alcohol has evaporated. Mix cream cheese with honey and cinnamon in food processor. Blend in cognac and raisins with a wooden spoon. Line a strainer with several layers of cheese cloth and place cream cheese mixture in the cheese cloth. Tie into a bag, being careful not to squeeze, and hang the bag over a bowl to drain for several hours. Place 1/2 cup cream cheese mixture in 8 individual bowls and place berries on top.

[Defenders of pasteurization] make little of enzymes and report that a large number of enzymes are completely destroyed in the process of pasteurization. They attribute little importance to this and point out that the complete destruction of the enzyme phosphatase is one method of testing to see if the milk has been adequately pasteurized. Phosphatase is essential for the absorption of calcium, *but the complete destruction of phosphatase is the aim of pasteurization!* William Campbell Douglass MD *The Milk of Human Kindness*

Know Your Ingredients

Name This Product #43

Skim milk, fructose, sugar, Dutch processed cocoa, gum arabic, partially hydrogenated soy oil, calcium caseinate, potassium citrate, lactic acid, artificial flavors, guar gum, soy fiber, oat fiber, carrageenan and the following vitamins and minerals: calcium phosphate, magnesium oxide, sodium ascorbate, vitamin E acetate, ferric orthophosphate, vitamin A palmitate, biotin, niacinamide, zinc oxide, calcium pantothenate, vitamin B12, manganese sulfate, vitamin D, copper gluconate, thiamine mononitrate, pyridoxine hydrochloride, riboflavin, folic acid, potassium iodide

See Appendix B for Answer

BAKED PEARS

Serves 8

8 whole pears
1/2 cup lemon juice
1 cup red wine
1/2 cup honey or maple syrup

Combine lemon juice, wine and honey or syrup in a small pan. Bring to a simmer. Peel pears and core from the bottom end. Set on sides in a pyrex dish and pour the wine mixture over them. Bake at 350 degrees for about 1/2 hour, turning and basting frequently. Carefully remove pears to a bowl and chill well. Meanwhile, pour syrup into a small saucepan and boil down until it thickens. Let cool.

To serve, place pears on individual plates and spoon sauce over. For a more elegant presentation, place pears on individual plates and place one large spoonful of thickened sauce on one side of the pear and one large spoonful of *creme anglaise* on the other side of the pear. Let the two sauces run together slightly for an interesting pattern.

Variation: Baked Peaches

Use *8 fresh peaches* instead of pears.

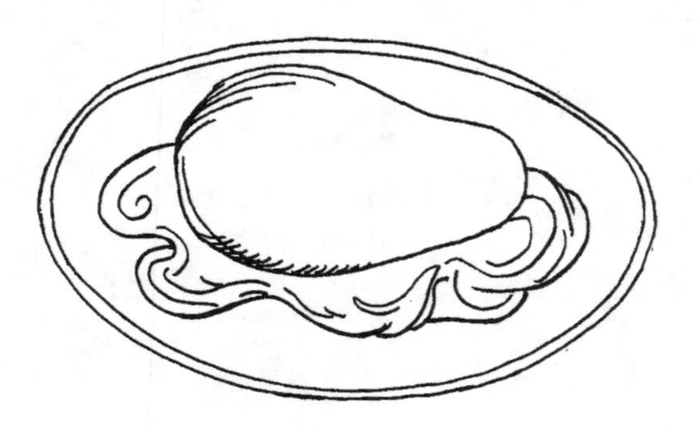

The pear is a relative of the apple and a native to the temperate regions of Europe and Asia. They are good sources of fiber and contain phosphorus and carotenoids as well as ellagic acid, a substance that acts against cancer. The ancient Chinese valued the pear for treatment of the stomach and lungs.
There are many delicious varieties of pears. The best for poaching and baking purposes are the bartletts. SWF

Know Your Ingredients

Name This Product #44

(Filling) milk, sugar, nonfat dry milk, corn syrup, microcrystalline cellulose, mono and diglycerides, natural and artificial flavor, sodium carboxymethylcellulose, guar gum, locust (carob) bean gum, polysorbate 80, carrageenan, salt (Wafer) enriched bleached flour (contains niacin, reduced iron, thiamine mononitrate, and riboflavin), sugar, mono- and di-glycerides (with BHA and citric acid), caramel color, dextrose, polydextrose, corn syrup, glycerine, leavening (sodium bicarbonate, sodium acid pyrophosphate), calcium sulfate, cocoa, cellulose fiber, food starch-modified, salt, water, artificial flavor, artificial color including FD&C yellow No. 6, sodium bisulfate.

See Appendix B for Answer

CREME ANGLAISE

Makes 3 cups

2 cups heavy cream, preferably raw
1/2 cup maple syrup or honey
1 tablespoon grated ginger (optional)
1 tablespoon vanilla extract
5 large egg yolks

Combine cream, syrup or honey, ginger and vanilla in a bowl. Heat until quite warm, but not burning to the touch, by placing in a pan of simmering water. Meanwhile, place egg yolks in a double boiler and beat for several minutes until pale. Over a low flame, add the warm cream mixture to yolks very gradually, stirring constantly, until the mixture thickens slightly. Chill well. Serve with fresh berries or other fruit

POACHED PEARS WITH CAROB SAUCE

(Poires Belle Helene)
Serves 8

8 ripe pears
1/2 cup fresh lemon juice
1/2 cup honey or maple syrup
1-2 quarts filtered water
1 tablespoon vanilla
2 1/2 cups warm carob sauce (page 518)
toasted slivered crispy almonds (page 487)

Peal pears, cut in half lengthwise, core and immediately brush with lemon juice. Bring water to a boil with honey and vanilla. Add pears and simmer, covered, for about 10 minutes until soft. Carefully transfer to a bowl, cover with cooking liquid and chill well.

To serve, remove pears from liquid, pat dry and place two halves on individual serving plates. Spoon carob sauce over them and sprinkle with almonds.

Know Your Ingredients

Name This Procuct #45

86% water, 4.8% corn syrup, 2.5% sucrose, 2.1% soy oil, 2.0% soy protein isolate, 1.4% coconut oil, 0.14% calcium citrate, 0.13% calcium phosphate tribasic, potassium citrate, potassium phosphate monobasic, potassium chloride, mono- and diglycerides, soy lecithin, magnesium chloride, carrageenan, ascorbic acid, l-methionine, potassium phosphate dibasic, sodium chloride, choline chloride, taurine, ferrous sulfate, m-inositol, alpha-tocopherol acetate, zinc sulfate, l-carnitine, niacinamide, calcium pantothenate, cupric sulfate, vitamin A palmitate, thiamine chloride hydrochloride, riboflavin, pyridoxine hydrochloride, folic acid, manganese sulfate, potassium iodide, phylloquinone, biotin, sodium selenite, vitamin D3 and cyanocobalamin.

See Appendix B for Answer

[In order to beat Britain's sugar blockade] Benjamin Delassert found a way to process the lowly Babylonian beet into a new kind of sugar loaf at Plassy in 1812. Napoleon awarded him the Legion of Honor. Napoleon ordered sugar beets planted everywhere in France, an imperial factory was established for refining; scholarships were granted to schools for starting courses in sugar beet crafts; 500 licenses were created for sugar refineries. By the very next year, Napoleon had achieved the herculean feat of producing eight million pounds of sugar from homegrown beets. When Napoleonic armies set out for Moscow, their sugar rations were ensured. Like the Moors before them, they were turned back while traveling north. The mighty French army, in the unaccustomed climate, had met their match and more, including the armies of a backward people who had not yet accustomed themselves to sugar in their tea. William Dufty *Sugar Blues*

BERRY GRATIN

Serves 4

3 cups mixed berries
2 cups creme anglaise (page 543)
2 tablespoons sucanat

Arrange berries on 4 flameproof dishes and place 1/2 cup creme anglaise on each. Sprinkle with sucanat. Place under broiler for 3 or 4 minutes until sucanat browns. Serve immediately.

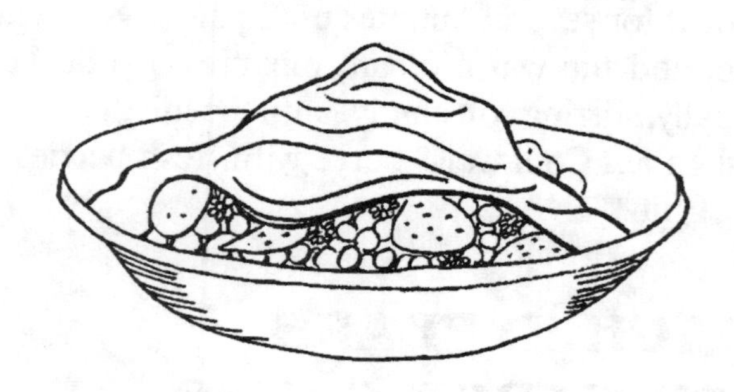

SUMMER FRUIT COMPOTE

Serves 8

1 1/2 cups filtered water
3 tablespoons honey
4-inch stick of cinnamon
freshly ground nutmeg
4 medium pears, peeled and quartered
4 medium peaches, peeled and quartered
2 cups dark cherries, pitted and halved

In a medium saucepan bring water to boil with honey, cinnamon and nutmeg. Add fruit and simmer, covered, for 3 minutes. Remove fruit to a bowl and chill in refrigerator. Remove cinnamon stick and reduce sauce to about one-third by boiling down. Let cool, pour over fruit and chill well. Divide among individual serving dishes and garnish with a dollop of whipped cream, creme fraiche or piima cream.

APRICOT SOUFFLE

Serves 4

1/2 pound dried unsulphured apricots,
cooked in water until tender
2 tablespoons honey or sucanat
2 egg yolks
2 tablespoons heavy cream
5 egg whites
pinch sea salt

The secret to a successful desert souffle is to make it in small quantities. This unusual souffle will fill a quart-sized souffle dish or 4 smaller souffle ramekins. If you double the recipe, use two quart-sized souffle dishes, not one larger one.

Transfer cooked apricots with a slotted spoon to food processor and process with honey, egg yolks and cream. In a clean bowl beat egg whites with pinch of salt until stiff. Fold in apricot mixture thoroughly, but as quickly and as lightly as possible. Pour into a buttered quart-sized souffle dish or 4 smaller ones and bake at 350 degrees for about 25 minutes. Check progress by peeking though the oven window—not by opening the door.

Variation: Fruit Souffle

Use *2 cups fresh berries or other fruit* instead of apricots. Sprinkle with *2 tablespoons sucanat* and macerate. Let stand about 1/2 hours. Meanwhile, blend honey, egg yolks and cream Using a slotted spoon, transfer fruit to egg yolk mixture and fold in. Proceed with recipe.

Know Your Ingredients

Name This Product #46

Reconstituted skim milk, graham cracker crumbs (enriched wheat flour {niacin, iron, thiamine mononitrate, riboflavin}, graham flour, sugar, partially hydrogenated soybean oil, water, corn syrup, salt, sodium bicarbonate), egg whites, fructose, polydextrose, modified food starch, hydrogenated coconut oil, cocoa powder (processed with alkali to enhance flavor), high fructose corn syrup, lactylated mono and diglycerides, partially hydrogenated soybean oil, soy protein, microcrystalline cellulose, egg white solids, dextrose, sodium caseinate, pear juice concentrate, sugar, gelatin powder, tapioca dextrin, carrageenan, natural and artificial flavors, sodium alginate, aspartame, beta carotene, artificial flavor, annatto and turmeric colors

See Appendix B for Answer

Know Your Ingredients

Name This Product 47

Sugar, modified cornstarch, salt, mono and diglycerides, carrageenan salts, polysorbate 60, artificial flavor, artificial color (including yellow 5), natural flavor.

See Appendix B for Answer

New evidence points a sharp finger at sugar as a food item that makes us older faster!

The quick rush of sugar into the bloodstream is probably what does it. . . In much the same way as a steak turns brown and toughens on the barbecue grill, a reaction between sugar and protein called the "browning effect"—sugar reacts with protein in human cells—occurs, particularly as human cells age. . .

Aging seems to be accelerated when the body must cope with excessive sugar and is unable to do it—as in diabetes.

[Scientists] now feel that collagen, which glues our trillions of cells together, and is affected by glucose, acts upon DNA causing mutations in this genetic material that permit the start and spread of cancer. . .

Any sudden rush of glucose into the bloodstream—from a candy bar, a glass of orange juice, or a couple teaspoons of granulated sugar in the coffee—stresses the pancreas to produce more insulin. Excessive sugar making the rounds of the bloodstream brings about cross-linking and aging. James F. Scheer *Health Freedom News*

LEMON MOUSSE

Serves 6

6 egg yolks, room temperature
1/2 cup honey
grated rind of 2 lemons
strained juice of 2 lemons
6 egg whites, room temperature
pinch sea salt
1/2 cup heavy cream, preferably raw, well chilled

Place egg yolks, honey, lemon rind and lemon juice in the top of a double boiler over simmering water. Whisk constantly for about 10 minutes until mixture thickens. Remove from heat and chill in refrigerator for about 1/2 hour. Beat cream until stiff. In a separate clean bowl beat egg whites with sea salt until stiff. Fold lemon mixture into cream and then egg whites into cream mixture. Spoon into individual parfait glasses and chill well before serving.

Variation: Lime Mousse

Use *zest and juice of 3 limes* instead of lemons.

BEVERAGES

BEVERAGES

It is difficult to think of a popular beverage that can qualify as a health food—tea, coffee, soft drinks, alcoholic beverages and even fruit juice—all should be avoided because they contain caffeine, concentrated sugars or large amounts of alcohol. Our collection of beverages offers unique alternatives to all of these. They feature dilute fruit juices, seeds, nuts and yoghurt, all enhanced by the process of lacto-fermentation to make their nutrients more available, and to supply lactic-acid and lactobacilli to the intestinal tract. The heartier drinks, made from grains and nuts, can qualify as foods; the others as refreshing pick-me-ups and digestive aids. We offer the theory that the craving for alcohol, as well as the craving for soft drinks, stems from an ancient collective memory of the kind of lacto-fermented beverages still found in traditional societies. These beverages give a lift to the tired body by supplying mineral ions depleted through perspiration, and contribute to easy and thorough assimilation of our food by supplying lactobacilli, lactic-acid and enzymes.

A survey of popular ethnic beverages will show that the fermentation of grains and fruits to make refreshing and health-promoting drinks is almost universal. Usually these drinks are very mildly alcoholic, the result of a fermentation process that is both alcoholic (by the action of yeasts on sugars) and lactic-acid forming (by the action of bacteria on sugars). Beers made from millet, corn, barley and wheat are ubiquitous: *tesquino*, an Aztec beer, is made from corn; *munkoyo*, a beer of Zambia containing less than .5% alcohol, is consumed in large quantities by young and old; *chicha*, a beer used by the Incas during religious festivals, is made from little balls of dough that have been chewed to inoculate them with saliva; very mildly alcoholic beers made from rice are found throughout Asia; *kvass*, the Russian national drink made from various cereal grains and fruits, contains less than 1% alcohol and is used to treat the sick; a similar Middle European drink called *kiesel* is made from oats or rye. Wines and ciders made from fruits such as grapes, bananas, apples, pears and watermelon are also found throughout the world: *pulque*, a Mexican drink, is made from juice of a cactus plant; palm wine, found throughout tropical countries, contains less that 2% alcohol and is made from spontaneous fermentation of palm sap; natives of British Guyana make a drink called *fly* from sweet potatoes and cassava; and fermented tea is found throughout Asia and Europe. The American Indians made a drink from crushed soaked pecans while European peasants made a similar beverage from walnuts. In Colonial America we find spruce beer, brewed from spruce leaves and a variety of seeds and berries. The explorer Cartier had earlier learned from the Indians that a brew made from hemlock leaves would relieve the symptoms of scurvy. It was for the same reason that Washington included "one quart of spruce beer per day" in the rations of the Continental Army.

Although most of these traditional beverages were mildly alcoholic, we have found that alcoholic fermentation can be completely avoided by the addition of whey and a little sea salt to our beverage preparations. The results are pleasantly acidic drinks with complex flavors, especially if allowed to age for several weeks in the refrigerator. Whey is easy to make (see page 80), and is superior to concentrated or powdered whey available at health food stores. Use only Celtic sea salt for lacto-fermentation (see Sources).

The use of whey to make nutritious drinks is not so much an innovation as a revival of an ancient method found throughout the British Isles, and probably in other European countries, since very ancient times. Medical treatises written during the 17th and 18th centuries extol the virtues of whey-based drinks including "wine whey" (wine mixed with whey), "whey whig" (a beverage made of whey flavored with herbs) and "small beer" (a non-alcoholic beverage brewed from whey and grain, as distinguished from "strong beer" in which yeast is added to promote the production of alcohol.)

Throughout the world, these lactic-acid-containing drinks have been valued for medicinal qualities including the ability to relieve intestinal problems and constipation, promote lactation, strengthen the sick, and promote overall well-being and stamina. Above all, these drinks are considered superior to plain water in their ability to relieve thirst during physical labor. Modern research has discovered that liquids containing dilute sugars and electrolytes of minerals (mineral ions) are actually absorbed faster than plain water. This research is used to promote commercial sports drinks, high-sugar concoctions containing small amounts of electrolytes. But natural lactic-acid fermented drinks contain numerous valuable minerals in suspension, a small amount of sugar, along with lactic acid and beneficial lactobacilli, all of which promote good health in many ways, while at the same time cutting the sensation of thirst.

Both soft drinks and alcoholic beverages—and even plain water—are poor substitutes for these health-promoting beverages. Taken with meals they promote thorough and easy digestion of food; taken after physical labor they rapidly replace lost mineral ions to give a needed lift that renews rather than depletes the body's reserves. The day when every town and hamlet in America produces its own distinctive lacto-fermented brew, made from the local products of woods and fields, will be the day when Americans see the dawning of a new age of good health and well-being, as well as a new era of economic vitality based on small-scale local production rather than on large-scale monopolistic control of the food-processing industry.

Equipment for beverages includes some 2-quart-sized containers with tops or lids that seal tightly; and cheesecloth for filtering. (A juicer is handy but not absolutely necessary for the production of grape cooler.)

GINGER ALE

Makes 2 quarts

3/4 cup ginger, peeled and finely chopped or grated
1/2 cup fresh lime juice
1/4-1/2 cup sucanat
2 teaspoons sea salt
1/4 cup whey
2 quarts filtered water

This is a most refreshing drink, taken in small amounts with meals, and as a restoring lift when doing hard work outside.

Place all ingredients in a 2-quart jug and fill with filtered water. Stir well and cover tightly. Keep at room temperature for 2 days before transferring to refrigerator. This will keep several months well chilled.

To serve, strain and mix half ginger ale with half filtered or carbonated water. Best drunk at room temperature, not cold.

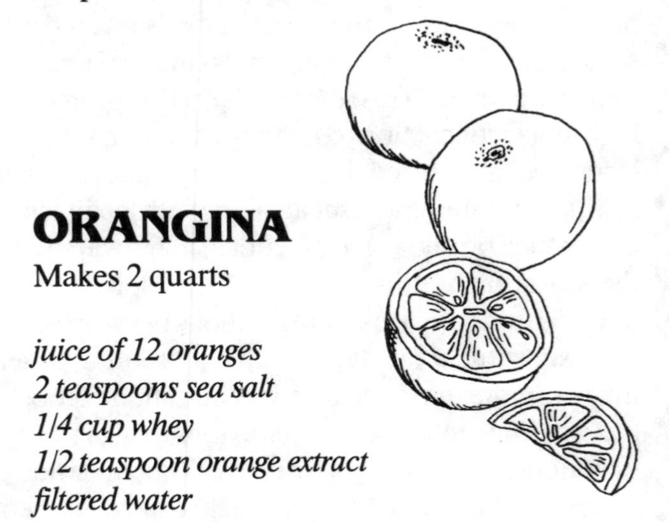

ORANGINA

Makes 2 quarts

juice of 12 oranges
2 teaspoons sea salt
1/4 cup whey
1/2 teaspoon orange extract
filtered water

Place all ingredients in a 2-quart container and stir well. Cover tightly. Leave at room temperature for 2 days before transferring to refrigerator. In several days the juice will develop an interesting banana-like flavor. Stir before pouring.

Now the sun and the wind were hotter and Laura's legs quivered while she made them trample the hay. She was glad to rest for the little times between the field and the stack. She was thirsty, then she was thirstier, and then she was so thirsty that she could think of nothing else. It seemed forever till ten o'clock when Carrie came lugging the jug half-full.

Pa told Laura to drink first but not too much. Nothing was ever so good as that cool wetness going down her throat. At the taste of it she stopped in surprise and Carrie clapped her hands and cried out, laughing, "Don't tell, Laura, don't tell till Pa tastes it!"

Ma had sent them ginger-water. She had sweetened the cool well-water with sugar, flavored it with vinegar, and put in plenty of ginger to warm their stomachs so they could drink till they were not thirsty. Ginger-water would not make them sick, as plain cold water would when they were so hot. Such a treat made that ordinary day into a special day, the first day that Laura helped in the haying. Laura Ingalls Wilder *The Long Winter*

Modern ginger ale has two ancestors. One is ginger beer, brewed and bottled at home like root beer. A fermented, bubbly drink, it was sometimes alcoholic, mostly not. The other is ginger water, or "switchel," as New Englanders called it, a non-alcoholic drink prepared for farmers during long hot days of scything in the hayfields. By Laura Ingalls Wilder's day, ginger drinks were flavored with sugar rather than with natural sweeteners such as maple syrup or honey; and the tart taste was obtained from vinegar rather than from lacto-fermentation. SWF

APPLE "CIDER"

Makes 4 quarts

1 gallon unfiltered, unpasteurized apple juice
1 tablespoon sea salt
1/2 cup whey

Place all ingredients in a large bowl. Cover and leave at room temperature for 2 days. Skim foam that rises to the top. Line a strainer with several layers of cheese cloth and strain juice into jars or jugs. Cover tightly and refrigerate. Flavors will develop slowly over several weeks. The "cider" will eventually develop a rich buttery taste.

If you wish to further clarify the cider, add lightly beaten egg whites to the jugs (1 egg white per quart.) Set aside a few hours and then filter again through several layers of cheesecloth.

RASPBERRY DRINK

Makes 2 quarts

2 12-ounce packages frozen raspberries
or 24 ounces fresh raspberries
juice of 12 oranges
1/4-1/2 cup sucanat
1/4 cup whey
2 teaspoons sea salt
2 quarts filtered water

Place raspberries in food processor and blend until smooth. Mix in a large bowl with remaining ingredients. Cover and let sit at room temperature for 2 days. Skim foam that may rise to top. Strain through a strainer lined with cheesecloth. Pour into jugs or jars, cover tightly and store in refrigerator. If you wish to further clarify the raspberry drink, add lightly beaten egg whites to the jugs (1 egg white per quart.) Set aside a few hours and then filter again through several layers of cheesecloth. To serve, dilute with sparkling mineral water.

What's inside the cupboard is competing strongly with what's inside the medicine cabinet for managing various physical ailments.

Now word from out of Denmark informs us that ginger has been found to be effective in relieving common symptoms of rheumatoid arthritis: pain, inflammation and stiffness.

Dr. Krishna C. Srivastava, of the Institute of Odense, gave arthritis patients a bit less than a tablespoon of ginger daily for three months, and patients reported "significant relief".

Doctor Srivastava fed the patients either five grams of fresh ginger root or from 1/2 gram to a gram and one-half of ginger powder. Both forms worked equally well. Every one of the patients noted marked improvement: ability to get around better, less swelling and less start-of-the-day stiffness.

Other natural ways of managing arthritis, reported in research literature, are eliminating nightshade plants form the diet—potatoes, tomatoes, peppers and desisting from tobacco (smoked or chewed)—reducing dietary fat [rancid and hydrogenated fats], eliminating common known allergens: wheat, corn, citrus fruits, beef, pork, sugar, coffee and alcohol; taking cod liver oil daily and, among other majors, using a supplement of yucca. Ginger ranks high among the foods that heal. It not only appears to be effective with rheumatoid arthritis, but also with motion sickness and morning sickness. A double blind study at Brigham Young University showed ginger root capsules to be more effective than Dramamine for preventing motion sickness. James F. Scheer *Health Freedom News*

Fruits contain protective substances, above all fiber and vitamin C. Berries (strawberries, raspberries, blackberries, gooseberries and cassis) are particularly rich. Grapes contain a phenol—ellagic acid—that reduces the effects of carcinogens. Johanna Brandt, author of a well known book, cured herself of metastasized cancer with grapes and fasting. Her book contains numerous testimonies of other cancer victims who were cured by her method. Claude Aubert *Dis-Moi Comment Tu Cuisines*

In an American Cancer Society study of 78,000 women, those who consumed artificially sweetened foods gained more weight over a one-year period than those who consumed sugar-sweetened products. In another study students were hungrier after drinking artificially sweetened liquids than sugared ones. If sugar is a substitute for "the sweet experience", then artificial sweeteners are a substitute for a substitute. It's like using counterfeit money to buy fake diamonds. David Marc *Nourishing Wisdom*

GRAPE COOLER

Makes 5-6 quarts

1 case organic red grapes, about 16 pounds,
1/2 cup whey
1 tablespoon sea salt

This beverage is best made with a vegetable juicer, although the food processor will do. It takes a bit of time but the results are worth it. This delicious and refreshing drink is an excellent substitute for wine, containing all the nutrients of grapes found in wine, including many enzymes, but none of the alcohol.

Remove grapes from stems, wash well and pass through the juicer. Place liquid in a large bowl with salt and whey and stir well. (Reserve pulp to make natural yeast bread, page 466). Cover and leave at room temperature for 2 days. Skim off scum and strain juice through a strainer lined with several layers of cheese cloth. Store grape cooler in airtight containers in refrigerator. Delicious flavors will develop over time. Best served diluted—half water, half grape juice.

If you wish to further clarify the grape cooler, add lightly beaten egg whites to the jugs (1 egg white per quart.) Set aside a few hours and then filter again through several layers of cheesecloth.

Know Your Ingredients

Name This Product #48

Water, sucrose, glucose syrup solids, citric acid, natural lemon flavor with other natural flavors, salt, sodium citrate, monopotassium phosphate, caramel color, ester gum, brominated vegetable oil.

See Appendix B for Answer

PUNCH

Makes 4 quarts

juice of 6 lemons
1/2 cup sucanat
1/2 cup whey
1/2 teaspoon grated nutmeg
2 quarts filtered water

Punch comes from the Hindu word meaning "five", because it was made with five ingredients. During colonial days in America, the five ingredients were water, sugar, lemons, tea and liquor. The earliest description, in a poem thought to have been written by Samuel Mather in 1757, calls for water, sugar, lemon juice, grated nutmeg and a small amount of "spirit". We substitute sucanat for sugar and whey for "spirit". The result is a delicious non-alcoholic fermented drink—a kind of Hindu lemonade.

Place all ingredients in a 2-quart glass jug. Cover and leave at room temperature for 2 days. Skim off any foam that may have risen to the top. Cover tightly and refrigerate. Punch will develop more flavor over time.

ROOT BEER

Makes 2 quarts

3-4 cups sassafras root shavings
1/4 cup whey
1 teaspoon sea salt
1/2 cup sucanat
1/4 cup molasses
1/2 cup fresh lime juice
1/2 teaspoon coriander seeds, crushed
1/4 teaspoon ground allspice

Sassafras, with its distinctive root-beer-like smell, grows all along the eastern seaboard. You'll need to dig up a piece of root and turn it into coarse shavings. Homemade root beer made from the root, rather than an extract, has little resemblance to syrupy sweet commercial varieties. Its taste is somewhat medicinal, but not unpleasant. You may wish to dilute it with sparkling mineral water.

Place shavings in a pan with about 4 cups of liquid, bring to a boil, reduce heat and simmer about two hours. Strain into a measuring cup. You should have about 1 cup of sassafras concentrate. Let cool and combine with remaining ingredients in a 2-quart glass jug. Cover tightly and leave at room temperature for about 2 days. Transfer to refrigerator for several weeks before serving.

Sassafras was one of America's first export crops, a bigger seller than even tobacco in the 17th century. Its leaves are in season from spring to fall, but the root is good all year. The Indians valued infusions of sassafras root for the blood and as a traditional spring tonic. American colonists and Europeans used it to treat a long list of complaints including arthritis, gout, colds, fevers, blood pressure, urinary problems, kidney stones, eczema and other skin disorders and intestinal problems. Safrole, an ester derived from the root, was valued for menstrual discomfort and the pain of childbirth. When research showed that astronomical quantities of artificial safrole caused cancer in rats, the US Food and Drug Administration had a convenient excuse to remove sassafras from the health-food stores. One suspects that the FDA was more concerned about eliminating competition for the drug and soft drink industries than in protecting the populace from a carcinogen. Americans had enjoyed sassafras as a tea and in root beer with no bad effects for centuries. SWF

You can eat a diet that has no enzymes and still live for many years, even to ripe old age, though each generation you would produce inferior offspring, and eventually reproduction would be impossible Would it not be better to let outside enzymes do some of the work and save your own enzymes for cellular work? Is it possible that cellular enzyme exhaustion is the root cause of what ails us? Victoras Kulvinskas *Introduction to Enzymes for Health and Longevity*

This supply [of enzymes], like the energy supply in your new battery, has to last a lifetime. The faster you use up your enzyme supply, the shorter your life. A great deal of our enzyme energy is wasted haphazardly throughout life. The habit of cooking our food and eating it processed with chemicals; and the use of alcohol, drugs, and junk food all draw out tremendous quantities of enzymes from our limited supply. Frequent colds and fevers and exposure to extremes of temperature also deplete the supply. A body in such a weakened, enzyme-deficient state is a prime target for cancer, obesity, heart disease, or other degenerative problems. A lifetime of such abuse often ends in the tragedy of death at middle age. Stephen Blauer *Introduction to Enzyme Nutrition*

Hominy Corn Drink—Shell corn, soak in lye until the skin can be removed. Beat the corn in the corn beater until it is the size of hominy. Sift the meal from the corn particles. Cook the corn particles until they are done, thicken this a little with meal. Drink this hot or wait until it sours and drink it cold. The drink may be kept for quite a while unless the weather is very hot. This was the customary drink to serve to friends who dropped by for a visit. *Cherokee Cooklore*

FERMENTED MINT TEA

Makes 2 quarts

1 cup bancha tea twigs
2 cups fresh mint leaves
1/4 cup sucanat or raw honey (optional)
1 quart filtered water
1 teaspoon sea salt
1/8 cup whey

Bancha tea is recommended for its high vitamin content and very low levels of theobromine (similar to caffeine.)

Bring water to a boil and pour over tea leaves. Let steep about 1 hour. Strain into a 2-quart jug. Add remaining ingredients and enough water to bring to fill the jug. Cover tightly and leave at room temperature for 2 days before transferring to refrigerator.

KVASS

Makes 2 quarts

4-5 slices whole grain sourdough bread (page 464)
2 quarts filtered water
1/4 cup whey
2 teaspoons sea salt
1/2 cup raisins
2 apples, peeled and quartered

Place bread in warm oven until dried out. Place in a large bowl. Bring water to a boil and pour over bread. Let cool and add salt and whey. Cover and let sit at room temperature for about 2 days. Remove bread and strain into a 2-quart container. Add raisins and apples, cover tightly and store in refrigerator for about 1 month before drinking. Kvass is ready when the fruit floats—a sign that sufficient lactic acid has been produced.

Variation: Kiesel

Use *2 cups freshly ground oat flour* in place of bread. To serve, strain through a strainer lined with several layers of cheese cloth.

ALMOND DRINK

Makes 2 quarts

2 cups blanched almonds
2 teaspoons sea salt
1/8 cup whey
1/8 cups sucanat or raw honey
1 teaspoon vanilla
1 teaspoon almond extract
filtered water

Soak almonds overnight in filtered water. Pour off water and process in food processor to a smooth paste. In a 2-quart jug mix almond paste with other ingredients and enough water to fill the jug. Cover tightly and leave at room temperature for 2 days before transferring to refrigerator. Stir well before serving.

Variation: Walnut Drink

Use *2 cups freshly shelled walnuts* instead of almonds

Variation: Pecan Drink

Use *2 cups pecan halves* instead of almonds

DAHI

Makes 3 quarts

1 quart plain yoghurt
juice of 12 limes
1/2 cup raw honey
filtered water

Place yoghurt, lime juice and honey in food processor and blend well. Dilute with filtered water to desired consistency.

No sooner had we concluded the formalities of taking possession of the island than people began to come to the beach. . . They are very well-built people, with handsome bodies and very fine faces, though their appearance is marred somewhat by very broad heads and foreheads, more so than I have ever seen in any other race. Their eyes are large and very pretty. . . These are tall people and their legs, with no exceptions, are quite straight and none of them has a paunch. They are, in fact, well proportioned. . . These people are very meek and shy. . .These lands are very fertile. They are full of *niames* [sweet potatoes] which are like carrots and taste like chestnuts. They have beans very different from ours. . .These fields are planted mostly with *ajes* [manioc, yuca or tapioca]. The Indians sow little shoots, from which small roots grow that look like carrots. They serve this as bread, by grating and kneading it, then baking it in the fire. More than 120 canoes came to the ships today. They all brought something, especially their bread and fish, small earthen jars of water, and seeds of many good kinds of spices. Some of these seeds they put in a gourd full of water and drank it, and the Indians with me said that is very healthy. . . I think that another 500 swam to the ships because they did not have canoes, and we were anchored 3 miles from land! Robert H. Fuson, trans. *The Log of Christopher Columbus*

The traditions that surround the life of Gautama Buddha include this one: that on the evening when he seated himself beneath the Bo tree and began the meditation that led to his enlightenment, he dined on rice milk offered to him by a peasant woman. His death occurred 45 years later, around 480 BC, when he ate some poisonous mushrooms that the smith Cunda served him by accident. In pain on his death bed, he commanded his companions to tell Cunda that of all the meals he had eaten in his lifetime, two brought him great blessings. One was the meal of rice milk that nourished him during his meditation under the Bo tree; the other was Cunda's meal that took him to Nirvana. SWF

Irish moss is a red algae that grows near the low-tide mark. It is gathered by the Irish and made into refreshing drinks and desserts. It contains a gel, similar to agar, called carrageenan that has many uses. Unfortunately some individuals have adverse reactions to carrageenan, in commercial preparations. This may be because, like all seaweeds, carrageen moss contains long chain sugars that some people have difficulty digesting.

But the Irish have always valued their seaweed as a health food, recommending it for digestive disorders, including ulcers, kidney ailments, heart disease and glandular irregularities. It promotes regularity and is used in cough preparations. It is high in carotenoids, iodine, iron, sulphur, sodium, copper and numerous trace minerals. It also contains B complex vitamins and protein. SWF

RICE MILK

Makes 2 quarts

1/2 cup brown rice
8 cups filtered water
1 teaspoon sea salt
1/8 cup whey
raw honey
cinnamon

This recipe comes from Egypt but similar recipes can be found throughout the Middle and Far East. Fermented grain drinks are traditionally prescribed to nursing mothers.

Cook rice in water, covered, for several hours until rice becomes very mushy. Pass rice and liquid through a moulin-a-legumes or a Foley Food Mill. Place in a 2-quart jug with salt and whey. Cover tightly and leave at room temperature for 2 or 3 days. Transfer to refrigerator. (A certain amount of separation is normal.)

To serve, blend with honey and cinnamon to taste and enough water to achieve desired consistency.

Variation:

Use other grains such as *oats, rye* or *barley.*

Variation: Nursing Mothers Tonic

Use *1/2 cup quinoa*, soaked 12 hours, rinsed and drained.

CARRAGEEN TEA

Makes 4 cups

1 cup carrageen moss (Irish moss)
3 cups filtered water
juice of 1 orange
juice of 1 lemon
1 tablespoon raw honey

Place Irish moss, water, orange and lemon juice in a pan and bring to a boil. Simmer for about 10 minutes. Let cool slightly. Strain into teapot and stir in honey. Serve in teacups or mugs.

FEEDING BABIES

FEEDING BABIES

Any effort to ensure optimal nutrition of your baby must begin long before he is conceived. The wisdom of primitive peoples has proved vastly superior to our own in this regard, in that a common practice among isolated groups is the feeding of special foods to both men and women for a period of time before conception occurs. Dr. Price's studies revealed that these foods were rich in fat soluble vitamins A and D as well as macro and trace minerals, such as organ meats, fish heads, fish eggs, shellfish, insects, and animal fats. Couples planning to have children should eat liberally of organic liver and other organ meats, fish eggs and other sea foods, eggs and the best quality butter, cream and fermented milk products they can obtain for at least six months before conception. A small daily cod liver oil supplement is also advised. (See note on cod liver oil, page 576.) Organic vegetables, grains and legumes should round out the diet, with a special emphasis on the leafy green vegetables with their content of folic acid, necessary for the prevention of birth defects like spinal bifida. A daily ration of superfoods such as evening primrose oil, bee pollen, kelp, spirolina, and rose hips will provide optimal amounts of nutrients for your unborn child. Beet kvass (page 586) and kombucha (page 572), with their liver cleansing properties, are useful in preventing future morning sickness—as are foods rich in vitamin B6, such as raw fish and other meats. A cleansing fast, undertaken several months before conception, is a good idea, but the period just before conception and during pregnancy should stress rich and nourishing foods. Every attempt should be made to enhance the digestibility of the diet through meat broths and the practice of lacto-fermenting grains, beverages and condiments. All empty calories and harmful substances should be eliminated—sugar, white flour, hydrogenated and rancid vegetable oils, excess of polyunsaturated oils, tobacco, caffeine and alcohol. Oral contraceptives should be avoided during this preparatory period as these deplete many nutrients, particularly zinc, the "intelligence mineral".

The importance of breast-feeding your baby, especially during his first few months, cannot be overemphasized. Breast milk is perfectly designed for your baby's physical and mental development. Breast-fed babies tend to be more robust, more intelligent and freer from allergies and other complaints, especially intestinal difficulties, than those on formula. In addition, colostrum produced by the mammary glands during the first few days of a baby's life, guards against colds, flu, polio, staph infections and viruses. It must be emphasized, however, that the quality of mother's milk depends greatly on her diet. Sufficient animal products will ensure proper amounts of vitamin B12, A and D as well as all important minerals like zinc in her milk. Pesticides and other toxins will be present in mother's milk if they are present in the diet so all care should be taken to consume organic foods, especially foods of animal origin, during pregnancy and lactation. Organic foods, of both animal and vegetable origin, also provide more omega-3 fatty acids needed for baby's optimal development

While breast feeding should ideally be continued for six months to a year, this is not usually practical for mothers in modern societies. It is a sad fact, however, that commercial infant formulas are highly fabricated foods, composed of milk or soy powders produced by high temperature processes that over-denature proteins and add many carcinogens. Milk-based formulas often cause allergies while soy-based formulas contain growth inhibitors and plant forms of female estrogen compounds that can have adverse effects on hormonal development in the infant. Soy-based formulas are also devoid of cholesterol, needed for the development of the brain and nervous system.

Fortunately it is possible to compose a formula that closely resembles mother's milk. Whenever possible this formula should be based on raw organic milk (preferably from Jersey or Guernsey cows, rather than Holsteins, so that it has a high butterfat content.) This may be purchased at the farm in some states. Of course such milk should be produced under the cleanest possible conditions and stored in sterilized containers. But the milk should be unheated. Raw milk does not pose a danger to your baby, in spite of what numerous public health propagandists may assert. Raw milk contains enzymes and antibodies that make it less susceptible to bacterial contamination than pasteurized milk, while many toxins that cause diarrhea and other ailments survive the pasteurization process. Your nose will tell you if raw milk is contaminated or spoiled—but pasteurized milk may be seriously contaminated with no tell-tale odor to warn the consumer. Raw milk is easier for your baby to digest than pasteurized, and less likely to cause cramps, constipation and allergies. If it is not possible for you to obtain raw milk, begin with the best quality pasteurized whole milk you can find, milk that is not homogenized, and culture it for 12 hours with piima culture to restore enzymes lost through pasteurization (page 77). Or you may prepare a milk-free formula made from organic liver.

Both recipes have been formulated to provide maximum possible correspondence with the various components of human milk. Our milk-based formula takes account of the fact that human milk is rich in whey, lactose, vitamin C, niacin, manganese and long chain polyunsaturated fatty acids compared to cows milk but leaner in casein (milk protein). The addition of gelatin to cow's milk formula will make it more digestible for the infant. The liver-based formula also mimics the nutrient profile of mother's milk. Use only Omega brand expeller expressed oils (see Sources) in the formula recipes, otherwise they may lack vitamin E.

A wise supplement for babies after they are weaned from breast milk —and even for babies still feeding from the breast—is a high omega-3 egg yolk per day, beginning at four months. Egg yolk supplies the cholesterol needed for mental development as well as important sulphur-containing amino acids. Egg yolks from free-range hens raised on flax meal, fish meal or insects are also rich in the kind of long chain fatty acids found in mother's milk, but which may be lacking in cow's milk. These fatty acids are essential for the development of the brain. Parents who institute the practice of feeding egg yolk to baby will be rewarded with children who speak and take directions at an early age. The white, which contains difficult-to-digest proteins, should not be given before the age of one year. Small amounts of grated raw organic liver may be added to the egg yolk after six months. This imitates the practice of African mothers who chew liver before giving it to their infants as their first food. Liver is rich in iron, the one mineral that tends to be low in mother's milk, possibly because iron competes with zinc for absorption. Liver should be given to baby occasionally, but not every day.

An unfortunate practice in industrial societies is the feeding of cereal grains to infants. Babies lack amylase needed for the digestion of grains and are not fully equipped to handle cereals, especially wheat, before the age of one year. (Some experts prohibit all grains before the age of two.) Baby's small intestine produces only one enzyme for carbohydrates—lactase, for the digestion of lactose. (Raw milk also contains lactase.) Many doctors have warned that feeding cereal grains too early can lead to grain allergies later on. Baby's earliest solid foods should be animal foods as his digestive system, although immature, supplies enzymes to break down both fats and protein.

Carbohydrate in the form of fresh, mashed banana can be added after the age of six months as bananas are rich in amylase enzymes and thus are easily digested by most infants. Some pre-industrial societies give a gruel of cereal grains, soaked 24 hours, to babies one year or older. Soaking in an acidic medium neutralizes phytates and begins the breakdown of carbohydrates, thus allowing children to obtain optimum nourishment from grains. It also provides lactic acid to the intestinal tract, to facilitate mineral uptake.

At the age of one year, meats, fruits and vegetables may be introduced, one at a time, so that any adverse reactions may be detected. Carbohydrate foods such as potatoes, carrots, turnips, etc., should be mashed with butter. (Don't overdo on the orange vegetables as baby's immature liver may have difficulty converting carotenoids to vitamin A. If your baby's skin develops a yellowish color, a sign that he is not making the conversion, discontinue orange vegetables for a time.) Lacto-fermented taro root or other roots (page 94) make an excellent carbohydrate food for babies. It is wise to feed babies a little buttermilk or yoghurt from time to time, to familiarize them with the sour taste. Above all, do not deprive your baby of animal fats—he needs these for physical growth and mental development. Mother's milk contains over 50% of its calories as fat. When we limit fats to children, we cheat them of what they need to grow and flourish.

It is unwise to give baby fruit juices, especially apple juice, which provide only simple carbohydrates and will often spoil an infant's appetite for more nutritious foods. Sorbitol, a carbohydrate in apple juice, is difficult to digest. Studies have linked failure to thrive in children with diets high in apple juice. High fructose foods are especially dangerous for growing children.

Keep your baby away from processed junk foods as long as possible —but do not think that you can do this indefinitely. Unless you lock your child in a closet—or live in a closed community of like-minded parents—he will come in contact with junk foods sooner or later. His best protection is the optimal diet that you have given him during his infancy, and your loving example and training in later years.

MILK BASED FORMULA

Makes 36 ounces

2 cups raw organic milk or piima milk (page 77), not homogenized
1/4 cup whey
4 tablespoons lactose (see Sources)
2 tablespoons good quality cream (not ultrapasteurized)
1 teaspoon cod liver oil (See note on cod liver oil, page 576)
1 teaspoon unrefined sunflower oil (see Sources)
1 teaspoon extra virgin olive oil
2 teaspoons coconut oil (see Sources)
2 teaspoons brewer's yeast
2 teaspoons gelatin (see Sources)
1 3/4 cup filtered water
1 100mg tablet vitamin C, crushed

Add gelatin to water and heat gently until gelatin is dissolved. Place all ingredients in a very clean glass or stainless steel container and mix well. To serve, pour 6 to 8 ounces into a very clean glass bottle, attach nipple, and set in a pan of simmering water. Heat until warm but not hot to the touch, shake bottle and feed baby. (Never heat formula in a microwave oven!) Note: We recommend only Omega brand oils for baby formula. (See Sources.)

Alexander and Bullowa made an extensive investigation of the action of gelatin on milk, employing the microscope and ultramicroscope in their studies. They observed that the casein of milk was an irreversible colloid and that it could be protected by the addition of a reversible colloid such as gelatin. They pointed out, moreover, that woman's milk was higher in albumen or protective colloid than cow's milk and that the curd obtained from the coagulation of woman's milk was softer and more easily digested. When gelatin was added to cow's milk, a curd of equally desirable characteristics was formed. In addition, gelatin exerted a very important influence on the milk fat. It served not only to emulsify the fat but also, by stabilizing the casein, improved the digestibility and absorption of the fat, which otherwise would be carried down with the casein in a lumpy mass. . .Experimental feeding tests show that milk containing gelatin is more rapidly and completely digested in the infant. N.R Gotthoffer *Gelatin in Nutrition and Medicine*

MILK FREE FORMULA

Makes 36 ounces

3 1/2 cups homemade broth,
(beef, lamb, chicken or fish)
2 ounces organic liver, cut into small pieces
5 tablespoons lactose (see Sources)
1/4 cup whey
1 tablespoon coconut oil (see Sources)
1 teaspoon cod liver oil
(See note on cod liver oil, page 576)
1 teaspoon unrefined sunflower oil (see Sources)
2 teaspoons extra virgin olive oil
1 100mg tablet vitamin C, crushed

Cook liver gently in broth until the meat is cooked through. Liquefy using a handheld blender or in a food processor. When the liver broth has cooled, stir in remaining ingredients. Store in a very clean glass or stainless steel container.

To serve, stir formula well and pour 6 to 8 ounces in a very clean glass bottle. Attach a clean nipple and set in a pan of simmering water until formula is warm but not hot to the touch, shake well and feed to baby. (Never heat formula in a microwave oven!) Note: We recommend only Omega brand oils for infant formula. (See Sources.)

During the process of digestion, lactose breaks up into two other sugars, glucose (dextrose), and galactose. . . In myelin there is a large amount of galactolipids in the nature of phrenocin (cerebrosides) of various kinds. Cerebrosides are compounds found in the brain . . . Galactose is one of the constituents of this material. . . Mother Nature must have intended that the young infant have this important substance, so amply provided for it in breast milk. . . I have long held the opinion that the tremendous use of various [other] sugars in milk formulas over the years could be an important factor in the high percentage of mental and nervous breakdowns in our civilian population, not to mention the alarming numbers of such cases that have been reported in the military. The demyelination of the nerves is what makes the dread disease multiple sclerosis, so crippling. This disease was quite rare in the days of breast feeding. Emory W. Thurston PhD *Nutrition for Tots to Teens*

In this paper we compare the fatty acid content of egg yolks from hens fed four different feeds as a source of docosahexaenoic acid (DHA, 22:6w3) to supplement infant formula. . . Two to three grams of Greek egg yolk may provide an adequate amount of DHA and arachidonic acid for a preterm neonate. Mean intake of breast milk at age 1 mo. provides 250 mg long-chain w3 fatty acids. This amount can be obtained from <1 yolk of a Greek egg (0.94), > 1 yolk of flax eggs (1.6) and fish

EGG YOLK FOR BABY

1 high omega-3 egg
1/2 teaspoon grated raw organic liver, frozen for 14 days (optional)

Supermarket eggs have only trace amounts of omega-3 fatty acids, as do most "free range" eggs. Look for eggs from chickens that have been fed fish or flax meal feed, or allowed to run free in areas where they can eat bugs and worms. One such producer is Country Hen, available on the East Coast. High omega-3 eggs will become more available with consumer demand.

Boil egg for 3 1/2 minutes. Place in a bowl and peel off shell. Remove egg white and discard. Yolk should be soft and warm, not hot, with its enzyme content intact.

If you wish to add liver, grate on the small holes of a grater while frozen. Allow to warm up and stir into egg yolk.

DIGESTIVE TEA FOR BABY

about 2 cups fresh anise leaves
about 2 cups fresh mint
2 quarts filtered water

This is a folk remedy for treating constipation and intestinal gas in infants.

Bring water to a boil and pour over the herbs. Let steep until water cools. Strain. Give tepid tea to baby, about 4 ounces at a time.

meal eggs (1.4) or 8.3 yolks of supermarket eggs. . . In previous studies, we showed that the w3 fatty acid content in eggs from range-fed Greek chickens was considerably higher than the w3 fatty acid content reported in eggs by the US Department of Agriculture and our own analysis of US supermarket eggs. In fact, the ratio of w6 to w3 fatty acids (w6:w3) for Greek eggs was 1.3 and that of the supermarket egg was 19.9. . . there is a lower ratio of w3 to w6 fatty acids in cultured than in wild fish. . . animals in the wild have more w3 fatty acids in their carcass than do domesticated animals. In another study we compared the a-linolenic acid. . . content of wild purslane with that of spinach and other cultivated plants and found that purslane was much richer in LNA. . . These studies indicate that industrialization and agricultural practices have systematically reduced the amount of w3 fatty acids in the plants, eggs, fish and meat that we eat. Most important, however, have been the studies indicating that infant formula is devoid of long-chain polyunsaturated fatty acids. . . including both the w6 and w3 families, whereas human milk contains both. . . studies . . . suggest that DHA is essential for the development of newborn infants and that preterm neonates who have deficient stores of DHA show deficits in visual function when not fed human milk or formula supplemented with marine oil containing eicosapentaenoic acid and DHA. Artemis P. Simopoulos and Norman Salem, Jr. *American Journal for Clinical Nutrition*

CEREAL GRUEL FOR BABY

Makes 2 cups

1/2 cup freshly ground organic flour of rye, barley, amaranth, quinoa or spelt
2 cups filtered water
1/4 teaspoon sea salt
2 tablespoons whey
cream, butter, yoghurt or cultured buttermilk

Mix flour with water, salt and whey, cover and let stand at room temperature for 24 hours. Bring to a boil over low heat, cover, stirring frequently, and then simmer for about 1 hour, stirring occasionally. Set aside to cool. Serve with cream, butter, yoghurt or cultured buttermilk.

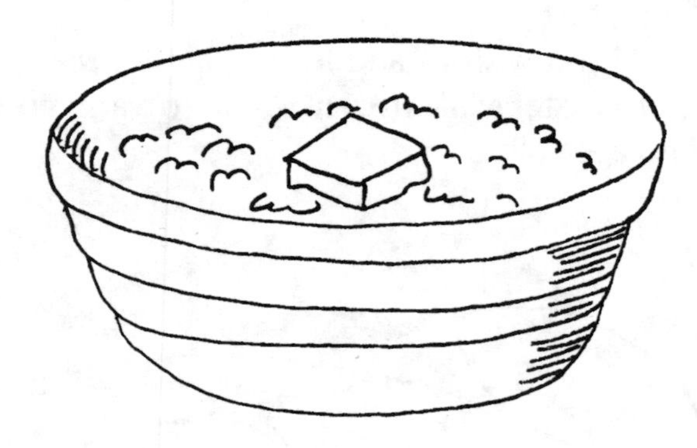

ARROWROOT BISCUITS

Makes 18

1 stick butter, preferably organic, softened, or 1/2 cup coconut oil
2 egg yolks
4 tablespoons water
1 cup arrowroot powder
1/2 teaspoon sea salt
1/4 teaspoon stevia powder

Cream butter or coconut oil with yolk and then with remaining ingredients. Spoon onto a well-buttered cookie sheet. Flatten biscuits with a fork. Bake at 200 degrees for about 2 hours or until slightly browned.

Both gelatin and [lactic] acid when added to cow's milk seem to make the milk more digestible to the ordinary infant. This is evidenced by the fact that both vomiting and constipation appeared to be reduced when either of these substances was added, and a better rate of gain was made on the low curd tension milks. Similarly, it was noted that a much smaller percentage of the children developed diarrhea on the modified milks than on the unaltered cow's milk. Attention is called to the lower incidence of upper respiratory infections in the gelatin milk group. N.R Gotthoffer *Gelatin in Nutrition and Medicine*

It is a remarkable fact that the young of most, including man, have weak digestive fluids; particularly do they have low amylase content in the saliva. The suckling animal or infant does not need to secrete a great quantity of enzymes because milk, its first food, does not demand so many of them for its digestion as it has quite a complement of its own enzymes. Edward Howell MD *Enzymes for Health and Longevity*

Soy-based infant formula may adversely affect hormonal development in neonatal infants and should not be sold commercially, according to scientists in New Zealand. Soya is the richest dietary source of phytoestrogens, a plant form of the female hormone estrogen. The scientists assert that neonatal infants are particularly vulnerable to estrogens and that insufficient research on the long-term health effects of phytoestrogens warrants a ban on the non-prescription sale of soy formula. *Community Nutrition Institute*

TONICS & SUPERFOODS

TONICS

The following tonics are offered for their medicinal rather than epicurean qualities. They are useful for strength-building and for fasting. Caution: Fasting should only be undertaken under a doctor's supervision. Consult a qualified health practitioner for the treatment of all serious disease conditions.

POTASSIUM BROTH

Makes 2 quarts

4 potatoes, well scrubbed
3 carrots, peeled and chopped
4 celery stalks, chopped
1 bunch parsley
4 quarts filtered water
whey

This is a wonderful pick-me-up, drunk warm like tea, a great rejuvenator for those who have been sick, or for recovery from childbirth.

Peel potatoes. Place peelings, carrots and celery in a pot with water. Bring to a boil, lower heat and simmer, covered, for about 1/2 hour. Add parsley and simmer 5 minutes more. Allow to cool and strain into a 2-quart container. Store in refrigerator and reheat in small quantities as needed. Add 1 tablespoon of whey to each cup of warm broth—this will greatly facilitate the absorption of potassium and other minerals.

BIELER BROTH

Makes 2 quarts

4 medium squash (zucchini, yellow or summer) washed, ends removed and sliced
1 pound wax beans, ends removed
2 stalks celery, chopped (optional)
2 bunches parsley, stems removed (optional)
fresh herbs such as thyme or tarragon, tied together with string (optional)
whey (optional)
1 quart filtered water

Maverick physician Henry Bieler recommended this broth for fasting, for energy and for overall health. He felt that this combination of vegetables was ideal for restoring acid-alkaline and sodium-potassium balance to organs and glands, especially the sodium-loving adrenal glands. Bieler broth is highly recommended for those under stress or suffering from stress related conditions, such as back pain and ligament problems. A more epicurean version is found on page 209.

Place water, vegetables and optional herbs in a pot. Bring to a boil, skim, lower heat and simmer, covered, for about 1/2 hour. Remove herbs. Vegetables may be eaten whole with cooking water, or blended into a thick soup with a handheld blender. Add 1 tablespoon whey to each cup of soup.

CARROT JUICE COCKTAIL

Makes 8 ounces

1 pound carrots, peeled
2 tablespoons cream

This recipe recognizes the fact that fat is needed for the body to efficiently convert carotene into vitamin A (retinol). This remedy is used with success in European clinics for the treatment of cancer, psoriasis and many other diseases. Use only the best quality cream you can fine—preferably raw, but never ultrapasteurized.

Process carrots in a juicer. Stir in the cream. Sip slowly.

When a toxemia is present without symptoms of a specific disease but with liver impairment, a short fast on vegetable broth or soup is a natural and efficient treatment that will relieve the liver of its congestion and restore it to normal function. Henry Bieler MD *Food is Your Best Medicine*

Sometimes the patient, unlike the horse, knows the "life-saving water" is there, but his professional life is so arranged that he cannot (or so he believes) stick to his therapeutic diet. Many of the motion-picture stars I have treated for instance, travel to far-away places or must attend many public functions and have meals at irregular hours; thus they find it difficult to eat properly. But when they return home, ill, exhausted, filled with tension, they immediately go on what they call "Bieler broth"—a combination of lightly cooked string beans, celery, zucchini and parsley . . . Even one correct meal aids a toxin-saturated body. Henry Bieler MD *Food is Your Best Medicine*

Accuse not Nature; she hath done her part; do thou but thine.
Milton

BEET KVASS

Makes 2 quarts

3 small or 2 medium organic beets,
peeled and chopped up coarsely
2 tablespoons whey
1 teaspoon sea salt
filtered water

Professor Zabel observed that sick people always lack digestive juices, not only during the acute phase of their illness but also for a longtime afterwards. In addition, he never saw a cancer victim that had a healthy intestinal flora. . . Thus the different lacto-fermented foods are a valuable aid to the cancer patient. They are rich in vitamins and minerals and contain as well enzymes that cancer patients lack. Of particular value are lacto-fermented beets which have a very favorable effect on disturbed cellular function. Many scientific studies have demonstrated that beets have a regenerating effect on the body. Annelies Schoneck *Des Crudites Toute L'Annee*

This drink is valuable for its medicinal qualities. Beets are just loaded with nutrients. One 4-ounce glass, morning and night, is an excellent blood tonic, promotes regularity, aids digestion, alkalizes the blood, cleanses the liver and is a good treatment for kidney stones and other ailments. Beet kvass may also be used in place of vinegar in salad dressings, and as an addition to soups.

Place beets, whey and salt in a 2 quart container. Add filtered water to fill the jug. Stir well and cover securely. Keep at room temperature for 2 days before transferring to refrigerator.

When most of liquid has been drunk, you may fill up the container with water and keep at room temperature another 2 days. The resulting brew will be slightly less strong than the first. After the second brew, discard beets and start again. You may, however, reserve some of the liquid and use this as your inoculant instead of the whey.

Note: Do not use grated beets in the preparation of beet tonic. When grated, beets exude too much juice resulting in a too rapid fermentation that favors the production of alcohol rather than lactic acid.

No Ukranian home was ever without its "beet kvas". The kvas was always handy and ready when a pleasing, sour flavour had to be added to soups and vinaigrettes. Lubow A Kyivska *Ukranian Dishes*

FLAX SEED DRINK

Makes 1 cup

1 tablespoon organic flax seeds
1 cup water

Grind flax seeds in a mini grinder and mix with water. Drink immediately. This supplies omega-3 fatty acids in the freshest possible state; the fiber is an excellent antidote to constipation.

VEGETABLE JUICE COCKTAIL

Makes 1 quart

1 green pepper
2 carrots, peeled
2 stalks celery
1 bunch parsley
1/2 zucchini or yellow squash
handful string beans
4 tablespoons whey

Run all vegetables through a juicer. Thin with a little filtered water if desired and stir in whey. Recommended for those with an acidic condition of the blood. Vegetable juice promotes a healthy alkalinity.

Truly the vegetable kingdom contains our best medicines. . . . [The vegetables] are not only beautiful to look at but filled with healthful properties, chief of which are their natural vitamins and trace elements. But only if they are used. Did you know that stalk of celery or a serving of fresh salad greens has more vitamins and minerals than a box of synthetic vitamin tablets? Henry Bieler MD *Food is Your Best Medicine*

POTTENGER LIVER COCKTAIL

Makes 1 cup

1 small chunk organic beef or lamb liver,
frozen for at least 14 days
4-6 ounces tomato juice
dash tabasco
squeeze of lime juice
1 tablespoon whey

Dr. Francis Pottenger, of Price Pottenger Nutrition Foundation fame, recommended this tonic for the health and stamina building properties of raw liver. This is a great tonic for athletes. The liver you use must be organic!

Grate liver finely to obtain about 1-2 teaspoons. Mix with tomato juice, whey and seasonings. Drink immediately.

Of course using food as medicine is ancient. The pharmacopeia of ancient Egypt, Babylonia, Greece and China as well as those of the Middle Ages, were based on food. Only in this century has society become almost exclusively dependent on manufactured pills to cure our miseries. But now that pharmaceutical model is breaking down as a panacea for today's plague of chronic diseases such as cancer, arthritis, and heart disease, and the ancient wisdom about food's medicinal powers, newly confirmed by twentieth-century scientific research, is increasingly infiltrating mainstream medicine. Jean Carper *The Food Pharmacy Guide to Good Eating*

For a civilization wracked with chronic disease, the traditional pharmaceutical model for the most part is bankrupt. What pill does one dispense to try to forestall cancer for example? or arthritis? diabetes? thrombosis? Flooding the populace with potent drugs to try to ward off maladies that develop over many years, strike erratically, and are of uncertain origin and course would subject millions to untold hazard and expense without clear-cut knowledge of risk or benefit. Generally prophylactic drugs are too risky and are too expensive and time-consuming to develop to use as scattershoot medicine to try to protect individuals from diseases that may never occur.

But food's medicinal powers mesh perfectly with the new imperative of preventive medicine. For they provide not single large jolts of curative medicine but a regular, steady regimen of low levels of nontoxic therapeutic chemicals over a lifetime. Such minute infusions of natural drugs, many scientists believe, provide cells with a shield of protection against everyday assaults, lessening the body's susceptibility to full-fledged illness in later years. Jean Carper *The Food Pharmacy Guide to Good Eating*

RAW LIVER DRINK

Makes 1 cup

1/4 pound raw beef liver,
frozen for 14 days and thawed
1/2 cup cold water
pinch sea salt
juice of 1 lime
1/2 cup freshly squeezed orange juice
1 teaspoon sucanat (optional)
1 tablespoon whey

Wash liver, chop finely and soak for two hours in water and sea salt. Press through a fine strainer. Mix remaining ingredients and drink immediately.

BARLEY WATER

Makes 1 quart

4 tablespoons pearl barley
1 quart water
juice of 1 lime
sucanat to taste
4 tablespoons whey

Wash barley, cover with cold water, heat to boiling and discard this water. Place barley and 1 quart water in top of double boiler and simmer for 2 hours. Strain and add remaining ingredients after barley water has cooled. May be drunk warm or cold.

REJUVELAC

2 cups organic, unsprayed wheat berries
filtered water

This tonic was popularized by Ann Wigmore, the first of American practical nutritionists to recognize the importance of enzymes and lacto-fermented food in the diet.

Soak wheat in 4 cups water for 24 hours. Pour off water and add another 4 cups. Repeat for 6 days. Strain out wheat and drink the liquid in small but frequent doses.

CABBAGE JUICE TONIC

Makes 2 quarts

1/4 organic green cabbage
1 tablespoon sea salt
2 tablespoons whey
filtered water

This should be taken in small amounts throughout the day to improve intestinal flora.

Shred cabbage finely with a stainless steel knife. Place in a 2-quart jug with salt, whey and enough water to cover. Cover tightly and leave at room temperature for 2 days before transferring to refrigerator.

Variation: Spiced Cabbage Juice

Add *1/4-1/2 teaspoon cayenne pepper* to 4 ounces cabbage juice tonic for a gargle and sore throat remedy.

Cabbage is an unusually rich source of vital nutrients, particularly vitamin C and carotenoids. Vitamin C is required by the body for the integrity of blood vessels, connective tissue, bones and every essential biochemical activity including immune function. Cabbage juice is highly valued as a folk remedy. Its healing powers may be related to its high sulphur and chlorine content which, in combination, exerts a powerful cleansing action upon the mucous membranes of the intestinal tract. Cabbage juice has been used in the treatment of arthritis, gastrointestinal ulceration, skin disorders and obesity. "Cabbage water for the complexion," is a truism among the Irish.

Even better than plain cabbage juice is the juice of fermented cabbage, with is content of lactic acid and enzymes. German folk wisdom values both cabbage juice and cucumber pickle juice for digestive disorders, infectious illnesses and many other complaints. SWF

IODINE GARGLE

Makes 1 cup

1 cup filtered water
2 teaspoons sea salt
7 drops atomidine, an iodine solution (see Sources)

Add salt to water and bring to a boil. Allow to cool and add atomidine. Use when the gargle is still quite hot, but not hot enough to burn. Great for sore throats, hoarseness and tonsillitis.

What a strange drink. . . a drink obtained by allowing an infusion of tea to ferment with the aid of a special inoculation and a little sugar. One finds this drink in many countries of Asia and Europe (China, Japan, Indonesia, Russia, Bulgaria, Poland and Germany) called by various names: *Tesschwamm, tea fungus, kombucha, wunderpilz, hongo, cajnij, teekvass*. This tea possesses antibiotic properties that are used in medicine in Russia. Claude Aubert *Les Aliments Fermentes Traditionnels*

KOMBUCHA

Makes 1 gallon

4 quarts filtered water
1 1/4 cups sugar or 1 cup raw honey
1 kombucha mushroom (see Sources)
3 tablespoons black or green tea tied up in cheesecloth or 5 teabags (may be decaffeinated tea)
1/2 cup kombucha from a previous culture (optional, but for best results)
1 teaspoon sea salt

It seems surprising, even ironic, to conclude a health food cookbook, in which we have warned against sugar, yeast and tea, with a tonic made from sugar, yeast and tea! But the kombucha mushroom acts on sugar and tea to produce not only lactic acid but also a potent detoxifying substance, glucuronic acid. Normally this organic acid is produced by the liver in sufficient quantities to neutralize toxins in the body—whether these are naturally produced toxins or poisons ingested in food and water. However, when liver function becomes overloaded, and when the body must deal with a superabundance of toxins from the environment—certainly the case with most of us today—additional glucuronic acid taken in the form of kombucha is a powerful aid to the body's natural cleansing process, a boost to the immune system and a proven prophylactic against cancer and other degenerative diseases. In addition, kombucha tastes delicious—we could well have included it in our beverage section for its epicurean qualities. A fizzy, dark colored, energizing beverage, at the same time acidic and slightly sweet, this gift to the world from the Ural mountain region of Russia qualifies as the soft drink of the New Age, the answer to the scourge of cola drinks that now wreaks havoc with the health of Western populations.

Our readers will immediately ask whether a natural sweetener can be used in place of white sugar. Experts in kombucha preparation have discovered through trial and error that white sugar actually gives the best results—it is the best food for the fungus. If

Taking a page from the police tactics of the KGB, Soviet cancer researchers determined to find out why, where and how this dread disease [cancer] had increased so dramatically following World War II. Using the probing techniques made infamous by the KGB, the Soviet researchers analyzed the cancer epidemiology community by community in minute detail—taking into detailed account all the environmental factors. There in the midst of dreadful cancer statistics two districts in the region of Perm on the Kama River in the central western Ural mountains stood out like neon lights. The districts of Solikamsk and Beresniki had hardly any cancer cases reported, and those few with cancer often turned out to be people who had only recently moved into the area from elsewhere.

How could this be? Environmental conditions were not any better than other districts—in fact the region had potassium, lead, mercury and asbestos mining with production facilities spewing plenty of pollution. In fact trees in the area and fish in the Kama were dying.

In typical KGB fashion, two teams of scientific investigators were set up, one in Ssolikamsk, the other in Beresniki. They probed into private lives and investigated and analyzed. In the end they were puzzled. . . the people of these two districts drank as much vodka as other Russians, but did not seem to have the social drunkenness problems, nor the poor work record usually associate with drinking. The problem was finding an explanation for this curious improvement.

the ferment is allowed to continue for the full 10-14 days, almost all of the sugar is converted to glucuronic acid and lactic acid. However purists may also use raw honey which imparts a distinctive flavor to the kombucha.

To prepare, bring 4 quarts filtered water to boil. Add sugar and salt and simmer until dissolved. Off heat, add the tea and allow to steep until water has completely cooled. Remove tea. (When preparing with honey, add honey to brewed tea after it has cooled enough to be touched. Stir well until honey is dissolved.) Pour cooled liquid into a 1 gallon glass jar (available at kitchen supply and container stores) and add 1/2 cup kombucha from previous batch. Place the mushroom on top of the liquid, cover loosely with a cloth or towel and transfer to a warm dark place. In 5 to 14 days the kombucha will be ready, depending on the temperature. It should be fizzy and rather sour, with no taste of tea remaining. Transfer to covered glass jugs and store in the refrigerator. (Always wash your one-gallon kombucha jars with mild soap—not in the dishwasher.)

When the kombucha is ready, your mushroom will have grown a second spongy pancake. This can be used to make other batches, or given away to friends. Store fresh mushrooms in the refrigerator in a glass or stainless steel container—never plastic. A kombucha mushroom can be used dozens of times. If it begins to turn black, or if the resulting kombucha doesn't taste good, it's time to throw the culture away.

A word of caution: In general individuals with yeast allergies tolerate kombucha; but we know of one case in which it provoked a severe reaction. If you have yeast allergies, start with a small taste to observe any adverse effects.

Variation: Ginger Kombucha

Add *1 cup fresh peeled ginger, coarsely chopped* to brewing kombucha.

Variation: Herb Tea Kombucha

Use *5-8 herb tea bags* in place of black tea.

Variation: Flavored Kombucha

Use *Twinings Black Current Tea* or other flavored tea.

Then it happened that one of the scientific team leaders personally visited the home of a family selected to be studied. It was a warm summer day and the family was away—only an elderly "babushka" was at home.

The old woman offered Dr. Molodyev a refreshing beverage. . . It turned out that Dr. Grigoriev in Beresniki also stumbled across tea kvass at about the same time and it was soon confirmed that nary a home in the region was without the fermenting crocks of kvass or Kombucha. . . . the Soviet experience is part of the large body of documentary evidence that the beverage made from kombucha fermentation of tea and sugar is, indeed, a dramatic immune system booster and body detoxifier. Tom Valentine *Search for Health*

The potentially large amount of glucuronic acid in the beverage is especially exciting to us, just as it was to Soviet scientists and cancer researchers. . . Glucuronic acid is not readily commercially synthesized, but the healthy human liver makes large amounts of it to detoxify the body. In the liver the glucuronic acid binds up all poisons and toxins—both environmental and metabolic—and rushes them to the excretory system. Toxins once bound by glucuronic acid cannot be resorbed into the system so we are rid of them. Tom Valentine *Search for Health*

SUPERFOODS

Superfoods—as opposed to vitamins or supplements—are foods that naturally concentrate important nutrients. Unlike dietary supplements, or vitamins taken in isolation, superfoods provide many nutrients at the same time which support each other and prevent the kind of imbalances that often occur when vitamins are taken singly.

Do we need superfoods? In theory, if the diet is good, we should need nothing more to supplement our daily fare; but can even the most conscientious among us say that our diet is or has been perfect? With the depletion of our soils, the widespread use of additives, and the prevalence of sugar, refined carbohydrates and rancid vegetable oils which all of us have invariably ingested, if not in adulthood, in our youth, no one living in an industrial society today can say that his diet has been perfect. For those unwilling or unable to give up bad habits like caffeine, alcohol or smoking, a daily supply of superfoods is essential.

Even those who live in isolated primitive societies seek out special foods for optimum health—foods high in fat soluble vitamins for enhancement of reproduction and strong healthy children, such as fish eggs and organ meats; soaked grains for strength and stamina; and herbs to prevent certain diseases.

The following short list is not meant to be exhaustive but only to provide a few examples of superfoods that can, in general, be taken by everyone. Other superfoods, such as glandular extracts and herb powders, are best taken with the advice of a wholistic health practitioner. To purchase superfoods, see Sources.

Bee Pollen: Bee pollen has been popularized by famous athletes who take it regularly for strength and endurance. It has been used successfully to treat a variety of ailments including allergies, asthma, menstrual irregularities, constipation, diarrhea, anemia, low energy, cancer, rheumatism, arthritis and toxic conditions. A Russian study of the natives of the province of Georgia, where many live to 100 years and a few to age 150, revealed that the majority of these centenarians were bee-keepers who ate raw, unprocessed honey with all its "impurities", that is with the pollen, every day. Bee pollen contains 22 amino acids including high amounts of the eight essential ones, 27 minerals, and the full gamut of vitamins, hormones, carbohydrates and fatty acids. Most importantly, bee pollen contains more than 5,000 enzymes and coenzymes. It is the presence of enzymes, many of which have immediate detoxifying effects, that sometimes provoke allergic reactions in those taking bee pollen for the first time. If this happens, start with very small amounts and slowly build up to a tablespoon or so per day. Some brands are more easily tolerated than others. Avoid pollen that has been dried at temperatures higher than 130 degrees. Bee pollen can be taken in powder, capsule or tablet form—or in raw unprocessed honey mixed with cereal or spread on toast.

Kelp: Like all sea vegetables, kelp provides minerals found in sea water, especially iodine and trace minerals that may be lacking in our depleted soils. For Westerners unaccustomed to including sea weeds in the diet, a small daily supplement of kelp in tablet or powdered form is a good idea.

Spirolina: Spirolina is a blue-green micro alga that grows on inland waters throughout the world—visible as greenish scum on still lakes and ponds. The Aztecs ate it as a staple food, spread on tortillas. Africans of the Sahara region also use dried spirolina with grains and vegetables. Spirolina is high in protein, carotenoids and minerals. Beware, however, of claims that spirolina can provide vitamin B12 in vegetarian diets—studies indicate that spirolina may in fact block the absorption of B12. Nevertheless, the high mineral and protein content of spirolina make it an excellent supplement, and a good source of protein during liquid fasts.

Rose Hips: In powdered or tablet form, rose hips provide vitamin C with numerous co-factors, including bioflavinoids and rutin, to optimize the body's uptake and use of vitamin C. Vitamin C is, of course, the vitamin of the century, popularized by Linus Pauling who recommends taking it in amounts up to 15 grams a day for a variety of ailments. But large quantities of vitamin C may be harmful to the kidneys. A gram or so of rose hips with its ancillary nutrients is a more prudent way of ensuring adequate vitamin C intake.

Trace Mineral Liquid or Powder: Dried mineral salts of ancient sea beds can be taken in water to provide the kind of milky, mineral-rich water found in areas noted for the longevity of the local populace—the valley of Hunza, in Kashmir, the village of Vilcabamba in Ecuador and the mountains of the province of Georgia in Russia. These regions are characterized by heavily mineralized water and soil. Look for a product that contains a full complement of trace minerals. Take 1/2 teaspoon powder per day in water or add mineral drops to drinking water according to directions.

Swedish Bitters: An herbal extract of bitter, mineral-rich herbs, originally formulated by Paracelsus, and later "rediscovered" by a Swedish scientist, Swedish bitters supply the nutrients from bitter leaves which are often lacking in the western diet that eschews bitter tasting foods. Many cultures including the Chinese and Hindu, value bitter herbs for their cleansing, strengthening and healing properties.

Cod Liver Oil: Once a standard supplement in traditional European societies, cod liver oil provides fat soluble vitamins A and D, which Dr. Price found present in the diet of primitives in amounts ten times higher than the typical American diet of his day. Cod liver oil supplements are a must for women *and* their male partners, to be taken for several months *before* conception, and for women during pregnancy. Growing children will also benefit greatly from a small daily dose. Cod liver oil is also rich in a tongue twister called eicosapentaenoic acid (EPA). The body makes this fatty acid from omega-3 linolenic acid as an important link in the chain of fatty acids that ultimately results in prostaglandins, localized tissue hormones. Those individuals who have consumed large amounts of polyunsaturated oils, especially hydrogenated oils, or who have impaired pancreatic function, such as diabetics, may not be able to produce EPA and will therefore lack important prostaglandins, unless they consume oily fish or take a cod liver oil supplement. Buy good quality oil containing anti-oxidants (we recommend Dale Alexander brand), in dark glass bottles, and store in the refrigerator. Some studies indicate that cod liver oil is toxic in large amounts so don't overdo —1 teaspoon per day is a good rule for adults, half that for children. It's easy to take when stirred into a small amount of water.

Gamma-Linolenic Acid: Found in certain oils of vegetable origin, this fatty acid is also produced in the body from omega-6 linoleic acid by the action of the delta-6 desaturase enzymes. In many individuals the production or effectiveness of this enzyme is compromised, especially as they grow older. Malnutrition, the consumption of hydrogenated oils and diabetes inhibit the action of delta-6 desaturase, thereby creating a deficiency of gamma-linolenic acid and the prostaglandins that result from this chain. Gamma-linolenic acid has been used to treat high cholesterol, cancer, premenstrual syndrome, breast disease, scleroderma, colitis, irritable bowel syndrome and cystic fibrosis and has also been shown to increase liver function and mental acuity. Sources include evening primrose oil, borage and black current oil.

Appendix A

LIMITED-TIME LIMITED-BUDGET GUIDELINES

No one in modern America who deserves more sympathy than the working parent on a limited budget. Finding the time, energy and means to prepare nutritious meals for oneself and one's children poses a real challenge, especially as the temptation to opt for convenience foods is very great. The first step needed to meet that challenge is the realization that fast foods are a terrible trap which, in the long run, lead to diminished vitality and hence even greater restrictions on one's time and budget, not to mention the tragedy of serious disease.

While it is not necessary to spend long hours in the kitchen in order to eat properly, it is necessary to spend *some* time in the kitchen. Simple wholesome menus require careful planning rather than long hours in the kitchen. Much can be accomplished in the way of advanced preparation by dedicating just one block of four to five hours per week to food, which might include shopping, starting a large pot of stock to last the week, putting up a jar of fermented vegetables, making a batch of cookies for school lunches, and preparing a large casserole of soup or stew that could last for several meals. Simple, nutritious meals can be prepared very quickly when one lays the groundwork ahead of time. If your present schedule allows no time at all for food preparation, you would be wise to reexamine your priorities.

- Don't buy fabricated breakfast cereals, even those made of whole grains. They are very expensive, poor in nutrients and difficult to digest. A serving of the best quality organic oatmeal costs half a serving of the average boxed breakfast cereal, and is infinitely more nutritious. For optimum nourishment, you need to think ahead and soak your oatmeal overnight. (Page 431)

- Make your own salad dressing. You can make your own dressing using the finest ingredients for about the same cost as the average bottled dressing, all of which contain rancid vegetable oils and numerous additives. With practice, it takes no more than a minute to produce a delicious dressing for your salad. (Pages 116-124)

- Always buy butter. Margarine may cost less but it is a false economy, one that leads to numerous impoverishing diseases. And the price of butter is coming down. Some discount markets now sell butter for about one dollar per pound.

- Make stock at least once a week. Meat stocks have formed the basis of nourishing peasant diets for millennia. They cost very little to make (often a good fishmonger will give you fish carcasses for free), are very nourishing, and have a protein-sparing effect. That means you can get by with very little meat in the diet when you use properly made stock for soups and stews. Use congealed fat from stocks for cooking, and leftover meat for soups, meat salads and other dishes.

- It's better to put your money into whole foods than vitamins. Most, however, benefit from a daily teaspoonful of cod liver oil, one of the most inexpensive supplements on the market. Lacto-fermented beet kvass (page 568) contains a large array of nutrients in easily assimilated form, and is simple and inexpensive to make.

- Good quality dairy products are worth the price. If you live in the country, keep a Jersey cow or goats.

- The less expensive vegetables include some of the most nourishing—potatoes, cabbage, carrots, zucchini, onions, broccoli, chard, beets and kale—and they are easy to prepare. Always prepare or serve with butter for best assimilation of the minerals they contain.

- If you can't afford caviar (and very few can) buy fish roe in the spring. Uncured roe from a variety of fish can be had from a good fish monger at a reasonable price. Use to make roe patties (page 294), or add to fish cakes (page 246). You can buy in quantity and store in the freezer to use throughout the year. Fish roe is just loaded with nutrients and was always prized by healthy primitive peoples.

- Don't forget eggs as a nourishing, low-cost alternative to meat. It pays to buy the best quality.

- Make soups part of your repertoire. Blended soups can be put together in very little time and are extremely nourishing. Invest in a handheld blender (which costs about $20) so you can blend your soups right in the pan, thereby saving time and pots to wash.

- Don't forget to eat liver occasionally. It is not expensive but worth its weight in gold, nutritionally speaking.

- Leftovers can be turned into delicious treats. Leftover pureed vegetables can be made into pancakes (page 390); leftover oatmeal is delicious fried (page 433); tender leftover meat from making broth can be added to soups or used for meat salads and sandwiches.

- A judicious choice of recipes will make a little go a long way. Budget stretchers include stir-fry stews (pages 264, 272 and 317), fish cakes (page 246), ground meat dishes, kidney rice casserole (page 284), chicken gumbo (page 267) and lamb shanks (page 324). For special meals, consider leg of lamb, one of the more economical meat cuts, which can provide several days of leftovers in the form of leg of lamb soup (page 191).

- Buy whole grains in bulk. Store in 5-gallon covered plastic buckets, available at paint stores.

- If you can't afford a grain grinder, buy whole grain flours at your health food store or supermarket and store in the refrigerator. Use to make easy and low cost pancakes, muffins, gingerbread, brownies, crackers, etc. If you have the time, you can save money by making your own bread. Otherwise, try to buy good quality sour dough or sprouted grain breads.

- Learn to make basic brown rice (page 441). It is delicious, economical and nutritious. Leftovers make wonderful salads (pages 447).

- Children love our cookies (pages 498-502)—adults do too. Peanut cookies are the most economical. Arrowroot powder is rather expensive. (Oriental markets often carry it at a good price.) Unbleached white flour or spelt flour are compromise substitutes.

- Make kombucha! It cost less than 20 cents per quart and the taste is better than the most expensive soft drink, beer or wine.

- Try not to over-economize on food. Instead cut out all the junk food —prepared cookies and cakes, soft drinks, frozen foods, fast foods, etc.—and use the savings to buy good quality whole foods. Above all use good quality fats—they keep you healthy during times of stress.

Appendix B

KNOW YOUR INGREDIENTS ANSWERS

Our "Know Your Ingredients" quizzes should demonstrate that certain ingredients recur in processed foods. The first of these is sugar in its many forms and guises—white sugar, corn syrup, fructose, etc. When sweeteners form the main ingredient of a processed food, manufacturers often use several so they do not need to list any one sweetener as the first ingredient. Next on the list is processed and hydrogenated vegetable oils, which allow the manufacturer to claim "no cholesterol"; third is refined flour, often listed as "wheat flour" which a careless reader may misinterpret as "whole wheat flour"; and finally, numerous additives, coloring agents and artificial flavors. Note that many so-called "diet" and "low-fat" foods are composed of skim milk (formerly considered a waste product by dairymen), sugar and hydrogenated or highly processed vegetable oil, a highly dangerous combination; and that MSG and hydrolyzed protein, both neuro-toxins, serve as substitutes for properly made meat broths. We hope that this exercise will convince our readers that when we enrich the food conglomerates by buying their impoverished concoctions, we jeopardize our own health and personal prosperity.

1. Cross and Blackwell Hot Mango Chutney
2. Wyler's Bouillon Cubes
3. Wish Bone Thousand Island Dressing
4. Seven Seas FREE Ranch Nonfat Dressing (Fat Free & Cholesterol Free)
5. Miracle Whip
6. Lipton Rice and Sauce (Asparagus with Hollandaise Sauce)
7. McCormick Green Pepper Sauce Blend
8. Town House Fancy Tomato Catsup
9. Thank You Brand Creamy French Onion Dip
10. Hearty Cup O'Noodles
11. Campbell's Homestyle Vegetable Soup
12. Campbell's Healthy Request Cream of Mushroom Soup (99% Fat Free, 1/3 less salt, low cholesterol, 60 calories, no MSG)
13. Farm Rich Non Dairy Breakfast Creamer (100% cholesterol Free)
14. Lean Cuisine Lasagna with Meat Sauce (98% fat free, 35% less sodium)
15. Weight Watchers Beef Broth Mix
16. McCormick Brown Gravy Mix

17. Hamburger Helper (Macaroni & Cheese Type)
18. Utz Sour Cream and Onion Flavored Potato Chips
19. Del Monte Vegetable Classics, Garden Duet
    (Less than 300 calories per package, no preservatives added, a source of fiber)
20. Kellogg's Poptarts (Strawberry with Smuckers Real Fruit; fortified with 6 vitamins and iron, complex carbohydrates 21 grams, sucrose and other sugars 16 grams)
21. Landolakes Light Sour Cream
22. Patio Chicken Burrito
23. Slender Diet Meal for Weight control (Chocolate Flavor)
24. Second Nature No Cholesterol Egg Product
25. Nature's Cupboard Hearty Granola Bread
26. Post Honey Bunches of Oats
27. General Mills Whole Grain Total
28. Rice-a-Roni, Long Grain and Wild
29. Mrs. Wright's Lite reduced calorie wheat bread (40 calories per slice, 33 1/3 less calories than regular wheat, 30% less carbohydrates than regular wheat)
30. Campbell's Baked Beans
31. Quaker Chewy Granola Bars, Raisin and Cinnamon, (no cholesterol, no tropical oils)
32. Hostess Twinkies
33. Nabisco Harvest Crisps, 5 grain crackers (lowfat, low salt, no cholesterol)
34. Santita's Corn Chips
35. Cheetos (Made with real cheese)
36. Kellogg's Low Fat Granola (Half the fat of leading granolas)
37. Nabisco's Oreo Cookies
38. Pepperidge Farm Wholesome Choice Soft Cookies, Cranberry Honey (low fat)
39. Hunts Snack Pack Pudding (No preservatives, no cholesterol)
40. Cool Whip
41. Keebler Ready Crust
42. Entemann's Fresh Baked Pineapple Crunch Cake
    (Fat free, cholesterol free, with less than 100 calories per serving)
43. Slim Fast (Chocolate Royal Flavor)
44. Weight Watchers Vanilla Sandwich Bar
45. Isomil Soy Protein Formula with iron
46. Weight Watchers Chocolate Mousse
47. Jello Pudding and Pie Filling
48. Gatorade Thirst Quencher, Lemonade Flavor

Appendix C

SOURCES

Arrowroot Powder: Mountain Ark Traders, P.O. Box 3170, Fayetteville, AR 72702, (800) 643-8909

Atomidine: (Iodine solution) The Apothecary, (301) 530-0800

Bee Pollen: L and H Vitamins, 37-10 Long Island City, NY 11101, (800) 221-1152

Breads: Sour dough breads made with Celtic sea salt can be ordered from A-Dough-B Bakery, 113 West Park Street, Livingston, MT 59047 (406) 222-3617

Creamed Coconut: This useful product can be found in Asian and Indian food shops; it may also be ordered wholesale from P.A. Tropical Products Brooklyn, NY 11236

Cutco Knives: (800) 633-8323

Dolomite (Calcium Carbonate): L and H Vitamins, 37-10 Long Island City, NY 11101, (800) 221-1152

Dr. Bronner's Sal Suds: L and H Vitamins, 37-10 Long Island City, NY 11101, (800) 221-1152

Gelatin: Bernard Jensen Gelatin (made from beef), L and H Vitamins, 37 10 Long Island City, NY 11101, (800) 221-1152

Grains, whole and organic: Mountain Ark Traders, P.O. Box 3170, Fayetteville, AR 72702, (800) 643-8909

Jet Stream Oven: Ozark (501) 298-3483

Jupiter Grain Mill: New Market Naturals (800) 873-4321

Kombucha Mushrooms: Kombucha Foundation, P.O. Box 882, Joshua Tree, CA 92252 (800) 579-0208. An informative book containing numerous tips and kombucha recipes is also available from the foundation.

Lactose: May be ordered from your pharmacist, who can obtain it from Drug and Chemical Co., Inc., Irvington, N.J. 07111. It may also be ordered by phone from The Apothecary, Bethesda, MD (301) 530-0800

Oils, Unrefined: Unrefined coconut, flax, olive, walnut and sunflower oils may be ordered from Omega Nutrition, 6505 Aldrich Road, Bellingham, WA 98226 (800) 661-352 9

Parchment Paper: James River Corporation, 800 Connecticut Avenue, Norwalk CT 06856-6000

Piima Culture: Price-Pottenger Nutrition Foundation, PO Box 2614, La Mesa, CA 91943 (619) 574-7763

Sea Salt: For natural, Celtic sea salt contact the Grain and Salt Society, Box DD, Magalia, CA 95954, (916) 873-0294

Seaweeds: Unsprayed seaweeds may be obtained from Maine Seaweed Company, P.O. Box 57, Steuben, ME 04680 (207) 546-2875

Stainless Steel Baking Pans and Cookie Sheets: Made by Fox Run Craftsmen, Ivyland, PA 18974, may be purchased in kitchen supply stores.

Supplements: L and H Vitamins, 37-10 Long Island City, NY 11101, (800) 221-1152

Sun Dried Tomato Bits: These are often found in gourmet stores but may be ordered from Timber Crest Farms, 4791 Dry Creek Road, Healdsburg CA 95448 (707) 433-8251

Trace Mineral Powder and Liquids: L and H Vitamins, 37-10 Long Island City, NY 11101, (800) 221-1152; and Mezotrace, 7426 129th Dr. SE, Snohonish, WA 98290 (800) 662-9966

Water Filters: Reverse osmosis filters available from Ozark (501) 298-3483; Multipure filters available from Multipure, 21339 Nordhoff Street, Chatsworth, CA 91311 (818) 341-7577

Appendix D

THE PRICE POTTENGER NUTRITION FOUNDATION

Accurate sources of up-to-date information in the field of nutrition are essential to those responsible for food choice and preparation, indeed for anyone who would take command of his own destiny and well being. The Price Pottenger Nutrition Foundation has supplied that information since its founding in the early Sixties. The foundation is both financially and intellectually independent from medical, government and industrial influence. Among all foundations for nutritional research in America, PPNF is unique in having maintained a relentless challenge to politically correct dictates on fats. It has been a lone warning voice on the dangers of processed vegetable oils, and the need for animal fats in the diet. The organization takes the nourishing traditions of non-industrialized peoples as its touchstone, emphasizing the prevalence of raw animal foods, meat stocks rich in hydrophilic colloids, and fermented foods in traditional ethnic cuisines.

PPNF serves as a repository for the research of two giants in the field of nutrition. The first is the late Weston A. Price, author of *Nutrition and Physical Degeneration*, the classic work on primitive diets. Described as the "Charles Darwin of Nutrition", Dr. Price made extensive studies of peoples untouched by civilization throughout the world, noting that their sound physical and mental health contrasted sharply with that of civilized persons subsisting on processed and devitalized foods. His work has inspired numerous subsequent researchers in the field of diet and nutrition

The other P in PPNF represents the late distinguished physician, Dr. Francis M. Pottenger. His studies with cats led him to the dramatic discovery of the importance of raw protein in the diet, a discovery that corroborated Dr. Price's observations; and his research on hydrophilic colloids demonstrated the need for gelatin-rich meat stocks with diets of cooked foods.

The nutrition foundation library maintains a collection of the Doctors Price's and Pottenger's complete papers and research data, as well as those of another scientific giant, the late William A. Albrecht, Ph.D., formerly Professor Emeritus, Department of Soils, University of Missouri.

Dr. Albrecht demonstrated that soil depletion profoundly affects animal and ultimately human nutrition. The foundation has also played a key role in disseminating the work of the late Dr. Edward Howell, who delineated the need for food enzymes in the diet; of the late John Myers who perfected the effective use of mineral ions for numerous disease conditions; and of the late Dr. Melvin Page who demonstrated the profoundly disturbing effects of sugar on the body's glandular systems. Recently the Foundation acquired the medical notes of the late Dr. Henry Bieler. PPNF has played a key role in educating Americans about disease conditions that establishment medicine has tended to ignore—hypoglycemia, candida albicans, allergies and chronic fatigue.

The Price Pottenger Nutrition Foundation provides access to this invaluable research, housed in their extensive archives; they have made films that give students and professionals immediate access to the findings of Dr. Price and Dr. Pottenger; their book sale program provides the most recent research of America's foremost independent nutritional specialists; they maintain a list of nutritionally-oriented doctors and other health care professionals that is available to members; and the foundation publishes a quarterly journal that keeps its members abreast of the latest discoveries in the field of diet and holistic medicine.

We urge you to join and support this fine organization. For a brochure and book list write Price Pottenger Nutrition Foundation. PO Box 2614, La Mesa, California 91943 or phone them at (619) 574-7763.

Appendix E
SUGGESTED READING

Periodicals: The following journals translate nutritional research into laymen's terms and have in common a history of balanced and rational presentation of the dietary fat issue. New discoveries and ideas often receive their first airing in these publications. *Health Freedom News* stresses political issues in the area of diet and nutrition.

Price Pottenger Nutrition Foundation Journal
Price Pottenger Nutrition Foundation
PO Box 2614, La Mesa, CA 91943

Health Freedom News
National Health Federation
PO Box 688, Monrovia, CA 91017

Search for Health
Valentine Communications Corporation
PO Box 11089, Naples, FL 33941

Second Opinion
Second Opinion Publishing, Inc.
Suite 100, 1350 Center Drive, Dunwoody, Georgia 30338

Books:

Nutrition and Physical Degeneration, Weston A Price, DDS (available from the Price Pottenger Nutrition Foundation, PO Box 2614, La Mesa, CA 91943 (619) 574-7763). The classic study of isolated populations on native diets, and the disastrous effects of processed foods and commercial farming methods on human health. Published in 1939, Dr. Price's findings have as much relevance today as they did 50 years ago. All who plan to bear children, and everyone in the practice of medicine, should read this book.

Your Body is Your Best Doctor, Melvin E. Page DDS and Leon Abrams, Jr. (available from the Price Pottenger Nutrition Foundation, PO Box 2614, La Mesa, CA 91943 (619) 574-7763). Of the many general books written on the subject of nutrition, this ranks among the most sensible. A good introduction to the subject of diet and health. Includes interesting findings on the role of the glands in determining body type.

Enzyme Nutrition, Dr. Edward Howell, (available from the Price Pottenger Nutrition Foundation, PO Box 2614, La Mesa, CA 91943 (619) 574-7763). Pioneering work on the role of food enzymes in diet and health. Reveals the dangers of diets composed entirely of cooked foods and problems posed by pasteurization of dairy products. Dr. Howell's work led to a renewed interest in lacto-fermented foods.

Cholesterol and Your Health, Chris Mudd (American Lite Co., PO Box 18662, Oklahoma City, Oklahoma 73118). Chris Mudd reveals the fallacies and dangers of the low-cholesterol, low-fat diet and therapies in this well-documented work.

Solved: The Riddle of Illness, Stephen Langer, M.D. (available from the Price Pottenger Nutrition Foundation, PO Box 2614, La Mesa, CA 91943 (619) 584-7763). Well documented work on the importance of a healthy thyroid gland. Dr. Langer itemizes the maladies that can result from the often-misdiagnosed problem of an underactive thyroid, and delineates important nutrients for the health of this all-important organ, including sufficient fat soluble vitamins.

Eat Right to Live Longer, Dr. Cass Igram (available from the Price Pottenger Nutrition Foundation, PO Box 2614, La Mesa, CA 91943 (619) 574-7763). Valuable information for layman and professional alike, from a doctor who never fell for the low-fat rhetoric.

Sugar Blues, William Dufty (Warner Books, New York, NY). Classic expose of the dangers of sugar, written in a highly entertaining style.

Nutrition Almanac, Lavon J. Dunne (McGraw Hill Publishing, New York) Competent primer on vitamins, minerals and other nutrients.

Kombucha, Healthy Beverage and Natural Remedy, Gunther Frank and *Tea Fungus Kombucha, The Natural Remedy*, Rosina Faschung (available from Search for Health (800) 321-0416). Fascinating story of kombucha tea including many testimonials on the healing powers of this unique beverage.

For those who read French, two excellent books by Claude Aubert are available from Terre Vivante, Domaine de Raud, PB 20, 38711 Mens Cedex, France. They are *Les aliments fermentes traditionnels. Une richesse meconnue* and *Dis-moi comment tu cuisines, je te dirai comment tu te portes*.

Appendix F
A CAMPAIGN FOR HEALTHY FATS

All of us pay a price for the widespread use of *trans* fatty acids—margarine, shortening and hydrogenated fats—in the food supply, even if we ourselves avoid processed and fast foods; because all of us collectively pay for the plague of cancer, heart disease and other chronic illness that the use of *trans* fatty acids has engendered. We pay with our pocketbooks in the form of increased health costs and lower productivity, and we pay with the lives of our loved ones. The health conscious may not eat potato chips, cookies, crackers, prepared foods and french fries, but their children and grandchildren probably do. The tragedy is that hydrogenated fats are unnecessary—food processors have many alternatives for fried foods, baked goods, cookies and other processed foods. These include the tropical oils—coconut, palm and palm kernel—butter and other animal fats. These are safe and healthy alternatives to *trans* fatty acids.

Does it make you angry that food processors and fast food outlets use dangerous hydrogenated fats to save money, while promoting them to the gullible consumer as health foods? If so, then join us in a letter-writing and phone-in campaign to the major food processing and fast food companies. No new laws are necessary to rid ourselves of the *trans* fatty acid menace—just the full weight of outraged public opinion.

Top Fast Food Companies

McDonald's Corporation
1 Kroc Drive, Oak Brook, IL 60521
(708) 575-3000, 575-5512 fax

Burger King Corporation
PO Box 52078, Miami, FL 33142
(305) 378-7011, 378-7262 fax

Pizza Hut Worldwide
9111 East Douglas, Wichita KS 67207
(619) 681-9000, 681-9869 fax

Taco Bell Worldwide
17901 Von Karmon, Irvine CA 92714
(714) 863-4500

Wendy's
PO Box 256, Dublin, OH 43017
(614) 764-3100, 764-3459 fax

Hardee's
1233 Hardee's Blvd., Rocky Mount, NC 27804
(919) 977-2000, 977-8655 fax

Kentucky Fried Chicken
PO Box 32070, Louisville KY 40232
(502) 456-8300

Little Caesar Enterprise, Inc.
2211 Woodward Avenue, Detroit, MI 48201-3400
(313) 983-6000, 983-6197 fax

International Dairy Queen, Inc.
PO Box 39286, Minneapolis, MN 55439-0286
(612) 830-0200, 830-0480 fax

Top Food Processing Companies

Nestle USA, Inc.
800 N. Brand Blvd., Glendale CA 91203
(818) 549-6000, 549-6952 fax
(Products containing hydrogenated fats include those under the Carnation, Raisonettes, Butterfinger, Chunky, Stauffers and Lean Cuisine labels.)

Philip Morris
120 Park Avenue, New York, NY 10017
(212) 880-5000
(Products containing hydrogenated fats include those under the Kraft, General Foods, Entemanns, Stove Top Stuffing and Coolwhip labels.)

Grand Metropolitan
30 St. James Square, London, England SW1Y4RR
(44-71) 321-6000
(Products containing hydrogenated fats include those under the Pillsbury and Hungry Jack labels.)

RJR Nabisco
1301 Ave. of the Americas, New York, NY 10019
(212) 258-5600

(Products containing hydrogenated fats include those under the Nabisco, Fleishman's, Planter's Peanuts, Stella d'Oro and Chun King labels.)

Sara Lee
Three First National Plaza, Chicago, IL 60602
(312) 726-2600
(Products containing hydrogenated fats include most baked goods with the Sara Lee label.)

Frito-Lay
7701 Legacy Drive, Dallas, TX 75035
(214) 351-7000
(Products containing hydrogenated fats include potato and corn chips.

CPC International
International Plaza Box 8000, Englewood Cliffs, NJ 07632
(201) 894-4000, 894-2186 fax
(Products containing hydrogenated fats include those with the Bran'nola, Arnold's, Hellman's, Mazola and Skippy labels.)

Kellogg's
PO Box 3599, Battle Creek, Michigan 49016
(619) 961-2000
(Products containing hydrogenated fats include breakfast cereals, pop tarts, snack bars and those with the Eggo, Le Gout and Mrs. Smith's labels.)

Campbell Soup
Campbell Place, Camden, NJ 08103
(609) 342-4800
(Products containing hydrogenated fats include those under the Swanson and Pepperidge Farm labels.)

Safeway
P.O. Box 28846, Oakland, CA 94604
(510) 891-3000
(Products containing hydrogenated fats include those under the Townhouse, Mrs. Wright's, Manor House, Bel Air and Lucerne labels.)

Continental Baking Company
Checkerboard Square, St. Louis, MO 63164
(314) 392-4700
(Products containing hydrogenated fats include those under the Wonderbread and Hostess labels.)

UTZ Quality Foods
900 High Street, Hanover, PA 17331
(717) 637-6644
(Products containing hydrogenated fats include potato and corn chips.)

Quaker Oats Company
321 North Clark Street, Chicago, IL 60610
(312) 222-7111
(Products containing hydrogenated fats include those with the Quaker Oats and Aunt Jemima labels.)

Proctor and Gamble
PO Box 599, Cincinnati, OH 45201
(513) 983-1100
(Products containing hydrogenated fats include those with the Duncan Hines label.)

Van Den Bergh Foods Company
2200 Cabot Drive, Lisle, Illinois 60532
(800) 955-5532
(Products containing hydrogenated fats include those with the Imperial Margarine, I Can't Believe It's Not Butter, Ragu and BakerSource labels.)

Lance, Inc.
PO Box 32368, Charlotte, NC 28232
(704) 554-1421
(Products containing hydrogenated fats include cookies and crackers.)

Keebler Company
One Hollow Tree Lance, Elmhurst, IL 60126
(708) 782-2630
(Products containing hydrogenated fats include cookies and crackers.)

Sunshine Biscuits, Inc.
100 Woodbridge Center Drive, Woodbridge, NJ 07095
(908) 855-4000
(Products containing hydrogenated fats include cookies and crackers.)

SUBJECT INDEX

H

I

J

K

O

P

Q

R

S

RECIPE INDEX

H

I

J

K

L

Y

Z

ABOUT THE AUTHORS

Sally Fallon, M.A. combines extensive background in nutrition with training in French and Mediterranean cooking. A creative and innovative cook, she has studied gourmet culinary techniques in both Paris and the United States, and has devoted many years to researching genuine versions of traditional cooking methods. She brings a wide range of knowledge drawn from the areas of literature, anthropology, history and comparative religion to the fascinating subject of ethnic and modern diets. She is a member of the Price Pottenger Nutrition Foundation Advisory Board and a regular contributor to the PPNF quarterly journal. She lives in Washington, D.C. with her husband and four children.

Mary G. Enig, Ph.D. is an expert of international renown in the field of lipid chemistry. She has headed a number of studies on the content and effects of *trans* fatty acids in America and Israel, and has successfully challenged government assertions that dietary animal fat causes cancer and heart disease. Recent scientific and media attention on the possible adverse health effects of *trans* fatty acids has brought increased attention to her work. She is a licensed nutritionist, certified by the Certification Board for Nutrition Specialists, a qualified expert witness, nutrition consultant to individuals, industry and state and federal governments, contributing editor to a number of scientific publications, Fellow of the American College of Nutrition and President of the Maryland Nutritionists Association. She is the author of over 60 technical papers and presentations, as well as a popular lecturer. Dr. Enig is currently working on the exploratory development of an adjunct therapy for AIDS using complete medium chain saturated fatty acids from whole foods. She is the mother of three children and lives with her husband in Maryland.

Patricia Connolly has been the guiding light of the Price Pottenger Nutrition Foundation for the past 20 years, as teacher, curator and executive director. Under her guidance, the Foundation has faithfully preserved and disseminated the research of Weston Price and Francis Pottenger, along with the writings of a number of other prominent nutritionists. She has been instrumental in bringing new information to public awareness, including the problem and treatment of candida albicans, enzyme and mineral ion therapies, and the importance of organic gardening and farming. She is the author of eight books, including the best selling *Candida Albicans Yeast Free Cookbook*, and has collaborated with well-known nutritional author Linda Clark on two other books. Mrs. Connolly is the mother of three. She lives with her husband in California.